1-10

Reapportionment:

The Law and Politics of

Equal Representation

BY ROBERT B. MCKAY

A CLARION BOOK

Published by Simon and Schuster

A Clarion Book
Published by Simon and Schuster
Rockefeller Center, 630 Fifth Avenue
New York, New York 10020
All rights reserved
including the right of reproduction
in whole or in part in any form

First Clarion printing 1970

SBN 671-20749-0
Manufactured in the United States of America

Foreword

IN THE spring of 1962, shortly after the Supreme Court ruled in *Baker v. Carr*, the Twentieth Century Fund held a conference to discuss the apportionment issue. The question put before the conferees — What is the proper basis of representation in a state legislature? — produced a surprising measure of agreement among the participants. The near-total assent to the principle that population is the sole legitimate criterion for apportioning representatives in a modern democracy led to the Fund's issuing a widely disseminated pamphlet, *One Man — One Vote*.

The decision of the Court in *Baker v. Carr* meant that this question could now be argued in the federal courts. The complexity of the issues, the lack of adequate information, and the significance of the Court's decision for social issues and political groupings prompted the Fund to sponsor this detailed study by Robert B. McKay, associate dean and professor of law of the New York University School of Law.

With the principle "one man, one vote" now established by the Court as the law of the land, it is hoped that this work will clarify the issues involved in the Court's decision and the significance this decision holds for the nation's political process. Information made available while the study was in progress has already proven valuable to those involved in state legislative reapportionment suits.

Dean McKay is a man dedicated to the cause of equal representation. We are grateful to him for having carried forward this work for the Twentieth Century Fund.

AUGUST HECKSCHER, *Director*
The Twentieth Century Fund

41 East 70th Street, New York
October 1965

Preface to the Clarion Edition

SINCE 1965, when *Reapportionment* was published, much has happened; but little has changed. The surprising fact is that the basic principles of the one-man, one-vote revolution in legislative representation were developed with remarkable speed. As soon as the Supreme Court announced its 1962 decision in *Baker v. Carr* that the federal courts would entertain voter challenges to malapportionment, the rest followed quickly, and decisively. By 1964, with decision in *Reynolds v. Sims* and *Wesberry v. Sanders*, the principle was established that substantial population equality was a constitutional requirement in state legislative apportionment and congressional districting.

By 1965, as reported in this volume, it was clear that the new doctrine had carried the day with the voters, even with the legislators; and there was less foot-dragging than might have been expected. Despite sour predictions of resistance and unworkability, the change-over was made with relatively little dislocation. After all, the new doctrine had a very American quality, combining as it did the two notions of majoritarianism and equality that had long been accepted as cardinal tenets of American-style democracy.

After substantial population equality was proclaimed as controlling principle, and after the test of popular appeal was met, much remained to be done in terms of definition and implementation. In particular, it was important to work off any rough edges about the new doctrine before disclosure of the 1970 census results would trigger the next round of reapportionment and districting.

The Supreme Court undertook this task with a diligence that was encouraged by litigants in state and federal courts pressing for answers to a number of large and small questions. Between 1965 and 1970 all the principal questions—save one to be discussed in a moment—were answered. Strikingly, there was no retreat from the bold outlines drawn in the original decisions. Rather, the Court extended those decisions very nearly to the permissible limits of their logic. Thus, in *Avery v.*

Midland County[1] the Court held that the population-equality principle applies to all local governmental units "with general governmental powers over an entire geographic area. . . ."

The other principal question that was answered during this period concerned the definition of "substantial population equality." The matter was developed in two steps. First, the Court held that where population variances are shown, the state has the burden of presenting "acceptable reasons for the variations among the populations of the various . . . districts. . . ."[2] This was logical enough; and then in 1969 the point was settled in *Kirkpatrick v. Preisler*[3] with a forceful insistence upon nearly precise equality:

> Unless population variances among congressional districts are shown to have resulted despite such effort, the State must justify each variance, no matter how small.

In mid-1970 one important question remains unanswered: the permissibility or not of gerrymandering. Unfortunately, the Supreme Court has shown little interest in developing guidelines on this vital issue. Now that legislative manipulation is no longer possible through malapportionment in terms of population inequality, the gerrymander to achieve partisan advantage or to accomplish racially discriminatory objectives has been applied with exquisite refinement. It seems entirely apparent that if the gains of the one-man, one-vote standard are not to be thwarted, other malevolent distortions of the electoral process must also be made impossible.

It is of course never easy to limit forces that seek to control the political process for selfish advantage. But once the Court has grasped the nettle of judicial intervention to protect the integrity of the political process, it scarcely seems possible to leave the task half done and in a posture that invites continuing abuse.

Other questions, perhaps less important, but nonetheless intriguing, also remain. For example, in view of increasing dissatisfaction with the representative character of the national party nominating conventions, the question has been raised whether the one-man, one-vote principle provides enforceable constitutional constraints. The problem is complicated by distinctions that must be drawn between the "interstate" apportionment of delegates to the states under national party rules and the "intrastate" aspect, involving the varied procedures under state law or state party rule for selecting each state's share of national convention delegates. Whether the matter is finally found to involve an issue subject to constitutional vindication or not, at least the population-equality decisions have heightened popular awareness of the fundamental equities involved. The old ways are likely to give way under modern majoritarian and egalitarian demands for change.

The remarkable achievement of the population-equality principle, previewed in this volume in 1965, and now confirmed in application, is a heightened awareness that the political process is too important to be left to the politicians. Equality of the franchise *is* important to majority rule and *is* realizable. Increasingly, state legislatures are looking toward the establishment of nonpartisan bodies to draw the district lines defining the districts from which legislators will be chosen. The process may be imperfect, as are all matters controlled by human intelligence, but it must at least be better than the venalities of the immediate past. The change to one man, one vote foretells a better future for the representative process on which so much depends for all of us.

ROBERT B. McKAY

1. 390 U.S. 474 (1968).
2. *Swann v. Adams,* 383 U.S. 440, 443–44 (1967).
3. 394 U.S. 526, 546 (1969).

Preface to the First Edition

THIS BOOK is not the first to appraise representative government in the United States from the perspective of state legislative apportionment and congressional districting. Current developments make especially appropriate renewed inquiry into these matters. Now that the equal-population principle has become established constitutional doctrine for state legislative representation and congressional districting, the relationship of apportionment and districting formulas to the fundamentals of representative government should be examined anew. This study seeks to raise the relevant questions and to suggest preliminary answers.

Surely it is significant that Title I (Voting Rights) of the Civil Rights Act of 1964 was being debated in Congress while the *Reapportionment Cases* of 1964 were working their way to the Supreme Court of the United States; and it is more than mere coincidence that the Voting Rights Act of 1965 was adopted by the same Congress that rejected a proposed constitutional amendment to limit the effect of the *Reapportionment Cases*. Although the legislation vindicating the right of franchise and the Supreme Court decisions invalidating malapportionment were stimulated in response to somewhat different problems, reasons for the converging emphasis are readily apparent. The congressional acts broaden the franchise and protect against discriminatory limitations on the exercise of that right; and the Supreme Court decisions require another measure of equality in the exercise of the same right. Together they represent a powerful new force to permit the voice of democracy to be heard effectively throughout the land.

To understand the contemporary implications for representative government of the constitutional principles announced by the Supreme Court in 1964, brief inquiry is first made into the political theory that undergirds the legislative aspects of representative government in the United States. The series of cases in which the equal-population principle was developed are next reviewed. Finally, the prospects for the future are examined to determine what choices are available and what may be the consequence of electing one alternative rather than another. It should be helpful to learn, for example, that a substantial majority of the apportionment formulas in the original constitutions of the 50 states were based primarily on population in both houses of the bicameral legislatures (as they nearly all were). It is now common knowledge that by 1962 nearly all the states had substantially abandoned the equal-population principle in one or both legislative houses, either by constitutional amendment or by legislative failure to satisfy state requirements for periodic reapportionment in accordance with population. Most revealing of all is the fact that by late 1965 the great majority of the states had returned to apportionment formulas in both houses based primarily on population; and in many cases, once the matter was settled, there appeared to be quiet relief and general satisfaction as with a job well done.

A major finding that deserves emphasis even in this prefatory note is that there is room for local diversity among state legislative apportionment formulas. Experience demonstrates that the equal-population principle need not be regarded as a straitjacket forbidding freedom of maneuver; rather it should be looked upon as a minimum constitutional condition designed to free the representative process from undemocratic restrictions, permitting substitution of creative devices that make more meaningful the exercise of the franchise.

As a matter of self-education for the preparation of the manuscript I found it necessary to examine the historical sources of the apportionment formulas in each of the 50 states, with particular reference to the emphasis on — or rejection of — the principle of equal population. To understand the significance of the various methods of legislative apportionment and congressional districting, I found it necessary also to investigate the various methods for constitutional amendment and the occasional provisions for use of the initiative and referendum. These inquiries led inevitably into the judicial challenges that have been made to particular apportionments, especially the large number of cases beginning in 1961 and later.

Once this preliminary study had been completed, it seemed probable that the same source material would be useful to others. Accordingly, the materials were updated to the extent possible in light of the ineluctable realities of a printing schedule; and they are here presented in the appendix.

No attempt has been made in the appendix to report all the refinements of apportionment and districting in each of the 50 states. The systems are too complex and varied to permit comprehensive summary even in the several pages devoted to some. Rather they are presented as an overview of the entire structure to permit comparison of the points of difference, some very marked. These materials have not been elsewhere collected; it is therefore hoped that they will serve as a useful point of departure for the further, more detailed studies that should now be undertaken in every state.

In this connection it is encouraging that in April 1965 the Ford Foundation announced a grant of nearly one million dollars "to improve and strengthen state legislatures." A large part of that grant will be used for precisely the purpose here recommended, namely, for state-by-state studies of the implications of legislative reapportionment and for programs to improve the effectiveness of state legislatures.

Because the information in this study, particularly the material in the appendix, was not conveniently available in any single location, its collection has required the cooperation of an unusually large number of individuals and agencies, both private and public. It is accordingly impossible to acknowledge individually the many persons who generously assisted in supplying data and in checking the accuracy of my interpretations; but I cannot leave unsaid how important is my debt to individual lawyers, legislative reference officials, and private organizations such as the always-helpful League of Women Voters. All assisted in countless ways.

Credit can and must be given by name to a few whose contributions were too direct and substantial to be left unidentified. I wish to recognize my particular debt to the National Municipal League, especially to William J. D. Boyd, the League's knowledgeable senior associate, for making available to me valuable information, in part collected by the organization and in part stored in Mr. Boyd's quick mind. Former students who prepared helpful memoranda for me were the following: Miss Judith Bader (preliminary drafts of all the state summaries and work on the bibliography and table of cases); Arthur L. Goldberg (judicial and other remedies for malapportionment); Merril Sobie (background studies of local government in general and in selected states). In addition, I am much indebted to my colleague in the Government Department of New York University, Professor H. Mark Roelofs, for his advice on sources of relevant materials in the area of political theory and specifically for his analysis of apportionment and districting in Great Britain. Similarly, I have been much benefited by an opportunity to study portions of a study of unicameralism soon to be published by Professor Calvin B. T. Lee, prepared while he was serving as assistant dean of Columbia College. The index was prepared entirely by my colleague, Professor Edward Bander, assistant librarian of New York University School of Law, and I am grateful indeed to have been so ably relieved of so difficult a task.

It is customary in this connection to absolve all such seeming collaborators for mistake of fact or interpretation. This I cheerfully do. While I have relied substantially on factual data thus made available to me, the conclusions are chargeable to me alone.

It is more than usually appropriate to express my gratitude and dependence upon the more than secretarial assistance supplied first by Mrs. Celina Gruenberg, who has since returned to her native Costa Rica, and later by Mrs. Dorothy Ryan, who saw me and manuscript through the critical stages of revision and updating.

Finally, and most important because essential to the project, was the support and guidance made available to me at the Twentieth Century Fund. I am particularly grateful to Morris B. Abram, a member of the board of trustees of the Fund, who suggested the study. Members of the staff to whom I most often turned for guidance include August Heckscher, the Director, Thomas R. Carskadon, and Ben T. Moore. By this enumeration I do not choose to omit, but only reserve for separate mention, Mrs. Elizabeth Blackert, who combines in superb degree those indispensable editorial qualities of patience and persistence.

ROBERT B. McKAY

New York, October 1965

Contents

Contents

Introduction

It is the proud boast of federalism in the United States that the governments of the fifty states and that of the nation can work together in common purpose rather than in a relationship of competition and mistrust. Moreover, it is a basic premise of representative democracy in the United States that qualified voters are entitled to representation somewhat in proportion to their numbers. The tradition of majority rule cannot otherwise be attained. Neither the division of sovereign powers prescribed in the federal system nor the fairness of the legislative representation formulas can be left long unattended. Vigilant superintendence by an informed electorate is essential.

John Quincy Adams observed in 1839 that the division of sovereign powers between the states and the nation, as set out in the Constitution of the United States, gave us "the most complicated government on the face of the globe." The twentieth century has proved how right he was. The interaction between increasingly potent national and state governments, frequently aggravated by friction arising out of competition for power, has produced a delicately balanced division of power and a complexity of relationships probably unsurpassed in the history of governmental institutions.

It is generally agreed that the state legislative process is not functioning properly, yet the cause is not lack of resources or even want of authority. State governments have grown in every measurable way — whether in terms of revenue, expenditures, or impact upon the lives of their residents. Indeed, state and local government expenditures are growing faster than those of the national government and threaten to overtake national expenditures even in absolute terms. There has nevertheless been a distinct loss of *relative* influence on the part of the states, largely to the gathering authority of the national government. The states, particularly the state legislatures, tend to view the matter in states' rights terms, deploring with varying degrees of rhetorical vehemence the federal "takeover" as an unwarranted grab for national power.

What the states have generally failed to recognize is their own indispensable contribution to the shift in the balance of authority. At least one of the major difficulties has been the all-too-common failure of state legislatures to provide adequately for the needs of the growing urban population. As a result of this neglect of the cities, urban governments have increasingly bypassed the states to make direct arrangements with the national government on such pressing matters as urban renewal, transportation, schooling, and antipoverty programs.

Every presidential commission that has studied the intergovernmental problems of federalism since 1950 has commented on the failure of the states to adopt and abide by fair reapportionment formulas as an important contributing factor to the decline of effective and responsible state government. The massive shifts of population to the cities in the twentieth century have aggravated the social problems of the urban areas; but the state legislatures during the same period — many elected on the basis of a population distribution of more than fifty years ago — have made no serious attempts to solve these problems. The failure to accomplish reapportionment and the decline in the prestige of state governments are not unrelated.

By the early 1960's state legislative malapportionment (the very word suggests unfairness) had become general. The constitutions of about two thirds of the states imposed significant restrictions on equitable apportionment in one or both chambers; and representation was further distorted by the failure of a number of state legislatures even to abide by the command of their own state constitutions for representation in proportion to population. The result was to inflate the relative influence of rural voters to the disadvantage of urban — and more recently suburban — residents. Malapportionment has seriously weakened the states' rights claim. It follows logically that the states must provide more equitable representation in their legislatures before they can rightfully reclaim the position of full partnership in the federal system to which they are otherwise entitled.

In the early years of the century the voters in the rapidly growing urban centers scarcely noticed their relative decline in legislative representation because the changes had occurred in almost imperceptible stages. By the time the imbalance was nearly everywhere substantial, and in some cases overwhelming, the power of correc- tion had usually slipped away from those most disadvantaged. The pattern was repeated in state after state. Where the state formula permitted some inequality, the legislators most benefited refused to approve any change that might jeopardize their control. Where the state constitution required equality, the not uncommon technique was simply to fail to reapportion at the periodic intervals specified.

Disregard of voter interests and flouting even of state constitu- tional provisions seemed both comfortable and safe to self-inter- ested legislators because both federal and state courts showed a gen- eral reluctance to intervene. The Supreme Court of the United States in 1946 had given the cue when it suggested in *Colegrove v. Green*[1] that the federal courts should not enter the "political thicket" of legislative representation. Not until 1962 was there any suggestion of relief, when the Supreme Court ruled in *Baker v. Carr*[2] that federal courts could and must decide constitutional chal- lenges to state legislative representation at the suit of qualified vo- ters who claimed impairment of their right of franchise.

Baker v. Carr decided only that there was power in the federal courts to decide these claims. Within less than twenty-seven months of that decision the standards for fair apportionment had been sub- stantially fixed in a series of cases. In *Gray v. Sanders*[3] the first step, short but unfaltering, was taken to assure equality of voter represen- tation in elections for statewide office; and in *Wesberry v. Sanders*[4] the Court required population equality "as nearly as is practicable" among each state's congressional districts. Then, on June 15, 1964, in *Reynolds v. Sims*[5] and a series of related cases, the Supreme Court completed the first round of the *Reapportionment Cases*, requiring substantial equality among state legislative representation districts in both houses of a bicameral legislature. Thus was the beginning made secure.

The principles formulated in these cases demonstrated that nearly all state legislative election districts, as well as most congres- sional districts, required revision to satisfy the constitutional man-

1. 328 U.S. 549 (1946).
2. 369 U.S. 186 (1962).
3. 372 U.S. 368 (1963).
4. 376 U.S. 1 (1964).
5. 377 U.S. 533 (1964).

date. In seeking to determine how revision should best be accomplished, this volume will examine the history of apportionment and districting; the meaning of the judicial guidelines now available; and what influence these changes will have on the future of American federalism.

Two preliminary points should first be made:

1. The *Baker* to *Reynolds* series of cases decided by the Supreme Court between 1962 and 1964 involved state legislative *apportionment* and congressional *districting*. Apportionment has ordinarily been described as the allocation of legislative seats by a legislative body to a subordinate unit of government, and districting as the process of drawing the final lines by which each legislative district is bounded. Thus, Congress apportions the number of congressional representatives to which each state is entitled, based on population figures disclosed in each decennial census. Each state legislature then draws lines that divide the state into as many congressional districts as are apportioned to it by Congress.

Formerly it was the practice of many state legislatures to apportion to local units — usually counties, sometimes towns — one or more electoral representative positions. Where more than one representative was apportioned to a particular unit of government, that local unit was frequently empowered to draw the district lines. Now that equality of population has been mandated among election districts, it will frequently not be possible to satisfy that requirement and at the same time confine election districts within local governmental unit lines. Accordingly, counties and towns should no longer be regarded as entitled to separate representation simply by virtue of their existence as local governmental units. Where two or more counties or towns, or parts thereof, must be combined to form a single election district, the state legislature is the only appropriate body for fixing the election district lines. Even where a county is entitled on a population basis to two or more whole election districts within its borders, it would probably be more logical for the legislature to draw the lines in order to fix responsibility for the almost inseparable functions of apportionment and districting in a single place.

In short, it appears that the apportionment and districting functions in the state legislative process will be merged into a single task to be performed by each legislature. It will therefore be proper at a later point in this study to examine the impact of this reallocation of duties upon state legislatures and the corresponding lessening of the role of counties and towns in this respect.

2. The *Reapportionment Cases* strike deep into the core of the social fabric of American society. Some commentators have criticized the decisions as an ill-advised judicial effort to resolve problems outside the competence of the judiciary. Others have praised the decisions for the boldness of the judicial contribution to the realization of the democratic principles of liberty, equality, and majoritarianism. Both praise and criticism are reminiscent of the initial reaction to the 1954 Supreme Court decision in the *School Segregation Cases* outlawing segregation in state-supported public schools. That decision also cut to the heart of the American social system; and it, like the *Reapportionment Cases*, was based on the equal protection of the laws clause of the fourteenth amendment to the Constitution of the United States.

Both cases involved problems of discrimination against individuals arising out of their situation in society — in the one case discrimination in education because of race and in the other case discrimination in the right of franchise based on the chance of geography. These were both ways of looking at the equal protection concept peculiarly appropriate to the second half of the twentieth century. Accordingly, criticism of the desegregation and apportionment decisions was not dissimilar. As to each the charge has been made that this is not judicial business at all, but rather a heady distillation of sociological experimentation (in the *School Segregation Cases*) or a tinkering with the political processes of the government (in the *Reapportionment Cases*) that should in both instances be foreclosed to the judiciary.

More than eleven years have now passed since the Court called for an end to public school segregation, and more than ten years since the Court's further announcement that school desegregation should be accomplished in "good faith" and "with all deliberate speed." We now know that the delays thus permitted made the ruling less effective than it might otherwise have been. The failures of the formula — the failures of temporizing — bear the unhappy names of Clinton High School, Tennessee; Central High School in Little Rock, Arkansas; the University of Alabama at Tuscaloosa; and the University of Mississippi at Oxford.

Perhaps more forceful and immediate demands for compliance would have been successful. We cannot now know. But certain it is that the Supreme Court now believes, as it said in 1964, that "There has been entirely too much deliberation and not enough speed"[6] in enforcing the constitutional right to nondiscriminatory education.

In the context of apportionment the Supreme Court has called upon each state to make an "honest and good faith effort to construct districts, in both houses of its legislature, as nearly of equal population as is practicable."[7] This time the necessity for prompt compliance was emphasized from the beginning. Once a legislative formula had been declared unconstitutional, "it would be the unusual case in which a court would be justified in not taking appropriate action to insure that no further elections are conducted under the invalid plan."[8]

The 1964 *Reapportionment Cases* were fortunate in their timing. Two years earlier *Baker* had been generally well received in the press, by the public as a whole, by the lower federal courts, and even by state legislators (except, understandably, those who saw their own seats threatened). Doubts as to the feasibility of judicial enforcement of an equal-population standard were advanced between 1962 and 1964. Some thought judicial intervention inappropriate because they believed that judicially manageable standards could not be devised or enforced. If those doubts can be resolved by discovery of a manageable standard in the equal protection clause, and if the availability of judicial remedies can be assured, those doubts disappear. The main body of this study will be devoted to an attempt to dissipate those doubts, particularly in terms of what has already been proved possible in satisfaction of the Supreme Court decision in the *Reapportionment Cases*.

6. Griffin v. County School Board of Prince Edward County, 377 U.S. 218, 229 (1964).

7. Reynolds v. Sims, 377 U.S. 533, 577 (1964).

8. Id. at 585.

CHAPTER I

Equality and the

Growth of Representative

Government

Even the wisest political theorists have difficulty in defining precisely the meaning of representative democracy. There is, however, general agreement that representative government in the United States includes something of liberty, equality, and majority rule. Even though these qualities are scarcely less abstract, it can surely be said, with Robert Dahl, that "democratic theory is concerned with processes by which ordinary citizens exert a relatively high degree of control over leaders; . . . ."[1] Debate has centered about the extent to which, and the ways in which, majority "control over leaders" should be exercised. That issue has been raised anew by the 1964 Supreme Court ruling in the *Reapportionment Cases*[2] that substan-

1. Dahl, A Preface to Democratic Theory 3 (1956). See also Krastin, The Implementation of Representative Government in a Democracy, 48 Iowa L. Rev. 549, 558–66 (1963).

2. The term *Reapportionment Cases* in this volume will refer to Reynolds v. Sims, 377 U.S. 533 (1964) and the five companion cases decided at the same time: WMCA, Inc. v. Lomenzo, 377 U.S. 633 (1964) (New York); Maryland Committee for Fair Representation v. Tawes, 377 U.S. 656 (1964) (Maryland); Davis v. Mann, 377 U.S. 678 (1964) (Virginia); Roman v. Sincock, 377 U.S. 695 (1964) (Delaware); Lucas v. Colorado General Assembly, 377 U.S. 713 (1964) (Colorado).

Other important cases popularly referred to as "reapportionment cases" are Baker

tial population equality among state legislative election districts is constitutionally required in both houses of a bicameral state legislature. The various proposals for constitutional amendment to limit the impact of those cases make necessary a careful examination of all the implications of legislative apportionment and districting in terms of history; the adjustments required by the Supreme Court decisions; and the significance of the proposed amendments.

The debate is not new. In the United States it goes back at least to the framing of the Constitution of the United States, and elsewhere even beyond that period. It is commonly assumed, for instance, that the principal draftsmen of the Constitution of the United States sought in that document to protect the United States against the "tyranny of the majority." What exactly the tyranny was may not have been altogether clear, but certainly many of those who played dominant roles in shaping the new government were to some extent mistrustful of unmitigated majority control. Alexander Hamilton's exaggerated fears on this score led him to propose what turned out to be a monumental irrelevancy, a constitutional monarchy. Others, less extreme, nonetheless sought to guard against unrestrained majority rule. James Madison, who well deserved the recognition he has been accorded as "Father of the Constitution," formulated the rationale, particularly in *The Federalist* No. 10, for the elaborate system of checks and balances incorporated into the Constitution. Writing in the middle of the nineteenth century, Alexis de Tocqueville and John Stuart Mill reported continuing manifestations of this same distrust of the majority. Not until the twentieth century, and particularly since the middle of the century, has much note been taken of the fact that even in a representative government precautions are necessary against abusive exercise of power by a minority which has somehow gained control. The "tyranny of the minority" also presents a danger not to be ignored.

The tension between these two views has been sharpened by the increasingly lively debate over proper standards for state legislative apportionment and for congressional districting. To give meaning to that debate, and to understand why the label "tyranny" in refer-

---

v. Carr, 369 U.S. 186 (1962) (upholding the jurisdiction of federal courts to decide certain apportionment matters); Gray v. Sanders, 372 U.S. 368 (1963) (invalidating the Georgia county unit system); and Wesberry v. Sanders, 376 U.S. 1 (1964) (requiring substantial population equality among congressional districts). All these cases will be discussed in some detail in Chapters III–VI, *infra*.

ence to either majority or minority groups may be nothing more than semantic shibbolethism, requires some exploration of the historical roots and present meaning of representative democracy in the United States.

While it may not be possible to obtain unanimous agreement on any completely satisfactory definition of representative democracy, we can at least examine the various strains from which it came to the United States and identify some of its goals. Knowing the varieties of American experience, we should not be surprised if some of the historical antecedents seem to point in opposite directions, and if some of the apparent objectives appear at times to cancel each other out. But at least, if we are to think realistically and rationally about the nature of the right of franchise and of the methods by which particular voters are required to cast their ballots in one election district for certain candidates rather than in another district for other candidates, we must reflect upon the nature of representative government in the United States. Only then can we hope to understand the extent to which the Constitution, in one place or another, prescribes a rigid rule or invites flexible interpretation of standards which are at best indefinite.

THE ORIGINS OF
REPRESENTATIVE GOVERNMENT

For our purposes the history of representative government before the eighteenth century is a story quickly told. While the drafters of the United States Constitution reviewed the experience of earlier states and were influenced by the views of earlier political philosophers, the United States nonetheless pursued an independent and somewhat different course from the beginning. Perhaps it is not getting too far ahead of the story to recall the simple fact that the American experiment was not only a building upon what had gone before; it was in significant part a specific and conscious rejection of much of the earlier, particularly the British, experience.

What follows is a kind of peering through the large end of a telescope to reduce the immense canvas of constitutional history to a manageable perspective, without loss of essential detail. The study will emphasize the strains of liberty and equality, which are, and have always been, the central themes of representative democracy in the United States. Even so, during the period between the promulgation of the Declaration of Independence in 1776 and the con vening of the Constitutional Convention in 1787, the notion that these two abstractions, liberty and equality, could be effectively combined into a single government was essentially novel. The English had emphasized liberty since the Revolution of 1688; and the French Revolution, yet to come, would depend mainly on the principle of equality. The point here is simply that, however large in history may have been writ the appeals to liberty and the demands for equality, and however clearly those cries were heard in eighteenth-century America, the particular genius of the Constitution, developed out of sometimes disparate and even contradictory sources, was the uniquely American contribution of successfully uniting the twin appeals for liberty and equality.

In and around these themes of liberty and equality is woven a third theme, tied principally perhaps to the concept of equality, but certainly not irrelevant to the concept of liberty. That is the issue of majority rule versus minority rights. Since the majoritarian aspects of equality are central to any discussion of apportionment, the linkage of these three — liberty, equality, and majority rule — to representative government must always be kept in mind.

The starting point, as for any analysis which involves political theory, is with Aristotle. He it was who did the original hard thinking in problems of democracy, particularly in the *Politics*; it is to that point of reference that one ordinarily turns for a secure beginning. Aristotle found in the idea of democracy an identification with political equality, popular sovereignty, and rule by majorities. He identified as the purest form of democracy

> the variety which is said to follow the principle of equality closest. In this variety the law declares equality to mean that the poor are to count no more than the rich: neither is to be sovereign, and both are to be on a level. . . . for if we hold, as some thinkers do, that liberty and equality are chiefly to be found in democracy, it will be along these lines — with all sharing alike, as far as possible, in constitutional rights — that they will most likely be found. A constitution of this order is bound to be a democracy; for the people are the majority; and the will of the majority is sovereign.[3]

Aristotle of course wrote not only of a world different from ours, but even of a different form of political organization. His experience was with the 160 or so city-states (*polis*) scattered over the Greek mainland, which he had studied. These governments-in-min-

3. Barker (ed.), The Politics of Aristotle 167 (1952 ed.).

iature were invariably small enough in area for their citizens to know one another personally; the citizens could be addressed by a single herald; a single orator could reach all the voters when they were assembled in their town meeting.[4] Pure democracy in this form scarcely exists in the United States today. Even the closest surviving approximation, the New England town meeting, seldom now serves that function in unadulterated form. Moreover, the equality Aristotle referred to was by no means the equality of modern constitutional democracy. His was a frankly class society in which only male citizens had the vote, while a large body of slaves and others thought unworthy of the political function were disenfranchised without distress to Aristotle or others of the ruling class. Equality was thus only an equality within the favored class.

The significance of Aristotle's comments in the fourth century B.C. is thus not a wisdom of direct parallels, but remains important because his acute perceptions profoundly influenced the later philosophers who in turn shaped modern political thinking, from St. Augustine, through St. Thomas Aquinas, to John Locke, Rousseau, and John Stuart Mill.

After the fall of Athens in the fifth century B.C. and the disappearance of its limited experiment in democracy, there was no further significant effort to achieve democracy until modern times. Even in Rome, despite a demonstrated genius for government, the government was not more than nominally democratic in republican times and not even formally democratic in imperial times.

The Romans did, however, further the notion of equality which was later to become an indispensable element of political democracy. Roman Stoics, Cicero, Seneca, Gaius, and Ulpian, sought to establish the identity of the reasoning part of one man, his soul, with that of any other man; and so they progressed to "astonishingly radical assertions that in this world of fact men are really alike."[5] During Roman times the slowly gathering forces of Christianity also played a part, particularly in the emergence of a theory of human rights distinct from the rationalist ideas of the Stoics. The Christian

---

4. Id. at xvii.

5. Brinton, Equality, in 5 Encyclopedia of the Social Sciences 574, 575 (1931). See also Laski, Democracy, id. at 76, 78.

It has even been suggested that the decline of the Roman Republic may perhaps be traced to the rejection in 124 B.C. by the Roman assembly of an electoral reform proposed by Gaius Gracchus which would have bestowed full suffrage rights on all Latins instead of restricting such rights to the 35 wards or "rotten boroughs," representing the original Latin tribes. See Frank, A History of Rome 207 (1923).

Church endorsed an equality more spiritual than worldly, for the equality asserted was that of all men before a single God. These Stoic and Christian ideals of equality did not, however, develop a synthesis capable of supporting an operative political doctrine, for at this time they went scarcely beyond the level of somewhat mystical generality.

Subsequent emphasis on the Augustinian doctrine of predestination changed the direction of the early Christian thinking into other avenues less clearly equalitarian in nature. Thomas Aquinas, for example, while maintaining the Christian doctrine of the equality of men before God, denied that men are equals on earth. The feudal social organization, which rejected equality and freedom alike, depended in large part on that rationale for its practices. The feudal view of the state was pragmatic: different men perform different functions for different rewards; and Church doctrine accepted, as a consequence of original sin, the notion that the unequal sufferings of men on earth were punishments in their various degrees.

The medieval period did contribute one idea of importance to the later-developed notion of representative government. The fundamental concept of representation, probably ecclesiastical in origin, was transferred to accepted notions of the state by the thirteenth century. In one sense the idea of representation antedated even this period. Almost universally, political rulers have been regarded in some important aspects as the spokesmen or agents of the people. Even during the Roman Empire the emperor was said to hold his powers, however absolute, as a representative of the Roman people. But not until the later Middle Ages did this concept of representation begin to take shape as a factor of more realistic limitation upon absolute rule. The theory that the group, secular or ecclesiastical, retained authority over its corporative head then gained general acceptance. The rise of parliamentary supremacy in England, which was essentially complete by the end of the Middle Ages, illustrated this development.

In a curiously undemocratic way the Renaissance provided immediate gains in equality that in time paved the way for the more truly democratic impulses of the seventeenth and eighteenth centuries. The very distance between the absolute monarch and all his subjects served to break down the hierarchical structure of feudalism and thus to emphasize the equality of the ruler's subjects in relation to each other.

The Reformation, particularly in its Calvinist aspects, ultimately supported the notion of equality, too. While its reaffirmation of pre-destination maintained the notion of human inequality, its removal of the distinctions between clerics and laymen and its rejection of distinctions based on rank or wealth led to concepts of greater unity and equality among men without regard to station in life. Indeed, an extraordinary degree of social uniformity was briefly mandated by Oliver Cromwell and demanded by the Levellers. They sought economic more than political equality; yet it is interesting that in 1649 even the most moderate revolutionists in Cromwell's army supposed that a reform of parliamentary representation was inevitable, making the same argument for that reform which ultimately prevailed in the nineteenth century.

As an exercise in government, Puritanism must be said to have failed; "the settlement in 1688 left Parliament unreformed and was so manifestly a compromise between the conflicting claims of Parliament and the Crown that it might be said to have set up compromise as a fundamental principle of English constitutionalism."[6] The English Revolution was, however, successful in another and important way; it established the uniquely English contribution to democracy, the idea of liberty, particularly religious toleration; and it provided a constitutional system to protect that freedom. From this root sprang the tree of liberty which grew to full maturity with the first amendment freedoms of the United States Constitution.

The eighteenth century saw the principal development of political equality, particularly in the American rejection of British rule in favor of a new government and, in different fashion, the later French insistence upon equality almost above all.

The American and French Revolutions had their own rather distinctive prophets. The work of John Locke, who had rationalized the English Revolution of 1688 in terms of liberty, played a similar part a century later in the formation of the new American government, although now with new overtones of equality as well. Thereafter, Rousseau was the proper instrument for the French insistence upon equality, suggesting as he did that no government is legitimate in which the general will of all the people does not control the effective lawmaking power. But through both there ran remarkably similar strains. Jefferson, after all, had postulated in the Declaration of Independence that "all men are created equal," while the French battle cry was for Liberté, Égalité, Fraternité.

6. Sabine, The Two Democratic Traditions, 61 Philosophical Rev. 451, 456 (1952).

Before examining more closely the American experience from and after 1776, let us review briefly the various forms which representative government has taken; for it will be significant to our ultimate inquiry, particularly as to the function of the bicameral system which became so predominantly the pattern in the United States.

Throughout most of the Middle Ages the only governments which might with any justification have been called representative were the royal councils, commonly composed of feudal lords, ecclesiastics, and royal officials, who usually served at the king's pleasure. They were at first consultative only, but gradually increased their authority as the rulers more and more often found it necessary to secure their consent to the levying and collection of taxes for the always-expensive business of government. Gradually the monarchs began to consult lesser nobility and such landed gentry as the knights of the shire in England. Since the larger numbers now involved made impractical the simultaneous consultation of the entire group membership, the representative device was increasingly employed. In some nations the persons called upon in this loosely representative capacity acted in behalf of estates of the realm, nobility, clergymen, and townspeople. This form continued in France until 1789 and in other countries into the nineteenth century. But in England the development was different. During the fourteenth century a bicameral legislature was formed, the high churchmen sitting with the nobility in a House of Lords, while the landed gentry and the townsmen met together in a House of Commons. From there the gradual accretion of parliamentary power to a point of ascendancy over the Crown is a well-known story not particularly relevant for present purposes.[7]

FROM COLONIES TO STATES

In the United States the idea of representative government was not only accepted but demanded, the memory of "no taxation without representation" still ringing in the ears of those who developed the earliest legislative patterns. To a surprising degree even the colonial legislatures had reflected this interest in representation in proportion to population. The Fundamental Orders of 1638–

7. Developments in the manner of representation in Great Britain, from "rotten borough" to boundary commission, are discussed infra at pages 29–34.

1639 in Connecticut, for example, after assuring equal representation to the three original towns, provided that new towns should send deputies in "a reasonable proportion to the number of Freemen that are in said towns . . . ." The 1663 Charter of Rhode Island and Providence Plantations provided for the election of deputies by freemen in the towns, chosen roughly in accordance with population figures of the time, six from Newport, four each from Providence, Portsmouth, and Warwick, and two from "each other place, towne, or city . . . ." With only minor adjustments Connecticut and Rhode Island continued these provisions into statehood, for neither adopted a written constitution until the nineteenth century, 1818 and 1842 respectively. In both instances the population referent in terms of town size, while not mathematically precise, represented a much closer approximation than anything then known in England.

Between 1775 and 1780 the other colonies turned to the task of drafting constitutions for their newly declared independence. The overall results produced a marked increase in the emphasis on representation in accordance with population. That absolute equality was not achieved is scarcely surprising. What is remarkable is that the emphasis on population should have been so significant so early. New York, for example, in its constitution of 1777, turned its back on the colonial legislative pattern in that state, which had given only limited recognition to population; instead, primary reliance was placed on population as the basis of apportionment in both houses. So it was destined to remain through successive New York constitutions until 1894.

Even where the formula chosen seemed not to be based on population, where, for instance, equal or nearly equal representation was provided for each county, city, or town, it must be remembered that the population differentials were not so striking then as they were later to become. New Hampshire, Massachusetts, and Rhode Island provided representation in one house by towns, but with adjustment upward for the more populous towns.[8] Georgia, Maryland, Pennsylvania, and South Carolina did somewhat the same in one

8. The Massachusetts formula for representation in towns was the following (Luce, *Legislative Principles* 337 (1930)):

Freeholders	Representatives
0–10	0
10–20	1
20–40	2
over 40	3

house[9] on the basis of counties or counties plus named cities. But even in those instances the pattern did not altogether ignore population. In Pennsylvania, for example, the constitution provided for reapportionment at seven-year intervals following an enumeration of "taxable inhabitants." Thereafter, the legislature was to fix representation "in proportion to the number of taxables" in such returns; for "representation in proportion to the number of taxable inhabitants is the only principle which can at all times secure liberty, and make the voice of a majority of the people the law of the land...."

There were also other variations among those first state constitutions. In Massachusetts and New Hampshire the seats in one house were apportioned in accordance with "public taxes paid" (the results turned out to be not very different from those on a pure population basis). Virginia's constitution of 1776 favored the older counties on the theory that the preponderance of property (particularly slaves) in that section required such security against the rising tide of democracy in the "new west."

Only in Delaware and New Jersey (and nearly so in North Carolina) was population rejected in both houses as a basis for apportionment. At that time, however, equality of voter representation was not severely distorted by the provision for equal representation from each county in those states. The 1790 census showed that the three Delaware counties ranged in population only from 18,920 to 20,488, while in New Jersey the range for twelve counties was between 8,248 and 20,153, and only one was substantially smaller with a population of 2,571.[10] Moreover, even in New Jersey there was an apparent recognition that another formula might be preferable in the event of substantial shifts of population. The New Jersey constitution of 1776 contained this interesting provision: "Provided always, that if a majority of the representatives of this Province, in Council and General Assembly convened, shall, at any time or times hereafter, judge it equitable and proper, to add to or diminish the number or the proportion of the members of Assembly for any county or counties in this [state], then, and in such case, the same

9. Technically, in Georgia and Pennsylvania legislative power was originally vested in a single house; a second house exercised primarily executive authority.

10. Advisory Commission on Intergovernmental Relations, Apportionment of State Legislatures 7 (1962). The 1790 census figures in the states which took population into account, however crudely, showed greater population differentials among the counties. Id. at 7–8.

may, on the principle of more equal representation, be done; . . . ."

Two lessons of prime importance emerge from this review. In the first place, no state constitution (or colonial charter) in effect between 1776 and 1787 established a legislature in which one house was apportioned entirely on the basis of population while representation in the second house was based exclusively on equal representation of political subdivisions. Clearly, the federal formula was not derived from the states.[11] Nor did the apportionment plan adopted in the United States Constitution lead to alteration of previously adopted state plans.[12] In the second place, the idea of equality in terms of voter representation made great gains during the period when the first state constitutions were being adopted.

THE CONSTITUTIONAL CONVENTION OF 1787

Long before 1787 the climate of opinion had begun to shift from emphasis on the political equality of localities to the equality of individuals. In June 1776 Thomas Jefferson had proposed a constitution for Virginia which provided for representation in proportion to qualified electors. Although his proposal was rejected, Jefferson never abandoned that ideal. In 1783 he wrote another constitution for Virginia with a lower house in which "The number of delegates which each county may send shall be in proportion to the number of its qualified electors."[13] The senate he favored would also have reflected population, since it would have included one senator for each six delegates in the lower house. Some years later he concluded "that a government is republican in proportion as every member composing it has his equal voice in the direction of its concerns . . . by representatives chosen by himself."[14]

At the Constitutional Convention of 1787 the conviction that the new government must be representative in character was foremost

11. The Maryland provision for the indirect election of senators was in part used as a model for the indirect election of United States Senators. See The Federalist No. 39 (Madison). The Maryland plan was abandoned in 1837. Radoff, The Old Line State 64 (1956). Indirect election of United States Senators was abolished by the seventeenth amendment, approved in 1913.

12. The irrelevance of the so-called federal analogy is more fully discussed *infra* at pages 162–203.

13. III Writings of Thomas Jefferson 322–23 (Ford ed. 1894).

14. X id. at 38 (1899).

in the minds of the principal draftsmen of the Constitution, as further evidenced in the arguments for its ratification advanced by James Madison and Alexander Hamilton in *The Federalist*.[15]

The somewhat rhetorical exhortation in favor of equality in the Declaration of Independence — "that all men are created equal" — was refined in the Constitution into more meaningful if perhaps more sober doctrine. The Virginia Plan, advanced early in the Convention, proposed that primary emphasis be placed on population as the basis of apportionment in both houses of the Congress. Rejection of that proposal was not for lack of belief in equality as an ideal. The decision involved highly pragmatic considerations relating to the feared loss of influence by the less populous states if they should submit to any formula in which they did not retain equal representation in at least one legislative chamber.[16] Since the proposed Constitution involved a consensual union of sovereign states, whose boundaries were to be assured against alteration, it was clear that agreement could be reached only on the basis of a formula which partially subordinated the favored equal-population principle in return for acceptance of the document as a whole.[17]

The proceedings of the Constitutional Convention also demonstrate the concern of those present with the participation of the electorate on an equal basis. As Robert McCloskey has observed:

> it is beyond doubt that the framers acknowledged popular consent as the indispensable basis for setting up that process of government in the first place. Though the government might take various forms and possess various powers, those characteristics were *derived* from the consent of the governed. If this central principle, so plain in the Declaration, was not ex-

15. Both Madison and Hamilton used the term "republic" to mean representative government as opposed to "democracy," which they reserved for the direct form of government of the Greek city-states or the New England town meetings. Madison defined a republic as "a government which derives all its powers directly or indirectly from the great body of the people . . . . It is *essential* to such a government that it be derived from the great body of the society, not from an inconsiderable portion or a favored class of it; . . . ." The Federalist No. 39 (Madison). See also id. No. 10 (Madison); No. 14 (Madison); No. 35 (Hamilton); No. 48 (Madison).

16. The story is more fully told in my pamphlet, Apportionment and the Federal Analogy (National Municipal League pamphlet 1962).

17. Madison explained his reluctant acceptance of the compromise in The Federalist No. 62 as follows: "A government founded on principles more consonant to the wishes of the larger States is not likely to be obtained from the smaller States. The only option, then, for the former lies between the proposed government and a government still more objectionable. Under this alternative, the advice of prudence must be to embrace the lesser evil . . . ."

pressed in the explicit language of the Constitution, it is because after 1776 it was taken for granted. Its claim to be a fundamental principle of the Constitution is about as solid as any claim could well be.[18]

That these views were widely shared at that time is indicated by the action of the Congress[19] which provided, in the Northwest Ordinance of 1787, that representation in the territorial legislatures to be created in that area should be based on population. "The inhabitants of the said territory shall always be entitled to the benefits . . . of a proportionate representation of the people in the legislature . . . ."[20]

On the one hand, John Locke, the philosopher who most influenced the American revolutionary movement, had made the classic statement in support of the principle of majority rule. He visualized a state of "perfect freedom . . . within the bounds of the law of Nature." It was, he said,

> A state also of equality, wherein all the power and jurisdiction is reciprocal, no one having more than another; there being nothing more evident than that creatures of the same species and rank, promiscuously born to all the same advantages of Nature and the use of the same faculties, should also be equal one amongst another without subordination or subjection . . . .[21]

As a result of this doctrine of natural equality, no man could legitimately claim superiority over any other; it followed that political decisions could be made only by majority rule. In this view the inherent equality of man legitimatized majority rule, which in turn derived its support from its equalitarian base.[22]

At the same time that these related notions of equality and majority rule were accepted as part of the basic theoretical apparatus of the period, there was, as there has always been in the United States, some uneasiness about allowing that majority to operate in all matters free of any restraint. One manifestation of this mistrust of the unchecked majority appeared in the several provisions in the Constitution denying popular election of persons upon whom governmental authority was to be conferred — President and Vice-Presi-

18. McCloskey, Foreword: The Reapportionment Case, 76 Harv. L. Rev. 54, 71 (1962).

19. Under the Articles of Confederation each state had but one vote.

20. Northwest Ordinance of 1787, art. II.

21. Locke, Of Civil Government 118 (Everyman's Library ed. 1924).

22. See Grimes, Equality in America 95–96 (1964).

dent, Senators, members of the federal judiciary. Further, the states were empowered to limit the exercise of the franchise in a variety of ways. Those restrictions have in time been almost entirely abandoned except that federal judicial positions have remained appointive rather than elective; but this is not so much because of lack of faith in the majority as in order to ensure that the judges need not respond to the popular passions of the moment in order to continue in office. Apart, then, from the concededly special reasons for denying election to the judiciary, direct election has almost entirely prevailed;[23] and universal suffrage is the rule rather than the exception.[24]

A second restraint on the power of the majority, central to the philosophy of the framers, has largely been retained even today. James Madison feared the "mischiefs of faction," which he proposed to control by providing for (1) representative government instead of pure democracy; (2) division of governmental powers between nation and states in a federal system; and (3) separation of powers at the national level, with an elaborate system of internal checks and balances.[25] All these restraints upon majority power — fractionalization of power and filtering of the decision-making process — remain very much a part of government in the United States in the twentieth century as they were in the eighteenth. In addition, the Bill of Rights, added in 1791 under the primary draftsmanship of Madison, imposed additional restraint upon the majority in specific protection of minority rights in matters deemed to be of primary importance. When the fourteenth amendment was added in 1868, as later reinforced by the absorption of the most important guarantees of the Bill of Rights into the due process clause as a limitation on the states, minority interests and individual rights received added protection.

It is important to view these developments in proper perspective. The near-elimination of indirect elections and the widespread acceptance of universal suffrage vindicated the principle of majority rule, as to which the original doubts have been largely overcome.

23. The selection of the President and Vice-President by electors rather than directly by the voters is a last, now almost anachronistic, vestige of the earlier view.

24. At the start of the Revolution all of the states except Pennsylvania had property qualifications for the suffrage. By 1800 only eight of the original states retained such restrictions, and by 1850 all states had abandoned the property qualifications. Grimes, Equality in America 101 (1964).

25. See particularly The Federalist No. 10 (Madison).

On the other hand, the increased protection accorded individual rights is a logical corollary of majoritarianism in its American context, with direct antecedents in the English Revolution of 1688, as implemented in the Bill of Rights. Majoritarianism in the United States involves at best a qualified acceptance of majority rule. Some values are considered so important that they may not be interfered with by the majority — even when that majority is very substantial in number and extremely insistent in its demands. In the American constitutional system these preferred values include freedom of speech, press, religion, the right of free association, separation of Church and State, the right to be free of unreasonable searches and seizures, habeas corpus, fair procedures in criminal actions, right to counsel, the privilege against self-incrimination, the right to be free of discrimination on grounds of race or color — and the free exercise of the right of franchise. In this last, the right to vote, both strains of American constitutionalism have been combined from the beginning: the insistent demand for equality as expressed in the concept of majority control, and the equally compelling demand for liberty, here in terms of freedom from arbitrary limitation upon the exercise of the right.

THE NINETEENTH AND TWENTIETH CENTURIES IN THE UNITED STATES

The Growth of Equality and Majoritarianism. The Age of Jackson brought a new emphasis upon equality and majority rule, manifested in the establishment of national nominating conventions for the selection of presidential party candidates, widened suffrage, and the popular election of presidential electors. As always, there were some who objected to the increased emphasis on majority rule. John Calhoun, for example, found insufficient the checks upon majority rule and the restraints upon factions which Madison had written into the Constitution. As new states were admitted, and as the population center shifted more and more to the North and West, Calhoun saw the South's share of representation in Congress declining in both houses and in absolute numbers in the House; and he feared the social and economic changes that this shift in power might portend for the South. The matter was particularly acute in the case of his own state, South Carolina, which went from nine to four seats in the House between 1830 and 1860 while the total number of House seats was on the rise.[26] The problem for Calhoun was not essentially different from that the framers had confronted: How can a government strong enough to control the governed itself be controlled to protect against abuse of the governed? But Calhoun, in his *Disquisition on Government,* would have denied virtually all power to the majority. The device he invented, under the phrase "concurrent majority," involved his conclusion that interests as well as numbers should be considered. In the Calhoun plan the concurrent majority, representing a concurrence of interests, would hold a veto power over the wishes of the numerical majority. But Calhoun's views, rejecting the essential premise of equality, were unacceptable to a nation which had accepted the tenets of majority rule, restrained only to the extent necessary to protect certain preferred freedoms.

Not until more than a hundred years after the ratification of the Constitution in 1789 did such states as California, Illinois, Michigan, New York, Ohio, and Pennsylvania, responding to new pressures, abandon the equal-population principle in one or both houses. So widespread had been the original acceptance of the equality principle that no fewer than 36 of the original state constitutions provided that representation in both houses of the state legislatures would be based completely, or predominantly, on population.[27] Between 1790 and 1889 no state was admitted to the Union in which the original constitution did not provide for representation princi-

26. In the eleven states which later constituted the Confederate States of America the percentage of Southern representation in the Senate declined between 1840 and 1860 from 40.8 to 33.3 per cent and in the House from 30.7 to 25.4 per cent. Grimes, Equality in America 104–105 (1964).

27. Advisory Commission on Intergovernmental Relations, Apportionment of State Legislatures 10–11, 35, 69 (1962).

The Commission's conclusion was challenged by Robert G. Dixon, Jr., who concluded that 21, not 36, states provided for representation in proportion to population for both legislative houses in their original constitutions. Reapportionment in the Supreme Court and Congress: Constitutional Struggle for Fair Representation, 63 Mich. L. Rev. 209, 239–42 (1964). He is clearly right in suggesting that classification standards are too variable to make agreement "a simple matter—or even possible." Id. at 239. Analysis of the two studies suggests that Dixon looked only at the formulas without noting the number of counties originally established, the size of the legislative body, and the population distribution at that time. Where the number of counties was at first substantially smaller than the number of legislators in a legislative body, accommodation to population differentials might well have been achieved even under a formula calling for at least one representative for each county.

For an analysis of the original state constitutional provisions relating to apportionment, see the state summaries and the chart summarizing those provisions, both in the appendix.

pally based on population in both houses of the legislature.[28]

To speak of those nineteenth-century legislatures in terms of acceptance of the principle of population as the basis for apportionment is not to suggest that there was mathematically precise equality among the districts at that time. As the state summaries in the appendix show, the newly added Western states commonly relied on county lines in drawing their apportionment formulas. The distortions which resulted from assuring each county at least one representative, for example, or from grouping whole counties to form election districts, were much less in agricultural and rural America than in present-day industrial and urban America. The population of the United States, outside the few great commercial centers in the East, was spread thinly across the face of the country. In percentage terms the dispersal was much more even than today.

Counties as Units of Government.[29] Most of the counties in the United States were created long after 1790, even most of those in existing states such as New York. The normal pattern for the creation of counties, particularly in the great agricultural states of the Midwest and West, was to lay them out in such a way that each farmer was no more than one day's wagon ride from his farm to the county seat and back. In this rural society, with counties established to meet the needs of the farmers, apportionment on the basis of population rarely caused much friction. Almost every county had a population large enough to warrant at least one representative in terms of the population ratio.

In the more sparsely settled states of the Far West and on the Pacific Coast, the county-making process continued well into the twentieth century. The old concept of the farmer's round trip to the county seat was not practical for these large, thinly settled areas; so, until the population grew, many of the counties were as large as the entire state of Connecticut and some were larger than New Jersey. Even today there are 61 Western counties and 15 Alaskan election districts larger than Connecticut; the state of New York could be swallowed whole in each of four of the present election districts in Alaska.

Another fact to be remembered is that most states entered the

28. Advisory Commission on Intergovernmental Relations, supra note 27, at 11.

29. For particular illustrations from the history of county development I have drawn upon the mimeographed text of a speech by William J. D. Boyd to the League of Women Voters of New York City on January 30, 1964.

Union with smaller legislatures than they have today. Therefore, as the need arose for granting greater representation to the faster growing areas of the state, it was common to expand the size of the legislature rather than reapportion the existing seats. "Thus, throughout the nineteenth century, the great majority of the counties in this country were sufficiently large to warrant their being assigned a representative *on the basis of population*."[30]

There was a practical limit beyond which legislative bodies could not be expanded to keep pace with the growth in population and, more particularly, its redistribution. During the latter half of the nineteenth century the United States began to change from an agriculture-based economy to an industrial economy; the nature of the population — and its concentrations — shifted to meet the new demands. Between 1821 and 1830 the United States admitted only about 140,000 people; but between 1881 and 1890 some 5,000,000 immigrants arrived, and between 1901 and 1910 almost 9,000,000. While the earlier group had been largely of Anglo-Saxon, Germanic, or Northwestern European stock, the immigrants toward the turn of the century were primarily from Eastern and Southern Europe. Moreover, the new immigrants settled primarily in the cities, wherever growing industry needed more workers.

Simultaneously, another trend began which became still more marked in the twentieth century. Many of the rural counties, in all sections of the country, started to decline not only in terms of their proportion of the statewide population, but even in absolute terms. Confronted with these facts and a growing distrust of cities as such, the legislatures began one by one to abandon their reliance on population as the principal basis for apportionment.

Montana heralded the new trend with its constitution of 1889, on the basis of which it was admitted to the Union. In establishing Montana as a territory in 1864 Congress had specified that apportionment of the members of the governing council and house of representatives was to be made "as nearly equal as practicable, among the several counties or districts . . . ." Congress also provided that the members of the constitutional convention of 1889 should be chosen in proportion to the population. But the convention itself worked out a different formula, retaining population as the basis of representation in the lower house but allotting one senator to each of the

30. Id. at 7.

sixteen counties in the upper house. The change was prompted by the rapid growth of population between 1880 and 1889, after the discovery of copper, and particularly the concentration of that population in three counties in the western part of the territory. As a result the fear was expressed, as it was soon to be expressed in other parts of the country, that a concentrated majority of the voters was not to be trusted with legislative power.

Thereafter, the same phenomenon recurred in a number of the already-established states. Not only did the state legislatures fail to adjust to the new population demands; many states actually abandoned long-established formulas based on population. The newly developing pattern can be explained in two ways which reinforce each other. In the first place, there were astonishingly frank expressions of distrust of majority control, particularly where a near-majority of the voters was concentrated in one or several cities within a state, although there had never been before, and certainly there was not then, any expression of mistrust of a *rural* majority. So it seemed for a time that the belief in equality and majoritarian principles was only as deep as the expectation of immediate advantage to the group previously in control. A second explanation perhaps more realistically suggests that the change may have been motivated less by an abandonment of democratic ideals than by the simple facts of political life. As individual legislators saw their own seats jeopardized by continued adherence to the equal-population principle, they were not long in finding various justifications for change to protect "the people" which would minimize their own risk of displacement or loss of influence.

Montana, then, was in 1889 the immediate harbinger of the future. Within seven years of the taking of the 1890 census Delaware and New York changed their state constitutions.[31] In Delaware "permanent" districts were established in both houses, while in New York the population base was relaxed if not abandoned and, to make doubly safe against any possibility of future city domination, limitations were placed on the proportion of the state legislature that could come from any one county.

After the census of 1900 Ohio adopted the Hanna amendment, which guaranteed each of its 88 counties at least one representative

---

31. Pennsylvania changed its constitution even earlier, in 1874, to assure each county at least one representative in the house of representatives. Pa. Const. 1874, art. II, § 17.

without regard to population. Other states, including Alabama, Illinois, Iowa, Michigan, Minnesota, and Tennessee, unable or unwilling to change their constitutions, neatly solved the problems of legislators who might have been displaced by reapportionment by ignoring the state constitutional command for periodic reapportionment.

Interestingly enough, when the population trends reversed so that the large cities declined in their percentage of state population — and in many cases lost actual population as well — there was no legislative enthusiasm for increasing the representation to which the suburbs accordingly became entitled. The 1960 census showed that, for the first time in fifty years, there was not one state with as much as half of its population in a single city. Only two states, Hawaii and New York, have even 40 per cent of their population in a single city. Of the ten largest cities in the United States only Houston has increased both in absolute size and in its percentage of the total state population, while eight of the ten have declined in actual population. As a result, today there are in many states three population groups which tend to be treated somewhat differently as to state legislative representation. In addition to the typically overrepresented less populous areas and the usually underrepresented urban areas, there is emerging a new class, the suburban area, which is often the most underrepresented of all. Thus, in the group of six *Reapportionment Cases,* voters who lived in the suburban counties surrounding Baltimore, Denver, New York, and Washington (including counties in Maryland and Virginia) were severely disadvantaged.

Twentieth-century urbanization has brought about other changes in the political structure. Sectionalism, the principal characteristic of politics in times past, gradually shaded into class-oriented politics.[32] More recently, the rise of the urban majority has produced a blend of sectional and class politics in which the urbanized areas tend to seek goals different from those of the less populous areas. Urbanization thus introduced a new dimension into the discussion of majority rule. In Calhoun's time the rural majority held firm control over the reins of political power. Accordingly, discussions of majority rule were not then confused, as they subsequently became, with issues of rural bias. But by the latter part of the nine-

32. See Holcombe, The New Party Politics (1933), The Middle Classes in American Politics (1940).

teenth century rural America concluded that urban America posed a threat to its continued control of the decision-making power.

The political manifestations were various. For example: (1) The Populist movement at the turn of the century represented in part the rural reaction to the rise of urbanism and the potential relocation of the balance of power. (2) In 1910, the last year in which rural America registered a majority in the census, the United States House of Representatives adopted the seniority system as the basis for selection of committee chairmanships. (3) After the 1920 census figures revealed the loss of rural dominance in terms of numbers, Congress failed to enact reapportionment legislation for congressional seats, the only time it has not acted in this respect. (4) In 1921 Congress adopted the first of a series of restrictive immigration statutes, based on a national-origins quota system, thus reducing the population influx into the urban centers.[33]

THE ENGLISH EXPERIENCE[34]

The emphasis on equality of voting rights came earlier and more emphatically to the United States than to England, which labored under the gradually worsening "rotten borough" system until the Reform Bill of 1832. Thereafter, democratization of the English electoral system made steady if slow progress while the United States was drifting away from guaranteed equality in the exercise of the right of franchise. England's ultimate reforms ensured near-equality among the election districts throughout England, Wales, North Ireland, and Scotland. The near-simultaneity of the reversal in trend in both countries is not without its ironies.

As the English Parliament gained ascendancy in control of the government during the Middle Ages, seats in the House of Commons came to be sought after rather than accepted as burdensome obligations. By the sixteenth century the active solicitation of seats was begun in earnest by courtiers, lawyers, and landowners. The residence requirement for members of Parliament was generally disregarded for more than a century before its repeal in 1774, and

33. See Grimes, Equality in America 110–12 (1963).

34. The summary of the early English experience which follows is largely based on the article on Rotten Boroughs by Emily Allyn in 13 Encyclopedia of the Social Sciences 443 (1934). The discussion of the reforms since 1944 is based on a study prepared for this volume by H. Mark Roelofs, Professor of Government at New York University.

the corrupt traffic in borough constituencies flourished during this entire period.

The electoral units represented in the House of Commons were counties, corporate towns, and universities. The difficulties arose through a combination of factors. For one thing the voting qualifications were not uniform.[35] Moreover, the decline of once prosperous towns accounted for a number of rotten boroughs, thus "creating new Gattons and Old Sarums in each generation."[36] Other rotten boroughs resulted from royal efforts to ensure the Crown's control of Parliament by the enfranchisement of villages which might return members of Parliament friendly to the Crown.

By 1793, when rotten boroughism was at its height, 157 members were returned directly by 84 individuals, and a majority of the members of the House were chosen by fewer than 15,000 voters. Boroughs were so commonly bought, sold, and inherited that the demands of the reformers were denounced by the boroughmongers as confiscation. Meanwhile, as a result of the opportunity thus afforded for corrupt manipulation of the elective process, George III had nearly succeeded in restoring to the Crown its independence of the popular will expressed through Parliament. Municipal life was contaminated, and bribery of the electorate became established practice, eliminated finally only with the introduction of the ballot in 1872 and the enactment of the Corrupt and Illegal Practices Prevention Act in 1883.

In these various ways the landed class continued its domination of Parliament well into the nineteenth century, denying any representation to the industrial towns of the north until 1832. In that year some of the rotten boroughs were eliminated, and the restoration of the democratic character of the franchise was begun. Further reforms throughout the nineteenth and early twentieth centuries continued the work thus begun, but the most significant recognition of the principle of representation in accordance with population took place in 1944.[37] In that year the British established per-

35. Among the 203 borough constituencies, for example, 59 had a resident householder franchise; in 39 the vote was attached to parcels of land called burgages; in 43 the mayor and council had the exclusive right of election; and in 62 the vote was conferred on freemen generally (as variously defined by the constituency corporations which controlled the admission of freemen to the franchise).

36. Allyn, supra note 34, at 443.

37. The legislation of 1944 was revised in 1949. Representation of the People Act, 1949, 12 & 13 Geo. 6, c. 68. Despite a number of subsequent changes of detail, this law remains the basic electoral law of Great Britain. For general discussion, see Butler, The Electoral System in Britain 1918–1951 (1953).

manent machinery for ensuring that the House of Commons constituencies would conform substantially to the principle of population equality and at the same time satisfy reasonable standards of political viability. After two decades of experience there is general agreement that the effort has succeeded. David Butler, the closest student of the British electoral process, has remarked that the problem of the redistribution of seats in the House of Commons is now "quietly dealt with as a matter of routine ...."[38] In 1961 the Hansard Society, in a survey of suggested reforms that might be made in the House of Commons, observed that "The question of constituency boundaries would appear to have been largely settled ...."[39]

The legislation of 1944, as implemented in 1949 and later modified, established four boundary commissions, one each for England, Scotland, Wales, and Northern Ireland. Each was to be a wholly impartial, nonpolitical body; and all four were chaired, *ex officio*, by the Speaker of the House of Commons, who is in England a judge-like figure without political affiliation once in office. In addition, each commission included two technical members, the Registrar-General of Births and Deaths and the Director-General of Ordnance Survey of the areas served, plus two other members to be appointed by the government. These last two could not be members of Parliament, and it was expected that they would be professional figures with intimate knowledge of local government and other regional problems. Provision was also made for special reports to be presented on particular areas to allow for the correction of anomalies and errors and to take notice of changes in local government boundaries or extraordinary shifts in population.

The procedure of the commissioners in drawing up their general reports was first to work out, in the light of their instructions, a complete set of boundary recommendations for the whole of the area for which they were responsible. Where these involved changes in existing boundaries, opportunity was to be given for expression

38. Butler, supra note 37, at 139.

39. The Hansard Society, Parliamentary Reform 1933–1960: A Survey of Suggested Reforms 2 (1961).

In Great Britain apportionment reform always included many other matters, such as extension of the franchise. In this sense apportionment reform did not reach its culmination until 1948 with the final abolition of the remnants of plural voting, double-member constituencies, and the nonterritorial university constituencies. Thus, it was not until that year that the boundary commissioners were instructed to divide the country, without exception, into single-member constituencies. Representation of the People Act, 1948, 11 & 12 Geo. 6, c. 65.

of the opinions of local citizens. At the completion of this stage the commissioners would again review the whole of their recommendations and submit them to Parliament. Upon an affirmative vote they became law.

The total number of seats to be filled in the House of Commons was originally fixed at "not substantially greater or less than 591."[40] In 1948, for a variety of reasons not related to the present matter, this figure was raised to 613.[41] By 1959 Wales had 36 seats, England 511, Scotland 54, and Northern Ireland 12. These figures resulted in some overrepresentation, relative to England, of Scotland and Wales and a somewhat more substantial underrepresentation of Northern Ireland. An average seat in England in that year had a population in excess of 80,000; in Scotland and Wales it was about 72,000; and in Northern Ireland it was 114,000.[42] Although these differences are not large compared to what is common in the United States, it is worth noting the reasons for which even these disparities have been tolerated in Great Britain. Northern Ireland, with its own parliament and a relatively large measure of local autonomy, may not need or deserve more than 12 seats. Scotland and Wales have less local autonomy; in addition, both are, by British standards, large, remote regions and have numerous special problems, mostly resulting from their having aging, intensely industrialized areas backed by vast, mostly wild hinterlands of declining population.

The first set of rules given the commissioners to guide them in drawing boundaries contained the following:

> So far as is practicable . . . the electorate of any constituency . . . shall not be greater or less than the electoral quota by more than approximately one quarter of the electoral quota.[43]

The commissioners were also instructed to draw constituency boundaries, again "in so far as practicable," to conform to those of existing local governmental units. Finally, the commissioners were instructed as follows:

> A Boundary Commission may depart from the strict application of the last two foregoing rules if special geographical considerations, including

---

40. House of Commons (Redistribution of Seats) Act, 1944, 7 & 8 Geo. 6, c. 41, p. 392.
41. Representation of the People Act, 1948, 11 & 12 Geo. 6, c. 65, p. 1646.
42. Jennings, Party Politics 38 (1960).
43. House of Commons (Redistribution of Seats) Act, 1944, supra note 40, at 393.

in particular the size, shape, and accessibility of a constituency, appear to them to render a departure desirable.[44]

In part this rule was intended to meet the problem of such off-shore islands as Anglesey in Wales, which, although small, may be more sensibly treated as single constituencies than as adjuncts of adjacent mainland areas. The commissioners have also considered this rule relevant in distinguishing between the compact urban constituency and the rural constituency whose population is widely dispersed. Application of this policy resulted in an average advantage of the rural constituencies of about 6,000 persons, about a 10 per cent deviation from the ratio, which is, after all, not large.

The boundary commissions found difficulty in working with these three rules, and Parliament modified the electoral quota rule in 1946 to read as follows:

> The electorate of any constituency shall be as near the electoral quota as is practicable having regard to the foregoing rules [requiring conformity of parliamentary constituency boundaries to those of existing local governmental units]; and a Boundary Commission may depart from the strict application of . . . [those rules] . . . if it appears to them that a departure is desirable to avoid an excessive disparity between the electorate of any constituency and the electoral quota, or between the electorate thereof and that of neighbouring constituencies . . . .[45]

Applying this rule, the English commissioners continued to adhere with remarkable fidelity to the equal-population principle. In their recommendations of 1947, they managed to put 358 (73 per cent) of the 489 constituencies considered within what they called "the normal range," that is, from 50,000 to 70,000 votes.[46] In 1954 they did even better: 410 out of 511 (80 per cent) were inside the normal range.[47]

What discussions of the present sort are almost always concerned with in the end is the exceptional case where a variety of factors conjoin to argue for a wide departure from the normal size. Probably

44. Id. at 394.

45. House of Commons (Redistribution of Seats) Act, 1947, 10 & 11 Geo. 6, c. 10, p. 23.

46. Boundary Commission for England, Initial Report 4 (1947). The quota that year for England was 59,312.

47. Boundary Commission for England, First Periodical Report 2 (1954). Because of the increase in the number of seats, the electoral quota was then 55,670, and the "normal range" 45,000 to 65,000.

the outstanding single advantage of the British rules as they now stand is that they make it possible to distinguish sharply between the normal cases, roughly 75 per cent of any total, and the exceptional ones. Moreover, it also follows from the current British rules that there is every right to expect that as the degree of exceptionality rises, there should be a corresponding decrease in the frequency of the cases.[48] Finally, the rules, together with the record, show that the British have relatively well-defined ideas of the factors that may justify exceptional size: the need to preserve "local unity" both in the sense of conformance to existing local boundaries and in the sense of recognition of local feeling and historic identity; geographic factors influencing the size, shape, and accessibility of a proposed constituency; concentration or dispersion of population or other comparable factors affecting capacity to "support" an electorate of a given size; and, in the light of the special treatment afforded Wales, Scotland, and Northern Ireland, the representational needs of an area as a whole.

Nevertheless, it is also clear that there is a critical limit beyond which the claims of exceptionality cannot be pushed. That limit appears when it becomes obvious that a large constituency could be divided into two small ones without either of them being "too small," or when two small ones are both so small that they could be reasonably combined.

48. The following table, taken from the Boundary Commissioners' Report of 1954, shows that fact bears out this expectation:

Range of Electorate	Seats
40,000–45,000	36
45,000–50,000	70
50,000–55,000	111
55,000–60,000	136
60,000–65,000	93
65,000–70,000	38
70,000–75,000	19
75,000–80,000	8

CHAPTER II

Malapportionment
and Federalism

> [T]he apportionment of representation in our Legislatures and (to a lesser extent) in Congress has been either deliberately rigged or shamefully ignored so as to deny the cities and the voters that full and proportionate voice in government to which they are entitled.
>
> SENATOR JOHN F. KENNEDY[1]

The American federal system began as an experiment; such it remains today. The framers of the Constitution had joined in a revolution that rejected the nonrepresentative structure of the then British government. When they gathered in Philadelphia in 1787 their purpose was to cast off the unsatisfactorily loose alliance of the Articles of Confederation. Although the ideas of liberty, equality, and majority rule which were infused into the new Constitution had their roots in earlier forms of government, the idea of a federal system was less the product of experience or doctrine than of hard necessity. There were then, as now, no fixed rules. The only immutable principle, originally and through the years, was that somehow a

1. Kennedy, The Shame of the States, N.Y. Times Magazine 12 (May 18, 1958).

meaningful partnership between nation and states must be created and maintained. Although general ground rules were provided in the Constitution, it has always been recognized that those were at best guidelines which admitted of considerable flexibility to accommodate to the varying needs of different times. Whether one talks in terms of powers "reserved to the States," in the language of the tenth amendment, or in terms of the "legislative powers granted" to the Congress by the first article, the perspective is the same. It was thus the *"constitution*-ness" of the basic charter which more than anything else characterized the highly pragmatic conception of federalism that emerged from the hands of the framers in 1787.

THE DECLINE OF STATE LEGISLATIVE RESPONSIBILITY

The unhappy truth is that American federalism is not functioning as well as it should. No one doubts the vital importance to healthy federalism of the continued strength of state governments.[2] Nor is there much disagreement with the proposition that many, perhaps most, state governments no longer satisfy that criterion of successful federalism.

State legislatures were once the most powerful and influential instruments of government in the United States. The average citizen looked primarily to his own state government for solution of immediate problems and for wise formulation of long-range governmental policies. Now, however, state legislatures have lost much of their power and influence, "primarily because they have not found effective solutions to problems that become more chronic and more difficult to cope with in a rapidly changing society."[3]

This simple truth has been somewhat obscured by complaints, however soundly based, against inefficiencies in the exercise of power at the national level as the central government has grown beyond any conception of what was originally contemplated. Ritualistic invocation of the demand for greater states' rights is nevertheless a poor substitute for analysis of the root causes of the rise in federal

2. House Committee on Government Operations, Federal-State-Local Relations: Federal Grants-In-Aid, H.R. Rep. No. 2533, 85th Cong., 2d Sess. 47 (1958). See also The Editors of Fortune, The Exploding Metropolis 1 (1957); Commission on Intergovernmental Relations, Report to the President 3, 38, 40 (1955).

3. Commission on Intergovernmental Relations, op. cit. supra note 2, at 38.

power and the alleged decline in state influence. The most cursory examination of readily available information discloses some striking facts about the two governmental systems, nation and state.

Despite the remarkable growth of the national government, it must be remembered that state and local expenditures have in recent years expanded at a faster rate than have the expenditures of the national government. In 1948, while the national government was spending more than $33 billion, state and local governments were spending less than half that amount, between $15 and $16 billion.[4] By 1961, while both had substantially increased total expenditures, the state and local governments had come perilously close to catching up. Their expenditures in 1961 exceeded $67 billion compared with national governmental expenditures of something over $81 billion.[5] When it is recalled that defense-related expenditures accounted for well over half the federal budget in that year and that something more than $7 billion was contributed by the nation to the states in the form of grants-in-aid,[6] it is apparent that the vast bulk of normal governmental services are furnished at the state and local level rather than at the national. Yet the depressing fact is that the state and local governments, while demonstrating remarkable capacity for expansion, have contributed disappointingly little to the solution of the pressing problems of the day.

The reasons for the relative loss of state influence are all too clear. The problem is not new, nor is the solution unknown. It has been evident ever since Thomas Jefferson warned that the only way in which the states can erect a barrier against the extension of national power into areas within the proper sphere of the states is "to strengthen the state governments: and as this cannot be done by any change in the federal constitution . . . it must be done by the states themselves. . . ."[7]

In 1906 Elihu Root warned: "It is useless for the advocates of states' rights to inveigh against the supremacy of the constitutional laws of the United States or against the extension of national authority in the fields of necessary control where the states themselves fail in the performance of their duty. The instinct for self-govern-

---

4. H.R. Rep. No. 2533, op. cit. supra note 2, at 77.

5. Statistical Abstract of the United States 391, 417 (1963).

6. Id. at 390, 418.

7. Letter to Archibald Stuart, Dec. 23, 1791, V The Writings of Thomas Jefferson 409–10 (Ford ed. 1894).

ment among the people of the United States is too strong to permit them long to respect anyone's right to exercise a power which he fails to exercise." Root prophesied that if the states fail in this respect, "sooner or later construction of the constitution will be found to vest the power where it will be exercised — in the national government."[8]

In 1928 H. L. Mencken ridiculed the long-continued control of the Maryland legislature in the hands of vastly overrepresented Eastern Shore counties of the state.

> The yokels hang on because old apportionments give them unfair advantages. The vote of a malarious peasant on the lower Eastern Shore counts as much as the votes of twelve Baltimoreans. But that can't last. It is not only unjust and undemocratic; it is absurd.[9]

Mencken's confident prediction that the demands of modern, effective government would not allow that anomaly long to survive was woefully wrong; the representation differentials became greater in succeeding years. Respect for the Maryland legislature, as for others, continued its long, steep decline without relief; for no relief was practicably available to the disadvantaged groups in the urban and suburban areas.

It is not possible to know precisely how to allocate blame for the debilitated condition of state and local governments. What is known is that when *Baker v. Carr* was decided in March 1962, malapportionment was the rule rather than the exception in state legislatures throughout the United States. The inequality of voter population among election districts had become alarmingly large and senselessly erratic in a substantial majority of the states. As population had grown and shifted, sometimes in expected ways and sometimes along uncharted paths, the slippage from the near-equality common to the states in earlier days had become a national disgrace. Moreover, it was clear that the situation was fast worsening.

The matter received surprisingly little attention as the national phenomenon it had become. In one way this was not unnatural. State legislators who completely understood the growing disparities in population representation were also those who had most to gain from not calling attention to the fact. It is scarcely to be expected

8. Address before the Pennsylvania Society, September 1906, quoted by Commission on Intergovernmental Relations, op. cit. supra note 2, at 56.

9. Mencken, A Carnival of Buncombe 160 (Moos ed. 1956) (reprinted from the Baltimore Evening Sun, July 23, 1928, p. 15, col. 4 (financial ed.)).

that a legislator who sees a decline in the population of the district he represents will complain that his campaigning has become too easy or that he "overrepresents" the voters in his election district. As this became true of an ever-larger proportion of the legislators in an ever-increasing proportion of the states, the resulting conspiracy of silence was entirely understandable.

The phenomenon of state legislative disrepair has been commented on extensively in recent years by various congressional committees, presidential commissions, and other study groups. They have unanimously agreed that state governments are not doing their assigned job; that the federal system is correspondingly endangered; and that corrective action must be taken promptly. The reports and studies have been quite frank in recognizing that the gradual accretion of federal power, much complained of by the states, is attributable to nothing less than the failure of the states to solve their own problems, leaving a vacuum of unfulfilled local demands into which the national government not only can, but almost inescapably must, move. In 1958 a congressional committee on federal-state-local relations reported that "Weaknesses in State governments, at a time when the responsibilities of government are being increased by rapidly changing conditions, help to facilitate the growth of Federal grant activities." Part of the blame was laid to malapportionment: "In many States the populous urban centers have not been given adequate authority to enable them to solve pressing local problems. In addition, they are often denied fair representation in State legislative bodies."[10]

The significance to sound state government of fair apportionment formulas fairly applied was emphasized by the Commission on Intergovernmental Relations, reporting to President Eisenhower in 1955:

> Reapportionment should not be thought of solely in terms of a conflict of interests between urban and rural areas. In the long run, the interests of all in an equitable system of representation that will strengthen State government is far more important than any temporary advantage to an area enjoying overrepresentation.[11]

Then, quoting with approval a study report prepared for it, the Commission stated bluntly:

10. H.R. Rep. No. 2533, op. cit. supra note 2, at 47.
11. Commission on Intergovernmental Relations, op. cit. supra note 2, at 39.

> If states do not give cities their rightful allocation of seats in the legislature, the tendency will be toward direct Federal-municipal dealings. . . . [The only] way to avoid this in the future . . . is for the states to take an interest in urban problems, in metropolitan government, in city needs. If they do not do this, the cities will find a path to Washington as they did before, and this time it may be permanent, with the ultimate result that there may be a new government arrangement that will break down the constitutional pattern which has worked so well up to now.[12]

It is only natural for the cities, which typically have not found an effective forum for their needs in the state capitals, to look to Washington for assistance in the planning for and the financing of housing, transportation, and schools, the three most costly and critical problems faced by every city. "Paradoxically enough, the interests of urban areas are often more effectively represented in the National legislature than in their own State legislatures."[13]

POPULATION MOBILITY AND FEDERALISM

The urbanization of the United States is an accomplished fact. In 1790 nineteen people lived on farms for every one who lived in a town. Today, the farm population is less than one-twelfth the total, and more than two thirds live in urban areas (cities or towns with a population in excess of 2,500).[14] Seventy per cent of the people now live on about 1 per cent of the land.[15] It can confidently be expected that the urban share of the population will exceed 85 per cent within a few years.[16] So rapid has been the movement from rural to urban areas that the urban population of the United States in 1960 was larger than the total population in 1930.[17] As James Reston observed, the "damn people won't stand still."[18]

The problem is further complicated by the fact that, as the population has concentrated more and more in an ever-smaller land mass, the governmental units competing to rule the urban and rural areas alike have steadily increased in number, complexity, and extent of

12. Id. at 39–40.
13. Id. at 40.
14. Statistical Abstract 20 (1963).
15. Schattschneider, Urbanization and Reapportionment, 72 Yale L.J. 1 (1962).
16. Weaver, The Future of the American City 4 (1962).
17. Id. at 4.
18. N.Y. Times, Aug. 15, 1962, p. 30, col. 3.

overlap one with another. By 1962 the local units of government (counties, towns, cities, villages, school districts, etc.) had reached the staggering total of 91,185, of which more than nine tenths had property-taxing authority.[19] Curiously enough, the largest number of governmental units is not necessarily in the more populous states. Kansas, for example, with a population slightly more than two million in 1962, had almost as many governmental units (5,410) as the states of Connecticut, New Jersey, and New York (5,595) with a combined population of more than thirty million;[20] and Kansas had many more than the 1,400 units of government which have proved far too cumbersome for the three-state metropolitan area of which New York City is the hub.[21]

Nonetheless, in the face of the demonstrated administrative and bureaucratic chaos which is the inevitable result of this governmental sprawl, the state legislatures have been unable or unwilling to take effective corrective measures.

THE STATISTICS OF MALAPPORTIONMENT

It is part of the customary wisdom of the times that nearly any proposition can be proved — or disproved — by an artful arrangement of figures without quite falsifying the statistical truth. But no one suggests that the facts of state legislative apportionment can be arranged or rearranged to prove anything but the bald truth that malapportionment has long been the rule.[22]

Although it is taken for granted that legislators are elected from districts defined along political subdivision lines or on some other geographic basis, that fact alone is not very illuminating. The district could be the entire state, as in the case of the Illinois lower house in the elections of November 1964, involving an at-large election of the 177 members of the house of representatives.[23]

19. Statistical Abstract 415 (1963). Of the total, 34,678 were school districts and the remaining 56,507 were divided among counties, municipalities, townships, and various special districts.

20. Ibid.

21. See Wood, 1400 Governments (1961).

22. The same is also true, although less dramatically, in congressional districting, which is discussed infra at pages 222–33.

23. That unusual case was the result of a political impasse within the state apportionment commission, as more fully explained in the Illinois summary in the appendix.

Most districts elect only one member; but in 1955, 45.4 per cent of all the lower house seats in state legislatures were chosen in multi-member districts.[24] Multimember districts have sometimes resulted from efforts to adjust representation to population or from state constitutional requirements which forbid the internal division of any county into separate election districts. As a result, the possibility of gerrymandering within those areas is eliminated. But the disadvantages of the multimember district probably outweigh the advantages, particularly as the number to be elected increases in metropolitan areas. The difficulty of providing adequate representation for political views held by a minority, always serious in a representative democracy, is substantially increased by the winner-take-all philosophy inherent in any multimember district election.

There are various statistical ways in which analysis can be made of existing inequalities, but all point to the same conclusion. Here it will suffice to enumerate the most common standards for measuring population disparities among election districts and to summarize the conclusions.

The simplest way of measuring state legislative malapportionment is to note the number of legislative bodies which are based entirely, partially, or not at all on population. Although the apportionment formulas present some problems of classification, generalizations can be drawn to make the point with considerable accuracy. This method showed these bases for apportionment in 1960 in the 99 state legislative chambers (49 bicameral legislatures plus the Nebraska unicameral legislature): 32 relied in large part on population; 8 used population but with weighted ratios; 45 combined population and area considerations; 8 granted equal representation to each unit; 5 had a fixed constitutional apportionment; and 1 (the New Hampshire senate) was based on state tax payments.[25] These conclusions somewhat understate the actual disregard of population as the basis of representation because this summary is drawn exclusively from the state constitutional requirements, without adjustment for violation of those provisions.[26]

24. Klain, A New Look at the Constituencies: The Need for a Recount and a Reappraisal, 49 Am. Pol. Sci. Rev. 1109 (1955).

25. Baker, State Constitutions: Reapportionment 5 (National Municipal League pamphlet 1960).

26. Another way of looking at existing apportionment formulas is to examine their consequences for particular urban and suburban areas to note the extent of underrepresentation. For this purpose Gordon E. Baker classified all the principal

More discriminating statistical methods permit the isolation of other relevant data. Perhaps the most commonly used have been the Dauer-Kelsay measures of representativeness, based on ingeniously simple calculations which effectively illustrate the varying degrees of apportionment inequality.[27] The method involves the computation of the theoretical minimum percentage of the state population that can elect a majority of each house. This percentage figure is arrived at by placing the various legislative districts in rank order from the smallest population per member to the largest. Beginning with the smallest population end of the scale the districts are cumulated to reach that portion of the population of the state that has the power to elect a majority of the house in question. While this method does not reflect the dramatic differentials between the least populous and the most populous election districts (the range is from 2 to 1 to 987 to 1), it has the advantage of dealing with averages rather than the possibly aberrational extremes.

No one claims that the least populous districts regularly act together to exercise their full potential for subordination of majority control; but equally it is not possible to deny the potential for minority veto of majority will. Indeed, it is clear that malapportionment not only confers the power of veto upon majority action, but in some instances actually bestows upon minority groups affirma-

---

metropolitan areas as of 1955 into five groups, ranging from severe underrepresentation to approximate equality. The extremes are interesting, as noted in this abridged extract of his study (Baker, Rural Versus Urban Political Power 16–17 (1955)):

States	Selected Urban Areas	Per Cent of State Population	Per Cent of Lower House	Per Cent of Upper House
		GROUP I — SEVERE		
Georgia	6 largest urban counties	32	9	7
Florida	9 most urban counties	60	23	24
Delaware	Wilmington urbanized area	59	23	24
Maryland	Baltimore & 3 largest urban counties	67	44	31
Connecticut	10 largest cities	46	7	46
Rhode Island	10 largest cities	77	67	34
New Jersey	8 largest urban counties	75	73	38
California	4 largest urban counties	59	59	10

* * *

GROUP V — EQUAL REPRESENTATION

States	Selected Urban Areas	Per Cent of State Population	Per Cent of Lower House	Per Cent of Upper House
Wisconsin	3 largest urban counties	50	50	50
Massachusetts	All cities over 50,000 population	33	32	33

27. For the original development, see Dauer and Kelsay, Unrepresentative States, 44 Nat'l Munic. Rev. 571–75, 587 (1955), 45 id. 198 (1956).

tive legislative power. Accordingly, the Dauer-Kelsay method provides a useful index of the general prevalence of inequalities in representation. Significantly, this was the index most commonly used by Chief Justice Warren in demonstrating the extent of the voter inequalities in the 1964 *Reapportionment Cases.*

Using this method, it was demonstrable that, shortly before these cases were decided, a voting majority could be elected in each of eight state senates by less than 20 per cent of the population, including California (10.7 per cent), Florida (12.3 per cent) and Nevada (8 per cent). In only thirteen was as much as 40 per cent of the population required for majority control. On the lower house side there were five states in which potential majority control was in the hands of fewer than 20 per cent of the voters, while only ten required more than 40 per cent for such control.[28]

Using the same system it is also possible to compile an "index of representativeness" by adding together the percentage figures required for control of each house of a bicameral state legislature. It is interesting to observe that, although Virginia was second most representative on that scale and New York twelfth, the Supreme Court found both apportionment formulas invalid.[29] This suggests either that the scale may not have been sufficiently discriminating by itself or that there were other constitutional difficulties with the particular formulas. A still more likely inference from the Supreme Court opinions would seem to be that *both* speculations are correct.

If the Dauer-Kelsay method is at all defective, it is that its conclusions are too general to reveal particular inequities which affect individual groups of voters in their own election districts. To supply this perspective Paul T. David and Ralph Eisenberg looked directly at the voter to see how his franchise was faring, using "methods that bring out differences in the relative value of the vote as it varies from place to place and changes from time to time."[30]

As a basis for these computations two stable factors were isolated for comparison: the average value of the vote on a statewide basis (here commonly referred to as the voter ratio); and the county as a

28. Advisory Commission on Intergovernmental Relations, Report on Apportionment of State Legislatures, App. B (1962).

29. Davis v. Mann, 377 U.S. 678 (1964); WMCA, Inc. v. Lomenzo, 377 U.S. 633 (1964).

30. I David and Eisenberg, Devaluation of the Urban and Suburban Vote 7 (1961). See also II id. (1962).

basic territorial unit. It was then possible to compute relative values of the vote for any county in comparison with the relative value of the vote in any other county in the same state.[31]

From the resulting calculations David and Eisenberg concluded that the overrepresentation of counties with a population under 25,000 in 1910 (the first year studied) was substantial compared with the underrepresentation of counties with a population over 500,000. The differential widened in each of the successive census years studied until in 1960 the value of the vote was down to 76 per cent of statewide norms for the larger counties and up to 171 per cent for the smaller counties.[32] They concluded: "The progressive disfranchisement of the urban voter has been going on in the country at large for at least 50 years on a scale that suggests that only some decisive change in the system could bring a general reversal."[33]

Another particularly interesting conclusion of the study is that the value of the vote actually increased in more than half of the central cities of the 27 largest metropolitan areas of the United States between 1910 and 1960; but in every case there was a corresponding decline, often quite severe, in the value of the vote in the adjacent suburban areas. Although the representation disadvantage to the cities remains substantial overall, the issue is now most sharply drawn between rural and suburban areas.

The statistics of state legislative apportionment, as of April 15, 1964, shortly before the Supreme Court's apportionment decisions in June 1964, are reproduced in the table at pages 46–47.

Statistics at large, however, do not tell the whole story. Particular instances of unconscionable inequality in voter representation are also useful in showing both the discriminations that were intended and those that were more the product of inadvertence than of design. Examples could have been taken in 1962 from almost every state, but a few will illustrate the variety of inequality.[34] At that time three New England states still provided representation for towns

31. Distorting factors peculiar to some states are summarized in the report, I id. at 7–8, but will not be repeated here because they are of minimal significance to the conclusions.

32. The 1960 figures were in most cases before redistricting on the basis of the 1960 census figures. Subsequent reapportionment enlarged the differences.

33. Id. at 10. See also Table 8, id. at 15.

34. See also Boyd, Patterns of Apportionment (National Municipal League pamphlet, 1962); Goldberg, The Statistics of Malapportionment, 72 Yale L.J. 90 (1962).

Comparative Data on the Composition of State Legislative Districts During 1963 and/or 1964 Sessions

State	Senate — Number of Senators (1963 and/or 1964)	Senate — Average Population per Senator	Senate — Largest District per Senator	Senate — Smallest District per Senator	Senate — Minimum Per Cent of Population That Can Elect Majority of Senators	Lower House — Number of Representatives (1963 and/or 1964)	Lower House — Average Population per Legislator	Lower House — Largest District per Legislator	Lower House — Smallest District per Legislator	Lower House — Minimum Per Cent of Population That Can Elect Majority of Lower House Members
Alabama	35	93,278	634,864	31,715	27.6	106	30,818	50,718	10,726	37.9
Alaska	20	11,308	88,021	4,603	41.9	40	5,654	7,174	2,945	47.3
Arizona	28	46,506	331,755	3,868	12.8	80	16,277	30,438	5,754	46.0a
Arkansas	35	51,036	80,993	35,983	43.8	100	17,863	31,686	4,927	33.3
California	39	392,930	6,038,771	14,294	10.7	80	196,465	306,191	72,105	44.7
Colorado	35	44,077	73,340	19,983	33.0	65	26,983	35,123	20,302	45.1
Connecticut	36	70,423	175,940	21,627	32.0	294	8,623	81,089	191	12.0
Delaware	17	26,252	64,820	4,177	22.4	35	12,751	58,228	1,643	18.5
Florida	45	115,152	467,523	12,276	14.1	124	44,210	66,788	2,868	22.9
Georgia	54	73,021	95,082	52,572	48.3	205	19,235	185,442	1,876	22.2
Hawaii	25	25,310	63,620	8,518	18.1	51	12,407	23,779	5,030	38.4
Idaho	44	15,163	93,460	915	16.6	63	10,590	15,576	915	32.7
Illinois	58	178,812	565,300	53,500	28.7	174	56,596	160,200	34,433	39.9
Indiana	48	93,250	171,090	39,011	38.5	99	46,625	145,824	14,804	36.5
Iowa	50	55,110	266,314	29,696	35.6	108	25,532	133,157	7,468	27.4
Kansas	39	54,125	323,574	16,280	27.5	125	17,378	64,423	2,241	19.0
Kentucky	37	79,951	120,700	62,048	46.6	99	30,382	40,480	20,166	44.8
Louisiana	39	83,513	248,427	31,174	33.0	105	31,019	57,622	6,909	33.1
Maine	34	28,508	45,687	16,146	46.9	151	6,418	13,102	2,394	39.7

Minnesota	67	50,953	99,440	20,458	40.1	135	26,060	99,446	8,343	34.5
Mississippi	52	44,452	187,045	20,987	37.2	122	15,558	26,361	3,576	41.2
Missouri	34	127,053	160,288	96,477	47.8	163	26,502	53,015	3,936	20.3
Montana	56	12,049	79,016	894	16.1	94	7,178	12,537	894	40.8
Nebraska	43	32,822	51,757	18,824	36.6	Unicameral Legislature				
Nevada	17	16,781	127,016	568	8.0	37	7,710	12,525	568	29.1
New Hampshire	24	25,288	41,457	15,829	45.3	400	1,517	1,779	8	43.9[b]
New Jersey	21	288,894	923,545	48,555	19.0	60	101,113	143,913	48,555	46.5
New Mexico	32	29,719	262,199	1,874	14.0	66	14,394	29,133	1,874	27.0
New York	58	280,014	650,014	168,398	41.8	150	108,272	314,721	15,044	34.7
North Carolina	50	91,123	272,111	45,031	36.9	120	37,968	82,059	4,520	27.1
North Dakota	49	12,907	42,041	4,698	31.9	113	5,499	8,408	2,665	40.2
Ohio	33	294,133	439,000	203,163	44.8	137	70,850	148,700	10,274	29.4
Oklahoma	44	52,916	346,038	13,125	24.5	121	19,402	62,787	4,496	29.5
Oregon	30	58,956	69,684	29,917	47.8	60	29,478	39,660	18,955	48.1
Pennsylvania	50	226,387	553,154	51,793	33.1	210	53,902	139,293	4,485	37.7
Rhode Island	46	18,684	47,080	486	18.1	100	8,594	18,977	486	46.5
South Carolina	46	51,796	216,382	8,629	23.3	124	19,214	29,490	8,629	46.0
South Dakota	35	19,443	43,288	10,039	38.4	75	9,074	16,688	3,531	38.6
Tennessee	33	108,093	133,448	83,031	44.5	99	36,031	50,105	22,275	39.7
Texas	31	309,022	1,243,158	147,454	30.3	150	62,864	105,725	33,987	38.7
Utah	25	35,625	64,760	9,408	21.3	64	13,916	32,380	1,164	33.3
Vermont	30	12,996	16,014	2,927	47.0	246	1,585	35,531	24	11.9
Virginia	40	99,174	163,401	61,730	41.1	100	39,669	95,064	21,825	40.5
Washington	49	58,229	145,180	20,023	33.9	99	28,820	57,648	12,399	35.3
West Virginia	32	58,138	126,463	37,192	43.9	100	18,604	39,615	4,391	38.9
Wisconsin	33	119,780	208,343	74,293	42.5	100	39,528	87,486	19,651	39.9
Wyoming	27	12,225	30,074	3,062	26.9	56	5,894	10,025	3,062	35.8

Source: Prepared by State Consultants for the National Municipal League.

a. Exact figure for per cent necessary to control lower house in Arizona not available, since exact boundary lines for districts are drawn by county, not state, agencies.

b. Only towns having 800 or more inhabitants are represented in every legislative session, and some of these with only minor consideration to population, a practice copied from England where it had long before been abandoned. Vermont simply assigned one representative to each town regardless of population so that a town of 38 people received the same representation as the state's largest city with a population of 35,531. Connecticut gave each town under 5,000 one representative; all above that figure were allowed two except that some older towns with populations below 5,000 also got two, for "historic" reasons. As a result, two towns, ranging in population from 383 (Union) to 162,178 (Hartford) chose two representatives each. On the other hand, some states fixed maximum limitations on the representation of political subdivisions. The most startling was California, in which no county was allowed more than one senator. As a result, Los Angeles County (population 6,038,771) had one senator — as did the twenty-eighth senatorial district (population 14,294).

In addition to inequalities produced by state constitutional provisions which require disproportionate representation, in 1962 there were also in most states strange, often unexplainable instances of inequality of the kind Justice Clark called "crazy quilt" in *Baker v. Carr*. Four of the cases decided by the Supreme Court on June 15, 1964, illustrate the point (although the facts related below were apparently not essential to the Court's determination of invalidity in each case).[35]

Alabama: On the eastern edge of Alabama, near the Florida line, are clustered five counties, all largely rural in nature, with 1960 population figures as follows: Barbour (24,700); Bullock (13,462); Lee (49,754); Macon (26,717); and Russell (46,351). Before the 1962 judicial reapportionment, Barbour, Lee, and Russell Counties were allotted two representatives and the others only one. Macon County, with one, had a larger population than Barbour County, with two. The population per representative in Macon County was more than twice that of Barbour County. On the senate side the picture was not different in the same counties. District number 24 consisted of Barbour County alone (24,700); district number 26 included Bullock and Macon (40,179); and district number 27 included Lee and Russell (96,105). The arrangement makes no sense at all.

Maryland: Washington County, with a 1960 population of 91,219,

35. See Brief for American Jewish Congress, American Civil Liberties Union, NAACP Legal Defense and Educational Fund, Inc. as Amici Curiae, pp. 21–23, Reynolds v. Sims (and related cases), 377 U.S. 533 (1964).

had one senator, as did Queen Annes County, with a population of 16,569, and Baltimore County, with a population of about half a million. The three suburban counties of Anne Arundel, Montgomery, and Prince Georges had three senators for about one million while the city of Baltimore, with a population of less than a million, had six senators. In this instance discrimination without rational pattern cut both ways. The rural counties were favored over urban and suburban alike, while the exclusively urban counties were favored at the expense of the suburban.

New York: Disparities of two to one were compelled by the state constitution, with respect to the size of assembly districts in a single county, entirely without regard to the rural or urban character of that county. This was the case, for example, in Onondaga County, where the assembly districts ranged in size (on the basis of the still-controlling 1950 citizen population) from 83,613 to 167,226.

Virginia: Adjacent districts with apparently similar voter compositions varied widely in terms of population represented by individual senators and delegates. To give a single example: Two senatorial districts at the remote western tip of Virginia differed in population ratio by more than two to one despite the fact that they were adjacent and both were essentially rural. Lee and Scott Counties made up a senate district with a 1960 population of 51,637, while Buchanan, Russell, and Tazewell Counties, also cumulated into a single district, had a population of 107,805. If Russell, for instance, had been joined to Lee and Scott, the differential between the two districts would have been less than 5 per cent.

THE CAUSES OF MALAPPORTIONMENT

The fact of malapportionment is clear. The causes are scarcely less evident. The root causes suggested above are essentially two, each of which works uniformly to the disadvantage of the urban-suburban complex and sometimes, but more erratically, to the disadvantage of particular low-population areas.

1. *State Constitutional Limitations.* A number of state constitutions provide that each county (town in three states) shall be assured at least one representative in one house (sometimes in both houses); other constitutions provide that no county shall have more than one representative in one chamber. Obviously, both types of provision, operating separately or in combination, produce dis-

tortions of the equal-population principle. To the extent that such provisions date from the early state constitutions, the distortion was originally not very great because large metropolitan centers did not exist, the entire population was rather evenly distributed, and there were at first a much smaller number of counties.

Kansas, a rather typical instance, illustrates the point. While still a territory, Kansas apportioned both houses on a population basis; but its original state constitution of 1861 provided that each county should have one representative, with the remaining members distributed according to population. Since the constitution provided for a house of 75 to 100 members and Kansas had only 34 counties, population was still the primary factor. However, by the time the western part of the state became organized, there were 105 counties and a constitutional maximum of 125 representatives. After the 1950 census Kansas' three largest counties contained 26 per cent of the population but were limited to 7 per cent of the seats in the lower house.

In other states legislators from areas of declining population could see that time and the shifting trends of population would eventually deprive them of their legislative seats so long as the population basis for representation should be continued. Accordingly, a rationale was constructed as a basis for denying equality of voter representation. Of the many states which took such action beginning with the latter part of the nineteenth century, New York is a good example.

When New York adopted its original constitution in 1777 there were only 14 counties, divided into four regional districts. Each district included from two to six counties, and from three to nine senators were apportioned to each of the districts, apparently in rough approximation to the estimated number of qualified electors.[36] The process of creating new counties began shortly thereafter, but was not complete until after the middle of the nineteenth century. Even then, the requirement of representation in accordance with population was maintained in both houses. Not until the constitution of 1894 was the formula changed to that invalidated in 1964 by the Supreme Court in *WMCA, Inc. v. Lomenzo.*[37] The reasons were made perfectly clear. As one delegate put it, "the average citizen in the rural district is superior in intelligence, superior in morality,

---

36. 3 Lincoln's Constitutional History of New York 168–69 (1906).

37. 377 U.S. 633 (1964).

superior in self-government, to the average citizen of the great cities . . . [and] your government will be safer in his hands than in the hands of the average citizen of the great cities."[38]

2. *Failure to Reapportion as Required.* Other legislatures, presumably unwilling to abandon formal allegiance to a constitutional requirement of equality in matters of voter representation, have reduced that protestation of belief in equality to a mere façade by failing to honor the state constitutional mandate. Aggravated instances of this failure to act came before the United States Supreme Court in *Baker v. Carr* and in *Reynolds v. Sims* where the Tennessee and Alabama legislatures respectively had failed to make any reapportionment for more than sixty years. While the failure to act in accordance with the state constitutional requirement for decennial reapportionment was not regarded as a denial of any federal constitutional right, the resulting "crazy quilt" disparities were held to deny the equal protection of the laws guaranteed by the fourteenth amendment to the United States Constitution.[39]

Legislative failure to act despite a state requirement of periodic reapportionment was so common that by 1961 at least one house of seventeen state legislatures was invalidly constituted as a matter of state constitutional law, simply through failure to take action required by state law.[40] In addition, the reapportionment actually accomplished in a number of other states was merely token and not in compliance with the equal-population requirements of the respective state constitutions. Finally, a number of the state constitutions either did not require reapportionment or were so restrictive in their provisions that little room was left for accommodation to the shifts in population which were everywhere taking place.

THE APPORTIONMENT PROCESS IN THE STATES

The Dilemma for the Individual Legislator. When every county or town is assured equal representation in one chamber of a legislature, population is disregarded entirely in that chamber. The

38. 4 Revised Records of the Constitutional Convention of the State of New York 10–11 (1900).

39. In the *Baker* case Justice Brennan noted that "It is primarily the continued application of the 1901 Apportionment Act to this shifted and enlarged voting population which gives rise to the present controversy." 369 U.S. 186, 192 (1962).

40. Advisory Commission on Intergovernmental Relations, Report on Apportionment of State Legislatures, App. A. (1962).

situation is not materially different in the states in which the number of counties assured at least one representative presses close against the number of seats authorized for the body. The size of the legislative body then imposes significant limitations upon any attempt at representation in proportion to population. The case of Iowa, prior to the 1964 Supreme Court decision in *Hill v. Davis*, was typical.[41] The Iowa constitution of 1857 established population as the controlling principle for both houses. Early in the twentieth century, however, the less populous counties secured amendments to limit the representation of the growing urban counties. The result was to guarantee each of the 99 counties one representative in the 108-member lower house, thus allowing only nine additional seats to be divided among the most populous counties.

The significance of these limitations is emphasized by the further fact that the state senates range in size from 17 to 67, while the lower houses vary from 35 to 400. It becomes axiomatic that the smaller the legislative body the less is the likelihood that the demand for equality of representation can be accommodated to the practice of giving representation to political subdivisions of the state. For example, if Georgia's 159 counties were each to receive separate representation and still meet the equal-population requirement, the house would have to consist of nearly 3,000 members.

State legislatures have always had difficulty with the task of reapportionment. The hard question has been this: Shall the areas of growing population be given the additional representation to which their enlarged numbers entitle them, or shall the areas of declining population be allowed to retain their control? The manner in which reapportionment questions are resolved is important to political parties, to interest groups, to the integrity of the governmental process, and to the people generally. But to the affected legislators the matter involves no less an issue than political survival. It is never easy to effect a genuine reapportionment that fairly takes into account shifts in population and logical district structure; it is far more tempting for legislators to carve up the districts of those not seeking re-election or to add new seats rather than to redistribute existing districts. "Redistricting proposals that dislodge a minimum number of sitting members, irrespective of party, will be favored over proposals that do not take into account sitting members."[42]

41. 378 U.S. 565 (1964).
42. Steiner and Gove, The Legislature Redistricts Illinois 5 (The Institute of Government and Public Affairs, University of Illinois, 1956).

The Partisan Element. Party politics is obviously a factor in determining the form any particular reapportionment will take, but it is difficult to assess the precise impact. The aphorism of Al Smith that the New York legislature was "constitutionally Republican" tells only part of the story. In statewide elections the state of New York has given its electoral votes almost evenly to Republican and Democratic presidential candidates in the half century before 1964, and has divided its electoral favor rather evenly between Republican and Democratic governors and United States Senators. Yet during that period the Democrats won control of the state legislature only twice before 1964. So New York has been described as "a two-party state with a one-party Legislature."[43] Unquestionably, the New York Constitution of 1894 has long made it easier for Republicans to retain control of the legislature. The 1964 election, in which the Democrats gained control of both houses, ended the Republican suzerainty. What would have happened in another election on the basis of that apportionment formula cannot now be known in view of changes later made in the formula.

There are many who believe that, as the central cities decline in proportion to the total state population in New York (and elsewhere), Republican advantage may well be found in giving full representation in proportion to population, which has been denied since 1894 in New York. The Republicans, however, do not seem convinced, in New York or elsewhere. It is the Republicans who are generally more apt to find judicial excess in the apportionment decisions, while the Democrats seem more inclined to voice cautious approval. It is not necessarily cynical to speculate that these relative hesitations and tentative enthusiasms are not based exclusively on high-minded considerations of the public weal or the proper role of the judiciary in the American scheme of government.

Intra-party politics inject a further imponderable into the already confused situation. Again New York may be representative.

> The position of Tammany legislators is illustrative of the politics of reapportionment in several states today where politicians of the city proper team up with rural county legislators to oppose redistricting along population lines because both are likely to lose some seats to the growing metropolitan area.[44]

43. Tyler and Wells, New York: "Constitutionally Republican," in Jewell (ed.), The Politics of Reapportionment 221 (1962).

44. Bone, States Attempting to Comply with Reapportionment Requirements, 17 L. and Contemp. Prob. 387, 401 (1952).

Similarly, California legislators from the metropolitan areas of northern California have not uncommonly joined forces with rural interests in order to block representation for southern California in proportion to population.[45]

Nonlegislative Reapportionment. By 1962 some thirteen states had sought to alleviate the personal and political difficulties that made fair reapportionment so nearly impossible. The usual technique was to remove that function partially or completely from the legislature. Ohio was the first to adopt this approach, in 1851; most of the others have taken this step only in recent years.

The thirteen states fall into two basic groups. The first, including California, Illinois, Michigan, North Dakota, Oregon, South Dakota, and Texas, provide for nonlegislative apportionment if the legislature fails to act within a designated time. The second group, including Alaska, Arizona, Arkansas, Hawaii, Missouri, and Ohio, have removed the legislature completely from the apportionment process.[46]

Both these plans for lessening the political passions which have so often endangered or defeated reapportionments undoubtedly produced greater compliance with state constitutional provisions. However, the political factors are not entirely removed where, as in Illinois in 1964, the apportionment commission, composed of an equal number of representatives from each of the two principal parties, could not reach agreement, with the result of an at-large election for 177 house seats. The more serious, because more typical, problem arises out of the fact that an apportionment commission or other similar body can act only within the framework of the state constitution. So long as state constitutions mandate inequality, the solution is at best partial.

By 1962 seven state constitutions — those of Alaska, Arkansas, Hawaii, New York, Oklahoma, Oregon, and Texas — specifically provided for court review of apportionment plans.[47]

45. See Way, California: "Brutal Butchery of the Two-Party System?", in Jewell (ed.), The Politics of Reapportionment 249 (1962). See also Advisory Commission on Intergovernmental Relations, Report on Apportionment of State Legislatures 19–22 (1962).

46. Advisory Commission on Intergovernmental Relations, op. cit. supra note 45, at 21–22. See also Report of the Governor's Reapportionment Commission, January 15, 1965, 49 Minn. L. Rev. 367, 420–45 (1964).

47. Advisory Commission on Intergovernmental Relations, op. cit. supra note 45, at 22.

THE CONSEQUENCES OF MALAPPORTIONMENT

In deciding the apportionment cases the Supreme Court quite properly analyzed the constitutional issue in terms of harm to the individual voter-plaintiffs who were before the Court. Once jurisdiction, justiciability, and standing had been agreed upon in *Baker*, the rest in a sense followed.[48] There was, for instance, little doubt that the right of franchise was a personal and present right. Therefore, once it was determined that the plaintiffs were suffering a dilution or diminution of that right, judicial intervention was almost assured.

As a result of that analysis, however, the Court necessarily treated the issue in individualized terms without having any occasion to inquire into the question whether the harms of malapportionment extended beyond the individual and worked as well to the detriment of underrepresented groups of voters. Although this issue is in a way extraneous to the constitutional question, there can be no doubt that if it can be established that malapportionment does bring such harms in its wake, that fact would add comforting assurance to the soundness of the constitutional conclusion and would buttress the arguments against constitutional amendments proposed to overturn the apportionment cases.

To the extent that urban and suburban dwellers find their voice in state government muted by malapportioned legislatures, the communities in which they live are short-changed in a variety of ways at the hands of legislators who primarily represent voters from the less populous areas of the state. The disadvantage may arise out of discrimination aimed directly at the underrepresented areas, such as denial of needed benefits, or it may result indirectly from simple inattention to the rather special, often uniquely complex, problems of the urban communities.

Discrimination by Design. The specifics of discrimination are difficult to identify with satisfactory precision, but it is at least clear that the more populous areas are to some extent disadvantaged by their lack of representation in proportion to population. The Conference of Mayors, referring to urban dwellers as "second-class citi-

48. The cases are discussed in chapters III–VI.

zens," has estimated, for example, that the nation's urbanites pay 90 per cent of all taxes, but at the state level have only about 25 per cent of the legislative representation.[49] More specific evidence is also available. Relevant here is the case of the Chicago metropolitan areas in relation to the downstate-controlled legislature. In 1925 the Cook County Board of Commissioners unanimously adopted a resolution directing the county treasurer to withhold state taxes collected by the county until the general assembly should have performed its reapportionment obligations. The treasurer did not comply, but in the same year the Chicago City Council called for a two-year campaign for reapportionment to be followed, if unsuccessful, by a move for secession. Although this too was a futile gesture, it does demonstrate the intensity of urban sentiments.[50]

In the New York case (*WMCA, Inc. v. Lomenzo,* supra) the plaintiffs offered at the trial to show in some detail the financial discrimination suffered by New York City. For example, despite the fact that New York City accounted at the time for 46 per cent of the total state population, the city received only 38 per cent of the combined aid funds distributed to local governments by the state. If New York City had been given its full share in 1961–62, it would have received another $108 million. Aid to education is particularly illuminating. Under the so-called "equalization" formula, New York City received $197 in school aid for each student in its public schools, while the average in the rest of the state was $314.[51] No one suggests that the public school problems are less complex or less costly in New York City than elsewhere, nor indeed that the problems of that metropolitan area are not in fact more complex and costly to deal with than in less populous areas. This obvious fact is further evidenced by the fact that New York City found it necessary to impose a 4 per cent sales tax to assist in meeting these heavy outlays long before a smaller tax was imposed in the rest of the state.

In the Tennessee case, *Baker v. Carr,* the plaintiffs alleged urban disadvantage in these terms:

> In the 1957–1958 apportionment of the county aid funds, the General Assembly permitted 23 counties to receive 57.9% more state aid than would be the case on a basis of state aid per capita, and it turns out that these counties had 23 more direct representatives than permitted under the state

49. Baker, Rural versus Urban Political Power 4, 27 (1955).
50. Id. at 27.
51. Transcript of Record 250–55, WMCA, Inc. v. Lomenzo, 377 U.S. 633 (1964).

constitution. Ten counties, having 25 less direct representatives than required by the Tennessee Constitution, among them Shelby, Knox, Hamilton, and Davidson, received 136.9% [*sic*] less state aid than on a per capita basis. Expressed another way, a voter in Moore County (with a voting population in 1950 of 2,340) has 17 times as much representation in the lower House as does a voter in Davidson County (1950 voting population 211,930), and Moore County receives 17 times the apportionment per vehicle of state gasoline taxes as does Davidson County.[52]

It has also been suggested that the overrepresentation of west Tennessee may be one of the explanations for adoption by the Tennessee legislature of resolutions condemning the Supreme Court decision on school desegregation, whereas such Tennessee cities as Nashville have been cited as models for their constructive methods of implementing those decisions.[53]

Other instances of disadvantage to the more populous areas in nonfinancial matters are found in recent Maryland experience. In 1963 the grossly unrepresentative state senate refused to abandon the unit vote system even after the decision in *Gray v. Sanders*[54] had invalidated the equivalent Georgia plan. Similarly, the 1963 Equal Accommodations bill contained exemptions for 12 counties, all rural, apparently the price of enactment.[55]

The Maryland legislature also illustrates how malapportionment of state legislatures can well lead to parallel discrimination in congressional districting. The Maryland legislature in 1963 approved a congressional districting bill establishing a district for the Eastern Shore counties with a population of 243,570, while another district, including populous Montgomery County, was fixed at 608,666 residents.[56] The experiences with congressional districting are of course similar throughout the nation.

Discrimination by Oversight. Malapportionment also damages the state governmental process by its impairment of effective relations between the state and local governments within the state. Many states have granted partial home rule to some cities or to

52. Brief for Appellants 13, Baker v. Carr, 369 U.S. 186 (1962). See also Transcript of Record 59, Maryland Committee for Fair Representation v. Tawes, 377 U.S. 656 (1964).

53. Crane, Tennessee: "Inertia and the Courts," in Jewell (ed.), The Politics of Reapportionment 314 (1962).

54. 372 U.S. 368 (1963).

55. See Note, Senate Reapportionment — The Maryland Experience, 31 Geo. Wash. L. Rev. 812, 822 (1963).

56. Id. at 821.

various classes of municipalities within those states. This has undoubtedly been useful in the solution of some kinds of local problems, but in many cases it has proved inadequate or worse. In the
first place, the growth of the metropolitan center as a complex of
different units of sometimes competing governments has meant
that, no matter how complete the home rule of the central city, it
often remained powerless to deal with what had become essentially
regional problems. Meanwhile, the state legislatures have generally
shown notable lack of concern for resolving the inevitable conflicts
between urban and suburban groups. The absence of adequate
authority has too often meant that no action is — or can be — taken
toward the solution of pressing problems.[57] In Kansas, for example, hardly a highly urbanized state, "The legislature actually ab-
dicates the general legislative function by yielding to any local government's request for a new or amended power as long as that
power is narrow in scope and is made special for that unit alone."[58]
The tendency is thus for a legislature to offer local governments
narrowly circumscribed authority and then to disclaim further responsibility for ensuing problems. Surely more attention would
be given such matters if the legislative representation were more
rationally and equitably distributed.

Finally, despite general agreement that county consolidation
would be desirable in many states, it is difficult to accomplish that
result where representation is tied to county units of government.
Where consolidation would reduce representation for the affected
area, it has been all but impossible to secure the necessary legislation.

The facts and figures in this chapter demonstrate that malapportionment is a fact; that it works to the actual disadvantage of the
groups underrepresented in the state legislatures; and that correction is not available through the legislatures themselves, too many
of whose members are beneficiaries of the ever-worsening situation. Next we will examine the gradual acceptance of the notion that
the apportionment of state legislatures is appropriate for judicial
inquiry.

57. Advisory Commission on Intergovernmental Relations, Report on Apportionment of State Legislatures 26–27 (1962).

58. Page, Legislative Apportionment in Kansas 136 (Bureau of Government Research, University of Kansas, 1952).

CHAPTER III

Apportionment and

Federal Judicial Power:

From Colegrove to Baker

Baker v. Carr[1] raised two questions: (1) May the federal courts pass on claims of voter discrimination arising out of legislative malapportionment? (2) If so, what standards should control? In Baker the Supreme Court answered the first question in the affirmative, thus necessitating an ultimate answer to the second question. The second question was answered two years later in the Reapportionment Cases.[2] The answer to the first question, which should have been easy, had been made to seem hard. The reasons for the seeming difficulty, and the straightforward answer of six members of the Court (increased to eight in 1964),[3] will be examined briefly here. The question of standards will be discussed in later chapters.

1. 369 U.S. 186 (1962).
2. Reynolds v. Sims, 377 U.S. 533 (1964) and companion cases.
3. Justice Whittaker did not participate, and Justices Frankfurter and Harlan dissented in the Baker case. Whittaker was replaced by Justice Byron R. White on April 16, 1962, and Justice Frankfurter was replaced by Justice Arthur J. Goldberg on October 1, 1962. In the 1964 cases both of the new Justices agreed with the majority on the question of the appropriateness of the exercise of judicial power (and on all other issues), leaving Justice Harlan the sole dissenter on the issue of justiciability.

Although it might ordinarily seem inappropriate, or at least unnecessary, to re-examine such preliminary jurisdictional questions
once they have been definitively settled to permit judicial review
of the merits, there are in this instance special reasons for at least a
cursory restatement of the issues and their resolution. In the first
place, the preliminary procedural issues of jurisdiction, justiciability, and standing are, in the context of apportionment, inescapably intertwined with the ultimate issues of substance having to
do with standards and remedies. Moreover, earlier cases in the
Supreme Court, in the lower federal courts, and in the state courts
could not fairly be said to speak with a single voice, or even in multi-
part harmony. One of the incidental but not inconsiderable benefits of the decision in *Baker* was that a new path was found through
the maze of seemingly (and sometimes actually) conflicting decisions. Both points deserve attention.

POLITICAL QUESTIONS AND
POLITICAL THICKETS

The principal argument against judicial intervention arose less
from any belief that there was an absolute lack of power than from
doubts about the ability of courts to make an effective contribution.
Such doubts prompted Justice Frankfurter's 1946 warning in *Col-
grove v. Green*[4] (a congressional districting case) that "Courts
ought not to enter this political thicket." Justice Frankfurter later
conceded that in that case there was "not in the strict sense [a] want
of power."[5] Apparently his doubts related more to the merits than to
the question of judicial power, for he said in *Baker*:

> Even assuming the indispensable intellectual disinterestedness on the
> part of judges in such matters, they do not have accepted legal standards
> or criteria or even reliable analogies to draw upon for making judicial
> judgments. To charge courts with the task of accommodating the incom-
> mensurable factors of policy that underlie these mathematical puzzles is
> to attribute, however flatteringly, omnicompetence to judges.[6]

It is necessary to separate the several distinct arguments that
have become intertwined. A contention occasionally advanced is
that the federal courts lack power to hear and decide allegations of

4. 328 U.S. 549, 556 (1946).
5. Baker v. Carr, 369 U.S. 186, 277 (1962) (Frankfurter, J., dissenting).
6. Id. at 268. See also id. at 269–70, 329–30; id. at 337 (Harlan, J., dissenting).

voter discrimination in connection with legislative apportionment and districting. No member of the Supreme Court has taken that position, nor is it defensible; the voter complaints manifestly claim deprivation of individual constitutional rights. Confusion arises because this rejected argument merges almost indistinguishably into the subtly different contention that these matters are so entangled in the political process that courts either should not (as a matter of voluntary withholding of intervention) or must not (because the matter is committed exclusively to state legislatures) accept jurisdiction. It is this contention, in one of its variant forms, that persuaded Justices Frankfurter and Harlan that the federal courts should avoid the "political thickets" for fear that, once they had become entangled, all exits would be barred by nettles. This view leads to the conclusion that apportionment issues are nonjusticiable and that the federal courts should therefore decline jurisdiction. The position has been supported also by some legal scholars who could simultaneously deplore the worsening pattern of legislative representation while finding no judicially acceptable way out of the deepening impasse.[7]

Those who doubt that the courts should act in these cases seem to say: No matter how great the inequities, the courts are not suited to the corrective process. Louis Pollak challenged that view with a pointed question: "Does not the answer lie elsewhere than in a quest for standards of justiciability? Does not the answer lie in the dissenters' apparent view that *on the merits,* taking their complaint at full value, the appellants in *Baker v. Carr* should not prevail?"[8]

Debate on this issue was joined in the Supreme Court in the *Reapportionment Cases* where the majority squarely ruled that the equal protection clause of the fourteenth amendment does include a command that the equal-population principle be substantially satisfied in both houses of bicameral state legislatures. Justice Harlan, dissenting, now argued explicitly that the equal protection clause could not be read to impose *any* limits on legislative freedom in the area of apportionment and districting. All other members of the Court agreed that jurisdiction was proper.

7. See the materials cited by Justice Stewart, dissenting, in Lucas v. Colorado General Assembly, 377 U.S. 713, 744, 746–47, n. 9 (1964).

8. Pollak, Judicial Power and "The Politics of the People," 72 Yale L.J. 81, 85 (1962).

Although the jurisdictional issue is thus settled, it will nonetheless be useful to review how there was for a time so much acceptance of what must almost be described as the myth of lack of judicial power in connection with matters of legislative apportionment.

The issue goes to the roots of American constitutionalism and the meaning of judicial review. To what extent must federal courts decide questions properly presented to them, and in what relatively exceptional circumstances may they avoid making decisions because they are difficult, because they are likely to be unpopular, or because they might aggravate some of the frictions the Constitution was intended to avoid?

The starting point is clear. When there is presented to a federal court in proper form a question "arising under this Constitution, the Laws of the United States, and Treaties made, or which shall be made, under their Authority,"[9] the federal court to which the question is presented is obligated to decide the case except in narrowly confined instances. Confusion has arisen out of attempts to define and delimit the extent of those exceptional circumstances. Justice Brandeis once observed that the Court "has developed, for its own governance in the cases confessedly within its jurisdiction, a series of rules under which it has avoided passing upon a large part of all the constitutional questions pressed upon it for decision."[10] For present purposes the most important of these doctrines of avoidance is the so-called "political question" doctrine. Until the decision in *Baker* this was possibly the largest and certainly the most unconfined of the exceptional bases for withholding jurisdiction.

Although the federal courts have refused from the beginning to decide particular types of cases in reliance on the political question doctrine, application of the principle to state legislative apportionment and congressional districting cases is of recent origin. The two principal cases, both involving aspects of congressional districting rather than state legislative apportionment, were *Colegrove v. Green*,[11] decided in 1946, and *MacDougall v. Green*,[12] decided in 1948; but neither of those cases, when carefully analyzed, holds that even congressional districting issues are not justiciable. Thus, the

9. U.S. Const., art. III, § 2.

10. Ashwander v. TVA, 297 U.S. 288, 346 (1936) (concurring opinion). See also United States v. Lovett, 328 U.S. 303, 320 (1946).

11. 328 U.S. 549 (1946).

12. 335 US. 281 (1948).

whole doctrine of judicial withdrawal in this area, arising out of a questionable reading of those two cases, became for a time a major obstacle to decision of the important questions of substantive constitutional law. The political question doctrine was re-examined in *Baker* and its misapplication to state legislative apportionment cases laid bare. It is nevertheless instructive to review the rise and decline of these misconceptions. One reason for the almost eager acceptance of the doctrine was the convenient excuse thus made available to judges seeking to avoid hard decisions. But there is more to it than that facile answer built on understandable human frailties.

Until the decisions in *Colegrove* and *MacDougall* neither state nor federal courts had developed any general doctrinal base for refusing to decide properly presented questions where denial, abridgment, or impairment of the right of franchise was alleged. It is a special irony that the application of the political question limitation to cases challenging legislative apportionment and districting should have developed as recently as 1946, during the very period when the need for judicial relief was becoming most acute. We have already noted that the distortions of the legislative process did not become grossly out of balance until toward the middle of the twentieth century. But until 1946 there had been no pattern, in federal or state courts, of judicial refusal to test particular apportionments and districtings against standards imposed by the United States Constitution or by state constitutions.

Testing the Right to Vote in Federal Courts Before 1946. Before 1932 the United States Supreme Court did not review any state legislative apportionment or congressional districting formulas as such. It is not surprising that for many years after the adoption of the fourteenth and fifteenth amendments in 1868 and 1870, the cases involving claimed discrimination against the exercise of the franchise arose in the context of discrimination on grounds of race.

The relevance of those cases to the justiciability of apportionment issues was noted by Justice Brennan in *Baker*:

> A citizen's right to vote free of arbitrary impairment by state action has been judicially recognized as a right secured by the Constitution, when such impairment resulted from dilution by a false tally . . . , or by a refusal to count votes from arbitrarily selected precincts . . . , or by stuffing of the ballot box . . . .[13]

13. Baker v. Carr, 369 U.S. 186, 208 (1962).

The argument may of course be made, as Justice Stewart did, dissenting in *Lucas v. Colorado General Assembly*,[14] that these cases of denial of the right to vote need not control the decision in a case in which the voting right is not claimed to have been denied as a result of malapportionment, but only impaired. But it is equally true that the Supreme Court had developed even before *Baker* an impressive body of law in support of the proposition that the right of franchise is an essential feature of the democratic process the integrity of which may not be interfered with; the Constitution "nullifies sophisticated as well as simple-minded modes of discrimination."[15]

The earlier cases established at least two propositions which are highly relevant to the apportionment cases:

1. Article I, section 4 of the Constitution provides that

> The Times, Places and Manner of holding Elections for Senators and Representatives, shall be prescribed in each State by the Legislature thereof; but the Congress may at any time by Law make or alter such Regulations, except as to the Places of Chusing Senators.

The pre-*Baker* voting cases had established that Congress could supersede state election laws where candidates for national offices were on the ballot and that the federal courts have jurisdiction over cases involving alleged infractions of those federally prescribed standards.[16]

2. There has never been any doubt that deprivation of the right to vote arising out of racially discriminatory action could be punished by Congress where the state directed the discrimination (fourteenth and fifteenth amendments) or where federal acts of discrimination were involved (fifteenth amendment).[17]

It is not a very long step from these undisputed propositions to the principle announced in *Baker* that allegations of other kinds of voter discrimination at the hands of the state, making citizen participation in the democratic process less effective, should also be within the competence of federal courts. Indeed, to hold otherwise

14. 377 U.S. 713, 744 (1964).

15. Lane v. Wilson, 307 U.S. 268, 275 (1939).

16. See, e.g., United States v. Classic, 313 U.S. 299 (1941). Cf. United States v. Harriss, 347 U.S. 612 (1954).

17. See, e.g., Ex parte Siebold, 100 U.S. 371 (1880); Ex parte Yarbrough, 110 U.S. 651 (1884); Smith v. Allwright, 321 U.S. 649 (1944); Terry v. Adams, 345 U.S. 461 (1953); Gomillion v. Lightfoot, 364 U.S. 339 (1960).

on the *jurisdictional* question would be an odd point at which to begin a retreat from the meaningful protection of the right of franchise which the Court has increasingly insisted upon.

Apart from this area of fully developed protection for the right of franchise, in the few instances before 1946 where the Court had occasion to pass directly upon alleged apportionment and districting abuses, the Court acted without hesitation, both in taking jurisdiction and in providing effective relief. The standing of private persons to bring an action in federal courts to challenge an illegal apportionment was specifically recognized in *Smiley v. Holm* in 1932.[18] There a unanimous Court took jurisdiction of a suit by a Minnesota "citizen, elector and taxpayer" and ruled that a contemplated congressional election could not be held pursuant to a Minnesota districting act which violated the federal statutory requirement that redistricting be carried out by the regular lawmaking power of the state, including approval by the governor. The Court also held a state districting law invalid (the governor had vetoed it) in *Carroll v. Becker*[19] and ordered an election at large. Similarly, in *Koenig v. Flynn*,[20] the Court rejected on the merits a suit by "citizens and voters" of New York who sought a writ of mandamus to compel the New York secretary of state to certify that congressional representatives were to be selected according to districts defined in a resolution of the state legislature.[21]

In *Wood v. Broom*,[22] which involved the Reapportionment Act of 1911, the Court took jurisdiction and decided the merits by holding that the 1911 act was no longer operative to the extent that it had required that congressional election districts be of contiguous and compact territory and, as nearly as practicable, of equal population. In a brief concurring opinion Justices Brandeis, Stone, Roberts, and Cardozo would have reversed "for want of equity" without passing on the merits, but there was no suggestion of a lack of jurisdiction.

Accordingly, until *Colegrove* and *MacDougall* were decided in 1946 and 1948 there was no reason to doubt the jurisdiction of fed-

18. 285 U.S. 355 (1932).

19. 285 U.S. 380 (1932).

20. 285 U.S. 375 (1932).

21. See also Hawke v. Smith, 253 U.S. 221 (1920); Leser v. Garnett, 258 U.S. 130 (1922); Stiglitz v. Schardien, 239 Ky. 799; 40 S.W.2d 315 (1931).

22. 287 U.S. 1 (1932).

eral courts to hear allegations of violation of the United States Constitution or of federal statutes regulating individual voter rights; to decide those claims on the merits; and to give appropriate relief. *Baker v. Carr* reasserted those propositions in unmistakably clear terms in 1962; but during the intervening sixteen-year period there was reason to wonder whether the older doctrine would prevail. Perhaps the doubts were groundless, insecurely based as they were on a reading — particularly of *Colegrove* — that was demonstrably erroneous. But it is incontestable that other courts, federal and state, read into *Colegrove* a restrictive meaning; and the Supreme Court itself, in a series of ambiguous per curiam opinions, not only failed to dispel the doubts, but may well have given some support to the belief that questions of apportionment and districting were not appropriate for judicial determination because of their involvement with political considerations.

To understand how this aberration occurred — and how it was at last set straight again — it is appropriate to look first at the decision in *Colegrove*, and particularly at the three separate opinions.

Colegrove v. Green arose out of a suit by three qualified voters resident in Illinois congressional districts with populations much larger than other congressional districts in Illinois, seeking a declaratory judgment of the invalidity of the districting act and an injunction against the conduct of elections under that act in November 1946. Justice Frankfurter, in an opinion for himself and Justices Reed and Burton, held that the relief must be denied on the basis of the 1932 decision in *Wood v. Broom* to the effect that the controlling federal statute, the act of 1929, contained no requirements "as to the compactness, contiguity and equality in population of districts." Frankfurter continued in an extended dictum to explain why he believed that the complaint should in any event be dismissed for want of equity. This dictum, not only unsupported by earlier case law but actually contrary to the case *holdings* still less than a generation old, was the principal basis for the doubts as to the jurisdiction of federal courts over apportionment matters.

In *Colegrove* Justice Frankfurter prefaced his "want of equity" argument in justification of the order of dismissal by expressing his agreement with the concurring opinion in *Wood v. Broom*, which had spoken of dismissal for want of equity. But that opinion was only a concurring opinion unsupported by citation of earlier cases. In short, the decision in *Wood v. Broom* was on the merits and thus consistent with the earlier cases in which apportionment and districting issues had been consistently heard and decided by the Supreme Court without any deference to political considerations in the guise of "want of equity." The Frankfurter opinion was nothing less than a judicial *coup de grâce*, for it managed to reverse, or at least cast doubt on, an established line of cases, announcing the new rule as a dictum in a minority opinion (as we shall see), supported only by an earlier concurring opinion which was itself undocumented. This might appropriately be described as triple bootstrap.

Justice Frankfurter spoke in *Colegrove* for only three of the seven members of the Court who participated in the decision.[23] This opinion for three expressed the view that the drawing of congressional district lines by a state is a matter "of a peculiarly political nature and therefore not meet for judicial determination."[24] Later in the opinion Frankfurter used language that has since been much quoted:

> To sustain this action would cut very deep into the very being of Congress. Courts ought not to enter this political thicket. The remedy for unfairness in districting is to secure State legislatures that will apportion properly, or to invoke the ample powers of Congress.[25]

The final sentence bears emphasis for its unrealistic recommendation that aggrieved voters "secure State legislatures that will apportion properly ...." If any one fact emerges starkly from the tangled efforts at apportionment reform, it is that the disadvantaged voters, by the very fact of their partial disenfranchisement, are disabled from any political remedy. It makes no difference whether there is a theoretically available initiative, a periodic constitutional convention, or other imagined remedy. The demonstrated fact is that, where the judicial remedy is not available, individual voters, or even groups of voters, are powerless.[26] For all the "practical politics" of Frankfurter's opinion, the stated reasons for judicial restraint demonstrated a surprising lack of political sophistication.

The foregoing is of course written on the assumption, which ap-

23. Chief Justice Stone had died in April 1946 before the *Colegrove* decision in June, and Justice Jackson was absent the entire term.

24. 328 U.S. at 552.

25. Id. at 556.

26. The reasons for which the political remedies have proved insufficient are discussed at pages 186–95 infra.

pears accurate, that Justice Frankfurter did not mean to deny that the federal courts have jurisdiction, in the sense of power, to take such cases and decide them on the merits. Justice Rutledge, whose concurring opinion provided the vote necessary to the order of dismissal, considered the jurisdictional issue foreclosed by the ruling in *Smiley v. Holm* that the federal courts have jurisdiction to decide such cases. He agreed to the dismissal solely in order to avoid too hasty decision of the difficult issues posed in the case, stating his reasons as follows:

> The shortness of the time remaining makes it doubtful whether action could, or would, be taken in time to secure for petitioners the effective relief they seek. To force them to share an election at large might bring greater equality of voting right. It would also deprive them and all other Illinois citizens of representation by districts which the prevailing policy of Congress commands.[27]

Justices Black, Douglas, and Murphy dissented in an opinion by Black that accurately forecast the results in 1962 and 1964.

> The assertion here is that the right to have their vote counted is abridged unless that vote is given approximately equal weight to that of other citizens. It is my judgment that the District Court had jurisdiction; that the complaint presented a justiciable case and controversy; and that appellants had standing to sue, since the facts alleged show that they have been injured as individuals . . . . Under these circumstances, and since there is no adequate legal remedy for depriving a citizen of his right to vote, equity can and should grant relief.[28]

Whatever doubts might have been entertained about the holding in *Colegrove* should surely have been dispelled by the Court's review of the merits of a subsequent case involving related questions. In *MacDougall v. Green*,[29] the Court took jurisdiction but found no constitutional defect in an Illinois election law requiring 200 signatures from each of at least 50 counties for an effective nominating petition.

27. Id. at 565–566 (Rutledge, J., concurring). See also Justice Brennan's disposition of Colegrove in his majority opinion in *Baker* (369 U.S. 186, 202):

"Two of the opinions expressing the views of four of the Justices, a majority, flatly held that there was jurisdiction of the subject matter. . . . Indeed, it is even questionable that the opinion of MR. JUSTICE FRANKFURTER, joined by Justices Reed and Burton, doubted jurisdiction of the subject matter. Such doubt would have been inconsistent with the professed willingness to turn the decision on either the majority or concurring views in *Wood v. Brown, supra,* 328 U.S., at 551."

28. Id. at 569 (Black, J., dissenting).

29. 335 U.S. 281 (1948).

The later per curiam orders are less clear, both because of the necessarily cryptic nature of rulings without reasoned opinion and because, quite frankly, they do seem to look in two directions. These are the cases on which Justice Frankfurter in part grounded his dissent in *Baker*; they also furnish the principal grist for the mills of the critics who, it may be added, grind exceeding fine.[30]

Between *Colegrove* and *Baker* the Supreme Court did affirm several lower court decisions refusing to exercise their equity powers; and the Court did dismiss some appeals for want of justiciability or equity, all looking at least indirectly back to the Frankfurter opinion in *Colegrove*.[31] The Solicitor General of the United States distinguished the cases in his substituted brief *amicus* submitted on the reargument of *Baker v. Carr*;[32] Justice Brennan borrowed some of those distinctions in the principal opinion in *Baker*;[33] and Justices Frankfurter and Harlan read the cases somewhat differently.[34]

There would be little gain in reviewing these necessarily tendentious matters once more. It is enough to remember that, whatever *Colegrove* was taken to mean — probably mistakenly where courts read it as imposing an obligation not to decide — it is now clear that the Supreme Court has returned to the pre-*Colegrove* mainstream in which decision of properly presented federal constitutional questions or issues involving the application of federal statutes is not only permissible but inescapable except for compelling reasons. There is no doubt that *Colegrove* represented a way of looking at apportionment and districting cases that gave encouragement to judges who were at best not eager to become involved with issues that cut to the core of the democratic premise on which the United States government is built. Equally, there is no doubt that

30. Whatever can be made of these cases is developed fully in two carefully wrought articles: Neal, *Baker v. Carr*: Politics in Search of Law, 1962 The Supreme Court Review 252; Lucas, Legislative Apportionment and Representative Government: The Meaning of *Baker v. Carr*, 61 Mich. L. Rev. 711 (1963).

31. Cook v. Fortson, 329 U.S. 675 (1946); Colegrove v. Barrett, 330 U.S. 804 (1946); MacDougall v. Green, 335 U.S. 281 (1948); South v. Peters, 339 U.S. 276 (1950); Tedesco v. Board of Supervisors, 339 U.S. 940 (1950); Remmey v. Smith, 342 U.S. 916 (1952); Cox v. Peters, 342 U.S. 936 (1952); Anderson v. Jordan, 343 U.S. 912 (1952); Kidd v. McCanless, 352 U.S. 920 (1956); Radford v. Gary, 352 U.S. 991 (1957); Hartsfield v. Sloan, 357 U.S. 916 (1958); Matthews v. Handley, 361 U.S. 127 (1959).

32. Brief for the United States as Amicus Curiae on Reargument, pp. 56–58, Baker v. Carr, 369 U.S. 186 (1962).

33. 369 U.S. at 202–204, 234–37. None of the concurring opinions expressed lack of agreement with this analysis.

34. Id. at 277–80 (Frankfurter, J., dissenting).

the *Colegrove* attitude is no longer available as a refuge to timorous judges. Fortunately, the fears that might have given pause to even the stoutest judicial heart have been much dissipated by the explicitness of the decisions in the *Reapportionment Cases*. Uncertainties about standards and about judicial power to implement the standards with effective remedies now appear much less formidable. Not all doubts have been resolved, of course, and judges will still be called upon to make difficult choices. They are, however, now free to act within the normal, relatively narrow arcs of judicial discretion rather than the wide-compass range of choice that formerly appeared all too available.

State Courts and Jurisdiction Over Suits for Reapportionment. Whatever may have been the hesitation in the federal courts to take jurisdiction over legislative apportionment and districting suits between 1946 and 1962, the state courts did not share those doubts to any substantial degree — either before or during that period of confusion. In some instances, of course, state courts were impelled to act by provisions of state constitutional or statutory law which required their review of apportionments challenged as being in conflict with requirements of *state* law. But even where that was not the case, state courts seem not to have shared the political question hesitations of the federal courts. In 1958 Anthony Lewis, Washington correspondent of the *New York Times*, reviewed the state cases, observing that

> The political thicket of malapportionment has not, as a rule, scared off the courts of the states. They have granted relief in a large number of lawsuits brought by private citizens against state officials to challenge apportionments. Districts have been held in violation of state constitutional requirements that they be of approximately equal population, be compact in shape, be made up of contiguous territory, or follow town boundaries. . . .
>
> There is virtually no discussion of justiciability in the state cases. The courts have not often articulated the political-question theory, nor cited *Colegrove*, as a ground for declining jurisdiction.[35]

The Solicitor General of the United States made a similar point in his brief *amicus* in *Baker*, calling attention to decisions from a

---

35. Lewis, Legislative Apportionment and the Federal Courts, 71 Harv. L. Rev. 1057, 1066–68 (1958). (Citations to cases are omitted.)

number of state courts in which jurisdiction was accepted and effective remedies were fashioned.[36]

BAKER v. CARR

The Tennessee constitution has required, since 1870, that the number of representatives and the number of senators in the two houses of the general assembly shall each "be apportioned among the several counties or districts, according to the number of qualified electors in each. . . ."[37] Thus, as the Court stated, "Tennessee's standard for allocating legislative representation among her counties is the total number of qualified voters resident in the respective counties, subject only to minor qualifications."[38]

Between 1901 and 1961, despite a requirement for decennial reapportionment in accordance with the required population standard,[39] the legislature had taken no action. Moreover, the complaint in *Baker* alleged that the 1901 statute itself failed to conform to the state constitutional mandate, "but instead arbitrarily and capriciously apportioned representatives in the Senate and House without reference . . . to any logical or reasonable formula whatever."[40] Meanwhile the number of persons eligible to vote more than quadrupled and at the same time there was a substantial shift in the centers of population, particularly from rural to urban areas. And so it was "primarily the continued application of the 1901 Apportionment Act to this shifted and enlarged voting population" which gave rise to the controversy.[41]

The action was brought under sections 1983 and 1988 of title 42 of the United States Code to redress alleged deprivation of federal constitutional rights, specifically claiming that plaintiffs, as eligible voters in urban areas, had been denied the equal protection of the laws "by virtue of the debasement of their votes."[42] This ultimate

36. Brief for the United States as Amicus Curiae on reargument, pp. 30–31, in Baker v. Carr, 369 U.S. 186 (1962).

37. Tenn. Const. art. II, §§ 5, 6. In the house of representatives it is further provided that the number "shall never exceed ninety-nine" (§ 5), while in the senate the number "shall not exceed one-third the number of representatives" (§ 6).

38. 369 U.S. at 189.

39. Tenn. Const. art. II, § 4.

40. 369 U.S. at 192.

41. Ibid.

42. Id. at 188.

question of substance was not decided. Instead, in Justice Brennan's words, the holding was narrow:

> In light of the District Court's treatment of the case we hold today only (a) that the court possessed jurisdiction of the subject matter; (b) that a justiciable cause of action is stated upon which appellants would be entitled to appropriate relief; and (c) because appellees raise the issue before this Court, that the appellants have standing to challenge the Tennessee apportionment statutes. Beyond noting that we have no cause at this stage to doubt the District Court will be able to fashion relief if violations of constitutional right are found, it is improper now to consider what remedy would be most appropriate if appellants prevail at the trial.[43]

Despite the Court's careful — and proper — limitation of the reach of its decision, the reader of the opinion is scarcely required to suspend his common-sense judgment that there is more between the lines. To suggest that a majority of the Court found no fault with the Tennessee apportionment structure would strain credulity. There were arguably two constitutional defects in the Tennessee scheme: (1) a severe imbalance between qualified electors and representation in both houses of the general assembly;[44] and (2) apart from population disparities, the absence of a rational basis for apportionment. That the two issues would raise for some of the Justices problems of differing constitutional magnitude was foretold by Justice Clark's suggestion that in his view even substantial disparity of population among voting districts "might not on its face be an 'invidious discrimination,'"[45] thus inviting further experimentation with preferential treatment of rural areas over urban or any other plan thought not "invidious."[46] But where there is not even *that* rationality in the allocation of representation, Justice Clark specifically found violation of equal protection, a proposition with which all members of the majority apparently agreed.

Justice Douglas, agreeing on jurisdictional issues with the majority opinion, nevertheless commented on the merits: "The traditional test under the Equal Protection Clause has been whether a

43. Id. at 197–98.

44. The record showed that 37 per cent of the voters of Tennessee elected 20 of the 33 senators, while 40 per cent of the voters elected 63 of the 99 members of the house. 369 U.S. at 253 (Clark, J., concurring).

45. Id. at 253.

46. As will be noted below (pages 136–37), Justice Clark persisted in this view of the meaning of equal protection in the *Reapportionment Cases.*

State has made 'an invidious discrimination,' .... Universal equality is not the test; there is room for weighting."[47] Accordingly, he agreed with "my Brother CLARK that if the allegations in the complaint can be sustained a case for relief is established."[48] But Douglas in *Baker* gave no indication as to his later-announced adoption of the principle of "one man, one vote" both in statewide primary elections[49] and among the election districts which make up each house of a state legislature.[50]

Justice Stewart also agreed with the majority ruling on the three points of jurisdiction, justiciability, and standing to sue; and he stated twice in the space of his two-page concurrence that nothing else was decided beyond these three matters.[51] He also suggested the point he was to develop more fully in the later cases:

> In case after case arising under the Equal Protection Clause the Court has said . . . that "the Fourteenth Amendment permits the States a wide scope of discretion in enacting laws which affect some groups of citizens differently than others."[52]

In combination Justice Brennan's opinion of the Court (joined by Chief Justice Warren and Justice Black) and the concurring opinions of Justices Douglas, Clark, and Stewart could scarcely be read with any comfort by a Tennessee legislature seeking to uphold the existing apportionment in that state. And so the Tennessee general assembly understood the opinions, as did the three-judge federal district court to which the Supreme Court remanded *Baker*; both concluded without great difficulty that the then-existing apportionment plan was constitutionally defective.[53]

Justices Frankfurter and Harlan, while recognizing "the gross inequality among legislative electoral units within almost every

47. Id. at 244–45.

48. Id. at 245.

49. Gray v. Sanders, 372 U.S. 368 (1963), discussed in chapter IV, infra.

50. Reynolds v. Sims, 377 U.S. 533 (1964), discussed in chapter V, infra.

51. Id. at 265–66.

52. Id. at 266, citing McGowan v. Maryland, 366 U.S. 420, 425 (1961).

53. Pursuant to the call of the governor of Tennessee the general assembly convened in extraordinary session on May 29, 1962, and enacted two separate reapportionment acts. Public Acts, Numbers 1 and 3, June 6, both approved by the governor June 7, 1962. Both acts, despite some improvements from the 1901 statute, were found still insufficient by the three-judge court on remand. Baker v. Carr, 206 F. Supp. 341 (M.D. Tenn. 1962). For the subsequent history of Tennessee attempts to satisfy the constitutional requirement, see the Tennessee summary in the appendix.

State,"[54] nevertheless dissented in all respects from this "umbrageous" decision.[55] Each wrote a dissenting opinion in which the other joined; and each opinion merits separate comment.

The essence of Frankfurter's opinion is simple, although the argument is comprehensive in coverage and meticulous in articulation. His concern was that, in holding that the federal courts could entertain such suits, the "uniform course of decision over the years is overruled or disregarded."[56] Although conceding that such "course of decision" had commenced "explicitly" only in 1946 when *Colegrove v. Green* was decided, and that even *Colegrove* was not grounded on denial of jurisdiction "in the strict sense of want of power," he found that "its roots run deep in the Court's historic adjudicatory process."[57] In short, he feared that the Court was violating its precept of self-restraint against participation in political questions.

To overcome the lack of "explicit" judicial precedent prior to the doubtful authority of *Colegrove* and its progeny, Justice Frankfurter recalled the English "rotten boroughs" from which he suggested the American constitutional traditions stemmed.[58] He concluded that the framers of the Constitution had not intended such a result[59] and that such had not been contemplated by those who proposed or those who ratified the fourteenth amendment.[60] Answers to these propositions are elsewhere suggested (see pages 120–28). Notice should be given, however, to the alternate prop to Frankfurter's "political question" argument. His position seems to come down to this: Apportionment cases should be regarded as nonjusticiable on the basis of a line of cases that hold "that Art. IV, § 4 of the Constitution, guaranteeing to the States 'a Republican Form of Government,' is not enforceable through the Courts."[61] The majority of the

54. 369 U.S. at 268 (Frankfurter, J., dissenting).

55. Id. at 267.

56. Id. at 277.

57. Ibid.

58. Id. at 302–307.

59. Id. at 268.

60. Id. at 297–301.

61. 369 U.S. at 289. The guaranty clause reads: "The United States shall guarantee to every state in this Union a Republican Form of Government, and shall protect each of them against Invasion; and on Application of the Legislature, or of the Executive (when the Legislature cannot be convened) against domestic Violence."

For a comprehensive discussion of the clause, see Bonfield, *Baker v. Carr*: New Light on the Constitutional Guarantee of Republican Government, 50 Calif. L. Rev. 245 (1962).

Court did not disagree with Frankfurter that cases arising under the guaranty clause are nonjusticiable as political questions, but only because that clause "is not a repository of judicially manageable standards which a court could utilize independently in order to identify a State's lawful government."[62]

The guaranty clause has never been held applicable as a barrier to federal court decision of apportionment or districting cases. Even where the Court declined jurisdiction, as in *Colegrove*, and even in the Frankfurter opinion, the reason for refusal was not grounded on the guaranty clause argument. The contention that these cases fall within the guaranty clause restriction comes too late to be seriously considered as a basis for rejecting without a hearing constitutional claims specifically based on the equal protection clause of the fourteenth amendment.

One further observation on this jurisdiction-justiciability issue is pertinent here. One of the aspects of the case which most troubled Frankfurter was his fear that the Court might find itself charged with a policing job impossible to administer. This unhappy event could result from either of two circumstances which he believed more than likely to come about. First, he feared that any decision in this area would be unenforceable because unpopular:

> The Court's authority — possessed neither of the purse nor the sword — ultimately rests on sustained public confidence in its moral sanction. Such feeling must be nourished by the Court's complete detachment, in fact and in appearance, from political entanglements and by abstention from injecting itself into the clash of political forces in political settlements.[63]

Those who shared these views must have been relieved to find how popular with the general public were the decisions in *Baker* and in *Reynolds* (see pages 218–21). The public of course has no ratification rights in connection with Supreme Court decisions on constitutional issues. Indeed, the Court has often interpreted the Constitution in ways it thought right but knew would be vastly unpopular. Nearly every decision in vindication of individual liberties has at first raised a public outcry; but the Court has not flinched from pronouncements in these areas, however unpopular, when it was believed necessary to protect minority rights. It is strange that protest should now be made against exercise of the power of decision in these cases, for once in vindication of the rights of the ma-

62. Id. at 223 (Brennan, J.).
63. Id. at 267.

jority. In any event, the expressed concern that the Court cannot protect its prestige and status in the face of adverse public reaction is shown to be groundless not only by the Court's historic willingness to stand up to criticism of unpopular decisions, but as well in this case for the added reason that these decisions *are* popular.

Frankfurter's second concern about the propriety of judicial intervention seemed meritorious to many when *Baker* was decided. His fear was that federal courts could not devise effective remedies even in cases of concededly severe malapportionment because there were no sufficiently objective standards.

> . . . . Considering the gross inequality among legislative electoral units within almost every State, the Court naturally shrinks from asserting that in districting at least substantial equality is a constitutional requirement enforceable by courts. Room continues to be allowed for weighting. This of course implies that geography, economics, urban-rural conflict, and all the other non-legal factors which have throughout our history entered into political districting are to some extent not to be ruled out in the undefined vista now opened up by review in the federal courts of state reapportionments.[64]

Ironically, the complete answer to this plausible-sounding argument was given two years later in *Reynolds* by the very majority whom Frankfurter thought incapable of devising appropriate standards. Six members of the Court, speaking through Chief Justice Warren, celebrated the logic of the equal protection clause by holding that "as a basic constitutional standard, the Equal Protection Clause requires that the seats in both houses of a bicameral state legislature must be apportioned on a population basis."[65] After that decision, if disagreement with the majority is to continue, other reasons must be assigned than those offered in *Baker*. The Court in *Reynolds* provided a definite, comprehensible standard, completely logical in terms of the equal protection clause. Deviations from the equal-population principle must now be justified by states, and approval of those deviations is to be anticipated only "[s]o long as the divergences from a strict population standard are based on legitimate considerations incident to the effectuation of a rational state policy. . . ."[66] Here is a standard more definite, far

64. Id. at 268–69.
65. Reynolds v. Sims, 377 U.S. 533, 568 (1964).
66. Id. at 579.

more precise, than such familiar and long-accepted constitutional norms as "commerce among the States" and the concept of due process as a basis for assurance of fair procedure in criminal proceedings.

Justice Harlan, who joined the Frankfurter dissent in *Baker*, also dissented in a separate opinion (with which Frankfurter joined) in which he went beyond the jurisdictional issue to the merits:

> appellants' allegations, accepting all of them as true, do not, parsed down or as a whole, show an infringement by Tennessee of any rights assured by the Fourteenth Amendment . . . .
>
> I can find nothing in the Equal Protection Clause or elsewhere in the Federal Constitution which expressly or impliedly supports the view that state legislatures must be so structured as to reflect with approximate equality the voice of every voter.[67]

Accepting the view that the equal protection clause permits considerable room for classificatory variation and experimentation in connection with economic and social matters subject to state regulation, Harlan would have applied the same standard to the voting right cases. Accordingly, he thought it "beyond argument that those who have the responsibility for devising a system of representation may permissibly consider that factors other than bare numbers should be taken into account."[68] For the moment it is sufficient to observe that the Harlan argument, as repeated and elaborated in more detail in *Reynolds*, was implicitly rejected by the Court in *Baker* and explicitly answered in *Reynolds*. Before turning to a discussion of that case, however, it is appropriate to comment on other cases raising similar issues that came to the Court after the decision in *Baker*.

67. Id. at 331–32.
68. 369 U.S. at 333.

CHAPTER IV

The Road to Equality:

From Baker to Reynolds

Baker v. Carr disposed of all the preliminary jurisdictional barriers which had earlier prevented Supreme Court determination of appropriate constitutional standards for state legislative apportionment. Thereafter, the Supreme Court worked cautiously toward decision of that important question, thus avoiding the danger of premature or ill-considered decision in an atypical case. When *Baker* was decided, two other cases, from Michigan and New York, were also pending. The Supreme Court sent all three cases back to the courts from which they had come: *Baker* was remanded to the three-judge federal district court in Tennessee for further proceedings "consistent" with the opinion of the Court; before the end of the term in June 1962 the Court remanded the Michigan case to the supreme court of that state and the New York case to the three-judge federal court in New York, both to be reviewed in light of the decision in *Baker*.

While these cases, and other state legislative apportionment cases decided after *Baker*, were working their way up, the Supreme Court heard and decided two further cases which did not, strictly speaking, involve state legislative apportionment but which were clearly relevant to some of the issues. The judicial action relating to apportionment during the two years between *Baker* and *Reynolds* is the subject of this chapter.

THE MICHIGAN CASE

Scholle v. Hare[1] was a suit to invalidate 1952 amendments to the 1908 constitution of Michigan and asked that subsequent elections be conducted pursuant to the relevant provisions of the state constitution as they were prior to 1952. The disputed amendments, adopted by initiative petition, had established 34 permanent state senatorial districts. At the time of the suit the disproportion among the election districts had grown to the point that 30 per cent of the state population could elect 53 per cent of the senate. The Michigan Supreme Court in 1960 dismissed the action in a five to three decision, relying on *Colegrove v. Green*. The United States Supreme Court vacated that decision and remanded "for further consideration in the light of *Baker v. Carr....*"[2]

On remand the Michigan Supreme Court, by divided vote, held that the 1952 amendments were invidiously discriminatory for want of a "rational, reasonable, uniform or even ascertainable nondiscriminatory legislative purpose ...."[3] The court said further that "Equal protection ... does not mean arithmetical equality .... It does mean that equality which fairly approximates, by the standards of reasonable minds exercising fair discretion, that which should have been done decennially between 1908 and 1952 and must now be done .... [W]hen any apportionment plan provides some elective districts having more than double the population of others, that plan cannot be sustained."[4]

The issues in the litigation described above were arguably mooted when, in 1963, the Michigan voters approved a new constitution with a different apportionment formula which became effective January 1, 1964. The 1963 constitution established a plan for the apportionment of senatorial election districts in accordance with a formula which gave weight to both area and population, as applied by a commission on legislative apportionment. Each county was assigned an "apportionment factor" computed as follows: (1) the percentage of the total state population in the county (as shown by the federal decennial census) multiplied by four, plus (2) the

---

1. 360 Mich. 1, 104 N.W.2d 63 (1960), vacated and remanded, 369 U.S. 429 (1962), 367 Mich. 176, 116 N.W.2d 350 (1962), cert. denied sub nom. Beadle v. Scholle, 377 U.S. 990 (1964).

2. 369 U.S. 429 (1962).

3. 367 Mich. at 185 116 N.W.2d at 353.

4. Id. at 188, 116 N.W.2d at 355.

percentage of the state land area in the county. The sum of these two figures became the county's apportionment factor, of which there were 500 in the state as a whole — 400 (80 per cent) based on population and 100 (20 per cent) based on area.

The 1963 constitution provided for a house of representatives of 110 members elected for two-year terms from single-member districts consisting of compact and convenient territory contiguous by land. The members were to be apportioned among the counties on the basis of population, except that any county with seven tenths of one per cent of the state population was allowed separate representation.[5]

The apportionment provisions in the 1963 constitution were unsuccessfully challenged before a three-judge federal district court in *Marshall v. Hare*.[6] However, on June 22, 1964, the United States Supreme Court reversed on the authority of *Reynolds v. Sims* and *Lucas v. Colorado General Assembly* and remanded for further proceedings consistent with the decisions in the *Reapportionment Cases*.[7] Thus was rejected a system which the dissenters thought perfectly "rational";[8] so it was, at least in the sense that the framers of the provisions intended exactly the result achieved, a "rule which frankly recognizes area in terms of square miles as a basis of apportionment."[9] The lesson to be learned is that "rationality" based on considerations of area is no substitute for equality. The Michigan formula in the 1963 constitution was thus insufficient.

THE NEW YORK CASE

WMCA, Inc. v. Simon[10] was the only other state legislative apportionment case raising equal-population issues which was reviewed in the United States Supreme Court after *Baker* and before *Reynolds*. The individual plaintiffs were qualified voters residing in

5. For more detailed analysis of the apportionment provisions of the 1963 constitution, see the Michigan summary in the appendix.

6. 227 F. Supp. 989 (E.D. Mich. 1964).

7. 378 U.S. 561 (1964).

8. Justices Clark and Stewart dissented "because the Michigan system of legislative apportionment is clearly a rational one and clearly does not frustrate effective majority rule"; Justice Harlan dissented "for the reasons stated in his dissenting opinion in *Reynolds v. Sims* . . . ." Ibid.

9. Pierce, Apportionment and Representative Institutions: the Michigan Experience 97 (1963).

10. 202 F. Supp. 741 (S.D.N.Y. 1961), vacated and remanded, 370 U.S. 190 (1962), 208 F. Supp. 368 (S.D.N.Y. 1962), reversed and remanded, 377 U.S. 633 (1964).

five of the six most populous counties of New York State; and WMCA was a New York corporation and taxpayer with its principal place of business in New York County. The complaint charged as violations of the due process and equal protection clauses of the fourteenth amendment those provisions of the New York constitution which (1) required enlargement of the senate by the number of senators to which the larger counties shall have become entitled since 1894; (2) prohibited any county from having four or more senators unless it had a full ratio for each senator; and (3) required that each of the 62 counties (except Hamilton) should always be entitled to one assemblyman, particularly in view of the overall membership limitation of 150. Because of these provisions, the complaint alleged, the apportionment formula resulted in a grossly unfair weighting of both houses in the state legislature in favor of the less populated rural areas to the disadvantage of the more heavily populated urban areas.

The three-judge court dismissed on the ground that the issue was not justiciable. The United States Supreme Court vacated that judgment and remanded the case for reconsideration in the light of *Baker*. Upon reconsideration the district court dismissed the complaint on the merits, concluding that the plaintiffs had not shown by a fair preponderance of the evidence that there was invidious discrimination; that the apportionment provisions were rational, not arbitrary; that they were of historical origin; that they contained no improper geographic discrimination; that they could be amended by an electoral majority of the people; and that they were therefore not unconstitutional. The United States Supreme Court reversed, concluding that under the New York constitutional provisions

> the weight of the votes of those living in populous areas is of necessity substantially diluted in effect. However complicated or sophisticated an apportionment scheme might be, it cannot, consistent with the Equal Protection Clause, result in a significant undervaluation of the weight of the votes of certain of a state's citizens merely because of where they might happen to reside. New York's constitutional formulas relating to legislative apportionment demonstrably include a built-in bias against voters living in the State's most populous counties.[11]

11. WMCA, Inc. v. Lomenzo, 377 U.S. 633, 653–54 (1964). The Supreme Court opinion is more fully discussed in chapter V, infra.

Here was another arguably rational plan; at least the formula was understandable and worked its discriminations in consistent patterns. This also was invalidated, once more over the dissents of Justices Clark and Stewart on the rationality ground, and of Justice Harlan on all grounds. The only question left open in the New York case was whether corrective action must be taken immediately, even before the elections scheduled for November 1964.[12]

The only other cases in that interim period from which hints might be secured as to the ultimate holding involved two right-of-franchise problems which the Court said explicitly were not controlling as to the legislative apportionment cases. Both cases arose in Georgia.

THE COUNTY UNIT CASE

The first of these was *Gray v. Sanders*,[13] which was not strictly an apportionment case, as the majority and concurring opinions spelled out with almost overanxious meticulousness;[14] yet the central issue was not unrelated to the issues raised in apportionment cases. The case involved an alleged impairment of the vote in a dispute between a claimed right to equal representation for all similarly situated voters against a contention that rural voters could be favored over urban voters as a matter of legislative preference. Appellants admitted candidly that the county unit system at issue was designed "to achieve a reasonable balance as between urban and rural electoral power."[15]

That the Supreme Court should select *Gray* for its first full-opinion decision after *Baker* is itself an interesting example of docket control and orderly progression in the development of a constitutional principle. *Baker* was a good "first case" because, once the preliminary issues were disposed of to permit adjudication of the equal

12. Subsequent developments are summarized in the appendix.

13. 372 U.S. 368 (1963).

14. "This case, unlike *Baker v. Carr*, . . . does not involve a question of the degree to which the Equal Protection Clause of the Fourteenth Amendment limits the authority of a State Legislature in designing the geographical districts from which representatives are chosen either for the State Legislature or for the Federal House of Representatives." Id. at 376 (Douglas, J.). See also id. at 378 (Douglas, J.), 381 (Stewart, J., concurring).

15. Id. at 370.

protection issue, the merits were relatively simple. The voter discriminations which had developed out of the Tennessee legislature's failure to reapportion were manifest, whether viewed vertically or horizontally, or (presumably) even if the viewer stood on his head. For similar reasons *Gray* was a good "second case" because, if ever the equal protection clause was to be applied in a meaningful way, the voter discriminations there laid bare fairly cried out for correction. Again, as in *Baker*, the risk of getting off to a premature or otherwise faulty start was minimal. The Court could say, as it did, that the decision was made without prejudice to later cases involving the fixing of appropriate equal protection standards for the more difficult apportionment cases. Despite this elaborate disavowal of prejudgment, there was no mistaking that the decision in *Gray* was highly relevant to at least some of the issues in the legislative apportionment cases which were soon to be granted review by the Supreme Court.[16] Certainly Justice Harlan in his dissenting opinion saw the way things were going; but his sharp protest was not joined by any member of the Court who had participated in *Baker* (Frankfurter had retired in the interim) nor by either of the new additions to the Court, Justices Byron R. White and Arthur J. Goldberg.

The election practice presented for decision in *Gray v. Sanders* was the so-called Georgia county unit system, which had, in one form or another, been challenged no fewer than four times in the Supreme Court, always without success.[17] Although none of these cases had received full-Bench consideration, there was much reason to believe that until *Baker* a majority of the Supreme Court had either not doubted the constitutional validity of the county unit system or had thought review inappropriate on grounds of presumed nonjusticiability. Indeed, that view was highlighted for Justice Harlan "by the dissenting opinion of Justices Black and Douglas in *South v. Peters* [339 U.S. 276, 277], in which they unsuccessfully espoused the very views which now become the law."[18]

In *Baker* Justice Brennan had explained these earlier refusals to

16. Gray v. Sanders was decided March 18, 1963. The Supreme Court did not grant review of the first of the *Reapportionment Cases* until June 10, 1963. 374 U.S. 802 (1963).

17. Cook v. Fortson, decided with Turman v. Duckworth, 329 U.S. 675 (1946); South v. Peters, 339 U.S. 276 (1950); Cox v. Peters, 342 U.S. 936 (1952); Hartsfield v. Sloan, 357 U.S. 916 (1958).

18. 372 U.S. at 383.

review or to upset the county unit system, which he thought left the question open.[19] Justice Douglas must have viewed the matter similarly, for in writing the majority opinion in *Gray* he did not cite any of the earlier per curiam dispositions by the Court of challenges to the Georgia scheme.

Under Georgia law applicable at the time *Gray* was decided, each county was given a specified number of representatives in the lower house of the general assembly. The county unit system at issue in *Gray* applied in this fashion in statewide primaries: A candidate for nomination who received the highest number of popular votes in a county was considered to have carried the county and to be entitled to two votes for each representative to which the county was entitled in the lower house of the general assembly. The majority of the county unit vote was required to nominate a United States Senator or state governor, while a plurality was sufficient for nomination to other offices. Because the most populous county (Fulton, with a 1960 population of 556,326) had only six unit votes, while the least populous county (Echols, with a 1960 population of 1,876) had two unit votes, "one resident in Echols County had an influence in the nomination of candidates equivalent to 99 residents of Fulton County."[20]

The three-judge federal district court before which the case was heard invalidated the county unit plan, including amendments adopted by the state legislature on the same day as the hearing in the district court.[21] But the district court did not hold that all weighted voting was outlawed. Rather the court sought to define the permissible deviations from equal representation which might be approved as not invidiously discriminatory. The district court would have permitted deviations from equality comparable to the distortions of the popular vote which may occur in the federal electoral college.[22]

The Supreme Court, however, would have none of this. It disavowed the analogy to the electoral college and rejected the district court's view that some weighting would be permissible. The rea-

19. 369 U.S. at 234–37.

20. 372 U.S. at 371.

21. The amendment modified the mathematics of the county unit system, but did not change its essential features of weighted representation and allocation of all county unit votes in each county to the front-running candidate. For an explanation of the amendment, see 372 U.S. at 372.

22. 203 F. Supp. 158, 170 (N.D. Ga. 1962).

sons were instructive. Analogies to the electoral college (along with other claimed analogies to districting and representation in state and federal legislatures) were found "inapposite."

> The inclusion of the electoral college in the Constitution as the result of specific historical concerns, validated the collegiate principle despite its inherent numerical inequality, but implied nothing about the use of an analogous system by a State in a statewide election. No such specific accommodation of the latter was ever undertaken, and therefore no validation of its numerical inequality ensued.[23]

While conceding that states "can within limits specify the qualifications of voters both in state and federal elections," the Court denied that a state is entitled to weight the votes "once the geographical unit for which a representative is to be chosen is designated . . . ."[24] Accordingly, the Court concluded: "The conception of political equality from the Declaration of Independence, to Lincoln's Gettysburg Address, to the Fifteenth, Seventeenth, and Nineteenth Amendments can mean only one thing — one person, one vote."[25] The fatal defect in the Georgia plan was that the votes were weighted on the basis of geography in recognition of a legislative preference for rural over urban votes.[26]

The significance of the holding can best be appraised by viewing it from several perspectives.

1. What lesson may be learned from examination of the alternative rulings which the Court necessarily considered and rejected? It is not without interest that the opinion of the Court did not even mention the several earlier per curiam opinions in which the Court had refused repeated invitations to upset the Georgia county unit system of conducting primary elections. Although it is true that none of these cases had been decided on the merits,[27] the refusal of decision had led many to believe that the system was not vulnerable to constitutional attack. *Baker v. Carr* necessarily dispelled the illusion of unassailability, but it did not necessarily point toward the

23. 372 U.S. at 378.

24. Id. at 379.

25. Id. at 381. See also the concurring opinion of Justices Stewart and Clark: "Within a given constituency, there can be room for but a single constitutional rule — one voter, one vote." Id. at 382.

26. Justice Douglas noted that the Georgia plan "weights the rural vote more heavily than the urban vote and weights some rural counties heavier than other larger rural counties." Id. at 379.

27. Baker v. Carr, 369 U.S. 186, 234–37 (1962).

invalidation of any weighting whatsoever. Indeed, the district court, while entirely persuaded that the existing system must fail, nonetheless was able to find that a less discriminatory plan might be rational and reasonable in its impact.[28] "Rational" the county unit system unquestionably was, at least in the sense of standing for an objective which was entirely clear: The "city" vote should not be allowed to control the choice of candidates for statewide office. But the demands of the equal protection clause are not satisfied by a plan which is rational only in terms of an improper legislative purpose. The system was an expression of confidence in the integrity of rural voters, the very voters who, under the Georgia legislative apportionment, were empowered until 1962 to select absolute majorities in both houses of the state legislature.[29] If the equal protection clause forbids any favoritism of rural over urban voters in statewide elections, as *Gray* unquestionably held, it does not seem a very long step to conclude that any other electoral system which inescapably favors rural dominance in both houses of a state legislature is also suspect.

2. What is the significance of the Court's rejection of the analogy to the practice in the federal electoral college? The Georgia state officials sought to draw an analogy between the county unit system and the voting procedure specified in the Constitution of the United States for the election of President and Vice-President. Article II, section 1 provides for the designation in each state of a "Number of Electors, equal to the whole Number of Senators and Representatives to which the State may be entitled in Congress . . . ." The federal election process established under this provision distorts the popular vote in two respects. One distortion arises from adding together the number of representatives to which the state is entitled in both houses of Congress, thus cumulating the over-representation of some states in each house. Alaska, for example, is entitled to 3 electoral votes whereas New York (the most populous state at the time of the 1960 census) is entitled to 41, a difference of less than fifteen to one, despite a population differential substantially in excess of one hundred to one. The other distortion

---

28. Compare Professor Dixon's contrasting of "reasonableness" with "rationality" in the context of apportionment. Apportionment Standards and Judicial Power, 38 Notre Dame Law. 367 (1963).

29. See Toombs v. Fortson, 205 F. Supp. 248 (N.D. Ga. 1962), holding the legislative apportionment in Georgia invidious and arbitrary.

arises out of the fact that all electors in each state customarily cast their ballots in favor of the plurality winner in the state, thus leaving unrecorded any fraction of votes cast for any other candidate in that state.[30]

Both these features of the federal electoral college were incorporated into the Georgia county unit system. In view of that federal precedent, however objectionable one may find the system, it is difficult to find it utterly devoid of rationality or reason. Accordingly, it becomes doubly significant that the Court should so readily reject the analogy as "inapposite." In a footnote explaining the non-relevance today of the historical motivations that prompted the adoption of the federal electoral system, Justice Douglas stated: "Passage of the Fifteenth, Seventeenth, and Nineteenth Amendments shows that this conception of political equality belongs to a bygone day, and should not be considered in determining what the Equal Protection Clause of the Fourteenth Amendment requires in state-wide elections."[31] The relevance of this remark to other analogies drawn from federal constitutional provisions is inescapable.

3. How, if at all, did the holding in *Gray* forecast the later-adopted equal-population principle announced in the *Reapportionment Cases* in 1964? The most obvious point is that the detractors from the concept of one man, one vote found no comfort in the opinion; the emphatic holding was that equality of voter influence is required once the geographic unit of representation has been designated. At the very least this means that all members of the state executive branch elected on a statewide basis (as well as any state legislators or congressmen chosen at large) must be selected without impairment of vote based on geography, taxes paid, economic factors, or any other group interest. The important result is that the equal-population principle won a clear and apparently easy victory which at least freed the executive branch from domination by any minority interest group.

The next question was to determine the extent to which this concept should be carried forward as a matter of logic to one or both houses of the state legislatures. Although that problem was not before the Court, and there was accordingly no precise ruling on the question, the language was at least more sweeping than was necessary: "We think the analogies to the electoral college, to dis-

---

30. For a more complete analysis, see the discussion of the federal analogy at pages 196–203 infra.

31. Gray v. Sanders, 372 U.S. 368, 377 n.8 (1963).

tricting and redistricting, and to other phases of the problems of representation in state or federal legislatures or conventions are inapposite."[32] It is difficult to read this to mean anything other than that in the state legislative context the Supreme Court denied the relevance of any analogy which has so far been drawn from practices established by the United States Constitution for the conduct of federal elections.

THE CONGRESSIONAL DISTRICTING CASE

The next franchise case decided by the Supreme Court with full opinion, *Wesberry v. Sanders*,[33] contained some surprises. This case also was not a state legislative apportionment case; it was a congressional districting case not too dissimilar from *Colegrove v. Green* — except in result. Plaintiffs were qualified voters of Fulton County, Georgia, and as such were entitled to vote in Georgia's fifth congressional district. That district had a 1960 population of 823,680, as compared with the 272,154 residents in the ninth congressional district and an average for the ten districts of 394,312. The complaint alleged that plaintiffs were deprived of the full benefit of their vote in violation of (1) article I, section 2 of the United States Constitution, which provides that "The House of Representatives shall be composed of Members chosen every second Year by the People of the several States . . . ."; (2) the due process, equal protection, and privileges and immunities clauses of the fourteenth amendment; and (3) that part of section 2 of the fourteenth amendment which provides that "Representatives shall be apportioned among the several States according to their respective numbers . . . ."

The three-judge district court before which the case was heard found unanimously that "It is clear by any standard that the population of the Fifth District is grossly out of balance with that of the other nine congressional districts of Georgia . . . ."[34] Notwithstanding these findings, a majority of the court dismissed the complaint

32. 372 U.S. at 378. Justice Douglas, in a footnote to this passage, observed that the Court did not reach "the questions that would be presented were the convention system used for nominating candidates in lieu of the primary system." Ibid., n.10. Where political decisions are made by a convention, the considerations are of course somewhat different because the basis for representation is differently conceived. Whatever problems of equal protection are posed by the use of conventions for the selection of primary candidates — and there may be some — need not be decided in order to pass upon the validity of what purports to be a direct election system.

33. 376 U.S. 1 (1964).

34. Wesberry v. Vandiver, 206 F. Supp. 276, 279–80 (N.D. Ga. 1962).

for "want of equity" in reliance upon *Colegrove*. Chief Judge Tuttle of the Fifth Circuit dissented from the disposition, believing that issues of voter inequality should be justiciable in congressional districting cases just as the Supreme Court had already ruled in *Baker* that they were in state legislative apportionment cases.

The United States Supreme Court, on review of *Wesberry*, made more explicit the point on which after *Baker* there should have been no doubt. Neither *Colegrove* nor any other decision can be read to deny to federal courts jurisdiction or justiciability of cases challenging state-imposed imbalance in state or congressional election districts. Justice Black stated for the Court:

> Mr. Justice Frankfurter's *Colegrove* opinion contended that Art. I, § 4, of the Constitution had given Congress "exclusive authority" to protect the right of citizens to vote for Congressmen, but we made it clear in *Baker* that nothing in the language of that article gives support to a construction that would immunize state congressional apportionment laws which debase a citizen's right to vote from the power of courts to protect the constitutional rights of individuals from legislative destruction, a power recognized at least since our decision in *Marbury v. Madison*, 1 Cranch 137, in 1803 . . . . The right to vote is too important in our free society to be stripped of judicial protection by such an interpretation of Article I. This dismissal can no more be justified on the ground of "want of equity" than on the ground of "nonjusticiability."[35]

Some myths die harder than others; the *Colegrove* myth has been one of the most durable of all,[36] whether the ruling be understood to deny jurisdiction, foreclose jurisdiction, or simply to permit judicial inaction for "want of equity." The myth has at last been laid; the ghost of *Colegrove* walks no more.

The surprise in *Wesberry* was not on the justiciability issue, which was hardly difficult to predict,[37] nor even that the Court found constitutionally excessive the population disparities among the Georgia congressional districts.[38] The surprise was rather that six members of the Court concluded that their authority for the invalidation of the congressional districting plan in Georgia stemmed

35. 376 U.S. at 6–7.

36. See Bickel, The Durability of Colegrove v. Green, 72 Yale L.J. 39 (1962); Note, Challenges to Congressional Districting: After *Baker v. Carr* Does *Colegrove v. Green* Endure?, 63 Colum. L. Rev. 98 (1963).

37. Only Justice Harlan dissented on this point.

38. Justice Harlan disagreed, and Justice Stewart did not reach this point because he dissented from the majority's reliance for decision on article 1, section 2 of the Constitution.

from article I, section 2 of the Constitution[39] and not from the equal protection clause of the fourteenth amendment.

The plaintiffs in *Wesberry* complained from the first that the inequality in congressional district representation deprived them of rights guaranteed by the equal protection clause of the fourteenth amendment and article I, section 2 of the fourteenth amendment;[40] and both issues were preserved throughout the litigation. By the time the case reached the Supreme Court, the plaintiffs had narrowed their constitutional reliance almost exclusively to the fourteenth amendment contention. In their brief to the Supreme Court the "Questions Presented" were said to be three in number: (1) whether the districting violated the equal protection clause; (2) whether the districting deprived plaintiffs of the privileges and immunities of national citizenship; and (3) whether the federal courts had jurisdiction to enjoin elections held pursuant to the current Georgia congressional districting statute.[41] Although the article I argument was preserved in the text of the brief, it was made faintly and without conviction, whereas the equal protection argument was forcefully urged upon the Court. The Solicitor General of the United States, in a brief amicus curiae on behalf of plaintiffs, stated the article I argument somewhat more fully, concluding that "the House of Representatives was plainly intended to represent people."[42] But the Solicitor General did not rely on that argument alone.

> Conceivably, [the constitutional provision in article I, section 2 for election of congressional representatives "by the People"] was merely the framer's [sic] intention rather than a binding requirement of the Constitution. However, the adoption of the Fourteenth Amendment — with its guarantee "of the equal protection of the laws" — strongly indicates that Congressional districting must be based on population.[43]

Nevertheless, the thrust of the Solicitor General's entire argument had a tentative quality: "we are not arguing that the Fourteenth Amendment imposes the substantive standard that Congressional

39. "The House of Representatives shall be composed of Members chosen every second Year by the People of the several States, and the Electors in each State shall have the Qualifications requisite for Electors of the most numerous Branch of the State Legislature."

40. Record, pp. 14–16, Wesberry v. Sanders, 376 U.S. 1 (1964).

41. Brief for Appellants, pp. 2–3, Wesberry v. Sanders, 376 U.S. 1 (1964).

42. Brief for the United States as Amicus Curiae, p. 31, Wesberry v. Sanders, 376 U.S. 1 (1964). See generally, id. at 30–35.

43. Id. at 35.

districting must be based on population even though we believe that this standard is correct."[44] He asked only that the Court uphold the jurisdiction of the federal court and remand to the district court for determination on the merits of this "question of first impression."[45]

Meanwhile, the argument based on article I, section 2 had not gained much momentum in the law reviews. There was general agreement that *Colegrove* should not bar the federal courts from deciding the merits of a case like *Wesberry*, and there were various views as to how such a case should be decided; but no one had given more than perfunctory attention to article I, section 2 before the Supreme Court focused all attention on that provision in *Wesberry*.[46]

Justice Black, writing for the majority, concluded that the command of article I, section 2, that representatives be chosen "by the People of the several States," construed in its historical context, means

> that as nearly as is practicable one man's vote in a congressional election is to be worth as much as another's. . . . To say that a vote is worth more in one district than in another would not only run counter to our fundamental ideas of democratic government, it would cast aside the principle of a House of Representatives elected "by the People," a principle tenaciously fought for and established at the Constitutional Convention.[47]

One might have thought that the history of the Constitutional Convention of 1787 and the state ratifying convention debates was ground sufficiently plowed that surprises would be unlikely. However, Black re-examined that history — as perhaps no one had before — from the perspective of learning what was meant by the requirement that representatives be chosen "by the People." As a result of that painstaking search he was able to report statements by many of the most influential delegates in support of the principle that, as James Wilson of Pennsylvania put it, "equal numbers of people ought to have an equal no. of representatives," and representatives "of different districts ought clearly to hold the same proportion to each other, as their respective constituents hold to each

44. Ibid.

45. Id. at 43.

46. See materials cited supra in note 36. See also, Black, Inequities in Districting for Congress: Baker v. Carr and Colegrove v. Green, 72 Yale L.J. 13 (1962).

47. 376 U.S. at 7–8.

other."[48] Others who spoke for the proposition of equality of voter representation in the House of Representatives included James Madison and George Mason of Virginia, Elbridge Gerry and Rufus King of Massachusetts, Alexander Hamilton of New York, Hugh Williamson of North Carolina, and Benjamin Franklin of Pennsylvania.[49] The Court concluded that

> The debates at the Convention make at least one fact abundantly clear: that when the delegates agreed that the House should represent "people" they intended that in allocating Congressmen the number assigned to each State should be determined solely by the number of the State's inhabitants.[50]

James Madison made the same point in *The Federalist* when he described the system of districting which he assumed the states would adopt: "The city of Philadelphia is supposed to contain between fifty and sixty thousand souls. It will therefore form nearly two districts for the choice of Federal Representatives."[51] Elsewhere in *The Federalist* he said that numbers are in any event "the only proper scale of representation."[52] The same point was echoed in the state ratification conventions.[53]

Soon after the Constitution was adopted, James Wilson of Pennsylvania, by then an Associate Justice of the United States Supreme Court, in a series of lectures at Philadelphia, stated that

> all elections ought to be equal. Elections are equal, when a given number of citizens, in one part of the state, choose as many representatives, as are chosen by the same number of citizens, in any other part of the state. In this manner, the proportion of the representatives and of the constituents will remain invariably the same.[54]

Justice Harlan wrote an elaborate dissent. Justices Clark and Stewart agreed with his main assertion, that article I, section 2 does not demand equality of representation in the choice of congress-

48. Id. at 11, quoting from 3 The Records of the Federal Convention of 1787, p. 180 (Farrand ed. 1911).

49. 376 U.S. at 10–14. Although some of the demands for equality of representation may have arisen in part out of the insistence that the number of representatives *apportioned* to each state be fixed in accordance with *state* population, the proposition emerges clearly that the prevailing view was that the districts within each state should also satisfy the principle of population equality.

50. Id. at 13.

51. The Federalist, No. 57, p. 389 (Cooke ed. 1961).

52. Id., No. 54, at 368.

53. 376 U.S. at 15–16.

54. Id. at 17, quoting from 2 The Works of James Wilson 15 (Andrews ed. 1896).

men. Justices Clark and Stewart both made clear, however, that they agreed with the majority that the matter was properly raised for decision on the merits in the federal courts. Justice Clark, believing that the equal protection clause of the fourteenth amendment was the relevant constitutional provision, would have remanded to the district court for further proceedings, while Justice Stewart agreed with Justice Harlan that the Constitution did not authorize judicial remedy.

The Harlan dissent was apparently based less on his disagreement with what the majority *said* than with the failure of the principal opinion to deal with other provisions of the Constitution which Harlan thought dispositive of the issue. He acknowledged that "many, perhaps most," of the delegates to the Constitutional Convention "believed generally — but assuredly not in the precise, formalistic way of the majority of the Court — that within the States representation should be based on population . . . ." However, the dissent continued, the delegates "did not surreptitiously slip their belief into the Constitution in the phrase 'by the People,' to be discovered 175 years later like a Shakespearean anagram."[55]

Justice Harlan accordingly read article I, section 2 in a much more limited fashion, observing that

> the very sentence of Art. I, § 2, on which the Court exclusively relies confers the right to vote for Representatives only on those whom *the State* has found qualified to vote for members of "the most numerous Branch of the State Legislature."[56]

Continuing, Harlan revealed his leave-it-to-the-state philosophy of the division of powers between nation and states.

> So far as Article I is concerned, it is within the State's power to confer that right [of franchise] only on persons of wealth or of a particular sex or, if the State chose, living in specified areas of the State. Were Georgia to find the residents of the Fifth District unqualified to vote for Representatives to the State House of Representatives, they could not vote for Representatives to Congress, according to the express words of Art. I, § 2.[57]

If Harlan is right in his belief that states may entirely disenfranchise voters on the basis of geography, then surely it follows that election "by the People" is empty rhetoric.

55. 376 U.S. at 27.
56. Id. at 25.
57. Id. at 25–26. The starkness of the quoted language seems at first to be muted somewhat by the following sentence: "Other provisions of the Constitution would, of

Even if Justice Harlan may have carried his argument beyond the threshold of reason in this respect, his main point was more carefully stated and more worthy of attention. The central Harlan contention seems to have been that, whatever article I, section 2 might have meant standing alone, it must be read in conjunction with other provisions of the same article, particularly section 4: "The Times, Places and Manner of holding Elections for Senators and Representatives, shall be prescribed in each State by the Legislature thereof; but the Congress may at any time by Law make or alter such Regulations, except as to the Places of chusing Senators."

This provision has always been understood to mean, as Harlan pointed out, that Congress retains a revisory power over state legislative decisions relating to "The Times, Places and Manner of holding Elections for Senators and Representatives . . . ." From this proposition, with which there is no disagreement, Harlan concluded as a corollary that the affirmative power of revision thus conferred on Congress excludes judicial power. For him this would involve two specific consequences: (1) state decisions relating to the exercise of the franchise involve political questions entrusted solely to the states (subject to approval or revision by Congress) which are not "meet for judicial determination" (shades of *Colegrove*); (2) even if federal courts have *power* to enter the "political thicket," they are foreclosed from remedy by the exclusive grant of reviewing power to Congress. Perhaps these are not two distinct arguments; certainly for Justice Harlan they are fused into the single command "No entry." But Justices Clark and Stewart apparently saw the two points as separable; each of them rejected the first while accepting the second, at least as to article I. Justice Clark may have escaped that particular dilemma by concluding in favor of jurisdiction and justiciability of the issue and finding a remedy in the standards of the fourteenth amendment. For Justice Stewart, however, the problem was more difficult. By agreeing with the majority that the issues are justiciable in the federal courts (while agreeing with Harlan that there is no clause of the Constitution which can be invoked by a federal court), he scaled the jurisdictional mountain only to descend at once into the pit of no remedy.

---

course, be relevant, *but so far as Art. I, § 2 is concerned,* the disqualification would be within Georgia's power." Id. at 26. (Emphasis in original.) But the qualification seems to have little meaning when it is recalled that Justice Harlan also reads the fourteenth amendment as not available as a basis for judicial relief. Apparently, then, he means that Congress alone has corrective power, a point discussed in the text immediately following.

The real difficulty with the Harlan proposition is that it implicates as an unspoken premise the faulty generalization that where Congress can go the federal courts cannot. That is certainly not true in other areas of constitutional grants of power, where Court and Congress often act in supplement to each other; and no precedent is cited to show that this area has ever before been regarded as different in this respect.

The problem involves the doctrine of the separation of powers, which is manifestly a doctrine of the first importance in American constitutionalism, for it provides in broad outline the limits beyond which the executive, legislative, and judicial branches may not intrude upon the specified domain of each other.[58] The doctrine of judicial review, however, has always limited the separation of powers concept in important ways.

In the first place, there are very few instances even of legislative *action* by Congress (opposed here to *inaction*) which are immune from judicial inquiry. Those rare instances of immunity of congressional action from judicial inquiry can be compendiously blanketed within the political question doctrine enunciated by the Court in *Baker v. Carr.* The principal argument against justiciability in that case was that the federal courts are barred by the provisions of article IV, section 4 of the Constitution, the guaranty clause,[59] from inquiring into questions of the distribution of electoral power. But all members of the present Court except Justice Harlan have rejected that argument. Justice Brennan put it this way:

> That review [of the "political question" cases reveals] that in the Guaranty Clause cases and in the other "political questions" cases, it is the relationship between the judiciary and the coordinate branches of the Federal Government, and not the federal judiciary's relationship to the States, which gives rise to the "political question."[60]

The fact that the political question doctrine does not limit judicial review of state legislative action bears also upon the second reason for concluding that the separation of powers doctrine does not preclude judicial review of congressional district lines drawn by state legislatures. The point is that the federal courts have never been foreclosed from testing state action against a properly pre-

---

58. See Youngstown Sheet & Tube Co. v. Sawyer, 343 U.S. 579 (1952). Cf. Vanderbilt, The Separation of Powers (1953).

59. "The United States shall guarantee to every State in the Union a Republican Form of Government . . . ."

60. Baker v. Carr, 369 U.S. 186, 210 (1962).

sented claim of violation of the United States Constitution simply because Congress could have acted but did not. The commerce clause is perhaps the best example. While it is clear that Congress could at any time ordain a single national rule for any activity affecting interstate commerce, the failure of Congress to do so certainly does not leave the states free of federal judicial supervision of their regulations of interstate commerce. At least since the 1851 decision in *Cooley v. Board of Wardens of the Port of Philadelphia*[61] the Court has never doubted its power to limit state regulation of interstate commerce even in the absence of congressional guidance. No less clear, and perhaps more directly relevant to the question here at issue, are the cases of judicial intervention to eliminate various kinds of state-supported racial discrimination in the absence of congressional action which would clearly have been within the power of Congress under the thirteenth, fourteenth, or fifteenth amendments.[62]

Whatever controversy the decision in *Wesberry* may have triggered within the Court, it seemed to present no problem of acceptability in Georgia, the state affected by the ruling. Within five days of the Supreme Court decision the Georgia general assembly redrew the congressional district lines, giving metropolitan Atlanta two representatives instead of one and making other adjustments to equalize the population among the ten districts. Because the new bill left a population discrepancy of 128,837 between the most populous and least populous districts, Governor Carl E. Sanders observed that there was "no guarantee that the Federal Courts will accept this plan . . . ." Accordingly, he indicated that he would favor keeping a legislative study committee in session to draw a revised plan if necessary.[63]

Shortly after the decision in *Wesberry* the Supreme Court disposed of an additional congressional districting case on the authority of the Georgia case. *Martin v. Bush*[64] involved a challenge to the

61. 53 U.S. (12 How.) 298, 318 (1851). "Now the power to regulate commerce, embraces a vast field, containing not only many, but exceedingly various subjects, quite unlike in their nature; some imperatively demanding a single uniform rule, operating equally on the commerce of the United States in every port; and some, . . . as imperatively demanding that diversity, which alone can meet the local necessities of navigation."

62. See, e.g., Brown v. Board of Educ., 347 U.S. 483 (1954), 349 U.S. 294 (1955); Cooper v. Aaron, 358 U.S. 1 (1958). Cf. Gomillion v. Lightfoot, 364 U.S. 339 (1960). See also Bickel, The Durability of Colegrove v. Green, 72 Yale L.J. 39, 39–40 (1962).

63. N.Y. Times, Feb. 23, 1964, p. 1, col. 2.

64. 376 U.S. 222 (1964).

congressional districts in Texas, where the deviation between the most populous and least populous districts was the largest in the country, from 951,527 to 216,371, a difference of 735,156. The district court, perhaps anticipating the decision in *Wesberry*, had ordered an at-large election of congressional representatives in the fall of 1964 in the absence of legislative action to correct the gross population imbalance among the existing districts.[65] But the district court invited an application for a stay pending Supreme Court review, which was granted by Justice Black.[66] The Supreme Court affirmed the district court order invalidating the existing districts, "without prejudice to the right of the appellants [the state officials] to apply by April 1, 1964, to the District Court for further equitable relief in light of the present circumstances, including the imminence of the forthcoming election and 'the operation of the election machinery of Texas....' "[67] Justice Clark joined in this disposition, as he had in *Wesberry*, but on the ground there stated of believing that the controlling constitutional provision was the fourteenth amendment rather than article I. Justices Harlan and Stewart dissented for the reasons stated in their dissenting opinions in *Wesberry*.

The reference to the "election machinery of Texas" was to the primary campaign for the Texas congressional races, for which filings had closed on February 3 for the primary to be held on May 2.[68] Thus, the order allowed the trial court to withhold its hand, as it did, because the election machinery was already in motion. Looking beyond Texas, the ruling appeared to suggest that the Supreme Court would not press for immediate redistricting in any state after the congressional election procedures had commenced.

Texas officials and members of Congress were reported "pleased" at the way the Court handled the matter. Governor John B. Connally, Jr., said that the Court had "recognized the difficulties" in the way of action in 1964. Representative Wright Patman, a Democrat who is dean of the Texas delegation in the House, said he wanted to make it "absolutely clear that nobody is resisting districting."[69]

65. Bush v. Martin, 224 F. Supp. 499 (S.D. Tex. 1963).
66. Martin v. Bush, 376 U.S. 222, 223 (1964).
67. Id. at 223.
68. N.Y. Times, March 3, 1964, p. 1, col. 1.
69. Ibid. For subsequent developments, see the Texas summary in the appendix.

CHAPTER V

Reynolds v. Sims:

One Man, One Vote

Wesberry v. Sanders was a congressional districting case rather than a state legislative apportionment case, so it was not played in the main ring. Moreover, in view of the Court's reliance on article I rather than the fourteenth amendment, nothing in the opinion necessarily foretold what action the Court would take on the state legislative cases, five of which by this time had been argued and were awaiting decision; and a sixth was scheduled for argument within six weeks of the decision in *Wesberry*. The six cases, destined for decision together on June 15, 1964, had been working their way through the lower federal courts, and in one case the state courts, since, in some instances, before the 1962 decision in *Baker*. These cases came from Alabama, Colorado, Delaware, Maryland, New York, and Virginia. Together they provided an especially appropriate spectrum of varied fact situations for judicial investigation of the whole question of state legislative apportionment. Among them they presented virtually every major variation of state apportionment arrangement and nearly every conceivable kind of judicial response. Although other cases were ripe for Supreme Court review by the spring of 1964, it seemed entirely probable that they did not present substantially different issues and therefore could be disposed of without oral argument after the guidelines for decision had been established in the six basic cases. That is exactly what the Court did on June 22, 1964, remanding to lower courts for appropriate disposition nine state legislative apportionment cases which had accumulated for Court review by the time of the decision in the *Reapportionment Cases*. The six cases decided with opinion on June 15 will be discussed in this chapter; the nine disposed of by order without opinion on June 22 will be discussed in the following chapter. Subsequent developments in all the cases are reviewed in the appendix.

Alabama: The Alabama litigation, which expanded into three cases before decision in the Supreme Court, began with a complaint filed in August 1961, seven months before the Supreme Court decision in *Baker*. The original plaintiffs — residents, taxpayers, and voters of Jefferson County (including Birmingham, the state's largest city) — sued in their own behalf and in behalf of other similarly situated Alabama voters to challenge the apportionment of the state legislature.

The complaint stated that the Alabama legislature then consisted of a senate of 35 members and a house of representatives of 106 members. Relevant portions of the Alabama constitution of 1901[1] provided that "The members of the House of Representatives shall be apportioned by the legislature among the several counties of the state, according to the number of inhabitants in them, respectively, as ascertained by the decennial census of the United States . . . ."; that the senate districts "shall be as nearly equal to each other in the number of inhabitants as may be . . . ."; that "Representation in the Legislature shall be based upon population, and such basis of representation shall not be changed by constitutional amendments"; that it is the duty of the legislature to reapportion after each census; that each of the 67 counties is entitled to at least one member of the house of representatives; and that each senate district shall have only one member and no county may be divided between two senate districts.

Plaintiffs alleged that the last legislative apportionment in the state was based on the 1900 federal census despite the state constitutional requirement for decennial reapportionment. Accordingly, since the population growth had been uneven, Jefferson and other

---

1. Art. IV, § 50; art. IX, §§ 197–203; art. XVIII, § 284.

counties were seriously discriminated against both as a result of the constitutional provisions and because of the legislative failure to reapportion. Plaintiffs alleged further that they had exhausted all remedies available other than in the federal courts: the legislative pattern of prolonged inaction was said to demonstrate the unavailability of legislative relief; the basis for representation at any future constitutional convention would be fixed by the same malapportioned legislature, making relief unlikely; and the state supreme court, while noting the legislative noncompliance with the constitutional requirement of decennial reapportionment, had indicated that it would not interfere.[2]

Upon the convening of a three-judge district court, additional groups of voters resident in Jefferson, Mobile, and Etowah Counties were permitted to intervene as intervenor-plaintiffs, and in general they adopted the allegations of the original plaintiffs.[3] On March 29, 1962, three days after the Supreme Court decision in *Baker*, the plaintiffs moved for a preliminary injunction requiring the defendant state officials to conduct at large the May 1962 Democratic primary elections and the November 1962 general elections for the state legislature. The district court, on April 14, found jurisdiction, justiciability, and standing; took judicial notice of the existing malapportionment; and indicated that if the legislature failed to take constitutionally sufficient corrective action, it would be the "clear duty" of the court to act prior to the November 1962 general elections.[4]

On July 12, 1962, the Alabama legislature in extraordinary session adopted two reapportionment plans to take effect for the elections of 1966. One was a proposed constitutional amendment, referred to as the "67-Senator Amendment," which provided for a house of representatives consisting of 106 members, one seat apportioned to each of the 67 counties and the remaining 39 distributed according to population by the 'equal proportions' method. The senate was to consist of one member from each of the 67 counties.

2. See Waid v. Pool, 255 Ala. 441, 51 So. 2d 869 (1951); Ex parte Rice, 143 So. 2d 848 (Ala. 1962).

3. The case in the Supreme Court bears the caption of the original suit, Reynolds v. Sims, 377 U.S. 533 (1964) (No. 23 on the Supreme Court docket for the October 1963 Term). Two of the intervening groups became cross-appellants in the Supreme Court in the other two cases decided in the same opinion, Vann v. Baggett (No. 27) and McConnell v. Baggett (No. 41).

4. Sims v. Frink, 205 F. Supp. 245 (M.D. Ala. 1962).

The proposed amendment was to be submitted to the voters for ratification at the November 1962 general election.

The other reapportionment plan was embodied in a statute known as the "Crawford-Webb Act." It was enacted as standby legislation to take effect in 1966 if the proposed constitutional amendment should not be approved by the state's voters or if the federal courts should deny the validity of the amendment even though approved by the voters. The act provided for a senate of 35 members, representing 35 senatorial districts established along county lines, largely the same as the existing districts; and it provided for a 106-member house, giving each county one representative and apportioning the remaining 39 on a rough population basis.

On July 21, 1962, the district court held, as had been "generally conceded" by the parties, that the inequality of the existing representation violated the equal protection clause of the fourteenth amendment, since population growth and shifts had converted the 1901 scheme, as perpetuated sixty years later, into an invidiously discriminatory plan completely lacking in rationality.[5] Based on the 1960 census figures, the number of persons represented by members of the lower house varied from 104,767 in Mobile County to 6,731 in Bullock County. The senatorial districts varied from 15,417 in district number 16 (Lowndes County) to 634,864 in district number 13 (Jefferson County). Under then-existing apportionment provisions, applying 1960 census figures, 25.1 per cent of the state's total population resided in districts represented by a majority of the members of the senate, and only 25.7 per cent lived in counties which could elect a majority of the members of the lower house.

The district court found both the 67-Senator Amendment and the Crawford-Webb Act constitutionally defective. The proposed amendment would have been "even more invidious" in its discrimination than existing law because (1) the percentage of voters necessary to control the senate would be reduced to 19.4 per cent; (2) the 34 smallest counties, with a total population less than that of Jefferson County, would have a majority of the total membership of the senate; and (3) senators elected by 14 per cent of the state population could prevent the submission of any future proposal to amend the state constitution. The district court found "totally unacceptable" the Crawford-Webb Act provision for the lower house,

5. Id., 208 F. Supp. 431 (M.D. Ala. 1962).

giving additional seats to the populous counties in diminishing ratio to their population (e.g., three for 90,000 to 150,000 people and four for 150,000 to 300,000). Each representative from Jefferson and Mobile Counties would represent over 52,000 people; representatives from eight "black belt" counties would each represent fewer than 20,000.

The district court then adopted as a provisional reapportionment the provisions relating to the lower house contained in the 67-Senator Amendment — one seat for each county and the other 39 distributed according to population — and the Crawford-Webb Act provisions for the senate. The court emphasized that this action was only a temporary expedient designed to break the stranglehold on the legislature and would not serve as a permanent reapportionment. Accordingly, the court retained jurisdiction and deferred any hearing on the motion for a permanent injunction "until the Legislature, as provisionally reapportioned by this order, has an opportunity to provide for a true reapportionment of both Houses of the Alabama Legislature."[6]

After the district court's decision, new primary elections were held as authorized by legislation adopted at the 1962 extraordinary session, to become effective if the district court ordered reapportionment. The general elections in November 1962 were likewise held on the basis of the court's apportionment.

On appeal the United States Supreme Court affirmed the judgment below and remanded the cases for further proceedings consistent with the Court's opinion. The holding was unequivocal in its demand for satisfaction of the equal-population principle.

> We hold that, as a basic constitutional standard, the Equal Protection Clause requires that the seats in both houses of a bicameral state legislature must be apportioned on a population basis.[7]

Justices Clark and Stewart concurred in brief separate opinions. Justice Harlan dissented by himself in an opinion which is discussed at pages 139–44.

Because the opinion in *Reynolds v. Sims* was in general applicable also to the five other cases decided at the same time, it is appropriate to note the facts of all those cases before detailing the specifics of the constitutional rationale relevant to all.

6. Id. at 442.
7. Reynolds v. Sims, 377 U.S. 533, 568 (1964).

New York: The New York case, *WMCA, Inc. v. Lomenzo*,[8] was filed in May 1961 by individual voters and residents of five of the six most populous New York counties (Bronx, Kings, Nassau, New York, and Queens), suing in behalf of all New York citizens similarly situated, and by WMCA, a radio station serving the New York metropolitan area.

The complaint was directed at those provisions of the New York constitution which provided for the apportionment of seats in the bicameral legislature. Article III, sections 1–4 provided that the senate should initially have 50 seats. However, as those provisions were interpreted by the New York courts, the 50 seats were subject to enlargement as follows. First, the total population of the state, excluding aliens, as determined by the last federal census, was divided by 50 to obtain a ratio. The counties which might necessitate an increase in the size of the senate were then identified — counties with three or more ratios, i.e., more than 6 per cent of the citizen population. Those counties (hereafter called the "populous counties") were then allocated as many seats as they had full ratios, disregarding fractions of ratios. Thereafter, each county was divided into the appropriate number of senate districts.

The second stage involved the apportionment of seats to the less populous counties — counties with less than 6 per cent of the citizen population. The 50 original seats were then increased by the number of seats added by reason of the growth of the populous counties since 1894, the date of adoption of the New York constitution. In short, the total number of seats gained by the populous counties since 1894 was added to the original total of 50 seats (for a total based on the 1950 census of 58 seats). Curiously, the populous counties were then denied any share in those additional senate seats, for the counties which had thus increased their proportion of the population shared only in the original 50 seats, and only to the extent of fully earned ratios.

From the current total of 58 the number assigned to the populous counties — 27 under the 1953 apportionment — was subtracted; and the remaining 31 under that apportionment were then divided among the less populous counties. A second ratio was obtained by dividing those 31 seats into the total citizen population of the less populous counties. A county entitled to two or three seats was then

8. 377 U.S. 633 (1964).

divided into senatorial districts on the basis of this smaller second ratio. Counties with substantially less than one second ratio were combined into multi-county districts.

The populous counties necessarily ended up with markedly less per capita representation in the state senate than the less populous counties. Under the 1950 census and 1953 apportionment a senator from one of the less populous counties represented, on the average, 195,859 citizens, while a senator from a populous county represented 301,178. The differential would have been still greater if reapportionment had been accomplished on the basis of the 1960 census.

Article III, section 2 of the constitution of 1894 established an assembly with a membership of 150. Each of the 62 counties (except Hamilton, which shared an assemblyman with Fulton County) was assured one seat by article III, section 5. The remaining 89 seats were apportioned among the counties in accordance with the ratio obtained by dividing the 150 seats into the citizen population. A county whose ratio was at least one and one-half times the base ratio was first given an additional assemblyman; and the remaining seats were then apportioned among those counties whose citizen population was three or more full ratios, any remaining seats being apportioned on the basis of "highest remainders." Finally, the counties were divided into the appropriate assembly districts. These provisions also consistently favored the less populous counties. Under that apportionment, applying 1960 census figures, the largest assembly district had 21 times as many citizens as the smallest; and the largest senate district had 3.9 times as many as the smallest. If reapportionment had been completed pursuant to the 1960 census figures, the smallest 44 counties would each have received one seat for an average of 62,765 citizens per seat; 3 counties would have received two seats each for a total of six, each representing an average of 93,478 citizens; and the 14 most populous counties would have been entitled to one hundred seats for an average representation figure of 129,183 citizens per seat.

The complaint alleged that application of the above provisions and the currently controlling statutes necessarily resulted in gross disproportion between population and representation in violation of the due process and equal protection clauses of the fourteenth amendment. Plaintiffs offered to prove (1) that the apportionment formula in the 1894 constitution was intentionally adopted to limit the representation of urban residents on the ground, among others, that such residents were believed to be morally and intellectually inferior; and (2) that as a result plaintiffs and others similarly situated suffered economic and other discriminations amounting to a denial of due process of law.

The three-judge court before which the case was heard dismissed the complaint, holding that the issue was not justiciable.[9] That was in January 1962. After the decision in *Baker*, the Supreme Court vacated the lower court decision in *WMCA* and remanded to the district court for reconsideration.[10] On rehearing the district court refused to receive evidence of the effect the reapportionment rules had on the representation of citizens in New York and Nassau Counties with respect to such matters as the collection of taxes and disbursement of state aid. It also excluded evidence proffered to show that the reapportionment rules were "devised for the very purpose" of creating a class of citizens whose representation was inferior to that of a more preferred class and that there was "intentional discrimination" against citizens of New York City. The district court concluded that there was no violation of the fourteenth amendment, saying in part that the New York apportionment provisions "are rational, not arbitrary, are of substantially historic origins, contain no geographical discrimination, permit an electoral majority to alter or change the same and are not unconstitutional under the relevant decisions of the Supreme Court."[11]

On appeal the United States Supreme Court reversed and once more remanded to the district court, this time "for further proceedings consistent with the views stated here and in our opinion in *Reynolds v. Sims*."[12] It is sufficient here merely to note the Court's conclusion about the New York apportionment formulas.

> Despite the opaque intricacies of New York's constitutional formulas relating to legislative apportionment, when the effect of these provisions, and the statutes implementing them, on the right to vote of those individuals living in the disfavored areas of the State is considered, we conclude that neither the existing scheme nor the forthcoming one can be constitutionally condoned.[13]

9. WMCA, Inc. v. Simon, 202 F. Supp. 741 (S.D.N.Y. 1962).
10. WMCA, Inc. v. Simon, 370 U.S. 190 (1962).
11. 208 F. Supp. 368, 380 (S.D.N.Y. 1962).
12. 377 U.S. 633, 655 (1964).
13. Id. at 654.

Justice Harlan dissented for the reasons stated in his opinion in *Reynolds*. Justices Stewart and Clark dissented in opinions filed in the Colorado case; their opinions are discussed in chapter V, infra.

Colorado: In March and July 1962, voters and residents of counties in the Denver metropolitan area filed two separate actions, later consolidated for trial and disposition, in behalf of themselves and all others similarly situated, challenging the constitutionality of the apportionment of seats in both houses of the Colorado general assembly pursuant to article V, sections 45, 46, and 47 of the Colorado constitution and relevant provisions of Colorado statutes. Sponsors of a referendum proposing a new apportionment for consideration by the voters in November 1962 were permitted to intervene along with state election officials, the original defendants. After trial the three-judge district court concluded in favor of jurisdiction and justiciability and decided that there was no basis for abstention. The court also stated that the then-existing population disparities among the various legislative districts were "of sufficient magnitude to make out a *prima facie* case of invidious discrimination . . . ."[14] However, because of the imminence of the primary and general elections, and because two constitutional amendments, proposed through the initiative procedure and prescribing rather different schemes for legislative apportionment, would be voted on in November 1962, the court continued the cases without further action until after the election.

At the November 1962 general election the Colorado voters adopted proposed Amendment No. 7, by a total vote of 305,700 to 172,725; it carried every county. Proposed Amendment No. 8 was defeated in every county, the total vote being 311,749 to 149,822. The rejected amendment would have prescribed an apportionment plan by which both houses of the legislature would have been apportioned on an approximate population basis; no senate districts, for example, with a population smaller than one half of the ratio secured by dividing total population by the number of senate seats would have been allowed.[15] The successful amendment provided for apportionment of the lower house generally on the basis of population, but essentially maintained the existing apportionment in the senate, in which population was only one of the factors.

14. Lisco v. McNichols, 208 F. Supp. 471, 478 (D. Colo. 1962).
15. Lisco v. Love, 219 F. Supp. 922, 925 (D. Colo. 1963).

The defeated amendment would have continued elections at large in counties entitled to more than one senator or representative, while the successful amendment established single-member districts. This issue, technically unrelated to apportionment on a population basis, was said to be influential in the decision of many voters from populous areas.

After the 1962 vote the parties amended their pleadings so that the cases thereafter involved solely the new Amendment No. 7. After trial the district court, dividing two to one, concluded that the new plan was valid and the deviations from a population basis in the apportionment of senate seats were rational. The court stated that the plan for the senate "recognizes population as a prime, but not controlling, factor and gives effect to such important considerations as geography, compactness and contiguity of territory, accessibility, observance of natural boundaries [and] conformity to historical division such as county lines and prior representation districts . . . ."[16] With reference to the statewide referendum the court stated: "By adopting Amendment No. 7 and by rejecting Amendment No. 8, which proposed to apportion the legislature on a per capita basis, the electorate has made its choice between the conflicting principles."[17]

On appeal the United States Supreme Court reversed the decision (for reasons to be discussed below) and remanded to the district court for reconsideration in view of *Reynolds*. Justices Stewart and Clark dissented in an opinion written by Stewart, and Clark wrote a brief separate dissent. Justice Harlan dissented in this case, as he did in all, in a separate opinion applicable to all the cases.

Maryland: Plaintiffs — residents and voters of four populous Maryland counties, the city of Baltimore, and an unincorporated association — originally filed suit in a state court in August 1960, seeking a declaratory judgment that article III, sections 2 and 5 of the Maryland constitution denied them and others similarly situated of rights protected by the equal protection clause. They also requested a declaratory judgment that the failure of the Maryland general assembly to convene a constitutional convention as approved by a majority of the state's voters in the general election of 1950 violated various provisions of the state constitution. Accordingly, the plaintiffs asked that unless the elections from and after

16. Id. at 932.
17. Ibid.

November 1962 were conducted at large, defendant election officials be enjoined from performing election duties until the general assembly should submit for popular vote a referendum measure seeking valid revision of the constitution.

In February 1961 the trial court sustained defendants' demurrers to the complaint; but in April 1962, after the decision in *Baker*, the Maryland Court of Appeals reversed and remanded the case for a hearing on the merits.[18]

Article III of the Maryland constitution of 1867 vested legislative power in a bicameral general assembly, providing for a senate of 29 members — one from each of the 23 counties and six from the city of Baltimore, and for a house of delegates of 123 members with a prescribed number of representatives from each of the counties and from each of the legislative districts in the city of Baltimore. Based on 1960 census figures the counties of Anne Arundel, Baltimore, Montgomery, and Prince Georges and the city of Baltimore had 76 per cent of the state's population, but when the suit was initiated they elected only 34 per cent of the state senators and 49 per cent of the members of the house of delegates. (The latter proportion was increased to 55 per cent by legislative action during the pendency of the litigation.) The largest senate district had 32 times the population of the smallest, and, even after the 1962 changes in the house of delegates, the ratio there was six to one.

At the trial defendants admitted that between 1951 and 1959 ten reapportionment bills had been introduced into the general assembly, but that all had failed to pass because of opposition of legislators from the less populous counties, and that in 1960 neither house passed bills incorporating reapportionment recommendations of a special commission created by the governor in 1959 to investigate and report on the question. Moreover, despite voter approval (by a vote of 200,439 to 56,998) in a statewide referendum in 1950 of the calling of a constitutional convention, the general assembly between 1951 and 1958 refused to enact the necessary enabling legislation.

In May 1962 the trial court judge ruled that the apportionment of the house of delegates invidiously discriminated against the people of Montgomery, Baltimore, and Prince Georges Counties (but not against the city of Baltimore or Anne Arundel County) in vio-

18. The Maryland Committee for Fair Representation v. Tawes, 228 Md. 412, 180 A.2d 656 (1962).

lation of the equal protection clause of the fourteenth amendment. The judge gave as his opinion, without a formal ruling, that the apportionment of the senate might "be constitutionally based upon area and geographical location regardless of population or eligible voters." The court also stated that the general assembly had the power to enact a statute providing for reapportionment of the house of delegates and to propose a constitutional amendment providing for reapportionment.[19]

At the end of May 1962 the Maryland legislature enacted a temporary reapportionment of the house of delegates providing, in a body of 123 members, that each of the 23 counties and each of the six legislative districts in the city of Baltimore should have a minimum of two delegates, and dividing the remaining 65 seats among the more populous counties.[20] The effect was to take 19 delegates from the less populous counties and divide them among the more populous counties, but still without achieving even approximate equality in the lower house and without altering the senate at all. The statute provided for its expiration on January 1, 1966, except that, if a superseding constitutional amendment should be submitted to the voters in the 1964 election and be rejected, the statute would continue in force until January 1, 1970. Upon its expiration the apportionment formula was to revert to that already held invalid by the state court. At that session the legislature failed to pass a proposed constitutional amendment which would have reapportioned the lower house.

Plaintiffs appealed from the trial court's failure to rule the senate apportionment invalid. The Maryland Court of Appeals promptly remanded for a decision of that question; with that urging, the trial court held that the senate apportionment was valid because an apportionment based on area and geography, regardless of population, protected minorities, prevented hasty (although popular) legislation, and accorded with history, tradition, and reason. The court relied heavily upon a comparison to the United States Senate. This decision was affirmed by the Maryland Court of Appeals by a vote of five to three, stating three grounds for the decision: (1) Since 1837 each county had had the same number of representatives except the

19. See The Maryland Committee for Fair Representation v. Tawes, 377 U.S. 656, 661–62 (1964).

20. Md. Ann. Code, art. 42, § 40 (1962 Supp.).

city of Baltimore, whose representation had been increased. (2)
One house should be apportioned on the basis of geography because
the idea of a bicameral legislature assumes two different methods
of apportionment in the two houses in order to check "hasty and ill-
conceived legislation." (3) The so-called federal analogy of different formulas for representation in the United States Senate and
House of Representatives justifies differences in state formulas between the two houses. Chief Judge Brune and Judges Prescott and
Marbury dissented. They pointed out that the house of delegates,
even under the new statute, was not apportioned in accordance with
population, and that the disparities in the senate were gross. They
concluded that neither history, the federal analogy (which they distinguished), nor the desirability of "a proper diffusion of political
restraint" furnished a rational basis for such gross disparities in per
capita representation as were found in the Maryland legislature.[21]

On appeal the United States Supreme Court reversed and remanded. Chief Justice Warren, writing for the Court, said in part:

> reliance on the so-called federal analogy as a sustaining principle for the
> Maryland apportionment scheme, despite significant deviations from pop-
> ulation-based representation in both houses of the General Assembly, is
> clearly misplaced. And considerations of history and tradition . . . do not,
> and could not, provide a sufficient justification for the substantial devia-
> tions from population-based representation in both houses of the Mary-
> land Legislature.[22]

For remedial action the Court placed "primary responsibility" on
the legislature, which was said to have "adequate time" to act.
"However, under no circumstances should the 1966 election of
members of the Maryland Legislature be permitted to be conducted pursuant to the existing or any other unconstitutional
plan."[23]

Justice Clark concurred for the reasons stated in his concurring
opinion in *Reynolds*. Justice Stewart would have vacated the judgment and remanded to the state court to determine whether the
Maryland apportionment "could be shown systematically to pre-

---

21. The Maryland Committee for Fair Representation v. Tawes, 229 Md. 406, 184
A.2d 715 (1962).

22. Maryland Committee for Fair Representation v. Tawes, 377 U.S. 656, 675 (1964).

23. Id. at 676.

vent ultimate effective majority rule."[24] Justice Harlan dissented.

Virginia: Plaintiffs — four residents and qualified voters of the Virginia counties of Arlington and Fairfax — filed suit in federal district court in April 1962, shortly after the Supreme Court decision in *Baker*, in their own behalf and in behalf of all similarly situated voters, challenging the apportionment of both houses of the state legislature. Defendants were officials charged with various duties in connection with administration of the election laws of Virginia, including the governor and the attorney general. A three-judge court was convened, and residents and voters of the city of Norfolk were permitted to intervene against the original defendants and against additional election officials of Norfolk.

Acting under sections 40–43 of the Virginia constitution of 1902, the Virginia general assembly in 1962 had established 36 senatorial districts from which 40 senators were to be elected, and 70 districts for the house of delegates, among which 100 seats were distributed. It was shown at the trial that the 1962 act produced disparities, in terms of voter representation by each member, of more than two to one in the senate and more than four to one in the house of delegates.

Defendants introduced various exhibits showing the number of military and military-related personnel in the city of Norfolk and in Arlington and Fairfax Counties, disparities from population-based representation among the various states in the federal electoral college, and the results of a comparative study of state legislative apportionment which showed Virginia ranking eighth among the states in population-based legislative representativeness.[25]

In November 1962 the district court, with one judge dissenting, sustained plaintiffs' claims and entered an interlocutory order. The court refused to stay its action pending initial ascertainment of the views of the state courts on the validity of the apportionment, finding instead that the relevant constitutional and statutory provisions were unambiguous. The court stated that, although population is the predominant consideration, other factors may be of some relevance, but that the inequalities in Virginia, if unexplained, showed an invidious discrimination. Although preferring legislative correction, the court concluded that decision could not be delayed because

24. Id. at 677.
25. Davis v. Mann, 377 U.S. 678, 682 (1964).

of the imminence of elections in 1963 for legislative terms not ending until 1968. Accordingly, the court enjoined conduct of elections
under the 1962 act, but stayed the operation of the injunction until
January 31, 1963, so that either the legislature could act or an appeal
could be taken to the Supreme Court. Jurisdiction was retained for
the entry of such orders as might be required.[26]

On appeal the United States Supreme Court affirmed and remanded the case. The Court, in its opinion by Chief Justice Warren, noted that, since no further election of Virginia legislators
would take place until 1965, "ample time remains for the Virginia
Legislature to enact a constitutionally valid reapportionment
scheme for purposes of that election."[27]

Justices Clark and Stewart agreed with the majority that the
Virginia apportionment did not satisfy equal protection standards,
but without adopting the full reach of the majority insistence that
both houses be apportioned substantially on a population basis.
Justice Harlan dissented.

Delaware: Shortly after the Supreme Court decision in *Baker*, an
action was filed challenging the apportionment of both houses of
the Delaware legislature. The plaintiffs in this action, *Roman v.
Sincock*,[28] were residents and qualified voters of New Castle County,
Delaware, suing in their own behalf and in behalf of all persons
similarly situated. Defendants were various officials charged with
the performance of duties in connection with state elections. Plaintiffs asserted that they had no adequate remedy except in the federal
courts because the existing apportionment was frozen into the Delaware constitution of 1897; because the legislature was dominated by
legislators representing the two less populous counties, to the disadvantage of the county of New Castle and the city of Wilmington;
and because it was, as a practical matter, impossible to amend the
state constitution or to convene a constitutional convention for the
purpose of reapportioning the legislature.

The constitution of 1897 apportioned ten representatives and
five senators to each of the three counties, Kent, Sussex, and New
Castle. The city of Wilmington, in the county of New Castle, was
given five representatives and two senators, even though at that time

26. Mann v. Davis, 213 F. Supp. 577 (E.D. Va. 1962).

27. Davis v. Mann, 377 U.S. 678, 693 (1964).

28. 377 U.S. 695 (1964).

the population of the city exceeded that of the rest of the county and was larger than the total population of either of the other counties.[29] The 35 representative districts generally followed the boundaries of the "hundreds," geographic subdivisions of the counties in Delaware since its founding.[30] Many of the representative districts coincided with a particular hundred; others consisted of a portion of a hundred, or of a hundred and a portion of another hundred, or of two or more hundreds or portions of hundreds. The city of Wilmington was divided into five representative districts. The 17 senatorial districts, also specified in the constitution, consisted either of two representative districts each (as was true in Kent and Sussex) or in New Castle County of two or more portions of hundreds or of portions of the city of Wilmington.

By 1962 the senate districts ranged in population from 4,177 to 64,820. On the basis of 1960 census figures, 22 per cent of the total population resided in districts electing a majority of the members of the senate. Representative districts ranged in population, as of 1960, from 1,643 to 58,228; and a majority of that body could be elected from districts including only about 18.5 per cent of the 1960 state population.

The three-judge federal district court, convened in response to the plaintiffs' request for an injunction to prevent the holding of further elections under the existing apportionment scheme, initially stayed the proceedings to August 7, 1962, to give the legislature an opportunity to take "some appropriate action."[31] On July 30 the general assembly approved a proposed amendment to the reapportionment provisions of the Delaware constitution, although under other provisions of that constitution it would not become effective unless again approved by the next succeeding session of the general assembly. On August 7 the district court refused to dismiss the suit

29. At the trial it was shown that in the six years preceding the suit, several bills providing for reapportionment or for the calling of a constitutional convention either were not reported or failed to pass.

30. Hundreds, as geographic units, had been used in England as subdivisions of counties or shires based on the number of families residing in the area. Each hundred consisted of ten towns or tithings, which in turn consisted of ten families of freeholders, 1 Blackstone, Commentaries 114–16 (1846 ed.). In Delaware the hundreds survive as subdivisions of counties established under the authority of William Penn. There are 11 hundreds in New Castle County (including Wilmington Hundred, which is coterminous with the city); 9 hundreds in Kent County; and 13 hundreds in Sussex County.

Hundreds were also used as geographic subdivisions in the early colonial days in Virginia, Maryland, and Pennsylvania; but they have survived only in Delaware.

31. Sincock v. Terry, 207 F. Supp. 205 (D. Del. 1962).

and stated the necessity of proceeding promptly to decision.[32] On October 16 the court denied plaintiffs' application for a preliminary injunction and defendants' application for a further stay.[33] As a result, the elections were held in November 1962 pursuant to the unrevised apportionment provisions of the 1897 constitution. In January 1963 the legislature gave the requisite second approval to the proposed constitutional amendment; but in April the three-judge court held that the Delaware apportionment provisions, even after amendment, resulted in gross and invidious discriminations in violation of the equal protection clause of the fourteenth amendment. "The uneven growth of the different areas of the State created a condition because of which the numbers of inhabitants in representative and senatorial districts differed not only on an intercounty basis but also on an intracounty basis."[34]

The district court ruled that at least one house of a bicameral state legislature must be based substantially on population and denied the relevance of the federal analogy as a justification for deviations from a population-based apportionment in either house. Nevertheless, the court thought it appropriate to allow the legislature a further opportunity to reapportion in accordance with the meaning of the fourteenth amendment, and so gave the general assembly until October 1, 1963, to adopt a valid plan.

In May 1963 the Delaware Supreme Court advised the governor that, notwithstanding the holding of the district court, he should proceed with the apportionment provided in the 1963 constitutional amendment, which the governor did. Thereupon, on May 20, 1963, the district court enjoined the holding of any election for the legislature, pursuant to the old or the new apportionment. However, on June 27, 1963, Justice Brennan stayed the operation of the injunction pending final disposition by the Supreme Court.

On appeal the United States Supreme Court affirmed and remanded the case. Justices Clark and Stewart concurred in the affirmance because the defendants had not shown any rational explanation for the gross inequalities; and Justice Harlan dissented for the reasons stated in his full dissent to all the cases.[35]

32. Id., 210 F. Supp. 395 (D. Del. 1962).
33. Id. at 396.
34. Sincock v. Duffy, 215 F. Supp. 169, 177 (D. Del. 1963).
35. Id. at 712.

THE EQUAL-POPULATION
PRINCIPLE ANNOUNCED

These were the six cases from whose factual variations the Court was conveniently able to extract examples of nearly all the variations of apportionment formulas and arguments in justification of deviations from equality of voter representation. Here, for example, was the elaborate plan of New York, with its explicit rationale of preference for the less populous counties in both houses, available for ready comparison with the voter-approved plan in Colorado based on population in one house and on other factors in the other house, both plans standing in sharp contrast to the relatively formless apportionment structures in Alabama, Delaware, Maryland, and Virginia. The Delaware and Maryland plans had some basis in history, but no adjustment had been made for population shifts, which threw whatever pattern there may have been far out of balance.

The New York and Virginia legislatures had been faithful to requirements of decennial reapportionment contained in their state constitutions. In contrast, the Alabama legislature had for sixty years ignored the constitutional requirement of periodic reapportionment. The Maryland legislature, somewhat similarly, had refused to call a constitutional convention despite an overwhelming popular vote to that effect. Still different was the situation in Delaware, in which the distribution of legislative seats had been frozen into the constitution before the turn of the century, while in Colorado the voters had exercised the power of initiative to effect a change in the provisions for apportionment in the state constitution.

In every case there was emphasis on local political subdivisions, counties, cities, towns — and even, in Delaware, the colonial relic of the hundred. In terms of an opportunity to test the constitutional definition of equal protection as applied to a variety of factual situations and against a host of conceptual justifications the cases were ideal. It was of course no accident that, of the fifteen or more state legislative apportionment cases in which jurisdictional statements were filed with the Court in the October 1962 and October 1963 terms, these particular cases were accepted for review, including briefing and oral argument. The conscious selection of cases for decision was most apparent in the grant of review in the Colorado case, *Lucas v. Colorado General Assembly*, on December 9, 1963, the day on which the last of the other five cases was argued. Several other cases were pending at the same time, but it was clearly not by inadvertence that the Court left all those cases for subsequent decision by per curiam order without oral argument. The reason was simple. The lower court decision in the Colorado case relied in large part on the federal analogy, an issue not so sharply presented in any of the other cases ripe for hearing. So the Court took that case out of sequence, as it were, and heard oral argument, on March 31 and April 1, 1964, more than three months after oral argument in the Delaware case, the last preceding case to be heard, and more than four months after the oral argument in the group of cases first heard — the Alabama, Maryland, New York, and Virginia cases. In short, the Court took the wise precaution of hearing every argument which could have been expected to shed any light on the problems on which a ruling was to be made. As a result, no matter how substantial the disagreement of any critic with the result, at least none could say that the Court had failed to inform itself of the consequences of its action. It was thus possible for Chief Justice Warren, in writing for the majority, to deal explicitly, in the factual setting of the cases before him, with every argument which had been advanced, or which was likely to be advanced, in opposition to the ruling he was about to make. Thus, almost uniquely in the enunciation of new and important constitutional principles, the opinions here could be shaped to dispose at one time of all the significant issues, leaving for future adjudication primarily questions of timing and the specifics of remedial techniques to deal with delays in compliance.

The Warren opinions are significant for another reason. In all six cases the opinions follow an established pattern characteristic of the Chief Justice. There is first a chronological history of the litigation, then a summary of the applicable apportionment formula and illustrations, primarily statistical, of the ways in which some groups of voters are disadvantaged in comparison with others in the state. Justifications advanced in support of these deviations are dealt with systematically and rejected one by one in straightforward, no-nonsense language the import of which can scarcely be mistaken. In short, the principal questions have now been given answers as clear as the subject matter permits. Short of success on

the part of those who propose constitutional amendments to overturn these rulings, the issue now appears to be one of simply getting
about the business of compliance. And, as will be noted, the process
of bringing the various state legislative apportionment formulas
into conformity with the Court's opinion began immediately after
the decision. There is every indication that substantial compliance
is likely to come rather quickly, compared with the notorious legislative foot-dragging after desegregation of the public schools was
mandated in 1954 by the Supreme Court in *Brown v. Board of Education*, even though that decision had the ostensible advantage of a
single opinion by a unanimous Court.

Probably the single most significant aspect of the Supreme Court
disposition of the state legislative apportionment cases is the literal-
istic, no-compromise reading given to the equal protection clause of
the fourteenth amendment as a command for nearly absolute equality, showing judicial respect for the right of franchise in terms nearly
as absolute as those formulated by the Court in the area of racial
discrimination. Where the Court earlier said in effect that *no* state-
supported racial discrimination is tolerable, it seems now to have
said much the same thing in connection with voter equality. The
state must assure "substantial" equality with only such deviations
as are justifiable on grounds that show no planned or even unintended unfairness. That the Court should have settled on this principle is particularly revealing in view of the fact that the Solicitor
General of the United States, as amicus curiae, although urging
invalidation of the state apportionment plan in each of the six
cases before the Court, had in each case supported the voter plaintiffs on grounds narrower than those settled on by the Court. Moreover, the plaintiffs themselves, while in each case urging adoption
of a principle calling for substantial equality of voter representation among the electoral districts in each of the houses of a bicameral legislature, had indicated in briefs and on oral argument a
willingness to settle for less than the whole loaf.

After the decisions in *Baker*, *Gray*, and *Wesberry*, for all their
factual distinctions, no particular clairvoyance was required to sense
that some state apportionment schemes were likely to be upset; and
the Solicitor General offered what many thought was a particularly
tempting lead into the "political thicket" which might avoid the
sharpest of the nettles until further testing could be had in lower
courts and state legislatures. Thus, the United States assumed argu-

endo in its amicus briefs in all six cases "that the Equal Protection Clause as applied to State apportionment, unlike Article I, Section 2, as applied to Congressional districting, does not require *per capita* equality."[36] Consistent with that assumption, the United States' analysis of the equal protection clause, as applied to state legislative apportionment, rested on these two principles:

> First, the basic standard of comparison, in applying the Equal Protection Clause, is the representation of qualified voters *per capita*. Second, discrimination in *per capita* representation accorded any group of voters is unconstitutional unless it has a rational basis in objectives relevant to the electoral process. The latter principle is, of course, the traditional rule in all kinds of cases under the Equal Protection Clause, although greater justification is required for discrimination in personal or political rights.[37]

No member of the Court adopted this seemingly reasonable invitation to judicial experimentation. Justice Harlan was not interested because even such a relatively moderate approach was inconsistent with his view of the necessity for judicial self-restraint and with his understanding of the meaning of equal protection. Justices Clark and Stewart were also not persuaded; each found rational

36. Brief for the United States as Amicus Curiae, p. 34, Lucas v. Colorado General Assembly, 377 U.S. 713 (1964).

37. Id. at 34–35. The latter principle was particularized in three corollary propositions formulated to cover all the cases then before the Court as most completely stated in the brief in the Colorado case.

"(a) The Equal Protection Clause is violated by an apportionment that creates gross inequalities in representation without rhyme or reason . . . .

"(b) The Equal Protection Clause is violated by a discriminatory apportionment based upon criteria which are contrary to express constitutional limitations, or otherwise invidious, or irrelevant to any permissible objective of legislative apportionment. We distinguish between (1) bases of apportionment which serve the purpose of making representative government work better, even though a collateral consequence may be *per capita* inequalities, and (2) methods of apportionment whose only function is to create classes of voters with political power disproportionate to their number, as by giving farmers more representation than wage earners, city dwellers more than suburbanites, shipping interests more representation than manufacturing communities, or Protestants more than Jews. . . .

"(c) The present case comes down to the question whether the permissible objectives can reasonably be deemed adequate to justify the inequalities in *per capita* representation resulting from Amendment No. 7. Circumstances or objectives that might, under our basic assumption, furnish a reasonable basis for small inequalities are utterly inadequate, even whimsical, when offered as support for grosser discrimination. Accordingly, we turn to the facts of the instant case. We show first that the equal *per capita* representation in Colorado's lower house is not alone enough to satisfy the requirements of equal protection. We then show that the discrimination in *per capita* representation in the Senate, even when weighed against every available justification, is too great to satisfy the requirements of equal protection in a matter so vital as participation in the processes of self-government." Id. at 35–38.

and not arbitrary the plans approved by the New York voters in 1894 and by the Colorado voters in 1962. In voting to invalidate other state formulas they did so only because they considered those plans irrational. The most striking fact is that none of the other six Justices was sufficiently tempted to follow the lead of the Solicitor General's suggestion to rest a while at that halfway house before making an irrevocable commitment to the hard principle. The Chief Justice, writing for six members of the Court, gave a firm answer to questions that had in part been only softly asked.

Since it is not given to those outside the Court to know with assurance why one approach to a threshold constitutional question is taken and another rejected, reasoned speculation is the only choice available.

Assuredly, the equal protection concept, until examined in its historical context and as fleshed out with Supreme Court interpretation, is at best an abstraction. Even after review of its origins and the substantial body of case law which surrounds it, the most astute student of the Supreme Court would have hesitated to predict with confidence the exact reach of the fourteenth amendment as a limitation upon state powers over legislative apportionment before the decision in *Baker*. Even after the Court made clear in *Baker* what should always have been clear — that the Court has not only the power of review but as well an obligation to decide — several avenues of decision were available. In addition to the course of decision taken by the Court, the equal protection clause could have been given the more limited reading suggested by the Solicitor General or the still more restrictive interpretation of Justices Clark and Stewart. Reasons will be suggested in the final chapters of this volume for believing that the Court fulfilled admirably its high obligation of wise choice in deciding as it did, in terms of history, experience, logic, and likelihood of success in enforcement.

The Majority Opinions and the Equal-Population Principle. The Chief Justice of the United States has the power of designating which member of the Court will prepare the opinion in those cases in which the Chief Justice has voted for the prevailing position. Chief Justice Earl Warren has divided the opinion-writing task with near-equality in terms of the numbers of cases assigned to the various Justices; but he has often reserved to himself the decisions most likely to be controversial, as he did in this instance.

The Chief Justice selected the Alabama case, *Reynolds v. Sims*, for the principal opinion in the *Reapportionment Cases*. It was a logical choice for several reasons: (1) The facts spoke overwhelmingly of discrimination in voter representation, not only as a result of the operative state constitutional provisions, but as well in terms of legislative refusal over a sixty-year period to comply even with the requirements of the Alabama constitution. The resulting aggravation of the already appreciable malapportionment presented a "crazy quilt" not unlike *Baker*, permitting agreement as to result by Justices Clark and Stewart. (2) The Supreme Court decision in *Reynolds* called for affirmance of the action of the lower court and indeed provided an opportunity for a little congratulatory pat on the back for the district court judges. (3) Only Justice Harlan dissented from the result.

With that much going for the decision, as it were, the Chief Justice was able to proceed directly to the large issues with which he was principally concerned. "Undeniably," he said, "the Constitution of the United States protects the right of all qualified citizens to vote, in state as well as in federal elections. A consistent line of decisions by this Court in cases involving attempts to deny or restrict the right of suffrage has made this indelibly clear. It has been repeatedly recognized that all qualified voters have a constitutionally protected right to vote."[38]

In making the point that "all qualified voters have a constitutionally protected right to vote," a proposition no one denies, the Chief Justice cited a familiar line of cases dealing principally with the long struggle to vindicate the right of franchise of the Negro in general elections and in primaries in the face of restrictive state laws and practices and hostile acts of individuals. The Chief Justice was naturally aware that the cases which he cited, and from which he quoted, affirmed the right of franchise primarily in the context of racial discrimination. Several of those cases involved the power of the United States, under article I, section 4, to "make or alter" state regulations as to the "times, places, and manner" of holding elections for federal officers.[39] In others the constitutional question turned on the fifteenth amendment's prohibition against official interference with the right of persons to vote on grounds of race, color,

38. 377 U.S. at 554.

39. Ex parte Siebold, 100 U.S. 371 (1880); Ex parte Yarbrough, 110 U.S. 651 (1884); United States v. Mosley, 238 U.S. 383 (1915) (semble); United States v. Classic, 313 U.S. 299 (1941); United States v. Saylor, 322 U.S. 385 (1944).

or previous condition of servitude.[40] In only two of the cited cases was the fourteenth amendment the decisive factor for the ruling; and in both of those there was blatant state action in specific denial of the right of Negro participation in the election process.[41]

In short, none of these cases did more than establish that the right of franchise is given preferred status in the hierarchy of constitutional values. Although this recitation does not, then, make inevitable any particular solution to the apportionment cases, it is indicative of a pervasive attitude of the Court in the past and exemplifies how that tradition can be carried forward. For example, when there was earlier presented to the Supreme Court evidence that, in order to protect the electoral process against discriminatory exclusions, the constitutional protection must be extended to eliminate the so-called "white" primaries, the Court did not hesitate to find a protected right even at the cost of overruling earlier case law.[42] It was in this spirit that the Court reminded of the primary values involved in the right of franchise and proceeded to inquire into the ways in which the now-complained-against practices might put in jeopardy that lofty principle.

Having said this much, the Chief Justice then moved immediately to the new question presented by the apportionment cases. That there was no significantly relevant judicial interpretation prior to 1962 was understandable. In the period during which the right-of-franchise cases were outlining new perimeters for the scope of the constitutionally protected area,[43] state legislative apportionment cases were not considered by the Court on their merits. In the few cases in which Supreme Court review had been sought during that same time, review had ordinarily been denied, usually for "want of equity" (see pages 68–71). *Baker v. Carr*, however, set the stage for a change, noting the fact of jurisdiction in the federal

40. Guinn v. United States, 238 U.S. 347 (1915); Lane v. Wilson, 307 U.S. 268 (1939); Smith v. Allwright, 321 U.S. 649 (1944); Terry v. Adams, 345 U.S. 461 (1953); Gomillion v. Lightfoot, 364 U.S. 339 (1960). See also Ex parte Yarbrough, 110 U.S. 651 (1884).

41. Nixon v. Herndon, 273 U.S. 536 (1927); Nixon v. Condon, 286 U.S. 73 (1932).

42. See Smith v. Allwright, 321 U.S. 649 (1944), overruling Grovey v. Townsend, 295 U.S. 45 (1935).

43. See particularly Smith v. Allwright, 321 U.S. 649 (1944) (invalidating the "white primary" conducted by a political party as part of the state election process); Terry v. Adams, 345 U.S. 461 (1953) (invalidating a pre-primary preferential ballot conducted by a "private" association, but which exercised effective choice over selection of candidates); Gomillion v. Lightfoot, 364 U.S. 339 (1960) (invalidating a racially motivated gerrymander of election district boundaries).

courts, justiciability there of the issues, and standing to sue of the voter-plaintiffs. The Chief Justice in *Reynolds* recalled the supremely important fact that in *Baker* the Court had made it clear that the issue in the state legislative apportionment cases was to be framed in terms of the equal protection clause, for which "well developed and familiar" judicial standards were said to be available to determine whether "a discrimination reflects *no* policy, but simply arbitrary and capricious action."[44] Progression in the development of the principle was evident, the Chief Justice suggested, in the 1963 decision in *Gray v. Sanders*, where the Court stated that "the Constitution visualizes no preferred class of voters but equality among those who meet the basic qualifications."[45]

However technically distinguishable that decision may have been from the problems later to be presented in the *Reapportionment Cases* (and the Court in *Gray* emphasized the differences), it was not readily possible to believe that *Gray* did not contain a lesson also for those cases to which it admittedly did not directly pertain. The Chief Justice made no effort to deny that relevance when he quoted from *Gray* where the Court had said that "there is no indication in the Constitution that homesite or occupation affords a permissible basis for distinguishing between qualified voters within the State."[46] Finally, the Chief Justice recited the holding in *Wesberry v. Sanders* that "as nearly as is practicable one man's vote in a congressional election is to be worth as much as another's."[47] And he noted, again quoting from *Wesberry*, that "Our Constitution leaves no room for classification of people in a way that unnecessarily abridges this right."[48]

Noting that *Gray* and *Wesberry* were "not dispositive" of the state legislative apportionment cases, the Chief Justice also observed that "neither are they wholly inapposite." *Gray* "established the basic principle of equality among voters within a State, and held that voters cannot be classified, constitutionally, on the basis of where they live . . . ."; and *Wesberry* "clearly established that the fundamental principle of representative government in this coun-

---

44. Baker v. Carr, 369 U.S. 186, 226 (1962).

45. 372 U.S. 368, 380 (1963).

46. Reynolds v. Sims, 377 U.S. 533, at 558 (1964), quoting from Gray v. Sanders, 372 U.S. 368, 381 (1963).

47. 377 U.S. at 559, quoting from Wesberry v. Sanders, 376 U.S. 1, 14 (1964).

48. 377 U.S. at 560, quoting from 376 U.S. at 18.

try is one of equal representation for equal numbers of people, without regard to race, sex, economic status, or place of residence within a State."[49] He concluded the historical review by stating that the problem "is to ascertain, in the instant cases, whether there are any constitutionally cognizable principles which would justify departures from the basic standard of equality among voters in the apportionment of seats in state legislatures."[50]

Consideration of this problem required explanation of the meaning of the equal protection clause in the context of state legislative apportionment. That inquiry was not necessarily an easy one; the words of constitutional prohibition are at best not self-defining; and the matter is further complicated by the fact that there have developed over the years two equal protection traditions, both stemming from the same clause but with substantially different results as applied. The matter is more fully developed at pages 169–80; a brief summary should suffice here. Perhaps the more traditional view, at least the one applied in the larger number of cases, is that state legislatures are entitled to considerable freedom in fixing classificatory schemes where economic or social policies of the state are the considerations involved. The other tradition, also of venerable standing, holds that where the classification challenged as a denial of equal protection "touches a sensitive and important area of human rights," and involves one of "the basic civil rights of man,"[51] the latitude for classification is narrowly confined.

In view of the importance of the right of franchise, already fully recognized by the Court, there was no particular hesitance to conclude that the dilution of the vote alleged in these cases involved an equal protection claim of the latter type, more nearly absolute in nature. The Court noted simply that "The right to vote is personal"[52] and that the political franchise is "a fundamental political right, because preservative of all rights."[53] Accordingly, the Court readily concluded that deliberate legislative malapportionment requires an application of the equal protection clause which borders on the absolute because rational classification is difficult if not impossible. The cases were in this sense comparable to other recent ap-

49. 377 U.S. at 560.
50. Id. at 561.
51. Skinner v. Oklahoma, 316 U.S. 535 (1942).
52. 377 U.S. at 561, quoting from United States v. Bathgate, 246 U.S. 220, 227 (1918).
53. Id. at 562, quoting from Yick Wo v. Hopkins, 118 U.S. 356, 370 (1886).

plications of the equal protection clause in similarly absolutist fashion to state-required racial discrimination in public schools[54] or discrimination against the indigent in criminal proceedings arising out of the fact of poverty.[55] The reasons given by the Chief Justice for this view of the equal protection clause gained force through positive statement.

> To the extent that a citizen's right to vote is debased, he is that much less a citizen. The fact that an individual lives here or there is not a legitimate reason for overweighting or diluting the efficacy of his vote. . . . Population is, of necessity, the starting point for consideration and the controlling criterion for judgment in legislative apportionment controversies. A citizen, a qualified voter, is no more nor no less so because he lives in the city or on the farm. This is the clear and strong command of our Constitution's Equal Protection Clause.[56]

With the hard question thus settled, the rest was easier, even if not absolutely inevitable. The holding itself was unequivocal.

> We hold that, as a basic constitutional standard, the Equal Protection Clause requires that the seats in both houses of a bicameral state legislature must be apportioned on a population basis. Simply stated, an individual's right to vote for state legislators is unconstitutionally impaired when its weight is in a substantial fashion diluted when compared with votes of citizens living in other parts of the State.[57]

The principal objection which has been advanced to the Court's ruling that the equal-population principle applies to both houses of a bicameral state legislature has been based on the so-called federal analogy. That question will be more fully discussed in a later chapter (pages 196–203), but the nature of the argument and the reasons for the Court's rejection of it should at least be mentioned here. The contention is that since one house of the United States Congress is apportioned on the basis of population, while membership in the other is allocated on an equal basis to all states, it should follow that the fourteenth amendment does not forbid a similar distribution of seats in state legislative bodies. The majority rejected the argument in *Reynolds* as "inapposite and irrelevant to state legislative districting schemes. Attempted reliance on the

54. Brown v. Board of Education, 347 U.S. 483 (1954).
55. Griffin v. Illinois, 351 U.S. 12 (1956); Douglas v. California, 372 U.S. 353 (1963).
56. 377 U.S. at 567–68.
57. Id. at 568.

federal analogy appears often to be little more than an after-the-fact rationalization offered in defense of maladjusted state apportionment arrangements."[58] In support of this proposition it was shown that both houses of most state legislatures were originally apportioned on the basis of population. Even in more recent years, when the trend has increasingly been to deny popular representation either through specific constitutional change or through disregard of constitutional requirements to that effect, the "federal analogy" has not been widely accepted by the states in principle, and not at all in precisely the same form as the United States Congress.

Moreover, the Court noted, the system of representation in the two houses of Congress is specifically provided for in the Constitution itself as part of the Great Compromise in order to permit the drafters of the Constitution to continue their work, which otherwise would have been aborted. Finally in this connection, the Court reminded of the difference between the sovereign states as governmental units entitled to direct representation and the counties and other local subdivisions of state governments, not possessed of sovereignty, but created solely to assist in the carrying out of such state governmental functions as may be delegated to them. On all these grounds, then, the federal analogy was put aside.

An alternative refuge for those who would permit nonpopulation factors to dominate one house of a bicameral state legislature is the contention that, if both houses are to be selected on essentially the same basis, there is no justification for continuing both houses. But the Court thought that the two houses would not become "anachronistic and meaningless" when the equal-population principle was applied to both houses.

> A prime reason for bicameralism, modernly considered, is to insure mature and deliberate consideration of, and to prevent precipitate action on, proposed legislative measures.[59]

Another argument sometimes made in support of the proposition that states should be allowed to fashion their legislatures as they wish is that, at least for those states admitted to the Union by Congress pursuant to article IV, section 3 of the Constitution (all ex-

58. 377 U.S. at 573.
59. Id. at 576. See also the discussion at pages 258–61 infra.

cept the original thirteen), Congress has at least implicitly approved the representation formulas, including any deviations from the equal-population principle included within those original constitutions. The contention is thus made that such arrangements are plainly sufficient in their establishment of a "republican form of government." The Court's answer was short:

> . . . congressional approval, however well-considered, could hardly validate an unconstitutional state legislative apportionment. Congress simply lacks the constitutional power to insulate States from attack with respect to alleged deprivations of individual constitutional rights.[60]

A final argument sometimes made in support of particular apportionment and districting arrangements is that they should be honored because approved by the voters and subject to alteration by majority vote whenever they prove unsatisfactory to a majority of the electorate. The argument was not even available to defendants in the Alabama,[61] New York,[62] Maryland,[63] Virginia,[64] and

60. Id. at 582.

61. "No effective political remedy to obtain relief against the alleged malapportionment of the Alabama Legislature appears to have been available. No initiative procedure exists under Alabama law. Amendment of the State Constitution can be achieved only after a proposal is adopted by three-fifths of the members of both houses of the legislature, and is approved by a majority of the people, or as a result of a constitutional convention convened after approval by the people of a convention call initiated by a majority of both houses of the Alabama Legislature." Reynolds v. Sims, 377 U.S. 533, 553–54 (1964).

62. "No adequate political remedy to obtain relief against alleged legislative malapportionment appears to exist in New York. No initiative procedure exists under New York law. A proposal to amend the State Constitution can be submitted to a vote by the State's electorate only after approval by a majority of both houses of two successive sessions of the New York Legislature. A majority vote of both houses of the legislature is also required before the electorate can vote on the calling of a constitutional convention. Additionally, under New York law the question of whether a constitutional convention should be called must be submitted to the electorate every 20 years, commencing in 1957. But even if a constitutional convention were convened, the same alleged discrimination which currently exists in the apportionment of Senate seats against each of the counties having 6% or more of a State's citizen population would be perpetuated in the election of convention delegates." WMCA, Inc. v. Lomenzo, 377 U.S. 633, 651–52 (1964).

63. "Maryland law makes no provision for the initiation of legislation or constitutional amendments by the people. Certain constitutional provisions provide, however, for the taking, at a general election each 20 years, of 'the sense of the People in regard to calling a Convention for altering this Constitution.' " But a statewide referendum in 1950, providing for the call of a convention on reapportionment, among other things, overwhelmingly approved by the voters, was never acted on by the legislature. Maryland Committee for Fair Representation v. Tawes, 377 U.S. 656, 668–69 (1964).

64. "No adequate political remedy to obtain legislative reapportionment appears

Delaware[65] cases, but it was the principal argument in the Colorado case. It was urged that the initiative and referendum were not only available to the electorate in Colorado, but had in fact been used in the November 1962 election.[66] The resulting apportionment established one house based on population and one in which nonpopulation factors were dominant. The amendment which so provided, the argument continued, was approved in every county, while an amendment which would have apportioned both houses according to a formula closely geared to population was rejected in every county.

The Supreme Court found the argument untenable in several respects. In the first place, the population-based amendment included objectionable features, such as election at large in multimember districts, which may have caused its defeat in the populous counties. "Thus, neither of the proposed plans was, in all probability, wholly acceptable to the voters in the populous counties, and the assumption of the court below that the Colorado voters made a definitive choice between two contrasting alternatives and indicated that 'minority process in the Senate is what they want' does not appear to be factually justifiable."[67] In the second place, and more significant as the constitutional rule of general applicability, the Court concluded that the equal-population principle must control even where a majority of the voters has indicated satisfaction with an unbalanced scheme of representation.

> While a court sitting as a court of equity might be justified in temporarily refraining from the issuance of injunctive relief in an apportionment case

---

to exist in Virginia. No initiative procedure is provided for under Virginia law. Amendment of the State Constitution or the calling of a constitutional convention initially requires the vote of a majority of both houses of the Virginia General Assembly. Only after such legislative approval is obtained is such a measure submitted to the people for a referendum vote." Davis v. Mann, 377 U.S. 678, 689 (1964).

65. "No initiative and referendum procedure exists in Delaware. Legislative apportionment has been traditionally provided for wholly by constitutional provisions in Delaware, and a concurrence of two-thirds of both houses of two consecutive state legislatures is required in order to amend the State Constitution. The Delaware General Assembly may also, by a two-thirds vote, submit to the State's voters the question of whether to hold a constitutional convention." Roman v. Sincock, 377 U.S. 695, 706 (1964).

66. "An initiated measure proposing a constitutional amendment or a statutory enactment is entitled to be placed on the ballot if the signatures of 8% of those voting for the Secretary of State in the last election are obtained. No geographical distribution of petition signers is required. Initiative and referendum has been frequently utilized throughout Colorado's history." Lucas v. Colorado General Assembly, 377 U.S. 713, 733 (1964).

67. Id. at 732.

in order to allow for resort to an available political remedy, such as initiative and referendum, individual constitutional rights cannot be deprived, or denied judicial effectuation because of the existence of a nonjudicial remedy through which relief against the alleged malapportionment, which the individual voters seek, might be achieved. An individual's constitutionally protected right to cast an equally weighted vote cannot be denied even by a vote of a majority of a State's electorate, if the apportionment scheme adopted by the voters fails to measure up to the requirements of the Equal Protection Clause.[68]

Compliance with the central holding of the apportionment cases, that the composition of both houses of a bicameral state legislature must satisfy the equal-population principle, will require adjustment of the apportionment formula in nearly all — certainly more than forty — of the states as they operated at the time of the decision in 1964.[69] In anticipation of the necessity for prompt action to accomplish these far-reaching changes, two questions of great importance emerge for the state legislatures and for state and lower federal courts which will be required to pass upon the proposed changes. (1) How much deviation, if any, is permissible from a mathematically precise apportionment according to population? (2) How quickly must the changes be accomplished? The Court was mindful of these questions and discussed both in the course of the six majority opinions. That judicial guidance is summarized below; further reflection on these questions will be presented in the final chapter.

Permissible Deviations from the Population Standard. Despite criticism of the decision based on an assumption that the Court in *Reynolds* demanded mathematical exactness among election districts, the Court explicitly disavowed any such requirement.

We realize that it is a practical impossibility to arrange legislative districts so that each one has an identical number of residents, or citizens, or voters. Mathematical exactness or precision is hardly a workable constitutional requirement.[70]

68. Id. at 736.

69. See the appendix for a review of state apportionment provisions through 1965. The sweeping nature of the changes called for was one of the reasons prompting Justice Harlan's dissent. "In these cases the Court holds that seats in the legislatures of six States are apportioned in ways that violate the Federal Constitution. Under the Court's ruling it is bound to follow that the legislatures in all but a few of the other 44 States will meet the same fate." Reynolds v. Sims, 377 U.S. 533, 589 (1964) (dissenting opinion).

70. 377 U.S. at 577.

The important consideration, putting aside the unattainable quest for mathematical precision, is that each state "make an honest and good faith effort to construct districts, in both houses of its legislature, as nearly of equal population as is practicable."[71]

Chief Justice Warren made it as clear as words can that various formulas may be acceptable in light of locally different situations among the several states, and that the testing is to be done, as in the cases first before the Court, in the usual fashion of a case-by-case approach, always giving the lead to state legislatures to devise apportionment formulas acceptable to them.

> For the present, we deem it expedient not to attempt to spell out any precise constitutional tests. What is marginally permissible in one State may be unsatisfactory in another, depending on the particular circumstances of the case. Developing a body of doctrine on a case-by-case basis appears to us to provide the most satisfactory means of arriving at detailed constitutional requirements in the area of state legislative apportionment.[72]

The most important problem for state legislatures making "honest and good faith" efforts to accommodate to the ruling is to ascertain how much, if any, reliance they can place upon the boundary lines of existing political subdivisions. The Court gave solid guidance. So long as "approximate" equality of the vote is satisfied,

> A State may legitimately desire to maintain the integrity of various political subdivisions, insofar as possible, and provide for compact districts of contiguous territory in designing a legislative apportionment scheme. Valid considerations may underlie such aims. Indiscriminate districting, without any regard for political subdivision or natural or historical boundary lines, may be little more than an open invitation to partisan gerrymandering. Single-member districts may be the rule in one State, while another State might desire to achieve some flexibility by creating multi-member or floterial districts.[73]

71. Ibid.

72. Id. at 578.

73. Id. at 578–79. In the Colorado case the Court referred to some of the practical, but presumably not constitutional, problems in the use of multimember districts. In populous districts the ballots become long and the voters are frequently unable to make intelligent selection among candidates not known to them. Thus, there are no identifiable constituencies within populous districts, and each legislator from a multi-member district represents the district as a whole. Lucas v. Colorado General Assembly, 377 U.S. 713, 731–32 (1964).

The term "floterial district" refers to a legislative district which includes within its boundaries several separate districts or political subdivisions which would not independently be entitled to additional representation, but whose aggregate population

A second important clue to the possibility of continued reliance by the states on political subdivision lines lies in the Court's discussion of the standards applicable to state legislative apportionment and those controlling in congressional districting. The Court would apparently approve wider use of political subdivision lines in state legislative apportionment than in congressional districting even though the requirements of "substantial equality" of the one and "equal as nearly as is practicable" of the other do not seem to the uninitiated very different. Differentiation, however, was drawn between the two as follows:

> Since, almost invariably there is a significantly larger number of seats in state legislative bodies to be distributed within a State than congressional seats, it may be feasible to use political subdivision lines to a greater extent in establishing state legislative districts than in congressional districting while still affording adequate representation to all parts of the State.[74]

A third consideration which the Court suggested could be taken into account in justifying some deviations from population-based representation in state legislatures was the assuring of some voice in state legislatures to political subdivisions, but presumably limited to those instances in which the local units of government are actually "charged with various responsibilities incident to the operation of state government."[75] However, the Court cautioned, "permitting deviations from population-based representation does not mean that each local governmental unit or political subdivision can be given separate representation, regardless of population. Carried too far, a scheme of giving at least one seat in one house to each political subdivision (for example, to each county) could easily result, in many States, in a total subversion of the equal-population principle in that legislative body."[76]

Finally, in dealing with the question of keeping apportionment up to date in view of population shifts, the Court noted that some forty-one of the states provide for reapportionment every ten years, which was described as a "rational approach to readjustment of

---

entitles the entire area to another seat in the legislative body being apportioned. The Court discussed floterial districts in Baker v. Carr, 367 U.S. 186, 256 (1962) (Clark, J., concurring) and in Davis v. Mann, 369 U.S. 678, 686 n.2 (1964).

74. 377 U.S. at 578.

75. Id. at 580.

76. Id. at 581.

legislative representation in order to take into account population shifts and growth."[77]

Timing of Changes to Comply with the Equal-Population Principle. In a technical sense the Supreme Court did not order immediate reapportionment of any state legislative body in any of the *Reapportionment Cases*; nor was there any command of immediate reapportionment in any of the nine cases disposed of the following week. Each case was remanded to the court from which review had been sought, and in each case the state court or lower federal court was directed to take further proceedings "consistent with" the general principles in *Reynolds* and the particularities in the applicable Supreme Court decision. The question in each case then became one of determining how the remand court should interpret its mandate.

Two propositions stand out, but they present their own problems of reconciliation. The Court seemed to require speedy implementation, but with deference to legislative judgment. First, "it would be the unusual case in which a court would be justified in not taking appropriate action to insure that no further elections are conducted under the invalid plan."[78] This is the caution against delay in implementation, perhaps a lesson learned from the failure of the "all deliberate speed" formula of the *School Segregation Cases*. Against this rather explicit demand for prompt action, however, is a second consideration which seems to run through all the opinions — less explicit perhaps, but nonetheless a matter of significance. This is a recognition of the judicial tradition against direct interference with the legislative process. It is in deference to this tradition that the courts ordinarily refuse to issue mandates directly to legislatures.[79] In accommodation of the two themes of speedy compliance and deference to legislative judgment, the Court again sounded a note of permissiveness in the solving of "the difficult question of the proper remedial devices which federal courts should utilize . . . ."[80] The locally variant factors which could be taken into account included the imminence of an impending election for which the machinery might already be in progress and general "equitable con-

77. Id. at 583.

78. Id. at 585.

79. "[L]egislative reapportionment is primarily a matter for legislative consideration and determination, and . . . judicial relief becomes appropriate only when a legislature fails to reapportion according to federal constitutional requisites in a timely fashion after having had an adequate opportunity to do so." Id. at 586.

80. 377 U.S. at 585.

siderations" in seeking "to avoid a disruption of the election process which might result from requiring precipitate changes that could make unreasonable or embarrassing demands on a State in adjusting to the requirements of the court's decree."[81]

The same formula was applied in all the cases before the Court, with slight variations appropriate to their varied fact situations. In the New York case, where the primary election machinery for the elections in November had commenced on June 2, 1964, almost two weeks before the Court's ruling in the case, the Court left to the district court decision as to whether corrective action should be attempted before those elections.

> Since all members of both houses of the New York Legislature will be elected in November 1964, the court below, acting under equitable principles, must now determine whether, because of the imminence of that election and in order to give the New York Legislature an opportunity to fashion a constitutionally valid legislative apportionment plan, it would be desirable to permit the 1964 election of legislators to be conducted pursuant to the existing provisions, or whether under the circumstances the effectuation of appellants' right to a properly weighted voice in the election of state legislators should not be delayed beyond the 1964 election.[82]

Although the district court was thus cautioned to look both ways before deciding, such discretion-granting language was calculated to permit, if not encourage, delay of implementation until after the 1964 elections. This is true for several reasons arising out of any realistic appraisal of the questions of timing, necessarily involving considerations of judicial, legislative, and executive convenience. For one thing, the Supreme Court mandate does not normally come to the remand court until twenty-five days after decision in the Supreme Court, thus postponing lower court consideration of the remedies questions until, in this case, July 10.[83] Moreover, as the case goes back to a court whose judgment has been reversed, as in the New York case, the combination of circumstances is unlikely to produce a climate for precipitate upsetting of state election machinery already in progress. Finally, where the governor promises a special session of the legislature, as Governor Rockefeller did in New York, but only after the report of a study commission not

81. Ibid.

82. WMCA, Inc. v. Lomenzo, 377 U.S. 633, 655 (1964).

83. Unless all parties to the litigation stipulate for an earlier issuance of the mandate. Predictably, however, the attorney general of New York preferred to "study" the mandate and so did not consent to advancement.

selected until July 12, 1964, the prospect for change before the 1964 elections came to seem more the exception than the rule.

Where no election was pending in 1964, the Court indicated willingness to permit the invalidly apportioned legislature to continue to sit, at least for the time and at least so long as no further election was held under the rejected apportionment provisions. In Maryland, for example, all legislators had been elected in 1962 for four-year terms. Accordingly, no further elections would be anticipated in normal course until 1966. The Court found delay in correction not impermissible.

> Thus, sufficient time exists for the Maryland Legislature to enact legislation reapportioning seats in the General Assembly prior to the 1966 primary and general elections. With the Maryland constitutional provisions relating to legislative apportionment hereby held unconstitutional, the Maryland Legislature presumably has the inherent power to enact at least temporary reapportionment legislation pending adoption of state constitutional provisions relating to legislative apportionment which comport with federal constitutional requirements.[84]

The Virginia case presented a potentially more serious problem, if permissive delay is thus the rule, because the legislative terms of the two legislative chambers in Virginia are different, four years for senators and two for delegates. While the next election for delegates was scheduled for 1965, the next regularly scheduled election for senators would not take place until 1967, for seating in 1968. The latter interval, nearly four years from the date of invalidation of the apportionment formula, seems an unduly long time for plaintiffs to be required to wait for the relief to which they are entitled. The Supreme Court's answer was somewhat ambiguous:

> Since the next election of Virginia legislators will not occur until 1965, ample time remains for the Virginia Legislature to enact a constitutionally valid reapportionment scheme for purposes of that election. After the District Court has provided the Virginia Legislature with an adequate opportunity to enact a valid plan, it can then proceed, should it become necessary, to grant relief under equitable principles to insure that *no further elections* are held under an unconstitutional scheme. [Emphasis supplied.][85]

---

84. Maryland Committee for Fair Representation v. Tawes, 377 U.S. 656, 675–76 (1964).

85. Davis v. Mann, 377 U.S. 678, 693 (1964).

The emphasized portion of this statement suggests that there might be no objection to allowing the present legislature to run its unconstitutional course for two years in one house and almost four years in the other. There are, however, other ways in which the imbalance could be corrected on a temporary basis. Thus, a system of weighted voting could be put into effect at once without provision for new elections, and this would accurately reflect population despite other problems that might make weighted votes unsatisfactory on a permanent basis. Alternatively, less precisely geared to population, but probably acceptable as a temporary measure, would be the provision of additional legislators for the underrepresented districts. These alternatives will be more fully discussed in the final chapter.

Justices Clark and Stewart, Concurring and Dissenting. In some ways the position of Justices Clark and Stewart in regard to state legislative apportionment is more difficult to accept, even to understand, than either the majority position or that of Justice Harlan, dissenting, both of which are logically clear, however far removed from each other in result and in conception of the role of the Court. Certainly, the majority's argument has about it the cool logic of saying that "equal" means "equal," and no two ways and no two houses about it. At the opposite pole the Harlan position is just as understandable when he said that this is not judicial business (as he did in *Baker v. Carr*), and, even if so, the equal protection clause of the fourteenth amendment does not speak to this point. Justices Clark and Stewart, on the other hand, appear to have attempted to straddle the concededly treacherous shoals of decision. With a bare foothold on either bank they run a serious risk of foundering on their own logic. Rejected by both the majority and the dissent, the concurring-dissenting Justices have only each other for support. The similarity, but not identity, of their views provided a workable basis for substantial agreement on the initial six cases so that they were able to accept without dissent the majority disposition in the Alabama, Delaware, Maryland,[86] and Virginia cases, while dissenting from the disposition of the Colorado and New York cases. That they differed somewhat between themselves on the meaning of the

86. Justice Stewart would have remanded the Maryland case to the state court to determine whether the apportionment "could be shown systematically to prevent ultimate effective majority rule." Maryland Committee for Fair Representation v. Tawes, 377 U.S. 656, 677 (1964).

equal protection clause as applied to state legislatures became apparent in their rather different views as to the proper disposition of the nine cases disposed of on June 22, 1964, which were for the majority easy and for Justice Harlan also perfectly clear. Justices Clark and Stewart agreed with the majority's disposition in three instances, albeit with slight variations in language;[87] disagreed in two instances;[88] and divided on the remaining four cases.[89] When two Justices join in a common dissent on June 15 and disagree as to its meaning in disposing of cases on June 22,[90] and when one Justice expresses his agreement with the majority by sometimes relying on his concurring opinion of the week before and once by citing his dissent of the previous week,[91] those not privy to the voting and decision-making process in the Supreme Court are apt to feel some bewilderment.

Despite, or perhaps because of, this uncertainty about the views of Justices Clark and Stewart, it is important to seek understanding of their "middle ground" position which has seemed to many to provide, in one or another variation, an appropriate solution.

Justice Clark's rationale appears to be two-pronged. In the first place, as he had indicated in *Baker v. Carr*, any apportionment plan which is a "crazy quilt" of irrationalities should be judged in violation of the equal protection clause as invidiously discriminatory. Second, where one house of a bicameral legislature "meets the population standard, representation in the other house might include some departure from it so as to take into account, on a rational basis, other factors in order to afford some representation to the var-

---

87. Williams v. Moss, 378 U.S. 558 (1964); Pinney v. Butterworth, id. at 564; Hill v. Davis, id. at 565.

88. Germano v. Kerner, 378 U.S. 560 (1964); Marshall v. Hare, id. at 561.

89. Swann v. Adams, id. at 553; Meyers v. Thigpen, id. at 554; Nolan v. Rhodes, id. at 556; Hearne v. Smylie, id. at 563.

90. In two cases Justice Clark agreed with the majority disposition, but on the grounds he had stated in his concurrence in Reynolds v. Sims, while Justice Stewart would simply have remanded for further proceedings consistent with the views which he stated in Lucas v. Colorado General Assembly, an opinion in which Clark had joined. Swann v. Adams, 378 U.S. 553 (1964); Meyers v. Thigpen, id. at 554.

In one case Justice Clark joined the majority in its disposition for the reasons stated in his *dissenting* opinion in Lucas v. Colorado General Assembly, while Justice Stewart would simply have remanded for further proceedings consistent with his dissenting opinion in Lucas v. Colorado General Assembly. Hearne v. Smylie, 378 U.S. 563 (1964).

In one case Justice Clark agreed with the majority disposition, while Justice Stewart dissented. Nolan v. Rhodes, 378 U.S. 556 (1964).

91. See discussion supra in note 90, of Swann v. Adams, 378 U.S. 553 (1964) and Meyers v. Thigpen, id. at 554.

ious elements of the State."[92] Putting the two points together, Clark seems to be saying that any logically consistent plan is valid so long as at least one house "meets the population standard." With that understanding, his dissent in the Colorado case is perfectly understandable, for that was precisely the situation there. But that statement does not at all explain the Clark dissent in the New York case where there was a "rational" formula (consistent favoring of the less populous counties at the expense of the more populous), but where neither house met the population standard. In that case, Justice Clark did not separately state why he dissented from the New York ruling, but simply joined in the dissent of Justice Stewart, who made it perfectly clear that he did not believe that *either* house in a bicameral legislature must be population-based. In any event, it was to become apparent one week after these views were announced that Justices Clark and Stewart were not as nearly in agreement as they had at first seemed to be.[93]

Although Justice Stewart, like Justice Clark, concurred in the majority's disposition of the Alabama, Delaware, and Virginia cases, and dissented in the Colorado and New York cases, it became clear in the disposition of the next group of cases that his views are somewhat farther away from those of the majority than those of Justice Clark.[94] The principal statement of the Stewart position is in his carefully drafted dissent to the New York and Colorado cases.[95] With considerable feeling he explained his belief that the majority was simply writing into the Constitution its own preference of political theory.[96] Rejecting what he believed to be an undesirable "locking" into the Constitution of a "particular political philosophy," Justice Stewart then outlined his own views as to the

92. Reynolds v. Sims, 377 U.S. 533, 588 (1964) (Clark, J., concurring).

93. For a fuller discussion of the cases decided on June 22, 1964, see chapter VI.

94. See note 90, supra, and discussion in text preceding the note. Justice Stewart's separate opinion in the Maryland case perhaps forecast his difference with Clark. See note 86, supra.

95. Lucas v. Colorado General Assembly, 377 U.S. 713, 744 (1964).

96. "The Court's draconian pronouncement, which makes unconstitutional the legislatures of most of the 50 States, finds no support in the words of the Constitution, in any prior decision of this Court, or in the 175-year political history of our Federal Union. With all respect, I am convinced these decisions mark a long step backward into that unhappy era when a majority of the members of this Court were thought by many others to have convinced themselves and each other that the demands of the Constitution were to be measured not by what it says, but by their own notions of wise political theory." Id. at 746–48.

proper function of representative government, particularly as safe-guarded by the equal protection clause.

> Representative government is a process of accommodating group inter-ests through democratic institutional arrangements. Its function is to chan-nel the numerous opinions, interests, and abilities of the people of a State into the making of the State's public policy. Appropriate legislative ap-portionment, therefore, should ideally be designed to insure effective rep-resentation in the State's legislature, in cooperation with other organs of political power, of the various groups and interests making up the elector-ate. In practice, of course, this ideal is approximated in the particular apportionment system of any State by a realistic accommodation of the di-verse and often conflicting political forces operating within the State.[97]

Proceeding more specifically to the equal protection clause, Stewart apparently rejected (though he did not refer to) the equal protec-tion interpretation commonly applied in individual rights cases, the line of cases which the majority thought most similar to the right-of-franchise problem here involved. Instead, he accepted as controlling the line of equal protection cases which permit the states wide latitude in experimental classifications within the social and economic welfare area. For example, he quoted with approval from *McGowan v. Maryland:*

> The constitutional safeguard is offended only if the classification rests on grounds wholly irrelevant to the achievement of the State's objective. State legislatures are presumed to have acted within their constitutional power despite the fact that, in practice, their laws resulted in some inequality. A statutory discrimination will not be set aside if any state of facts reasonably may be conceived to justify it.[98]

But in that case the only equal protection issue to which these re-marks were addressed was the question whether Sunday closing laws violated the equal protection clause in permitting certain merchants in Maryland (operators of bathing beaches and amuse-ment parks, for example) to sell merchandise while forbidding its sale to other vendors. That case scarcely sheds much light on the power of the states to regulate the fundamental principle of repre-sentative government, which Stewart thought was involved in the apportionment cases.[99]

97. Id. at 749.
98. 366 U.S. 420, 425–26 (1961).
99. On the equal protection point Justice Stewart cited only one other case, New

When Justice Stewart defined what he described as the two basic attributes of any plan of state apportionment, it was by no means clear that he had not rejected the Court's "particular political philosophy" only to substitute in its place one of his own. The attributes of apportionment which he thought the fourteenth amendment required were these:

> First, it demands that, in the light of the State's own characteristics and needs, the plan must be a rational one. Secondly, it demands that the plan must be such as not to permit the systematic frustration of the will of a majority of the electorate of the State. I think it is apparent that any plan of legislative apportionment which could be shown to reflect no policy, but simply arbitrary and capricious action or inaction, and that any plan which could be shown systematically to prevent ultimate effective majority rule, would be invalid under accepted Equal Protection Clause standards. But beyond this, I think there is nothing in the Federal Constitution to prevent a State from choosing any electoral legislative structure it thinks best suited to the interests, temper, and customs of its people.[100]

How he could reject "the particular political philosophy" of the majority while finding this still less definite standard in the equal protection clause was a mystery left unexplained by the Stewart opinion. The majority interpretation of the clause was clear, indeed simplistic, and therein may have lain its inability to attract Justice Stewart. Perhaps it is just too easy to say that "equal" means "equal" when individual rights are involved.

The Harlan Dissent. Justice Harlan's dissent was a very different thing. Anguished, fearful for the future of federalism and concerned with the danger of a judicial takeover, Harlan disagreed with everything the majority said and with nearly everything in the opinions of Justices Clark and Stewart. Repeating his disagreement with the idea of judicial intervention in the area of state legislative apportionment, as approved by the Court in *Baker v. Carr*, he now described that case as "an experiment in venturesome constitutionalism."[101] Even assuming the correctness of the jurisdictional reach of *Baker*, Harlan explained why he thought plaintiffs had failed to

---

State Ice Co. v. Liebmann, 285 U.S. 262, 280 (1932), in which Justice Brandeis, dissenting, extolled the virtues of permitting states "to try novel social and economic experiments without risk to the rest of the country." It is no denigration of that worthy statement to think it not relevant to the issues of the apportionment cases.

100. 377 U.S. at 753–54.

101. Reynolds v. Sims, 377 U.S. 533, 625 (1964).

state a cause of action in any of the cases. So far-reaching was his denial of the power of remedial action by the federal courts, however, as to make that argument almost indistinguishable from his and Justice Frankfurter's denial of jurisdiction and justiciability in *Baker*. Indeed, there would not have been much point in ruling first that legislative malapportionment was subject matter within the competence of the federal courts only to hold, as Justice Harlan argued in *Reynolds*, that even the most egregious malapportionment would not be sufficient to state a cause of action. Even if there may be some instances which illustrate the subtle distinction between presence of jurisdiction and absence of any conceivable remedy for a claimed constitutional injury,[102] that seems scarcely to be this case. This is not to say that Harlan's argument should accordingly be disregarded; indeed, the contentions advanced in *Reynolds* are, as he quite frankly noted, based on "materials now called to [the Court's] attention for the first time."[103] Presumably, if the dissenters in *Baker* had been aware of the arguments now advanced for the first time, the arguments would have been made at that time.

Essentially, Justice Harlan made three points in his dissent:

1. The fourteenth amendment must be read as a unit. When so regarded, section 2[104] withdraws from the federal courts any supervisory power over matters of state legislative apportionment and suffrage which the equal protection clause in section 1 might otherwise appear to have conferred upon those courts. This result was said to be ascertainable, despite the absence of any textual guidance one way or the other, because the drafters of the fourteenth amendment intended to confer on Congress the exclusive power to impose sanctions on any state which "denied . . . or in any way abridged" the right of any of its male inhabitants to vote for federal or state

---

102. See, e.g., Bell v. Hood, 327 U.S. 678 (1946).

103. 377 U.S. at 593.

104. "Representatives shall be apportioned among the several States according to their respective numbers, counting the whole number of persons in each State, excluding Indians not taxed. But when the right to vote at any election for the choice of electors for President and Vice-President of the United States, Representatives in Congress, the Executive and Judicial officers of a State, or the members of the Legislature thereof, is denied to any of the male inhabitants of such State, being twenty-one years of age, and citizens of the United States, or in any way abridged, except for participation in rebellion, or other crime, the basis of representation therein shall be reduced in the proportion which the number of such male citizens shall bear to the whole number of male citizens twenty-one years of age in such State."

elected officials. The contemplated sanction was a proportionate reduction in the basis for the offending state's representation in Congress.

There are difficulties with the argument. In the first place, it seems probable, and no evidence is cited to the contrary, that section 2 was intended to prevent the outright disenfranchisement of whole classes of persons whom Congress intended to have the right to vote, particularly of course the newly freed Negroes, who were presumptively protected from voting abridgment by section 1 as well. Certainly, there was nothing in section 2 or in the legislative debates to indicate that the remedy of section 2 was at that time intended to permit proportionate reduction of a state's representation in Congress because of inequities in legislative apportionment.[105]

Similarly, it must be admitted that the legislative history of the fourteenth amendment does not affirmatively show any intention that the equal protection clause should be the instrumentality for judicial review of state legislative apportionment; but application of a provision of the Constitution to situations not specifically contemplated by its drafters is not novel. That has been well-understood constitutional doctrine at least since the Chief Justiceship of John Marshall.

Even if, contrary to what seems the more persuasive evidence in an area at best clouded with uncertainty, section 2 was designed to give Congress the power to reduce congressional representation from states which failed to provide population-based representation, it would still not follow that the congressional remedy was intended to be exclusive. The areas of authority shared between Congress and the federal judiciary are very substantial, as has been already noted (pages 59–71). The fourteenth and fifteenth amendments furnish particularly vivid illustrations in view of frequent congressional implementation of those amendments[106] without any doubt as to the retained power of the federal courts to strike down

105. But see Bonfield, The Right to Vote and Judicial Enforcement of Section Two of the Fourteenth Amendment, 46 Corn. L.Q. 108 (1960), arguing that section 2 might *now* be invoked as a congressional remedy as to those states with seriously malapportioned legislatures.

106. The various Civil Rights Acts, dating from the period immediately after the adoption of the fourteenth amendment through the Act of 1965, have all relied to some extent on the enabling powers of section 5 of the fourteenth amendment and section 2 of the fifteenth amendment.

state legislation which interfered with the rights guaranteed in those amendments.[107] To suggest that the possibility that Congress might take corrective action in this area negates the always-assumed judicial power is to disregard history.

The contention that the equal protection clause was not intended to be used for the correction of discriminatory state practices in connection with the exercise of the franchise has been previously raised and specifically rejected by the Supreme Court. In *Nixon v. Herndon*[108] and *Nixon v. Condon*,[109] decided respectively in 1927 and 1932, the Court explicitly held the equal protection clause applicable in holding unconstitutional the state statutes there involved restricting the exercise of the franchise by Negroes. Contrary to the suggestion of Justice Harlan that these holdings have been implicitly rejected by more recent cases grounded on the fifteenth amendment,[110] the Court has continued to cite *Herndon* and *Condon* with approval.[111] The reliance on the fifteenth amendment in other cases is entirely explained by the fact that that amendment

107. The cases that struck down various aspects of state-required segregation or state-enforced discrimination, too numerous to cite comprehensively, can be symbolically represented by Brown v. Board of Education, 347 U.S. 483 (1954) and more recent cases involving state-supported acts of private discrimination such as Peterson v. Greenville, 373 U.S. 244 (1963) and Lombard v. Louisiana, 373 U.S. 267 (1963).

108. 273 U.S. 536 (1927).

109. 286 U.S. 73 (1932).

110. "Before and after these cases, two cases dealing with the qualifications for electors in Oklahoma had gone off on the Fifteenth Amendment, Guinn v. United States, 238 U.S. 347; Lane v. Wilson, 307 U.S. 268. The rationale of the Texas cases [Nixon v. Herndon and Nixon v. Condon] is almost certainly to be explained by the Court's reluctance to decide that party primaries were a part of the electoral process for purposes of the Fifteenth Amendment. See Newberry v. United States, 256 U.S. 232. Once that question was laid to rest in United States v. Classic, 313 U.S. 299, the Court decided subsequent cases involving party primaries on the basis of the Fifteenth Amendment, Smith v. Allwright, 321 U.S. 649; Terry v. Adams, 345 U.S. 461 [and] Gomillion v. Lightfoot, 364 U.S. 339 . . . ." 377 U.S. at 614–15 n.72 (Harlan, J., dissenting).

111. Both cases were cited approvingly by the majority in Reynolds v. Sims, 377 U.S. at 555. See also (to note only recent cases citing either Herndon or Condon or both) Snowden v. Hughes, 321 U.S. 1, 11 (1944); Smith v. Allwright, 321 U.S. 649, 658 (1944); Screws v. United States, 325 U.S. 91, 115 (1945) (Rutledge, J., concurring); Ray v. Blair, 343 U.S. 214, 226 n.14 (1952); Terry v. Adams, 345 U.S. 461, 480 (1953) (Clark, J., concurring); Gomillion v. Lightfoot, 364 U.S. 339, 347 (1961); Monroe v. Pape, 365 U.S. 167, 211, 213 n.19 (1961) (Frankfurter, J., dissenting on another point); Baker v. Carr, 369 U.S. 186, 247 (1962) (Douglas, J., concurring).

Justice Frankfurter, in his dissenting opinion in Baker v. Carr (with which Justice Harlan joined), observed that "An end to discrimination against the Negro was the compelling motive of the Civil War Amendments. The Fifteenth expresses this in terms, and it is no less true of the Fourteenth . . . . Nixon v. Herndon, 273 U.S. 536, 541." 369 U.S. 186, 286.

deals explicitly with denial of the right of franchise, whereas the fourteenth forbids in generic manner all invidious inequalities.

Moreover, the Court has made it clear that the fourteenth amendment protections are not to be limited by historical research into the intent of the framers, even if that intent could be more clearly ascertained than is in fact the case. In *Brown v. Board of Education* the Court had asked for comprehensive briefing and reargument as to the circumstances surrounding the adoption of the fourteenth amendment. The briefs and oral argument carefully re-examined the debates in Congress, contemporaneous practices relating to racial segregation, and the ratification debates in the states. After all the evidence was in, the Court nonetheless concluded that history was "inconclusive."

> The most avid proponents of the post-War Amendments undoubtedly intended them to remove all legal distinctions among "all persons born or naturalized in the United States." Their opponents, just as certainly, were antagonistic to both the letter and the spirit of the Amendments and wished them to have the most limited effect. What others in Congress and the state legislatures had in mind cannot be determined with any degree of certainty.[112]

In short, as the Court concluded, "In approaching this problem, we cannot turn the clock back to 1868 when the Amendment was adopted, or even to 1896 when *Plessy v. Ferguson* was written."[113]

In the debates on the fourteenth amendment there was no explicit discussion of state apportionment, so there is even less room for speculation here as to the intention of the framers beyond the always-accepted generalization that the failure of a state to act in evenhanded fashion would be presumptively within the prohibitory reach of the fourteenth amendment.[114]

2. Justice Harlan's second argument in dissent was that many, perhaps most, of the states which ratified the fourteenth amendment had at that time provisions in their constitutions permitting reliance on nonpopulation factors in one or both houses of their legislatures. Accordingly, as to the so-called "loyal" states he could only imagine a negative answer to his rhetorical question: "Can it be seriously contended that the legislatures of these States, almost two-

112. 347 U.S. 483, 489 (1954).
113. Id. at 492.
114. See generally Harris, The Quest for Equality (1960).

144 *One Man, One Vote*

thirds of those concerned, would have ratified an amendment which might render their own States' constitutions unconstitutional?"[115] He found it equally hard to believe that when Congress readmitted the "reconstructed" states to the Union it could have found their constitutions "republican" in form if the equal-population principle was then thought of as a federal constitutional requirement.[116] However, neither the ratifying states nor Congress adverted to questions of reapportionment. At that time, unlike the period leading to the adoption of the original Constitution, and unlike recent decades, apportionment was not a major issue. But, for reasons already discussed, even if the issue had been considered, a congressional determination at that time of nonapplicability would not have been binding on the federal courts then, and certainly not now. To the extent that Congress examined the provisions of the "reconstructed" states' constitutions, the inquiry seems to have been solely into the question of whether they were "republican in form,"[117] conceivably a very different question from that now decided by the Court, that legislative districts must be population-based in deference to the equal protection clause. But that inquiry as to whether state constitutions satisfied the "Republican Form of Government" requirement of article IV, section 4 of the Constitution has little bearing on whether Congress, in readmitting the reconstructed states into the Union, had tested all provisions of each state's constitution against the ultimate standard of the United States Constitution. Congress never purported to pass that kind of judgment upon the constitutions of the states seeking re-entry to the Union; and of course, if Congress had sought to do so, it could not have foreclosed subsequent Supreme Court judgment to the contrary. Again, the *School Segregation Cases* are relevant. Many of the states which ratified the fourteenth amendment provided at that time, by constitutional provision or by statute, for various kinds of racial discrimination which would now be forbidden by the equal protection clause. The same thing could be said equally

115. 377 U.S. at 603.
116. Id. at 604–607.

117. The only cited evidence that Congress ever considered the apportionment formula of any state seeking readmission was an objection by Congressman Farnsworth to the apportionment of representatives in Florida. Cong. Globe, 40th Cong., 2d Sess., 3090–91 (1868). The response of Congressman Butler is revealing for its indication that Congress had inquired only as to whether the provision was "republican and proper" and had found it so. Id. at 3092.

as to post-1868 interpretations of numerous other provisions of the Constitution, notably the commerce and due process clauses, pursuant to which many long-established state practices have been held to be no longer constitutionally permissible.

3. Not unrelatedly, Justice Harlan also noted that Congress, after adoption of the fourteenth amendment, had admitted several states to the Union whose apportionment formulas would not have satisfied the Court's newly stated requirements. This he thought confirmed his view that the fourteenth amendment should never have been interpreted to limit state legislative malapportionment. Perhaps it is enough to make again the point that the Constitution is a living, flexible document as to which Congress has no power of final interpretation. Where the express words permit a particular interpretation, as the words of the fourteenth amendment clearly do, and where no other words expressly foreclose that interpretation, even long-standing practice far less ambiguous than that on which Justice Harlan relied might well have to give way.

Finally, and perhaps most important, although intangibly nonspecific, is the fact that the Harlan argument comes too late; if sustained, it would require overturning too much else that is well established. If such a literal reading were to be placed on such scattered bits and pieces of legislative history as are here relied upon, then surely doubt would be cast upon much else, much indeed with which Justice Harlan has himself agreed. Distinctions cannot readily be drawn between finding in the equal protection clause a prohibition against segregation of the races in public schools — which was not clearly within the intent of the drafters of the fourteenth amendment — and malapportioned state legislatures, however ambiguous may have been the intent of the drafters on that score. School segregation and severe distortions in the system of legislative representation are alike destructive of the democratic process because based on invidious discrimination of the fundamental rights of individuals, and, worst of all, endorsed by the very state governments to which those individuals must inevitably look for protection.

CHAPTER VI

Equality in Action:

The Orders of June 22, 1964

In *Reynolds v. Sims* and the companion cases decided on June 15, 1964, the Supreme Court set forth in some detail the principles which were thereafter to control state legislative apportionment. One week later, on June 22, the principles there announced were applied to resolve nine additional cases from as many states. The Court, not having had briefs on the merits[1] and not having heard oral argument in any of these cases, disposed of each case with a brief per curiam order. Again, as the preceding week, each state apportionment scheme was found invalid, and each case was remanded to the court from which review had been sought for further proceedings "consistent with the views stated in our opinions in *Reynolds v. Sims* and in the other cases relating to state legislative apportionment decided along with *Reynolds*."[2] Thus, on those two Mondays of June 15 and June 22 the Supreme Court had held unconstitutional the apportionment formulas for nearly one third of all the state legislatures. It was immediately clear that if every one of the

1. In each case there had been filed with the Court a jurisdictional statement and a reply brief. Although such statements and briefs are supposed to deal only with the question as to whether the Court should grant review, they are often very similar in form and scope of argument to briefs on the merits. The Solicitor General did not file a brief amicus curiae in any of these "second-round" cases.

2. Quoting from the order in Swann v. Adams, 378 U.S. 553 (1964), which was typical.

first fifteen cases to reach the Court resulted in a ruling of invalidity as to the state formula at issue, most of those not yet reviewed would also fail to satisfy the equal-population test now formulated by the Court.

However apparent that proposition may be, the answer to the next question was less self-evident; but it was an inquiry relevant to every state legislature: What formula, short of absolute mathematical equality (which is likely to find favor with few), would suffice? The nine cases summarily disposed of by the Court suggest preliminary answers. They are discussed below in alphabetical order of the states involved.[3]

Connecticut: The concept of representation by towns, not uncommon in seventeenth-century New England, was continued in the Connecticut house of representatives, guaranteeing each town at least one and no more than two representatives. In the resulting body of 294 members there was a differential of 424.5 to 1 between the number of voters represented by one representative from the most populous town and one representative from the least populous town. A majority of the house members could be elected from constituencies with 11.9 per cent of the population. The 36 senate districts were fixed with a "regard" to population, but the representation differential remained approximately eight to one.

In *Butterworth v. Dempsey*[4] the plaintiffs were residents and voters of six urban and suburban Connecticut towns, and the defendants included the governor and others charged with administration of the election laws. Other voters were permitted to intervene, including the chairmen of the Republican and Democratic state central committees. A three-judge federal district court held that the districting of the senate and the apportionment of the house debased the voting rights of plaintiffs in violation of the equal protection clause. In its decision of February 10, 1964, the court allowed all parties additional time to file proposals for a decree, which was entered on March 26, 1964, and review was promptly sought in the United States Supreme Court under the case name of *Pinney v. Butterworth*.[5] The Supreme Court affirmed and re-

---

3. See also the state summaries in the appendix.

4. 229 F. Supp. 754 (D. Conn. 1964).

5. The district court had denied at the same time a petition for intervention by a group of small towns on behalf of the defendants. The Supreme Court unanimously affirmed that judgment. Town of Franklin v. Butterworth, 378 U.S. 562 (1964).

manded to the district court, with only Justice Harlan dissenting.[6]

Florida: Between 1924 and 1962 the Florida constitution provided for a senate of 38 members, chosen from districts "as nearly equal in population as possible, but no county shall be divided in making such apportionment...." The house of representatives during the same period was to have "not more than 68" members, apportioned as follows: three representatives to each of the 5 most populous counties, two to each of the 18 next most populous counties, and one to each of the remaining counties. In *Sobel v. Adams*[7] the three-judge federal district court held these provisions invidiously discriminatory, noting that each of the three representatives from Dade County represented the equivalent of 311,000 people, while the representative from Gilchrist County represented 2,866 residents. The court found similar disparity in the senate. It concluded, moreover, that a proposed constitutional amendment then pending was also invalid. Meanwhile, the governor had convened a special legislative session in the summer of 1962. Another amendment was proposed in that session, and the court found it rational;[8] but the voters rejected it in November 1962. In a further special session in February 1963 the legislature adopted a proposal for a senate of 43 members and a house of 112 members.[9] More than half of the senatorial districts under the new statute were to be one-county districts, and no district was to include more than three counties, thus preserving the basic principle of the earlier apportionments, representation of political divisions. The federal district court, which had retained jurisdiction, found the new plan rational. "The present plan gives more weight to the population factor than did the rejected plan. But if it be required that both branches of the legislature, or either branch, must be apportioned on a strict population basis, then, admittedly, neither the rejected amendment nor the statutory enactment would pass the test."[10]

On appeal to the United States Supreme Court the judgment of the district court was reversed and the case was remanded to that

---

6. 378 U.S. 564 (1964).

7. 208 F. Supp. 316 (S.D. Fla. 1962).

8. Id. at 324.

9. The Florida Supreme Court had meanwhile ruled that the legislature might provide reapportionment by statutory enactment notwithstanding the limitations in the state constitution. In re Advisory Opinion to the Governor, 150 So.2d 721 (Fla. 1963).

10. Sobel v. Adams and Swann v. Adams, 214 F. Supp. 811, 812 (S.D. Fla. 1963).

court for further proceedings. Justice Clark agreed with that disposition by the majority of six, and Justice Harlan dissented. Justice Stewart would simply have remanded "for further proceedings consistent with the views expressed in his dissenting opinion in *Lucas v. Colorado General Assembly*, 377 U.S. 713, 744."[11] Apparently he believed further data were needed to determine whether the plan was invidiously discriminatory or not.

Idaho: The apportionment of both houses of the Idaho legislature was challenged in *Hearne v. Smylie*,[12] an action brought in federal district court by residents and qualified voters of Ada and Bannock Counties. The Idaho senate then consisted of 44 senators, one from each of the 44 counties, which in 1960 ranged in population from 915 to 93,460. As a result, 17 per cent of the population could elect half of the senators, and 33 per cent could choose three fourths of the senate membership. The seven most populous counties, with a majority of the population, chose only 16 per cent of the senators. Apportionment of the house of representatives, as revised in 1963, assigned at least one representative to each county. If the county population exceeded 5,000, another representative was alloted for each additional full 10,000 of population; and a ceiling of 132 was imposed on the size of the house.

The district court, by a vote of two to one, concluded that it lacked "omnicompetence and prescience," and dismissed without consideration of the merits. Moreover, the majority believed that dismissal was necessary for want of equity because of its inability to devise any effective remedy for the claimed injustices. Apparently untroubled by similar concerns, the Supreme Court reversed and remanded for further proceedings. Justice Clark agreed with the disposition; Justice Harlan dissented; and Justice Stewart, as in the Florida case, would simply have remanded for further proceedings without either affirming or reversing.[13]

Illinois: Article IV, section 6 of the Illinois constitution, as

11. Swann v. Adams, 378 U.S. 553 (1964). At the same time the Supreme Court unanimously affirmed another three-judge federal court judgment which had unsuccessfully challenged the 1963 apportionment statute for failure to provide for identifiable districts within Duval County to which four representatives were apportioned, apparently for at-large election. Presumably, plaintiffs wanted district lines drawn within the county so that they and other Negro voters in the county could elect one of their own number as a representative. Lucas v. Adams, No. 63–51–Civil–J (N.D. Fla. 1963), aff'd per curiam, 378 U.S. 555 (1964).

12. 225 F. Supp. 645 (D. Ida. 1964).

13. Hearne v. Smylie, 378 U.S. 563 (1964).

amended in 1954, provided for 58 senatorial districts; the lines were to be drawn by the legislature in 1955 and to be permanent thereafter.[14] By that apportionment Cook County was allotted 24 districts, 18 within the corporate limits of the city of Chicago and 6 in the county outside the city. The remaining 101 counties of Illinois were allotted 34 senatorial districts. Article IV, section 7 of the Illinois constitution, as amended in 1954, provided for 177 representatives in the lower house, to be elected from 59 districts of three members each. The apportionment was principally based on population. In *Germano v. Kerner*[15] plaintiffs, as residents and qualified voters of metropolitan areas of Illinois, sought to restrain state election officials from certifying the election of any candidates for state senator chosen in accordance with those provisions. It was shown that 29 per cent of the voters, largely resident in rural or "downstate" areas, could control the senate and that there were "irrational" disparities even within the three classes of districts, the 18 in Chicago, the 6 in Cook County outside Chicago, and the 34 in the remainder of the state. By a two to one vote the federal district court rejected the argument, finding that apportionment not irrational, particularly in view of the essentially population basis for apportionment of the house, and in view of the fact that the challenged provision had been approved by a referendum of the voters in 1954. The United States Supreme Court reversed and remanded for further proceedings, but this time with only five votes because Justice Goldberg did not participate in the case. Justice Harlan dissented as before; and Justices Clark and Stewart, in agreement this time, would have affirmed because "the Illinois system of legislative apportionment is entirely rational and does not frustrate effective majority rule."[16]

Iowa: Article III, section 34 of the Iowa constitution provided for a senate of 50 members to be elected from as many senatorial districts, but no county was to have more than one senator. As a result, "A single county district may have a population greater than the average in multiple county districts."[17] Article III, section 35 provided for a house of representatives of not more than 108 members, with two representatives for each of the nine most populous coun-

14. People ex rel. Giannis v. Carpentier, 30 Ill. 2d 24, 195 N.E.2d 665 (1964).
15. 220 F. Supp. 230 (N.D. Ill. 1963).
16. Germano v. Kerner, 378 U.S. 560 (1964).
17. Selzer v. Synhorst, 253 Ia. 936, 943, 113 N.W.2d 724, 728 (1962).

ties and one representative allotted to each of the ninety-nine least populous counties. These provisions were challenged in *Davis v. Synhorst*[18] by plaintiffs who were residents and voters in Polk County, the most populous in the state. The three-judge federal district court found the existing provisions invidiously discriminatory, noting that the nine most populous counties together had about 37 per cent of the state population, but only one sixth of the house membership (and less than one fifth of the senate membership). "The House is at least potentially controlled by the 55 smallest counties; 27.4 per cent of Iowa's total population elect a majority of the representatives . . . . The 26 least populous [senate] districts . . . elect a majority of the Senate although they include only 35.6 per cent of all Iowans."[19] Moreover, the court found insufficient the amending processes as a basis for relief. "[T]he amendment machinery permits a malapportioned General Assembly to perpetuate the inequality of representation. When amendments are accomplished through the legislative proposal method the initiative is with the legislature; and when the people vote for a constitutional convention, the legislature determines how the convention will be constituted."[20] However, because a proposed constitutional amendment was pending, the court declined immediate relief, but retained jurisdiction. After the voters rejected the proposed amendment, the court entered its final order of invalidation of the existing constitutional provisions in January 1964.[21] The court ruled that at least one house must be chosen on a strict population basis, and any departure from population in the other house must be on a "rational basis." In terms of a timetable for further action the district court was specific: "[A] new apportionment plan in accordance with these standards shall be enacted by a special session of the legislature which will govern the composition of the General Assembly commencing with its regular session in 1965 . . . ."[22] The United States Supreme Court affirmed; only Justice Harlan dissented, although Justices Clark and Stewart briefly stated their separate reasons.[23]

18. 217 F. Supp. 492 (S.D. Iowa, 1963).
19. Id. at 496.
20. Id. at 499–500.
21. Davis v. Synhorst, 225 F. Supp. 689 (S.D. Iowa 1964).
22. Id. at 693.
23. Hill v. Davis, 378 U.S. 565 (1964).
After the January 1964 decision in the district court the governor of Iowa con-

Michigan: The apportionment provisions of the Michigan constitution of 1963, which became effective January 1, 1964, had a short and largely unhappy life. After early and repeated attack in state and federal courts, those provisions succumbed to a double-barreled blast on June 22, 1964, from the United States Supreme Court and from the state supreme court.

That constitution provided for 38 senate districts which were to have been apportioned in accordance with a formula giving weight to both population and area, roughly in a proportion of four to one. The house of representatives was to consist of 110 members apportioned among the counties more nearly in accordance with population. Separate representation was guaranteed to each county or group of counties having as much as seven tenths of one per cent of the state population; and the remaining seats were to be distributed by the method of equal proportions. In *Marshall v. Hare*[24] plaintiffs, as residents and voters of metropolitan areas of Michigan, challenged the validity of the apportionment of both houses, a position in which the state attorney general, representing the secretary of state, joined. Intervening defendants included state senators and, interestingly, the chief assistant attorney general. The three-judge federal district court, by a divided vote, upheld the validity of the constitutional provisions as "neither invidious nor irrational, but . . . a most remarkable result, openly and fairly reached, with ample facility for correction if need therefor arises."[25] In reaching that result the majority sought to apply the tests suggested by the Solicitor General of the United States in his briefs amicus curiae in the *Reapportionment Cases*. Those tests, defined by the district court as follows, were said to have been satisfied: "(1) whether the basis for departure from the principle of equal population can be discerned, (2) whether it represents a legitimate objective in legislative apportionment, and (3) whether the principle of equal representation is subordinated to an excessive degree." As to the first test, the court observed that "the substantial departure [from the prin-

---

vened a special legislative session beginning on February 24, 1964. After a new plan was approved by the legislature, the district court upheld its validity; but the correctness of that decision was not at issue in the appeal to the Supreme Court. Accordingly, that Court "did not consider or pass upon this matter." Ibid. The district-court-approved plan permitted 45 per cent of the people to select a majority of the representatives, and 39 per cent to choose a majority of the senators. Davis v. Synhorst, 231 F. Supp. 540 (S.D. Iowa 1964). See also N.Y. Times, June 23, 1964, p. 16, col. 4.

24. 227 F. Supp. 989 (E.D. Mich. 1964).
25. Id. at 994.

ciple of equal population] in the Senate and the possibility of a slight departure in the House result from a determination deliberately made to increase the representation of the people of Northern Michigan." The second and third tests were also said to have been met. "The assurance of adequate representation to a sparsely populated and impoverished region constitutes a proper objective, and the provisions of the new Constitution do not subordinate the principle of population to an excessive degree."[26]

The United States Supreme Court, which, it will be remembered, had not accepted the Solicitor General's proffered standards, simply reversed and remanded for further proceedings consistent with the *Reapportionment Cases.*[27]

On the same day, June 22, 1964, the Supreme Court put an end to the original, much-buffeted apportionment litigation in Michigan by denying certiorari in *Beadle v. Scholle.*[28] This was the final stage in the litigation which had presented the most substantial challenge to the Michigan apportionment scheme as it existed between 1952 and 1964.[29] The denial of certiorari left standing the 1962 decision of the Michigan Supreme Court in which the 1952 amendment was held to be invidiously discriminatory for want of a "rational, reasonable, uniform or even ascertainable nondiscriminatory legislative purpose . . . ."[30]

Acting on the same day, the Michigan Supreme Court ordered into effect an apportionment plan based strictly on population which had been proposed by the state apportionment commission. Relying on the United States Supreme Court decision of the previous week in the *Reapportionment Cases,* the court, by a six to two vote, ruled that the new plan would control the 1964 elections for the state legislature.[31]

Ohio: Since 1903 the Ohio constitution has assured each of the 88 counties at least one representative, even though by 1960 more than half of the counties had a population of less than one half of

26. Id. at 993. It may be doubted that the Solicitor General would have agreed that this was a valid application of the tests he had suggested. For a discussion of the position of the United States as amicus curiae, see pages 188–20 supra.

27. Marshall v. Hare, 378 U.S. 561 (1964).

28. 377 U.S. 990 (1964).

29. For a discussion of that litigation, see the Michigan summary in the appendix.

30. Scholle v. Hare, 367 Mich. 176, 185, 116 N.W.2d 350, 353 (1962).

31. In the Matter of Apportionment of the Michigan Legislature, 373 Mich. 247, 250, 128 N.W.2d 721, 722 (1964).

the population ratio. In that year the 69 least populous counties had 29.4 per cent of the state's population, but a majority of the seats in the house; the 7 most populous counties, with 51.9 per cent of the population, had 37.2 per cent of the representation in the house. The senatorial ratio was to be determined "forever" by dividing the whole population of the state by 35; and the state was divided into 33 senatorial districts, each entitled to one senator except that the district of Hamilton (Cincinnati) was allotted three. Senatorial districts were composed of undivided counties. When any senatorial district had a fraction of the ratio such that, after multiplication by five, the result would equal one or more full ratios, an additional senator was to be elected by that district for a two-year term to a proportionate share of the decennial period. (Similar "fractional" representation was also provided in the representative districts.) A majority of the senate could be elected by 41 per cent of the population.

The constitutionality of the provision guaranteeing one representative to each county was challenged in *Nolan v. Rhodes*[32] and *Sive v. Ellis*[33] by plaintiffs who were residents and voters in the two most populous Ohio counties. Despite the fact that plaintiffs alleged disparities in voter ratios of almost fifteen to one, the three-judge federal district court found no invidious discrimination, concluding that it is not irrational to allow separate representation for each county. "There does not seem to be much reason for a bicameral legislature if both houses are required to be apportioned on the same basis."[34] The court also pointed out that the 1903 amendment had been adopted by an overwhelming (98 per cent) majority of the voters and had been in effect for sixty years.[35] "Ohio's constitutional apportionment takes into account the varying interests of its citizens engaged in different occupations in the 88 counties of the state. It reflects a determination of the people to give representation to each of the counties even though some of them are thinly populated. It seeks to protect the masses by giving them control of the Senate. The system is one of checks and balances designed to protect minority as well as majority interests, but neither in control.

32. 218 F. Supp. 953 (S.D. Ohio 1963).
33. Ibid.
34. Id. at 957.
35. Id. at 956.

Such an apportionment, in our judgment, cannot be said to be irrational."[36]

The United States Supreme Court reversed and remanded for further proceedings consistent with the opinion in the *Reapportionment Cases.* Justice Clark joined in the reversal; Justice Harlan dissented; and Justice Stewart would have affirmed "because the Ohio system of legislative apportionment is clearly a rational one and clearly does not frustrate effective majority rule."[37]

Oklahoma: In 1962 article V, section 10 of the Oklahoma constitution provided for apportionment of the house of representatives with population as a primary factor. However, by way of limitation on the primacy of population the constitution also provided for one representative for each county with a population equal to one half of the ratio, two representatives for every county with a population equal to one-and-three-fourths ratios, "and so on, requiring after the first two an entire additional ratio for each additional representative: Provided that no county shall ever take part in the election of more than seven representatives." The state constitution also provided for floterial representation in the house (a representative elected from a county or district with an excess of population over that required for its assigned representation, but not enough to justify an additional full-time representative). By a prescribed formula additional representation was authorized for one or more of the five legislative sessions in any decennial period.[38] The foregoing provisions were honored by the state legislature principally in the breach between 1921 and 1962. During that period each apportionment statute allocated at least one seat to each county regardless of population, thus further emphasizing the population imbalance already required by the constitution. On the other hand, the maximum limit of seven representatives for any county was adhered to. Counties were sometimes also permitted to retain floterial representatives without regard to the constitutional limitation of their service to only some of the sessions.

The constitution of 1907 established 33 senatorial districts (22 to elect one senator and 11 to elect two senators for a total of 44), to remain in effect until reapportionment should be made after the next

36. Id. at 958.
37. Nolan v. Rhodes; Sive v. Ellis, 378 U.S. 556, 557 (1964).
38. For more details, see the Oklahoma summary in the appendix.

decennial census. Until 1961, however, no comprehensive reapportionment of the senate was accomplished; instead, there were only "piecemeal" acts which effected minor shifts in the composition of a few districts and created three new districts.

These apportionment provisions were challenged by Oklahoma residents and voters in *Moss v. Burkhart*.[39] The three-judge federal district court held that the provisions in combination were invidiously discriminatory, but it initially denied relief, noting the pendency of an initiative proposal which would have vested the power of reapportionment in an independent commission (later declared not approved).[40] The initial stay of corrective action was also thought appropriate in order to give the Oklahoma legislature an opportunity to enact a constitutionally valid system, but reserved the power to undertake judicial apportionment "as a last resort."[41] By way of emphasizing the lack of equality the court pointed to the fact that a majority of the house membership could be elected by 26 per cent of the population and that in the senate 9 members represented 52 per cent of the people, while the remaining 48 per cent were represented by 35 senators.

By the time the case came back to the court for rehearing in March 1963 the legislature had approved and the governor had signed a reapportionment act. Although it was not technically effective at the time of the court's decision on July 17, 1963 (because of the possibility of referral to the voters), the court concluded that it was necessary to clarify what would be the applicable law for the next elections in Oklahoma. The proposed apportionment was held invalid because it provided little or no improvement over the already-invalidated existing formula.[42] Thus, the population disparities among senate and representative districts alike were almost five to one. Accordingly, the court "reluctantly" decided to reapportion the Oklahoma legislature by judicial decree because it was convinced "from all that has transpired in this prolonged proceedings, that the Legislature, as now constituted, is either unable or unwilling to reapportion itself, in accordance with our concept of the re-

39. 207 F. Supp. 885 (W.D. Okla. 1962).

40. The proposal received a majority of the votes on the petition, but was declared not approved because it was not endorsed by a majority of all the votes cast in the election. Allen v. Burkhart, 377 P.2d 821 (Okla. 1962).

41. Moss v. Burkhart, supra note 39, at 892.

42. Moss v. Burkhart, 220 F. Supp. 149 (W.D. Okla. 1963).

quirements of the equal protection clause of the Fourteenth Amendment."[43] The court divided the state into 44 districts: Oklahoma, Tulsa, and Comanche Counties were allotted eight, seven, and two senators respectively, while the remaining 71 counties were combined in various groupings to constitute the other 27 districts. The house membership was fixed initially at 109, but, through various floterial arrangements, was to be reduced to 107 in the last four years of the decennial period for which the apportionment was made.[44]

Review in the United States Supreme Court was sought in three cases: *Williams v. Moss*, in which the attorney general of Oklahoma represented the state treasurer as appellant; *Baldwin v. Moss*, in which the primary appellants were a group of state senators who had intervened in the district court as defendants; and *Oklahoma Farm Bureau v. Moss*, in which the appellant was the intervening Farm Bureau. The United States Supreme Court affirmed the judgment below on the merits in all cases and remanded "for further proceedings, with respect to relief, . . . should that become necessary." Justices Clark and Stewart agreed with that disposition in brief separate concurrences, and Justice Harlan dissented.[45]

Washington: Since 1889, when Washington was admitted to the Union, the state constitution has provided for the apportionment of both houses in accordance with population; but by 1964 this requirement had never been satisfied. At least one representative had been regularly given to each county regardless of population. Since 1901 the legislature had neither reapportioned nor redistricted the house or senate on its own; and the state supreme court held in 1916 that the legislature could not be compelled to redistrict the state in accordance with the state constitutional requirement.[46] However, in 1930 and 1956 reapportionment was accomplished by means of the initiative (although the 1956 apportionment was so substantially altered by the legislature that it amounted virtually to re-establishment of the pre-existing apportionment).

In November 1962 an initiative which would have reapportioned the state legislative districts in accordance with 1960 population

43. Id. at 155.
44. Id. at 157–60.
45. Williams v. Moss, 378 U.S. 558 (1964).
46. State ex rel. Warson v. Howell, 92 Wash. 540, 159 Pac. 777 (1916).

figures was defeated by the voters. Meanwhile, in June 1962, plaintiffs, as residents and voters of Washington, had challenged the existing formula in *Thigpen v. Meyers*.[47] The three-judge federal district court found that the existing legislative apportionment was invidiously discriminatory, but continued the case to give the legislature an opportunity to act at its forthcoming session in January 1963. The district court held that under the Washington constitution "the principle of numerical equality is the rule" and that both representative and senatorial districts "must be reasonably proportionate according to the number of inhabitants, in order to stand the test of the constitutional mandate. . . . There may be relevant countervailing factors, such as geography, economics, mass media and functional or voting strength. But none of these factors, whether considered separately or collectively, can overcome the basic principle underlying the right of an individual to cast an effective vote . . . ."[48] In support of its conclusion of invidious discrimination the court noted that 38 per cent of the state population elected a majority of the house, and 35.6 per cent elected a majority of the senate. "The lines of inequality run the length and breadth of the State, from east to west and from north to south, between contiguous districts and between different districts in the same cities."[49]

The Washington legislature met in regular session and in special session in the early months of 1963, but failed to enact any apportionment legislation. The federal court in May 1963 entered its decree declaring the 1957 reapportionment act unconstitutional as to both house and senate. In effect, the decree provided that the only alternative to reapportionment by the legislature would be an at-large election in 1964, although the court did not specifically order an election at large.

On appeal the United States Supreme Court affirmed on the merits and remanded for further proceedings, with respect to relief, consistent with the opinions in the *Reapportionment Cases*. Justice Clark joined in the affirmance on the basis of his separately stated reasons from the earlier cases; Justice Stewart would have

47. 211 F. Supp. 826 (W.D. Wash. 1962). The action also challenged the congressional districting in the state; that portion of the complaint was dismissed by the court. The United States Supreme Court, in its order of June 22, 1964, noted specifically that the Court was not then passing on the validity of the congressional districting, which had not been "presented in this appeal." Meyers v. Thigpen, 378 U.S. 554 (1964).

48. 211 F. Supp. at 831–32.

49. Id. at 832.

remanded for further proceedings, presumably to test rationality and preservation of effective majority rule; and Justice Harlan dissented.[50]

PRELIMINARY CONCLUSIONS

Study of the majority, concurring, and dissenting opinions in the six state legislative apportionment cases decided on June 15, 1964, and the nine cases summarily decided on June 22, 1964, reveals much as to the future composition of state legislatures.

1. The most important point to emphasize, however obvious, is the remarkable sweep of the holding. Although the Supreme Court order was an affirmance of lower court decisions in almost half the cases,[51] that is not at all to say that the Supreme Court order should be read as an approval of what the lower courts had said even in those cases; only in the most general way can the Supreme Court action be taken as an approval of the action of the lower courts in invalidating particular state legislative apportionment formulas. In every instance of Supreme Court affirmance of the judgment below, there was in the lower court opinion some kind of temporizing language which was in apparent approval of some variation from the equal-population principle in both houses, which is now the constitutional standard. Thus, in each case invalidation in the lower court was grounded on failure to meet even the more flexible population standards which those lower courts had applied.

2. As a corollary to the first proposition, there is no mistaking the fact that when the Supreme Court stated as a requirement of the equal protection clause that "the seats in both houses of a bicameral state legislature must be apportioned on a population basis," it meant just that. Not only did the Court explicitly reject the federal analogy argument — requiring instead that both houses be closely based on population — there was more as well. In two of the six cases decided with opinion, Chief Justice Warren made the point explicit where, if there had been any wish to keep the issue a little on the vague side to leave room for future maneuver, a judicious silence would have been indicated. In *Maryland Committee for Fair Representation v. Tawes*[52] the appellants had centered their

50. Meyers v. Thigpen, 378 U.S. 554 (1964).
51. Alabama, Connecticut, Delaware, Iowa, Oklahoma, Virginia, and Washington.
52. 377 U.S. 656 (1964).

attack on the state senate and, at least arguably, had conceded that the house of delegates apportionment, at least since the 1962 changes, was not unconstitutional. But the Court insisted on examining the apportionment of both houses because of the unity of the whole formula.

> Regardless of possible concessions made by the parties and the scope of the consideration of the courts below, in reviewing a state legislative apportionment case this Court must of necessity consider the challenged scheme as a whole in determining whether the particular State's apportionment plan, in its entirety, meets federal constitutional requisites. It is simply impossible to decide upon the validity of the apportionment of one house of a bicameral legislature in the abstract, without also evaluating the actual scheme of representation employed with respect to the other house. Rather, the proper, and indeed indispensable, subject for judicial focus in a legislative apportionment controversy is the overall representation accorded to the State's voters, in both houses of a bicameral state legislature . . . . We cannot be compelled to assume that the Maryland House is presently apportioned on a population basis, when that is in fact plainly not so.[53]

Lucas v. Colorado General Assembly,[54] presented a somewhat similar issue. The district court had assumed, "and the parties apparently conceded," that the 65 representative districts in Colorado were "apportioned sufficiently on a population basis to comport with federal constitutional requisites." But the Court would not accept such a concession. "We need not pass on this question, since the apportionment of Senate seats . . . clearly involves departures from population-based representation too extreme to be constitutionally permissible, and there is no indication that the apportionment of the two houses of the Colorado General Assembly, pursuant to the 1962 constitutional amendment, is severable."[55]

3. Where an existing apportionment fails to satisfy the equal-population principle in both houses, aggrieved voters are entitled to prompt relief; "it would be the unusual case in which a court would be justified in not taking appropriate action to insure that no further elections are conducted under the invalid plan."[56] Apparently, the only justifiable reason for delay in implementation would be in the "unusual" case in which "an impending election is

53. Id. at 673.
54. 377 U.S. 713 (1964).
55. Id. at 734–35.
56. Reynolds v. Sims, 377 U.S. 533, 585 (1964).

imminent and a State's election machinery is already in progress.
. . ."[57] That limited exception offers little room for maneuver. The
time is at hand for nearly all states, for whom the bell tolls now, not
at some comfortably remote time. Even though direct impact upon
the 1964 elections was not required in some of the cases before the
Court because of the time exigencies, it must nonetheless be remembered that the Court did not disapprove the implied threat of
an at-large election sounded by the district court in the Washington
case[58] and that it approved explicitly the technique of judicial reapportionment in the circumstances of the Alabama and Oklahoma
cases. The Supreme Court has apparently learned well the potential
error in assuming willing compliance with a flexible mandate to be
accomplished "with all deliberate speed."

4. While apportionment is clearly a legislative function in the
first instance, not only may the federal courts test the validity of the
legislative end-product against the standards of the United States
Constitution as formulated by the Supreme Court. but the courts
may intervene directly in exceptional cases where a legislature has
not made an "honest and good faith effort" at compliance. In the
Alabama case the Supreme Court expressly approved the action
taken by the district court to put into operation a temporary apportionment on the basis of which elections were actually held in
Alabama in 1962:

> We feel that the District Court in this case acted in a most proper and
> commendable manner. It initially acted wisely in declining to stay the im-
> pending primary election in Alabama, and properly refrained from acting
> further until the Alabama Legislature had been given an opportunity to
> remedy the admitted discrepancies in the State's legislative apportionment
> scheme, while initially stating some of its views to provide guidelines for
> legislative action. And it correctly recognized that legislative apportion-
> ment is primarily a matter for legislative consideration and determination,
> and that judicial relief becomes appropriate only when a legislature fails to
> reapportion according to federal constitutional requisites in a timely fash-
> ion after having had an adequate opportunity to do so.[59]

5. The Court was apparently satisfied that the opinions in the six
cases in the *Reynolds* group should serve as a sufficiently compre-

---

57. Ibid. See also WMCA, Inc. v. Lomenzo, 377 U.S. 633, 655 (1964). Cf. Martin v.
Bush, 376 U.S. 222, 223 (1964).

58. Thigpen v. Meyers, 211 F. Supp. 826 (W.D. Wash. 1962), aff'd, 378 U.S. 554
(1964).

59. Reynolds v. Sims, 377 U.S. 533, 586 (1964).

hensive textbook for the guidance of legislatures and lower courts. Those six cases raised in some form every argument so far made in support of or in opposition to the equal-population principle. Those arguments were patiently dealt with one by one in the opinions of the Chief Justice, both in terms of the specifics of the cases in which they arose and as more broadly stated general principles adaptable to other cases. The majority of the Court found in that body of principles sufficient doctrine to permit decision one week later of nine cases, with substantially varied facts, in as many brief per curiam orders. No member of the Court can be unaware of the danger (and the likelihood of criticism) in per curiam opinions that are not adequately explainable in terms of previous adjudications of the Court. But here that risk seems minimal because the central proposition was stated so crisply and with so little qualification. Accordingly, the opportunity for agreement as to the implications of the rule in regard to any particular fact situation is correspondingly enhanced.

The point should not be overemphasized, however, at the risk of misunderstanding of a different kind. The initial guidelines fixed by the Court were in large part negative — *thou shalt nots*, as it were — without fixing a single rigid mold to which all state legislatures must conform. There is room for differentiation, subject to review by federal and state courts under the broad standard announced. The extent of that room for maneuver is the matter next discussed.

6. Without relaxation of its insistence upon "good faith" application of the equal-population principle to both houses of a bicameral state legislature, the Court recognized the impracticality — indeed, the undesirability — of rigid mathematical precision in the effectuation of that standard. "We realize that it is a practical impossibility to arrange legislative districts so that each one has an identical number of residents, or citizens, or voters."[60] The possibility of using political subdivision lines was recognized as a matter of practical convenience, to prevent gerrymandering, and to ensure some voice to local governmental entities charged with implementation of state governmental operations.[61]

Application of the foregoing principles commenced immediately upon the announcement of the decisions. The Colorado legis-

60. Reynolds v. Sims, 377 U.S. 533, 577 (1964).
61. Id. at 578–80.

lature acted promptly to effect a reapportionment, which was said to be based on population in both houses, to be effective in the primary elections held on September 8, 1964. The Michigan Supreme Court directed the Michigan Commission on Legislative Apportionment to submit a plan for reapportionment to the court within forty-eight hours.[62] The governor of New York indicated his intention to call a special legislative session and appointed a special commission to study the matter and report back promptly. The federal district court to which the New York case was remanded was convened on July 15, 1964, five days after the issuance of the mandate to that court, and on the same day entered as its order a judgment that the New York apportionment plan was invalid, and adjourned the matter for nine days to allow the state to come up with a revised apportionment to be effective in 1964, or to give reasons for believing that the court should not impose a temporary reapportionment by its own order. Other appropriate action has been taken in other states.[63]

The process of implementation is under way. An examination of some aspects of that process, the legal questions, and the implications for a representative democracy, will be examined in a final chapter. But first, because there has been considerable uneasiness about the assertion of judicial power in these cases, even from persons not routinely hostile to any action of the Supreme Court, it is appropriate to look further into the role of the Court in these cases, including explanation of the basis for the ruling beyond what the Court could properly articulate within the confines of judicial opinions even of the relative fullness of those in the apportionment cases.

62. Matter of the Apportionment of the Michigan State Legislature, 373 Mich. 247, 250 128 N.W.2d 721, 722 (June 17 and 22, 1964).

63. The first-round legislative and judicial reaction to the Supreme Court decisions is summarized on a state-by-state basis in the appendix.

CHAPTER VII

Apportionment and

Majority Rule

When Winston Churchill described Russia as "a riddle wrapped in a mystery inside an enigma," he might almost as well have been expressing the bewilderment that Americans must feel in trying to understand their own system of government. Even within the United States agreement is lacking as to whether the governmental system should be called representative democracy, constitutional federalism, both, or neither. The three branches of the national government, legislative, executive, and judicial, coexist in a state of perpetual and precarious balance in which no one can say for sure what hidden alchemy keeps the constitutionally separated branches sufficiently together to make a functioning whole and sufficiently apart to keep them from destroying one another. Even more tension-ridden is the shifting division of authority between nation and states which is somehow maintained in working, but always-uneasy, equilibrium. Politicians have engaged in self-analysis; political scientists have described and dissected the process; other social engineers have used every technique known to empirical research. But we still cannot be certain what we have and why it works as well as (usually) it does.

SUPREME COURT AND SUPREME LAW

The Supreme Court of the United States, although only one relatively small part of the complex whole, has always held a special fascination for Americans. Whether the judiciary is "the weakest of the three departments of power," as Alexander Hamilton believed,[1] or whether judicial usurpation is the real danger,[2] is a question never settled and endlessly engrossing. The Supreme Court does not provide a dramatic show nor does it issue press releases in the conventional sense; the Justices are not widely known to the public and their opinions are read by only a few. Yet there is no doubt that Supreme Court decisions, no matter how imperfectly understood, exert an influence in even the remotest communities of the land. Almost every citizen has an opinion, usually rather rigidly held, as to whether the Court is adequately fulfilling the function its partisans assign it of protecting against governmental abuse or whether, as others believe, the Court is disrupting the division of powers through disregard of its limited function.

The two positions sometimes seem irreconcilable, leaving little common ground for discussion beyond the level of assertion. However, the issue to be debated never quite stands still, as perhaps it cannot in view of the nature of the basic charter which the Supreme Court is required to interpret. The Supreme Court is asked to define the indefinable: freedom, equality, and due process among others; and it is asked to solve contemporary problems in terms of a document fashioned with deliberate nonspecificity in times as remote as 1787 and 1866. As Paul Freund has written in connection with the superbly indefinite phrase "due process," "it is one thing to slam the door of the due-process clause, and another to keep it shut."[3]

The Flexible Constitution. The problem is scarcely new. The arguments about the proper role of the Court have all been made many times and from varied perspectives.[4] One thing at least is per-

---

1. The Federalist No. 78 (Hamilton), at 523 (Cooke ed. 1961).

2. See, e.g., Boudin, Government by Judiciary (1932); Cf. Hand, The Bill of Rights (1958).

3. Freund, The Supreme Court of the United States 47 (1961).

4. For a sampling, see Bickel, The Least Dangerous Branch (1962); Black, The People and the Court (1959); Cahn (ed.), Supreme Court and Supreme Law (1954); Clayton, The Making of Justice (1964); Frank, The Marble Palace (1958); Freund,

fectly clear. No one dissents from the proposition that the Constitution was intended to be adaptable "to the various crises of human affairs,"[5] as Chief Justice Marshall observed in 1819. This is the kind of Constitution Justice Cardozo had in mind when he described the constitutional ideal:

> A *constitution* states or ought to state not rules for the passing hour, but principles for an expanding future. In so far as it deviates from that standard, and descends into details and particulars it loses its flexibility, the scope of interpretation contracts, the meaning hardens.[6]

The difficulty, then, is not with the principle of flexibility, broadly enough stated to accommodate widely varying interpretations, but with its application to particular situations in various periods of history.

The crucial issue in apportionment involves the same central question: Is the "adaptable" Constitution sufficiently flexible to provide hospitable shelter for application of the equal protection clause to matters not before considered within its scope? If apportionment meets that test, the next question follows: Does the concept of adaptability demand constitutional tolerance of a wide range of departures from equality?

Flexibility and Activism. When the Supreme Court was regarded as "activist" in its use of the due process clause to strike down state legislation in regulation of business activities, it was condemned by Justice Holmes for attempting "to enact [into the fourteenth amendment] Mr. Herbert Spencer's Social Statics"[7] and by Justice Brandeis for seeking "to erect our prejudices into legal principles."[8] The decisions of which Justices Holmes and Brandeis complained have since been overruled or rendered impotent. More recently, the complaint of activism has been advanced in connection with different areas of decision. When the commerce clause is read to invalidate state regulation or taxation of business, or when police practices are held unconstitutional because violative of individual

---

The Supreme Court of the United States (1961); Hand, The Bill of Rights (1958); Lewis, Gideon's Trumpet (1964); Rostow, The Sovereign Prerogative (1962); Wechsler, Principles, Politics and Fundamental Law (1961).

5. McCulloch v. Maryland, 17 U.S. (4 Wheat.) 316, 415 (1919).
6. Cardozo, The Nature of the Judicial Process 83–84 (1921).
7. Lochner v. New York, 198 U.S. 45, 75 (1905) (dissenting opinion).
8. New State Ice Co. v. Liebmann, 285 U.S. 262, 311 (1932) (dissenting opinion).

liberty, the claim is heard again that state sovereignty or personal safety is jeopardized by judicial excess. The point is simply that issues change, and the Constitution accommodates the changing necessities of the times under the guidance, hopefully skillful, of the Supreme Court.

The equal protection of the laws clause of the fourteenth amendment provides an even more vivid illustration of this point. After the adoption of the amendment, and for a number of years thereafter, the Court doubted "very much whether any action of a State not directed by way of discrimination against the negroes as a class, or on account of their race, will ever be held to come within the purview of this provision. It is so clearly a provision for that race and that emergency, that a strong case would be necessary for its application to any other."[9] Even as applied to the Negro the equal protection clause was long regarded as at best a limited protection against racial discrimination. The "separate but equal" formula of *Plessy v. Ferguson*[10] recognized what most of the nation was willing at the time to accept — that there was no constitutional barrier to state-required segregation in transportation accommodations. Moreover, there was little reason to believe that the equal protection clause at the time of its adoption sought to erase segregation in the public schools.[11]

Meanwhile, despite the fact that there was also "no contemporary understanding of the relation of equal protection to business regulation,"[12] it was not long before the Court found in equal protection a quite explicit prohibition upon unreasonable classificatory schemes imposed on businesses in the interest of state regulation of matters having to do with economic and social welfare. The turning point is interesting because of the casual way in which major new constitutional doctrine was introduced. In 1886 Chief Justice Waite said from the bench that the Court did not wish to hear argument on the question whether the equal protection clause applied to corporations. "We are all of the opinion that it does."[13]

9. The Slaughter-House Cases, 83 U.S. (16 Wall.) 36, 81 (1873).

10. 163 U.S. 537 (1896).

11. Bickel, The Original Understanding and the Segregation Decision, 69 Harv. L. Rev. 1 (1955).

12. Frank and Munro, The Original Understanding of "Equal Protection of the Laws," 50 Colum. L. Rev. 131, 143 (1950).

13. The case was Santa Clara County v. Southern Pac. R.R., 118 U.S. 394 (1886).

THE TWO FACES OF
EQUAL PROTECTION[14]

Between 1886 and the late 1930's the equal protection clause was applied to more than 400 cases involving state legislation in regulation of economic interests,[15] although during that same period the clause was seldom used in vindication of individual rights, including protection against racial discrimination, and not at all in challenges to apportionment formulas. This suggests in a preliminary way the variety of uses to which the equal protection clause has been put at varying times in its first century of constitutional history. Analytically, the seemingly diverse cases may be grouped into two principal categories, each of which has generated its own distinctive application of the equal protection concept. So different is the doctrinal base for the two that one might almost say that there are two equal protection clauses or, at least, since some kinds of discriminatory classification are more readily forbidden than others, that there is something akin to a scale of preferences within the equal protection clause itself.

The two faces of equal protection may be generalized in these terms: (1) Where the state, in the exercise of its police power authority over health, morals, and general welfare, imposes a classification scheme for the regulation of economic or social welfare matters, there is room for differentiation under the comfortably loose coverage of "reasonableness." The classification in these situations carries with it a presumption of constitutionality difficult to overcome. (2) But where the classification impinges upon the "basic civil rights of man,"[16] the latent libertarianism that always lies close to the surface of equal protection emerges either to forbid all classification, because none is permissible, as in the case of state-supported racial discrimination, or at the least to overcome the presumption

---

The quoted remark of the Chief Justice was made in the presence of, and apparently with the acquiescence of, Justice Miller, who had in 1873 denied the likely application of equal protection concepts to anything except matters of racial discrimination. See Magrath, Morrison R. Waite: The Triumph of Character 222–24 (1963).

14. The ideas expressed in this section are developed in more detail in my article, Political Thickets and Crazy Quilts: Reapportionment and Equal Protection, 61 Mich. L. Rev. 645, 659–81 (1963). See also Tussman & tenBroek, The Equal Protection of the Laws, 37 Calif. L. Rev. 341 (1949).

15. Harris, The Quest for Equality 59 (1960).

16. Skinner v. Oklahoma, 316 U.S. 535, 541 (1942).

of constitutionality and to demand rigorous examination of the standards set.

Before more specific illustration of these rather separate aspects of equal protection is advanced, this caveat should be entered. Although these divergent implications emerge clearly from the decided cases, the Supreme Court itself has not in any formal opinion acknowledged the division. Rather the common practice has been, when equal protection is invoked and the claim is destined for rejection, to deal with the question in generalized terms, fortified by a string of now-familiar citations dealing with classification in the regulation of economic interests. Thus, Chief Justice Warren, speaking of a state's exemption of certain businesses from Sunday closing laws, said that "A statutory discrimination will not be set aside if any state of facts reasonably may be conceived to justify it."[17] Similarly, in *Baker v. Carr* two Justices, in their separate concurring opinions, each referred to the applicable equal protection standard in terms of "invidious discrimination,"[18] a phrase drawn from *Williamson v. Lee Optical Co.*,[19] in which a clearly unequal classification of economic interests was sustained for lack of a showing of "invidious discrimination."

Study of the cases decided under the equal protection clause reveals a more orderly pattern than these imprecise generalizations seem to indicate. When the Supreme Court applied the equal protection clause in the *Reapportionment Cases* to require adherence to the equal-population principle, this was a perfectly logical and natural application of principles already established in the line of equal protection cases involving the "basic civil rights of man." As Justice Brennan, writing for the majority in *Baker*, had said, the controlling standards were "well-developed and familiar,"[20] even though the immediate line of cases raised issues not yet tested against those standards.

Regulation of Economic Interests. The equal protection and the due process clauses of the fourteenth amendment had a somewhat

17. McGowan v. Maryland, 366 U.S. 420, 426 (1961). The equal protection point in the case did not involve either religious freedom or separation of Church and State, but only the power of the state to regulate some businesses while exempting others.

18. 369 U.S. 186, 245 (1962) (Douglas, J., concurring); id. at 253 (Clark, J., concurring).

19. 348 U.S. 483, 489 (1955).

20. Baker v. Carr, 369 U.S. 186, 226 (1962).

parallel history for some years after the adoption of the amendment. As the Reconstruction period drew to a close both due process and equal protection became chiefly identified with substantive rights, particularly with judicially imposed limitations on the power of states to regulate economic affairs. Both aspects of that story have been well chronicled and will not be repeated here.[21] It is sufficient now to recall that since the mid-1930's the Court has ordinarily refused to review state economic regulation under either the due process or the equal protection clause. Due process claims appear to be altogether unavailing in the area of economic regulation,[22] and equal protection claims have been successful only rarely.[23]

Morey v. Doud[24] was the only important case in the last quarter of a century to apply the equal protection clause to invalidate state legislation regulating economic activity. The act in question created a closed class by exempting money orders issued by the American Express Company from regulations applicable to all other issuers of like orders. For such a statutory discrimination to be sustained, Justice Burton said, it "must be based on differences that are reasonably related to the purposes of the Act in which it is found."[25] No such relationship was found, only a special exemption in behalf of one favored company. Even on that premise the decision evoked three dissents, one by Justice Black and one by Justices Frankfurter and Harlan. Justice Frankfurter feared that the holding represented a return to a discarded past, stating his view of the equal protection clause in these words:

21. *Due process*: Frankfurter, Mr. Justice Holmes and the Supreme Court, appendix (1938). For a more recent statement, see Lewis, A Newspaperman's View: The Role of the Supreme Court, 45 A.B.A.J. 911 (1959). For the somewhat different regard which many state courts have for due process provisions in their own constitutions, see Carpenter, Our Constitutional Heritage: Economic Due Process and the State Courts, 45 A.B.A.J. 1027 (1959); Paulsen, The Persistence of Substantive Due Process in the States, 34 Minn. L. Rev. 92 (1950).
Equal protection: Harris, The Quest for Equality (1960).

22. Since Nebbia v. New York, 291 U.S. 502 (1934), substantive due process has been applied mainly in connection with claimed violation of individual liberty. For illustrative denials of due process claims, see West Coast Hotel Co. v. Parrish, 300 U.S. 379 (1937); Olsen v. Nebraska, 313 U.S. 236 (1941).

23. Mayflower Farms, Inc. v. Ten Eyck, 297 U.S. 266 (1936); Hartford Co. v. Harrison, 301 U.S. 459 (1937); Hillsborough v. Cromwell, 326 U.S. 620 (1946); Wheeling Steel Corp. v. Glander, 337 U.S. 562 (1949) (distinguished in Allied Stores, Inc. v. Bowers, 358 U.S. 522, 526-30 (1959)); Morey v. Doud, 354 U.S. 457 (1957).

24. 354 U.S. 457 (1957).

25. Id. at 465.

Legislation is essentially empiric. It addresses itself to the more or less crude outside world and not to the neat, logical models of the mind. Classification is inherent in legislation; the Equal Protection Clause has not forbidden it. To recognize marked differences that exist in fact is living law; to disregard practical differences and concentrate on some abstract identities is lifeless logic.[26]

Justice Black, dissenting separately, agreed that state power over state domestic economic affairs should not be narrowly restricted. Then, noting the separate uses to which equal protection may be put, he continued:

I think state regulation should be viewed quite differently where it touches or involves freedom of speech, press, religion, assembly, or other specific safeguards of the Bill of Rights. It is the duty of this Court to be alert to see that these constitutionally preferred rights are not abridged.[27]

Whether *Morey v. Doud* and its few companions are regarded as rare examples of invidious discrimination unsupported by any legislative purpose or merely as judicial sports, it is clear at least that they are very exceptional. The volume and variety of cases in which state economic regulation has been upheld against an equal protection challenge is impressive in size and in the summary nature of the judicial response to the issue.[28]

Regulation of "Basic Civil Rights of Man." Equal protection and due process alike got off to a slow start as defenders of individual liberty. But as the restraining power of these clauses upon state economic regulation has declined almost to zero, substantive content on the side of individual liberty has been poured into them at an accelerating rate. This is not the place to recount this aspect of the development of the due process clause except to note the role played by the due process clause in the absorption of the fundamental human rights in the Bill of Rights into the fourteenth amendment as a limitation upon the states. That process was accelerated

26. Id. at 472.
27. Id. at 471.
28. See, e.g., Kotch v. Board of River Port Pilot Comm'rs, 330 U.S. 552 (1947); Goesaert v. Cleary, 335 U.S. 464 (1948); AFL v. American Sash Co., 335 U.S. 538 (1948); Railway Express Agency v. New York, 336 U.S. 106 (1949); Salsburg v. Maryland, 346 U.S. 545 (1954); Williamson v. Lee Optical Co., 348 U.S. 483 (1955); McGowan v. Maryland, 366 U.S. 420 (1961); Braunfeld v. Brown, 366 U.S. 599 (1961); Gallagher v. Crown Kosher Mkt., 366 U.S. 617 (1961); Two Guys from Harrison-Allentown, Inc. v. McGinley, 366 U.S. 582 (1961); Florida Avocado Growers v. Paul, 373 U.S. 132 (1963).

by significant Supreme Court decisions between 1961 and 1965 in *Mapp v. Ohio*,[29] *Gideon v. Wainwright*,[30] and *Pointer v. Texas*.[31] In *Malloy v. Hogan*, for example, the Court held that "the Fifth Amendment's exception from compulsory self-incrimination is also protected by the Fourteenth Amendment against abridgement by the States."[32] Although that result was reached by a divided vote, it is significant for the present discussion to note that there was no disagreement within the Court on the proposition that the due process clause does not have an immutably fixed content. Justice Brennan for the majority made the point thus:

> The Court has not hesitated to re-examine past decisions according the Fourteenth Amendment a less central role in the preservation of basic liberties than that which was contemplated by its Framers when they added the Amendment to our constitutional scheme.[33]

Justice Harlan, dissenting from the extension of the privilege against self-incrimination as a limitation on the states under the facts of this case, did not deny the central proposition of constitutional growth. He said:

> I accept and agree with the proposition that continuing re-examination of the constitutional conception of Fourteenth Amendment "due process" of law is required, and that development of the community's sense of justice may in time lead to expansion of the protection which due process affords.[34]

The parallel development of the equal protection clause as a guardian of individual liberty was, until the 1950's, less dramatic, but nonetheless significant. With decision of the series of cases that have finally eradicated "separate but equal" as an excuse for segregation, and the series of apportionment cases, from *Baker* through *Reynolds*, the equal protection clause moves strikingly into the forefront in the struggle for the advancement of individual liberty.

29. 367 U.S. 643 (1961).

30. 372 U.S. 335 (1963).

31. 380 U.S. 400 (1965). See also Brennan, The Bill of Rights and the States, 36 N.Y.U.L. Rev. 761 (1961); Henkin, "Selective Incorporation" in the Fourteenth Amendment, 73 Yale L.J. 74 (1963).

32. 378 U.S. 1, 6 (1964). The case also contains a valuable review of the "absorption" question.

33. Id. at 5.

34. Id. at 15.

Significant cases in this nearly century-long development are enumerated in the margin,[35] and the highlights are noted in the text.

The developing significance of the equal protection clause as a guardian of individual liberty has been demonstrated most comprehensively and dramatically in the case-by-case erection of a total barrier against state-supported racial discrimination. In the early years following the adoption of the fourteenth amendment little protection against racial discrimination was found in the clause save as a limitation on discrimination in the selection of jurors. Originally, even here, only overt discrimination by statute or participation in the discrimination by judges was condemned.[36] By the middle of the twentieth century, however, forbidden discrimination was found even in long-standing patterns of jury composition where Negroes were not excluded by formal rule.[37]

The gradually evolving role of the equal protection clause in con-

35. *Malapportionment*: Baker v. Carr, 369 U.S. 186 (1964); Gray v. Sanders, 372 U.S. 368 (1963); Reynolds v. Sims, 377 U.S. 533 (1964).

Racial discrimination: (a) *Segregation*: Missouri ex rel. Gaines v. Canada, 305 U.S. 337 (1938); Sweatt v. Painter, 339 U.S. 629 (1950); McLaurin v. Oklahoma, 339 U.S. 637 (1950); Brown v. Board of Educ., 347 U.S. 483 (1954); Mayor & City Council v. Dawson, 350 U.S. 877 (1955); Holmes v. City of Atlanta, 350 U.S. 879 (1955); Gayle v. Browder, 352 U.S. 903 (1956); State Athletic Comm'n v. Dorsey, 359 U.S. 533 (1959); Johnson v. Virginia, 373 U.S. 61 (1963); Peterson v. Greenville, 373 U.S. 244 (1963); Wright v. Georgia, 373 U.S. 284 (1963); Watson v. Memphis, 373 U.S. 526 (1963); Goss v. Board of Educ., 373 U.S. 683 (1963); Griffin v. Prince Edward County School Board, 377 U.S. 218 (1964).

(b) *Restrictive covenants*: Shelley v. Kraemer, 334 U.S. 1 (1948); Barrows v. Jackson, 346 U.S. 249 (1953).

(c) *Jury service*: Virginia v. Rives, 100 U.S. 313 (1880); Neal v. Delaware, 103 U.S. 370 (1881); Pierre v. Louisiana, 306 U.S. 354 (1939); Smith v. Texas, 311 U.S. 128 (1940); Hill v. Texas, 316 U.S. 400 (1942); Akins v. Texas, 325 U.S. 398 (1945); Patton v. Mississippi, 332 U.S. 463 (1947); Cassell v. Texas, 339 U.S. 282 (1950); Shepherd v. Florida, 341 U.S. 50 (1951); Coleman v. Alabama, 377 U.S. 129 (1964).

(d) *Other forms of racial discrimination*: Yick Wo v. Hopkins, 118 U.S. 356 (1886) (limitation of livelihood); Oyama v. California, 332 U.S. 633 (1948) (limitation of land ownership); Takahashi v. Fish & Game Comm'n, 334 U.S. 410 (1948) (limitation of livelihood). See also Truax v. Raich, 239 U.S. 33 (1915) (discrimination against aliens). But cf. Hirabayashi v. United States, 320 U.S. 81 (1943); Korematsu v. United States, 323 U.S. 214 (1944).

Discrimination by reason of indigence: Griffin v. Illinois, 351 U.S. 12 (1956); Burns v. Ohio, 360 U.S. 252 (1959); Smith v. Bennett, 365 U.S. 708 (1961); Douglas v. California, 372 U.S. 353 (1963); Lane v. Brown, 372 U.S. 477 (1963); Draper v. Washington, 372 U.S. 487 (1963).

Sterilization of "habitual criminals": Skinner v. Oklahoma, 316 U.S. 535 (1942).

36. Virginia v. Rives, 100 U.S. 313 (1880); Ex parte Virginia, 100 U.S. 339 (1880); Neal v. Delaware, 103 U.S. 370 (1881).

37. See, e.g., Hill v. Texas, 316 U.S. 400 (1942); Akins v. Texas, 325 U.S. 398 (1945); Patton v. Mississippi, 332 U.S. 463 (1947); Cassell v. Texas, 339 U.S. 282 (1950); Hernandez v. Texas, 347 U.S. 475 (1954); Reece v. Georgia, 350 U.S. 85 (1955); Eubanks v. Louisiana, 356 U.S. 584 (1958); Arnold v. North Carolina, 376 U.S. 773 (1964); Coleman v. Alabama, 377 U.S. 129 (1964).

nection with segregation is similar. While the clause was being given a wide-ranging application to strike down economic classifications, segregation was considered a rational classification so long as the facilities provided, though "separate," were "equal."[38] Although the doctrine was not destined to survive, its demise was, to say the least, lingering. Hints along the way, ever stronger, were offered in 1917,[39] 1938,[40] and 1950.[41] Finally, the turnabout came in 1954 and 1955 with the invalidation of segregation in public schools and the requirement of its elimination "with all deliberate speed."[42] In 1964 the Court impatiently remarked that "There has been entirely too much deliberation and not enough speed in enforcing the constitutional rights" to nonsegregated public school education.[43]

The equal protection concept has had a similarly expansionist history in relation to state action whose hostile thrust was aimed at noncitizens because of the fact of alienage, as often further distorted by racial bias as well. The earliest of these cases, and still the doctrinal base for most that have followed, was *Yick Wo v. Hopkins*.[44] The San Francisco ordinance involved in that case, apparently fair on its face, required the licensing of all laundries within the corporate limits of the city and county except those built of brick or stone. Presumptively the ordinance was designed as a police measure to reduce the hazard of fires in wooden, perhaps ramshackle, laundry structures. Yet the undisputed facts were that, although permission to continue operation in wooden buildings was denied to petitioners and 200 others, all of whom happened to be Chinese subjects, 80 others, not Chinese subjects, were permitted to carry on the same business under similar conditions. Justice Matthews, writing for a unanimous Court, concluded that no reason for this unequal treatment existed "except hostility to the race and nationality to which the petitioners belong, and which in the eye of the law is not justified."[45] In short, the facts provided vivid testimony of the administration of a law, however fair on its face, "with a mind so unequal

---

38. Plessy v. Ferguson, 163 U.S. 537 (1896).
39. Buchanan v. Warley, 245 U.S. 60 (1917).
40. Missouri ex rel. Gaines v. Canada, 305 U.S. 337 (1938).
41. Sweatt v. Painter, 339 U.S. 629 (1950).
42. Brown v. Board of Educ., 347 U.S. 483 (1954); 349 U.S. 294 (1955).
43. Griffin v. Prince Edward County School Board, 377 U.S. 218, 229 (1964).
44. 118 U.S. 356 (1886).
45. Id. at 374.

and oppressive as to amount to a practical denial by the State of that equal protection of the laws" secured by the fourteenth amendment.[46] Two things about the case should be observed for their relevance today. First, the Court looked at the pattern of administration under the ordinance and unhesitatingly found in that performance sufficient evidence of discriminatory purpose to invoke equal protection. Second, upon a demonstration of the fact of unequal administration of the ordinance, any presumptive validity that might otherwise have attached disappeared; and the failure of the city to offer justification apart from racial hostility required invalidation of the ordinance.

A further matter of special interest about *Yick Wo* is a dictum of great relevance to the current apportionment cases. Emphasizing that a person's right to earn a livelihood should not be held "at the mere will of another," Justice Matthews analogized from a related proposition which he apparently believed was beyond contest.

> There are many illustrations that might be given of this truth, which would make manifest that it was self-evident in the light of our system of jurisprudence. The case of the political franchise of voting is one. Though not regarded strictly as a natural right, but as a privilege merely conceded by society according to its will, under certain conditions, nevertheless it is regarded as a fundamental political right, because preservative of all rights.[47]

Later cases have confirmed and strengthened the proposition that state legislation which displays, on its face or in its administration, a hostility to aliens as a class is at least subject to "strict scrutiny of the classification"[48] and, if racial hostility is present, to the probability of invalidation. *Truax v. Raich*[49] involved an attack upon an Arizona law which required all Arizona employers of more than five workers to hire not less than 80 per cent of their staff from qualified electors or native-born citizens of the United States. Raich, an alien who worked as a cook in a restaurant which had more than five employees, was about to lose his job solely because of the state law's coercive effect on his employer. The Court invalidated the law and declared that Raich, as a lawfully admitted alien, had a federal priv-

46. Id. at 373.

47. Id. at 370. The last portion of the quotation above was repeated by the Court in Reynolds v. Sims, 377 U.S. 533, 562 (1964).

48. Skinner v. Oklahoma, 316 U.S. 535, 541 (1942).

49. 239 U.S. 33 (1915).

ilege to enter and abide in any state and thereafter a right to enjoy the equal protection of the laws where he resided. Accordingly, the state could not restrict the right of all lawfully resident aliens to engage in otherwise lawful employment. Although the Court conceded that in some respects the state could treat aliens differently than citizens, special justification was required in each such case. Here that burden had not been met:

> [U]nderlying the classification is the authority to deal with that at which the legislation is aimed. The restriction now sought to be sustained is such as to suggest no limit to the State's power of excluding aliens from employment if the principle underlying the prohibition of the act is conceded.[50]

The most recent of the restriction-on-employment cases, *Takahashi v. Fish and Game Comm'n*,[51] held invalid a California statute barring issuance of commercial fishing licenses to persons "ineligible to citizenship," a classification which included resident-alien Japanese and precluded such persons from earning a living as commercial fishermen in the California coastal waters. The Court held that the state of California had failed to show, as required in *Truax*, a "special public interest with respect to any particular business . . . that could possibly be deemed to support the enactment . . . ."[52]

The other principal class of cases in which discrimination on grounds of race or alienage is involved relates to laws restricting ownership or occupancy of land to citizens. The root case was *Terrace v. Thompson*,[53] in which the Court upheld a classification restricting ownership of land in the state of Washington to citizens and aliens eligible for citizenship who had in good faith made a declaration of intent to become citizens as required by the naturalization laws. *Truax v. Raich* was distinguished, the Court concluding that the requisite showing of the state's special interest was sustained by the fact that "The quality and allegiance of those who own, occupy and use the farm lands within its borders are matters of highest importance and affect the safety and power of the State itself."[54] That case, however, was sharply limited in *Oyama v.*

50. Id. at 43.

51. 334 U.S. 410 (1948).

52. Truax v. Raich, 239 U.S. at 43.

53. 263 U.S. 197 (1923). See also Frick v. Webb, 263 U.S. 326 (1923); Webb v. O'Brien, 263 U.S. 313 (1923); Porterfield v. Webb, 263 U.S. 225 (1923).

54. 263 U.S. at 221.

California[55] and *Takahashi v. Fish and Game Comm'n.* The California Alien Land Law construed in *Oyama* in effect forbade aliens ineligible for American citizenship to acquire, own, occupy, lease, or transfer agricultural land. In a proceeding by the state to escheat two parcels of land said to have been acquired in violation of the statute, the Court recognized the potentiality for discrimination in the statute and that such discrimination could be sustained only if there was "compelling justification."[56] But under the facts no justification was shown where the escheat, if permitted, would take away land recorded in the name of an American citizen, a minor, solely because the land had been paid for by his father, a Japanese alien ineligible for naturalization. The Court could only conclude that "the discrimination is based solely on his parents' country of origin . . . ."[57] Although *Terrace v. Thompson* was not specifically overruled, state courts have interpreted the later decisions in *Oyama* and *Takahashi* to repudiate the doctrine that ownership of land could be limited to citizens and aliens eligible for citizenship.[58]

Skinner v. Oklahoma[59] involved a very different kind of situation, but again one in which the Court recognized that legislation is on its face suspect when it involves limitation of "one of the basic civil rights of man," and is accordingly subject to "strict scrutiny."[60] At issue was the validity of Oklahoma's Habitual Criminal Sterilization Act, which defined habitual criminals to include any person convicted two or more times of felonies involving moral turpitude and thereafter convicted and sentenced in Oklahoma for such a crime. Although this definition included larceny, embezzlement was specifically exempted by statute, and in this the Court found "a clear, pointed, unmistakable discrimination. Oklahoma makes no attempt to say that he who commits larceny by trespass or trick or fraud has biologically inheritable traits which he who commits embezzlement lacks."[61] One may doubt whether any classification

55. 332 U.S. 633 (1948). Four members of the Court would have overruled Terrace v. Thompson outright. Id. at 649, 672.

56. 332 U.S. at 640.

57. Ibid.

58. See Sei Fujii v. California, 38 Cal. 2d 718, 242 P.2d 617 (1952); Namba v. McCourt, 185 Ore. 579, 204 P.2d 569 (1949).

59. 316 U.S. 535 (1942).

60. Id. at 541.

61. Ibid.

would survive which contemplated sterilization of some habitual criminals but not of others,[62] but the Court was not required to reach that ultimate proposition where, as in this case,

> We have not the slightest basis for inferring that that line [between larceny by fraud and embezzlement] has any significance in eugenics, nor that the inheritability of criminal traits follows the neat legal distinctions which the law has marked between those two offenses.[63]

In 1956 still another facet of equal protection was uncovered. In *Griffin v. Illinois*[64] the Court ruled that in a criminal case a state may not administer its law "so as to deny adequate appellate review to the poor while granting such review to all others."[65] That case involved the demand that the transcript of the trial proceedings necessary under state law for appellate review be furnished without cost to an indigent defendant. Failure to make provision for such transcript was held to violate both due process and equal protection. Since that time, comparable state practices have been found similarly vulnerable in a series of cases expounding the basic proposition announced in *Griffin*, and making clear that its reach was retroactive as well as prospective.[66] Principal reliance on equal protection seems also to follow from the later cases. In *Burns v. Ohio*,[67] for example, Chief Justice Warren stated that "The imposition by the State of financial barriers restricting the availability of appellate review for indigent criminal defendants has no place in our heritage of Equal Justice Under Law."

While it may seem that there is little logical identity among the matters thus far discussed, freedom from discrimination on grounds of race or alienage, the right to have offspring, the right to an appeal in a criminal case free of the handicap of poverty, and the right not to have one's vote diluted by malapportionment, yet there is also a strong kinship in each as "one of the basic civil rights of man." In

62. But cf. Buck v. Bell, 274 U.S. 200 (1927).

63. 316 U.S. at 542.

64. 351 U.S. 12 (1956).

65. Id. at 13.

66. Eskridge v. Washington State Prison Bd., 357 U.S. 214 (1958); Ross v. Schneckloth, 357 U.S. 575 (1958); Douglas v. Green, 363 U.S. 192 (1960); Burns v. Ohio, 360 U.S. 252 (1959); McCrary v. Indiana, 364 U.S. 277 (1960); Smith v. Bennett, 365 U.S. 708 (1961); Douglas v. California, 372 U.S. 353 (1963); Lane v. Brown, 372 U.S. 477 (1963); Draper v. Washington, 372 U.S. 487 (1963). But cf. Norvell v. Illinois, 373 U.S. 420 (1963).

67. 360 U.S. 252, 258 (1959).

this is found the rationalizing principle which explains the two sides of equal protection. Where the matter subject to regulation is economic in nature or pertains to social welfare, the presumption of constitutionality will outride all but the most exigent claims of legislative discrimination. But where preferred freedoms are involved, the presumption is liable to reversal; the state's rationale for any unequal treatment will be subjected to "strict scrutiny" and will be sustained only upon a showing of "compelling justification."

Equal Protection: A Contemporary Meaning. With the decisions in *Brown, Baker,* and *Reynolds,* the libertarian side of the equal protection clause has fully matured. As a shield against limitation of individual liberties at the hands of state governments, it must be ranked second in importance only to the due process clause; and there is indeed a marked relationship between the two. Neither clause any longer has much to say about the state's power to regulate economic activities. On the other hand, both clauses are strongly partisan in protection of the preferred freedoms relating to individual liberty. The due process clause sometimes speaks through portions of the Bill of Rights and sometimes of its own force, while the equal protection clause speaks always in its own name to forbid segregation, to require equality in rights of appeal in criminal cases, to limit eugenic experiments in limitation of the right of procreation, and now, to forbid irrational arrangements of voters into election districts.

THE RIGHT OF FRANCHISE AS A "BASIC CIVIL RIGHT"

The applicability of the equal protection clause to voting discriminations is entirely apparent if exercise of the right of franchise is recognized as a "basic civil right of man." Of this there can surely be no doubt. In a constitutional democracy, where the power of decision is vested in representative government, the right of franchise is all-important. The individual member of the body politic has no opportunity to participate in the governing process except through the ballot. This simple truth was reaffirmed in straightforward terms in *Reynolds*:

> The right to vote freely for the candidate of one's choice is of the essence of a democratic society, and any restrictions on that right strike at the heart of representative government. And the right of suffrage can be denied by a

debasement or dilution of the weight of a citizen's vote just as effectively as by wholly prohibiting the free exercise of the franchise.[68]

No one doubts that the right of franchise is a fundamental right which deserves in full measure whatever protections the Constitution affords. But some, while not disagreeing with the proposition stated thus generally, have suggested that the less restrictive side of the equal protection clause should be applied to apportionment, that the issue should be framed in terms of "reasonableness" or of "invidious discrimination."[69] To accept this version of equal protection would be to deny the centrality of equality, to downgrade the importance of the right of participation in the representative process, and to concede to the states a latitude for experimentation with the processes of democratic government comparable to matters within the conventional understanding of the police power. The strength of the equal protection clause, as compared in this setting to the due process clause, is that the former provides a definite standard, whereas the latter affords no stopping place.

Of the Supreme Court membership only Justice Harlan would go the whole distance of denying any meaning to the equal protection clause in this area, based on his reading of the original understanding of the equal protection clause. This limitation is somewhat curious in view of his willingness to give the same clause, in the context of racial discrimination, an expanded meaning beyond the intention of the framers. One wonders why, if the clock cannot be turned back to 1868 for a reading of equal protection in the area of racial discrimination,[70] the hands of the clock must be forever fixed in a timeless limbo when the issue is apportionment. Moreover, Justice Harlan has not been unsympathetic to a flexible and expanding reading of due process to permit absorption of provisions from the Bill of Rights into the due process clause of the fourteenth amendment, whence those provisions may emerge as limitations on the states.[71]

A different argument, on its face more appealing because conceding the applicability of equal protection as a safeguard against "unreasonable" interference with the franchise, proposes that the

68. Reynolds v. Sims, 377 U.S. 533, 555 (1964).

69. See, e.g., Dixon, Reapportionment Perspectives: What Is Fair Representation?, 51 A.B.A.J. 319 (1965).

70. Brown v. Board of Educ., 347 U.S. 483, 492–3 (1954).

71. See text preceding note 34 supra.

states be required to advance a "rational" apportionment plan and that they be restrained from "the systematic frustration of a majority of the electorate of the State."[72] These were the standards suggested by Justice Stewart (with whom Justice Clark joined) in disagreement with the equal-population standard for both houses adopted by the majority of the Court.

Justices Clark and Stewart disagreed with the majority disposition of the Colorado and New York cases. In the New York case they found "certainly rational" a "policy guaranteeing minimum representation to each county,"[73] even though that policy had the intended effect of creating substantial population disparities among districts. They also concluded that majority control was not frustrated because the ten most populous counties in the state, with 73.5 per cent of the citizen population, chose a majority of the senators and representatives.[74] However, they failed to point out — or did not find significant — the fact that the six most populous counties, with well over half of the population, were represented by less than a majority in each house of the legislature; and they were unmoved by the fact that the underrepresentation of the urban and suburban areas would have increased further if the New York legislature had been reapportioned in accordance with the 1960 census figures.

The dissenters thought the Colorado plan, too, was rational, but for a different reason. There the lower house was apportioned on a basis closely approximating population, while the senate apportionment was principally based on factors of geography and economic interests. The conclusion that the senate apportionment was rational was based on an undocumented assumption:

> The fact is, of course, that population factors must often to some degree be subordinated in devising a legislative apportionment plan which is to achieve the important goal of ensuring a fair, effective, and balanced representation of the regional, social, and economic interests within a State.[75]

In explaining why it was assumed "of course, that population factors must often to some degree be submerged," Justice Stewart shifted emphasis from concern for "balanced representation of the

72. Lucas v. Colorado General Assembly, 377 U.S. 713, 753–54 (Stewart, J., dissenting).

73. Id. at 762.

74. Id. at 763.

75. Id. at 751.

regional, social, and economic interests" to an admitted concern for the integrity of the county as a unit:

> It is clear from the record that if per capita representation were the rule in both houses of the Colorado Legislature, counties having small populations would have to be merged with larger counties having totally dissimilar interests.[76]

This frank expression of concern for "counties having small populations" becomes understandable in light of the fact that the animating principle in the 1962 reapportionment of the Colorado senate involved more clearly an interest in county representation than in the so-called regional groupings. This is apparent from an examination of the senate districts, as outlined in an appendix to the opinion of the district court. The four regions were:[77]

	Square Miles	Counties	Senators	Population	Population per Senator
Western Region	47,412	30	8	227,841	28,480
Eastern Region	27,322	16	5	142,033	28,407
South Central Region	14,580	8	3	66,554	22,185
East Slope Region	14,933	9	23	1,317,519	57,283
Totals	104,247	63	39	1,753,947	44,973

It is apparent that considerations of area did not provide a rational explanation for what was done. The south central region, with the smallest area, was also the region most overrepresented. Nor is it easy to believe that the senatorial apportionment provisions represented a realistic appraisal of the social or economic interests of the regions (even if those considerations were valid) in light of the contemporary structure of Colorado. As Judge Doyle pointed out in his dissenting opinion in the district court, "Amendment No. 7 arbitrarily froze existing apportionment and at the same time furnished one additional senator to each of four populous metropolitan counties by writing into the Colorado organic law disparities which had long existed and which we held were gross. It cannot be said that it was rational. The unpleasant truth is that it was particularly designed and dictated not by factual differences, but rather by political expediency. Simplicity and success at the polls overrode considerations of fairness and justice."[78]

The conclusion that political expediency and the preservation of

76. Id. at 757.
77. Lisco v. Love, 219 F. Supp. 922, 935–38 (D. Colo. 1963).
78. Id. at 941–42.

existing representation patterns determined the result is further demonstrated by two additional points. First, the four seats given to more populous counties were simply added to the existing 35 districts for a new senate membership of 39, without taking away, or altering, the representation from the other regions.[79] There was no updating of the economic interests of the state, no recognition of the decline in importance of the mining, cattle, and farming interests that had in fact occurred since the last substantial reapportionment. "It is foolish to say that because an area sustained a substantial mining industry at some previous time, it deserves greater representation today; or, because one area has cattle or a surplus of water, that it deserves greater representation."[80] In the second place, an examination of the actual districts rather than the general grouping of regions raises further doubts of rationality. For example, senate district number 32, consisting solely of Mesa County in the western region, had a 1960 population of 50,715 and a larger area than district number 25, consisting of Fremont and Custer Counties also in the western region, with a combined total population of 21,501. In fact, in the western region five of the seven districts other than district number 32 had populations of less than one half the population of that district.[81] If formula there was, the only rationalizing factor was a bias against populous counties, regardless of the region in which located. The formula apparently was that unless a county had reached a population in 1960 of more than 70,000 it should neither be divided into two senatorial districts nor combined with another county to provide multiple representation among the two or more counties thus combined. In short, grouping of counties was permitted only to form a single senatorial district. This is not apportionment based on social and economic interest groupings, but apportionment based on county representation. Perhaps Justice Stewart would be willing to defend it as that; but that is not the ground on which the claim of rationality was based.

That the devising of a rational plan based on population was not so difficult as some had thought is attested by the fact that, within less than a month after the decision in the Supreme Court, the Colorado legislature enacted, the federal court approved, and the

79. Except that sparsely populated Elbert County was joined to Kit Carson, Cheyenne, Lincoln, and Kiowa Counties rather than to Arapahoe County. Id. at 937.

80. Id. at 943.

81. Id. at 935–36.

governor signed, a plan for representation based more nearly on population in the senate as well as in the house.[82]

The second point in Justice Stewart's argument in favor of upholding the Colorado senatorial apportionment related to his minimal equal protection standard, that there be no frustration of effective majority control. Since the Colorado voters had approved the challenged plan in 1962, he could see no reason to set it aside. "Thus the majority [of Colorado voters] has consciously chosen to protect the minority's interests, and under the liberal initiative provisions of the Colorado Constitution, it retains the power to reverse its decision to do so. Therefore, there can be no question of frustration of the basic principle of majority rule."[83]

Justice Stewart's position will appeal to many as being within the best judicial tradition of both moderation and forward movement. He would not relinquish to state legislatures the power to alter as they will, or to destroy, the representative character of American democracy; at the same time he would avoid the charge that the Court is bent on becoming a super-legislature.[84] Thus, distortion of the admittedly important population base for representation should be permitted, in his judgment, so long as the electorate has the power to change the representation formula.

Others have made the same argument in various forms. Representative of these views is the suggestion of Robert G. McCloskey that the only question proper for judicial inquiry is the essentially "procedural" one of determining "whether the ultimate constituent power was being allowed an adequate opportunity to express itself .... But no constitutional question could be raised as to the actual, substantive nature of the apportionment, if the popular will had expressed itself or possessed adequate means for doing so."[85]

The Supreme Court, however, rejected all temporizing solutions and insisted on population as the nearly exclusive factor in both houses. In so doing the Court confounded the prognosticators, con-

82. Colo. Sess. Laws 1964, 2d Extra. Sess., c. 2.

83. Lucas v. Colorado General Assembly, 377 U.S. 713, 759 (1964) (Stewart, J., dissenting).

84. Justice Stewart expressed the fear in these words: "I am convinced these decisions mark a long step backward into that unhappy era when a majority of the members of this Court were thought by many to have convinced themselves and each other that the demands of the Constitution were to be measured not by what it says, but by their own notions of wise political theory." Id. at 747–48.

85. McCloskey, Foreword: The Reapportionment Case, 76 Harv. L. Rev. 54, 71 (1962).

fused and divided its critics, and addressed its argument directly to the majority of the voting public, who were, after all, the beneficiaries of the ruling. Nonetheless it is not irrelevant to look at what the Court rejected and, so far as can be determined, why the Court turned aside the proffered aids to expression of majority will, the initiative and referendum, the constitutional convention, and other devices designed to accommodate change of state constitutions to conform to popular will. Then it will be possible to examine as well the other principal argument made against application of the equal-population principle in both houses of a bicameral legislature, based on the so-called federal analogy.

MALAPPORTIONMENT AND POLITICAL REMEDIES

Amendments to state constitutions, whether proposed by the legislature or by initiative, are submitted to the voters for approval in all states except Delaware, where action by two successive legislatures is sufficient.[86] Vastly the most important means by which the frequent amendments to state constitutions are proposed is through action of the legislature, usually by a specified extraordinary majority vote in both houses, by two successive legislatures, or both. It is scarcely necessary to repeat the fact that malapportioned legislatures have been notably reluctant to propose changes in apportionment which would transfer power to emerging areas of population strength to the electoral disadvantage of present members. As a result, experts in the state governmental system have commonly believed that the voters should have some more direct means of bringing about constitutional amendment.[87]

The Initiative: Story of a Failure. The initiative was devised to permit direct voter action to overcome legislative inertia or disregard of popular will; for a time it seemed likely that an initiative provision would be incorporated in most state constitutions. However, that initial enthusiasm was tempered by the difficulties en-

86. Del. Const. art. XVI, § 1.

87. The Model State Constitution proposed by the National Municipal League (6th ed. 1963) includes a provision for the initiative (§ 12.01) in the belief that "Some way should be provided by which the people may directly effect constitutional change without depending on existing governmental institutions." Id. at 106. However, no extensive use of the initiative is "expected." Ibid. See also Wheeler (ed.), Salient Issues of Constitutional Revision 165–72 (National Municipal League pamphlet 1961).

countered in practical operation; now only thirteen states have provisions for the initiative for constitutional amendments,[88] while seven more provide the initiative for statutory change.[89] Even in these states, experience with the initiative has been disappointing, particularly in connection with attempts to obtain reapportionment. It has not proved a particularly helpful means of preventing "frustration of effective majority rule." Before telling that story, however, it will be useful first to note how the initiative ordinarily operates.

An amendment proposed by initiative must ordinarily be proposed by its sponsors in an initiative petition signed by a prescribed percentage of the qualified voters of the state, ranging in 12 states from 3 to 15 per cent, while North Dakota requires 20,000 signatures.[90] The signature provision has a further restrictive bite in some states; Ohio, for example, requires that in at least half of the state's 88 counties 5 per cent of the voters must sign the petition.[91] Thus, any attempt to change Ohio's lower house by initiative would require signatures from a number of overrepresented counties which would lose representation as a result of any reapportionment in satisfaction of the equal-population principle. Where, then, is the "effective majority rule"?

Moreover, it has been estimated that the cost in Ohio of attempting to get an initiative proposal on the ballot is prohibitive for any individual citizen, and indeed for all but the wealthiest groups. In recent initiative efforts in Ohio the cost has been considerably in excess of $100,000, without considering the substantially larger out-

---

88. Arizona, Arkansas, California, Colorado, Massachusetts, Michigan, Missouri, Nebraska, Nevada, North Dakota, Ohio, Oklahoma, and Oregon.

89. Alaska, Idaho, Maine, Montana, South Dakota, Utah, and Washington. Legislation adopted by statutory initiative ordinarily stands on equal footing with ordinary legislation and is therefore subject to legislative repeal or amendment. See Luker v. Curtis, 64 Idaho 703, 136 P.2d 978 (1943); Bottomly v. Ford 117 Mont. 160, 157 P.2d 108 (1945); State v. Houge, 67 N.D. 251, 271 N.W. 677 (1937); Kadderly v. Portland, 44 Or. 118, 74 Pac. 710 (1903); People ex rel. Zimmerman v. Herder, 122 Colo. 456, 223 P.2d 197 (1950). There appear to be two reasons for the rule. First, unlike a legislative act there is no debate, in the formal sense, on an initiated measure. It is not subject to change by anyone but the initiators before adoption. Second, the courts adhere to the political question doctrine in refusing to enjoin the legislature from repealing or amending the measure in question. But see Beneficial Loan Soc. v. Haight, 215 Cal. 506, 11 P.2d 857 (1932), where the court interpreted the California constitution as requiring the consent of the electorate for the repeal or amendment of any initiated legislation.

90. National Municipal League, Model State Constitution 107 (6th ed. 1963).

91. Ohio Const. art. II, § 1.

lay which would be required for the campaign itself.[92] That difficulty was recognized explicitly by the district court in a case challenging the apportionment formula in the unicameral Nebraska legislature.

> To say that such a remedy is adequate for one ordinary voter, and we are here concerned with the rights of an individual voter, for concededly one ordinary voter could maintain this action, is being impractical. In addition, the expense of putting an initiated proposal on the ballot in Nebraska is prohibitive for the ordinary voter.[93]

The court's conclusion is well justified. The initiative procedure, in other states as well as in Ohio and Nebraska, is better suited to efficient organizational effort than to independent action.[94]

The difficulties involved in securing a place on the ballot are only part of the problem. Even if an initiated proposal gains a place on the ballot, it is often not easy to interpret the significance of the vote as to any particular matter. In seeking to determine the significance of the Colorado vote on amendments 7 and 8 in 1962, the Supreme Court noted that in all probability neither of the proposed plans was wholly acceptable to the voters in the populous counties, and that it was not justifiable to assume that the voters chose between two distinct alternatives.[95] Similarly, the district court in the Washington case rejected the argument that a "no" vote on an initiated apportionment proposal should preclude relief. The court pointed out that the vote might have indicated disapproval of the choice presented or lack of understanding of the issues no less than satisfaction with the existing apportionment.[96]

92. Jurisdictional Statement of appellant, pp. 24–25, Sive v. Ellis (Nolan v. Rhodes), 378 U.S. 556 (1964).

93. League of Nebraska Municipalities v. Marsh, 209 F. Supp. 189, 193 (D. Neb. 1962). Article III, section 2 of the Nebraska constitution requires that 5 per cent of the electors in two fifths of the state's counties must sign the initiative petition.

94. See Brief of J. Howard Edmonson, Governor of Oklahoma, as amicus curiae, pp. 14–17, Baker v. Carr, 369 U.S. 186 (1962). See also Lisco v. Love, 219 F. Supp. 922, 942 (D. Colo. 1963), rev'd sub. nom. Lucas v. Colorado General Assembly, 377 U.S. 713 (1964): "This possible remedy is not merely questionable, it is for practical purposes impossible."

95. Lucas v. Colorado General Assembly, 377 U.S. 713, 732 (1964). See also the discussion at page 191 infra.

96. Thigpen v. Meyers, 211 F. Supp. 826, 832 (W.D. Wash. 1962), aff'd per curiam, 378 U.S. 554 (1964). See also Davis v. Synhorst, 217 F. Supp. 492, 500 (S.D. Iowa 1963), aff'd per curiam sub nom. Hill v. Davis, 378 U.S. 565 (1964); Moss v. Burkhart, 220 F. Supp. 149, 154–55 (W.D. Okla. 1963), aff'd per curiam sub nom. Williams v. Moss, 378

The initiative has accordingly been little used as a means of effecting reapportionment. The legislative reform issue has not been glamorous enough to overcome the very substantial procedural and financial obstacles to success. There are only five states — Arkansas, California, Colorado, Michigan, and Oregon — in which reapportionment has been achieved by constitutional initiative and one, Washington, in which reapportionment was accomplished by statutory initiative.[97] Because each instance is instructive, the experience in those states is summarized below (plus Nebraska where a federal court commented on the theoretical availability of the initiative).

Arkansas: In Arkansas reapportionment was achieved by constitutional initiative in 1936 after nearly half a century of legislative failure to act. The amendment provided for decennial reapportionment by a board of apportionment and vested in the state supreme court the power to review action of the board. The old basis for representation was retained and brought up to date — population for the senate and one representative for each of the 75 counties, with the remaining 25 seats allocated on a population standard. In 1956 the Arkansas Farm Bureau Federation sponsored a successful initiative measure which froze permanently the senate districts laid out by state supreme court order in 1952, taking away from the apportionment board any jurisdiction over senate districts.[98] Even if due credit be given the operation of the initiative to overcome a long period of legislative inaction, the 1956 decision seems by any standard unfortunate in its permanent establishment of legislative districts regardless of population shifts certain to occur in later years. Undoubtedly, the change was presented to the voters as no more than a ratification of the existing formula without calling to

---

U.S. 558 (1964); Toombs v. Fortson, 205 F. Supp. 248, 256 (N.D. Ga. 1962), vacated in part and remanded, 379 U.S. 621 (1965).

Voters in Oklahoma were told that an earlier proposed reapportionment "eliminated homestead exemption, reduced pension checks, stopped school busses, eliminated rural road care, . . . helped labor, hurt labor, and a number of other untruths and half truths." Brief of J. Howard Edmonson, Governor of Oklahoma, as amicus curiae, p. 16, Baker v. Carr, 369 U.S. 186 (1962).

97. In a few other states the initiative to secure reapportionment was attempted but failed to get sufficient signatures to get on the ballot or was defeated at the general election. For general discussion of the initiative, see Baker, State Constitutions: Reapportionment 20, 38, 47–50 (National Municipal League pamphlet 1960).

98. The history is reviewed in Pickens v. Board of Apportionment, 220 Ark. 145, 246 S.W.2d 556 (1952). See also Baker, supra note 97, at 48.

their attention the way in which it would operate to magnify the inequalities over the years.

California: The original California constitution of 1849 provided for representation in both houses of the legislature in accordance with population. For at least three decades northern California, with more than nine tenths of the state's population, held firm control of the legislature. Even after the balance began to shift south, population continued dominant until about 1930. Reapportionments were made in 1883, 1891, and 1902 to reflect the gradual shift of population to the south. But conflicts between north and south developed in the early years of the twentieth century, and the Los Angeles interests joined with rural interests to secure for Los Angeles the representation to which it was entitled by population (except one assemblyman).[99] But that alliance broke down with further population gains in southern California. "By 1920 rural groups were determined to control at least one house of the legislature, while the decline of San Francisco tended to encourage an alliance with other northern groups to prevent southern California majorities in both houses."[100] The respective interests turned to the initiative and placed two measures on the ballot in 1926. The proposal to continue a population base and to establish a reapportionment commission was defeated by a margin of about three to two, while the so-called (but somewhat misnamed) federal plan, initiated by the California Farm Bureau Federation and supported by other farm groups and by the San Francisco Chamber of Commerce, was approved by a margin of about five to four. Since that time Los Angeles County has had only 1 of 40 senators, the same as the least populous senatorial district, with a 1960 population of 14,294, for a ratio of almost 500 to 1. It is hard to believe that this result promotes "effective majority rule," engineered as it was by a combination of interest groups normally antagonistic to one another, united only in their desire to prevent effective representation of a great urban center.

Subsequent events in California bear out the same pattern. In 1948, 1960, and 1962 initiative measures were qualified for the ballot for the purpose of providing a greater measure of representation in the state senate for the populous counties, although never on a

99. Report of California Study Commission on Senate Apportionment 4–6 (1962).
100. Id. at 6.

strict population basis. Each was defeated, again largely as a result of the unwillingness of this oddly aligned majority to relinquish even in part its selfishly aggrandized power.

Colorado: In 1962 the Colorado electorate adopted proposed Amendment No. 7 by more than three to two and defeated proposed Amendment No. 8 by more than two to one. The rejected amendment prescribed an apportionment plan pursuant to which seats in both houses of the Colorado legislature would have been apportioned substantially in accordance with population, while Amendment No. 7 provided for apportionment of the house on the basis of population, but essentially maintained the existing apportionment in the senate, which was based on a combination of population and other factors.

To understand the voters' choice it is necessary to examine the immediately preceding apportionment situation and some of the side effects of Amendments 7 and 8 apparently unrelated to the population question. The apportionment formula adopted in 1953, which was in effect prior to the 1962 amendment, provided for the election at large of senators and representatives chosen from counties entitled to more than one senator or representative. Thus, for example, the city and county of Denver had 8 senate seats and 17 house seats, while Pueblo County had two senators and four representatives. Voters in the more populous counties, particularly members of minority groups (racial, religious, ethnic, or political), commonly felt disadvantaged by the elections at large within their counties. Accordingly, when Amendment No. 7 proposed that all seats in both houses should be chosen on a single-member basis, and No. 8 proposed continuance of the objectionable elections at large in the populous counties, it is not surprising that in the minds of many the disadvantages of elections at large outweighed the advantages of enlarged representation. As the Supreme Court observed, "the choice presented to the Colorado electorate, in voting on these two proposed constitutional amendments, was hardly . . . clear-cut."[101]

Michigan: Until 1952 the Michigan constitution had required representation substantially in accordance with population in both houses, but the requirement had been sadly neglected for many years; and in 1930 the voters rejected an amendment which would

---

101. Lucas v. Colorado General Assembly, 377 U.S. 713, 731–32 (1964).

have given the secretary of state the duty of reapportionment in accordance with the state constitution if the legislature failed to act promptly after each United States decennial census.

In 1952 the Michigan voters approved the so-called "balanced legislature" plan, which provided for apportionment of representatives in accordance with population, increased senatorial districts from 32 to 34, and froze those 34 districts into the constitution without provision for reapportionment. This reflected the increased tensions between Wayne County, where the proposal was disapproved almost two to one, and the rest of the state, where it carried by substantial margins. At the same election in 1952 the voters rejected about three to two a proposal to guarantee apportionment on a population basis, with mandatory provisions for decennial adjustment. The petition for this proposal had been initiated by the Michigan Committee for Representative Government, supported largely by the CIO. Because of the attitude of Democrats in the upper peninsula, the Democratic party was divided; and the "balanced legislature" proposal, supported energetically by the Michigan Farm Bureau and Republicans generally, was approved. As in the case of California in 1926, various interest groups in the state joined in what would have been a strange alliance for any purpose except that of putting populous Wayne County at a disadvantage in the state legislature. But that objective at least was effectively accomplished.

Nebraska: Although the initiative has never been used to accomplish reapportionment in Nebraska, the initiative provisions in that state merit comment because their very existence was urged by defendants in a challenge to existing apportionment as a sufficient protection against malapportionment. In rejecting the argument, the federal district court explained the procedures for use of the initiative, which it said was not "an adequate remedy" to correct existing malapportionment. The proponent of an initiative proposal in Nebraska is required first to clear his petitions with the secretary of state. Then he must secure the signatures of 10 per cent of the electors of the state if he is proposing a constitutional amendment, or of 7 per cent if he proposes enactment of a law. Moreover, the signatures must be distributed to include 5 per cent of the electors of each of two fifths of the 93 counties of the state. The court continued with examples demonstrating the inadequacy of the initiative as a means of securing even relatively noncontroversial changes:

The Nebraska State Bar Association with its over 2000 members failed recently to secure sufficient signatures to place on the ballot an amendment relating to the judiciary. The court of its own knowledge knows that in 1957 an attempt was made to place on the ballot a proposal to elect rather than appoint the State Commissioner of Education. Petitions with 58,548 signatures were presented. 56,793 were required. 4,884 were struck by the Secretary of State following examination. This reduced the number of qualified signatures below the number required to put the proposal on the ballot.[102]

Oregon: By initiative in 1952 the Oregon constitution was amended to provide enforcement for the apportionment provisions after nearly half a century of legislative inaction. The basis of representation, primarily population in both houses, was retained from the original constitution of 1857, and a temporary reapportionment was approved to begin in 1954. The amendment provided for decennial redistricting by the legislature beginning in 1961, subject to direct review in the state supreme court upon the petition of any qualified voter. If the legislature should fail to act by July 1 of the year of the legislative session following the federal census, the secretary of state was directed to prepare a plan to be filed with the governor by August 1 of the same year, which would then become law. This is the one example of an initiated change in apportionment formula which satisfied both the equal-population principle and a broadly based combination of interest groups. The initiative campaign was supported by Young Democrats, Young Republicans, the League of Women Voters, and even by agriculture and labor organizations.[103]

Washington: The state legislature did not reapportion either house on its own after 1901, in defiance of state constitutional requirements. Despite the burdensome state procedures for the initiative, necessitating the signatures of 8 per cent of the registered voters, the statutory initiative was employed in 1930 and 1956 to overcome the legislative failure to act. Although the measure was approved, the 1956 act illustrates another defect in the statutory initiative as a reapportionment device; for in 1957 the legislature sharply restricted the population base of the initiated measure, and the state supreme court upheld its power to do so.[104]

102. Nebraska League of Municipalities v. Marsh, 209 F. Supp. 189, 192–93 (D. Nebr. 1962).

103. Baker, supra note 97, at 31–32, 49.

104. State ex rel. O'Connell v. Meyers, 51 Wash. 2d 454, 319 P.2d 828 (1957). See also Baker, supra note 97, at 49.

In 1962, Initiative No. 211 sought to redraw the state legislative districts according to 1960 population figures (as required by the state constitution). But it was defeated by the voters, perhaps because they now sensed the futility of their action where the legislature had proved willing to upset a similar vote only five years earlier. When the federal district court was asked to decline jurisdiction of a suit challenging the malapportioned state legislature, the court's answer was, in its words, "concise and direct."

> We have no way of knowing whether the measure was defeated because a majority did not desire reapportionment or whether they didn't approve of the proposed method or whether they didn't understand it (there were numerous other complicated matters on the ballot) or whether the opponents were better organized than the proponents. It makes no difference. The inalienable constitutional right of equal protection cannot be made to depend upon the will of the majority.[105]

The Constitutional Convention. States that do not have the initiative frequently provide for voter-initiated proposals to call a constitutional convention for constitutional revision or provide for periodic review by the voters of the question whether a constitutional convention should be called. The New York constitution is representative of the latter group in providing for a referendum every twenty years on the question whether a constitutional convention should be called.[106] In 1957 the voters rejected such a call, but there is no reason to believe that this was in any way a ratification of existing malapportionment. Although Governor Harriman urged a "yes" vote, he went no further on the apportionment issue

105. Thigpen v. Meyers, 211 F. Supp. 826, 832 (W.D. Wash. 1962).

106. N.Y. Const. art. XIX, § 2. Apart from this method of amendment after constitutional convention, the New York constitution cannot be amended except by popular vote after an amendment is approved by a majority of the members of each house of the legislature at two successive regular sessions, a general election of the legislature having intervened. Id., art. XIX, § 1. But this route has produced no reapportionment in New York, despite the fact that as far back as 1950 the joint legislative committee on reapportionment had concluded that "The cities, particularly the City of New York, do not have equitable representation in either House," and that the present method of obtaining the ratio for apportioning senators is "unfair to urban districts." See Preliminary Report to the Joint Legislative Committee on Reapportionment, N.Y. Legis. Doc. No. 3144, 12 (1950). Averell Harriman, during each of the years he was governor (1955 through 1958), recommended the initiation of a constitutional amendment on apportionment, always unsuccessfully. See brief of Paul R. Screvane, in support of appellants, p. 74, WMCA, Inc. v. Lomenzo, 377 U.S. 633 (1964). See also Scholle v. Hare, 367 Mich. 176, 116 N.W.2d 350 (1962).

than to say that it was one of the important issues. At the same time former Governor Thomas E. Dewey was urging a "no" vote, not on the ground that revision was not needed, but because a convention was an outmoded, unwieldly, and costly instrument for revision. The same view was expressed by other leading figures in the state, and other groups came out for or against the constitutional convention on various grounds, usually unrelated to the need for reapportionment.[107]

The possibility of a constitutional convention at the call of the voters under a system like that in New York is clearly not a practical political remedy. Moreover, the possibility of apportionment relief from a convention called by a malapportioned legislature, whose membership selection is likely to mirror the legislature itself, is scarcely a reliable vehicle for the correction of voter imbalance.

Majority Rule and Minority Rights. There is a more fundamental difficulty with the suggestion that it is possible by majority vote, even if accurately representative of majority sentiment on issues clearly understood, to transfer control of the governmental process to some particular minority group. No one would suggest that segregation could be reimposed by the "will of the people" manifested through constitutional amendments, whether proposed by legislature, initiative, or constitutional convention. Equally, religious discrimination could not be imposed by initiative. Similarly, it could scarcely be contended that it would be possible by popular vote to give one group of voters half a vote while others were given a full vote.[108] "The inalienable constitutional right of equal protection cannot be made to depend upon the will of the majority."[109]

Finally, if the doctrine were to prevail that the availability of the initiative as an expression of "effective majority rule" would satisfy the requirements of the equal protection clause, we might anticipate that states which do not now have the initiative would "accept the implicit invitation to bypass the [Supreme Court rulings] by adopting such devices."[110]

---

107. See brief of Paul R. Screvane, *supra* note 106, at 73–84.

108. Cf. Colegrove v. Green, 328 U.S. 549, 569–71 (1946) (Black, J., dissenting).

109. Thigpen v. Meyers, 211 F. Supp. 826, 832 (W.D. Wash. 1962), aff'd per curiam, 378 U.S. 554 (1964).

110. Sindler, Baker v. Carr; How to "Sear the Conscience" of Legislators, 72 Yale L.J., 23, 32 (1962).

APPORTIONMENT AND
THE FEDERAL ANALOGY

For a time after the decision in *Baker v. Carr* much was made of the so-called federal analogy as one possibly acceptable basis for decision of the ultimate issue on the merits. The theory was readily understood and seemed plausible on its face. The suggestion was simple. If one house of a bicameral legislature must be apportioned in close approximation to the population standard, which nearly all conceded was the minimum required of equal protection, then why should it not be permissible for the other house to be apportioned without regard to population? The prime example was of course the United States Congress with its apportionment of representatives geared as closely as possible to population, while the Senate consisted of two senators from each state without regard to population. Justice Harlan thought the matter clear: "It is surely beyond argument that those who have the responsibility for devising a system of representation may permissibly consider that factors other than bare numbers should be taken into account. The existence of the United States Senate is proof enough of that."[111] There are several difficulties with the analogy which made its appeal more superficial than substantial. Nonetheless, the federal analogy, as illustrated by the very fact of its misnomer, makes an almost mystical appeal to what seems the rationality of real political life and to a beguiling historical fallacy. Accordingly, the argument, despite its spurious attraction — perhaps because of it — deserves careful attention.

The Historical Fallacy. The appeal to history is not sound. As the Supreme Court properly observed, "Attempted reliance on the federal analogy appears often to be little more than an after-the-fact rationalization offered in defense of maladjusted state apportionment arrangements."[112]

---

111. Baker v. Carr, 369 U.S. 186, 333 (1962) (dissenting opinion).

112. Reynolds v. Sims, 377 U.S. 533, 573 (1964). See also Gray v. Sanders, 372 U.S. 368, 376–77 n.8 (1963); Sincock v. Duffy, 215 F. Supp. 169, 186–87 (D. Del. 1963), aff'd sub. nom. Roman v. Sincock, 377 U.S. 695 (1964); Mann v. Davis, 213 F. Supp. 577, 584–85 (E.D. Va. 1962), aff'd, 377 U.S. 678 (1964); McKay, Reapportionment and the Federal Analogy (National Municipal League pamphlet 1962); McKay, the Federal Analogy and State Apportionment Standards, 38 Notre Dame Law. 487 (1963); Merrill, Blazes for a Trail Through the Thicket of Reapportionment, 16 Okla. L. Rev. 59, 67–70 (1963).

The thirteen colonies which became the original states all carried over into statehood precisely or in some modified form the governmental structure they had during the Revolutionary War, often based on a constitution adopted in 1776 or 1777 when statehood was first proclaimed. All the predecessor colonial governments had to some extent been influenced by the English model, including all the inequalities of representation which existed in the mother country in the eighteenth century. Significantly, as the colonies became states there was a marked trend toward greater reliance on population in one or both houses of the legislature when bicameralism became common. The successor constitutions in those states, adopted in the late eighteenth and early nineteenth centuries, as well as the constitutions in states admitted thereafter until late in the nineteenth century, reflected increasing reliance on population.

Not one of the states represented at the Constitutional Convention in 1787, and not one of the states at the time of the ratification of the Constitution, had in its own state legislature a representation formula comparable to that adopted in the United States Constitution for the Congress of the United States (see pages 16–23). The reasons for the failure of the states to copy the federal plan are clear. The gifted individuals who drafted the United States Constitution, and most of those who voted for its ratification in the various states, were committed to the democratic ideal of equality and even, perhaps less explicitly, to the concept of majority rule. Both ideas shine through the Declaration of Independence and the debates leading to the approval of the Constitution as transmitted to the states for ratification. The writings of such men as Thomas Jefferson[113] and, in more restrained vein, the contributors to *The Federalist*, demonstrate similar concern for equal treatment in a democratic, essentially majoritarian context. Thus it is not surprising that the so-called Virginia Plan, out of which emerged the basic pattern of the Constitution during the Convention in 1787, originally provided

113. Thomas Jefferson was particularly disturbed that the Virginia constitution of 1776 did not provide for apportionment in both houses on the basis of population. In 1816 he wrote that "a government is republican in proportion as every member composing it has his equal voice in the direction of its concerns . . . by representatives chosen by himself . . . ." Letter to Samuel Kercheval, X Writings of Thomas Jefferson 38 (Ford ed. 1899). In 1819 he wrote: "Equal representation is so fundamental a principle in a true republic that no prejudice can justify its violation because the prejudices themselves cannot be justified." Letter to William King, Jefferson Papers, Library of Congress, vol. 216, p. 38616.

for representation in accordance with population in both houses of Congress.[114] But the drafters of the Constitution were also practical men who recognized that insistence on that principle would make impossible the ratification by a sufficient number of states of any constitution containing such a proposal. As a consequence, the favored equalitarian principle was in part set aside in the so-called Great Compromise under which Congress still operates.

Even at the time the Constitution was being drafted to include these partial restrictions on equality in the federal establishment, Congress was demonstrating its interest in promoting equality of representation in the political subdivisions over which it had directive authority. The Northwest Ordinance, adopted in 1787, provided for the apportionment of seats in the territorial legislatures solely on the basis of population. "The inhabitants of the said territory shall always be entitled to the benefits . . . of a proportional representation of the people in the Legislature."[115] That command was largely satisfied in the various territorial legislatures as they were established one by one. Moreover, the states ultimately created out of the Northwest Territory also provided in their original state constitutions for apportionment in both houses with principal reliance on population.

There can be no mistaking the fact that the federal analogy has no roots in the history of state legislative apportionment in the United States. It was not the pattern in the original states; Congress for more than one hundred years encouraged, where it did not require, equal population in both houses of bicameral legislatures. States that have more recently turned in part away from population as a basis for representation have done so for reasons more selfishly pragmatic than philosophic. The representation formula for the United States Senate and House of Representatives was unique when proposed in 1787, drawn from neither earlier history nor contemporary experience.[116] Unique it remained for nearly a century

114. Farrand, The Framing of the Constitution of the United States, 74–75 (1913). For an illuminating collection of statements from the Convention and from contemporaries, see Brief for the United States as amicus curiae, appendix B, Maryland Committee for Fair Representation v. Tawes, 377 U.S. 656 (1964).

115. Northwest Ordinance of 1787, art. II, § 14.

116. The federal analogy argument was advanced in presumed defense of the pre-1962 apportionment in Maryland and in the plan adopted by initiative in Colorado in 1962, which survived only until 1964. However, in Maryland neither house was based on equal representation for all counties (or even all counties plus the city of Balti-

thereafter. At the time of the 1964 Supreme Court decisions, at most ten states could fairly be described as having a legislative apportionment formula even closely approximating that in the United States Congress.[117]

Apart from the inappropriateness of reliance upon the federal analogy for the reasons already stated, there is yet another historic reason for rejecting the analogy. The constitutional decision which established the Senate without reference to population was made by sovereign states in an act of consensual union. But counties, cities, towns, and other subdivisions of the states are not sovereign; they neither have nor need the perquisites of sovereignty. The power of altering local political lines rests with the parent state, not with the dependent units. Unlike the states, which are protected by the Constitution from boundary changes,[118] the lesser subdivisions within a state have no constitutional protection against state legislative decisions to reduce, enlarge, alter, or abolish them[119] except, for example, where the redrawing of political lines is motivated by racial discrimination intended to make ineffectual the right of franchise of Negroes.[120]

Federal Elections and Voter Equality. The United States Constitution permits departure from the equal-population principle in the federal election process in three respects. Although none of these bears directly upon the state legislative apportionment process, the persistence of the federal analogy argument suggests that those examples of nonreliance on population should be examined for any possible relevance by analogy or otherwise.

1. The most extreme departure from the equal-population principle is of course the provision for the choice of two senators from each state without regard to population. As a result, each senator from Alaska represents fewer than 120,000 constituents, while each

---

more), and neither house was based even approximately on population. See Maryland Committee for Equal Representation v. Tawes, 377 U.S. 656 (1964). The initiated plan in Colorado, while providing for apportionment in one house approximately in accordance with population, did not attempt equal representation among the counties in the other.

117. Arizona, Connecticut, Idaho, Montana, Nevada, New Mexico, New Jersey, Rhode Island, South Carolina, and Vermont. But each of those states departed to some extent from the alleged federal model. See the table of state apportionments supra at pages 46–47.

118. U.S. Const. art. IV, § 3.

119. See Hunter v. City of Pittsburgh, 207 U.S. 161, 178–79 (1907).

120. See Gomillion v. Lightfoot, 364 U.S. 339 (1960).

senator from California represents more than 8,000,000. The resulting differential is thus more than 65 to 1 in terms of the relative
influence of each voter. The fact that authority for this inequality
of representation is found in the Constitution provides such justification as there is, in terms of that analogy to federal practice, for
similar differentials within state legislatures. The reasons for which
the Court unhesitatingly rejected this argument are discussed further below.

2. A much less extreme departure from the equal-population
principle arises from the provision that assures each state one representative in the House regardless of population. Thus, in the House
Alaska is again overrepresented, with one representative for its
1960 population of 226,157, compared with the 1960 apportionment ratio of 410,000 used as the basic figure for computing the apportionment of representatives to the states. Here the differential
is more than two to one, compared with some underrepresented
states.[121] Disparities of this nature occur similarly in state legislatures where district lines are drawn in accordance with political
lines; but the disparities in state legislatures thus occasioned are
ordinarily far greater than those in the United States House of
Representatives.

3. In addition to the two constitutionally authorized deviations
just described, a third falls somewhere between the first two in
severity of impact, compounded as it is of features of both. Article
II, section 1 of the Constitution provides for the designation in each
state of "a number of Electors, equal to the whole Number of Senators and Representatives to which the State may be entitled in the
Congress . . . ." who thereafter cast votes for the President and Vice-
President.[122]

The defendants in *Gray v. Sanders*,[123] the Georgia county unit
case, made their appeal by analogy to this provision. To recapitu-
late briefly what was discussed before (see pages 83–85), the system
applied as follows in statewide primaries: A candidate for nomination who received the highest number of votes in a county was con-

121. E.g., Maine and New Mexico. In 1960 each had a population of nearly 1,000,000
but was allotted only two representatives. Thus, each representative in those states has
between two and three times as many constituents as does Alaska's single representative.

122. The original procedure was somewhat revised by the specifics of the twelfth
amendment.

123. 372 U.S. 368 (1963).

sidered to have carried the county and to be entitled to two votes for each representative allotted to that county in the lower house of the general assembly. Since no county was given more than three seats in that house, the most populous county (Fulton, with a 1960 population of 556,326) had only six unit votes, while the least populous county (Echols, with a 1960 population of 1,876) had two. The United States Supreme Court summarily rejected this branch of the federal analogy argument.

> We think the analogies to the electoral college, to districting and redistricting, and to other phases of the problems of representation in state or federal legislatures or conventions are inapposite. The inclusion of the electoral college in the Constitution as the result of specific historical concerns, validated the collegiate principle despite its inherent numerical inequality, but implied nothing about the use of an analogous system by a state in statewide elections.[124]

By footnote the Court explained the reasons for the adoption of the electoral college device in the first place; it was "designed by men who did not want the election of the President to be left to the people." However, "Passage of the Fifteenth, Seventeenth, and Nineteenth Amendments shows that this conception of political equality belongs to a bygone day, and should not be considered in determining what the Equal Protection Clause of the Fourteenth Amendment requires in statewide elections."[125]

The "Tyranny of the Majority." The argument is sometimes made that minority interests need and deserve special representation as a protection against the tyranny of the majority. And certainly the Constitution recognizes the need to protect various groups against majority pressures which might otherwise make intolerable the situation of racial, religious, or politically unpopular minority groups. But to endorse the desirability — and the necessity — of those provisions is not at all the same as to demand, in the name of minority rights, that some minority groups be empowered to act as though they were in fact the majority. To urge that the popular majority should be restrained from fulfilling its goals because of the objections of economic or social interest minority groups is to confuse high principle with cynical expediency.

Yet that is exactly what those dissatisfied with the equal-popula-

124. Id. at 378.
125. Id. at 376–77 n.8.

tion principle have urged. Justice Harlan, dissenting in *Reynolds*, argued that "legislators can represent their electors only by speaking for their interests — economic, social, political . . . ."[126] Similarly, Justice Stewart wrote that "population factors must often to some degree be subordinated in devising a legislative apportionment plan which is to achieve the important goal of ensuring a fair, effective, and balanced representation of the regional, social, and economic interests within a state . . . ."[127] And Alexander Bickel has offered a frank justification for ethnic-group constituencies as follows: "I believe the Silk Stockings should be represented by a man specially responsive and congenial to them, ... I think the same of Negroes, Puerto Ricans, farmers, and other distinguishable groups of reasonable size."[128] The proposition is untenable for at least two reasons. In the first place, any American majority is itself composed of various minority groups that overlap and intersect, whether the perspective is race, religion, ethnic origin, economic interest, urban, rural, or other special-interest group. There is no practical or defensible way of determining which minority interest is to be preferred over which majority interest, and indeed over which other minorities. In the second place, if it be suggested that a particular minority interest deserves protection today against some majority assumed to be antagonistic to that minority, there is no assurance of permanent security. That which the legislature can give it can also withdraw.

The simple truth is that the opinions in the *Reapportionment Cases* reaffirmed the basic ideals of a representative democracy in which universal suffrage is the nearly realized objective. As Carl Auerbach has observed: "Nothing is more fundamental to representative government — and therefore more constitutional — than the rules governing the electoral process itself . . . . No reason consistent with the democratic ideals of equality and majority — or minorities' — rule has been advanced for not effectuating" the equal-population principle.[129]

No matter how forthright the rejection of the federal analogy, and almost without regard to how persuasive the reasons that estab-

---

126. 377 U.S. at 623–24.

127. Id. at 749–51.

128. Letter to Editor, 36 Commentary 344 (1963).

129. Auerbach, The Reapportionment Cases: One Vote, One Value, 1964 Supreme Court Review 1, 66–67.

lish its nonrelevance, the analogy has a way of not quite staying down. Even when it is established that the argument from history is fallacious, the proponents of unequal representation in at least one house are likely to argue that it can hardly be irrational for states *now* to propose an apportionment formula comparable to the plan long employed in the national legislature. However, as suggested earlier, the equal protection clause is not to be given such a loose reading when the "basic civil rights of man" are involved. The equal protection clause must be read in the light of contemporary experience, rather than with an over-the-shoulder glance at a different practice by a different sovereign whose representation formula is specified in provisions of the Constitution unaffected by the command of an equal protection clause.

CONGRESSIONAL ATTEMPTS TO RESTRICT VOTER EQUALITY

As soon as the decision in *Reynolds v. Sims* was announced on June 15, 1964, the argument that legislatures should be free to apportion without regard to population took a new turn. The earlier contention that state legislatures should be altogether free to act as they chose in this regard was largely abandoned in favor of the compromise proposition that one, but only one, house of a state legislature must represent people as such. Since the Supreme Court had rejected that argument in light of the logic of the equal protection clause, the desired result could be achieved only by constitutional amendment or by leaving control of reapportionment to the exclusive control of the legislatures, as nearly as possible immune from judicial review. Both approaches were promptly attempted.

In July 1964 the Republican National Convention approved a plank in the party platform condemning the apportionment decisions and calling for some limitation by constitutional amendment or statute. By mid-August more than a hundred resolutions and bills had been introduced in Congress calling for either constitutional amendment or some kind of statutory limitation on the exercise of jurisdiction by the federal courts.

There is no mistaking the fact that these proposals raise questions of the utmost seriousness in terms of long-accepted principles of American contitutionalism, particularly in connection with the concept of federalism. Some of the proposals sought no less than to restore to the unrestrained control of state legislatures the authority to continue along the old ways of malapportionment in the service of narrow self-interest.

Some of the statutory proposals present larger problems as well. If Congress should be allowed today, by mere legislative act, to deny or to control the exercise of jurisdiction by federal courts in apportionment cases, then tomorrow it may do the same in any other area to which there is transitory objection. The issue may be discrimination against racial or religious minorities, protection of first amendment freedoms, extension of fair procedures to state court criminal proceedings, or any other matter which, like all of these, has on occasion prompted congressional criticism. If this should become the rule, the system in which we have long taken rightful pride would no longer be so stable and secure as it once was.

To reinforce these objections with greater specificity it is necessary to analyze the three principal kinds of proposals advanced to limit the effect of the *Reapportionment Cases*.[130]

1. *Denial of Jurisdiction to Federal Courts.* H.R. 11926 was introduced during the summer of 1964 by Representative Tuck of Virginia and routed to the floor of the House by the Rules Committee in an unusual bypass of the Judiciary Committee. It proposed to withdraw jurisdiction from all federal courts to prevent their entertaining any proceeding "seeking to apportion or reapportion the legislature of any State of the Union or any branch thereof." This bill was probably the most drastic, the most dangerous, and the most clearly invalid of the various proposals. Although it was readily approved by the House on August 19, 1964, the Senate did not concur — indeed, the Senate never seriously considered enactment of the Tuck bill.

An unspoken premise of the bill as it passed the House was that Congress may selectively withdraw from the federal courts all jurisdiction over particular matters, even though Congress has never before attempted a complete denial of jurisdiction in a specified class of cases. Presumably, the claim that Congress could thus validly withdraw specified classes of cases from the jurisdiction of the federal courts was based on a claimed similarity to the post-Civil War

130. The 1964 attempts in Congress to limit the Reapportionment Cases are reviewed in my article, Court, Congress, and Reapportionment, 63 Mich. L. Rev. 255 (1964).

case of *Ex parte McCardle*.[131] That was a case in which the Court upheld an act of Congress that withdrew Supreme Court jurisdiction to review a class of habeas corpus cases, one of which had already been argued before the Court.

There are at least two difficulties in drawing a parallel between *McCardle* and the proposal in the Tuck bill. One is that *McCardle* involved only congressional withdrawal of jurisdiction from the Supreme Court as to appeals from lower federal courts. Congress had not attempted to withdraw the exercise of original habeas corpus jurisdiction either from the lower federal courts or from the Supreme Court. Even more important, Congress had not attempted the much more critical interference with the judicial branch and with the functioning of the federal system that is now suggested — a denial of appellate jurisdiction in review of *state* court decisions. To take away this power would render impotent what has always been considered the most important aspect of judicial review and to alter fundamentally the character of the federal system. As Justice Holmes long ago observed, "I do not think the United States would come to an end if we lost our power to declare an act of Congress void. I do think the Union would be imperiled if we could not make that declaration as to the laws of the several states."[132] The proposal should be regarded as unconstitutional even assuming that *McCardle* was correctly decided on its facts. But that, too, is doubtful. Justice Douglas has stated that "There is a serious question whether the *McCardle* case could command a majority view today."[133] In the same case Justice Harlan, while not so specifically disavowing *McCardle* on its narrow facts, observed that "The authority [of Congress] is not, of course, unlimited."[134]

Even apart from the constitutional objections to the Tuck bill, there are further undesirable features. By withdrawing all judicial power from the federal courts, the state courts would necessarily become courts of last resort on matters of apportionment. Under article VI of the Constitution, the supremacy clause, state courts would be bound to apply the same constitutional doctrine as would the federal courts if permitted to act; and of course there would be no lack of suitors willing to test the issue in the state courts if the fed-

131. 74 U.S. (7 Wall.) 596 (1869).
132. Law and the Court, in Collected Legal Papers 295–96 (1920).
133. Glidden Co. v. Zdanok, 370 U.S. 530, 605 n.11 (1962) (dissenting opinion).
134. Id. at 568.

eral courts should be closed to them. Apparently the proponents of that bill and others like it either did not see that possibility or, less worthily, assumed that the state courts would be willing to flout the already announced rule of constitutional law applicable to apportionment matters. It seems both unwarranted and gratuitously disrespectful to imply that if these matters should be left in the hands of the state courts, those courts would disregard the pronouncement already laid down by the Supreme Court of the United States as to the meaning of the constitutional command. It is hard to believe that state courts would reject clearly enunciated principles simply because they might be relieved of the likelihood of explicit reversal.

Even assuming, however, that the state courts would conscientiously apply the rules laid down by the Supreme Court, there remain areas of doubt which can only be clarified by more Supreme Court decisions rather than by fewer. The Constitution should be permitted to speak with a single voice rather than in the potential dissonance of fifty interpreters, however conscientious.

2. *Stays of the Exercise of Jurisdiction by Federal Courts.* Senator Dirksen of Illinois was the principal proponent in 1964 of various efforts to limit the exercise of jurisdiction by the federal judiciary in all apportionment matters, ostensibly without quite denying all jurisdiction. The purpose, as Senator Dirksen quite frankly stated, was to gain time to seek approval of a constitutional amendment limiting the reach of the Supreme Court decisions along lines discussed in point (3) below. The technique, however, was quite irregular. Despite the obvious importance of the matter, a bill to this effect was rushed through the Senate Judiciary Committee without hearings. Then, in apparent recognition that the bill would not be approved on its own merits, Senator Dirksen proposed it as a rider to the foreign aid bill, the passage of which was urgently sought by the Administration and presumably favored by a majority of the Senate. It is a testimonial to the integrity of the Senate that the device did not succeed out of hand. The initial proposal was opposed by the Department of Justice and, among others, by a group of law school professors and deans who said that it "unwisely and indeed dangerously threatens the integrity of our judicial process."[135]

That defective and probably unconstitutional bill was withdrawn

135. N.Y. Times, Aug. 10, 1964, p. 36, col. 1.

and another substituted in its place. The later proposal was, however, scarcely less objectionable. That version would have required any federal court having jurisdiction of a challenge to a state legislative apportionment, upon application of an authorized person, to stay the entry of any order "for such period as shall be in the public interest."[136]

There were additional constitutional objections to the proposal. Although dressed in procedural form, in reality it seemed little more than an attempt to prescribe the decision to be entered in an important class of cases. The vital area of apportionment, always in flux, is manifestly an area in which justice delayed may well be justice denied. Each denial of the exercise of the franchise on a valid basis is a loss never regained. That which is lost through even one session of a malapportioned legislature cannot be recaptured by a constitutionally correct legislature at a later date.

The proposal was uncomfortably close to an 1870 act of Congress invalidated by the Court in *United States v. Klein*,[137] distinguishing that case from the *McCardle* case decided three years earlier. In *Klein* the Court passed upon an act by which Congress purported to withdraw jurisdiction from the Court of Claims and the Supreme Court on appeal over cases seeking indemnification for property captured during the Civil War, so far as eligibility therefor might be predicated upon an amnesty awarded by the President, as both courts had previously held that it might. The Court refused to apply the statute to a case in which the Court of Claims had already held the claimant entitled to recover, calling it an unconstitutional attempt to invade the judicial province by prescribing a rule of decision in a pending case. In mildly sardonic vein the Court said: "We must think that Congress has inadvertently passed the limit which separates the legislative from the judicial power."[138] The proposed rider to the foreign aid bill might have been similarly unconstitutional because the Constitution gives to the courts the responsibility for deciding when an order staying

136. The "public interest" was in turn defined to include, "in the absence of highly unusual circumstances," a stay (1) to permit the completion of any state election regularly scheduled before January 1, 1966, "to be conducted in accordance with the laws of such State in effect immediately preceding any adjudication of unconstitutionality" and (2) a stay to allow the legislature or the people "a reasonable opportunity" to complete the reapportionment required by the Constitution.

137. 80 U.S. (13 Wall.) 128 (1872).

138. Id. at 147.

proceedings shall issue. Such an order is a necessary adjunct of the judicial power, without which the judicial power is something less than entire.

The weight of these objections to the proposed limitations or delays in the exercise of federal court jurisdiction in apportionment matters persuaded a small band of United States Senators to oppose the Dirksen amendment in what they said was an "education debate" rather than a filibuster. Although their numerical strength was small, cloture was defeated, and the original proposal was substantially revised. Finally, on September 24, 1964, the Senate approved by a vote of 44 to 38 a sense-of-Congress resolution much milder in tone than any predecessor. Suggested by majority leader Senator Mansfield, who wanted to get on with other Senate business, it said merely that courts "could properly" (1) "allow" the legislatures additional time for reapportionment, not exceeding six months, and (2) "permit" the next election of state legislatures to be conducted in accordance with the laws in effect on September 20, 1964. Moreover, the resolution specifically approved reapportionment by the federal courts in the event of legislative failure to act within any time specified by court order.

After differing versions of the foreign aid bill were passed by both houses, the apportionment rider was eliminated altogether by the Conference Committee convened to resolve the differences between the Senate and House versions of the foreign aid legislation.

Thus, the whole fight to deny, restrict, or even temper the jurisdiction of the federal courts on apportionment matters at last came to nothing. However substantial may have been the sentiment in Congress that the *Reapportionment Cases* went too far — clearly the view of many — the ultimately prevailing view was that such disagreement with the Court should be expressed in a constitutional amendment rather than by legislation, particularly legislation of doubtful constitutionality.

3. *Constitutional Amendment.* With the failure of the attempts to deny or limit the jurisdiction of federal courts in connection with apportionment matters, opponents of the equal-population principle of the *Reapportionment Cases* enlarged their efforts to secure constitutional amendment to reverse in whole or in part the force of those decisions.

Article V of the Constitution of the United States provides two ways for accomplishing that result. The only method by which the

Constitution has been amended in its first nearly two hundred years is through the proposal of an amendment by two-thirds vote of each house of the Congress plus ratification by three fourths of the states (normally by legislative action, although Congress may authorize conventions for the purpose). This is the amendment route now most seriously proposed; it will be discussed below at pages 211–13. The previously untried method, also now being proposed, provides that Congress shall call a *national* convention "on the application of the Legislatures of two thirds of the several States . . . ."[139] Current efforts to amend the Constitution via this route are discussed immediately below.

a. *Constitutional Convention on the Application of Thirty-Four States.*[140] On December 1, 1964, the Board of Managers of the Council of State Governments adopted a resolution urging amendment of the Constitution to permit states with bicameral legislatures to use factors other than population in apportioning one house — the apportionment plan in any state to be submitted to the electorate before becoming effective. On December 3, 1964, the Seventeenth Biennial General Assembly of the States called for a similar amendment, but added the text of a joint resolution submitted for action by the state legislatures, applying to Congress for a constitutional convention to propose such an amendment.[141]

Analysis of the unresolved problems that lie in the path of proposals to amend the Constitution in this fashion suggests that novelty may be the only thing to be said in its favor. Arthur Earl Bonfield has pointed out a number of difficulties, which may be summarized as follows:[142]

1. It is by no means certain that the resolution proposed for adoption by the state legislatures satisfies the constitutional require-

---

139. See generally Black, The Proposed Amendment of Article V: A Threatened Disaster, 72 Yale L.J. 957 (1963).

140. See the symposium on this subject in 38 State Government (spring 1965), including articles by Robert G. Dixon, Jr., Alfred de Grazia, and myself. I have drawn upon those materials in the discussion in the text of this subsection.

141. The essence of the resolution suggested for state legislative adoption was this:

"RESOLVED . . . that the Congress propose an amendment to the United States Constitution which would provide that (1) any state which has a bicameral legislature may utilize factors other than population in apportioning one house of its legislature if the plan of apportionment is specifically approved by vote of the electorate of the state and (2) any state may determine how governing bodies of its subordinate units shall be apportioned . . . ."

142. Bonfield, Proposing Constitutional Amendments by Convention: Some Problems, 39 Notre Dame Law. 659 (1964).

ment for an "application" to Congress. The Constitution specifies that Congress is to "call a Convention for proposing amendments." If, as has been assumed, the "Convention" contemplated by Article V was intended to be a fully deliberative body for the consideration of various alternatives, a resolution which offers no alternative choices may not satisfy the "application" requirement. Moreover, the amendment proposed for uniform state adoption specifies that, if approved by Congress, it shall be ratified by "the state legislatures." Since Article V gives to Congress the power to determine the method of ratification, the proposed "application" form seems defective in this respect, too, as an intrusion upon authority conferred exclusively on Congress.

2. It is by no means clear how nearly contemporaneous with each other the state legislative applications must be. Is it essential that each state have acted within that most recent period during which all state legislatures had an opportunity to consider the question during a full regular session? Would a five-year period be too long? Ten years? Have the federal courts authority to prescribe a limitation period?

3. May states withdraw applications once tendered? The question, which probably should be answered in the affirmative, may have special relevance in the context of apportionment. It is not inconceivable that an application for constitutional amendment approved by a malapportioned legislature might be withdrawn by a later-elected legislature constituted in accordance with the equal-population principle.

4. If requisite "applications" are submitted to Congress within a "reasonable" time, presumably Congress is obligated to call a convention; but there is probably no way to force a reluctant Congress to take the necessary action. Indeed, Congress alone has the authority to prescribe the terms on which a convention would be constituted, how it would operate, and what would be its authority. Congress would have to decide such important matters as whether the vote in convention should be by states (which seems undesirable and unlikely) or in accordance with population, as well as the majority necessary for approval.

Admittedly, the foregoing problems are not the central objections to the proposed amendment. After all, similar proposals have been introduced in Congress, where they are free of any problems arising under Article V. Objections to amendments proposed in the normal manner are discussed below.

b. *Proposals to Restore Nonpopulation Factors in State Apportionment Formulas.*[143] The proposals which have received most attention, of which Senator Dirksen's is representative,[144] include these features: (1) authorization for apportionment of one house of a bicameral legislature "upon the basis of factors other than population" and (2) apportionment of unicameral legislatures by giving "reasonable weight" to nonpopulation factors, so long as (3) the apportionment has been submitted to popular vote and approved by a majority of those voting on the issue.

Examination of the various suggested amendments indicates that their authors may have shown more enthusiasm for unthinking reversal of the Supreme Court than for consideration of the consequences. A charitable view of the problems presented by the various proposals leads to the conclusion that the difficult question of how to amend the Constitution without accomplishing undesirable — and unintended — results was not adequately studied.

The original Dirksen proposal left open the possibility (one would hope unintended) that judicial review would not be available to superintend state legislative compliance with provisions whose meaning was at best clouded with doubt. In the absence of any standards to govern the apportionment of the "non-people" house, the way would be open for apportionment and districting based on arbitrary criteria with racial or other discriminatory overtones. Moreover, by providing that "reasonable weight" could be given to nonpopulation factors in unicameral legislatures, an invitation might seem extended for adoption of unicameralism simply as a means of perpetuating minority rule.

The original Dirksen amendment, as modified several times during the course of Senate debate in the summer of 1965, would have

143. The principal proposals are carefully analyzed — and disapproved — in a Report of the Federal Legislation Committee of The Association of the Bar of the City of New York. Proposed Constitutional Amendments and Jurisdictional Limitations on Federal Courts With Respect to Apportionment of State Legislatures, 4 Reports of Committees of The Association of the Bar Concerned with Federal Legislation 1 (April 1965).

144. "The right and power to determine the composition of the legislature of a State and the apportionment of the membership thereof shall remain in the people of that State. Nothing in this Constitution shall prohibit the people from apportioning one house of a bicameral legislature upon the basis of factors other than population, or from giving reasonable weight to factors other than population in apportioning a unicameral legislature, if, in either case, such apportionment has been submitted to a vote of the people in accordance with law and with the provisions of this Constitution and has been approved by a majority of those voting on that issue." S.J. Res. 2, 89th Cong., 1st Sess. (1965).

permitted one house of a legislature to be apportioned on the basis of population, geography, or political subdivisions. The legislatures would have been allowed to give "each factor such weight as they deem appropriate." However, this general principle would have been conditioned in the following ways: (1) An apportionment plan based on factors other than population would have had to be approved by the voters of the state. (2) When a nonpopulation plan was submitted to the voters, it would have had to be accompanied by an alternative plan based on "substantial equality of population." (3) Two years after each decennial census the voters were to be given the right to decide whether to retain the plan previously approved or to adopt a new plan.

Unable to get the proposed amendment out of the Senate Judiciary Committee, Senator Dirksen brought it to the floor as a substitute for a pending resolution to designate August 31 to September 6 as National American Legion Baseball Week. Although on August 4, 1965, he secured the majority vote necessary for the substitution, the vote on his resolution did not gain the two-thirds vote required for a constitutional amendment.[145]

The House had taken no action, so the matter seemed ended. But the ever-resourceful Senator Dirksen modified his proposal further in an effort to meet the criticisms. Now he provided that any proposal for reapportionment of one house of a bicameral legislature must be approved by both houses, one of which must itself satisfy the equal-population standard. The stated objective was to insure "effective representation in the State's legislature of the various groups and interests making up the electorate."[146] This resolution was reported out of the Senate Judiciary Committee on September 8, 1965, for debate in 1966.[147]

As in the earlier version it was not clear to what extent judicial review would be available, if at all. In any event, the difficulties of judicial definition might well be insuperable if courts should be called upon to determine whether "effective representation" had been achieved in a state "of the various interest groups and interests making up the electorate."

Many state legislators are the beneficiaries of continuing malapportionment. It seems therefore unfortunate to submit to them for

---

145. N.Y. Times, Aug. 4, 1965, p. 1, col. 1.
146. S.J. Res. 103, 89th Cong., 1st Sess. (1965).
147. N.Y. Times, Sept. 9, 1965, p. 1, col. 3.

ratification proposed amendments which would allow them to vote in accordance with their own self-interest. Yet that is exactly what is contemplated in the Dirksen and other principal proposals. Even if Congress were to provide that an amendment be ratified by convention in three fourths of the states, a fairer result would not be assured if the malapportioned legislatures should be permitted to determine the composition of those conventions free of any congressional specifications.

Apart from the above-outlined objections to the proposed constitutional amendments, there are reasons more deep-seated — reasons that bear upon the nature of representative democracy and the concept of majority rule in the United States. The equal-population principle, or as it is popularly known, the concept of "one man, one vote," is now part of the Constitution of the United States. Whether the Supreme Court decision was "right" or not is a relatively abstract question not subject to proof in any conventional manner. When amendment to the Constitution is proposed, the issue is no longer one of determining whether the decision sought to be overturned was correct as a matter of constitutional interpretation. Rather the question is whether the constitutional requirement of substantial population equality among legislative representation districts in both houses of a bicameral legislature is so intolerable as to require resort to the drastic and seldom-exercised device of constitutional amendment.

The burden of persuasion accordingly rests heavily upon the proponents of this sweeping change. That obligation is reinforced in this instance by the specifically anti-democratic character of the proposal, which quite frankly suggests the desirability of subverting majority rule.

CHAPTER VIII

Apportionment and

the Future of Federalism

To make a government requires no great prudence. Settle
the seat of power; teach obedience: and the work is done.
To give freedom is still more easy. It is not necessary to
guide; it only requires to let go the rein. But to form a
free government; that is, to temper together those opposite elements of liberty and restraint in one consistent
work, requires much thought, deep reflection, a sagacious,
powerful, and combining mind.

EDMUND BURKE[1]

The equal protection of the laws clause of the fourteenth amendment is not self-defining; it does not even speak with a single voice.
Rather it provides a vessel into which can be poured interpretations
of the command for equality appropriate to the varied contexts in
which the concept of equality may apply. The *Reapportionment
Cases* filled the cup of equal protection to the brim of meaning with
the requirement of substantial equality among state legislative election districts, along with an approving reference to the phrase "one

1. 1 Burke, Works 474 ("Reflections on the Revolution in France") (1834).

person, one vote."[2] Meanwhile, the Court had emphasized in *Wesberry v. Sanders*[3] that near-equality is the basic constitutional standard for congressional districting, as derived from the requirement in article I, section 2 that Representatives be elected "by the People."

Wesberry and *Reynolds* left as nearly unambiguous as is possible in the nature of a complex subject the meaning to be ascribed to equality in relation to congressional districting and state legislative apportionment. State legislatures, in drawing congressional district lines, must satisfy equality of population among those districts "as nearly as is practicable." In the apportionment of state legislative representation, "the seats in both houses of a bicameral state legislature must be apportioned on a population basis." Even so, since "Mathematical exactness or precision is hardly a workable constitutional requirement,"[4] questions remain. These are not, to be sure, the hard questions of judgment which made Justice Frankfurter, in *Baker v. Carr*, seek to avoid the judicial task which he foresaw and which, in those dimensions, he believed impossible of accomplishment. The Justice, however, made an erroneous forecast. He assumed that on reaching the merits the Court would shrink "from asserting that in districting at least substantial equality is a constitutional requirement enforceable by courts." He believed that the Court would allow the legislatures to continue to rely substantially on "geography, economics, urban-rural conflict, and all the other non-legal factors which have throughout our history entered into political districting . . . ."[5]

The choices which Justice Frankfurter thought would confront federal courts under any meaning of equality he could envisage

2. 377 U.S. 533, 558 (1964). The aphorism "one man, one vote" strikingly makes the point that the ultimate issue is one of fairness. Literally and historically, however, "one man, one vote" should be regarded either as a protest against plural voting or as a demand for broadening the franchise. Brinton, "Equality," in 5 Encyclopedia of the Social Sciences 574, 577 (1935). Important as both those matters have been at various times in the struggle to protect against abuses of the democratic process, the question of fair apportionment really involves other considerations. In shifting from contentions that each person shall be entitled to vote, and that no person shall be allowed to vote more than once, to the issues of malapportionment, the phrase should be modified to read "one man, one vote, *one value*," emphasizing the last clause in recognition that here is the issue. See also Baker, One Vote, One Value, 47 National Municipal Review 16 (1958).

3. 376 U.S. 1 (1964).

4. Reynolds v. Sims, 377 U.S. 533, 577 (1964).

5. Baker v. Carr, 369 U.S. 186, 268–69 (1962) (Frankfurter, J., dissenting).

were indeed hard questions for judicial resolution. But when the Court concluded that election of Congressmen "by the People" does require equality "as nearly as is practicable" and that state election districts must also satisfy a population test, the underlying premise of the Frankfurter opinion was largely cut away. While problems of interpretation and judgment remain, they are not at all of the order anticipated by Frankfurter. Once equality is defined to mean equality, the hardest questions disappear, and the remaining issues are seen to be entirely manageable within the accustomed competence of the judicial experience.

The range of questions remaining for decision is not unlike the problems of enforcement which arose in the wake of the *School Segregation Cases*, originally decided in 1954. The cure for segregation in public schools was of course to be found in nonsegregation, and that, at least in concept, was a relatively unambiguous idea. Similarly, when the equality concept is applied to malapportionment of state legislatures or to inequality among congressional districts, the cure is rather clearly to be found in correct apportionment and districting; and nothing short of substantial equality will do. In determining where lies the line between substantial equality and something less, however, there will be areas of doubt and, properly enough, room for individual adjustment by states which claim local diversities. Chief Justice Warren recognized that fact in *Reynolds*: "What is marginally permissible in one State may be unsatisfactory in another, depending on the particular circumstances of the case."[6]

In one other respect the districting and apportionment cases draw from the analogy of the *School Segregation Cases* and the Supreme Court's experience in that area. The idea that public school segregation should be eliminated "with all deliberate speed," as the Court specified in 1955, seemed at first to be a judicial recognition of equitable considerations which might justify avoidance of precipitate disruption of a long-established social order. With the advantage of twenty-twenty hindsight it later came to seem that the opportunity for delay thus provided may have been a mistake. The apportionment issue, however, was clearly different, and the Court identified that difference at once. Malapportionment is like state-supported segregation in one respect: each is a continuing breach of

6. 377 U.S. at 578.

guaranteed equality, and persons affected by either have a present right to correction of that inequality. In the case of segregation other factors were at first thought sufficiently important to justify postponement of the inevitably wrenching dislocations believed likely to follow any drastic reordering of the system. The consequences of reapportionment in satisfaction of the equal-population principle are entirely different. After the change has once been made, no continuing disruption is involved. Even the initial change involves no dislocation except for the substitution at the next election of new legislators from formerly underrepresented areas in replacement of legislators from areas previously overrepresented. It is no more upsetting either to the system or to the individuals involved to make the change at one time than at any other. No doubt having these considerations in mind, the Supreme Court made it perfectly plain in *Wesberry* and in *Reynolds* that the changeover should be prompt except in "unusual" circumstances.

This final chapter will examine briefly the timetable of reapportionment and redistricting; review the factors which may permissibly be taken into account in any proposed deviations from equality; and evaluate the significance of these changes for federalism and for representative democracy in the United States.

THE TIMETABLE OF REAPPORTIONMENT

In *Reynolds* the Supreme Court made explicit its requirement of prompt action in correction of existing state legislative malapportionment:

> It is enough to say that, once a State's legislative apportionment scheme has been found to be unconstitutional, it would be the unusual case in which a court would be justified in not taking appropriate action to insure that no further elections are conducted under the invalid plan.[7]

The public reaction to the 1964 decision was generally favorable, as had been the case when *Baker* was decided two years earlier.[8] The editorial reaction of the press was on the whole not unsympathetic either to the idea of substantial equality among election districts or to the proposition that the principle should be made operative at

7. Id. at 585.
8. See Newland, Press Coverage of the United States Supreme Court, 17 W. Pol. Sci. Q. 15, 29–30 (March 1964).

once.[9] Individual voters also seemed receptive to the prospect for judicial enforcement of the principle of equality in the fashioning of election districts. In a Gallup poll released in August 1964 the Court's ruling was endorsed by a three to two ratio.[10] About the same time the mayors of a number of important cities expressed to the White House their support for the apportionment decisions and their resulting opposition to legislative efforts then being made in Congress to curb the jurisdiction of the federal courts in apportionment matters.[11]

Popular support for the Supreme Court decisions was scarcely surprising. Those decisions promised relief from the worsening underrepresentation suffered by the majority of American voters, those living in the more populous areas. This popular reaction was at first, however, largely nonvocal. For a time the anguished protests of legislators who saw in the decisions an immediate threat to their source of power were the most audible response. The complaints against the apportionment decisions, according to Senator Joseph S. Clark of Pennsylvania, came "only from the politicians in the State legislatures, their friends, their sycophants, their supporters."[12] Or, as Anthony Lewis of the *New York Times* analyzed the opposition, "This would seem to be strictly a politician's rebellion."[13]

Another important test for the Supreme Court rulings depended upon the way in which the state legislatures and the courts, both state and federal, would react to the decisions. There the Supreme Court must be judged to have passed the test with remarkable success. Not merely was judicial and legislative foot-dragging conspicuously not the typical reaction; significantly, a number of the courts and legislatures showed remarkable good faith in calling for com-

9. Senator Lee Metcalf of Montana read into the Congressional Record sixty-eight newspaper editorials (which he described as a random sample), more than two thirds of which opposed then-pending congressional efforts to curb the federal courts on apportionment matters. 110 Cong. Rec. 20716–33 (daily ed. Sept. 2, 1964).

10. As reported by Senator Paul Douglas of Illinois. 110 Cong. Rec. 19742 (daily ed. Aug. 19, 1964).

11. N.Y. Times, Aug. 19, 1964, p. 16, col. 1. In July 1965 delegates to the annual meeting of the National League of Cities expressed overwhelming opposition to the Dirksen proposal to amend the Constitution to reverse in part the *Reapportionment Cases*. N.Y. Times, July 29, 1965, p. 15, col. 4.

12. 110 Cong. Rec. 19383 (daily ed. Aug. 18, 1964).

13. N.Y. Times, Aug. 16, 1964, p. E3, col. 1.

pliance both more prompt and more complete than the Supreme Court would necessarily have required.

In appraising this threshold reaction to the Supreme Court decisions it is important to note exactly what the Court had to say on the important and related issues of (1) the proper relationship between legislature and court and (2) the timetable for corrective action, whether by legislature or court. The starting point is the Court's recognition that

> legislative apportionment is primarily a matter for legislative consideration and determination, [so] that judicial relief becomes appropriate only when a legislature fails to reapportion according to federal constitutional requirements in a timely fashion after having had an adequate opportunity to do so.[14]

Not only did the Court recognize the pre-eminent role of the legislature in the reapportionment process, but it indicated as well considerable flexibility on the question of timing. In the Alabama case the Court said:

> With respect to the timing of relief, a court can reasonably endeavor to avoid a disruption of the election process which might result from requiring precipitate changes that could make unreasonable or embarrassing demands on a State in adjusting to the requirements of the court's decree.[15]

In the New York case the Court similarly indicated a disposition toward tolerant acceptance of one more election from malapportioned districts, at least where the election machinery was already in operation.[16]

Nonetheless, initial reaction was more in the direction of prompt compliance than in efforts to search out special justifications for further delay. Even before the *Reynolds* decision the Wisconsin Supreme Court had directed a reapportionment based on popula-

14. Reynolds v. Sims, 377 U.S. 533, 586 (1964).

15. Id. at 585. In March 1964 the Court had affirmed a lower court decision requiring that the congressional district lines in Texas be redrawn to provide substantial equality, but had continued the stay of the effective date of that order previously granted by Justice Black. The majority observed that the district court, in deciding whether to continue the stay, should consider "the imminence of the forthcoming election [then eight months away] and 'the operation of the election machinery of Texas'...." Martin v. Bush, 376 U.S. 222, 223 (1964).

16. WMCA, Inc. v. Lomenzo, 377 U.S. 633, 655 (1964).

tion in both houses, effective for the 1964 elections.[17] Shortly after the equal-population principle was announced by the Supreme Court, complete or substantial compliance was accomplished by regularly established state procedures in several states.[18]

The striking fact that emerges from these early and prompt reactions to the ruling is that before November 1964 the election machinery was recast, in furtherance of the equal-population principle, in no fewer than six states: Colorado, Delaware, Michigan, Oklahoma, Washington, and Wisconsin.[19] In a substantially larger number of additional states the legislative and judicial machinery had been set in motion, probably irreversibly, for reapportionment before another election could be held after 1964. The speed and apparent good faith of the early compliance was nothing short of remarkable in a matter as complex and emotion-ridden as the fixing of state legislative election districts. These were auspicious omens for a relatively prompt acceptance and smooth accommodation to what many had honestly thought would be a severely disruptive process.

PERMISSIBLE DEVIATIONS
FROM EQUALITY

There has been much misunderstanding of the actual significance of the equal-population principle. There is of course room for some uncertainty; but interpretation has to some extent been made more difficult than necessary because of the unwillingness of some to read the decisions with a realistic flexibility. The Court has been charged with a mathematical rigidity which simply does not exist. Opponents of the apportionment decisions, particularly supporters of constitutional amendments designed to modify or overturn the decisions, have been especially inclined to read the Court's opinions

17. On February 28, 1964, the Wisconsin Supreme Court, holding that the then-existing apportionment formula was invalid, allowed the state until May 1 to enact a new plan. When the legislature failed to comply, the state court ordered a complete re-apportionment of both houses. State ex rel. Reynolds v. Zimmerman, 22 Wis. 2d 544, 126 N.W.2d 551 (1964), 23 Wis. 2d 606, 128 N.W.2d 16 (Wis. 1964).

18. For these and other developments through the early fall of 1965, see the appendix.

19. In a few states, notably Alabama and Virginia of the originally decided group of cases, no state legislative elections were scheduled for the fall of 1964.

to require rigid adherence to absolute equality. The decisions do not lend themselves to such a restrictive reading.

Because of the misunderstanding as to the proper meaning of the decisions in this respect, it becomes especially important to analyze the application of the equal-population principle to congressional districting and to state legislative apportionment. The most obvious conclusion is that greater equality among election districts is required in connection with congressional districting than in connection with state election districts. Suggested meanings for the equal-population principle are discussed below, first in the context of congressional districting and then in connection with state legislative apportionment.

Congressional Districting and the Equal-Population Principle. The Georgia congressional districting case, *Wesberry v. Sanders*, has been analyzed in some detail in chapter IV; here it is only necessary to remind of the Court's holding that

> the command of Art. I, § 2, that Representatives be chosen "by the People of the several States" means that as nearly as is practicable one man's vote in a congressional election is to be worth as much as another's.[20]

The critical words are those requiring equality "as nearly as is practicable." In 1964 the Court applied the test in only two cases. In the Georgia case itself a population disparity among congressional districts which ranged from 823,680 to 272,154 (with an average of 394,312) was held to be excessive; and in the Texas case, *Martin v. Bush*,[21] the Court affirmed the holding of a three-judge federal district court which had found excessive a range of 951,527 to 216,371 (with an average of 416,507).[22] The differentials between the largest and smallest districts in Texas and Georgia were respectively the largest and the third largest variations among the states. So the result in these two cases was not necessarily decisive as to the lesser deviations in other states, which ranged down to as little as 41,665 between the two congressional districts in Maine.[23] However, as

20. 376 U.S. 1, 8 (1964).

21. 376 U.S. 222 (1964).

22. Bush v. Martin, 224 F. Supp. 499 (S.D. Tex. 1963).

23. In an appendix to his dissenting opinion Justice Harlan summarized the relevant figures as revealed by the 1960 census. Wesberry v. Sanders, 376 U.S. 1, 49–50 (1964).

Justice Harlan pointed out in his dissent in *Wesberry*, of the 42 states with more than one single-member congressional district in 1962,[24] all but five had a population differential between the most populous and the least populous districts in excess of 100,000.[25] It is hard to disagree with his conclusion that, since the average population of the districts in each state is under 500,000,[26] a difference in excess of 100,000 persons is "not equality among districts 'as nearly as is practicable'...."[27] One can also agree, then, with Harlan's conclusion that redistricting may be necessary in 37 or more states.

Reynolds confirmed what had been intimated in *Wesberry* as to the more exacting standard of equality required in congressional districting than in state election districts.

> ... some distinctions may well be made between congressional and state legislative representation. Since, almost invariably, there is a significantly larger number of seats in state legislative bodies to be distributed within a State than congressional seats, it may be feasible to use political subdivision lines to a greater extent in establishing state legislative districts than in congressional districting while still affording adequate representation to all parts of the State.[28]

Study of the composition of congressional districts, as compared with state election districts, discloses further reasons in support of the Court's demand for greater population equality in congressional districts. No state has as many representatives in Congress as it has political subdivisions at the next level of authority below the state, such as the county. Thus, no state legislature has suggested that each county (or any other political subdivision) should be entitled to at least one congressional representative. It follows that all states are quite accustomed to the cumulation of several (or many) counties to make up a single congressional district. Moreover, the states have in general not been troubled by the notion of adding together parts of two or more counties to make a single congres-

24. Representatives were elected at large in Alabama (8), Alaska (1), Delaware (1), Hawaii (2), Nevada (1), New Mexico (2), Vermont (1), and Wyoming (1). In addition, Connecticut, Maryland, Michigan, Ohio, and Texas each elected one Representative at large in 1962.

25. The five states were Iowa, Maine, New Hampshire, North Dakota, and Rhode Island. Together, they elected 15 Representatives in 1962.

26. Except Connecticut, whose 1960 population of 2,535,234 was divided into five districts; the sixth Representative was elected at large in 1962.

27. 376 U.S. at 21.

28. Reynolds v. Sims, 377 U.S. 533, 578 (1964).

sional district. Of the 42 states which in 1962 elected two or more
Representatives from single-member congressional districts, there
was of course no state which did not cumulate several counties into
individual congressional districts. More significant is the fact that
in 1964 no fewer than 12 states had one or more districts made up of
parts of two or more counties.[29] Examples are interesting and pertinent:

1. In California the ninth congressional district (1960 population 383,498) consisted of part of Alameda County and part of Santa
Clara County, while the thirty-fifth district (473,511) consisted of
part of Orange County and part of San Diego County. When it came
to the division of Los Angeles County into 15 congressional districts, the legislature was unable to get closer to population equality
among districts *within* the county than that provided by a range
from 588,933 to 360,558. Reasons for that result are more readily
understood than justified.

2. The second congressional district in Kansas consisted of 14
whole counties plus part of Wyandotte County, the smallest county
in the state in terms of area. Interestingly enough, more than half of
the counties in the state (and more than half the area) were placed
in a single district, which was also the most populous of the five Kansas congressional districts. That districting, working to the apparent
disadvantage of the more rural portions of the state, might seem at
first a curious one to have been adopted in an essentially rural state,
whose legislature was then dominated by rural interests. The explanation is not difficult. Wyandotte County (Kansas City, Kansas)
ordinarily votes Democratic, so its division between two ordinarily
Republican districts was logical to a Republican legislature even if
another Representative would have to travel more than half the
state to meet his underrepresented constituents.

3. Ten of the twelve Massachusetts congressional districts included parts of two or more counties. Despite the manifest willingness to disregard county lines, the population disparity was 102,626.
Speculation becomes inevitable that the legislature may have been
moved by partisan considerations.

4. The two congressional districts in New Hampshire roughly
bisect the state along a north-south axis; in the process the counties

---

29. California, Connecticut, Florida, Kansas, Maryland, Massachusetts, Minnesota,
New Hampshire, New Jersey, New York, Ohio, and Washington.

of Hillsborough and Merrimack were both divided between the two districts. As a result of this division, the population differential between the two districts was in 1962 next to the smallest in the nation, 56,715. Each district was within 10 per cent of the mean ratio for the two districts.

5. In New York the twenty-fifth, thirty-sixth, thirty-seventh, and fortieth congressional districts all consist of from one to four complete counties plus part of an adjacent county. Although no congressional district in New York in 1964 varied by more than 15 per cent from the mean ratio for the 41 congressional districts, as will be noted later, even these differentials are likely to be significant. While not so marked as the population differentials among congressional districts in many other states, the political use of the gerrymander was a significant factor in the most recent New York districting, both as to numbers of Republicans and Democrats in the various districts and in respect to district shape.

As revealed in the above representative examples, the substantial population differentials among congressional districts in the various states are almost never produced by state legislative attempts to preserve the integrity of local political subdivisions or the homogeneity of interests of persons grouped together in particular districts. To the extent that county or other political subdivision lines have been retained as the basis for the drawing of congressional district lines, it is apparent that the reason has been to serve political convenience, and that the lines have been drawn in state after state — adhering to county lines or disregarding county lines — with no other purpose than partisan advantage.[30]

Despite the fact that these political considerations have in the past played a powerful and distorting role in congressional districting, the state legislatures have shown an almost surprising willingness to conform to the demand for equality "as nearly as is practicable." One reason may be that the redrawing of congressional district lines in satisfaction of the equality requirement does not immediately affect the seat of any legislator who is called upon to

---

30. This is not to say that there has been no discrimination against populous areas in the drawing of congressional district lines, but only that partisan considerations have also been important. Urban areas which were notably underrepresented in Congress in 1962 included the following: Phoenix, Arizona (first district: 663,510); Denver, Colorado (first district: 653,954); Atlanta, Georgia (fifth district: 823,680); Indianapolis, Indiana (eleventh district: 697,567); Dallas, Texas (fifth district: 951,527).

act; so it becomes correspondingly less painful for legislators to comply with their constitutional duty.

Three-judge federal courts in Alabama,[31] Kansas,[32] Maryland,[33] and Texas[34] held invalid the existing congressional districting formula, but allowed the 1964 elections to proceed under the disapproved plans. In a number of other states the redistricting was accomplished in time for the 1964 elections. In Georgia, whose districting statutes were invalidated in *Wesberry*, new legislation was approved within less than three weeks of that decision.[35] In terms of population, the resulting districts were much more nearly equal than under the previous legislation, although a population differential of more than 125,000 remained between the most populous and the least populous districts; and the variation from the mean ratio was 20 per cent below for the ninth district and 9 per cent above for the sixth district. Interestingly, the aggregate populations of the two districts which include the most populous area of the state, the Atlanta metropolitan area (whence came the *Wesberry*

31. Following the 1960 census Alabama's congressional delegation was reduced from nine to eight. The legislature, however, did not draw new district lines, but provided for a double primary system whereby candidates would be nominated from each of the old districts in a preliminary primary, and in the runoff one candidate would be eliminated. After the decision in *Wesberry* this system was held invalid, but the court allowed delay until after the 1964 elections. Moore v. Moore, 229 F. Supp. 435 (S.D. Ala. 1964). Perhaps not surprisingly, the candidate eliminated in the second primary in 1962 was Carl Elliott, who had served eight consecutive terms and was considered the most liberal of the Alabama Representatives. The state administration thus engineered defeat on a statewide basis of a man who was the clear choice of his own region of the state. See 53 National Civic Review 379 (1964).

32. In Meeks v. Anderson, 229 F. Supp. 271 (D. Kans. 1964), the court held excessive differentials of 38 per cent among the five congressional districts in the state, but permitted the 1964 elections to be held on the old basis until the reapportioned state legislature should have an opportunity to correct the inequities.

33. The Maryland legislature, itself still malapportioned in terms of the Supreme Court decision affecting that state (Maryland Committee for Fair Representation v. Tawes, 377 U.S. 656 (1964)), failed to agree upon new congressional district lines in 1964, and the three-judge court allowed the 1964 election to be conducted under the system held invalid. Maryland Citizen's Committee for Fair Congressional Redistricting v. Tawes, 226 F. Supp. 80, 228 F. Supp. 956 (D. Md. 1964). Thereafter, in seeking agreement on a plan for 1966 the legislature continued its struggle amid bitter charges of gerrymander. See N.Y. Times, Sept. 13, 1964, p. 73, col. 1.

34. For a time it appeared that all 23 Texas Representatives might have to run at large in 1964, as required in the order of a three-judge federal court. Bush v. Martin, 224 F. Supp. 499 (S.D. Tex. 1963). Although the Supreme Court affirmed the holding of invalidity of the existing districting, the lower court was allowed to "consider the imminence of the forthcoming election and 'the operation of the election machinery of Texas' . . . ." Martin v. Bush, 376 U.S. 222, 223 (1964). The lower court took the hint and permitted the 1964 elections to proceed without alteration.

35. Ga. Laws 1964, No. 923, p. 478.

challenge), were each adjusted to within less than 4 per cent of the mean ratio.[36]

Other states in which new plans became effective in 1964 made a closer approach to equality. In Connecticut, for example, the new act[37] divided the state into six districts which ranged in population from 404,201 to 482,135.[38] The makeup of the districts was quite varied. The first and fourth consisted of selected towns in a single county; the second consisted of three whole counties; the third and fifth included towns from two different counties; and the sixth included one whole county and towns from three different counties.

When the existing Colorado plan was challenged by a suit in federal court, the legislature was called into special session and adopted a new plan in which the variation from the most populous to the least populous district was about 87,000.[39]

The developments in Michigan were especially significant. On March 26, 1964, a three-judge federal district court invalidated the current (1963) congressional districting statute for the state.[40] The act struck down had established districts which, with two exceptions, were within approximately 15 per cent of the population norm; and the average deviation was less than 10 per cent. However, the most populous district (in the Detroit area) contained approximately 200,000 more persons than the least populous district (in the Northern Peninsula); the average district size for Wayne County (Detroit area) was 444,000, while other districts averaged 397,000; and even within Detroit the districts varied by more than 100,000. The court thought these deviations excessive in the absence of a rational explanation by the state. On the question of timing the court held, with one judge dissenting, that the redistricting should be accomplished in time for the 1964 elections:

> We do not read the *per curiam* opinion in Martin v. Bush, supra, as a nationwide directive to the District Courts to leave things be . . . . In our case . . . there is ample time to act, should the Legislature be so minded, as we believe they should be and are.[41]

36. Id. at 482 (Conference Report).
37. Conn. Gen. Stat. Ann., tit. 9, § 9 (1964).
38. N.Y. Times, April 24, 1964, p. 1, col. 7.
39. Colo. Sess. Laws 1964, 1st Extra. Sess., c. 1.
40. Calkins v. Hare 228 F. Supp. 824 (E.D. Mich. 1964).
41. Id. at 830.

The Michigan legislature responded promptly with legislation which was made applicable to the 1964 elections. To achieve near-equality of population among the new election districts, the new act cut across county lines in 12 of the 19 congressional districts.[42]

In Wisconsin, congressional district lines were redrawn in 1963.[43] Even without judicial prodding, the legislature managed to construct ten districts among which the maximum population variation was less than 27,000, and no district deviated more than 3.4 per cent from the population norm.[44]

What conclusions, then, are to be drawn after the early response to the *Wesberry* requirement of equality in congressional districting? At the least, these points deserve mention:

1. Equality "as nearly as is practicable" in the context of congressional districting must be read to require near-exactness of population equality among election districts, certainly more so than among state legislative election districts. The reasons are apparent: Representatives chosen from congressional districts play no part in the state legislative process. They do not in any way "represent" political subdivisions of the state. They are chosen "by the People," and their only constituency is "the People" of the district from which they are chosen. In this context population is peculiarly the factor of central, almost exclusive importance.

2. Although the Supreme Court initially ruled only in cases of the most severe imbalance in Georgia and Texas, the lower courts soon began to interpret those opinions to require the invalidation of plans which showed a much narrower population differential. As of the 1964 elections, there were only nine states with a population spread of less than 100,000 from the most populous to the least populous congressional district.[45] It may well be that all those with a larger spread are vulnerable to attack. This would include the 1964 redistricting in Georgia with a spread of 125,837; and of course there is no assurance that the 1964 Colorado act will be sufficient with its deviation of 87,988, or that of Connecticut with a spread of 77,934. Once it is established that county and township

42. Mich. Stat. Ann. § 4.24(1) (1964).

43. Wis. Laws 1963, Ch. 63.

44. See Steiger, Form or Substance?, 53 National Civic Review 182 (1964), in which the chairman of the Wisconsin Assembly Elections Committee effectively explained the legislative modus operandi in working out the details of the redistricting.

45. Colorado (87,988), Connecticut (77,934), Iowa (89,250), Maine (41,665), Michigan (13,911), New Hampshire (56,715), North Dakota (34,134), Rhode Island (59,924), and Wisconsin (26,847). See 53 National Civic Review 322 (1964).

lines are not to be rigidly adhered to, justification for deviations from nearly exact equality become increasingly difficult.

3. Rational justification for substantial population differentials is difficult to construct in the case of congressional districts. County lines and other political subdivision lines have no intrinsic significance for congressional elections. It has always been accepted that congressional districts must sometimes cumulate counties or towns and must sometimes cut across county and township lines. Moreover, there are no political party organizations formed along congressional district lines, except those created for the ad hoc purpose of electing individual Representatives. In short, political subdivision lines have no significance in congressional districting except as a matter of legislative convenience and to limit gerrymandering, a matter noted below.

Congressional Districting and the Gerrymander. The conclusions already summarized suggest a final observation. Equality by itself does not assure ultimate fairness in the electoral process, whether in connection with congressional districting or state legislative election districts. So long as representation is primarily based on single-member election districts, a legislature bent upon distortion of democratic institutions can satisfy the equal-population principle while at the same time indulging in severe gerrymandering.

The Supreme Court has not answered the question as to whether the gerrymandered congressional district or state legislative election district is constitutionally vulnerable (see pages 255–58). Two propositions are clear, however. First, gerrymandering for political advantage is disruptive of the democratic process and should be curtailed by whatever orderly procedures are available. Second, Congress *can* act rather effectively to prevent gerrymandering of congressional districts pursuant to its unchallenged powers under article I, section 4 to "make or alter" the regulations governing the "Manner of holding Elections for Senators and Representatives ...."

It is familiar history that Congress has in the past exercised exactly that power on a number of occasions, beginning as early as 1842. Before that time many of the states had elected all of their Representatives on a statewide, or at-large, basis.[46] Nothing in the Constitution specifically forbade the at-large election of Represent-

46. Hacker, *Congressional Districting* 48 (rev. ed. 1964).

atives, and at least there was no way of weighting one vote more heavily than another when each voter was permitted to vote for as many candidates as there were congressional seats to be contended for. However, there were also substantial disadvantages. In states where one party could command a disciplined majority of voters on a statewide basis, that party could sweep the state's entire congressional delegation, leaving a possibly substantial minority of the electorate unrepresented by any candidate of their choosing. The Apportionment Act of 1842 was enacted by Congress to limit this winner-take-all method of choosing Representatives. It provided that Representatives must "be elected by districts composed of contiguous territory equal in number to the number of Representatives to which said state may be entitled, no one district electing more than one representative."[47] Although it was thus required that each state be divided into distinct geographic units, each with its own Representative, there was no statutory requirement of equality.

The act of 1842, however, was not continued in subsequent apportionment acts of Congress. At-large elections have been held from time to time since then, but ordinarily in response to particular problems of the moment rather than as a reflection of any consciously adopted long-range policy.[48]

In 1872 Congress directed that all Representatives "be elected by districts composed of contiguous territory, and containing as nearly as practicable an equal number of inhabitants, . . . no one district electing more than one Representative."[49] In 1901 Congress additionally required that each district should consist of "compact territory."[50] These provisions were carried forward through 1911; but there was no reapportionment following the

47. 5 Stat. 491 (1842).

48. In 1964 twenty Representatives were elected at large from eleven states. Alaska, Delaware, Nevada, Vermont, and Wyoming are entitled to only one Representative, who is therefore elected at large. Alabama elected eight at large, and Hawaii and New Mexico each elected two at large. In addition, Maryland, Ohio, and Texas each elected one of their Representatives at large.

When the Alabama legislature complies with the order to redistrict prior to the 1966 elections, presumably the state will be divided into eight districts. See Moore v. Moore, 229 F. Supp. 435 (S.D. Ala. 1964). As to whether single-member districts are constitutionally required, see pages 262–64, infra.

49. 17 Stat. 28 (1872).

50. 31 Stat. 733 (1901).

1920 census; and the provision for equality among districts was dropped in 1929[51] and not revived thereafter.

When the Supreme Court later considered the significance of that legislative change, it stated:

> It was manifestly the intention of the Congress not to re-enact the provision as to compactness, contiguity, and equality in population with respect to the districts to be created pursuant to the reapportionment under the Act of 1929.[52]

Efforts were made between 1929 and the *Wesberry* decision in 1964 to reinstate as requirements the trinity of compactness, contiguity, and equality, but without success.[53] The significance of that legislative impasse has now been altered by the fact that the Supreme Court is no longer inhibited from deciding these questions by the political question doctrine. When the "want of equity" restraint upon judicial decision was lifted by the decisions in *Baker v. Carr* and *Wesberry v. Sanders*, the Court for the first time declared its judgment as to the meaning of the applicable constitutional language.

Now that the Constitution has been read to require equality of population "as nearly as is practicable," the question arises as to what there remains for Congress to do, if anything. The answer is that the need for congressional action continues. Surely it would be appropriate for Congress to reinstate the requirement that districts be compact and contiguous, on which the Court has expressed no constitutional judgment, but which is clearly within the congressional power of regulation.[54]

To the extent that earlier regulation of compactness and contiguity had proved largely ineffectual, it was probably because of judicial unwillingness at that time to deal with a subject matter over which Congress had its own direct means of enforcement. That is, Congress could at any time have refused to seat any Representative chosen in violation of congressional mandate.[55] When

51. 46 Stat. 21 (1929).

52. Wood v. Broom, 287 U.S. 1, 7 (1932).

53. For a careful review of the entire history, see Celler, Congressional Apportionment — Past, Present, and Future, 17 Law & Contemp. Prob. 268 (1952).

54. H.R. 5505, 89th Cong., 1st Sess., discussed infra at pages 232–33, would require compactness and contiguity in congressional districting.

55. "Each House shall be the Judge of the Elections, Returns and Qualifications of its own Members ...." U.S. Const. art. I, § 5. See also note 58, infra.

Congress chose not to act where it had ample authority and primary responsibility, the Court was reluctant to fill that particular vacuum of authority. There is, however, no reason why Congress could not now require compactness and contiguity and give to the federal courts the authority to pass upon the validity of state congressional districting plans in these respects as well as in connection with the equality requirement, which is now clearly within the judicial domain.

Congress and the Definition of Equality. There remains the question whether Congress might validly, or should desirably, exercise its regulatory powers under article I, section 4 to amplify the meaning of equality as defined by the Court. It must be taken as a starting point that Congress cannot now redefine the concept of election of Representatives "by the People" to mean something other than did the Court when it called for equality "as nearly as is practicable." But that does not necessarily mean that Congress cannot now amplify the Court-announced constitutional standard with some specifics to serve as guidelines for the states. Any act of Congress which sought to provide such definitional guidance would itself be subject to testing in the Supreme Court; but it is not unlikely that the Court would welcome congressional participation in this task.

Congressional action of this character appears to be a real possibility. Representative Emanuel Celler, the chairman of the House Judiciary Committee, has advocated such legislation since the early 1950's. With the aid of the *Wesberry* decision he secured passage in the House of Representatives in March 1965 of H.R. 5505, which represents the distillation of his thinking over the years.[56] It contains the following elements essential to a congressional districting statute:

1. Each state must establish as many districts as the state is authorized Representatives in Congress, "no district to elect more than one Representative."

2. Each district shall be "composed of contiguous territory."

3. Each district shall be "in as compact form as practicable."

4. The maximum permissible variation in population from the population norm is prescribed in percentage terms. H.R. 5505

56. 111 Cong. Rec. 4960 (daily ed. March 16, 1965).

fixed the permissible deviation at 15 per cent. However, as noted by the Committee on Federal Legislation of The Association of the Bar of the City of New York, "in view of the pronouncements in *Wesberry*, it would seem highly doubtful that a variation of as much as 15% from the average — which could mean a 30% variation between districts from the average — is permissible."[57]

Earlier versions of the congressional districting bill had provided for enforcement through judicial review in the federal courts "at the suit of any citizen" of a district alleged not to satisfy the standards. But H.R. 5505 contained no specific provision for judicial review. Other enforcement procedures have been suggested, including direct congressional enforcement by refusing to seat Representatives from a state which violates the statute;[58] giving Congress — or some other body — the power to redistrict when states fail to comply with the act;[59] and requiring election at large where the congressional criteria are not satisfied. None of these enforcement suggestions seems as likely to produce a fair result, with maximum freedom from political considerations, as the proposal for judicial review in the federal courts.[60]

State Legislative Apportionment and the Equal-Population Principle. In order to determine the permissible deviations from equality among state legislative election districts within a state, it is necessary to examine not only the affirmative standard laid down

57. 3 Reports of Committees of The Association of the Bar Concerned with Federal Legislation 65, 68 (1964).

58. The question of congressional enforcement of districting requirements has twice come before the House of Representatives in connection with earlier legislation. In Davison v. Gilbert (1901), Rowell, Digest of Contested Election Cases in the House of Representatives, 1789–1901, at 603–06 (1901), the House of Representatives Committee on Elections held it to be "not politic" to deny a seat to a candidate on the ground that the district from which he was elected was illegally constituted. In Persona v. Sanders (1910), Rowell, id., 1901–17, at 43–49 (Moore's ed. 1917), the House took no action, despite a committee recommendation that a Virginia districting act be held void as violating the reapportionment law.

59. See Report of American Political Science Association, Committee on Reapportionment, reprinted in Hearings Before Subcommittee No. 2 of the House Committee on the Judiciary, 86th Cong., 1st Sess. 26–29 (1959).

60. It might be desirable, as suggested by the Federal Legislation Committee of the Association of the Bar of the City of New York (supra note 57, at 69), that districting legislation should make explicit provision for judicial review, including a determination whether or not the jurisdiction to review conferred on the federal district courts is intended to be exclusive of review by state courts. See General Investment Co. v. Lake Shore & Michigan State Railway, 260 U.S. 261, 286–88 (1922); Hart & Wechsler, The Federal Courts and the Federal System 373–74 (1953).

by the Supreme Court but also the negative warnings as to what factors would not be acceptable in justification of departures from equality. The affirmative proposition was perfectly straightforward:

> We hold that, as a basic constitutional standard, the Equal Protection Clause requires that the seats in both houses of a bicameral state legislature must be apportioned on a population basis. Simply stated, an individual's right to vote for state legislators is unconstitutionally impaired when its weight is in a substantial fashion diluted when compared with votes of citizens living in other parts of the State.[61]

Although this emphasis on equality should not be read as a requirement of mathematical exactness (see pages 128–32), it is true that factors extraneous to the representative function in the democratic process may not be weighted into the system as though they had some intrinsic significance. It was with this in mind that the Court warned that

> neither history alone, nor economic or other sorts of group interests are permissible factors in attempting to justify disparities from population-based representation. . . . Again, people, not land or trees or pastures, vote. Modern developments and improvements in transportation and communications make rather hollow, in the mid-1960's, most claims that deviations from population-based representation can validly be based solely on geographic considerations. Arguments for allowing such deviations in order to insure effective representation for sparsely settled areas and to prevent legislative districts from becoming so large that the availability of access of citizens to their representatives is impaired are today, for the most part, unconvincing.[62]

On the other hand, the Court did offer suggestions as to factors which the states might legitimately take into account, so long as the resulting plan did not submerge the "overriding objective . . . of substantial equality of population among the various districts . . . ."[63]

> A State may legitimately desire to maintain the integrity of various political subdivisions, insofar as possible, and provide for compact districts of contiguous territory in designing a legislative apportionment scheme. Valid considerations may underlie such aims. Indiscriminate districting, without any regard for political subdivision or natural or historical

61. Reynolds v. Sims, 377 U.S. 533, 568 (1964).
62. Id. at 579–80.
63. Id. at 579.

boundary lines, may be little more than an open invitation to partisan gerrymandering. Single-member districts may be the rule in one State while another State might desire to achieve some flexibility by creating multimember or floterial districts.[64]

The principal area for legislative choice left to the states, some utilization of political subdivision lines, is also the most significant distorting factor in existing apportionment formulas. Obviously, then, the Court was not committing to the states anything like the essentially uncontrolled discretion in this matter which had previously been theirs. In assessing the significance of the new and more limited role which political subdivisions could play, some propositions stood out clearly.

1. All formulas must be discarded which provide that no more than one representative shall be chosen from any political subdivision for either house of the legislature. This would apply alike to those states which specify a single senator from each county; those which provide for a single representative from each town; and those which provide that no county may have more than one senator.

2. Existing formulas which provide for at least one representative from each county (or town) will almost certainly all require revision. It is theoretically possible for a state with a small number of political subdivisions, and a narrow population spread among them, to achieve substantial equality of population among its election districts by assuring each county one representative and providing for enlarged representation of the other counties (or towns) in proportion to population. Very few states, however, have a small enough number of counties (or towns) and a narrow enough population range to use such a formula except at the price of an unmanageably large legislature.[65]

3. From the foregoing propositions it follows that, in order to satisfy the equal-population principle, it will frequently be neces-

64. Id. at 578–79. The somewhat separate issues of gerrymandering and multi-member districts are discussed at pages 254–58 and 262–64 respectively.

65. Arizona, for example, has only 14 counties; but in 1960 Maricopa County (Phoenix) had 60 times the population of Santa Cruz County. A legislative body well in excess of 100 would have been required to meet the population standard in 1960, without taking into account the continuing rapid growth of Phoenix. Kansas, on the same basis, would require a legislative body with more than 1,000 members to satisfy the population standard using its pre-1965 formula of at least one representative from each of its 105 counties.

sary to cumulate the less populous counties or towns to make a single district, while the more populous units will frequently be entitled to representation by two or more legislators. Moreover, in most states it will often be impossible to achieve substantial equality without cutting across political subdivision lines — much in the manner now commonly utilized in congressional districting, as already discussed.

The Meaning of "Substantial" Equality. The critical question now emerges with sharp clarity. What is "substantial" equality? Is it to be determined in terms of percentage deviation from a population norm? That standard has been suggested as one possible test to measure the more demanding standard of equality required in congressional districting. In state legislative apportionment, however, any purely mechanical test may lack the flexibility which is appropriate for realistic appraisal of various state formulas. Nevertheless, it should be possible to use a mathematical scale in determining whether a prima facie showing of malapportionment can be made requiring state justification. Thus, if all the election districts for a legislative body fall within a narrow percentage range of the norm (10 or 15 per cent should be close enough), the apportionment and districting could be judged sufficient on the equality point, and the state might not be required to justify those deviations.[66]

On the other hand, the failure of a state's apportionment system to satisfy the percentage deviation test need not mean that substantial equality has not been achieved. In the case of deviation from the norm beyond an established percentage, a state might then be allowed to show that in the great majority of the districts the deviation was small, while in one or a few a larger deviation was justified because of peculiarities of geography or of population dispersal. In other words, the element of district homogeneity need not be altogether submerged in the interest of seeking near-equality of population. Examples may help to illustrate the issue and possible solutions.

1. Where one portion of a state is specifically cut off from other portions of the state by water (ocean, bay, lake, or river), by moun-

66. In such a case it would take about 50 per cent of the votes to elect a majority of the legislative body in question. Accordingly, the state would show up well on the Dauer-Kelsay index computed on that basis.

tains, or by other natural barriers, the state may be justified in preserving the physical integrity of such an isolated unit in one house of the legislature. The case that comes most readily to mind involves the popular resort islands lying off the Massachusetts shore at the outermost end of Long Island Sound. Dukes County (including Martha's Vineyard Island) had a 1960 population of about 6,000, and Nantucket County (comprising Nantucket Island) in 1960 had a population of about 4,000. It is instructive to note how they have been treated by the Massachusetts legislature for various election district purposes. For congressional district purposes both counties are joined with Plymouth and Barnstable Counties plus enumerated towns in Bristol and Norfolk Counties to form the twelfth district. In the state senate the two counties share a senator with Barnstable County and enumerated towns in Bristol and Plymouth Counties. In the state house of representatives, however, each county has its own representative, resulting in substantial overrepresentation. *Perhaps* this is justified, but one wonders if the interests of those two counties could not be represented by a single representative rather than two separate representatives.[67]

2. Until 1964 the Upper Peninsula of Michigan, separated by water from the principal part of the state, had long been specially favored in terms of congressional representation and in terms of representation in the state legislature. The combined population of the eleventh and twelfth congressional districts (the Upper Peninsula plus nine Lower Peninsula Counties) was almost exactly equal in 1960 to the median district size for all 19 of the congressional districts in Michigan. In the state legislature the favoritism in behalf of the Upper Peninsula counties was even more marked, both before and after the effective date of the 1963 state constitution. Remarkably enough, the reapportionment which became effective in 1964 eliminated the disparities almost completely. The population of the 38 senatorial districts varied only from 205,118 to 207,094, while in the house the range was from 69,118 to 72,200. In both cases county lines were followed to the extent possible (in the senate apportionment only one Upper Peninsula county was divided); but of course it was sometimes necessary to cross county lines in order to avoid substantial continuing population differen-

67. Or it might be argued that the 10,000 population of these two counties should be joined with the representatives sent to the state legislature from Cape Cod (Barnstable County), whose interests might not be very different.

tials among the districts. Where it was thought essential to divide counties, the lines were drawn almost entirely along city and township lines, thus avoiding the division of an essentially unitary community between two or more districts. Perhaps the most unusual is senate district number 39, which consists of Flint City plus a portion of adjoining Genesee Township, the whole carved right out of the center of Genesee County. The logic is apparent; the metropolitan center of the county may well have interests in part distinct from the surrounding countryside. Michigan has demonstrated that equality is possible where it had long been thought least likely to be attained.

3. Colorado has frequently been cited as an example of a state in which the irregularities of terrain make unreasonable any attempt at substantial equality among the election districts. And it may be that equality to the extent achieved in Michigan, as just described, would be neither practical nor desirable. That is very different, however, from accepting the wide disparities in representation which existed in Colorado when the Supreme Court, in *Lucas v. Colorado General Assembly*,[68] ruled invalid the then-existing state apportionment plan.

The reconstituted senatorial and representative districts in the state legislature now comport much more nearly with the population distribution in the state. But the still not inconsiderable variations in both houses may require more justification than has yet been forthcoming.[69]

These illustrations indicate the remaining range of problems. They also provide an encouraging demonstration that the equal-population principle can be implemented without undue strain on the integrity of the electoral process or on the realities of the political process. On the surface it would have seemed that no state had a more complex problem than Michigan in seeking to attain equality among election districts. But there it was accomplished with surprising ease and with apparently minimal complaint — except of course from legislators who anticipated personal displacement. Similarly, reapportionments approaching equality were worked out in other states in 1964, notably Oklahoma and Wiscon-

68. 377 U.S. 713 (1964). The lack of rationality of that plan, even in terms of the asserted deference to terrain, has been discussed supra at pages 182–85.

69. The 1964 act was held valid for the 1964 elections. Lucas v. Colorado General Assembly, 232 F. Supp. 797 (D. Colo. 1964).

sin, where the problems might have been expected to be severe. In Oklahoma the 48 senate districts under the 1964-approved reapportionment varied from 42,347 to 61,866 (without crossing any county lines), and the 99 house districts varied from 21,040 to 26,462 (also without disturbing county lines).[70] In Wisconsin considerable equality was achieved, again without crossing county lines in the formation of any district in either the house or senate. As the Wisconsin Supreme Court noted, in commenting on the extent of equality among the districts:

> For no assembly district does the 1960 population exceed by more than one-third the state-wide average population of assembly districts: 39,528. . . .
> For no senate district does the 1960 population exceed by more than one-sixth the state-wide average population of senate districts: 119,780.[71]

In both Oklahoma and Wisconsin greater equality could of course have been attained if it had not been thought advisable to follow county lines. In any event, compactness of districts was well satisfied, better in both cases than in Michigan with its almost mathematical exactness. And it may be that even these deviations are not too great if the state can make an adequate case in support of the significance of the counties as integral and significant units in the state governmental process, a matter to which we now turn.

Local Political Subdivisions and the Governmental Process. It is commonly believed that the county (or, in New England, the town) has essentially the same relation to the state as does the state to the nation. As a consequence, it is popularly believed that counties and towns should be accorded a position in the state governmental structure comparable to that of the states in a federal system. But this is a misconception built upon mistake of fact. These erroneous conclusions are not supported in terms of theory, practice, or any commonsense view of the realities.

The theory of the federal system involves a division of power between two sovereign entities, each of which must treat the other with the respect appropriate to the knowledge held by each partner of its own limited authority. In the federal partnership the unique ingredient of sovereignty is granted solely to the nation and the states. The state systems are different in two significant ways.

70. See Reynolds v. State Election Board, 233 F. Supp. 323 (W.D. Okla. 1964).
71. State ex rel. Reynolds v. Zimmerman, 128 N.W.2d 16, 17 (Wis. 1964).

In the first place, no subordinate unit of government has any authority, sovereign or otherwise, which is not committed to it by the state and subject to withdrawal by the same command. Second, and perhaps more important, is the fact that there is not one, but a multitude of local units of government, each with its own authority, ordinarily overlapping other units of local government in terms of area, and often in terms of authority. In addition to the county, there is in every state a confusing array of other units of local government, often possessing equal or greater authority than the counties. These include, in various combinations, cities, towns, villages, school districts, and numerous other kinds of districts with special purposes, such as sanitation or fire protection, and, finally, authorities with powers relating to bridges, tunnels, water ports, and airports, among many others. Some governmental power has been committed to each of these, usually including some power of taxation and appropriation.

To understand the curious fact that representation formulas for state legislatures have often been built around counties and New England towns, it is necessary to examine somewhat the background of the county — its rise and more recent decline — and the growing importance of other units of government.

The primacy of the county in the popular mind, if not in its actual role in the governmental process, is undoubtedly in part a product of historic development. The county as a unit of government was a well-developed concept in colonial America, while the early city charters, granted by the governors or proprietors in the name of the British crown, were relatively few. It has been estimated that only about twenty municipal charters were granted prior to the Revolution.[72] Thereafter, the charter-granting authority was recognized as an adjunct of the legislative power, so that charters of municipal corporations in effect became statutes, subject to amendment or repeal by legislative act. Although the same was technically true as to the existence and powers of counties, undoubtedly the two were regarded somewhat differently. Indeed, there may have been an original justification for this difference in popular regard. Only a small proportion of the population was concentrated in the few cities, and special-purpose districts in the modern sense were unknown. Moreover, what cities there were

72. Kauper and Stason, Municipal Corporations 3 (3d ed. 1959).

provided only the most limited governmental services, a minimum of police protection, local courts, regulation of trading activities, and a limited device for the collection of revenues.[73] Accordingly, the vast bulk of the citizens of each state looked primarily to the towns in New England or the counties elsewhere for local governmental services.

Gradually, almost imperceptibly, these relationships changed, both in terms of operative theory and in practice. Analysis can be sharpened by dividing local governments into two broad classes with several lesser subdivisions. First, municipal corporations have definite geographic areas with essentially urbanized populations and relatively broad powers of local self-government. This category includes cities, boroughs, villages, and towns (except New England towns). Second, quasi-public corporations include the less highly organized units, such as counties, townships, New England towns, school districts, sanitary districts, and other special-purpose districts and authorities. While these corporations, like municipal corporations, ordinarily operate within prescribed geographic areas, unlike municipal corporations, "they do not necessarily embrace urban populations, and their corporate powers are much less comprehensive."[74] It is strange that from this heterogeneity of local governmental units there should have been extracted for primary emphasis in terms of representation only those particular units, counties and New England towns, which are no longer necessarily the most significant units of local government. If representation of local units of government in state legislatures were to be developed along logical lines, cities, school districts, and even occasional special-purpose districts could make a better claim than counties. But this claim is nowhere advanced. Comprehension of the reasons for this anomalous situation is important to an understanding of the proper role of local units of government in reapportionment. The following brief analysis of the modern role of the county is intended to open the way to the rethinking of that question.

The County and the New England Town as Units of Local Government. The county is the most traditional and universal unit of

73. Id. at 7.
74. Id. at 1.

local government in the United States. The idea of the county orig-
inated in England, where after the Norman Conquest the local
unit of government, the shire, came to be called the county. The
chief executive was known as shire-reeve, or later as sheriff. It was
only natural that the English who settled in America brought their
county organization with them; and it took deep roots, especially
in the Southern colonies. The concept of the New England town
was not essentially different.[75] In the United States, counties en-
joyed a substantial degree of autonomy for many years; but in the
latter part of the nineteenth century the state legislatures began to
assume more control. Reasons for the shift in power included the
widespread corruption of local officials and the increased demand
for governmental services, particularly on a statewide basis.[76]
What the legislatures once assumed they have ordinarily not relinquished. State control was for a time somewhat diminished by pro-
hibitions against special and local acts; but these limitations have
been commonly avoided by the classification of statutes along population or area lines. The one genuine movement toward return of
some control to local governmental units has been the slow trend
in favor of local home rule. Twenty-seven state constitutions now
provide for municipal home rule.[77] But it is significant that the
states have been much less inclined to offer home rule to counties
than to cities, and even where the opportunity for home rule has
been extended to the counties, the option has not been much exercised.

There are more than 3,000 counties in the United States. Texas
has 254, the largest number; Delaware has only 3. Approximately
two thirds of the counties have an area between 300 and 900
square miles; but the variations are large, ranging at least from the
22.6 square miles of New York County to the 20,160 square miles
of San Bernardino County, California; and the four great regions
of Alaska are even larger. Most counties fall in a population range
of 10,000 to 30,000 inhabitants; but again the variations are spec-

75. For a discussion of the history of the New England town, see Bryce, American
Commonwealth, c. 48 (on Local Government) (1921 ed.). For a contemporary analysis, in terms of apportionment, see Note, Small Town Representation: Invidious Discrimination? The Reapportionment Problem in Rhode Island, Vermont and Connecticut. 43 B.U.L. Rev. 523 (1963).

76. Sandalow, The Limits of Municipal Power Under Home Rule: A Role for the
Courts, 48 Minn. L. Rev. 643, 646 (1964).

77. Id. at 645.

tacular. In 1960 Armstrong County, South Dakota, had a population of 52, while Cook County, Illinois, and Los Angeles County, California, respectively exceeded five and six million inhabitants.

Counties for the most part exercise only administrative functions such as the collection of taxes and the building of roads. Except for the New England states (in which the counties play almost no role) the county is typically governed by an elected board of supervisors or commissioners. Other important local officials, such as sheriffs and district attorneys, are also frequently elected directly by the voters, and there is a resulting fragmentation of power and responsibility. Most important of all is the proliferation of independent and semi-independent special-purpose districts and authorities.

All these elements in combination — the weakening of county government, the growth of municipal home rule, and the development of new quasi-governmental bodies — make less meaningful the historic central position given the county in determining the allocation of state legislative representation. The point can be made more explicit by an examination of the complex local government situation in several representative states: California, Illinois, New York, Texas, and Wisconsin.

California:[78] Of California's 18 million people, 90 per cent live in ten metropolitan areas, and the intergovernmental relationships are exceedingly varied and complex. There are 58 counties, nearly 400 cities, and more than 3,000 special districts, without including nearly that number of local school districts. The problem is more than simply one of numbers. The still more difficult issue involves the question of how to plan comprehensively and intelligently for the great metropolitan areas, which have unfortunately been no respecters of established political boundaries. Many hundreds of thousands of residents in unified metropolitan areas must look to a variety of cities for essential services; and additional thousands of metropolitan area residents actually live in unincorporated areas. Intergovernmental cooperation, difficult at best, is scarcely made easier at the state level by legislators who may consider themselves responsible to particular units of government.

Under the California constitution counties are of two classes,

78. In addition to official sources, the following were helpful in preparing this summary: Hall, County Supervisorial Districting in California (Bureau of Public Administration, Univ. of California: Berkeley, 1961); League of Women Voters of California, California Voters' Handbook (8th ed. 1964).

those governed under general law and those governed by charter, the so-called home-rule counties. Ten of California's 58 counties have elected home rule, and San Francisco County, by special provision in the constitution, is both a county and a city. Although the charter counties may extend their functions somewhat beyond those of the general law counties, the scope of their activities must remain consistent with their position as administrative agencies of the state; and their powers are more limited than those of charter cities. The remaining 47 counties have not availed themselves of home rule and so remain general law counties. Counties of both types are typically governed by an elected board of supervisors (usually five) chosen from geographical districts within the county.[79] There are also ordinarily about a dozen other elected officials in each county, in addition to locally elected judges and boards of education.

California cities, like the counties, may be either charter (home rule) or general law, the former having somewhat greater independence of the state legislature. In all cities the voters elect a legislative body (the council) to make and enforce local ordinances. These governments provide fire and police protection; fulfill the health, recreation, and cultural needs of the citizens; construct and maintain streets; provide sanitation facilities; furnish public transportation; control land utilization; and sometimes provide public utilities — all subject to the limitation that the cities may not act where the state has pre-empted the field. Cities also have considerable power to annex adjoining land.

The gross overlap of county and city jurisdiction has of course produced considerable confusion, some conflict, but also an appreciable measure of cooperation, fostered no doubt by necessity. Thus, counties usually provide such services as welfare, probation, and recording of vital statistics on a county-wide basis, and counties ordinarily furnish outside the incorporated areas the services usually given by cities. Moreover, some counties and cities have contracted together for the county to furnish some of those services even within the city limits; but there is no uniform pattern.

---

79. In 1963 the California Supreme Court ruled that the state constitution required that the supervisorial districts of the general law counties must be approximately equal in population. Yorty v. Anderson, 33 Calif. Rptr. 97, 384 P.2d 417 (1963). The impact of the equal-population principle on local governmental units is discussed infra at pages 264–66.

Within cities special-purpose districts are commonly formed to provide services not offered by the city itself. Although the school district is the most important of these, numerically there are more special districts of other kinds. The widely varied special districts include cemetery districts, sewer districts, hospital districts, irrigation districts, reclamation and soil conservation districts, smog and air pollution districts, and many others. The size of a special district may vary from a few city blocks to a multi-county, region-wide district, such as those in the San Francisco Bay area. There is no limit to the number of districts which may operate within a given geographic area, with the result that most California property owners pay taxes or service charges to several governmental units in addition to the city, county, and state.

The governmental problems of California are as varied as its population, its resources, and its topography. Partial solutions have been worked out in different ways in different areas. In Los Angeles County a functional consolidation has been in part accomplished; most of the more than seventy cities arrange to have some of their services furnished by the county on a contractual basis. In the multi-county San Francisco Bay area regional cooperation has been more the pattern. For example, the Bay Area Air Pollution District and the Bay Area Rapid Transit District both include several counties. There is also a research and planning unit (which has no governing functions) known as the Association of Bay Area Governments, now including eight of the nine eligible counties and 64 of the 84 eligible cities.

Manifestly, the governmental problems of California transcend local units of government, however important individual counties, cities, or local and regional special districts may be for some purposes. To think in terms of representation tied solely to any one of those units is to think in terms of governmental anachronism.

Illinois:[80] There are three kinds of county in Illinois: those organized on a township basis, those not so organized, and Cook County. In all three types the governing body is the elective county board, which has both legislative and executive functions. Non-township counties and Cook County have boards of commissioners, while in

80. Especially helpful in summarizing local government patterns and problems in Illinois were various pamphlets of the League of Women Voters of Illinois and a book published by the Citizens Information Service of Metropolitan Chicago, The Key to Our Local Government (1960).

township counties there are boards of supervisors. In addition to these officials 12 other county officers are elected because of constitutional requirements, and others are elected in compliance with statutory requirements.

County functions, similar in all three types of county, include assessment and collection of taxes, law enforcement, conduct of elections, welfare responsibility (both as a matter of local responsibility and as an agent for state and national programs), highway maintenance on a similar basis, protection of public health, zoning in unincorporated areas, and regional planning. Unlike Illinois cities, counties do not have any specific home-rule option.

Of the 102 counties in Illinois, 85 have adopted the township form of organization. In each of the nearly 1,500 organized townships the voters elect the supervisors and ordinarily a clerk, assessor, collector, highway commissioner, and member of a board of auditors as well. The townships have increasingly been caught in a squeeze between the expanding powers of the cities and villages on the one hand and the increased centralization of county functions on the other. It has been suggested that the principal remaining functions of the township — administration of public assistance and maintenance of local roads — could often be done more efficiently and economically by another unit of government. Despite this range of local governmental units, it has been found necessary in Illinois, as in other states, to create in addition a large number of special-purpose districts. There are at least 32 kinds of special districts in Illinois, totaling about 1,800.

The eight metropolitan areas in Illinois have tended to aggravate the already pressing problems of local government. Thus, in the six counties that constitute the Chicago metropolitan area there is a population of more than six million; and there are 978 local governments, 201 of which are municipalities. The city of Chicago is governed by the same general statutory provisions as other cities in the state, except that special legislation may be adopted by the simple expedient of making a statute applicable only to cities over 500,000 (Chicago is the only one in Illinois), which is sometimes an advantage, sometimes not. In addition to the city, five other governmental bodies are directly supported by Chicago taxpayers (as well as many special-purpose districts): Cook County; the Forest Preserve District (coterminous with the county); the Chicago Park District and the Board of Education (both coterminous with the city); and the Metropolitan Sanitary District of Greater Chicago (with an area larger than the city but smaller than the county). Within the county, local government is conducted by Cook County, by townships (except Chicago), cities, villages, school districts, special boards, commissions, and districts. To take but a single example of the inevitable confusion, responsibility for street and road maintenance is shared by the state, counties, cities, villages, and townships. Streets are a municipal responsibility. Roads are financed jointly from local taxes, state and federal aid, and bond issues. The motor fuel tax is collected by the state and divided among municipalities, counties, and the state.

Illinois has obviously not solved its problems of intergovernmental relationship. Equally apparent is the fact that it is meaningless to organize a state system of representation around the county as a principal unit of government when "county" itself means at least three distinctly different things in the state, and when the county is not intrinsically more important than — perhaps not as important as — other units of local government.

New York:[81] The 62 counties of New York are each further divided into cities and towns (except the counties comprising New York City). Moreover, a town may have within its borders one or more incorporated villages, and a village may lie in two or more towns. In addition, there are, as in other states, numerous school districts, fire districts, improvement districts, and other districts and authorities created for various special purposes. Nassau County, to take a single example, consists of three towns and two cities. Within the towns there are 64 incorporated villages. There are also 269 special districts and 57 school districts in the county.

The five counties that constitute New York City have no direct governmental power as such. In each of the remaining 57 counties there is a board of supervisors made up of the supervisors of the cities and towns in the county. Town supervisors are also executive and legislative officers of their towns, while in the cities supervisors are officials of the county only and have no function to perform in the city government. The board of supervisors adopts local laws; creates and abolishes county departments and agencies; makes ap-

81. Two publications by New York League of Women Voter groups are especially illuminating: New York State: A Citizen's Handbook (1963) and This is Nassau County (1963). For a discussion of the three-state complex in the New York metropolitan area, see Wood, 1400 Governments (1961).

propriations and levies taxes; manages county property; and fixes county salaries except for the judiciary. Each county elects a district attorney, sheriff, county clerk, county treasurer; and sometimes a few other county officials are appointed or elected. County home rule has been available since 1959, but only a few counties availed themselves of the option; a few others had earlier secured home rule by special legislation.

Cities have in general been permitted more home rule in New York than have other units of local government, which accounted in the past for some reincorporation of villages as cities. But the seeming autonomy has also been limited by various statutes. Only one new city, Rye, was incorporated between 1940 and 1963.

There are 932 towns in New York State, varying in population from more than 700,000 to only 65. Towns are divided into two population classes with different numbers of elected officials. Each town elects a supervisor, who is the chief executive officer and also represents the town on the county board of supervisors. The town board has charge of town finances, establishes fire and other special districts, adopts zoning ordinances, regulates the use of streets, protects the peace, and performs other similar local activities.

There are some 550 incorporated villages in New York, ranging in population from 19 persons to more than 36,000. Home rule is frequently available, always subject to the limitation that a village may not act in specified areas committed to state control.

Special improvement districts may be created by towns and/or counties where there are special needs and in conformity with state law. In addition, there are no fewer than seven different kinds of school districts meant to serve different needs.

To comprehend the confusion at the local government level in New York State, it should be recalled that everyone who lives in the state is a resident of the state, a county, a city or town, and a school district. If he lives in a village, that adds one unit to the list without displacing another. In addition, there are multiple special-purpose districts in counties and in towns. The problem of New York City, with its tristate metropolitan area, is of course immeasurably more complex, even though there the counties have no governing function at all. In short, for nearly half the state's population the county has no meaning as a unit of government, while for the remainder of the state's residents the county is but one, and not necessarily the most important, of a complex hierarchy of confusingly interrelated governmental units.

Texas:[82] Article IX, section 1 of the Texas constitution authorizes the state legislature "to create counties for the convenience of the people." The counties already in existence when the constitution was adopted in 1846 were continued, and the number has since grown to a total of 254, the highest in the nation. All Texas counties have the same organizational structure. Each county elects a county judge and four county commissioners who together constitute the county commissioners' court, a body with legislative and executive functions. The county judge is a member of the commissioners' court and in addition is chief magistrate of the county court. Other officials in each county whose election is required by the constitution are the county clerk, county attorney, sheriff, tax assessor-collector, four justices of the peace, and constables. In counties with more than 10,000 population a county treasurer and a county surveyor are also elected. Election of other officials is required by statute, including a county board of trustees, county superintendent, public weigher, and inspector of hides and animals. Others are appointed, depending on the size and property valuation in the county.

Legally, the county is a political subdivision of the state which exists for the administration of matters of state concern. However, "from a practical administrative point of view the county is assumed to be a local corporation,"[83] to which is committed substantial authority over maintenance of law and order, supervision of schools, county finance, construction and maintenance of county highways, responsibility for administration of state welfare programs, and collection of state taxes. Clearly, these are important responsibilities. But the counties are almost entirely unaided by home rule, which has been considered too ambiguous and cumbersome for any significant utilization by the counties. As of late 1963 no county had adopted a home-rule charter.

Texas cities are classified as general-law cities or home-rule cities. The provision for home rule, one of the most liberal in the nation, has been operative since 1912. It appears to confer upon cities all governmental and proprietary power that the legislature could have exercised prior to the adoption of home rule, including lib-

82. In addition to official sources, the following materials were especially helpful: Symposium on Constitutional Revision in Texas, 35 Tex. L. Rev. 901–1089 (especially the articles by Will Wilson, John M. Claunch, Wilfred D. Webb, and James A. Hankerson) (1957); League of Women Voters of Texas, A Guide to Understanding State-Local Relations (mimeo. 1962).

83. Claunch, Toward a More Effective Government, 35 Tex. L. Rev. 986, 988 (1957).

eral powers of annexation until somewhat curtailed by statute in 1963. The cities, whether general-law or home-rule, provide fire and police protection, health services, and certain welfare services. They provide such physical services as zoning, construction and maintenance of streets, communications, and transportation systems. All cities regulate public utility systems, and some operate them, as well as public markets, airports, tunnels, recreational activities, etc.

As in other states, special-purpose districts have expanded greatly in Texas, beginning with the best known, the school district. Special districts have also been commonly created for the development and conservation of natural resources, hospital districts, and for many other purposes.

More than half of the population of Texas now lives in only 18 counties, and there are at least 15 metropolitan areas in the state, but each of the 254 counties retains the same basic governmental structure without significant variation. It is not surprising that important governmental functions may be regulated at several different levels of local government. The problem arises in connection with tax assessment and collection, police and fire protection, health functions, water supply, and regulation of airports, as well as elsewhere.One example will make the point. "Thus, it becomes apparent that when the full authority provided by the constitution and statutes of Texas is exercised, there may be upwards of six or seven autonomous local police authorities operating within the bounds of any given metropolitan county."[84]

Texas, like other states, has not resolved the problems of confusion inherent in overlapping authority of local units of government. Important as are the functions committed by law to the counties, the fact remains that their operations have in fact often been superseded by the needs and demands of the burgeoning metropolitan areas. Once again, it is demonstrated that reliance upon the county as *the* unit of local government about which representation patterns should be formulated does not fit twentieth-century facts.

Wisconsin: [85] The county board in each of Wisconsin's 71 coun-

84. Wilson, Toward a More Effective Division of Powers in Local Government, 35 Tex. L. Rev. 975, 977 (1957).

85. In addition to official sources relevant materials include the following: Bradbury, A Recapitulation of Home Rule, 59 The Municipality 201 (1964); Donaghue,

ties consists of the chairmen of town boards, a supervisor for each city ward, and a supervisor for each village or part of a village within the county. There are approximately 2,600 county supervisors, an average of about 36 per county.[86] In addition, the state constitution requires the election in each county of a county sheriff, coroner, recorder of deeds, and district attorney. The authority of the county board, however, apparently remains primary. Supervisors are authorized to acquire, hold, maintain, and convey property, apportion taxes, perform zoning functions, levy the school tax for distribution among school districts, organize towns, and provide police protection.

> However, the few available facts indicate that most local services of the county are oriented toward the rural or unincorporated areas and that urban residents pay a substantial portion of the costs of these services and receive little or no return for them. . . . Municipal residents in addition paid the cost of like services within their own borders.[87]

There is no county home rule in Wisconsin, partly because of strict interpretation of the state constitutional provision that the legislature shall establish only one system of county government, which shall be as nearly uniform as practicable.[88]

Wisconsin has provisions for municipal home rule both on a constitutional and on a statutory basis. By 1961, after nearly thirty years of such authorization, no city or village had adopted a complete home-rule charter under the constitutional authority; the failure to adopt home rule is attributable in part to restrictive judicial interpretation of the powers delegated and in part to the cumbersome machinery prescribed for adoption. Legislative home rule has also not been widely utilized, despite the view that "a city operating under the general charter finding no limitations in express language has . . . all the powers that the Legislature could by any possibility confer upon it."[89] It has also been difficult to apply the accepted test of "paramount interest" in determining which unit of government, state or local, may exercise particular

County Government and Urban Growth, 1959 Wis. L. Rev. 30; Hagensick, Wisconsin Home Rule, 50 National Civic Review 349 (1961).

86. Donaghue, supra note 85, at 45.

87. Id. at 50–51.

88. Wis. Const. art. IV, § 23.

89. Hack v. City of Mineral Point, 203 Wis. 215, 219, 233 N.W. 82, 84 (1931).

regulatory authority. As the Wisconsin Supreme Court noted in 1964, "the problem of drawing the line [is] difficult for the reason that the functions of state and local governments necessarily overlap."[90]

Wisconsin has apparently not solved even to its own satisfaction the acute problems arising out of the complex interrelationship among the local units of government, with the state, and with each other. However unsatisfactory may be the arrangement, many important functions have remained with the counties, a fact resented by the cities, but not as yet effectively overcome. It is especially instructive that in Wisconsin, with its strong tradition of county government, it was nonetheless possible in May 1964, before the decision in *Reynolds*, for the state supreme court to approve a plan of reapportionment which combined some counties and divided others, the latter along established town, village, ward, and assembly district lines, to achieve near population equality.[91]

What is the significance of these summaries of various ways in which local governments operate? In the first place, it is not here suggested that the five local government structures above described illustrate by any means all of the various combinations and permutations. Nor is there any aim here to criticize the form and operation of counties and other units of local government. That has been sufficiently done elsewhere.[92] Rather the purpose has been to examine the division of authority among local government units to observe to what extent counties may justifiably be adopted as the basic units in apportionment formulas. Several conclusions emerge.

1. Legally, counties are administrative units of the state in which they are located. States ordinarily assign to counties such important functions as the collection of taxes, construction and maintenance of roads, administration of public health, public education, and justice. The powers and duties of counties derive exclusively

90. Milwaukee v. Milwaukee Amusement, Inc., 22 Wis. 2d 240, 251–52, 125 N.W.2d 625 (1964).

91. See State ex rel. Reynolds v. Zimmerman, 23 Wis. 2d 606, 128 N.W.2d 16 (Wis. 1964).

92. See, for example: "It is characteristic of Americans to strain every effort to find improved methods of running industry, business and scientific pursuits but to cling to out-dated methods of operating government until pressures for improvement become overwhelmingly demanding. This has been particularly true of county government." National Municipal League, Model County Charter V (1956).

from state constitutions and statutes and may be withdrawn or limited at any time by the same route.

2. Cities, towns (except in the New England sense), and villages were originally much less important than counties as units of government. However, as the majority of the population has settled in urban areas, which have developed without respect to county or even state lines, the urban centers — and now the metropolitan areas — have taken on new importance and new powers. The pattern of change in governmental structure has been uneven; sometimes the cities have assumed or been given authority at the expense of the counties; sometimes cooperation has been arranged by contract or other mutually satisfactory arrangement. But everywhere the patterns have shifted; the search continues for new and more viable arrangements.

3. The growth in importance of the special-purpose district, whether a school district, irrigation district, or a Port of New York Authority, has dramatically affected all local government concepts. Neither county nor city nor town nor village can ever be quite the same again.

4. The infinite variety among the local government patterns in the fifty states necessitates careful analysis to determine in each state the local relevance of political subdivision lines in relation to representation of voters in the state legislature. If any one proposition emerges clearly, it is that the county should no longer be regarded as the sole or nearly exclusive unit of local government upon which election district lines can logically be based. Even if it would be too strong to describe the county as irrelevant for apportionment purposes, it is difficult to conceive that it is inherently more significant than cities, villages, or even special-purpose districts. School districts, for example, probably touch political emotions and the voters' pocketbooks more than any other body with governmental authority.

5. Finally, the county has historically played one role in the apportionment process which should not be minimized, although it has not been previously discussed and will be only briefly noted here. It is obviously necessary that each political party build from some local geographic base unit, and the county has often proved a convenient unit for that purpose. Obviously, there is some convenience, if only historic, in retaining that structure. But it has repeatedly been demonstrated that political organizations can also

function within other units, in the cities, assembly districts, wards, and the like. It is correspondingly difficult to believe that substantial deviation from population as a basis for representation can be justified by such political considerations.

THE CONSEQUENCES OF EQUALITY

The burden of the argument thus far has been that there is nothing particularly mysterious about the concept of substantial equality as a constitutional requirement for state legislative representation. Obviously, the task of reapportionment, now made necessary in most states, has not suddenly become a game to be won or lost by mathematical incantation. In the commonsense view of the Supreme Court, certain enumerated factors are not relevant: "neither history alone, nor economic or other sorts of group interests, are permissible factors in attempting to justify disparities from population-based representation."[93] On the other hand, in allowing states to "maintain the integrity of various political subdivisions"[94] against a background of substantial equality, the Court simply reserved to the states the traditional room for experimentation and maneuver.

The *Reapportionment Cases* should demonstrate the need in each state for careful analysis of the functional operation of the various local government units and their relationship to each other. It appears likely that such study will often lead to a conclusion that the political subdivision lines of local units of government, whether counties, cities, towns, villages, or special-purpose districts, are only marginally relevant to the logic of apportionment in state legislatures. The Supreme Court, however, was not dogmatic or even assertive on the question, leaving the matter open to individual state experimentation. Wherever a case can be made for adherence to political subdivision lines, the Court has indicated willingness to accept the local legislative judgment.

Apportionment formulas must begin somewhere; there must be some convenient means of measuring the population confined within such districts in order to know when equality has been achieved; and the units of substantially equal population should be described in terms that are not unknown to political usage. Ac-

93. Reynolds v. Sims, 377 U.S. 533, 579–80 (1964).
94. Id. at 578.

cordingly, it can scarcely be suggested that political lines be alto-gether disregarded as irrelevant to apportionment and districting. There would appear to be no reason not to use existing lines drawn about counties, cities, towns, villages, and even assembly districts and wards, so long as the caveat against too great deviation from population equality is not violated.

Where existing political units do not readily lend themselves to viable election districts, division can also be made along the boundary lines of census tracts, the geographic areas from which United States census tabulations are made every ten years. The census tracts have the advantage of being politically neutral: the lines are not drawn for partisan advantage, but to include within a compact territorial area as nearly as possible a homogeneous population grouping which, in a city for example, might be a neighborhood. The number of persons in each census tract is small enough (typically from a few hundred to a few thousand) that maximum flexibility is available in seeking to satisfy both the equal-population principle and the appropriate demand for logical arrangement of voters into reasonably homogeneous units.

Satisfaction of the equal-population principle is the only constitutional requirement in state legislative representation which the Supreme Court originally specified. But equality alone may not suffice. Even the most literal satisfaction of the equality principle, without the leaven of common sense, might prove at best an incomplete victory.

Other relevant considerations, to be discussed in this final section, include the ever-present threat of the gerrymander; the decision as to one house or two in a fairly apportioned legislature; the permissibility and desirability of multimember election districts; the impact of the equal-population principle upon representation formulas in local government below the state level; and the consequences for the two-party system.

Equal Population and the Gerrymander. It would probably not be difficult to reach a consensus on the proposition that, apart from malapportionment, the gerrymander is the device currently most destructive of fairness in the electoral process. Nor are malapportionment and gerrymandering unrelated. Even though the equal-population principle does not of its own force forbid gerrymandering, malapportionment and gerrymandering are nonetheless of the same family. Both arise out of the instinct for partisan advantage in defiance of the democratic ideal. There is, however, an important difference between the two. Malapportionment of state legislative election districts and inequality in congressional districting have been held forbidden by the Constitution, but there is no Supreme Court ruling that gerrymandering of state election districts or of congressional districts is invalid as a matter of federal constitutional law. While gerrymandering has on a few occasions been invalidated for violation of state constitutional or statutory requirements of compactness, those rulings have not been based on any explicit command or any inference drawn from the Constitution of the United States;[95] and between 1929 and 1965 there was no federal requirement that congressional districts be compact and contiguous.

The only case in which the constitutional issue has been considered by the Supreme Court was *Wright v. Rockefeller*,[96] decided on the same day in 1964 as *Wesberry v. Sanders*, which established the requirement of near-equality in congressional districting. But the *Wright* case did not directly raise the issue of gerrymandering for political advantage. Plaintiffs in that case had alleged that New York's 1961 congressional districting statute "segregates eligible voters by race and place of origin" in New York County.[97] The complaint alleged:

> The 18th, 19th and 20th Congressional Districts have been drawn so as to include the overwhelming number of nonwhite citizens and citizens of Puerto Rican origin in the County of New York . . . .[98]

The case was tried before a three-judge court whose members read the evidence in as many ways, although two voted to dismiss

95. In Matter of Orans, 257 N.Y.S.2d 839 (N.Y. Sup. Ct.), aff'd, 15 N.Y.2d 339 (1965), Judge Matthew Levy of the New York Supreme Court concluded that prima facie evidence of invalid gerrymandering had been shown by petitioners in their challenge to the Reapportionment Compliance Act enacted by the New York legislature in 1964. However, he did not have to rule on the ultimate question because he held the act otherwise violative of the state constitution, on which point the decision was affirmed by the New York Court of Appeals.

96. 376 U.S. 52 (1964).

97. Id. at 53, quoting from the complaint.

98. Id. at 54. The racial and ethnic distribution of the four districts was as follows (id. at 59):

District	White as Per Cent of District	Negro and Puerto Rican as Per Cent of District
17th	94.9	5.1
18th	13.7	86.3
19th	71.5	28.5
20th	72.5	27.5

the complaint.[99] Judge Moore concluded that there was no proof that the boundaries were drawn on racial lines. Judge Feinberg, believing the case closer, stated that plaintiffs' evidence might justify an inference that racial considerations motivated the reapportionment, but concluded that plaintiffs had not met the requisite burden of proof. Judge Murphy, dissenting, concluded that the statistical evidence demonstrated that Negroes and Puerto Ricans were fenced out of the seventeenth district, thus establishing a prima facie case of legislative intent to discriminate on racial lines.

The Supreme Court affirmed the dismissal because "appellants have not shown that the challenged part of the New York Act was the product of a state contrivance to segregate on the basis of race or place of origin."[100] Justice Harlan concurred on the explicit premise that "the only issue in this case involves racially segregated districts."[101] Justices Douglas and Goldberg, dissenting, also treated the case as one involving allegations of racial gerrymandering, charges which they thought established.

Wright did not hold that racial gerrymandering is permitted by the Constitution. Indeed, the inference is quite the reverse; only three years before, the Supreme Court held that the boundary lines of a municipality could not be redrawn to exclude Negroes from the city limits.[102] *Wright* held only that the proof was insufficient in the circumstances of that case. Without speculating how much more proof might be demanded to make such a showing, it is enough here to observe that the opinion intimated no view at all on the more usual kind of gerrymander, that for purely political advantage.[103] That issue might have been reached in *Wright*, although the plaintiffs did not push it. An argument could have been made that the irregularities in the district boundaries were designed primarily for political advantage rather than essentially to achieve racially discriminatory objectives. In light of the well-known patterns of residential segregation, it could have been

99. Wright v. Rockefeller, 221 F. Supp. 460 (S.D. N.Y. 1962).

100. 376 U.S. at 58.

101. Ibid.

102. Gomillion v. Lightfoot, 364 U.S. 339 (1960).

103. That the Court intended to leave the issue open is further supported by the dictum in Fortson v. Dorsey, 379 U.S. 433, 439 (1965). "It might well be that, designedly or otherwise, a multi-member constituency apportionment scheme, under the circumstances of a particular case, would operate to minimize or cancel out the voting strength of racial or political elements of the voting population."

suggested that political advantage was sought in one of two ways: (1) It might have been contended that, by concentrating Negro and Puerto Rican voters in one district, the aim was to assure at least one Representative from one of those racial or ethnic groups; or (2) it might have been a straight political party gerrymander, in which the lines were drawn to exclude Negroes and Puerto Ricans from one district and to concentrate them in another on the assumption that, as a class, they were more likely to vote for one party than another.

The latter explanation would comport exactly with the classic theory of the gerrymander in terms of the placement of "excess" votes and of "wasted" votes. Andrew Hacker has described it as follows:

> If the aim of gerrymandering is for one party to obtain the maximum voting advantage at the other's expense, there are several methods by which this can be done. In each, the gerrymandering party (henceforward to be called Party A) intends to make the votes of the opposition (Party B) as ineffective as possible. One method is for Party A to set up a district in which Party B will have "excess" votes — that is, considerably more votes will be cast for Party B's candidate than he needs to win. A second method is to create a district where Party B's "wasted" votes — those cast for a predictable loser — will be increased. And the third is to design a district so that Party A's "effective" votes will be increased — usually by putting its own known followers into small districts compared to much larger districts for Party B's known followers.[104]

Until the Supreme Court provides definitive guidance on the constitutional status of the political gerrymander, it follows that restraint of such disruptive schemes must first be sought within the political process itself. Re-enactment of a congressional requirement of compactness and contiguity among congressional districts is urgently desirable, as would be similar legislation at the state level in limitation of the gerrymander in state legislative representation.

One House or Two?[105] The bicameral legislature has always

---

104. Hacker, Congressional Districting 55 (rev. ed. 1964). See also Wells, Legislative Representation in New York State 20–28 (mimeo. published by I.L.G.W.U., March 1964 ed.).

105. For background study and interpretation of the significance of early American experience with unicameral and bicameral legislatures, I am indebted to Calvin B. T. Lee, Assistant Dean of Columbia College, in an unpublished paper. Useful published studies include the following: Senning, The One-House Legislature (1937); Hagan, The Bicameral Principle in State Legislatures, 11 J. Pub. L. 310 (1962).

overwhelmingly dominated the state legislative field in the United States. The reasons are by no means clear, but the fact is that only four states have ever experimented with unicameralism even for brief periods. Georgia had a unicameral legislature in the years 1777 and 1778, and Pennsylvania between 1776 and 1790. But in both instances there was during that period a plural executive with at least quasi-legislative powers, which made the unicameralism less than pure; and both were abandoned with more enthusiasm than regret. The Vermont one-house legislature survived until the constitution of 1835. None of these three states has intimated any desire to return to the unicameral system. Nebraska is the only state since 1835 to perform its legislative functions in a one-house legislature, which has operated there since 1937, apparently to the reasonable satisfaction of the people.

Despite the overwhelming acceptance in practice of the bicameral principle, its origins are by no means clear. It is sometimes suggested that bicameralism in the colonies, and later in the original state constitutions, most of which were adopted between 1776 and 1780, followed the example of the British Parliament. But representation in the House of Commons was based on population, while in the House of Lords it was based on nobility, an idea clearly not acceptable to the drafters of the original state constitutions. Nor were the state constitutions patterned on the two houses of Congress, for that plan was not adopted until 1787, long after most of the states had settled on a bicameral system. It cannot even be said that the congressional representation formula was drawn from the states. As a result of the so-called Great Compromise, Congress adopted for itself a plan radically different from that which then prevailed in most of the states (see pages 196–99). Despite the solid acceptance of the bicameral principle in state legislatures in the United States, students of government have been generally unenthusiastic. Illustrative is the fact that the Model State Constitution of the National Municipal League, in its current (sixth) edition, as in its first, favors the unicameral legislature.[106] Criticism of bicameral legislatures is reported on the ground of "complexity and confusion" and "frustration at the inability to obtain prompt passage of important programs by two houses operating with an overloaded legislative calendar and an adjournment date fixed either by law or tradition." On the other

106. National Municipal League, Model State Constitution § 4.02 (6th ed. 1963).

hand, the National Municipal League comments on the Nebraska unicameral legislature as follows:

> Most of the claimed virtues of unicameralism have been realized in the Nebraska experience during the past 25 years. Nebraska's single house with 43 members has permitted more easily the pinpointing of legislative responsibility than in sprawling two-house legislatures. Fewer bills have been introduced and a higher percentage of them passed. The prestige of membership has risen and in the view of many observers so has the quality of candidates.[107]

The constitutional necessity of reapportioning both houses in satisfaction of the equal-population principle has raised again, with new emphasis, the question of one house or two. The inquiry is commonly made: Why should there be two houses if population is the principal factor to be taken into account in apportionment? Although the issue is not one of constitutional dimension, but rather one of political preference, the Supreme Court commented on the matter at some length in *Reynolds*:

> We do not believe that the concept of bicameralism is rendered anachronistic and meaningless when the predominant basis of representation in the two legislative bodies is required to be the same — population. A prime reason for bicameralism, modernly considered, is to insure mature and deliberate consideration of, and to prevent precipitate action on, proposed legislative measures. Simply because the controlling criterion for apportioning representation is required to be the same in both houses does not mean that there will be no differences in the composition and complexion of the two bodies. Different constituencies can be represented in the two houses. One body could be composed of single-member districts while the other could have at least some multimember districts. The length of terms of the legislators in the separate bodies could differ. The numerical size of the two bodies could be made to differ, even significantly, and the geographical size of districts from which legislators are elected could also be made to differ. And apportionment in one house could be arranged so as to balance off minor inequities in the representation of certain areas in the other house. In summary, these and other factors could be, and are presently, in many States, utilized to engender differing complexion and collective attitudes in the two bodies of a state legislature, although both are apportioned substantially on a population basis.[108]

107. Id. at 43.
108. Reynolds v. Sims, 377 U.S. 533, 576–77 (1964).

Little more can be said for the present. The decision whether to have one house or two must be made individually in each state. While states are involved in reconsideration of their apportionment formulas, they should re-examine from that perspective the advantages and disadvantages of unicameralism as compared with bicameralism. The Chief Justice is surely right in stating that the population standard does not eliminate many of the commonly accepted virtues of bicameralism, particularly the popular, but somewhat untested, belief that two houses protect against ill-considered action. Where change is considered, it should be on the merits as to which structure offers greater promise for the legislative process. On this question of judgment it is clear that further study by students of the governmental process is urgently needed.[109]

We already know that bicameralism does not operate in the same fashion in all states. The two houses may already think alike in a one-party state.[110] Even in a two-party state in which one party has ordinarily controlled the legislature, and where party discipline is strict, the result may not be very different.[111] Negotiations take place off the floor, and decisions are transmitted to the two houses for ratification. "The rare revolt against the leaders only emphasizes the extent to which, operationally, the bicameral scheme in New York fails to secure a second legislative consideration."[112] These instances should be compared with others in which the two houses do in fact represent different views on many matters, sometimes to the actual point of inability to act in any direction, which may also not be much of a recommendation for the bicameral system.

After study of the problem from the perspective of a number of individual instances, Charles B. Hagan concluded: "It is altogether likely that little change would occur in any of the American states if a shift were made from one form of legislative body to the other."[113]

---

109. In the spring of 1965 several states initiated serious study of unicameralism, most notably Missouri and Rhode Island. See also Fordham, A Spur for the States, 53 Nat'l Munic. Rev. 474, 478, 502 (Oct. 1964).

110. Farmer, The Legislative Process in Alabama 304–305 (1949).

111. Straetz and Munger, New York Politics 61 (1960).

112. Hagan, The Bicameral Principle in State Legislatures, 11 J. Pub. L. 310, 320 (1962).

113. Id. at 326.

Single-Member and Multimember Constituencies. The equal-population principle, as formulated by the Supreme Court, does not in so many words address itself to the question whether state legislators and Representatives to Congress may be chosen, at each state's pleasure, from single-member constituencies or from multi-member districts. Indeed, the Court suggested that it might be a matter of constitutional indifference. In commenting on the possible ways in which varied bases of representation could be achieved between the two houses of a bicameral legislature, Chief Justice Warren observed, in what at first appeared to be an unstudied dictum, that "One body could be composed of single-member districts while the other could have at least some multimember districts."[114] In 1965 the Court made it clear that this was more than a casual dictum, holding in *Fortson v. Dorsey*[115] that provision for election of state legislators from a multimember constituency does not violate the fourteenth amendment. The case involved legislation adopted in Georgia in 1962 pursuant to which 33 of the state senatorial districts were made up of from one to eight counties each, while the remaining 21 districts were allotted in groups of from two to seven among the seven most populous counties, all the latter involving elections at large. Only Justice Douglas dissented from the holding that, so long as population equality was substantially satisfied among the 54 senatorial districts, there was no objection on equal protection grounds. The ruling is important, not only for what is said about the permissibility of using multimember districts but as confirmation of the Court's willingness to approve state experimentation in devising representation formulas in satisfaction of the equal-population requirement.

It is of course important to have the constitutional question settled promptly. There remain, however, important questions of wisdom which should be carefully considered in each state that has or contemplates multimember districts.

It is commonly assumed that the great bulk of the election districts are single-member constituencies, and, numerically, that is true. In most districts only one member is elected. But when Maurice Klain counted the districts and the representatives in 1955, he found that "only nine states choose all legislators in single-mem-

114. Reynolds v. Sims, 377 U.S. 533, 577 (1964).
115. 379 U.S. 433 (1965).

ber elections . . . ."[116] He found further that 12 per cent of the state senators and 45.4 per cent of the state representatives were chosen in multimember elections.[117]

Multimember districts have sometimes offered useful ways around state constitutional requirements forbidding the internal division of any county into districts. In the absence of constitutional inhibition on the enforcement of such a provision (discussed below), there may have been no other way of securing representation in proportion to population except by allowing the election at large of all the representatives to which such an undivided district would be entitled on a population basis. If such state constitutional restrictions are held invalid or are otherwise discarded, the impetus for multimember districts will be reduced, but not necessarily eliminated. Where agreement on the specifics of district line-drawing is politically difficult, it remains tempting to patch over the differences with at-large elections in the disputed areas. But clearly there are dangers, as evidenced by the election at large on a state-wide basis of all 177 members of the Illinois lower house in the fall of 1964. That was the result of an unexpected political impasse within the state apportionment commission, and it was deplored by everyone involved. The obvious undesirability of this particular instance of multimember elections, however, does not necessarily establish either the undesirability or the unconstitutionality of using a multimember district for the choice of a small number of legislators.

Students of government ordinarily prefer single-member districts,[118] especially when the districts are large. In support of the single-member district it is urged that "it is far easier for the average citizen to judge the qualities and performance of a limited number of candidates for a single office than of a mass of candidates for several offices . . . ."[119] Moreover, multimember districts do not adequately reflect the diversity of political views in the area. The majority party in such a district may sweep all, or nearly all, the seats. One device to avoid this consequence has been devel-

116. Klain, A New Look at the Constituencies: The Need for a Recount and a Reappraisal, 49 Am. Pol. Sci. Rev. 1105, 1106 (1955).

117. Id. at 1107, 1109.

118. The sixth edition of the Model State Constitution (1963) proposes "one member to represent each legislative district" (§ 4.02).

119. Id. at 44.

oped in Illinois, which has approved a plan for cumulative voting — allowing the voter to distribute his votes as he pleases, giving them all to one candidate if he so desires. (This was rejected as not feasible in the 1964 statewide election at large.) On that basis the minority party can ordinarily secure some representation. Another suggestion is proportional representation, often recommended but seldom tried.[120]

Despite these disadvantages, which many have thought sufficient reason to oppose all multimember districting, something may be said in its favor in special circumstances. Multimember districts in some heavily populated areas might avoid gerrymandering; but the National Municipal League cautions that "Voters should not, however, be called upon to pass judgment on more than three or four legislative positions."[121]

Equal Population and Local Government. Reynolds and the related apportionment cases involved only state legislative representation; but it is hard to believe that the equal-population principle there announced does not apply in much the same manner to the legislative branches of the units of local government, the counties, cities, towns, and villages. There are of course important differences in structure and function among these units as well as between them and state legislatures. Almost all the local governmental units are governed by unicameral bodies. Moreover, some of the local governing bodies may perform functions which are more realistically described as quasi-executive than as quasi-legislative. However, where the legislative function can be isolated from the nonlegislative, it would be very difficult indeed to argue that the equal protection clause of the fourteenth amendment does not apply to require substantial equality among whatever election districts there may be.[122]

Presumably because *Baker v. Carr* and *Reynolds v. Sims* applied specifically only to state legislative representation, the implications for counties, cities, and other local governments were not immedi-

120. See Hallett, Proportional Representation — The Key to Democracy (National Municipal League 1940).

121. National Municipal League, Model State Constitution 49 (6th ed. 1963).

122. For an excellent and comprehensive survey, see Weinstein, The Effect of the Federal Reapportionment Decisions on Counties and Other Forms of Municipal Government, 65 Colum. L. Rev. 21 (1965).

ately recognized. But change is in the offing there as well as in state legislatures. The California Supreme Court, acting between *Baker* and *Reynolds*, ruled that the supervisorial districts in each of the forty-seven general law counties must be apportioned on a population basis.[123] Although the decision was based on state law, it is worth noting that the relevance or not of *Baker v. Carr* was argued by both parties. Moreover, the court did overturn a 1925 decision which had held that the boards need not redistrict in accordance with population, despite inconsequential intervening change in the applicable state law. It is not impossible that the California Supreme Court had in mind the already-decided case of *Baker* and that it may even have anticipated a little the still-to-be-decided *Reynolds* case.

Somewhat similarly, a case in the federal district court in Minnesota, challenging the apportionment in Hennepin County (Minneapolis), was in effect mooted when the Hennepin County Board indicated its intention to redraw the district lines on a population standard. The court held that exercise of jurisdiction was no longer appropriate, but granted a continuance so that the plaintiffs could, if necessary, reassert their claims at a later time.[124]

The Supreme Court had one opportunity in 1964 to pass on a claim of malapportionment in county government, in a case arising out of Hancock County, Mississippi. The appeal was not properly presented, however, and it was dismissed for want of jurisdiction.[125] Other challenges to county apportionment formulas were ordinarily successful in lower federal courts and in state courts.[126]

123. Griffin v. Board of Supervisors of Monterey County, 33 Cal. Rptr. 101, 384 P.2d 421 (1963). See also State ex rel. Scott v. Masterson, 173 Ohio St. 402, 183 N.E.2d 376 (1962). But cf. Davis v. Dusch, 205 Va. 676, 139 S.E.2d 25 (1964).

124. Hedlund v. Hanson, 213 F. Supp. 172 (D. Minn. 1962).

125. Glass v. Hancock County Election Comm'n, 156 So. 2d 825 (Miss. 1963), appeal dismissed, 378 U.S. 558 (1964). The allegations of the complaint, if otherwise properly presented, demonstrated substantial malapportionment. One of the five districts in the county (known as beats) had a larger population than the other four combined.

126. See, e.g., Bianchi v. Griffing, 238 F. Supp. 997 (E.D. N.Y. 1965), in which plaintiffs challenged the validity of the county governmental structure in Suffolk County, New York. The county is divided into ten townships, which vary in population from 1,367 to 191,280. For the facts see an earlier opinion, Bianchi v. Griffing, 217 F. Supp. 166 (1963). Each town elected a supervisor, who was not only chief executive of the town but was also a member of the county board of supervisors, with one vote. The resulting disparity in voter representation was 150 to 1. The court retained jurisdiction to allow an opportunity for corrective legislative action to be sought. See also Sonneborn v. Sylvester, 132 N.W.2d 249 (Wis. 1965). But cf. Reed v. Mann, 237 F. Supp. 22 (N.D. Ga. 1964).

The most interesting challenge to the apportionment formula of a city body with legislative power is that involving the New York City procedure for the election of councilmen-at-large.[127] The procedure was adopted with the commendable purpose of ensuring enlarged representation in the city council for the minority (Republican) party. The device was to elect two councilmen-at-large from each of the five boroughs, while permitting each party no more than one nomination for each position. As a result, the two councilmen-at-large elected from each borough are necessarily members of different parties. The challenge was made primarily on state grounds; there was, for example, no reference to the fact that the borough of Richmond is substantially overrepresented under this formula, compared with the four other boroughs. The majority of the New York Court of Appeals found that the plan was similar to proportional representation and upheld its validity, making only passing reference to the fourteenth amendment. Chief Judge Desmond dissented on the state ground, but also expressed serious doubts on the federal constitutional question, even though *Reynolds* had not yet been decided. Clearly, the last word has not yet been heard on this matter. If the issue should be squarely presented to the Supreme Court, reversal might well be anticipated.

Finally, one case in 1964 raised a question as to the impact of the fourteenth amendment on the composition of state conventions. In *West v. Carr*[128] the Tennessee Supreme Court refused to invalidate a provision that delegates to a state constitutional convention should be chosen from the same malapportioned districts as then (June 1962) established for the state legislature. The United States Supreme Court denied certiorari in June 1964, so resolution of this question, too, must be postponed for later determination on the merits. Again it must be emphasized that it is not easy to see how any of these units, county or city governing bodies and state constitutional conventions, can be considered immune from the fourteenth amendment command of equality whenever the legislative function is sufficiently implicated.

127. Blaikie v. Power, 13 N.Y.2d 134, 193 N.E.2d 55 (1963), appeal dismissed, 375 U.S. 439 (1964). See also Ellis v. Mayor and City Council of Baltimore, 234 F. Supp. 945 (D. Md. 1964); McMillan v. Wagner, — F. Supp. — (S.D.N.Y. 1964).

In July 1965 the New York Court of Appeals held that the membership of the Binghamton city council must be reapportioned in accordance with population. Seaman v. Fedourich, 16 N.Y.2d 94, — N.E.2d — (1965).

128. 370 S.W.2d 469 (Tenn. 1963), appeal dismissed, 378 U.S. 557 (1965).

Equal Population and Partisan Advantage. Political advantage or disadvantage resulting from application of the equal-population principle is irrelevant to the constitutional requirement that such an adjustment be made. But speculation concerning the possible political implications of reapportionment and redistricting cannot be easily confined to questions exclusively constitutional. There has been much loose talk, but very little objective study, about the consequences to the two-party system, and specifically the gain or loss to the Republican and Democratic Parties, which might result from faithful adherence to the equal-population standard. The popular belief is that the Democrats will gain from correction of urban underrepresentation because of Democratic strength in the cities, particularly in the Northeast and Midwest, and that the Republican Party may find advantage in equal representation in the suburban areas and in the South, Southwest, West Coast, and Mountain States. Senator Paul Douglas, a Democrat, argued on the Senate floor in August 1964 that the Republican Party would benefit in his home state of Illinois, but stated that he favored reapportionment "even if it does help the Republican Party."[129] The benefit to the state would come in other ways, he thought:

> We have a big water problem in Chicago and the suburbs . . . . We also have a problem of smoke abatement, a problem of zoning, a problem of taxation, a problem of relief, and a housing problem. These problems affect the urban and suburban areas alike.[130]

Most Republicans, however, have not been persuaded, including the Republican Senator from Illinois, Everett Dirksen, who led the Senate drive in the summer of 1964 to restrict the jurisdiction of federal courts in apportionment matters; and, when he was unsuccessful in that effort, Senator Dirksen in 1965 masterminded the campaign for a constitutional amendment.

One student of the political process has avoided idle talk and has instead made a specific and persuasive study of the political consequences likely to flow from representation in accordance with population in congressional districting. Andrew Hacker concluded that if equal-sized districts were created at random, the Republicans would profit more than the Democrats. He declared that "Re-

129. 110 Cong. Rec. 19002 (daily ed. Aug. 14, 1964).
130. Id. at 19003.

publicans would be well-advised to work for the equalization of districts: they can only profit by such a move."[131]

Regardless of political impact, other consequences of the shift to equality of representation may be anticipated, some very significant. At the very least it should be expected that state legislators will show greater concern for the critical urban and suburban problems of education, housing, and transportation, to mention only the most acute. Since the more populous areas have always contributed a proportionately larger share of the state revenues, while receiving a significantly smaller share in return, some readjustment may be anticipated.

Reapportionment in satisfaction of the equal-population principle will not automatically correct all the weaknesses of the state and local legislative process — even if a consensus could be reached as to the nature of those deficiencies. Final assessment of the practical consequences of reapportionment must in large part await further experience following the return of the decision-making power to the hands of the majority. Nevertheless, even by the conclusion of 1965 legislative sessions in which action was taken by legislatures after reapportionment, preliminary assessment of those sessions was favorable.

The Colorado legislature, at its 1965 session, enacted into law a number of proposals which had long had substantial support in the state, but which had never been able to command a legislative majority. The most important was increased support for education, particularly higher education. In addition, there were such varied items as a fair housing act; legislation to support dissemination of birth control information through health and welfare departments; repeal of sales taxes on food and drugs; institution of daylight savings time (over the opposition of farmers and after-dark recreational establishments in the cities); billboard control; increase in workmen's compensation; and regulation of debt adjusters. One legislator observed that "We passed things which should have been passed 10 years ago. The rural bloc simply sat on the lid too long — and now it's off."

The speaker of the house stated that "the results of reapportionment disproved the worst fears of its opponents. There was no anti-rural campaign or punitive actions, nor did the urban and suburban

131. Hacker, Votes Cast and Seats Won, Trans-Action 7, 29 (Sept.–Oct. 1964).

control turn out to be that of dangerous radicals, even from the Republican point of view. . . . The need for change and modernization in the social order was recognized and change itself was no longer as frightening a concept." Another representative commented that "the first good, strong annexation law . . . in Colorado has been passed, in addition to broad new legislative expenditures to upgrade the entire educational program in the suburban and urban Denver area. All of these bills passed very easily and had been heavily defeated in previous sessions."

In Delaware the reapportioned legislature, after a thirteen-year campaign, approved the state's first minimum wage law, a wage payment and collection law, and improved workmen's compensation legislation.

In Michigan the following legislation was enacted which in each case had been rejected before reapportionment: an increase in unemployment benefits; amendments designed to improve the workmen's compensation law; and enlarged support for mental health, including ratification of an interstate compact on mental health. In addition, the largest school supplement bill in state history was approved, as well as the most substantial advance in state conservation programs. Interestingly enough, much legislation was approved benefiting rural areas. The legislative counsel for the Farm Bureau in Michigan said the legislative record demonstrated a friendliness to agriculture's needs and was "especially productive of good farm legislation." Finally, the legislature even took steps to increase its own efficiency. The speaker of the house said: "For the first time, we truly have a committee system in operation. Committees are no longer functioning as rubber-stamp, bill-passing groups; they have learned the particular area of state government assigned to them."

Despite the somewhat self-serving nature of the above testimonials, and the fact that not all would approve the apparent extension of legislation aimed at social welfare, it cannot be doubted that these actions, comparable to developments in Congress and in other states, reflect present-day majority preferences. And who is to deny that legislatures should ordinarily serve those ends?

WHAT OF THE FUTURE?

It has been the theme of this volume that the *Reapportionment Cases* have opened the way for revitalization of representative democracy in the United States at the national, state, and even local levels. The requirement of substantial equality among election districts is a matter of the first importance, but obviously does not resolve all problems. The solution must ultimately lie in the return to responsible government by legislative bodies at every level. With this in mind, it is here suggested that the procedures for apportionment and districting should be substantially insulated from the seriously distorting pressures of partisan politics. Manifestly, the process should not be — and could not be — entirely divorced from political considerations. Yet surely it should now be possible, in light of the constitutional requirement of equality and the desirability of anti-gerrymander provisions, to turn much of the apportionment and districting process over to nonpartisan bodies. The following criteria are suggested for a nonpartisan apportionment commission at the state level:

1. Representation should be accorded to the leading political parties so long as persons not specifically involved in political pursuits are represented in adequate numbers. Such nonpolitical representatives might be nominated to the appointing authority by presidents of leading universities or other respected bodies.

2. Less than a majority of the entire commission membership should be drawn from legislative or other official positions.

3. The commission should be entrusted with complete responsibility for the apportionment and districting functions, subject only to adequate opportunity for judicial review to test compliance with whatever standards are specified (see below).

4. Standards to govern apportionment and districting should include the following:

   a. Each district should be as nearly equal in population as practicable.

   b. Each district should be composed of as compact and contiguous an area as practicable.

   c. To the extent practicable and consistent with the foregoing standards, local political subdivision lines should be followed.

   d. Districts should be drawn without respect to the strength of any political party as reflected by enrollment, votes for candidates in any election, or any similar criteria.

There is nothing intrinsically difficult about drawing legislative representation district lines to satisfy the equal-population principle even while following local political subdivision lines to a substantial extent. Indeed, these already-existing lines make the task simpler so long as rigid adherence to any one such set of lines, such as county lines, is not required. City, township, village, census tract, or even ward and precinct lines may sometimes be more meaningful. The practice of adhering to existing lines is also helpful in minimizing the always-present risk of the gerrymander.

Mechanical help is available, and will probably be more widely used in the future, at least to draw preliminary lines in conformity with whatever standards are predetermined as basic. It has already been demonstrated that computers can do this task;[132] and some courts have indicated willingness to use the services of computer experts.[133]

It is not suggested that adoption of these procedures would immediately cure all the ailments that now afflict the legislative process. But at least two of the besetting problems — malapportionment and gerrymandering — could be sufficiently limited to provide an opportunity for representative democracy to assert once more its potential for effective government. It should be given the opportunity.

132. Extensive computer studies have been conducted by James B. Weaver and Sidney W. Hess in Wilmington, Delaware. See Hess and Weaver, A Procedure for Nonpartisan Districting: Development of Computer Techniques, 73 Yale L.S. 288 (1963). See also Nagel and Kaiser, Simplified Computer Redistricting (mimeo. 1964).

133. See Sincock v. Roman, 233 F. Supp. 615, 619, (D. Del. 1964); Butterworth v. Dempsey, 237 F. Supp. 302, 313 (D. Conn. 1965).

ple even while following local political and litigation lines to a
significant degree. Indeed, these already existing functional networks
simply so long as local adherence to any one such set of lines had
account was not required. They newship village could meet
or comprised and present—that may sometimes be born meaningful.
The practice of adhering to existing lines is also helpful in maintaining the slowly increasing trust of the gainmaker.

Technical help is available to and will probably be more widely
used in the future, at least to many preliminary lines to confront
with weaker and larger production in the bill. It has already
been demonstrated that computers can do this task, and some
courts have indicated their readiness to use the services of competent
persons.

It is not suggested that adoption of these procedures would immediately cure all the difficulties in our society. And availability of
aids that assist most of the resolving problem of communication and
and power interests. It will thus substantially limited to provide im-
portunity that presumably are either seriously negotiated or resolved at the level of the nation — should be given the opportunity.

40. For comparative discussions have been considered to appear in the record and
report. This will balance between industrial and scientific ... 1950. Also consider Coney Seen
Frugal Distinguishing Directions of Commerce. In Aparicio (ed.) Vol. 1.5 of the Section
of the source and references to Disputants Facts. Sch. Nairobi (eg.)
41. Range considerations, with Chapter 5 ... ...Disputants, and 1995 Source with
Disputants Advances Sciences as the Commission.

Appendix:

State Summaries

ALABAMA

By act of Congress in 1819 the inhabitants of the territory of Alabama (formerly the eastern part of the territory of Mississippi) were authorized to form a constitution and state government. All white male citizens over twenty-one years of age were authorized to participate in the choice of 44 delegates to a constitutional convention, to be selected from the then 22 counties, each of which was allocated from one to eight representatives in the convention depending on population. Congress specified that the government, "when formed shall be republican, and not repugnant" to the principles of the Northwest Ordinance of 1787 (art. II), which provided for "a proportionate representation of the people in the Legislature." The constitution of 1819, adopted by the convention, ratified by the people, and approved by Congress, provided for single-member senate districts which were to be "as nearly equal, in the number of white inhabitants, as may be" and for a house of representatives whose districts should be fixed on the basis of an apportionment "among the several counties, cities, or towns, entitled to separate representation, according to their respective numbers of white inhabitants," so long as "each county shall be entitled to at least one representative." Ala. Const. of 1819, art. III, §§ 9, 10. These provisions continued essentially unchanged through the succeeding constitutions of 1861, 1865, 1868, 1875, and into the present constitution of 1901, except that the maximum number of representatives was increased over the years from 60 to 100 and finally to 105 (plus one for any newly created county), and the maximum number of senators was increased from 20 to 35. The merits of the final increase, in the constitution of 1901, from 100 to 105 in the house, and from 33 to 35 in the senate, were debated with candor in the constitutional convention of 1901. The primary purpose seems to have been to make the white population distribution more nearly equal among the election districts, a matter more readily achieved with the larger number in each house. Moreover, as one delegate stated in regard to the increase in the house: "I want to say further that these five representatives will go to the white counties. Something has been said about the black belt getting a majority. I want to say that everyone [sic] will go to white counties." Proceedings of the Constitutional Convention of 1901, p. 2345.

The constitution of 1901 provided for a house of representatives of not more than 105 members except in the event of the creation of new counties, each of which was allocated one representative. Art. IX, § 198. Each county (now 67) was assured at least one representative. Art. IX, § 199. Only one new county, Houston, has been created since 1901. Accordingly, in 1962 the membership of the house of representatives was 106. See Comment, Alabama's Unrepresentative Legislature, 14 Ala. L. Rev. 403, 404 (1962).

The constitution provides for apportionment of the house of representatives by the legislature according to the number of inhabitants in the counties of the state as ascertained by the United States decennial census. Art. IX, § 198. The legislature has a duty to apportion at its first session after each decennial census (art. IX, § 199); and the apportionment, once made, is not "subject to alteration" until the legislative session after the next United States decennial census (art. IX, § 198).

The number of senators cannot be

less than one fourth nor more than one third of the whole number of representatives (art. IX, § 197), and therefore the senate can be no more than 35. The legislature is to divide the state into senatorial districts which "shall be as nearly equal to each other in the number of inhabitants as may be, and each shall be entitled to one senator, and no more . . . ." Art. IX, § 200. "No county shall be divided between two districts, and no district shall be made up of two or more counties not contiguous to each other." Art. IX, § 200. Section 284 further provides that "Representation in the legislature shall be based upon population, and such basis of representation shall not be changed by constitutional amendments."

Sections 202 and 203 of article IX fixed the apportionment of representatives among the counties and the senators among the senatorial districts "[u]ntil the legislature shall make an apportionment" for the house and "divide the state into senatorial districts . . . ." However, the legislature did not reapportion or redistrict until 1962. In July of that year the legislature advanced two reapportionment plans to become effective in 1966. One was a constitutional amendment proposed for submission to the voters in November 1962, known as the "67-Senator Amendment," which provided for a house of 106 members, allocating one seat to each of the 67 counties and distributing the others according to population by the equal proportions method. The senate was to be composed of 67 members, one from each county.

The "Crawford-Webb Act" was approved by the legislature to take effect in 1966 if the "67-Senator Amendment" should not be approved either by the voters or by the courts. Under this act the senate would have had 35 members

chosen from an equal number of districts, established along county lines, but somewhat different from the then-existing districts. The statute apportioned the 106 house seats along county lines, giving 48 counties one representative each with varying numbers for the remaining 19 counties, ranging up to 12 for Jefferson County.

Before the Supreme Court decision in *Baker v. Carr*, 369 U.S. 186 (1962), every effort to compel legislative compliance with the state constitutional requirement for reapportionment every ten years substantially in accordance with the population distribution was rejected in the courts. In 1951 the supreme court of Alabama dismissed a bill to enjoin the secretary of state from issuing certificates of election to candidates for the house, holding that recourse "should be made to the legislature and to the people of the State, not to the Court." *Waid v. Pool*, 255 Ala. 441, 443, 51 So.2d 869, 870 (1951). A suit in federal court, alleging denial of due process and equal protection of the laws, as well as violation of federal civil rights statutes, was dismissed for lack of jurisdiction because of the "political nature" of the controversy. "The duty of apportioning representation in the legislature is thus made to rest exclusively with the legislature itself." *Perry v. Folsom*, 144 F. Supp. 874, 876 (N.D. Ala. 1956), quoting from *Opinion of the Justices of the Supreme Court of Alabama, No. 145*, 263 Ala. 153, 81 So. 2d 697, 698 (1955).

Meanwhile, the state supreme court interpreted some of the apportionment provisions of the constitution in nonbinding advisory opinions. In *Opinion of the Justices of the Supreme Court of Alabama, No. 117*, 254 Ala. 185, 47 So.2d 714 (1950) the court gave its opinion that the legislature cannot initiate amendments to the constitution which would change the basis of representation to other than a population basis; the legislature may apportion itself in a special extraordinary session; and the duty to apportion is not limited to the first session of the legislature after the United States decennial census. In *Opinion of the Justices of the Supreme Court of Alabama, No. 148*, 263 Ala. 158, 81 So.2d 881 (1955) a majority of the court gave somewhat different advice, this time to the effect that the legislature has the power to propose a constitutional amendment to repeal the last sentence of article XVIII, section 284, providing that "Representation in the legislature shall be based upon population, and such basis of representation shall not be changed by constitutional amendments." The court concluded that ultimate sovereignty rests with the people, who can thus lawfully remove any provision which they previously put in the constitution. In the same case the court advised that the legislature cannot delegate its duty of reapportionment to a board of reapportionment.

There is no provision in the Alabama constitution for initiative and referendum as to constitutional provisions, and no provision for the convening of a constitutional convention. Only the legislature can propose constitutional amendments, even though article I, section 2 of the constitution provides that "all political power is inherent in the people . . . and . . . therefore, they have at all times an inalienable and indefeasible right to change their form of government . . . ."

In August 1961 fourteen citizens and taxpayers, residents and registered voters of Jefferson County, Alabama, filed suit in their own behalf and in behalf of all other voters similarly situated,

against the secretary of state, the attorney general, and other elected officials charged in various ways with responsibility for the state election process. The complaint alleged deprivation of rights under the Alabama constitution and under the equal protection clause of the fourteenth amendment, asserting jurisdiction under the Civil Rights Act, 42 U.S.C. §§ 1983, 1988, and under 28 U.S.C. § 1343. The three-judge federal district court which was convened to hear the case granted leave to intervene as intervenor-plaintiffs to three groups of Alabama voters from Jefferson, Mobile, and Etowah Counties. Three days after the decision in *Baker v. Carr* plaintiffs moved for a preliminary injunction requiring defendants to conduct at large the May 1962 primary elections and the November 1962 general elections of the legislature. In April 1962 the court denied relief "until the Legislature has had a further reasonable but prompt opportunity to comply with its duty" of reapportionment; and the case was reset for hearing in July 1962. *Sims v. Frink*, 205 F. Supp. 245, 247 (M.D. Ala. 1962).

By the time of the July hearing the legislature had met in special session and had enacted the two proposals to become effective in 1966, discussed above. However, the court found the existing apportionment and each of the proposals constitutionally defective.

Based on the 1960 census figures the disparity in number of persons represented by members of the lower house varied from 104,767 in Mobile County to 6,731 in Bullock County; and the senatorial districts varied from 15,417 in district number 16 (Lowndes County) to 314,301 in district number 33 (Mobile County). Accordingly, the court concluded that the existing apportionment was invalid. The court called attention to the fact that section 284 of the Alabama constitution provides for representation in the legislature to be based on population. Moreover, the court ruled that neither the proposed constitutional amendment nor the 1962 legislative act met the standards of the United States Constitution. The court noted that the "67-Senator" proposal was even more discriminatory than the existing apportionment because it provided for one senator from each county without regard to population. The Crawford-Webb Act, while "a step in the right direction," was found too short a step to satisfy ultimate constitutional requirements in that it would still leave substantial imbalance. But it was accepted in regard to the senate as a temporary expedient for the 1962 election, pending later legislative correction. As to the house the court adopted as a part of its order those portions of the "67-Senator Amendment" relating to the house of representatives which proposed apportionment of seats in that house by the equal proportions method, thus eliminating the most gross inequalities. The court retained jurisdiction pending more equitable apportionment by the legislature. *Sims v. Frink*, 208 F. Supp. 431 (M.D. Ala. 1962).

On June 15, 1964, the Supreme Court of the United States affirmed the judgment of the three-judge district court and remanded the case to that court for such further proceedings as might be necessary before the next (1966) election of Alabama legislators "should the reapportioned Alabama Legislature fail to enact a constitutionally valid, permanent apportionment scheme in the interim . . . ." *Reynolds v. Sims*, 377 U.S. 533, 587 (1964). (That decision is fully discussed in chapter V of the text.) The legislature, during its 1964 session, took no action other than to memorialize

Congress to propose a constitutional amendment to limit the effect of the decision (Ala. H.J. Res. 5, Aug. 13, 1964) and to enact "stop-gap" legislation to stay further court rulings until a constitutional amendment could be proposed (Ala. H.J. Res. 12, Aug. 13, 1964).

On September 23, 1965, the Alabama legislature, in an effort to satisfy the equal-population standard, approved legislation to reapportion both houses. The act was sent to the governor and to the federal court to review for compliance with its earlier order. The act provided for some districts of more than one county in both houses. For the lower house it was provided that in specified multi-county districts, no more than one representative could come from a single county. Mobile Register, Sept. 24, 1965, p. 1, col. 1.

On the basis of the 1960 census the congressional delegation from Alabama was reduced from nine to eight, thereby making inoperative the existing congressional districts. The Alabama legislature was unable to agree in 1961 on new district lines and therefore provided for election at large for the eight congressional seats on the basis of a "9-8 plan." Each of the nine previous districts was retained for the purpose of conducting primaries. The nine thus nominated then ran at large in a primary run-off to eliminate the low man in determining the eight party nominees for the general election. In *Alsup v. Mayhall*, 208 F. Supp. 713 (S.D. Ala. 1962) the validity of this act was challenged by a voter of Mobile County. Rejecting plaintiff's arguments, the court concluded that elections at large did not amount to arbitrary action in violation of the fourteenth amendment. In 1964, after the United States Supreme Court decision in *Wesberry v. Sanders*, 376 U.S. 1 (1964), a three-judge federal district court held the "9–8" plan unconstitutional and enjoined its use after 1964, although not necessarily forbidding its use for the congressional elections in that year for which the election machinery was already in motion. *Moore v. Moore*, 229 F. Supp. 435 (S.D. Ala. 1964).

In August 1964 the legislature enacted a new districting statute providing for eight single-member districts to be effective beginning with the 1964 congressional elections. County lines were not crossed; the population differential between the largest and smallest was 149,635 for a ratio of 1.4 to 1 between the most populous and the least populous districts. Ala. Laws, 1st Spec. Sess. 1964, Act No. 21. Interestingly, five Republicans were elected in 1964. On April 16, 1965, a three-judge federal court held this differential too great and advised that it would provide its own remedy if corrective action were not taken at the 1965 legislative session. N.Y. Times, April 17, 1965, p. 9, col. 4.

In August 1965 the Alabama legislature approved, and the governor signed, a congressional redistricting act with population differentials among the eight districts ranging between zero and 7.3 per cent from the population ratio. Ala. Laws 1965, S.B. 208. Jefferson County (Birmingham) was divided among three districts, prompting claims of gerrymander and revival of the federal court action in *Moore v. Moore*, supra.

REFERENCES

Alabama Legislative Reference Service. Reapportionment. Montgomery: August 1954.
Havens, Murray C. City Versus Farm? Urban-Rural Conflict in the Alabama Legislature, Bureau of Public Administration, University of Alabama: 1957.
Larsen, James E. Reapportionment in Alabama. Bureau of Public Administration, University of Alabama: 1955.
——. Reapportionment and the Courts. Bureau of Public Administration, University of Alabama: 1962.
Comment, Alabama's Unrepresentative Legislature, 14 Ala. L. Rev. 403 (1962).

ALASKA

Although purchased from Russia in 1867, the Alaska territory was not given any legislative authority of its own until 1912 in the Organic Act of 1912 (37 Stat. 513). That act provided for a bicameral legislature consisting of a house of representatives of 16 members and a senate of 8 members. For thirty-two years two senators and four representatives were elected at large from the four judicial divisions into which the territory was divided, and the remaining legislators were divided equally among the four divisions. By a 1942 amendment to the Organic Act (56 Stat. 1016), effective for the election of 1944, the senate was increased to a membership of 16, and the house to a membership of 24, the latter apportioned on the basis of estimated civilian population. The 1942 act also provided for reapportionment of seats by the United States Director of the Census after the 1950 decennial census; and the territorial legislature was authorized to provide for legislative districting within the judicial divisions.

In 1951 the Director of the Census reapportioned the house seats on the basis of the civilian population reported in the 1950 census, with the following results:

Judicial Division	Apportionment 1944–1951	Apportionment 1952–1958
First	8	6
Second	4	3
Third	7	10
Fourth	5	5
	24	24

The apportionment and districting for the election of the 55 delegates to the constitutional convention of 1955–1956 anticipated the provisions of the Alaska constitution on that point. The 22 election districts were of three types: (1) The 17 one-member districts were based on existing districts or combinations of those districts. (2) Each of the four judicial divisions constituted a multimember district, as follows: first division 7; second division 4; third division 12; and fourth division 8. (3) The territory as a whole constituted one district from which seven delegates-at-large were elected.

Alaska was admitted to statehood by proclamation dated January 3, 1959, on the basis of the constitution drafted in the 1955 constitutional convention. Pursuant to that constitution the Alaska legislature is divided into a house of representatives of 40 members and a senate of 20. Alaska Const., art. II, § 1. Reapportionment is an executive function, to be performed by the governor immediately following each United States decennial census. Art. VI, § 3. The governor can appoint a reapportionment board of five members to act in an advisory capacity, which must include one member from each of the four senate districts. Art. VI, § 8. The board must submit a report to the governor within ninety days following the official reporting of each census; and the governor must, by proclamation, reapportion or redistrict within ninety days thereafter. Art. VI, § 10. Any qualified voter may apply to the superior court to compel the governor, "by mandamus or otherwise," to perform his reapportionment duties. Art. VI, § 11.

Apportionment of the house is primarily by population. "Reapportionment shall be by the method of equal proportions." Art. VI, § 4. Originally the state was divided into 24 election districts. Art. XIV, § 1. Then the total civilian population was divided by 40

and "each election district having the major fraction of the quotient obtained" was allotted one representative. Art. VI, § 4. If "the total civilian population of any election district falls below one-half of the quotient," provision is made for attaching the district to another election district "within its senate district, and the reapportionment for the new district shall be determined as provided in Section 4 of this article." Art. VI, § 5. After publication of the 1960 census results, the governor accepted the recommendations of his advisory board on apportionment and reduced the number of districts to 19, thereby meeting more nearly the population standard fixed in article VI, section 4.

Apportionment of the senate is a combination of area and population, with the emphasis on area. The state was originally divided into 16 senate districts (art. XIV, § 2), which were continued in the 1961 reapportionment.

The governor is allowed to change the size and area of election districts, but each district must "be formed of contiguous and compact territory containing as nearly as practical a relatively integrated socio-economic area. Each shall contain a population at least equal to the quotient obtained by dividing the total civilian population by forty. Consideration may be given to local government boundaries. Drainage and other geographic features shall be used in describing boundaries wherever possible." Art. VI, § 6. Senate districts may be modified to reflect changes in election districts. Art. VI, § 7.

The report of the committee on suffrage, elections, and apportionment to the Alaska constitutional convention stated in a letter of December 17, 1955, to the president of the convention that "These [election] districts are economic units of the Territory and may be compared in a sense to Swiss cantons. Their boundaries are watersheds wherever possible; waterways and steamship routes are not used as boundaries, but are considered as highways piercing valleys." Alaska Legislative Council, *Legislative Apportionment in Alaska 1912–1961*, Appendix B, p. 2.

Despite substantial population disparities in the senate (19 to 1) and in the house (2.5 to 1), no legal action had been instituted by September of 1965. On September 3, 1965, the governor promulgated a new reapportionment plan for the senate designed to satisfy the equal-population principle. Each of the 11 senate districts (composed of one or two election districts) was given one senator except Anchorage (seven) and Fairbanks (four). No change was made in the house districts as promulgated in 1961.

Amendments to the constitution are proposed by the legislature. Art. XIII, § 1. The legislature may also call constitutional conventions at any time. Art. XIII, § 2. However, if a constitutional convention has not been held in ten years the secretary of state is directed to place a referendum on the ballot asking "Shall there be a Constitutional Convention?" If a majority of voters answer in the affirmative, a convention of plenary powers will be called. Art. XIII, § 3. Amendments or revisions proposed by a constitutional convention must be proposed to the people for ratification. Art. XIII, § 4.

The initiative and referendum (for statutes) are provided for in article XI, sections 1–8.

The whole of Alaska constitutes a single congressional district.

REFERENCES

Alaska Legislative Council. *Legislative Apportionment in Alaska 1912–1961*. Juneau: April 1962.

ARIZONA

By act of Congress in 1910 the qualified electors of the territory of Arizona were authorized to organize a constitutional convention consisting of 52 delegates to be apportioned "as nearly as may be, equitably among the several counties in accordance with the voting population . . . ." Sec. 19. It was further provided that "The constitution shall be republican in form and . . . shall not be repugnant to the Constitution of the United States and the principles of the Declaration of Independence." Sec. 20. The convention so provided for was held in 1911, and the resulting constitution was approved by the voters, including an amendment insisted upon by Congress. On February 14, 1912, Arizona was proclaimed a state of the Union "on an equal footing with the other States . . . ."

As originally adopted, the Arizona constitution established a house of representatives of 35 members and a senate of 19 members, providing that each of the 14 counties should have at least one senator and one representative, the additional seats being apportioned in accordance with the then population distribution. Art. IV, pt. 2, § 1. Although the section was amended in 1918, 1932, and 1948, it was not until 1953 that section 1 took its present form (there having been no senate reapportionment since 1912), providing for the election of two senators at large from each of the 14 counties. The house of representatives was also increased in numbers, but "not to exceed eighty members, to be apportioned to the counties according to the number of ballots cast in each county at the preceding general election for governor . . . ." Apportionment is to be every four years "on the basis of one Representative for each county and one additional

Representative for each thirty-five hundred and twenty ballots cast at the last preceding general election, according to the official canvass of the votes cast in each county." If the above formula results in more than 80 representatives, the 3,520 unit of apportionment is to be increased by ten or a multiple of ten to reduce the number of representatives to 80. Art. IV, pt. 2, § 1(1).

Apportionment is an executive function in that the secretary of state is to notify the board of supervisors in each county of the number of representatives it will be entitled to elect, and the board is to "divide the county into as many legislative districts as there are Representatives to be elected. The district shall have as nearly as may be an equal voting population, be compact in form, and include no non-contiguous territory." Ibid.

Amendments to the Arizona constitution may be proposed by the legislature or by initiative petition. Art. XXI, § 1. Provisions for initiative and referendum appear in article IV, part 1, sections 1(1), (2), (3). However, constitutional conventions cannot be called by the legislature unless the people, by referendum, first approve laws providing for the convention. Art. XXI, § 2.

Article XXII, section 12 provides for one congressional representative to be elected from the state at large. Arizona Revised Statutes § 16-727A provided for two congressional districts, while § 16-727B divides the state into three congressional districts "if and when" Arizona becomes entitled to three representatives in Congress, as it did in 1960. Three representatives were elected from the prescribed districts in 1962 and 1964. The first district, consisting of Maricopa County, had a 1960 population of 663,510, and the second and

third districts respectively had 1960 populations of 440,415 and 198,236.

The invalidity of the apportionment formula in the Arizona legislature and of the congressional districting plan was readily apparent after the Supreme Court decision in *Reynolds v. Sims*, 377 U.S. 533 (1964) and *Wesberry v. Sanders*, 376 U.S. 1 (1964). However, in light of the already-commenced election procedures a three-judge federal district court in June 1964 stayed the proceedings in an action challenging the existing plan. *Klahr v. Fannin*, Civ. No. 5112, Phoenix (D. Ariz. 1964). Shortly thereafter the Governor's Committee on Legislative Reapportionment began regular meetings leading to its report and recommendations of December 1964. The committee recommended (1) that reapportionment and redistricting be based on voter registration figures rather than population, in part because it would then be possible to reapportion and redistrict every two years rather than every ten years; (2) that the congressional districts be equalized by crossing county lines, including division of Maricopa County (Phoenix) between two congressional districts; (3) that each congressional district be divided into 9 senatorial and 27 representative districts for a senate of 27 and a house of representatives of 81; (4) that a state board of elections be established by statute with authority to fix the election districts by March 31 of each election year.

In preparation for a special session of the legislature contemplated for the fall of 1965, the Joint Committee of the Senate and the House agreed to leave the house apportionment unchanged until after the 1970 census (because of substantial, but uncharted population shifts since 1960). In the special session the legislature reapportioned the senate, allotting 13 senators to Maricopa County, 5 to Pima County, 2 to Pinal County, and 1 to each of the other 11 counties. Plaintiffs in the federal suit renewed their challenge to both houses.

REFERENCES

Bingham, David A. Arizona's New "Third": A Look at Congressional Reapportionment, 12 Arizona Review of Business and Public Research 1 (May 1963).
———. "Legislative Apportionment: The Arizona Experience," 11 Arizona Review of Business and Public Administration 1 (Oct. 1962).
Mason, Bruce, B. Congressional Redistricting in Arizona. Study No. 2. Tempe. Bureau of Government Research, Arizona State University: 1962.
Mason, Bruce B., and Hink, Heinz R. Constitutional Government in Arizona. Tempe. Bureau of Government Research, Arizona State University: 1963.

ARKANSAS

The land which is now the state of Arkansas was originally ceded by France in a treaty of purchase in 1803 and became successively part of the district (later territory) of Louisiana, the territory of Missouri, and finally, in 1819, the territory of Arkansas. In January 1836 a convention of delegates of the people of the territory of Arkansas prepared a constitution and petitioned Congress to admit the territory into the Union as a state. Congress, having found the constitution and government so formed to be republican, admitted Arkansas as a state by an enabling act and a supplemental enabling act, both approved in 1836.

That first constitution of Arkansas provided for division of the state into 17 senatorial districts (with authorization to expand the membership to a maximum of 33), "based upon the free white male inhabitants of the State,

each Senator representing an equal number as nearly as practicable . . . ." Ark. Const. of 1836, art. IV, § 31. On that basis the county of Washington was originally allotted two senators in a single district, while each of the other 16 districts included either two or three counties. The house of representatives was to consist originally of 54 representatives (with authorization for expansion to a maximum of 100), "to be apportioned among the several counties in this State, according to the number of free white male inhabitants therein, taking five hundred as the ratio, until the number of representatives amounts to seventy-five; and when they amount to seventy-five, they shall not be further increased until the population of the State amounts to five hundred thousand souls . . . ." Each of the then 34 counties was assured one representative; and the original allocation varied from one to six representatives for each county. Id., § 34. In addition, provision was made for an enumeration of the population every four years, to be followed by reapportionment of each house in accordance with the population changes reported. Id., §§ 32, 34.

In 1861 the constitution of 1836 was amended by a state convention, principally by substituting the words "Confederate States" in place of "United States." But this revision was declared null and void by a convention in January 1864, after occupation of a portion of the state by armed forces of the United States; that action was subsequently ratified by the people. The apportionment provisions were essentially unchanged, even the provision that "free white male inhabitants" should be the population measure. Ark. Const. of 1864, art. IV, §§ 31, 32.

In the constitution of 1868 the membership of the legislature was fixed at 26 senators and 82 representatives, with power in the legislature, after ten-year enumerations of population, to "re-arrange the senatorial and representative districts according to the number of inhabitants . . . ." Ark. Const. of 1868, art. IV, §§ 7, 8. It was further provided that senatorial districts "shall be composed of convenient contiguous territory, and no representative district shall be divided in the formation of a senatorial one." Id., § 9.

In the constitution of 1874, flexibility in the size of the legislature was again introduced, providing for a house of 73 to 100 members and a senate of 30 to 35 members. With each of the 73 counties entitled to one representative, provision was included for "the remainder to be apportioned among the several counties according to the number of adult male inhabitants . . . ." Ark. Const. of 1874, art. VIII, § 1. On that basis only one county, Pulaski, was entitled to as many as four representatives in the 93-member house provided for until the next enumeration. Ibid. The 30 senatorial districts initially established included one to four counties, all entitled to one senator except the district composed of Pulaski and Perry Counties, which was allotted two senators. Id., § 2. It was also provided that "no county shall be divided in the formation of a senatorial district." Id., § 3.

By constitutional amendment in 1936 the number of senators was fixed at 35 and representatives at 100. The requirement for one representative to each county and the prohibition against division of counties in the formation of senatorial districts were continued; the mandate to conform otherwise "as nearly as practicable" to population was also continued. In addition, the 1936 amendment established a board of ap-

portionment consisting of the governor, secretary of state, and attorney general to make the apportionment in both houses. Failure to act or abuse of discretion was made subject to correction by an original suit for mandamus in the state supreme court. Art. VIII, § 5. This provision was utilized in *Smith v. Board of Apportionment*, 219 Ark. 611, 243 S.W.2d 755 (1951) to secure a third senator for Pulaski County, the 13th senatorial district. After that decision the board of apportionment made further changes, affecting districts in western and southwestern parts of the state. In *Pickens v. Board of Apportionment*, 220 Ark. 145, 246 S.W.2d 556 (1952), the state supreme court sustained a challenge to that action and ordered reapportionment in accord with its own plan. Thereafter, by initiative petition the decision in the *Pickens* case was written into the state constitution by constitutional amendment in 1956. As a result, the board of apportionment was denied any role in reapportioning the state senate. "Senatorial districts as now constituted and existing, as heretofore directed by the Supreme Court of Arkansas in the case of *Pickens v. Board of Apportionment*, 220 Ark. 145, 246 S.W.2d 556, shall remain the same and the number of Senators from the districts shall not be changed." Art. VIII, § 3.

In apportioning the house of representatives the board of apportionment formerly assigned one representative to each of the present 75 counties. The remaining 25 were to be apportioned by the method of equal proportions, as required in *Shaw v. Adkins*, 202 Ark. 856, 153 S.W.2d 415 (1941). See also the more recent case of *Stevens v. Faubus*, 234 Ark. 826, 354 S.W.2d 707 (1962), where the court stated that "it is to be regretted that no plan has been or ever can be formulated in a situation like this that will be so mathematically balanced that no disparity will exist. But the method of equal proportions is the fairest that has yet been devised to meet the situation that confronts us here." 234 Ark. at 833, 354 S.W.2d at 711.

In January 1965 a three-judge federal district court held invalid the state constitutional provisions for apportionment of the senate (with a population spread from 81,765 to 35,983) and of the house of representatives (with a population spread from 37,087 to 4,927). The defendants, members of the state board of apportionment, who took the position that they had power to make a valid reapportionment, were ordered to do so by June 15, 1965, unless the legislature should take earlier corrective action. *Yancey v. Faubus*, 238 F. Supp. 290 (E.D. Ark. 1965).

The 1965 general assembly adjourned without acting on the matter, whereupon the board of apportionment was granted a one-month delay by the federal court. On July 14, 1965, the board promulgated a new apportionment dividing the state's 75 counties into 44 house districts and 25 senate districts. For the first time in the state's history some counties will have to share a representative with another or other counties. For example, Pulaski County (population 242,980) and adjoining Perry County (population 4,927) will constitute one district with 13 representatives. The senate reapportionment is similar to earlier plans except for rearrangement of counties. The entire plan will require approval of the three-judge federal court before it becomes effective; and at least one small county that is joined to a large county in a multimember district is objecting to approval. Ark. Gazette, July 15, 1965.

Constitutional amendments can be proposed by either house of the legislature and are presented to the people for vote if approved by a majority of both houses, though not more than three amendments may be proposed by the general assembly in one biennium. Art. XIX, § 22. An unlimited number of amendments may also be proposed by initiative petitions. Art. V, § 1 (amendment VII, § 1).

As a result of the 1950 and 1960 census figures, Arkansas lost one representative in Congress after 1950 and two after 1960. In each instance the legislature promptly redistricted by statute. Ark. Stat. Ann. §§ 3-509 to 3-515 (1951) and §§ 3-516 to 3-520 (1961). The four districts created in 1961 varied in 1960 population from 332,844 to 575,385. The differential of 242,541 was found excessive by a three-judge federal district court in February 1965, which enjoined the holding of further elections based on the invalid districts. The court indicated that it would not itself draw district lines and would indeed not object if future congressional elections should be held at large, as authorized by 2 U.S.C. § 2a(c)(5) (1958). *Park v. Faubus*, 238 F. Supp. 62 (E.D. Ark. 1965).

The 1965 general assembly, in a special session, divided the state into four congressional districts without crossing county lines. The population differential among the districts was less than 10,000 Ark. Gazette, May 28, 1965.

CALIFORNIA

After the cession of California to the United States by Mexico in 1848 in the Treaty of Guadalupe Hidalgo, the provisional governor of California called a constitutional convention in Monterey in 1849. The resulting constitution was presented to, and accepted by, Congress, which found the form of government to be "republican" and admitted California into the Union in 1850. That constitution provided for periodic enumerations of the population to "serve as the basis of representation in both houses of the legislature." Cal. Const. of 1849, art. IV, § 28. The assembly was to have from 24 to 36 members until the state population should increase to 100,000, the number of members thereafter to be not less than 30 nor more than 80 (the present number). Id., § 29. The number of senators was fixed as a proportion, neither less than one third nor more than one half the number of members in the assembly. Id., § 6. Both were to be "apportioned among the several counties and districts to be established by law, according to the number of white inhabitants." Id., § 29. Originally, and until 1930, as noted below, both houses of the legislature were apportioned primarily on the basis of population, even though for three decades more than nine tenths of the population was concentrated in northern California. Report of California Study Commission on Senate Apportionment, p. 4 (1962). Reapportionments were made in 1883, 1891, and 1901 to reflect the gradual shift of population to the south. But conflicts between north and south developed in 1911, and the Los Angeles interests joined with rural interests to give Los Angeles all the representation to which it was entitled by population except one assemblyman. Id. at 5–6. "By 1920 rural groups were determined to control at least one house of the Legislature, while the decline of San Francisco tended to encourage an alliance with other northern groups to prevent southern California majorities in both houses." Id. at 6. No reappor-

tionment proved possible; so the respective interests turned to the initiative and placed two measures on the ballot in 1926. The proposal to continue a population base and to establish a reapportionment commission was defeated by a margin of about three to two, while the so-called federal plan, initiated by the California Farm Bureau Federation and supported by other farm groups and by the San Francisco Chamber of Commerce, was approved by a margin of about five to four. Id. at 6–7. The provisions of that amendment, as incorporated into the constitution, are described below.

California was divided into 80 assembly districts which "shall be composed of contiguous territory, and . . . shall be as nearly equal in population as may be." Furthermore, "In the formation of assembly districts no county, or city and county [San Francisco is the only consolidated city and county in the state], shall be divided, unless it contains sufficient population within itself to form two or more districts." In addition, it was forbidden to have a district consisting of a county and a part of another county because section 6 further provided: "nor shall a part of any county, or of any city and county, be united with any other county, or city and county, in forming any assembly or senatorial district." Only citizens are counted in computing the population of any district. Cal. Const., art. IV, § 6.

The Report of the California Assembly Interim Committee on Elections and Reapportionment (1959–1961) made the point (page 38) that "the growth of semi-metropolitan counties is going to force greater inequality of population. More counties are going to fall in the category of having population that easily justifies one full district, but having surplus population not sufficient for two districts. Unless county lines are ignored, surplus populations cannot be attached to underpopulated counties or districts."

California was divided into 40 senatorial districts. In the formation of the districts no county, or city and county, could be divided, nor could parts of counties be united with other counties. No county, or city and county, could contain more than one senatorial district. Not more than three counties of small population could be grouped in a district. Art. IV, § 6. Effective with the apportionment of 1961 there were 27 one-county districts, 8 two-county districts, and 5 three-county districts. The four most populous California counties had 4 of the 40 senators and 47 of the 80 assemblymen.

The legislature is charged with the responsibility of reapportionment every ten years. Until 1965 the senate was apportioned with only the slightest regard to population, as indicated above, while the assembly was apportioned "so as to preserve the assembly districts as nearly equal in population as may be." Art. IV, § 6.

If the legislature should fail to reapportion, a reapportionment commission consisting of the lieutenant governor (chairman), attorney general, state controller, secretary of state, and state superintendent of public instruction is authorized to reapportion according to the provisions of article IV, section 6; and such reapportionment becomes effective immediately as if it "were an act of the legislature." This commission has never functioned. Cal. Interim Report, p. 85.

Amendments to the constitution are proposed by the legislature and ratified by the people. Art. XVIII, § 1. Two thirds of each legislative branch may recommend to the voters the calling of a constitutional convention; if a majority approves, the legislature is to provide for calling the convention. The delegates "shall be chosen in the same manner, and have the same qualifications, as members of the Legislature." Art. XVIII, § 2.

The initiative and the referendum are provided for in article IV, section 1. Signatures of 8 per cent of the number of voters in the last gubernatorial election are required for the initiative. The referendum is made specifically applicable to the reapportionment of assembly and senatorial districts in article IV, section 6. There is no such specific provision as to congressional districts; but the United States Supreme Court, in *Davis v. Hildebrant*, 241 U.S. 565 (1916), held an Ohio congressional districting act subject to a referendum; and the California reapportionment commission assumes the same would be true in California. Cal. Interim Report, p. 86.

The constitutional apportionment formula for the senate was challenged in *Yorty v. Anderson*, 33 Cal. Rptr. 97, 384 P.2d 417 (1963), appeal dismissed for want of jurisdiction, 379 U.S. 8 (1964), by taxpayers and qualified voters resident in Los Angeles in an original proceeding in mandamus in the state supreme court to compel defendants, as members of the reapportionment commission, to convene and reapportion the state senatorial districts. Although the court did not rule on the validity of article IV, section 6, it dismissed the petition on the ground that the reapportionment commission lacked power to act *after* the legislature had reapportioned in 1961 for the period following the 1960 census. Instead, the power of the commission to act is conditioned upon the *failure* of the legislature to act. The court made it clear that the validity of the 1961 apportionment could be tested "in an appropriate proceeding against [the secretary of state] such as mandamus . . . ." 33 Cal. Rptr. at 100, 384 P.2d at 420. In fact, as the court further noted, a suit of that precise nature had been instituted in federal court in July 1962. After the court ruled in that case that it had jurisdiction, plaintiff filed a stipulation agreeing to dismissal of the suit if a pending initiative petition (providing for apportionment of the senatorial districts in accordance with population) should be approved by the voters in November 1962. The initiative proposal was defeated, and the case was ultimately heard on the merits. After the decision in *Reynolds v. Sims*, 377 U.S. 533 (1964) the three-judge federal district court inevitably concluded that the California senate formula was invalid. *Silver v. Jordan*, 241 F. Supp. 576 (S.D. Calif. 1964). The court ordered the California legislature to take corrective action by July 1, 1965; and the court retained jurisdiction to prescribe its own remedy if the legislature failed to act. The Supreme Court of the United States affirmed on June 1, 1965. 381 U.S. 415 (1965). When the California legislature did not meet its July 1 deadline, the court extended the time to October 1, 1965, to permit the state supreme court to act.

Meanwhile, the California Constitutional Revision Commission, consisting of 20 legislators and 43 other citizens, continued its review begun in 1963 of recommendations for constitutional change for submission to the legislature in 1965, including a new draft of article IV, the article dealing with the legislature and the initiative and referendum.

The necessity for legislative reapportionment brought forth several proposals, presumably ironic, for dividing California into two states, along the line of the Tehachapi Mountains, so that Los Angeles and 6 counties (population 10.5 million) would be one state and San Francisco and 51 counties (population 8.1 million) would be another. N.Y. Times, Feb. 14, 1965, p. E 10, col. 1. In May 1965 the senate approved a reapportionment bill, continuing the senate membership at 40, but dividing the state into 24 districts based more or less on population. N.Y. Times, May 11, 1965, p. 28, col. 1. But the two houses were unable to agree on this or any other plan, and the legislature adjourned *sine die*.

On September 1, 1965, the state supreme court announced "temporary" reapportionment plans for both houses to be effective in 1965 if the legislature should fail to enact valid plans by December 9, 1965. On October 21, 1965, the legislature completed reapportionment of the senate, cutting northern California's seats from 31 to 18 and increasing southern California's share from 9 to 22. Lesser changes were made in 58 of the 80 house districts. N.Y. Times, Oct. 24, 1965, p. 55, col. 3. Although the principle of equality was approximately satisfied, charges of partisan gerrymander were advanced.

In *Griffin v. Board of Supervisors of Monterey County*, 33 Cal. Rptr. 101, 384 P.2d 421 (1963), decided the same day as *Yorty v. Anderson*, supra, the California Supreme Court directed the board of supervisors of Monterey County to reapportion the five supervisorial districts of the county to satisfy the statutory requirement that the district be "as nearly equal in population as may be." Although the board was permitted to give "subsidiary effect" to "(a) topography, (b) geography, (c) cohesiveness, contiguity, integrity, and compactness of territory, and (d) community of interests of the districts," (33 Cal. Rptr. at 102–103. 384 P.2d at 422–423), the court found excessive the population disparities ranging from 938 voters in the least populous supervisorial district to 34,059 in the most populous.

The legislature responded to *Griffin* by enacting in 1964 a bill requiring that after each decennial census each general-law county board of supervisors shall adjust district boundaries to be "as nearly equal in population as may be." The bill also provides that the population in any three of the five districts must always equal at least 50 per cent of the total county population. If the board of supervisors fails to act by a specified date (including an initial date in 1965 for most counties), a commission consisting of the county assessor, the district attorney, and the county clerk (if an elected official) shall perform the task. Cal. Code Ann. §§ 25001–25001.4 (Supp. 1964).

The legislature also proposed a constitutional amendment, which was approved by the voters in November 1964, making the provisions of the law applicable to charter home-rule counties as well as to the general-law counties.

Article IV, section 27 provides for congressional districting subject to the following limitations: (1) congressional districts composed of two or more counties cannot be separated by any county belonging to another district; (2) counties may be divided into as many congressional districts as justified by population; (3) parts of counties may be attached to contiguous counties only after at least one entire congressional district has been formed, leaving a residue of population; (4) in dividing a county, or city and county, into congressional districts, no assembly district shall be divided so as to form a part of more than one congressional district; and (5) "every such Congressional district shall be composed of compact contiguous assembly districts."

Periodic redrawing of congressional district lines is not required by the constitution, and the reapportionment commission has no duties in this connection. But so long as California's population increases at a greater rate than that of other states, it is likely that congressional districts will be redrawn every ten years to provide for the new representatives.

The 1961 districting, based on 1960 census figures, left a population differential among the districts of 287,761. In September 1965 the state supreme court dismissed without prejudice a challenge to the congressional districts, but indicated the necessity for redrawing of district lines and invited resubmission if the legislature should fail to act by the end of its regular session in 1967. *Silver v. Brown*, — Cal. Rptr. —, — P.2d — (1965).

REFERENCES

Assembly Committee on Elections and Reapportionment. Reapportionment in California: Consultants' Report to the Assembly. Vol. 7, No. 9. Sacramento: 1965.

Assembly Interim Committee on Elections and Apportionment. Report for 1959–1961. Vol. 7, No. 5. Sacramento: 1961.

Assembly Interim Committee on Elections and Apportionment, Final Report to the Assembly. Vol. 7, No. 8. Sacramento: 1965.

Study Commission on Senate Apportionment. Report. Sacramento: 1962.

Hall, Stuart. County Supervisorial Districting in California. Bureau of Public Administration, University of California: 1961.

Baker, Gordon E. "The California Senate: Sectional Conflict and *Vox Populi*," in Jewell, Malcolm E. (ed.). The Politics of Reapportionment. New York: Atherton Press. 1962.

Gallagher, John F. Supervisorial Districting in California Counties 1960-1963. Institute of Governmental Affairs, University of California, Davis: October 1963.

Hinderaker, Ivan and Waters, Laughlin E. A Case Study in Apportionment — California 1951, 17 Law & Contemp. Prob. 440 (1952).

Pitchell, Robert J. Reapportionment as a Control of Voting in California, 14 W. Pol. Q. 214 (1961).

Stoffers, William H. Reapportionment in California Counties, 4 Santa Clara Law. 201 (1964).

Way, Frank H. California: "Brutal Butchery of the Two-Party System?" in Jewell, Malcolm E. (ed.). The Politics of Reapportionment. New York: Atherton Press. 1962.

COLORADO

The territory of Colorado, composed of portions of the territories of Kansas, Nebraska, New Mexico, and Utah, was organized and provided a territorial government by act of Congress in 1861. Legislative power was vested in the governor and a bicameral legislative assembly consisting of a council of 9 (to 13) members and a house of representatives of 13 (to 26) members. Provision was made for an apportionment "as nearly equal as practicable, among the several counties or districts for the election of the council and house of representatives, giving to each section of the Territory representation in the ratio of its population (Indians excepted) as nearly as may be . . . ." Sec. 4. By 1865 a congressional enabling act had been approved, a constitution drafted, ratified, and approved by the people and by Congress; but the act of admission was vetoed by President Johnson in 1866 and, on repassage, again in 1867. A further congressional enabling act was approved in 1875, providing for a constitutional convention to be "apportioned among the several counties in said Territory in proportion to the vote polled in each of said counties at the last general election, as near as may be . . . ." Sec. 3. The convention completed its work in March 1876 after which the proposed constitution was ratified in July, and Colorado was proclaimed a state August 1, 1876. The general assembly was directed to provide by law for an enumeration of inhabitants in 1885 and every tenth year thereafter, adjusting the apportionment "on the basis of such enumeration, according to ratios to be fixed by law" (Colo. Const. of 1876, art. V, § 45), at the next session following each enumeration as well as after each United States decennial census. Meanwhile, the senate was fixed at 26, divided among 20 senatorial districts. Id., § 48. The districts included from one to four counties and were assigned from one to four senators on a population basis. The 49 representatives were similarly divided among the 28 counties on a population basis, including one house district made up of two counties. Id., § 49. The 1876 constitution, amended as indicated below, remains effective.

In 1950 article V, section 46 was amended to provide for a senate and a house of representatives of "not more than" 35 and 65 members, respectively. Colo. Const., art. V, § 46. The population basis of representation was modified by the use of a "weighted ratio" (also called a "differential" or "multiple" ratio) of population. Each county or governmental unit was allocated one seat and the additional seats were distributed according to a progressively higher ratio of population requirement.

The "ratios to be fixed by law" were established by statute in 1953: The ratio for the apportionment of senators was one seat for the first 19,000 population plus another seat for each additional 50,000 or any fraction over 48,000. The ratio for the apportionment of representatives was one seat for the first 8,000 population plus another seat for each additional 25,500 or any fraction over 22,400. Colo. Rev. Stat. § 63-1-2.

These ratios favored sparsely settled areas by denying heavily populated districts additional representation in proportion to their population growth. As a result rural areas were overrepresented in both houses. League of Women Voters of Colorado, Representative Government in Colorado—The Challenge of Reapportionment 19 (1961).

Article V, section 47 provides that "No county shall be divided in the formation of a senatorial or representative district." Until 1964 this was interpreted to mean that a single county could not be divided into two or more districts for the purpose of electing legislators. Hence, elections of delegates in multimember legislative districts were at large. Representative Government in Colorado, p. 18. Moreover, the same constitutional provision was thought to forbid combining a part of one county with another county or part of another county to form a legislative district. Ibid.

Article V, section 45 provides for reapportionment not only after the federal census, but also after a state census taken in every year ending in "5"; but this requirement has not been followed. Representative Government in Colorado, p. 19. Since the adoption of the constitution in 1876, Colorado has been reapportioned only six times: in 1881, 1901, 1913, 1932 (initiated measure), 1953, and 1962 (initiated measure). The 1962 provisions and resulting litigation will be discussed below.

In 1910 Colorado adopted a constitutional provision permitting the initiative and referendum as to both "Laws and Amendments to the Constitution." Art. V, § 1. An initiated reapportionment law was adopted in 1932. At its next session the legislature passed its own reapportionment law and the conflict between it and the initiated measure went to the Colorado Supreme Court (*Armstrong v. Mitten*, 95 Colo. 425, 37 P.2d 757 [1934]), which set aside the legislative apportionment and revived the initiated measure, holding the initiative and referendum power broad enough to include the power to reapportion. Furthermore, the court found the legislative act invalid because not based on population and not according to ratios fixed by law.

In 1954 the voters rejected a referred apportionment measure and in 1956 rejected an initiated constitutional amendment proposing the reapportionment of both chambers of the legislature on a straight population basis. Representative Government in Colorado, p. 23. An effort early in 1962 to compel state court action failed. *In Re Legislative Reapportionment*, 150 Colo. 380, 374 P.2d 66 (Colo. 1962). Petitioners had sought to have the state supreme court issue a writ requiring the general assembly to reapportion the legislature in accordance with the constitutional provisions in article V, section 45, specifying that the general assembly reapportion at the "session next following" the enumeration of the inhabitants of the state by the United States census which the forty-third general assembly had failed to do. The court held that legislative apportionment does not have to occur in the session immediately following the census and that such legislation would not be mandatory until the forty-fourth session of the general assembly. "[S]ince in Colorado, as distinguished from *Baker v. Carr* [369 U.S. 186], all power has been reserved by the people through the initiative and referendum, there is no need for the judiciary to take action until it is determined that both the people and the Legislature have failed to act." Leave was granted to reopen the case if no constitutional amendment or legislative apportionment should be adopted by the next session of the legislature, and further consideration was postponed until June 1, 1963.

Citizens and voters of Denver, declining to wait for the 1963 legislature to act, sought injunctive relief against the governor, treasurer, secretary of state, and the general assembly of Colorado to restrain enforcement of the existing 1953 apportionment statutes. *Lisco v. Mc Nichols,* 208 F. Supp. 471 (D. Colo. 1962). The three-judge court held that the evidence established disparities in apportionment "of sufficient magnitude to make out a *prima facie* case of invidious discrimination" and that the defendants had shown no rational basis for the disparities. Id. at 478. The court, however, declined to enjoin the pending primary and general elections and continued the case until after the general election.

At the 1962 general election two initiated constitutional amendments were submitted to the electorate. Amendment No. 7 provided for a house of representatives of 65 members apportioned on a population basis and for a 39-member senate apportioned according to fixed area districts, but in the counties apportioned more than one senator the single-member senatorial districts were to be "as nearly equal in population as may be." Mandatory provisions required the revision of representative districts and of senatorial districts within counties apportioned more than one senator after each federal census.

Amendment No. 8 would have apportioned both the house and the senate upon a population basis with limited permissible variations therefrom, but it would have provided local option on subdistricting in multimember counties. No. 8 also proposed a three-man com-

mission to apportion the legislature periodically; its actions were to be reviewed by the Colorado Supreme Court.

Amendment No. 7, the "little federal plan," carried in every county of the state and amendment No. 8 was defeated in every county. Following the approval of amendment No. 7 the plaintiffs in *Lisco* amended their complaint to assert the invalidity of the amendment, contending that the equal protection clause of the United States Constitution requires that each house of a bicameral state legislature be apportioned on a per capita basis. However, the district court, by a two to one vote, upheld the constitutionality of the amendment. *Lisco v. Love,* 219 F. Supp. 922 (D. Colo. 1963).

Despite the recognition of population disparities among the senatorial districts varying from 3.6 to 1, the court found amendment No. 7 to be rational because it "recognizes population as a prime, but not controlling, factor and gives effect to such important considerations as geography, compactness and contiguity of territory, accessibility, observance of natural boundaries, conformity to historical divisions such as county lines and prior representation districts, and 'a proper diffusion of political initiative as between a state's thinly populated counties and those having concentrated masses.'" Id. at 932.

The court emphasized that the electorate freely adopted amendment No. 7. "[A] proper recognition of the judicial function precludes a court from holding that the free choice of the voters between two conflicting theories of apportionment is irrational or the result arbitrary . . . . At the most [plaintiffs] present a political issue which they lost." Id. at 932–933.

The Supreme Court of the United

States reversed the lower court in an opinion now captioned *Lucas v. Colorado General Assembly*, 377 U.S. 713 (1964). The Court noted that the senatorial apportionment under amendment No. 7 involved little more than adding four new senate seats (the senate membership was raised from 35 to 39) and distributing them to four populous counties in the Denver area, but otherwise "in substance perpetuates the existing senatorial apportionment scheme. Counties containing only 33.2% of the State's total population elect a majority of the 39-member senate [and] the maximum population-variance ratio, under the revised senatorial apportionment, is about 3.6-to-1." Id. at 728. Without passing on the validity of the apportionment in the house of representatives (where the ratio was 1.7 to 1), the Court held the "overall legislative representation in the two houses" deficient because of the substantial population disparity in senatorial districts.

The Court rejected the argument that the initiative constituted an adequate remedy for underrepresented voters. "Courts sit to adjudicate controversies involving alleged denials of constitutional rights .... An individual's constitutionally protected right to cast an equally weighted vote cannot be denied even by a vote of a majority of a State's electorate, if the apportionment scheme adopted by the voters fails to measure up to the requirements of the Equal Protection Clause." Id. at 736. (The opinion is more fully discussed in chapter V.)

The decision was announced on June 15, 1964. The governor convened a special session of the legislature on July 1; and by July 8 a new statute had been enacted for the 1964 elections. Colo. Sess. Laws 1964, 2d Extraordinary Sess., c. 2. The act established a senate of 35 members and a house of 65 members, all to be elected from specified single-member districts. Without crossing any county lines the population disparities were greatly reduced. Five days later the three-judge federal district court on remand held that for purposes of the 1964 election the new law satisfied federal constitutional standards. In addition, it upheld the division of populous counties into single-member election districts despite state constitutional provisions to the contrary. *Lucas v. Colorado General Assembly*, 232 F. Supp. 797 (D. Colo. 1964).

On July 17, 1964, four days after the federal court decision, the state supreme court, in an original proceeding brought to test the validity of the legislative act, held it violative of the state constitution's requirement that "No county shall be divided in the formation of a senatorial or representative district." *White v. Anderson*, 394 P.2d 333 (Colo. 1964). See also *MacDonald v. Love*, 394 P.2d 345 (Colo. 1964). However, in view of the action of the federal court and the imminence of the 1964 election, the court stayed the effect of its judgment. The 1965 legislature eliminated subdistricts within multimember counties. Colo. Sess. Laws 1965, c. 173.

In February 1965 the Supreme Court of the United States affirmed the judgment of the federal district court as to its decision of the *federal* issues, but vacated the judgment and remanded for reconsideration of the *state* issues "in light of the supervening decision of the Colorado Supreme Court in *White v. Anderson.* . . ." *Colorado General Assembly v. Lucas*, 379 U.S. 693 (1965).

A constitutional convention may be called upon the recommendation of two thirds of the general assembly and the concurrence of a majority of the voters. Art. XIX, § 1. An amendment to the constitution may be proposed by a two-thirds vote of both houses. If approved by a majority of voters, such amendment becomes part of the constitution. Id., § 2, as amended, 1901. Initiative and referendum provisions appear in article V, section 1, as amended in 1910.

Article V, section 44 provides that "[w]hen a new [congressional] apportionment shall be made by congress the general assembly shall divide the state into congressional districts accordingly." The population disparity among the four congressional districts into which the state was divided until 1964 was 458,403, one of the highest in the nation. After the decision in *Wesberry v. Sanders*, 376 U.S. 1 (1964) and the filing of a federal court challenge to the Colorado districting, the governor called a special session of the legislature, which promptly drew new lines. The population differential was reduced to 87,988 without crossing any county lines. Colo. Sess. Laws 1964, 1st Extraordinary Sess., c. 1.

REFERENCES

Colorado Legislative Council. Reapportionment of the Colorado General Assembly. Research Publication No. 52. Denver: 1961.
Klemme, Howard C. The Powers of Home Rule Cities in Colorado, 36 Colo. L. Rev. 321 (1964).
League of Women Voters of Colorado. Representative Government in Colorado. Denver: 1961.
Note, 35 Colo. L. Rev. 431 (1963).

CONNECTICUT

The Fundamental Orders of 1638–1639 provided representation in the unicameral legislature to the three original towns of Hartford, Windsor, and Wethersfield, which were to "send four of their Freemen as their deputies to every General Court." New towns were to "send so many deputies as the Court shall judge meet, a reasonable proportion to the number of Freemen that are in said towns . . . ." Fundamental Orders, § 8. The Charter of 1662, granted by Charles II, laid down the basic pattern which persisted until 1965 in the house of representatives, providing that the general assembly should have not more than "two persons from each Place, Town or City . . . ." The second house was added in 1698 as an outgrowth of the governor's council, a form of appointed cabinet which had existed for some time. Thereafter, the pattern of apportionment was not altered until the adoption of the first state constitution in 1818. Of this earlier period the Supreme Court of Errors of Connecticut had this to say: "Prior to 1818 the whole sovereign power was exercised by the people, unrestrained by anything except their present will, through a body of magistrates chosen annually, and deputies chosen semi-annually. This was a democracy, as close to a pure democracy as it is possible for a representative government to be. There were certain forms established by legislation, and certain fundamental principles generally acknowledged as true and important; but there was no power that could enforce them. They depended on the unrestrained will of the people, as expressed semi-annually. This body of laws and customs might be broadly called a 'constitution.' But they were not, and the government was not a constitutional government, in the American sense . . . ." *Appeal of Norwalk St. Ry. Co.*, 69 Conn. 576, 37 Atl. 1080, 1083, rehearing denied, 69 Conn. 576, 38 Atl. 708 (1897).

The constitution of 1818 provided for two separate houses, but retained in the house of representatives the seventeenth-century concept of representation by towns, preserving representation in the same numbers "as at present practiced and allowed." New towns were to have one representative only, unless made up from pre-existing towns, in which case the representation of the pre-existing town should not be reduced without the consent of any town so affected. Conn. Const. of 1818, art III, § 3. The senate was originally fixed at a membership of 12 on the basis of the number of votes cast throughout the state, without provision for separate election districts. Id., §§ 4–6. The foregoing provisions were modified in many respects over the years up through and including the changes incorporated into the constitution of 1955, whose provisions are described below. Further changes, also noted below, were effected by statute in 1965, and additional changes may be anticipated as a result of the constitutional convention in 1965.

The constitution of 1955 continued reliance on the town as the unit of apportionment in the house of representatives. "Every town which now contains or hereafter shall contain a population of five thousand, shall be entitled to send two representatives, and every other one shall be entitled to its present representation . . . ." A new town was entitled to a representative only if (1) it had a population of 2,500 and (2) the town from which the major portion of the new town's territory had been taken also had at least 2,500 inhabitants. Otherwise, any new town (with less than a 2,500 population) for purposes of representation was to be attached to and deemed part of the town from which the major portion of its territory had been taken. Art. III, § 3.

The 1955 constitution provided that "The number of senatorial districts shall not be less than twenty-four nor more than thirty-six, and each district shall elect only one senator." Art. III, § 5. However, the senatorial apportionment was primarily based on pop-

ulation; in forming the districts "regard shall be had to population . . . that the same may be as nearly equal as possible under the limitations of this section." The limitations were that the senatorial districts shall "always be composed of contiguous territory"; that "neither the whole or a part of one county shall be joined to the whole or a part of another county to form a district"; that "no town shall be divided, unless for the purpose of forming more than one district wholly within such town"; and that "each county shall have at least one senator." Districts could be altered by the general assembly only "at a session . . . next after the completion of a census of the United States, and then only in accordance with the principles hereinbefore provided." Ibid. *Cahill v. Leopold*, 141 Conn. 1, 103 A.2d 818 (1954) struck down a 1953 bill to redistrict the senate upon the ground that this section only allowed reapportionment at the session of the general assembly immediately following the taking of the census. Under that interpretation, failure to act at that first opportunity would mean that no action could be taken until the next census ten years later.

The last general redistricting of the senate before 1965 was accomplished in 1903 when the general assembly divided the state into 35 districts. In 1941 Greenwich became the 36th district. Aside from the addition of Greenwich and some shifting of the boundaries of New Haven, no redistricting had taken place between 1903 and 1965. Report of Bi-Partisan Committee to Study the Problem of Redistricting the Senate 7 (1961). The population disparity between the largest and smallest senate districts was eight to one.

In *Valenti v. Dempsey*, 211 F. Supp. 911 (D. Conn. 1962) plaintiffs as Connecticut citizens and voters sought to enjoin defendants from convening the 1963 assembly and to command them instead to reconvene the 1961 assembly to take action with respect to the senate alone. The court denied the preliminary injunction since plaintiffs were residents of New Haven, which was overrepresented in the senate. Accordingly, plaintiffs did not show irreparable harm.

In *Butterworth v. Dempsey*, 229 F. Supp. 754 (D. Conn. 1964) a three-judge federal district court held that the districting of the senate and the apportionment of the house so debased the voting rights of plaintiffs as to result in invidious discrimination amounting to a denial of the equal protection of the laws. Plaintiffs were resident citizens and voters of six urban and suburban Connecticut towns, and the defendants included the governor and others charged with administration of the election laws. Other voters were permitted to intervene, including the chairmen of the Republican and Democratic state central committees, who intervened as individuals rather than as political leaders. The court was unanimous in its finding as to the senate where the population disparity between the most populous and the least populous district was in a ratio of eight to one, and deviations from the population norm were as high as 226.8 per cent. Accordingly, the court ruled that "the Senate must be redistricted promptly in such a way as to achieve substantially equal weighting of the votes of all voters . . . ." Id. at 760.

By a two to one vote the court held invalid the town representation formula in the house, noting deviations from the population norm as high as 573.4 per cent, and pointing out that a majority of the house is elected by 11.9 per cent of the population. Rejecting the "federal analogy" the court ruled that the house, as well as the senate,

"must be reapportioned promptly in such a way as to achieve substantially equal weighting of the votes of all voters . . . ." Id. at 764. Provisions were made for later formulation of an appropriate decree, and counsel were asked for further briefs and arguments on how to satisfy the guidelines laid down in the separate opinion of the late Judge Charles E. Clark. Id. at 773.

On June 22, 1964, the Supreme Court of the United States affirmed the three-judge court. *Pinney v. Butterworth*, 378 U.S. 564 (1964). On remand the federal district court, on July 29, 1964, amended its original order to stay execution of the injunctive provisions in that order, provided a special session of the general assembly should enact by September 10, 1964, a temporary reapportionment for the election of the 1965 general assembly and an appropriate statute for the convening of a constitutional convention by November 5, 1964. Although a special session was convened, it failed to complete the required action by September 10. Accordingly, the court order enjoining the conduct of the November election became effective; and the court extended to January 30, 1965, the time for legislative action, but cautioned that it would act if the legislature did not. With that possibility in mind the court appointed a special master to advise the court, pursuant to judicially announced guidelines, as to the fixing of district lines if that should become necessary. The court appointed as master Morris S. Davis, director of the Yale University Computer Center, and authorized him to consider "the feasibility and advisability of utilizing an appropriate electronic computer technique to minimize partisanship in redistricting the senate and reapportioning the house . . . ." *Butterworth v. Dempsey*, 237 F. Supp. 302, 313 (D. Conn. 1965).

Thus encouraged to act, the general assembly met the new deadline with a bill continuing the senate membership at 36, but reducing the size of the house from 294 to 177 members. It was provided that all members should be elected from districts of about 14,200 persons, discarding representation in the house by towns. The first election under the new procedure was fixed for November 1966. Conn. Pub. Act. No. 2, Nov. 1964 Spec. Sess.

On January 22, 1965, the day the bill was approved, the three-judge court announced that the reapportionment act and the act providing for a convention satisfied its earlier order. Accordingly, all restraint on the carrying on of the legislative function by the general assembly was lifted pending election of its successor in 1966; and the special master was instructed to suspend further action. *Butterworth v. Dempsey*, 237 F. Supp. 302, 313 (D. Conn. 1965).

Constitutional amendments may be proposed by a majority of the house of representatives. If approved by two thirds of each house at the next session of the legislature, such an amendment is presented to the town clerks for approval by the electors present at town meetings across the state. Art. I, § 1. There is a statutory right of referendum for the approval or disapproval of constitutional amendments (Conn. Gen. Stat. Ann. c. 152, § 9-369), but no provision for the initiative. There is no provision for the convening of a constitutional convention, although conventions have been called on three occasions in the twentieth century at the call of the legislature. The most recent of these was authorized by the general assembly in January 1965 by Public Act. No. 1. That act directed the election of 84 delegates, no more than one half to be from any one political party. Fourteen delegates were chosen from each of the six congressional districts in an election held on June 15, 1965, for the convention that began on July 1, 1965. The delegates were charged with the responsibility of preparing proposals to amend or revise the constitution, to be submitted to the secretary of state no later than November 1, 1965, for consideration at a special referendum on December 14, 1965. Conn. Pub. Act. No. 2, Nov. 1964 Spec. Sess.

Statutory provisions for congressional districting prior to 1964 authorized the election at large of one representative and the election of five from specified congressional districts. Conn. Gen. Stat. Ann. c. 142, § 9-9. The population differential among the five districts, based on 1960 population figures, was 370,613. In February 1964 the districting was challenged in federal district court. N.Y. Times, Feb. 23, 1964, p. 49, col. 1. Before the case could be decided the Connecticut general assembly, in a special session, approved a redistricting act dividing the state into six districts, with a population differential of 77,934. Conn. Gen. Stat. Ann., tit. 9, § 9 (1964).

REFERENCES

Connecticut General Assembly. Report of Bi-Partisan Committee to Study the Problem of Redistricting the Senate. Hartford: 1961.
Connecticut Public Expenditure Council. Districting and Redistricting the Connecticut Senate. Hartford: 1961.
Valenti, James J., and Galiette, Richard T. The Problem of Representation, a Review of Connecticut's General Assembly. New Haven: League of Independent Voters. 1963.

DELAWARE

The three counties of the present state of Delaware had their beginnings in the early Dutch judicial districts in Delaware, of which there were two when the land passed out of Dutch hands in 1673. The Duke of York continued these and in 1680 created the third county. In 1682 the duke conveyed the counties to William Penn, who later that year joined them to his own province of Pennsylvania; and by 1683 the counties had acquired their present names, Kent, New Castle, and Sussex. The three counties were not then a separate colony; instead they shared representation with other counties in the Pennsylvania assembly, in which each county had equal representation. But in the Charter of Liberties of 1701 Penn permitted within three years "a distinct Assembly for the Territories," with equal representation for each county.

The subsequent history is succinctly related by the court in *Sincock v. Duffy*, 215 F. Supp. 169, 183 (D. Del. 1963): "In 1704, the three lower counties separated completely from the Province of Pennsylvania except for the office of Governor General. The people who resided in the three counties joined together in 1776 and created an organization completely independent of the colony and the Commonwealth of Pennsylvania. Delaware existed as a State prior to the creation of the United States. For at least one hundred years prior to 1776 the three Counties had been in existence. From time to time there was a Colonial Assembly and later a state assembly or legislative body for the three lower Counties on the Delaware River in which there was equal representation from each one of the three Counties. That system continued to exist until the adoption of the Constitution of 1897, having been embodied in the Constitution of 1776, the Constitution of 1792 and the Constitution of 1831.

"In 1896 the population of each of the three Counties, excluding Wilmington, was approximately equal. The Constitution of 1897 varied the pattern of equal representation from the three Counties by adding five representatives for New Castle County and two for the City of Wilmington. The basis for this addition is not clear from the constitutional debates."

The provisions of the constitution of 1897, as amended in 1962 (effective in January 1963), are outlined below, although in *Sincock v. Duffy*, supra, the three-judge district court held invalid both the basic provisions and the amendment and enjoined further elections under the existing law. The court allowed the legislature through October 1, 1963, to make correction (215 F. Supp. at 192). Before the legislature completed action on a further proposal, the injunction was stayed by Justice Brennan, and the legislature did not further act before the case was heard in the United States Supreme Court in December 1963.

Article II, section 2 of the constitution of 1897 provided for a house of representatives of 35 and a senate of 17 members divided among the three counties (including a special representation for the city of Wilmington). New Castle County was assigned 15 representative districts and 7 senatorial districts, and Kent and Sussex counties were each allotted 10 representative and 5 senatorial districts.

The foregoing provisions were amended effective in January 1963 by (1) increasing the senatorial districts in Kent and Sussex Counties from five each to seven each for a total senate membership of 21 and (2) adding ten additional representative districts by dividing the more populous districts and by providing additional representation for each increment of 15,000 population residing therein, or any major fraction thereof. The amendment provided additional representation in the senate for each of the two least populous counties of the state, thus increasing the disparity between population and representation in that house. The changes in the house (affecting only New Castle County) left untouched the disparities in the other two counties, while giving rise to population disparities in population per representative of about twelve to one.

There is no provision in the constitution or state statutes for reapportionment of the general assembly; and there is no procedure for either initiative or referendum. Amendments may be proposed by a two-thirds vote of each house of the assembly, which must be published three months prior to the next general election, and then agreed to once more by a two-thirds vote of each legislative chamber. Art. XVI, § 1. The general assembly may also propose, by a two-thirds vote of each house, that the voters decide upon the holding of a constitutional convention, which would be composed of one delegate from each representative district and two delegates from each county. Art. XVI, § 2.

On April 17, 1963, a three-judge federal district court held unconstitutional the apportionment provisions of the constitution of 1897 as well as the amendment of 1963 in *Sincock v. Duffy*, 215 F. Supp. 169 (D. Del. 1963). (Earlier proceedings in the same case appear under the caption, *Sincock v. Terry*, 207 F. Supp. 205, 210 F. Supp. 395, 210 F. Supp. 396 (D. Del. 1962).) Plaintiffs in that case, residents and qualified voters of New Castle County, claimed invidious discrimination as to the inhabitants of that county and the city of Wilmington. This argument was sustained by the court. Circuit Judge Biggs, in his opinion, found no rational or reasonable basis for the apportionment either before or after amendment. Although the court concluded that reapportionment was basically a legislative function, and thus favored additional opportunity for legislative reconsideration, it noted that minimal constitutional standards required that at least one house be apportioned on an "equal population basis." 215 F. Supp. at 191.

On June 15, 1964, the Supreme Court of the United States affirmed the three-judge federal district court. *Roman v. Sincock*, 377 U.S. 695 (1964). The Court noted that the population disparities among the senatorial districts were about fifteen to one and among the representative districts about twelve to one. Constitutional change was shown to be difficult in that the constitution could be amended only by a two-thirds vote of both houses, but under the 1963 amendment a majority of house members could be elected by about 28 per cent of the state's population and a majority of the senate could be elected by about 21 per cent of the state's population. After determining that those provisions violated the equal protection clause, the Court remanded the case to the federal district court to determine whether the 1964 elections should be allowed to proceed under the invalid plan or whether corrective action must sooner be taken. (The case is more fully discussed in chapter V, supra.)

Before the district court could act the Delaware legislature adopted two reapportionment statutes, on July 6 and 8, 1964. S.B. 332 provided for a house of 35 members to be elected for two-year terms from single-member districts, and a senate of 18 members to serve four-year terms, also elected from single-member districts. S.B. 336 established the boundaries of the senatorial and representative districts. 29 Del. Code c. 6 (Supp. 1964).

The new legislation was promptly challenged by the plaintiffs in the original proceeding, claiming violation of the equal-population principle and asserting that the plan involved an impermissible gerrymander.

The court heard evidence on these arguments, but refused to rule definitively before the November 1964 election. It would, the court suggested, be too disruptive to change the election districts so close to the election date. Accordingly, the court held that the 1964 election should be conducted in accordance with the newly drawn lines, but retained jurisdiction for further proceedings. *Sincock v. Roman*, 233 F. Supp. 615 (D. Del. 1964).

Delaware's single congressman is elected at large.

FLORIDA

The territories of East and West Florida were ceded to the United States in 1819 by a treaty of amity, settlement, and limits with Spain. In 1822 Congress vested the legislative power over the territory of Florida in a governor and legislative council of 13 to be appointed by the President of the United States. A constitution for the proposed state of Florida was completed in convention in 1839, but was not submitted to the people at that time, for Congress did not enact enabling legislation until 1845. Article IX of that constitution provided for a state census every ten years beginning in 1845, providing that "to the whole number of free white inhabitants shall be added three-fifths of the number of slaves . . . ." The house of representatives was to have 1 representative from each of the then 20 counties to an initial total of 41, the additional 21 to be apportioned on a population basis. Fla. Const. of 1838, art. IX, §§ 1, 5. The senate was to be composed of 16 senators from as many

districts, each including one, two, or three counties. Id., §§ 2, 5.

In 1861 the constitution was changed only by the substitution of "Confederate States" for "United States." The constitution of 1865, replacing that of 1861, retained the essentials of the earlier apportionment formula except that the house was enlarged to a membership of 59 and the senate to 29, to be chosen as before out of the then 39 counties. Fla. Const. of 1865, art. IX. The constitution of 1868, in article XIII, continued the same basic structure but limited the number of representatives from any county to four and authorized the legislature to fix the size of the senate.

The constitution of 1885, which, as amended, has survived to the present, fixed the size of the houses at not more than 32 in the senate and not more than 68 in the house. Fla. Const. of 1885, art. VII, § 2. The representatives were to be apportioned "among the several counties as nearly as possible according to population," but with the limitation that each county should have one representative and no county more than three. The provision for legislative apportionment of the senatorial districts was also continued. Id., § 3.

By constitutional amendment in 1924 slightly greater flexibility was allowed for the accommodation of the increasingly sharp population differentials among the counties, although this was held invalid in *Sobel v. Adams*, 208 F. Supp. 316 (S.D. Fla. 1962), as discussed below. The apportionment formula between 1924 and 1962 consisted of a senate of 38, "to be as nearly equal in population as practicable, but no county shall be divided in making such apportionment . . . ." Fla. Const. of 1885, as amended, art. VII, § 3. Section 4 of article VII further provided that "[w]here any senatorial district is composed of

Appendix: State Summaries

301

two or more counties, the counties of which such districts consist shall not be entirely separated by any county belonging to another district."

The house of representatives was fixed at "not more than" 68 members. Id., § 2. The legislature when apportioning the house was to allow three representatives to each of the 5 most populous counties, two representatives to each of the 18 next most populous counties, and one to each of the remaining counties. Art. VII, § 3. The legislature was to apportion the house and the senate according to the last preceding federal decennial census (id., § 5); and if the legislature failed to apportion the house and the senate as required, the governor was charged to call a special session which was then "mandatorily required" to reapportion. Id., § 3.

The foregoing provisions were held to be invidiously discriminatory in *Sobel v. Adams*, 208 F. Supp. 316 (S.D. Fla. 1962), the court noting that each of the three representatives from Dade County represented the equivalent of 311,000 people, while the representative from Gilchrist County represented only 2,868 residents. The court found similar disparity in the senate. It concluded, moreover, that a proposed apportionment amendment submitted at the 1961 session of the legislature (S.J.R. No. 216, Laws of Fla. 1961, p. 1165) was also invalid. Thereupon, between the first hearing of the case in July 1962 and a later hearing in August 1962, the governor convened a special session of the legislature which proposed a further amendment to establish a house of 135 members and a senate of 46. Although the court held this plan to be rational (id. at 324), it was rejected by the voters in November 1962. The legislature was again convened in special session; and on February 1, 1963, the legislature

passed senate bill 10-X(63), providing for a senate of 43 members and a house of 112 members. Meanwhile, the Florida Supreme Court had ruled in an advisory opinion to the governor that the legislature might provide for reapportionment by statutory enactment notwithstanding the limitations in the constitution. 150 So.2d 721 (Fla. 1963). The federal district court, which had retained jurisdiction, examined the new plan and found it rational. "The present plan gives some more weight to the population factor than did the rejected plan. But if it be required that both branches of the legislature, or either branch, must be apportioned on a strict population basis, then, admittedly, neither the rejected amendment, nor the statutory enactment would pass the test." *Sobel v. Adams*, 214 F. Supp. 811, 812 (S.D. Fla. 1963).

The 1963 apportionment statute (Fla. Stat. Ann. §§ 10.01–10.03) provided for a senate of 43 members. The counties of the state were to be apportioned among 42 senatorial districts, with 1 district added "by superimposing over district thirteen (13) district forty-three (43) representing Dade County. The forty-three (43) districts shall be apportioned among the several counties of the state to provide equitable representation based upon similar economic interests, geographic area and population." In addition, "no county except Dade shall be divided in creating a senatorial district. Every district shall consist of contiguous counties."

The provisions of section 10.01 of the Florida code enumerated the senatorial districts. More than half were single-county districts, and no district included more than three counties. Hence, the apportionment was essentially based on area.

Section 10.03 of the Florida code, as

amended in 1963, provided for a house of 112 representatives "which shall be apportioned among the counties by the method of equal proportions; that is, each county shall have one representative and the remaining representatives shall be assigned to the counties in proportion to population."

On June 22, 1964, the Supreme Court of the United States reversed the 1963 judgment of the federal district court in *Swann v. Adams*, 378 U.S. 553 (1964), and remanded for further proceedings consistent with the opinion in *Reynolds v. Sims*, 377 U.S. 533 (1964). On remand the three-judge court was asked to enjoin the secretary of state from placing on the November 1964 ballot a proposed constitutional amendment which also would not satisfy the equal-population test. The court took no action before the election; and the voters defeated the proposal.

In January 1965 the three-judge federal district court gave the legislature a deadline of July 1, 1965. In response to a challenge to the regularity of the Florida legislative action under the terms of the state constitution, the supreme court of Florida ruled in April 1965 that existing provisions of the Florida constitution could be disregarded as a result of the federal rulings invalidating the state apportionment formula. *Jordan v. Green*, 173 So.2d 448 (Fla. 1965). Thus free to act, the state legislature adopted a new plan for a 109-member house (with population disparities from 19,029 to 76,895) and a 58-member senate (with disparities from 65,723 to 101,688). Fla. Laws of 1965, c. 65-2440. The following day the plan was challenged in the original proceeding in federal court, where jurisdiction had been retained.

The 1963 apportionment statute was also challenged in *Lucas v. Adams*, Case No. 63-51-Civil-J (M.D. Fla. 1963). Plaintiffs, residents and qualified voters of Duval County, to which four representatives were allotted by the 1963 act, claimed that identifiable districts should be drawn within the county, presumably so that Negro voters in the county, including plaintiffs, could elect a representative from their own number. The three-judge federal district court refused equitable intervention to halt the state election to be held the following week. The Supreme Court of the United States affirmed in a brief per curiam order without opinion. 378 U.S. 555 (1964).

Article XVII of the Florida constitution provides for its revision as follows: (1) Section 1 allows either branch of the legislature at a regular or special session to propose an amendment by a three-fifths vote. The amendment is referred to the voters at the next election. (2) If the legislature by a two-thirds vote determines that a constitutional revision is necessary, and if a majority of electors favor such a revision, a constitutional convention can be called pursuant to section 2 of article XVII. (3) Section 3 outlines the procedures for amending the constitution at a special election.

The state is divided by statute into 12 congressional districts. Fla. Stat. Ann. § 8.01. Section 99.091(2) provides that "when Florida is entitled to additional representatives according to the last census, representatives are elected from the State at large thereafter until the state is redistricted by the legislature."

In *Lund v. Mathas*, 145 So.2d 871 (Fla. 1962), the validity of this congressional reapportionment act (§ 8.01) was unsuccessfully attacked. The plaintiffs claimed that the districts were so unequal in population as to deny the equal protection of the laws. The lower court dismissed the complaint and the supreme court of Florida affirmed, holding that "Neither the federal nor state constitutions, nor the federal nor state statutes, require that the Florida legislature apportion congressional districts upon the basis of numerical equality . . . and in *Wood v. Broom*, the United States Supreme Court has held that the requirements of compactness, contiguity and equal number of inhabitants were no longer in effect." 145 So. 2d at 873.

In addition the court said that "population is one of several important factors in apportionment. The varying interests of an area, including economic, elements of topography, geography, means of transportation and industrial, agricultural and resort activities, together with numerous other regional characteristics are to be considered. Neither the Congress nor the courts are qualified by intimate knowledge of any given area to mark out reasonable boundaries calculated to best serve the public welfare." Ibid.

In *Gong v. Bryant*, 230 F. Supp. 917 (S.D. Fla. 1964) the federal district court noted the population disparities existing among the 12 Florida congressional districts in 1960, ranging from 237,235 to 660,335. Despite the conceded invalidity of the districting that produced that result, the court reserved judgment until 60 days after adjournment of the next session of the Florida legislature. In a second extra session in July 1965 the legislature approved a new congressional districting act. Nine of the 12 districts consisted of one or more entire counties, and each of the three remaining districts included a portion of Dade County (Miami). The tenth district was all of Broward County plus part of Dade County, the eleventh a portion of Dade County, and the twelfth all of Monroe County plus part of Dade County. Fla. Laws 1965, c. 65-2441.

REFERENCES

Froemke, Robert L. Non-Political Remedies of the People, 20 Intra. L. Rev. 274 (1965).
Gathin, Douglas S. and Mason, Bruce B. Reapportionment: Its History in Florida. Civic Information Series No. 23. Gainesville: Public Administration Clearing Service, University of Florida. 1956.
Havard, William C., and Beth, Loren P. Representative Government and Reapportionment: A Case Study of Florida. Studies in Public Administration No. 20. Gainesville: Public Administration Clearing Service, University of Florida. 1960.
———. The Politics of Mis-Representation: Rural-Urban Conflict in the Florida Legislature. Baton Rouge: Louisiana State University Press. 1962.
McQuown, Ruth. Reapportionment and Other Constitutional Amendments of 1962. Gainesville: Public Administration Clearing Service, University of Florida. 1962.
Price, Hugh Douglas. "Florida: Politics and the 'Pork Choppers,'" in Jewell, Malcolm E. (ed.). The Politics of Reapportionment. New York: Atherton Press. 1962.

GEORGIA

Under the original Charter of Georgia in 1732 the colony was governed by the governor and his council. When the Continental Congress in 1776 recommended the preparation of individual state constitutions as a part of the independence movement, Georgia moved quickly to comply, holding a convention in Savannah beginning October 1, 1776. The resulting constitution of 1777 provided for a house of the assembly to consist of 10 members from each of the eight counties, except that Liberty was given 14, and Glynn and Camden were given 1 each with provision for enlargement as population should grow. In addition, the towns of Savannah and Sunbury were allowed 4 and 2 members respectively to "represent their trade." The executive powers were shared by the governor and an executive council chosen from among the members of the assembly. Ga. Const. of 1777, arts. II–V.

The constitution of 1789 abandoned the unicameral legislature and provided for a senate made up of 1 member from each of the then 11 counties and a house of representatives of 34 members, the counties having been assigned from two to five representatives. Ga. Const. of 1789, art. I, §§ 2, 6. The legislature was empowered to alter the boundaries of present counties and to fix new counties, the representation in the new counties to be apportioned out of the existing representation in the counties from which the new ones were created. Id., § 17.

The constitution of 1798 preserved the senate membership formula without change (art. I, § 3) but provided in the house a more specific tie to population, "according to their respective numbers of free white persons, and including three-fifths of all the people of color .... Each county containing three thousand persons ... shall be entitled to two members; seven thousand, to three members; and twelve thousand, to four members; but each county shall have at least one and not more than four members." Id., § 7. By an 1843 amendment 47 senatorial districts were created, and the number of representatives was fixed at 130, each county to have no more than two. McElreath, Treatise on the Constitution of Georgia 277 (1912).

After secession in January 1861, a revision of the constitution was completed in March and ratified in July of that year. That was in turn supplanted by the constitution of 1865. In that constitution the then 132 counties were divided into 44 senatorial districts of 3 counties each; and the house of representatives was established with two representatives from each of the 37 most populous counties and one from each

of the remaining counties for a total chamber of 169. Ga. Const. of 1865, art. II, §§ 2, 3. The constitution of 1868 continued the same formula of three counties for each senatorial district, but provided for a house of 175 members composed of three members from each of the 6 most populous counties, two from each of the 31 next most populous, and one from each of the remaining 95 counties. Ga. Const. of 1868, art. III, §§ 2, 3. In the constitution of 1877 this basic formula was retained except that only 26 counties were given two representatives and 105 counties were allowed only one representative for a total chamber of 175. Ga. Const. of 1877, art. III, §§ 2, 3. Changes in the total number of representatives were made from time to time because of the creation of new counties to a total of 159 in 1917. *Sanders v. Gray*, 203 F. Supp. 158, 162 (N.D. Ga. 1962).

In the present Georgia constitution, the constitution of 1945, the same principles control except as modified by the United States Supreme Court and lower federal court decisions in 1962 and later. The provisions as they stood before those decisions are discussed first and then the modifying decisions.

Under the constitution of 1945 the senate consisted of "not more than" 54 members from "not more than fifty-four senatorial districts with one senator from each district." Ga. Const. of 1945, § 2-1401. This provision neither enumerated the districts nor named the counties in each, but left the districts "comprised of the counties now provided," giving the general assembly (the house and senate) "authority to create, rearrange and change these Districts within the limitations herein stated." Ibid. Section 47-102 of the Georgia code distributed the 54 senatorial districts among the counties so that three contiguous counties comprised each senatorial district with exceptions for district number 1, which was composed of only two counties (Effingham and Chatham), and district number 52, which was composed of only Fulton County. These were the two most populous senatorial districts. Otherwise, the districts bore no relation to population. According to the 1960 census the population varied from 13,050 in the smallest senatorial district to 556,326 in the largest.

In addition, section 47-102.1 of the Georgia code required rotation of each senatorial position among the counties comprising each district. As a result, no senator could succeed himself, nor could he be succeeded by a resident of the same county. Other provisions of the Georgia statutes stipulated that where a county's candidate for election to the senate was to be chosen by a primary election, only those voters from the county which was to provide the senator under the rotation system could vote in the primary. Thus, residents of two out of the three counties were ordinarily unable to participate in the primary which chose candidates for their own senatorial district. The provisions for rotation were held invalid in *Toombs v. Fortson*, 205 F. Supp. 248 (N.D. Ga. 1962).

The 1945 constitution provided that the 8 most populous counties should have three representatives each, the 30 next largest counties should have two each, and the remaining counties (121) should have one each. Art. III, § 2-1501. It was further provided that "the above apportionment shall be changed by the General Assembly at its first session after each census taken by the United States Government . . . ." Reapportionment has taken place after each decennial census.

Toombs v. Fortson, supra, stated that

(1) representatives from the 103 least populous counties of a total of 159 comprised a constitutional majority of the 205 members of the house, although representing counties having approximately 22.5 per cent of the population of the state; (2) the 8 most populous counties, with 41 per cent of the population, elected 24 of the 205 representatives, constituting only 11.7 per cent of the total number of representatives; and (3) the 69 least populous counties, with 12.17 per cent of the total population, were able to block the two-thirds vote of the house required for the submission of a constitutional amendment to the people of the state.

In *Toombs v. Fortson* residents of the two most populous counties in Georgia (Fulton and DeKalb) sought declaratory and injunctive relief to cause the legislature to apportion its members on a population basis. Defendants were the secretary of state and six ordinaries of selected Georgia counties (the ordinary is the county officer whose duty it is to supervise primary and general elections). The three-judge federal district court took jurisdiction and found the system "arbitrary in any sense of that term." 205 F. Supp. at 254. "Viewing the extreme disparities existing in both Houses of the Legislature . . . the present composition of the Georgia Legislature amounts to invidious discrimination against the plaintiffs . . . . It follows, therefore, that the continued operation of the Georgia State government under a legislative system as presently constituted violates plaintiffs' right to equal protection of the law . . . ." Id. at 256.

In declining to issue an injunction the court decided to postpone further proceedings until the state legislature had had an opportunity to reconstitute itself to meet the constitutional standards outlined in the court's opinion.

The governor called an extraordinary session of the general assembly, which met in September 1962 and enacted the following legislation:

(1) Section 47-102.1 of the Georgia code, requiring senators to be furnished by counties in rotation, was repealed.

(2) Section 47-102 of the Georgia code, which divided the state into 54 senatorial districts, was completely superseded by a new reapportionment and redistricting. Ga. Code Ann. § 47-102 (1963 Supp.). This act was subsequently proposed as a constitutional amendment and ratified by the electors on November 6, 1962. Ga. Const. of 1945, art. II, § 2-1401(b) (1963 Supp.).

(3) Article II, section 2-1401(a) of the constitution was further amended to vest authority to reapportion the senate in the legislature "in such manner as the General Assembly may deem advisable." Section 47-121 of the code outlines the standards of reapportionment which the assembly is to apply: (a) Apportionment is to be effected after each federal census "if necessary to conform to changes in population." (b) Entire counties may be combined to form senatorial districts, but parts of counties may not be so combined. (c) Counties in senatorial districts composed of more than one county must adjoin at least one other county in the same senatorial district. (d) "[D]istricts shall be arranged so as to be as compact as practicable." (e) A county may have more than one senatorial district within that county. Ga. Code Ann. 47-121 (1963 Supp.).

(4) "Nothing herein shall be construed as an expression of intention by the General Assembly of Georgia to apportion both houses thereof according to population, rather, the General Assembly hereby expressly declares its intention to be that the Senate of Georgia be apportioned on population and that the House be apportioned on geography." Ga. Laws, Sept.–Oct. 1962, Extra. Sess., § 12, p. 7.

Section 9 of the 1962 senatorial reapportionment act also provided for the election at large of all senators in the seven counties authorized to choose two or more senators. A state court held this provision invalid under the Georgia constitution and ordered that elections in Fulton and DeKalb Counties be held solely on a district-wide basis. *Finch v. Gray*, No. A 96441 (Fulton County Super. Ct., Oct. 30, 1962). But this provision was incorporated into the state constitution by amendment approved by the voters in November 1962. Ga. Const., art. III, § 2, par. 1. Meanwhile, the same provision was challenged before a three-judge federal district court, the contention now being that the at-large election violated the equal protection of the laws clause of the fourteenth amendment. Plaintiffs' argument was sustained by the district court in *Dorsey v. Fortson*, 228 F. Supp. 259 (N.D. Ga. 1964), but rejected by the Supreme Court of the United States with only Justice Douglas dissenting. *Fortson v. Dorsey*, 379 U.S. 433 (1965). Justice Brennan, writing for the majority, said: "There is clearly no mathematical disparity . . . . The statute uses districts in multi-district counties merely as the basis of residence for candidates, not for voting or representation. Each district's senator must be a resident of that district, but since his tenure depends upon the county-wide electorate he must be vigilant to serve the interests of all the people in the county, and not merely those of people in his home district; thus in fact he is the county's and not merely the district's senator." Id. at 437-38.

On the same day that the Supreme

Court decided *Fortson v. Dorsey*, it dealt with another aspect of the earlier litigation in which the district court had in 1962 invalidated the senatorial structure. *Toombs v. Fortson*, supra. In the earlier opinion the district court had enjoined state election officials from placing on the ballot any constitutional amendments proposed by the legislature so long as it remained malapportioned. The 1964 election, however, substantially changed the composition of the legislature before the case was ready for decision on appeal to the Supreme Court. Accordingly, that Court, in a brief and somewhat cryptic per curiam order, vacated the complained-of portion of the district court's decree and remanded to that court for reconsideration, allowing "a wide range" of discretion in moulding a new decree in light of the results of the 1964 elections. *Fortson v. Toombs*, 379 U.S. 621, 622 (1965).

Meanwhile, the validity of the basic apportionment formula continued to be challenged in the federal district court which had retained jurisdiction of *Toombs v. Fortson*, supra. In June 1964 that court held invalid the apportionment formula for the Georgia house of representatives, but allowed the election scheduled for November 1964 to take place, and provided that the representatives then chosen should serve only one year. Pursuant to that order the legislature adopted a new formula for a 205-member house of representatives. H.B. 281, 367, 580. However, the court found the plan still defective because of population deviations of more than two to one and variances above the average district population of more than 36 per cent above and 24 per cent below. The deviations of 1.81 to 1 in the senate were also considered excessive. However, because of the good-faith progress

made by the Georgia legislature, the court agreed to accept the formula on an interim basis, allowing the general assembly until 1968 for final corrective action. *Toombs v. Fortson*, 241 F. Supp. 65 (N.D. Ga. 1965).

In the special election required because of the partially redrawn house districts 17 Republicans won seats in the house of representatives (an increase of 13); and 7 Negroes, all Atlanta Democrats, won election as the first of their race to sit in that house since early in the century. N.Y. Times, June 17, 1965, p. 20, col. 7.

Gray v. Sanders, 372 U.S. 368 (1963), while not strictly an apportionment case, nonetheless involved issues central to the election process in Georgia, specifically to the so-called county unit system of voting in statewide primaries. Under that system a candidate for nomination who received the highest number of popular votes in a county was considered to have carried the county and to be entitled to two votes for each representative to which the county was entitled in the house of representatives. For a complete history of the county unit system, see *Sanders v. Gray*, 203 F. Supp. 158, 161–64 (N.D. Ga. 1962). The United States Supreme Court held the system invalid, rejecting the notion that weighting of votes is permissible "once the geographical unit for which a representative is to be chosen is designated . . . ." Id. at 379. Accordingly, the Court concluded: "The conception of political equality from the Declaration of Independence, to Lincoln's Gettysburg Address, to the Fifteenth, Seventeenth, and Nineteenth Amendments can mean only one thing — one person, one vote." Id. at 381.

A constitutional convention may be called by a two-thirds vote of each house; and any changes there proposed must be referred to the people. Ga. Const. of 1945, art. XIII, § 2-8102. Other amendments may be proposed by a two-thirds vote of each house of the legislature and must then be referred to the people. Id., § 2-8101. There are no provisions for initiative or referendum.

The general assembly divided the state into ten congressional districts in 1931. Ga. Code Ann. § 34-2301. On the basis of 1930 census figures the most populous district was nearly twice as large as the least populous. Although the disparities continued to increase, no reapportionment was accomplished; by 1960 the census figures showed a differential of almost three to one between the most and the least populous congressional districts. The validity of this districting was challenged by residents and qualified voters of the most populous district, the fifth, in *Wesberry v. Vandiver*, 206 F. Supp. 276 (W.D. Ga. 1962). The three-judge federal district court found that the statute in question reflects "a system which has become arbitrary through inaction when considered in the light of the present population of the Fifth District and as measured by any conceivable reasonable standard." 206 F. Supp. at 282. But the court did not retain jurisdiction. In a two to one vote the majority concluded that, although the question presented was justiciable, *Colegrove v. Green*, 328 U.S. 549 (1946) remained a valid precedent; accordingly, the case was dismissed for want of equity.

On February 17, 1964, the Supreme Court held that claims of inequality in congressional districting are justiciable in the federal courts and that accordingly the district court's dismissal of the complaint was erroneous. *Wesberry v. Sanders*, 376 U.S. 1 (1964). Finding that the 1931 districting "grossly discrimi-nates against voters in the Fifth Congressional District," a majority of the Court held that "the command of Art. I, § 2, that Representatives be chosen 'by the People of the several States' means that as nearly as is practicable one man's vote in a congressional election is to be worth as much as another's." Id. at 8. The Court recognized that "it may not be possible to draw congressional districts with mathematical precision," but nonetheless found "no excuse for ignoring our Constitution's plain objective of making equal numbers of people the fundamental goal for the House of Representatives. That is the high standard of justice and common sense which the Founders set for us." Id. at 18. Accordingly, the lower court judgment was reversed and remanded for further judicial action if the Georgia legislature should fail to redraw the congressional district lines. Justice Harlan, who alone believed that the complaint did not state a justiciable claim, would have affirmed the judgment below which dismissed the complaint. Justice Stewart stated his agreement with the majority that the issue is justiciable and that the Court has power to afford relief, but dissented from the majority holding because, like Justice Harlan, he believed that the basis for the judicial power does not lie in article I. Justice Clark also agreed that the issue is justiciable, but believed the relevant constitutional provision to be the equal protection clause of the fourteenth amendment. Accordingly, he would have sent the case back for a hearing in the trial court on the merits of that issue in the light of *Baker v. Carr*, 369 U.S. 186 (1962). The opinions are more fully discussed in chapter IV.

In March 1964 the Georgia legislature enacted a new districting plan for the November 1964 elections. Ga. Code § 34-2301 (Supp. 1964). The population range in these districts, in terms of 1960 census figures, ranged from 329,-738 to 455,575. Conference Report, Ga. Laws 1964 Sess., p. 482. Governor Sanders commented at the time: "There is no guarantee that the Federal Courts will accept this plan." N.Y. Times, Feb. 23, 1964, p. 1, col. 2.

In *Stokes v. Fortson*, 234 F. Supp. 575 (N.D. Ga. 1964) a three-judge federal district court rejected a challenge to the method of electing judges and solicitors general of the judicial circuits in Georgia. State law permits candidates for these offices to be nominated from their respective judicial circuits, but requires election on a statewide basis, thus making difficult the local election of persons not on the ballot of the party with the strongest statewide support. Ga. Const., art. VI, § 3; Ga. Code §§ 24-2601 and 2602. The court found no inequality in the way the votes were cast and concluded further that the principle of one man, one vote, does not apply to judicial positions.

In *Reed v. Mann*, 237 F. Supp. 22 (N.D. Ga. 1964) a three-judge federal district court dismissed a claim that the method of electing the county commissioners in DeKalb County violated the equal protection of the laws clause of the fourteenth amendment. The statutory procedure specified that the chairman and four members of the commission should be elected from the county at large, although the members other than the chairman were required to be residents of the commissioner district they were chosen to represent. Plaintiffs claimed that the county-wide vote could override the will of those residing in the district. The district court held that the relevant unit for equal protection purposes was the county, and all electors within the county were treated equally.

REFERENCES

McElreath, Walter. Treatise on the Constitution of Georgia. Atlanta: Harrison & Co. 1912.
Saye, Albert B. A Constitutional History of Georgia, 1732–1945. Athens: University of Georgia Press. 1948.

HAWAII

"Hawaii is unique is many respects. It is the only state that has been successively an absolute monarchy, a constitutional monarchy, a republic, and then a territory of the United States before its admission as a state." *Holt v. Richardson*, 238 F. Supp. 468, 470 (D. Haw. 1965).

The Hawaiian Islands were annexed to the United States by joint resolution of Congress in 1898 (30 Stat. 750) and were designated as the territory of Hawaii in 1900 (31 Stat. 141). In the act of 1900 Congress provided for a territorial legislature of two houses to consist of a senate of 15 members selected from four senatorial districts, and a house of representatives of 30 members selected from six representative districts. Section 55 of the Organic Act of Hawaii (31 Stat. 141 [1900], as amended, 48 U.S.C. § 562 [1958]) required that "The legislature, at its first regular session after the census enumeration shall be ascertained, and from time to time thereafter, shall reapportion the membership in the senate and house of representatives among the senatorial and representative districts on the basis of the population in each of said districts who are citizens of the Territory . . . ." But there was no reapportionment between 1900 and 1956. The provision was amended by Congress in the latter year (and again in 1958) after the successful attack on the existing apportionment in *Dyer v. Abe*, 138 F. Supp. 220 (D. Haw. 1956), rev'd as moot, 256 F.2d 728 (9th Cir. 1958). That case concerned apportionment under the Organic Act while Hawaii was still a territory. Section 55 of the Organic Act of Hawaii provided for periodic reapportionment of territorial legislatures on the basis of population "from time to time." The court took judicial notice of the fact that neither branch of the legislature was evenly apportioned although, when the apportionment was drawn in 1900, the geographic representation was "roughly fair." 138 F. Supp. at 225. However, the court held that " 'Time to time' indisputably requires affirmative action within a span of fifty-five years," and that "Biased inaction has had the same result as biased action. It is a denial of the equal protection of the law." Id. at 226. The court also found a deprivation of due process. Id. at 227. *Colegrove v. Green*, 328 U.S. 549 (1946) was held inapplicable because an act of Congress was involved, and Hawaii then had no sovereignty of its own.

The court also stated that "A classification which discriminates geographically has the same result [as discrimination by reason of race]. It deprives a citizen of his constitutional rights . . . . Any distinction between racial and geographic discrimination is artificial and unrealistic. Both should be abolished." Id. at 236.

After this decision in the district court, Congress reapportioned the legislature of Hawaii, and the case was reversed as moot by the United States Court of Appeals for the Ninth Circuit. 256 F.2d 728 (9th Cir. 1958).

By constitutional convention in the territory of Hawaii a new constitution

was approved in 1950, to become effective "upon the admission of Hawaii into the Union as a State." The apportionment provisions of that constitution (described below), destined to become effective in 1959, were incorporated into the United States Code in all essential features by act of Congress in 1956. 70 Stat. 907 (1956). Then, in 1959, Congress adopted an admission act (73 Stat. 4, as amended, 74 Stat. 422), approving the 1950 constitution as "republican in form and in conformity with the Constitution of the United States and the principles of the Declaration of Independence," and admitted the former territory as the state of Hawaii.

Article III, section 3 of the constitution provided for a house of representatives of 51 members to be chosen initially from the 18 representative districts specified in article XVI, section 1. Reapportionment was made an executive function to be performed by the governor "on or before June 1 of the year 1959, and of each tenth year thereafter . . . ." Art. III, § 4. The house reapportionment system was as follows: The state was divided into four "basic areas": (1) the island of Hawaii, (2) the islands of Maui, Molokai, Lanai, and Kahoolawe, (3) the island of Oahu and all other islands not specifically enumerated, and (4) the islands of Kauai and Niihau. The 51 representatives were to be apportioned among these four basic areas "on the basis of the number of voters registered at the last preceding general election in each of such basic areas and computed by the method known as the method of equal proportions, no basic area to receive less than one member." After determination of the total number of representatives allotted to each basic area, that total was to be apportioned "among the one or more representative districts within each basic area on the basis of the number of voters registered at the last preceding general election within each of such representative districts and computed by the method known as the method of equal proportions, no representative district to receive less than one member." However, "should the total number of voters registered in any representative district be less than one-half of the quotient obtained by dividing the total number of voters registered in the State by the total number of members to which the house is entitled, then, as part of such reapportionment, the basic area within which such representative district lies shall be redistricted by the governor in such manner that the total number of voters registered in each new representative district therein shall be more than one-half of such quotient." The governor was then to issue a proclamation showing the results of the reapportionment which was to be effective for the election of representatives for the next five succeeding legislatures. Any registered voter was empowered to compel the governor, by mandamus or otherwise, to perform his reapportionment duties or to correct errors in them. Original jurisdiction to hear such suits was vested in the Hawaii Supreme Court. Ibid.

Senate membership was fixed at 25, chosen from six senatorial districts which were allotted from two to five senators, all enumerated in the constitution. Art. III, § 2. The short of it was that the senate was apportioned by geography and the house by registered voters. Unlike the constitutional and statutory provisions relating to the house of representatives, there was no mention of a "population" or equiva-

lent factor to govern the composition of the senate, nor was there a constitutional or statutory provision concerning reapportionment of the senate.

After the decision in *Reynolds v. Sims*, 377 U.S. 533 (1964), no one doubted that change in the constitutional formula was necessary at least in the senate. The state supreme court promptly so ruled in *Guntert v. Richardson*, 47 Haw. —, 394 P.2d 444 (1964), but refused to order reapportionment before the 1964 elections. Meanwhile, the governor called a special session to begin on July 23, 1964, seeking immediate reapportionment of both houses of the legislature. In the absence of a court order it was not possible to overcome long-established patterns so quickly. In particular, incumbents from the neighbor (outer) islands who controlled the senate were reluctant to relinquish their authority in favor of the island of Oahu.

When the matter was brought to the federal court, the three-judge district court, as expected, ruled invalid the senate apportionment formula. In addition, it held invalid the restrictive amendment provision forbidding change in the senate formula except with the concurrence of a majority of the voters in each of a majority of the four basic areas or counties. However, the court did not hold invalid, as plaintiffs had urged, the reliance in the house apportionment formula on registered voters rather than on citizen population or total population. The court observed: "Not only does the fluctuating military population of the State make representation on the basis of total population politically suspect, but large numbers of tourists who continually flow in and out of the State and who . . . , for census purposes are initially at least, counted as part of Hawaii's census population (10,000 estimated, 1960 census), would likewise result in gross inequity to citizens of the State eligible to vote, if total population were held to be the only constitutional basis for reapportionment in Hawaii." *Holt v. Richardson*, 238 F. Supp. 468, 475 (D. Haw. 1965).

To ensure that the legislature would take effective reapportionment action the court enjoined all parties to the litigation (state officials and members of the legislature) from taking final action on any legislation except that necessary to organize the legislature until passage of legislation asking for a 1965 vote on the question: "Shall there be a convention to propose a revision of or amendments to the Constitution?" The court also specified that, in the event of an affirmative popular vote, the convention should be convened in the fall of 1965 and in turn should present its proposals to the voters for approval no later than January 30, 1966. The court retained jurisdiction if the legislature should fail to act in constitutional fashion or if the voters should reject any satisfactory legislative proposal. Id. at 478–79. To accomplish all the steps suggested by the court for reapportionment of the senate, it has been observed that six elections would be required during 1965 and 1966. 54 National Civic Review 206–207 (April 1965).

Upon request by the legislature, the court modified the above order to permit the legislature to adopt a provisional reapportionment for the senate and a proposed constitutional amendment, and to postpone to 1966 the popular vote on the holding of a constitutional convention. The legislature, then in regular session, adopted legislation designed to accomplish those purposes. H.B. 773, 986, and 987. H.B. 987, the

provisional plan for reapportionment of the senate, divided the state into eight senatorial districts from each of which one to four senators were to be elected at large for a total senate of 25. Without considering the proposed constitutional amendment (H.B. 773) or the proposal for submission to the electorate of a constitutional convention call (H.B. 986), the court rejected the provisional senate reapportionment in H.B. 987 and reinstated its more restrictive order in the earlier opinion. The principal difficulty with the new plan, in the judgment of the court, was that no justification was given for establishing multimember districts in the senate, as had already been done in the house (whose formula had been approved by the court). The court found that the multimember senate districts "resulted in a material part at least, from gerrymandering." *Holt v. Richardson*, 240 F. Supp. 724, 732 (D. Haw. 1965). Moreover, said the court, "There can be no truly representative government without a system of apportionment which provides potentially equal representation to the divergent factors incorporated within the body politic." Id. at 729.

On May 21 Justice Douglas granted the governor's request for a stay of the prohibition on legislative action other than apportionment. N.Y. Times, May 22, 1965, p. 12, col. 2. On October 11, 1965, the Supreme Court granted review of what had now become three cases. *Burns v. Richardson, Cravalho v. Richardson*, and *Abe v. Richardson*, 86 Sup. Ct. 74 (1965).

Amendments to the constitution may be proposed by constitutional convention or by the legislature, in accordance with procedures set forth in article XV, sections 2 and 3. Both types of amendments must be referred to the people.

There are no provisions for the initiative.

Article XVI, section 10, as amended in 1959, provides for one representative to be elected to Congress. However, under the census of 1960 Hawaii became eligible for two representatives, both elected at large.

IDAHO

In 1863 Congress established a temporary government for the newly created territory of Idaho. Legislative power was vested in a governor and a legislative assembly consisting of a council of 7 members (which could be raised to 13) and a house of representatives of 13 members (which could be raised to 26). Provision was made for an apportionment "as nearly equal as practicable among the several counties or districts for the election of the council and representatives, giving to each section of the Territory representation in the ratio of its qualified voters as nearly as may be." Sec. 4. The authority given to the governor to fix the apportionment to undefined "counties or districts" was made somewhat more specific in a congressional amendment of the following year; and from this apparently developed the practice that was put into the constitution of 1889, which Congress recognized in 1890 as republican in form and sufficient to justify entry into the United States as a full member of the Union. Article III, section 2 of that constitution fixed the size of the original legislature at 18 senators and 36 representatives, with authority in the legislature to enlarge the bodies to their respective maximum memberships of 24 and 60. Again there was the provision for choice of senators and representatives by electors of the "counties or districts" into which the state should be divided by law. However, now the meaning was clarified in article XIX, which laid down the specifics of the election districts for both houses. The then 18 counties of the state were divided among 16 senatorial districts, 2 districts being allotted two senators each. Moreover, in a further attempt to even out population disparities, electors in each of two counties participated in the choice of senators in two different districts. Thus, the fifth district was Latah County, and the second district included Kootenai *and* Latah Counties. Idaho Const. of 1889, art. XIX, § 1. The 36-member house used the same device even more extensively; no fewer than ten counties shared in the election of two representatives. Thus, the counties of Alturas and Logan were each entitled to elect two representatives directly, and the county of Bingham was allotted three; and the three counties together chose an additional representative. Id., § 2. With seeming inconsistency, article III, section 4 assured each county one representative; and section 4 provided that no county could be divided in the formation of senatorial or representative districts. But the Idaho Supreme Court reconciled these provisions by holding that so long as any representative is elected from a district composed of more than one county, that county is represented. *Sabin v. Curtis*, 3 Ida. 662, 32 Pac. 1130 (1893).

In another early Idaho case the state supreme court, commenting on the apportionment provisions, observed that "One of the very foundation principles of our government is that of equal representation, and the legislature is prohibited from enacting an apportionment law which does not give to the people of one county substantially equal representation to that given each other county in the state . . . . The reservation of rights by the people is broad enough to prohibit the legislature from passing an apportionment act which is manifestly unequal and unjust to the people of any portion of the state." *Ballantine v. Willey*, 3 Ida. 496, 506, 31 Pac. 994, 997 (1893).

That mandate has long been disregarded in Idaho. See *Caesar v. Williams*, 84 Ida. 254, 371 P.2d 241 (1962), rejecting a challenge to the 1951 formula. As a result of amendments to the constitution and statutory implementations of authority there contained, the senate in 1965 consisted of one senator from each of the 44 counties, which in 1960 ranged in population from 915 to 93,-460. Idaho Code Ann. § 67-202. In consequence, 17 per cent of the population elected half of the senators, and 33 per cent of the population elected three fourths of the senators. The seven most populous counties contained 52 per cent of the population but elected only 16 per cent of the senators.

Apportionment of the house of representatives, as outlined in 1963 legislation, provided for at least one representative in each county. If the county population exceeded 5,000, another representative was allotted for the next complete 10,000. That is, one representative was provided for a population of 0 to 4,999, two representatives for a population of 5,000 to 14,999, etc. Ida. Sess. Laws 1963, c. 15, ¶1, p. 149. A limitation on size was imposed by a provision that the house could not exceed 132 (three times the size of the 44-member senate). Ida. Const. of 1889, art. III, § 2.

In 1963 the entire state legislative structure was challenged on fourteenth amendment grounds as well as on state grounds (improper submission of the 1911 amendment to the voters for ratification). Plaintiffs in the class action were residents and qualified voters in Ada and Bannock Counties who alleged that the 1911 amendment to the constitution and the apportioning laws of 1917, 1933, 1941, 1951, and 1963 were part of "a continuing, purposeful and systematic plan of aggressive disenfranchisement of persons living in the more populous areas of the state . . . ." Moreover, "it is alleged that the least populated one-half of the counties of the state represent only 13½ per cent of the disposable personal income of the state, yet control over half of the Representatives and 80% of the Senators . . . ." Plaintiff's Opening Brief, pp. 3, 4, *Hearne v. Smylie*, 225 F. Supp. 645 (D. Ida. 1964). Relief was denied by a two to one vote, the majority doubting its ability to fashion any effective relief in a suit for declaratory judgment.

The Supreme Court of the United States reversed and remanded for further proceedings. *Hearne v. Smylie*, 378 U.S. 563 (1964). On remand the three-judge federal district court noted that the primary election was scheduled for August 4, 1964, and so declined to interfere with the election machinery for the November 1964 elections. The court stayed all further proceedings until thirty days after the adjournment of the next legislative session scheduled to begin in January 1965.

Plaintiffs were dissatisfied with the court's failure to act and took a direct appeal to the Supreme Court. They complained of the lower court's failure to declare invalid the constitutional and statutory provisions regulating apportionment in Idaho and the failure to suggest guidelines for legislative action.

Before the Supreme Court took action, the Idaho legislature adopted a new reapportionment plan and adjourned on May 25, 1965. One week later the Supreme Court noted the existence of the new legislation and the expiration of the stay order by its own terms. Accordingly, the appeal was dismissed with the observation that the district court and the parties could now "proceed promptly" with the litigation. *Hearne v. Smylie*, 381 U.S. 420 (1965).

The 1965 legislation divided the state into nine senatorial districts for the election of 44 senators. It is presumably no coincidence that the same number of senators were to be elected from each district as there were counties included within the district. The act further provided that each political party should nominate one senatorial candidate from each county. Ida. Code Ann. § 67-202 (Supp. 1965).

More attention was paid to population in the house where provision was made for the election of the 67 representatives from 27 districts, each consisting of from one to four counties to be represented by from one to nine representatives. Ida. Code Ann. § 67-203 (Supp. 1965).

The legislature may propose constitutional amendments by a two-thirds vote of each house, subject to approval by a majority of the electors. Ida. Const. of 1889, art. XX, § 1. Similarly, by a two-thirds vote of each house the legislature may put to the voters the question whether to call a constitutional convention. Id., § 3. There is reserved to the people the power of initiative and referendum, but only as to statutory matters. Id., art. III, § 1.

The congressional districting provisions, dividing the state into two districts, appear in sections 34-1901 to 34-1904 of the Idaho code, as last amended in 1965. Based on 1960 census figures, the two districts in the 1965 act had populations of 364,984 and 299,207.

ILLINOIS

What is now the state of Illinois was originally included in the Northwest Territory whose government was prescribed in the Northwest Ordinance adopted by the Congress of the Confederation in 1787. Legislative power was vested in a governor (appointed by Congress), a five-member council (chosen by Congress from a list of ten names submitted by the territorial house of representatives), and a house of representatives chosen from the counties and districts in the number of one "for every five hundred free male inhabitants . . . ." The ordinance specified that "The inhabitants of the said territory shall always be entitled to the benefits of . . . a proportionate representation of the people in the legislature . . . ." Art. II. The provision in the ordinance for the division of the territory into "not less than three nor more than five States" (art. V) began to take shape with the division of the area into separate territories as early as 1800, when the Indiana territory was created as a governmental entity separate from the remainder of the land mass. In 1809 the Indiana territory was itself divided to create the Illinois territory. This in turn led to enabling legislation in 1818 permitting the inhabitants of the latter to form a constitution and state government; and Congress specified how the 33 delegates to the convention thus authorized should be divided among the 15 counties. The delegates, who were bound to the principles of the ordinance of 1787, fixed the representation in both houses of the first legislature (Ill. Const. of 1818, Schedule, § 8); provided for a census in 1820 and every five years thereafter (id., art. II, § 31); and provided that at the first session after those returns "The number of senators and representatives shall ... [be] apportioned among the several counties or districts to be established by law, according to the number of white inhabitants." Id., art. II, § 5. Similar fidelity to the ordinance-mandated adherence to the principle of proportionate representation was preserved in the constitution of 1848 (art. III, § 6) and the constitution of 1870 (art. IV, §§ 6, 7). Although the 1870 constitution remains the current constitution, the apportionment provisions have been substantially changed, as will be noted below.

Article IV, section 6 of the Illinois constitution (as amended in 1954) established 58 senatorial districts, the district lines to be drawn by the general assembly in 1955 in accordance with the following formula. Cook County was allotted 24 districts, 18 located within the corporate limits of the city of Chicago and 6 in the territory of Cook County outside of Chicago. The remaining 101 counties were allotted 34 senatorial districts. "All senatorial districts shall be formed of contiguous and compact territory. In their formation, area shall be the prime consideration." No provision was made for reapportionment of the senate after 1955; and the Illinois Supreme Court held that the lines drawn in 1955 were intended to be permanent. *People ex rel. Giannis v. Carpentier*, 30 Ill. 2d 24, 195 N.E.2d 665 (1964).

The constitutionality of a reapportionment act based on the above section was challenged in *Donovan v. Holtz-*

man, 8 Ill. 2d 87, 132 N.E.2d 501 (1956), where plaintiffs, as taxpayers and voters of Chicago, claimed the 1955 apportionment act (Ill. Stat. Ann. §§ 158-1 to 158-8) was unconstitutional because the senatorial districts in Chicago were neither compact nor uniform in area. The court observed that the legislature's reluctance to redistrict "can be attributed almost entirely to the fact that the General Assembly was opposed to giving control of both houses of the legislature to population-heavy Cook County." Id. at 91, 132 N.E.2d at 504. But the court had held as early as 1895 that "it was without power to compel the legislature to act affirmatively to perform its constitutional duty." Id. at 90–91, 132 N.E.2d at 503. In *Donovan v. Holtzman* the court held that "On this record we cannot conclude that the legislature did not apply the principal [*sic*] of compactness nor give 'prime consideration' to area." 8 Ill. 2d at 97, 132 N.E.2d at 507. In short, the area figures for the 18 Chicago districts were not thought sufficiently out of line to amount to a violation of article IV, section 6 of the Illinois constitution. Area differentials in Cook County and in downstate districts were not involved; nor were population differentials or the fourteenth amendment at issue.

Article IV, section 7 of the Illinois constitution, as amended in 1954, provided for a population-based house of 177 representatives to be elected from 59 districts, 3 representatives to be elected from each district. In the 1955 redistricting Cook County was given 30 districts, 23 within the corporate limits of Chicago and 7 outside of Chicago. The remaining 101 counties were given 29 districts. In redistricting subsequent to the 1960 census (required by the constitution to be accomplished in 1963 and decennially thereafter) "the fifty-nine representative districts shall be divided among (1) that part of Cook County that is within the present corporate limits of the City of Chicago, (2) that part of Cook County that is outside such corporate limits, and (3) the remaining one hundred and one counties of the state, as nearly as may be, as the population of each of these three divisions bears to the total population of the state."

In addition, section 7 provided that the districts "shall be formed of contiguous and compact territory, and shall contain, as nearly as practicable, a population equal to the representative ratio; outside of Cook County, such districts shall be bounded by county lines unless the population of any county entitles it to more than one representative district. The representative ratio for the entire state shall be the quotient obtained by dividing the population of the state by fifty-nine. No representative district may contain less population than four-fifths of the representative ratio."

Under sections 6 and 7 of article IV the duty to redistrict and reapportion was imposed on the legislature. If, however, the general assembly should fail to meet its reapportionment obligation, section 8 directed that the redistricting be accomplished by a commission selected as follows. Within thirty days after July 1 the state central committee of each of the two political parties casting the highest votes for governor in the last gubernatorial election was to submit a list of ten persons to the governor. Within thirty days thereafter the governor was directed to appoint a commission of ten members, five from each list. The commission was charged with redistricting the state in a plan approved by at least seven commission members to become effective as though enacted by the general assembly. If the commission should not file a plan within four months after its appointment, the commission was to be discharged and all candidates elected at large. Unfortunately, that is precisely what happened in 1963, necessitating election at large in 1964 of the entire 177 members of the house. In January 1964 the legislature established procedures to control the primaries preceding the at-large election. Each party nominating convention consisted of 118 delegates, 2 from each of the 59 districts, the delegates' votes weighted according to their party vote for state representatives in the 1962 general election. The conventions nominated 118 candidates for each party; and cumulative voting was abolished. Ill. Laws, 1st Spec. Sess. 1963, H.B. 1. In the November 1964 election all 118 Democratic candidates were elected in a sweep that saw that party's weakest candidate outpoll the strongest Republican. The Republicans, however, retained control of the senate. N.Y. Times, Dec. 4, 1964, p. 24, col. 1.

Cumulative voting has been permitted in Illinois since adoption of the constitution of 1870. The 1954 amendment to article IV, section 7 continued this manner of voting for members of the house of representatives, providing that "each qualified voter may cast as many votes for one candidate as there are representatives to be elected [3 in each district], or may distribute the same, or equal parts thereof, among the candidates as he shall see fit; and the candidates highest in votes shall be declared elected." Cumulative voting works in the following manner: Each voter has three votes to cast for candidates of his choice, and he can cast these votes in four different ways: (1) all three can be cast for a single candidate; (2) three votes can be divided equally between two candidates — a vote and a half for each; (3) one vote can be cast for each of the three candidates; (4) two votes can be cast for one candidate and one vote for another candidate.

Cumulative voting aims to assure minority representation in the house. Members of a minority party, by casting all votes for one candidate, can assure their representation in the legislature provided that their total votes exceed one third of the total votes of the majority party. For more detail concerning cumulative voting see Hyneman and Morgan, Cumulative Voting in Illinois, 32 Ill. L. Rev. 12 (1937) and Blair, The Case for Cumulative Voting in Illinois, 47 Nw. U.L. Rev. 344 (1952).

Amendments to the constitution of Illinois may be proposed by the legislature by two-thirds vote of both houses and submission to the electors for majority ratification (art. XIV, § 2); or by constitutional convention if two thirds of both houses vote to call a convention and a majority of the electors concur. Art. XIV, § 1. There is no provision for the initiative and referendum in Illinois.

The principal challenge to the state legislative apportionment and districting system in Illinois subsequent to *Baker v. Carr* was in the case of *Germano v. Kerner*, 220 F. Supp. 230 (N.D. Ill. 1963), rev'd, 378 U.S. 560 (1964). Plaintiffs, as residents and qualified voters of metropolitan areas of Illinois, sought to restrain state election officials from certifying the election of any candidates for state senator chosen in accordance with the provisions of article IV, section 6 of the state constitution. It was shown that 29 per cent of the voters, largely resident in rural or "downstate" areas, could control the

senate and that there were "crazy-quilt" disparities in senatorial districts even within the three classes of districts, the 18 in Chicago, the 6 in Cook County outside Chicago, and the 34 districts in the rest of the state. By a two to one vote the federal district court rejected the argument, finding the apportionment not irrational, particularly in view of the districting in the essentially population-based house and the fact that the provision here at issue had been approved by a referendum of the voters in 1954.

On June 22, 1964, the Supreme Court of the United States reversed and remanded for further proceedings. The three-judge federal district court, to which the case was remanded, took no action until after the 1964 election described above. When the Illinois legislature convened on January 6, 1965, for its regular session the Democratic governor presented a plan for reapportionment that was not acceptable, at least immediately, to the Republican-controlled senate. N.Y. Times, Jan. 7, 1965, p. 22, col. 5. Later that month, on January 22, the three-judge court held invalid the provisions of the state constitution calling for apportionment of the senate "on the basis of area." The court enjoined the holding of further elections for state legislators pursuant to the provisions held invalid and threatened an at-large election for the 58 senate seats if the legislature failed to adopt a valid reapportionment. The court also specified that any such legislation be submitted to it before any election should be held pursuant to its terms. In February 1965 the Illinois Supreme Court, in a separate proceeding, also held invalid the composition of the state senate; and it too retained jurisdiction. *People ex rel. Engle v. Kerner*, 32 Ill. 2d 212, 205 N.E.2d 33 (1965).

In light of that decision the federal court was asked to vacate its January order and stay further proceedings; but it declined to do so. *Germano v. Kerner*, 241 F. Supp. 715 (N.D. Ill. 1965). On appeal from that decision the Supreme Court of the United States vacated the order of the federal court which "should have stayed its hand." The Court observed that "The power of the judiciary of a State to require valid reapportionment or to formulate a valid redistricting plan has not only been recognized by this Court but appropriate action by the States in such cases has been specifically encouraged." *Scott v. Germano*, 381 U.S. 407, 409 (1965).

In a unique proceeding, the state and federal courts in August 1965 agreed on an apportionment formula that gave 21 senators to Chicago, 9 to Cook County outside Chicago, and 28 to the rest of the state. Failure of commission agreement on a house plan could produce a similar order there. N.Y. Times, Oct. 17, 1965, p. 84, col. 1.

Illinois was districted into 24 congressional districts by legislation enacted in 1961. Ill. Stat. Ann., c. 46, § 156f.1 (Supp. 1963). Challenges to earlier congressional districting statutes of the Illinois general assembly were uniformly unsuccessful before the decision in *Baker v. Carr*. The most celebrated was *Colegrove v. Green*, 328 U.S. 549 (1946). See also *Keogh v. Horner*, 8 F. Supp. 933 (S.D. Ill. 1934); *Daly v. Madison County*, 378 Ill. 357, 38 N.E.2d 160 (1941). For another unsuccessful assault upon a different feature of Illinois election laws, the requirement of 200 signatures from each of at least 50 counties for an effective nominating petition, see *MacDougall v. Green*, 335 U.S. 281 (1948).

On October 13, 1965, the state and federal courts, apparently pleased with their cooperative efforts at state legislative reapportionment, agreed upon a congressional districting plan. N.Y. Times, Oct. 14, 1965, p. 29, col. 7.

REFERENCES

Barker, Twiley W., Jr. A Long, Long Ballot, 53 National Civic Review 170 (April 1964).
———. Illinois Tries Again, 54 National Civic Review 417 (Sept. 1965).
Blair, George S. Cumulative Voting: An Effective Electoral Device in Illinois Politics. Urbana: University of Illinois Press. 1960.
Grove, Samuel K., and Steiner, Gilbert Y. The Illinois Legislative Process. Urbana: Institute of Government and Public Affairs, University of Illinois. 1954.
———. The Legislature Redistricts Illinois. Urbana: Institute of Government and Public Affairs, University of Illinois. 1956.
Illinois Legislative Council. Legislative Apportionment in Illinois. Springfield: 1952.
Illinois State Constitutional Convention (1869). Debates and Proceedings. 2 Volumes. Springfield: E. L. Merritt & Brother, 1870.
Juergensmeyer, John E. The Campaign for the Illinois Reapportionment Amendment. Urbana: Institute of Government and Public Affairs, University of Illinois. 1957.
Wimberly, William Carl. The Direct Primary in Illinois. Unpublished doctoral thesis. Urbana: University of Illinois. 1957.
Blair, George S. The Case for Cumulative Voting in Illinois, 47 Northwestern University Law Review 344 (1952).
———. Cumulative Voting: An Effective Electoral Device in Illinois Politics, 34 S.W. Soc. Sci. Q. 3 (1954).
———. Cumulative Voting in Illinois, 42 Nat'l Munic. Rev. 410 (1953).
———. Cumulative Voting: Patterns of Party Allegiance and Rational Choice in Illinois State Legislative Contests, 52 Am. Pol. Sci. Rev. 123 (1958).
Hyneman, Charles S. Legislative Experience of Illinois Lawmakers, 3 U. Chi. L. Rev. 104 (1935).
——— and Morgan, Julian D. Cumulative Voting in Illinois, 32 Ill. L. Rev. 12 (1937).
Olson, Russell E. Illinois Faces Redistricting, 43 Nat'l Munic. Rev. 343 (1954).

INDIANA

The land within the present state of Indiana was originally included in the Northwest Territory whose government was prescribed in the Northwest Ordinance adopted by the Congress of the Confederation in 1787. Legislative power was vested in a governor (appointed by Congress), a five-member council (chosen by Congress from a list of ten names submitted by the territorial house of representatives), and a house of representatives chosen from the counties and districts in the number of one "for every five hundred free male inhabitants . . . ." The ordinance specified that "The inhabitants of the said territory shall always be entitled to the benefits of . . . a proportionate representation of the people in the legislature . . . ." Art. II. The provision in the ordinance for the division of the territory into "not less than three nor more than five States" (art. V) began to take shape with the division of the area into separate territories as early as 1800 when the Indiana territory was created as a governmental entity separate from the remainder of the land mass. From that territory Congress carved out the territory of Illinois in 1809 and, five years later, set Indiana on the path to becoming a state of the Union. In 1814 Congress empowered the territorial house of representatives to divide the territory into five districts for the election of members of the legislative council of the territory. In 1816 Congress authorized the inhabitants of the territory to form a constitution and state government. Apportionment of the 33 delegates to the convention was provided by the congressional enabling act among the 13 counties, varying from one to five delegates allotted to each county. The resulting constitution of 1816, as approved by resolution of Congress, established a bicameral legislature, both houses of which were to be apportioned in accordance with a census "of all the white male inhabitants above the age of twenty-one years." Ind. Const. of 1816, art. III, § 2. Pro-

vision was made for a house initially of 25 to 36 members which might later be raised, as the population increased, to a maximum of 100 (the present number). Ibid. Senators, in a number from one third to one half the number of representatives (50 is the present number), were also to be "apportioned among the several counties or districts . . . according to the number of white male inhabitants of the age of twenty-one years in each . . . ." Id., § 6.

The constitution of 1851, which, as amended, is the present constitution, also provided for apportionment of both senators and representatives "among the several counties, according to the number of male inhabitants . . . ." Ind. Const. of 1851, art. IV, § 5. There were also added at this time two provisions, one specifically allowing the cumulation of counties in both senatorial and representative districts, so long as the counties were contiguous, and the other providing that "no county, for Senatorial apportionment, shall ever be divided." Id., § 6. All of the above provisions of the constitution of 1851 have remained essentially unchanged, even, curiously, the provision for apportionment "according to the number of *male* inhabitants, above twenty-one years of age" (emphasis supplied), despite the intervening nineteenth amendment to the United States Constitution which would seem to make this provision inoperative.

Reapportionment is made a responsibility of the general assembly at six-year intervals. Id., § 4. However, the last apportionment prior to 1963 was in 1921. Ind. Gen. Stat. §§ 34-101 to 34-104. As a result, in 1962 39.5 per cent of Indiana voters could elect a majority of the senate, and 38 per cent could elect a majority of the house. The variance in the house was four to one; for example, 14,875 persons in Parke County elected one representative, and 62,795 persons in Clark County also elected one representative. Indiana has 92 counties.

Apportionment bills were enacted in 1857, 1867, 1879, 1885, 1891, 1893, 1895, 1897, 1903, 1905, 1915, and 1921; five of these twelve acts were declared unconstitutional. *Parker v. State ex rel. Powell*, 133 Ind. 178, 32 N.E. 836 (1892), 33 N.E. 119 (1893) invalidated the 1891 and 1879 acts. *Denny v. State ex rel. Basler*, 144 Ind. 503, 42 N.E. 929 (1896) invalidated the 1893 and 1895 acts. *Brooks v. State ex rel. Singer*, 162 Ind. 568, 70 N.E. 980 (1904) invalidated the 1903 act. See also Note, Reapportionment in the Indiana Legislature: Judicial Compulsion and Legislative Duty, 32 Ind. L. J. 489 (1957).

The courts in the above cases held that the duty of the legislature with respect to periodic apportionment was mandatory and not discretionary and that the constitution was designed to secure an equal voice to all electors of the state. It was also decided that questions relating to the validity of apportionment acts were judicial and not political questions and that courts could pass upon the validity of apportionment acts in the same manner as upon the validity of all other legislative actions. *Parker v. State ex rel. Powell*, supra. *Brooks v. State ex rel. Singer*, supra, held that only one valid apportionment act could be passed for each six-year enumeration period. *Brooks* also settled the question of standing to sue by deciding that any qualified voter could bring an action to declare an apportionment act invalid regardless of whether the inequalities complained of existed in his own senatorial or representative district or in another. *Denny*

v. State ex rel. Basler, supra, decided that if one reapportionment act failed, the state should fall back upon the latest noninvalidated act; and it ordered election officials to follow such a procedure. But in *Fesler v. Brayton*, 145 Ind. 71, 44 N.E. 37 (1896) the court held that a challenge to the one remaining apportionment act which had not been repealed or invalidated could not be considered by the courts.

More recent cases have challenged the constitutionality of the 1921 apportionment act, and have sought to have the court order the legislature to reapportion itself according to the state constitution.

(1) *Matthews v. Handley*, 179 F. Supp. 470 (N.D. Ind. 1959), aff'd per curiam, 361 U.S. 127 (1959) was a taxpayers' suit against the governor wherein plaintiffs sought a declaratory judgment and injunction to restrain collection of the state income tax, alleging their right to have the entire membership of the Indiana legislature reapportioned as required by the constitution. The federal district court dismissed the petition for lack of jurisdiction after admitting that the Indiana legislature had flagrantly disregarded its duty: "We are here concerned with two distinct, sovereign bodies: the State of Indiana and the United States of America. As stated above, we are here presented with a state judicial question in which the plaintiffs seek to invoke the Equity jurisdiction of this Federal Court. This court has no jurisdiction to determine this question as the plaintiffs have adequate remedies at law available to them, and, what is more important, the Federal sovereignty must not and shall not invade this bulwark of state sovereignty." 179 F. Supp. at 471. See also *Grills v. Gardner* (John-

son County Cir. Ct. 1964), denying an injunction to restrain the payment of legislators' salaries and expenses because of the alleged invalidity of the method of selection.

(2) In *Grills v. Anderson*, 29 U.S. L. Week 2443 (March 28, 1961) the Marion County Superior Court of Indiana found that the failure of the members of the general assembly to make a reapportionment for more than thirty-four years constituted a violation of their sacred oath of office "and strikes down the legislature of the state of Indiana." However, the court did not exercise its equity power to take any action to restrain or prevent the election of members of the legislature. It merely declared that the failure to reapportion constituted a denial of equal protection under both the state and federal constitutions. Defendants failed to perfect an appeal from that decision.

(3) In *State ex rel. Welsh v. Marion Superior Court, Room 5*, 243 Ind. 307, 185 N.E.2d 18 (1962) the trial court had ordered the elections board to reapportion the state and to conduct elections accordingly. The question on review was whether the trial court had the jurisdiction to enter such an order. The supreme court of Indiana held that it did not, because the state election board was merely an administrative body created by the legislature to perform the limited function of administering the election laws of the state without discretion to reapportion.

(4) In *Stout v. Hendricks*, 228 F. Supp. 568 (S.D. Ind. 1963) the state attorney general, on behalf of the defendants, stipulated with the plaintiffs that "no rational explanation of the present apportionment in Indiana can be given in terms of the equal protection clause of the Fourteenth Amendment to the Constitution of the United States." Ac-

cordingly, the sole issue before the court related to the choice of remedy. The three-judge federal district court accepted the stipulation and found the existing apportionment invalid, but withheld affirmative relief to give the 1965 legislature an opportunity to act.

Meanwhile, a reapportionment act passed by the legislature in 1963 was vetoed by the governor. Ind. S.B. 160, 1963 Spec. Sess. However, in a suit challenging the timeliness of a similar veto the state supreme court held that the veto came too late, thus reviving the legislation. *Hendricks v. State ex rel. Northwest Indiana Crime Commission*, 196 N.E.2d 66 (Ind. 1964). Accordingly, a similar result followed as to the apportionment statute. *State ex rel. Bogard v. Hendricks*, Cause No. S63-7713 (Super. Ct., Marion County, Room 3, 1964). Because the act now declared operative had repealed the acts held unconstitutional by the three-judge federal district court, a single member of that panel refused to hear challenges to the constitutionality of the 1963 act and so dismissed the federal court case. *Stout v. Hendricks*, 228 F. Supp. 613 (S.D. Ind. 1964).

Thereafter, plaintiffs in the now-dismissed federal court case secured permission from the *three*-judge panel to file a second supplemental complaint challenging the constitutionality of the 1963 act. *Stout v. Hendricks*, 235 F. Supp. 556 (S.D. Ind. 1964). On the merits the court noted that under the provisions of the 1963 act the most populous house district was 2.16 times larger than the least populous district and that comparable ratios in the senate were 2.66 to 1. The court held the 1963 act violative both of the equal protection clause of the fourteenth amendment and of article IV, section 5 of the Indiana constitution. Since the predecessor act of 1921 had previously been held invalid, the court stated in its ruling on February 26, 1965, that "no valid apportionment . . . now exists in Indiana, and it is the duty of the 94th General Assembly now in session to enact a valid and constitutional law . . . in compliance with the standard of representation in each house on the basis of 'substantial equality' of population." *Stout v. Bottorff,* No. IP 61-C-236 (S.D. Ind. 1965).

The legislature responded with new legislation asserted to meet those standards. Chapter 230 of the Indiana Acts of 1965 provided that 100 representatives should be elected from 58 districts composed of from one to four counties, each to be represented by from one to 15 representatives. Floterial districts were liberally used to even out population differentials, with the result that in a number of cases one county was allowed to participate in the selection of representatives from two districts. By the same act the 50 senators were divided among 38 districts. Multiple-county districts and floterial districts were again used. For example, Marion County (Indianapolis) was allotted seven senators in the 28th district and also shared one senator with Hendricks and Morgan Counties in the 29th district.

Additional plaintiffs from counties included in floterial districts created by the 1965 act joined the *Stout* litigation in federal court to challenge the constitutionality of the floterial districts; and the claim was sustained on September 20, 1965. The court held that the act produced "substantial and unjustified debasement, devaluation, and impairment of the right of voters within said special joint districts and in relation to voters in other districts within the State." *Stout v. Bottorff,* Cir. No. IP 61-C-236 (S.D. Ind. 1965). The legislature

was given until December 1, 1965, to enact a valid plan for the 1966 elections.

Article XVI, section 1 provides that amendments to the constitution may be proposed by either branch of the legislature, and, if agreed upon by a majority of both branches of two consecutive general assemblies, may be submitted to the electors for approval by a majority of those voting. There are no provisions for a constitutional convention, nor for the initiative and referendum.

In 1942 the state was divided into 11 congressional districts, the present number. Ind. Gen. Stat. §§ 24-201 to 24-213. In terms of 1960 census figures the population differential between the most populous and least populous district was 406,971. Redistricting was completed in 1965 to accomplish greater equality. 1965 Ind. Laws, c. 205.

REFERENCES

McPherson, Edwin B. and Roberts, George C. Apportionment and Reapportionment in Indiana. Bloomington: Bureau of Government Research, Indiana University. 1957.

Seltzer, Robert D. Rotten Boroughism in Indiana. Unpublished doctoral dissertation. Bloomington: Indiana University. 1952.

Hamilton, Howard D., Beardsley, Joseph E., and Coats, Carleton C. Legislative Reapportionment in Indiana, 35 Notre Dame Law. 368 (1960).

Hyneman, Charles S. Tenure and Turnover of the Indiana General Assembly, 32 American Political Science Review 51, 311 (1938).

League of Women Voters, Reapportionment of the Indiana General Assembly (1963).

Note, Reapportionment in the Indiana Legislature: Judicial Compulsion and Legislative Duty, 32 Ind. L.J. 489 (1957).

Note, The Significance of Baker v. Carr for Indiana, 38 Ind. L.J. 240 (1963).

IOWA

By act of Congress in 1834 the region which became the territory and later the state of Iowa was attached to and made a part of the territory of Michigan. Within two years the population of the entire territory increased, Michigan became a state, and the future Iowa was incorporated into the territory of Wisconsin. In the act of 1836 the provisions of the Northwest Ordinance of 1787 were reaffirmed, including article II of that document, which guaranteed "a proportionate representation of the people in the legislature." The territory of Wisconsin was itself divided in 1838, and Congress established the territorial government of Iowa. The legislative power was vested in the governor and a legislative assembly to consist of a council of 13 members and a house of representatives of 26 members. An apportionment was to be made "as nearly equal as practicable, among the several counties, giving to each section of the Territory representation in the ratio of its population, Indians excepted, as nearly as may be." Sec. 4.

Article III of the constitution of 1846 provided for an enlarged legislature, a house of 26 to 39 members initially, with provisions for increase to 75 as population expanded (§ 31), and a senate "not less than one third, nor more than one half the representative body . . . ." (§ 6). The number of senators and representatives was to be apportioned "according to the number of white inhabitants" among the several counties, on the basis of an enumeration to be completed every other year over an initial period of eight years. Iowa Const. of 1846, art. III, § 31.

The constitution of 1857 provided for a senate of not more than 50 members and a house of not more than 100 members to be "apportioned among the several counties and representative districts in the State according to the number of white inhabitants in each . . . ; but no representative district shall contain more than four organized counties, and each district shall be entitled to at least

one Representative. Every county and district which shall have a number of inhabitants equal to one-half of the ratio fixed by law, shall be entitled to one Representative; and any one county containing, in addition to the ratio fixed by law, one-half of that number, or more, shall be entitled to one additional Representative. No floating district shall hereafter be formed." Iowa Const. of 1857, art. III, § 35. Despite this first concession to representation by political units, it was clear that the basic unit of representation continued to be the district, which could be cumulated from as many as four counties.

The constitutional requirements for equal representation were faithfully adhered to by the state legislature until 1886, when the tradition of redistricting to achieve equality was replaced by legislative inaction. Specific reversal of the equality principle was accomplished by two constitutional amendments in the twentieth century, in 1904 and 1928. The 1904 amendment provided one representative for each county regardless of population, with an additional nine seats for the nine most populous counties. The amendment of 1928, providing that no county be granted more than one senate seat, largely abandoned the principle of equality of representation in the senate. That system, more fully described below, "insures a minimum of representation for small political units in one house, and at the same time affixes maximum limits to the representation of populous areas in the other house." Note, Judicial Intervention in Legislative Reapportionment — Applicability to Malapportionment in Iowa, 49 Iowa L. Rev. 109, 118 (1963).

Article III, section 34 of the Iowa constitution established a senate of 50 members elected from senatorial districts established "at the next session of the general assembly held following the taking of the state and national census." Although the apportionment of senators is to be based on population "as shown by the last preceding census," the 1928 limitation provided that "no county shall be entitled to more than one (1) senator." Iowa Const. of 1857, art. III, § 34. Two further qualifications were imposed by article III, section 37: Senatorial districts composed of two or more counties were not to be entirely separated by any county belonging to another district; and no county was to be divided in forming a senatorial district (qualifications which applied also to the fixing of congressional and representative districts). Section 41.1 of the Iowa code (effective 1961) divided the state into 50 senatorial districts. The consequences of these provisions were noted by the Iowa Supreme Court in *Selzer v. Synhorst*, 253 Ia. 936, 943, 113 N.W.2d 724, 728 (1962), as follows: "Because of the provision that no county shall have more than one Senator, it is impossible to apportion the seats in the senate into units of equal population. A single county district may have a population greater than the average in multiple county districts."

Article III, section 35 of the Iowa constitution established a house of representatives consisting of "not more than one hundred and eight members." Apportionment in the house was primarily based on representation by political unit (at least one representative per county), allowing one additional representative only to each of the nine most populous counties.

The Iowa legislature is authorized to propose constitutional amendments for ratification by the people, if passed in identical form by two successive legis-

latures. Art. X, § 1. Acting pursuant to that power, the 59th general assembly in 1961 and the 60th general assembly in 1963 proposed an entirely new apportionment plan providing for a senate of 58 members to be chosen on a population base with no more than 10 per cent deviation from the population ratio in each district, and a house of 99 members, 1 for each county. However, the proposal was rejected by the voters on December 3, 1963, by a vote of 271,214 in opposition and 191,421 in favor. The urban counties voted heavily against the plan, assuring its defeat, although the proposal carried in 64 of the 99 counties.

The urban negative may have been stimulated by the prospect for judicial relief of their underrepresentation in both houses. In *Davis v. Synhorst*, 217 F. Supp. 492 (S.D. Iowa 1963), plaintiffs were residents and qualified voters in Polk County, the most populous in the state. The three-judge federal district court found the existing provisions invidiously discriminatory, noting that the nine most populous counties together had about 37 per cent of the state population, but only one sixth of the house membership (and less than one fifth of the senate membership). "The House is at least potentially controlled by the 55 smallest counties; 27.4 per cent of Iowa's total population elect a majority of the representatives. . . . The 26 least populous [senate] districts . . . elect a majority of the Senate although they include only 35.6% of all Iowans." Id. at 496. Moreover, the court found insufficient the amending processes as a basis for relief. "[T]he amendment machinery permits a malapportioned General Assembly to perpetuate the inequality of representation. When amendments are accomplished through the legislative proposal method the initiative is with the legislature; and when the people vote for a constitutional convention, the legislature determines how the convention will be constituted." Id. at 499–500. However, because of the then pendency of the proposed constitutional amendment, the court by a two to one vote declined to give immediate relief, although retaining jurisdiction. After the voters rejected the proposed amendment, the court entered its final order of invalidation of the existing constitutional provisions in January 1964. The court ruled that at least one house must be chosen on a strict population basis, and any departure from population in the other house must be on a "rational basis." The court suggested a special session of the legislature and said that "if a special session of the Legislature is not called within a reasonable time, or if the Legislature is convened and it becomes apparent that no substantial progress has been made to provide for constitutional apportionment, this court reserves jurisdiction to consider prescribing an interim plan of reapportionment." *Davis v. Synhorst*, 225 F. Supp. 689, 694 (S.D. Iowa 1964).

The Supreme Court of the United States affirmed the decision of the three-judge federal district court and remanded the case to that court for further proceedings. *Hill v. Davis*, 378 U.S. 565 (1964). The Supreme Court did not, however, pass on the validity of an apportionment plan which had in the meanwhile been enacted by the Iowa legislature in a special session convened by the governor after the January decision by the district court. The act had been approved as an "interim" plan of apportionment by the three-judge court on March 27, 1964; but that decision was not before the Supreme

Court when it issued its brief order affirming the decision invalidating the earlier legislation. The district court noted that by the 1964 act "the malapportionment in both houses of the General Assembly has been materially reduced." *Davis v. Synhorst*, 231 F. Supp. 540, 541 (S.D. Iowa 1964). The maximum population disparity among representative districts was reduced to 2.23 to 1 and among senatorial districts to 3.2 to 1.

When the district court considered the matter in 1965, after the Supreme Court ruling in the *Reapportionment Cases* in June 1964, it held the senate formula invalid; but two members of the three-judge court thought it unnecessary to rule on the validity of the house formula — which they thought "arguably close" — because the apportionment scheme as a whole was at issue and thus held defective. The third judge would have held the house formula also invalid. *Davis v. Cameron*, 238 F. Supp. 462 (S.D. Iowa 1965).

The court also divided on the appropriate remedy. The majority was content to enjoin the use of the 1964 legislation for the next election in 1966, but fixed no exact deadline for legislative compliance. Judge McManus, dissenting, would have preferred a deadline during the 1965 legislative session in time to allow judicial review before adjournment. If necessary, he said, "this court should do the job." Id. at 468.

In June 1965 a temporary reapportionment act (to control the 1966 elections pending popular vote on a proposed constitutional amendment in 1967) became effective. No change was made in the house apportionment, but two additional senatorial positions were created, both to go to Polk County, which would then have five of 61 seats instead of three of 59. Iowa Laws 1965,

Sen. File 568. The entire plan was attacked in state court on the ground of disadvantage to counties with multiple representation for which election was to be at large. The way was cleared for state court decision of this issue when the federal court agreed to withhold its own judgment pending the state court interpretation of this question. Des Moines Register, Sept. 3, 1965, p. 1, col. 8.

Although there is in Iowa no provition for initiative or referendum, changes in the Iowa constitution may be proposed by two successive legislatures, as noted above, and by constitutional convention, as provided in article X, section 3. Provision is there made for the question to be put to the voters every ten years, "Shall there be a Convention to revise the Constitution, and amend the same?" (In November 1964 an amendment to the constitution requiring voter approval before any revision of the constitution by convention can become effective was approved by a vote of about two to one).

Section 40.1 of the Iowa code provides for the division of the state into seven congressional districts (effective 1961). Article III, section 37 of the constitution provides that when a congressional district shall be composed of two or more counties, it shall not be separated by any county belonging to another district; and no county shall be divided in forming a congressional district. The population differential in 1964 between the most populous and the least populous districts (based on 1960 census figures) was 89,250.

REFERENCES

Report of the Governor's Reapportionment Action Committee. Des Moines: State of Iowa. 1959.

Iowa Legislative Research Bureau. A Look at State Apportionment and Reapportionment. Bulletin No. 4. Des Moines: 1956.

League of Women Voters of Iowa. A Study of State Legislative Representation. Des Moines: July 1962.

League of Women Voters of Iowa. What About the Shaff Plan for Legislative Reapportionment? Des Moines: August 1962.

Mather, George B., and Ray, Robert F. The Iowa Senatorial Districts Can be Reapportioned, A Possible Plan, 39 Iowa L. Rev. 535 (1954).

Stoyles, Robert L., and Kennedy, Frank R. Constitutional and Legal Aspects of the Plan, 39 Iowa L. Rev. 557 (1954).

Note, Judicial Intervention in Legislative Reapportionment — Applicability to Malapportionment in Iowa, 49 Iowa L. Rev. 109 (1963).

KANSAS

What later became the state of Kansas was established as the territory of Kansas by act of Congress in 1854. Legislative power was vested in the governor and a legislative assembly consisting of a 13-member council and a 26-member house of representatives, both to be apportioned "as nearly equal as practicable, among the several counties or districts . . . giving to each section of the Territory representation in the ratio of its qualified voters as nearly as may be." Sec. 22. Between 1854 and the act of 1861 by which Congress admitted Kansas into the Union as a state, four constitutional conventions were held, and as many constitutions proposed, in 1855, 1857, 1858, and 1859. The apportionment provisions of the first three of those, although differing considerably in detail one from another, were in general conformity with the equal-population principle in both houses of the legislature. Kan. Const. of 1855, Schedule, Sixth Part; Kan. Const. of 1857, art. V, § 23 and unnumbered section entitled Election Districts; Kan. Const. of 1858, Schedule, §§ 9, 10. Congress found the constitution of 1859 to be "republican in form" and in 1861 admitted Kansas to the Union. The constitution then approved, as amended, remains the present constitution of the state.

The legislature was originally fixed in size at 75 representatives and 25 senators (Kan. Const. of 1859, art. 2, § 2), to be selected from 14 election districts. The original apportionment was specified in the constitution. Adherence to the principle of population representation is indicated by the way in which the districts were drawn among the then 40 counties. For example, the 3d district, consisting of three counties, was allotted two representatives and one senator; the 7th district, consisting of a single county, was allotted nine representatives and three senators; and the 14th district, consisting of seven counties, was allotted one representative and (curiously) no senator. Id., art. 10, § 3. For the future it was provided that each organized county should be entitled to at least one representative. Id., art. 10, § 1.

In 1873 the apportionment provisions took their present form with a constitutional amendment which fixed the maximum membership of the senate at 40 and of the house at 125. In addition, it was provided that each county in which at least 250 votes were cast at the last preceding general election should be entitled to one representative. Kan. Const. of 1859, as amended, art. 2, § 2. With the present 105 counties this means that there were only 20 house seats to be divided among the most populous counties on the basis of population.

Article 10, section 2 requires reapportionment as a legislative duty every five years after 1866, "based upon the census of the preceding year," language which has been construed by the Kansas courts to mean that the periodic reapportionments must satisfy the test of substantial equality. See *Harris v. Shan-*

ahan, 192 Kan. 183, 389 P.2d 771 (1963). However, from 1886 to 1963, when a new apportionment act was passed (later invalidated, as noted below), only limited readjustments were made in senatorial and representative districts. Drury and Titus, Legislative Apportionment in Kansas: 1960, p. 31; The Wichita Sunday Eagle and the Wichita Beacon, July 28, 1963, p. B1, col. 1.

Harris v. Shanahan, supra, attacked both the senatorial and representative apportionments. An injunction was sought to restrain the secretary of state and other election officials from conducting further elections under existing laws and, instead, to conduct elections for senators on an at-large, statewide basis and for representatives from multi-district counties on an at-large county-wide basis because of the legislature's failure to reapportion every five years. The trial court granted the injunction. While the case was on appeal to the Kansas Supreme Court, a further reapportionment was enacted by the legislature then in session, changing the 40 senate districts to conform to population with no more than a 10 per cent differential in any district from the population norm. This was achieved by the drawing of district lines to some extent without regard to existing county lines. Thus, 11 western Kansas counties were combined into a single district, while Sedgwick County, the most populous county, was allotted five complete districts and shared in parts of four other districts made up in part of other adjoining counties.

In December 1963 the Kansas Supreme Court held the entire apportionment scheme invalid. The 1963 apportionment of the senate was held invalid because of a flaw in the enactment process (the enrolled bill signed by the governor was not identical with the bill passed by the legislature). The house apportionment, although not changed by the 1963 act, was also invalidated for failure to satisfy the state constitutional requirement that the house districts must be as substantially equal in population as the constitution's geographic requirements permit. With a 125-member house to be apportioned among the 105 counties of the state, substantial equality is not possible so long as each county is assured one representative. *Harris v. Shanahan*, supra.

At a special session the legislature in early 1964 adopted legislation apportioning the state into 40 senatorial districts of approximately equal population and retaining the 125-member house. As before, one representative position was apportioned to each of the 105 counties and the 20 remaining seats were distributed by population in accordance with the method of equal proportions. Kan. Laws 1964, Spec. Sess., cc. 1 and 2. This apportionment was promptly upheld by the state supreme court in *Harris v. Shanahan*, 192 Kan. 629, 390 P.2d 772 (1964). However, after the decision of the Supreme Court of the United States in the *Reapportionment Cases*, the state supreme court held invalid the 1964 apportionment act and the provisions of the Kansas constitution calling for at least one representative for each county — a task which the court found "distasteful." *Harris v. Anderson*, 400 P.2d 25 (Kan. 1965). The court promised, in reviewing future reapportionment legislation, "to exercise all the patience and understanding it is permitted within the limitations of *Reynolds*, and will approve any reasonable plan of the legislature which does not result in arbitrary classification or unreasonable departure from the equal population principle recently

declared to be a federal constitutional requisite." Id. at 32. The court fixed no deadline for legislative action, but felt "certain" that the legislature would act long enough before April 2, 1966, to permit the secretary of state time to implement the legislation. Review of this decision was sought in the Supreme Court of the United States by petition for writ of certiorari. The petition was denied by the Court on October 26, 1965.

The legislature by a two-thirds vote of both houses may propose constitutional amendments to be submitted, after publication, to the electors for majority ratification. Art. 14, § 1.

By a two-thirds vote of both houses, the legislature may also recommend to the electors the calling of a convention to revise, amend, or change the constitution. If a majority of the electors vote for a convention, the legislature shall provide for one at its next session. Id., § 2. There is no provision to indicate how delegates to such a convention would be chosen.

As a result of national population shifts since 1950, the 1960 census showed that Kansas would lose one congressional seat. The legislature completed the necessary redistricting in 1961, dividing the state into five congressional districts. Interestingly enough, the resulting first district was the largest both in area (more than one half the state) and in population (23.8 per cent above the population norm). See Titus, How Kansas Was Reapportioned, 17 Your Government (pamphlet, 6 pp. Apr. 15, 1962). It is also worth noting that Wyandotte County, the smallest in terms of area, was divided into two parts, each assigned to a different congressional district. This division was made by a Republican legislature, which, it may be speculated, was not unmindful of the fact that the county had gone Democratic by substantial majorities for at least fifteen years. Id. at 3.

REFERENCES

Drury, James W., and Titus, James E. Legislative Apportionment in Kansas: 1960. Lawrence: Governmental Research Center, University of Kansas. 1960.
Page, Thomas. Legislative Apportionment in Kansas. Unpublished doctoral dissertation. Minneapolis: University of Minnesota. 1951. All except chapters 2 and 4 published as Governmental Research Series No. 8, Lawrence: Bureau of Government Research, University of Kansas. 1952.
Titus, James E. How Kansas Was Reapportioned, 17 Your Government 1 (Apr. 1962).
Recent Case (Harris v. Shanahan), 77 Harv. L. Rev. 1526 (1964).

KENTUCKY

The commonwealth of Virginia in 1789 consented to the severance from its boundaries of the district of Kentucky for the formation of a new state. Thereafter, in 1791, Congress, upon petition from the people of the district of Kentucky, approved admission of the state of Kentucky to become effective in 1792. The first constitution thus approved provided for a general assembly of 40 to 100 representatives (Ky. Const. of 1792, art. I, § 6) and a senate of 11 members "until the number of counties is equal to the number of senators; after which, when a new county is made, it shall, as to the choice of senators, be considered as being a part of the county or counties from which it shall have been taken." Id., § 9. The number of representatives was originally fixed at 40; and the apportionment of that number among the then nine counties in section 3 of the schedule of that first constitution shows the attempt to conform to the existing population dispersal. The allotment of representatives ranged from nine for Fayette County to two for Mason County. It was also provided that within two years after the first meeting of the general assembly, and every four years thereafter, an enumeration should be made of "the free male inhabitants above twenty-one years of age," and the number of representatives "apportioned among the several counties, according to the number of free male inhabitants above the age of twenty-one years in each . . . ." Id., art. I, § 6.

The constitution of 1799 specifically stated that "Representation shall be equal and uniform in this Commonwealth; and shall be forever regulated and ascertained by the number of qualified electors therein." Apportionment of the 58 (to 100) representatives, based on a census every fourth year, was to be made "among the several counties and towns, in proportion to the number of qualified electors." Ky. Const. of 1799, art. II, § 6. Similarly, the 24 senate districts were to be allotted "to contain, as near as may be, an equal number of free male inhabitants in each, above the age of twenty-one years," permitting cumulation of counties to form a district, but forbidding division of counties. Id., §§ 11, 12.

The constitution of 1850 was even more insistent upon equal election districts for the choice of senators and representatives, providing against the division of ward or municipal divisions "unless it be necessary to equalize the elective, senatorial or representative districts." Ky. Const. of 1850, art. II, § 5. In that constitution the number of representatives was fixed at 100 and the number of senators at 38 (id., § 13), the former to be chosen from 10 election districts (§ 6), and the latter from 38 single-member districts (§ 14).

These provisions were slightly modified in the most recent constitution, that of 1890, although the size of the two houses was not changed. Ky. Const. of 1890, §§ 33, 35. The districts were to be "as nearly equal in population as may be without dividing any county, except where a county may include more than one district . . . . Not more than two counties shall be joined together to form a Representative district: Provided, in doing so the principle requiring every district to be as nearly equal in population as may be shall not be violated . . . . If, in making said districts, inequality of population should be unavoidable, any advantage resulting therefrom shall be given to districts having the largest territory." Id., § 33. These provisions have remained constant.

It is of course not possible to satisfy both the constitutional requirement of near-equality of population among the representative districts and the apparent prohibition against joining more than two counties to form a single district. With that problem in mind the Kentucky Court of Appeals, as long ago as 1906, offered in dictum its belief that "more than two counties may be joined in one district, provided it be necessary in order to effectuate that equality of representation which the spirit of the whole section so imperatively demands." *Ragland v. Anderson*, 125 Ky. 141, 161–162, 100 S.W. 865, 870 (1907). In fact, between 1893 and 1918 there were four districts consisting of more than two counties each. But after 1918 no district included more than two counties, with the result that by 1963, 37.5 per cent of the state's population in 93 counties (of 120) elected 53 representatives; and the population disparity among the districts was 17 to 1 in

the house. As a result of the failure of the legislature to make any reapportionment between 1942 and 1963, the situation in the senate was little better. A senator in Kentucky's most populous district then represented six times as many people as his counterpart in the least populous district. See Report of Commission on Reapportionment, pp. 1, 2 (Dec. 4, 1962). There were also wide disparities within some metropolitan counties as well as between urban and rural areas.

In view of these inequalities the governor called the legislature into an extra session in 1963 to consider only the question of apportionment. To test the legality of his proposed action he brought a declaratory judgment action in the state court, *Combs v. Matthews*, 364 S.W.2d 647 (Ky. 1963). The defendant, the commissioner of finance, whose department would have to approve salaries and expenses for the assemblymen and senators, claimed that under section 33 of the constitution the general assembly could not consider reapportionment until 1964. The trial court held that there was no justiciable issue. The court of appeals reversed, noting that "[w]hen [reapportionment] has not been undertaken for twenty years, the emphasis is clearly on promptness in correcting accumulated inequalities, for pervading the whole section [33] is the 'principle requiring every district to be as nearly equal in population as may be.'" Id. at 649.

The most important question decided in *Combs v. Matthews* was that concerning the apportionment limitation in section 33 that "not more than two counties shall be joined together to form a representative district . . . ." The court, relying in part on the 1906 *Ragland* case, specifically held that the general assembly may include more than two counties in a representative district if it is deemed necessary to effect a reasonable equality of representation among the districts.

As a result of the decision in *Combs v. Matthews*, permitting cumulation of more than two counties in a single representation district, the Kentucky legislature was able in 1963 to enact a reapportionment statute in which the maximum population disparity in each house was about two to one as between the most and the least populous districts. In the senate 44.8 per cent of the population was necessary to elect a majority of the senators, and in the house 46.6 per cent. Ky. Rev. Stat. Ann. §§ 6.010, 6.030 (3d ed. 1963).

Amendments to the constitution may be proposed by the legislature by a three-fifths vote of both houses and submitted to the electorate for majority ratification. Ky. Const., § 256. Provisions for the convening of a constitutional convention are found in section 258 of the constitution. There are neither constitutional nor statutory provisions for the initiative or referendum.

The 1964 session of the Kentucky legislature created the Kentucky Constitution Revision Assembly, authorizing continuing review of the state constitution and providing for submission of proposals for constitutional change as appropriate. The act creating the assembly provided that its members be chosen jointly by the governor, the lieutenant governor, the speaker of the house, and the chief justice of the court of appeals. One delegate was appointed from each of the 38 state senatorial districts; five were appointed from the state at large; and each of the state's seven living former governors was made a delegate by the act. Ky. Rev. Stat. Ann. § 7.170 (Supp. 1964).

After the results of the 1960 census became known, Kentucky was forced to reduce its congressional districts from eight to seven. Ky. Rev. Stat. 1962, § 120.070. Jefferson County was made the third congressional district with a population of 610,947, while the least populous first district consisted of 20 counties with a 1960 population of 350,839. Hence, the value of a vote in the first district was 1.75 times that of a vote in the fifth district. The state court of appeals in *Watts v. Carter*, 355 S.W. 2d 657 (Ky. 1962) held the act to be valid. The court stated that "[c]onsidering . . . the special problems and disadvantages inherent in splitting up a single densely-populated county and grafting a slice of it onto another and dissimilar district, we are unable to say that the solution . . . was clearly arbitrary and unreasonable . . . . As to the shape of the new district, compactness was formerly, but is no longer, a statutory requirement imposed by Congress." Id. at 658-59.

In August 1962 the citizens of Jefferson County brought a class suit in federal district court, *Clark v. Carter*, 218 F. Supp. 448 (E.D. Ky. 1963), claiming the inequality violated the equal protection clause of the fourteenth amendment. That court also held the statute not to be arbitrary. "Since it is clear from the record in this case that the Third District contains the thickly populated city of Louisville, the largest city in the State, and its populous surrounding area, the Fourth District contains the thickly populated cities of Covington and Newport with their suburbs, and the other districts contain many thinly populated rural areas, in view of the slight difference in respect to the value of individual votes in the largest district as compared with the smallest district, it seems quite apparent that the enactment of [the statute] was the result of legislative consideration as to the proper diffusion of political initiative as between the thinly populated districts and those having concentrated masses in view of the fact that the latter have practical opportunities for asserting their political weight not available to the former." Id. at 452.

REFERENCES

Jewell, Malcolm E. "Kentucky: A Latent Issue," in The Politics of Reapportionment 111–19. New York: Atherton Press. 1962.
————. The 1962 Congressional Redistricting in Kentucky, 51 Ky. L.J. 16 (1962).
Note, Legislative Reapportionment — the Kentucky Legal Context, 51 Ky. L.J. 722 (1963).

LOUISIANA

The present state of Louisiana, originally part of the land ceded to the United States by treaty of purchase with France in 1803, became in 1804 the territory of Orleans. The legislative power was vested in the governor and a council of 13 "persons of the territory" who were to be appointed annually by the President of the United States. In 1811 Congress authorized the calling of a constitutional convention, to which not more than 60 delegates were to be apportioned "amongst the several counties, districts and parishes in the said territory of Orleans in such manner as the legislature of the said territory shall by law direct." Sec. 2. The resulting constitution of 1812, which was approved by Congress as the basis for admission of Louisiana into the Union in the same year, provided that "Representation shall be equal and uniform in this state, and shall be forever regulated and ascertained by the number of qualified electors therein." The enumeration of the electors was to be made in 1813 and every fourth year

thereafter. The number of representatives was to be fixed at not less than 25 and not more than 50. La. Const. of 1812, art. II, § 6. The senate was to have a membership of 14 chosen from single-member districts. Most of the original districts comprised individual counties; but population differentials were taken into account as well. The city and county of Orleans was divided to form two districts, and two parishes were united into a single district. Id., § 10.

The constitution of 1845 preserved the requirement of "equal and uniform" representation in the house of representatives, then increased to a membership of 70 to 100. There was, however, a provision that each parish should have at least one representative, although this in turn was qualified by a prohibition against the creation of any new parish (1) with fewer electors than the norm for a representative, or (2) whose creation would leave any other parish with fewer than the requisite number of electors. La. Const. of 1845, tit. II, art. 8. Thus, the principle of equality was satisfied. The provisions for the senate were more complex, but essentially provided for 32 senatorial districts, allowing cumulation of parishes, but no division thereof except in the case of Orleans. Population was the controlling factor, subject to the following rules to be applied after each enumeration: (1) After deduction of the population of New Orleans from that of the state, the remainder was to be divided by 28 (since New Orleans was limited to one eighth (4) of the senators); (2) the resulting figure became the senatorial ratio; and (3) single or contiguous parishes could be formed into districts having a population as nearly as possible that of the senatorial ratio. Id., arts. 15, 16. Reapportionment was to be completed after each enumeration, to be made in 1847, 1855, and every ten years thereafter. Id., arts. 7, 15.

The constitution of 1852 did not significantly change the method of apportionment and did not change at all the size of the two houses. That constitution was carried over virtually without change during the secession period except that in 1861 the words "Confederate States" were substituted for "United States."

The constitution of 1864 preserved essentially the same principles, but provided in the constitution itself the apportionment for both representative and senatorial districts. Of the 118 representatives to be divided among the then 48 parishes, it was specified that 44 should go to the parish of Orleans, which in turn was divided into ten plural-member representative districts on the left bank of the Mississippi and one on the right bank; and the other parishes were assigned from one to four representatives each. La. Const. of 1864, tit. III, art. 12. The state was divided into 22 senatorial districts composed of as many as four parishes or as little as a part of the parish of Orleans (ibid.), "according to the electoral population contained in the several districts; *Provided*, That no parish shall be entitled to more than nine senators." Id., art. 22.

The constitution of 1868 carried forward the same basic principles, but with a reduced number of representatives (101 rather than 118); and the parish of Orleans was reduced in representation even more (from 44 to 23). La. Const. of 1868, tit. II, art. 22. The representation of the left-bank portions of the parish of Orleans in the senate was also reduced, from nine to eight, although the number of senators remained constant at 36. Ibid. This pattern was largely preserved as well in the

constitution of 1879. As before, the legislature was required to change the apportionment in the first legislative session after each census, at ten-year intervals beginning in the year 1890. La. Const. of 1879, arts. 16–18.

The constitution of 1921 (the present constitution, last amended in 1960) provided originally for a house of representatives of 100 members. Art. III, § 5. Article III, section 2 continued the historic provision that representation in the house "shall be equal and uniform, and shall be based upon population." However, that section limited strict equality by providing that each parish and each ward of the city of New Orleans must have at least one representative. There are 63 parishes (in addition to the parish of Orleans) and 17 wards in New Orleans. Consequently, only 20 of the 100 representative seats were left to be distributed in accordance with population. This is in marked contrast with the constitution of 1864, discussed above, which allotted 44 of 118 seats in the house to the parish of Orleans.

In 1954 a second member was added for Jefferson Parish, and in 1960 the number of house seats was increased to 105 by constitutional amendment to article III, section 5, which also apportioned those seats, giving two additional seats to the parish of East Baton Rouge and two seats to the parish of Jefferson.

Attacks on the 1960 house apportionment formula were unsuccessful in both federal and state courts in 1963. *Daniel v. Davis*, 220 F. Supp. 601 (E.D. La. 1963); *LeDoux v. Parish Democratic Executive Committee*, 156 So.2d 48 (La. 1963).

Article III, section 3 of the Louisiana constitution provides that the "number of senators shall not be more than thirty-nine." The principal limitation upon apportionment of senatorial districts is that "No parish, except the parish of Orleans, shall be divided in the formation of a senatorial district." Art. III, § 3. In addition, whenever a new parish is created, "it shall be attached to the senatorial district from which most of the territory is taken, or to another contiguous district, but shall not be attached to more than one district." Ibid. Consequently, only whole parishes may be added together to form senatorial districts. The provision of contiguity when adding parishes to form districts is express in the case of new parishes, and it can be argued that the section implies that only contiguous counties may be added together to form senatorial districts.

It is the duty of the legislature to divide the state into senatorial districts "in every year in which it shall apportion representation in the House of Representatives," that is, every ten years after 1930. Art. III, § 3. As noted above, the constitution explicitly requires that the house of representatives be apportioned on the basis of population; but there is no such constitutional provision relating to apportionment of the senate. Article III, section 3 provides only that the senate be reapportioned at the same time that the house is reapportioned and article III, section 6 that the "apportionment of senators and representatives shall not be changed or altered in any manner until after the enumeration shall have been taken by the United States." Article III, section 4, amended in 1956, established the composition of the 39 senatorial districts. It also provided that "whenever more than one senator is apportioned to any district composed of more than one parish not more than one senator shall be elected from any parish."

The 1960 census disclosed the population of Louisiana as 3,257,022, which, divided by 39, gives the senatorial mean of 83,513. The most populous senatorial district then contained 248,477 persons while the least populous had 31,175. A majority of the senate could be elected by 33 per cent of the population. The house mean was 31,019; the most populous house district had 120,205 persons while the least populous had 6,909.

In *Bannister v. Davis*, Civ. No. 2818 (E.D. La.) plaintiff in 1963 sought reapportionment of the state senate before the elections to the 1964 legislature or, alternatively, an election at large. In April 1965 plaintiff sought an order requiring the legislature to submit a plan for senate reapportionment in time to permit nominations to be held on that basis for the 1968 legislature to be nominated in November 1967. In September 1965 no date had been set for a hearing.

The legislature may propose amendments to the constitution by a two-thirds vote of both houses. Amendments become effective upon ratification by a majority of the electors voting thereon (except where five or fewer political units are affected, then requiring also a majority vote in the affected units). Art. XXI, § 1.

There are no provisions for a constitutional convention nor for the initiative or referendum.

Article VIII, section 9 of the Louisiana constitution provides that congressmen shall be chosen in the manner and at the time prescribed by law. Louisiana Revised Statutes, tit. 18, § 1431 divides the state into eight congressional districts. This act was passed in 1912 and there have been no changes since that time. As a result of intervening population shifts the districts are grossly out of proportion according to the 1960 census. The mean is 407,128 persons per district. However, the largest congressional district, one of the two in New Orleans, consisted of 536,029 persons while the smallest upstate district had only 263,850 persons.

REFERENCES

Louisiana Legislative Council. Legislative Apportionment in Louisiana. Report to the Council No. 29. Baton Rouge: 1961.
Havard, William C. The 1958 Proposals to Amend the Louisiana Constitution, 19 La. L. Rev. 128 (1958).
———. The 1960 Proposals to Amend the Louisiana Constitution, 21 La. L. Rev. 109 (1960).
Comment, Congressional Reapportionment: The Theory of Representation in the House of Representatives, 39 Tulane L. Rev. 286 (1965).
Note, Reapportionment — The Louisiana Situation, 38 Tulane L. Rev. 173 (1963).

MAINE

The province of Maine was the subject of various royal English grants between 1606 (the first charter of Virginia) and 1691 when it was included within the Massachusetts Bay Colony under the terms of the second charter of Massachusetts Bay. In 1820 the commonwealth of Massachusetts agreed to the separation of the district of Maine for the purpose of forming the latter into a state of the Union. With the concurrence of Congress, as required by article IV, section 3 of the United States Constitution, Maine was separated from Massachusetts and admitted to the Union to be governed under the terms of the constitution prepared at a convention assembled in 1819, and approved thereafter by the people. That constitution, as amended from time to time, remains the instrument of government today. Although the number of senators and representatives has changed from the original provisions in 1819, the emphasis on population as the principal factor in determining representation has remained constant as outlined below in connection with the present constitution.

Legislative power in Maine is vested in two "distinct" branches of government, a house of representatives and a senate, "each to have a negative on the other," but the people reserve to themselves the power to propose laws (the initiative) and to reject laws (the referendum) at the polls independent of the legislature. Me. Const. of 1819, art. IV, pt. 1, § 1. See also art. IV, pt. 3, §§ 17, 18, discussed below.

The house of representatives consists of 151 members to be apportioned by the legislature not more often than every five years nor less frequently than every ten years among the several counties according to the number of inhabitants "exclusive of foreigners not naturalized." Art. IV, pt. 1, § 2. The legislature has the duty of causing the number of inhabitants of the state to be ascertained (ibid.), a duty which may be discharged in any reasonable manner, including the adoption of the latest federal census. *Opinion of the Justices*, 148 Me. 404, 94 A.2d 816 (1953). When an apportionment of representatives has been made it must remain in force without alteration for at least five years. *Opinion of the Justices*, 33 Me. 587 (1851). The duty to apportion is a continuous one, and if it is not made within the period prescribed by the constitution, that duty "devolves upon the legislature then next sitting and upon each following legislature until that duty is performed." *Opinion of the Justices*, 148 Me. 404, 407, 94 A.2d 816, 818 (1953).

After enumeration the number of representatives shall be "apportioned among the several counties, as near as may be, according to the number of inhabitants, having regard to the relative increase of population." Art. IV, pt. 1, § 2.

In *Opinion of the Justices,* 3 Me. 477 (1821) the last clause quoted above was interpreted as follows: "It was unquestionably the intention of the framers of our Constitution, that each of the counties should be fairly and equally represented according to its population; but it must have been foreseen that no arrangements could produce a representation precisely proportioned to numbers." Id. at 479. Since in the irregularities of settlement some counties would increase in numbers more rapidly than others, and since every apportionment must continue for five years and may continue for ten, inqualities in representation would necessarily arise during the intervals of successive apportionments. Therefore, the legislature was encouraged to anticipate the population of each county at an appropriate point between the two periods of enumeration and thus to allocate to such county additional representation if the ratio of its increase of population justified increase. Ibid. This unique provision for legislative 'regard to the relative increase of population" was repealed by constitutional amendment approved by the voters in 1963, as discussed below.

Representation in Maine is ascertained by a double process described in Article IV, part 1, sections 2 and 3, as amended in 1963 and 1964. First, the representatives are apportioned to the respective counties as outlined above; then a constitutional ratio (the unit base number) is applied to the cities, towns, and plantations within the counties. The process works as follows:

(1) The 151 representatives are equally apportioned among the 16

counties according to the number of inhabitants, "fractional excesses over whole numbers to be computed in favor of the counties having the larger fractional excesses." Art. IV, pt. 1, § 2. (The last clause represents a change made by amendment in 1963.)

(2) These representatives are then apportioned within each county by use of the unit base number, a constitutional ratio determined by dividing the county population by the number of seats allotted to the county.

(3) The 1963 amendment clarified the procedure as follows: "Each city or town having a number of inhabitants greater than the unit base number shall be entitled to as many representatives as the number of times the number of its inhabitants fully contains the unit base number; and the remaining cities, towns and plantations within the county which have inhabitants in numbers less than such unit base number shall be formed into representative class districts in number equal to the remainder of county representatives unallocated under the foregoing procedure by grouping whole cities, towns and plantations as equitably as possible with consideration for population and for geographical contiguity." Art. IV, pt. 1, § 3.

The above provisions are basically the same as previous provisions. However, the rest of the amended section 3 contains provisions which tend to make the representative districts within the counties more equitable.

(4) No representative district "shall contain fewer inhabitants than the largest fraction remaining to any city or town within such county after the allocating of one or more representatives under the foregoing procedure." Ibid.

(5) Section 3 also enables the legislature by a two-thirds vote of both

houses to organize towns or cities entitled to two representatives into single-member districts "provided that all such cities and towns are so organized."

(6) The last paragraph of amended section 3 authorizes the supreme judicial court of Maine to make an apportionment in the event the legislature fails to do so.

The present Maine senate consists of 34 members, apportioned by a fixed population formula. Each county with a population of 30,000 inhabitants or less is entitled to one senator; counties with populations between 30,000 and 60,000 are entitled to two; those between 60,000 and 120,000 shall have three; those between 120,000 and 240,000 shall have four; and counties with a population over 240,000 shall have five (the maximum). Me. Const., art. IV, pt. 2, § 1. No county has over 240,000 according to the last senatorial apportionment in 1961. See Me. Sess. Laws 1961, c. 120, pp. 1266–1267. "For the purpose of representation, foreigners not naturalized and Indians not taxed shall not be counted as inhabitants." Me. Const., art. IV, pt. 2, § 1.

There is no express constitutional statement providing for reapportionment of the senate by the legislature as there is in the sections relating to the house. It appears that changes are only to be made whenever a county's population entitles it to an additional senator. Thus, the only change in existing senate membership made by the 1961 act, supra, was to increase the legislature from 33 to 34 members by allotting an additional (fourth) senator to Penobscot County. This was the first change since 1931.

The 1960 population of Maine, divided by 34 senate seats, gives a population senate mean of 28,508. On that basis the most populous senate district in 1961 had 45,687 persons, while the least populous district had only 16,146 and 46.9 per cent of the population was able to elect a majority in the senate.

The legislature, by a two-thirds vote of both houses, may propose amendments to the constitution, to be referred to the people for ratification by a majority of the electors voting. Art. X § 4. The legislature may also, by a two thirds "concurrent" vote of both branches, call a constitutional convention. Art. IV, pt. 3, § 15.

Electors comprising 10 per cent of the total vote for governor cast in the last gubernatorial election may request (within ninety days after the recess of the legislature) that one or more acts or bills passed by the legislature be referred to the people for approval or rejection by a majority of electors voting thereon at a general or special election (the referendum). Art. IV, pt. 3, § 17 The electors also have the right of direct initiative except that it does not extend to amendments to the state constitution. Art. IV, pt. 3, § 18.

After the 1960 census Maine had to reduce the number of its congressional representatives from three to two. Me. Sess. Laws 1961 c. 196, p. 1165. The 1960 population divided by two gives a congressional population mean of 484,633. The larger district contains 505,465 persons and the smaller 463,800. Maine had previously been districted generally along vertical (north–south) lines. The new act essentially switched the axis placing the seven counties in the southern tier in the first district.

REFERENCES

Maine Constitutional Commission. Fourth Report (Leg. Doc. 1476, 101st Legislature Augusta: 1963.

Mawhinney, Eugene A. Maine's Legislative Apportionment — Present and Future, Maine Manager's Newsletter 1 (April 1963

Note, State Apportionment — the Wake of Reynolds v. Sims, 45 B.U.L. Rev. 88, 92–98 (1965

MARYLAND

Between 1632 and the inception of the revolution in 1776, Maryland was governed in the manner authorized by the royal charter of 1632 through which King Charles granted the "Province of Maryland" to Caecilius Calvert, Lord Baltimore. Throughout the colonial period the upper house of the Maryland legislature consisted of the governor and council. The council, modeled after the English House of Lords, was appointed by the proprietor. Members of the house of delegates during this period were selected on a county basis, four from each of the 18 counties and two from each of 2 cities.

The constitution of 1776 provided for the indirect election of the senate. Two electors were chosen by the people of each county and one each from the town of Baltimore and the city of Annapolis (as they then were). The electors chose 15 senators, of whom 9 had to be from the western shore and 6 from the eastern shore. On the basis of the 1790 census this resulted in 40 per cent of the people choosing a majority of the electors. An 1837 amendment to the constitution ended the indirect election of senators and provided for one senator from each county and one from the city of Baltimore. By this time the senate was subject to the control of 33 per cent of the population.

The 1851 constitution kept the same formula in the senate, which resulted, under the 1860 census, in reducing the percentage of the population necessary to elect a majority of the senate to 29 per cent. At this time it was specified that the house of delegates should be apportioned "among the several counties of the State, according to the population of each . . . ." Md. Const. of 1851, art. III, § 3. Limitations were imposed in that the city of Baltimore was assured "four more delegates than are allowed to the most populous county, but no county shall be entitled to less than two members, nor shall the whole number of delegates ever exceed eighty, or be less than sixty-five; . . . ." Ibid.

The constitution of 1864 gave each county one senator and divided the city of Baltimore into three districts, each of which was given one senator (Md. Const. of 1864, art. III, §§ 2, 3), a pattern continued in the constitution of 1867 (Md. Const. of 1867, art. III, § 2). Amendments to that constitution in 1900 and 1922 increased the number of senators and legislative districts in the city of Baltimore to four and six respectively. Md. Laws, 1900, c. 469; id., 1922, c. 7. Despite the increased numerical representation for the city of Baltimore, the proportion of the populace with power to elect a majority dropped considerably between 1860 and 1960: 1860, 29 per cent; 1900, 23 per cent; 1922, 21 per cent; 1940, 17 per cent; 1960, 14 per cent.

In the successive constitutions noted above the house of delegates was apportioned with some attention to population, but always to the disadvantage of the city of Baltimore and more recently to the disadvantage also of the county of Baltimore and the counties adjacent to the District of Columbia, principally Anne Arundel, Montgomery, and Prince George's. Until the Maryland state courts held invalid the apportionment provisions as to the house of delegates, article III, section 5 of the constitution had since 1950 provided for 123 delegates, 36 to be chosen from the city of Baltimore (6 from each legislative district), 6 from each of seven named counties, 4 from each of four counties, 3 from each of five counties, and 2 from each of seven counties.

The above-described provisions for the apportionment of both houses of the Maryland general assembly were challenged and, as to the house of delegates, upset in *Maryland Committee for Fair Representation v. Tawes*, 228 Md. 412, 180 A.2d 656; 229 Md. 406, 184 A.2d 715 (1962). In that case plaintiffs — residents and voters of the city of Baltimore and three urban and suburban counties, and an unincorporated association on behalf of its members — had filed a complaint in the circuit court of Anne Arundel County against the governor and other state officials who have duties in connection with election proceedings. At the initial hearing the trial judge sitting as chancellor dismissed the complaint. But on appeal that decision was reversed, and the case was remanded for a hearing on the merits. The evidence at that hearing showed that, while the city of Baltimore and the counties of Anne Arundel, Baltimore, Montgomery, and Prince George's had 75.3 per cent of the total 1960 state population, they had only 10 of the 29 senators and 60 of the 123 delegates. In addition, there were substantial further inequalities even within the disfavored population groups. The trial court concluded that the apportionment of the house of delegates was invidiously discriminatory, but said that the senate apportionment might be "constitutionally based upon area and geographical location regardless of population or eligible voters," although he did not at that time rule formally on that point. Subsequently, the Maryland Court of Appeals directed the chancellor to determine that issue, whereupon he issued a supplemental opinion holding that the composition of the Maryland senate did not violate the fourteenth amendment. On July 23, 1962, the Maryland Court of Appeals, in a four to three decision, affirmed the lower court's ruling that the

senate formula was valid. 229 Md. 406, 184 A.2d 715 (1962).

Meanwhile, the Maryland legislature enacted temporary legislation reapportioning the house of delegates. Md. Ann. Code art. 40, § 42 (Supp. 1962). Under that statute the membership of the house of delegates remained at 123. Each county and each of the six legislative districts of the city of Baltimore was assured a minimum of 2 delegates (total of 58); the remaining 65 delegates were to be apportioned "on a basis of relative population," by proclamation of the governor after each federal decennial census in accordance with the formula set out below.

The total population of the state was divided by 65, and the resulting quotient became the unit of population necessary for an additional delegate. The unit of population, as divisor, was then to be divided into the population of each county in the state and of each legislative district of the city of Baltimore whose population exceeded the unit of population. Each county (and legislative district) was to have an additional number of delegates equal to the resulting quotient in each instance, dropping any fractional remainder. If the total number of delegates so apportioned should be less than 123, the additional delegates were to be awarded in descending order to those counties or legislative districts "having the highest fractional share of a unit of population as a remainder" after the quotient has been computed, until all of the 123 delegates were apportioned. Id., § 42(a)–(c).

Subsection (d) of article 40, section 42 made this apportionment formula effective in 1966. During the four-year term of members of the house of delegates elected in November 1962 each county and legislative district was continued with the number of delegates it had on January 1, 1962. "For those four years [1962–1966], the formula for membership in subsection (c) based upon the federal census of 1960 shall be applied as to those counties and legislative districts for which it provides an increase in representation, but the formula shall not be applied as to those counties and legislative districts for which it would provide a decrease in representation, or as to which it leaves representation unchanged." Id., § 42(e). In accordance with that formula additional members in the house of delegates were given to Baltimore County (13 instead of 6), Montgomery and Prince George's Counties (10 each instead of 6 each), Anne Arundel County (7 instead of 6), the third legislative district of Baltimore (8 instead of 6), and the fifth legislative district (7 rather than 6). Id., § 42(f). Thus, the only practical effect of the 1962 temporary legislation was to add 19 seats to the membership of the house of delegates, increasing its membership from 123 to 142 for the four-year terms beginning in 1962.

When the Supreme Court of the United States reviewed the 1962 decision of the Maryland Court of Appeals, which had upheld the senate apportionment formula, the Court considered as well the above-discussed 1962 legislation relating to the house of delegates, even though its validity had not been specifically passed on by the Maryland high court. The Supreme Court noted the impossibility of deciding "the validity of the apportionment of one house of a bicameral legislature in the abstract, without also evaluating the actual scheme of representation employed with respect to the other house. . . . We cannot be compelled to assume that the Maryland House is presently apportioned on a population basis, when that is in fact plainly not so." *Maryland Committee for Fair Representation v. Tawes*, 377 U.S. 656, 673 (1964). In a full opinion (discussed in chapter V) the Court held invalid the apportionment in both houses of the general assembly. Observing that no further elections were due until 1966, the Court thought that there was "sufficient time" for the general assembly to act.

In October 1965 the legislature approved, and the governor signed, two reapportionment plans, apparently leaving the choice to the federal court.

The legislature may propose constitutional amendments by a three-fifths vote of both houses, to be referred to the electors for majority ratification. Md. Const., art. XIV, § 1. The constitution can also be amended by a constitutional convention. The general assembly is empowered at the general election in 1970 and every twenty years thereafter to "take the sense of the people" in regard to calling such a convention. Any changes which may be adopted at the convention must be ratified by a majority of electors. If called the convention must consist of delegates from each county and legislative unit equal to its legislative strength. Id., § 2. Sections 1 and 2 of article XVI prescribe the referendum powers of the people. There is no provision for the initiative.

In 1963 Maryland was divided into eight congressional districts (Md. Sess. Laws 1963, c. 380, pp. 618–620), effective June 1, 1963, for the primary and general elections scheduled in 1964. Since the population of Maryland by the 1960 census was 3,100,689 the congressional population mean was 387,586 for each district. However, the districts so created ranged in population from 711,045 to

243,570. In a suit challenging this legislation a three-judge federal district court on February 3, 1964, suggested that if the legislature failed to act, election at large might be ordered. *Maryland Citizens Committee for Fair Congressional Redistricting, Inc. v. Tawes,* 226 F. Supp. 80 (D. Md. 1964). On March 26, 1964, the same court specifically held the existing congressional districting statute unconstitutional, as well as the 1963 enactment, described above, then pending on referendum. But the court allowed the 1964 elections to be held under the existing statute (Md. Ann. Code art. 33, §§ 159–66 [1957]), providing for seven Congressmen to be elected from districts and one to be elected at large. *Maryland Citizens Committee for Fair Congressional Redistricting, Inc. v. Tawes,* 228 F. Supp. 956 (D. Md. 1964).

In *Ellis v. Mayor and City Council of Baltimore,* 234 F. Supp. 945 (D. Md. 1964) a three-judge federal district court held invalid the apportionment of city councilmen, both as prescribed in the Baltimore city charter and as proposed for revision. Noting that no further elections would be held for the council positions until 1967, the court indicated its confidence that the city council would take timely corrective action.

REFERENCES

Radoff, Morris Leon (ed.). The Old Line State, A History of Maryland. Hopkinsville, Ky.: Historical Record Association. 1956.

Lukas, J. Anthony. Barnyard Government in Maryland, Reporter 31 (April 12, 1962).

Pettengill, Dwynal B. "Frustration of One-Party Control," in Jewell, Malcolm E. (ed.). The Politics of Reapportionment. New York: Atherton Press. 1962.

Tabor, Neil. The Gerrymandering of State and Federal Legislative Districts, 16 Md. L. Rev. 277 (1956).

Note, Senate Reapportionment — The Maryland Experience, 31 Geo. Wash. L. Rev. 812 (1963).

MASSACHUSETTS

In 1629 Charles I of Great Britain granted a proprietary charter for the colony of Massachusetts Bay. The charter designated a governor, deputy governor, and eighteen "assistants" for the governing of the body there created to be known as the "Governor and Company of the Massachusetts Bay in Newe England." Legislative power was conferred upon the governor or his deputy and any seven or more of the assistants, to act as "a full and sufficient Courte or Assemblie" of the company.

Although the freemen of the colony were at least in theory entitled to participate in the legislative process of this general court, the government was in fact dominated by the company for some years. As the number of freemen increased, and as they asserted their rights more vigorously, a form of government evolved that was new to the colonies. By 1644 the general court was divided into two branches, one the original court of assistants and the other the general court, both chosen by the freemen. Thereafter, the two bodies sat as separate and coordinate branches of the general court, thus constituting the first bicameral legislature in the American colonies. Perry (ed.), Sources of Our Liberties 80–81 (1959).

Official recognition of representative government in a two-chamber assembly continued in the charter of Massachusetts Bay, granted in 1691 by William and Mary, which combined the provinces of Massachusetts Bay, including Maine, New Plymouth, and the territory of Acadia or Nova Scotia into a single colony. Legislative power was conferred upon a "Great and Generall Court of Assembly" to consist of the governor and his council and of two freeholders elected from each of "the respective Townes and Places." Thereafter, that legislative body was itself to choose 28 members for the council (at least 18 from Massachusetts Bay, at least 4 from New Plymouth, at least 3 from Maine, and at least 1 from Nova Scotia) and to fix the number of delegates to be elected from each "County Towne and Place."

These provisions were in large part confirmed by George I in 1725, while reserving to the governor the right of rejection of any person selected as speaker of what was by then known as the house of representatives.

The Massachusetts constitution of 1780 has survived to the present, although with considerable change in the apportionment provisions. Initially, the constitution provided for a senate of 40 members to be chosen from districts fixed by the general court (as the legislature is still known) in accordance with "the proportion of the public taxes paid by the said districts . . . provided that the number of districts shall never be less than thirteen; and that no district be so large as to entitle the same to choose more than six senators." Mass. Const. of 1780, c. I, § II, art. I. Until the legislature could act the seats were divided among the then 14 counties, giving each county from one to six senators except that Dukes and Nantucket Counties were combined into a single senatorial district. Ibid.

Apportionment of the house of representatives has from 1780 been directed to be "founded upon the principle of equality." Id., c. I, § III, art. I. The constitution provided for representation by corporate towns, originally authorizing the selection of one representative for 150 "ratable polls," thereafter adding one representative for each 225 additional ratable polls. Id., art. II.

The number of ratable polls sufficient to justify additional representation was increased several times in the mid-nineteenth century; and provisions were added for a census every ten years "to provide for a representation of the citizens of this commonwealth, founded upon the principles of equality . . . ." A provision of special interest was that dealing with the representation to be accorded towns with less than the minimum ratio for one representative and to those towns with any number of ratable polls in excess of the number needed to qualify for their authorized representation. In such cases representation was authorized for part of the years of each ten-year period in proportion to the number of unrepresented voters divided by the whole number of voters required for one additional representative. See, for example, amendments XII (1836), XIII (1840), and XXI (1857) of the constitution of Massachusetts. Amendment XXI also made special provision for the town of Cohasset to be added for apportionment purposes to the county of Plymouth, which completely surrounds it *physically*, rather than to Norfolk County in which it was, and is, *politically* situated; and provisions were made for the drawing of district lines within multiple-member county districts "according to the relative numbers of legal voters in the several districts of each county . . . ."

Under the terms of amendment XXII (1857) a census was to be taken in 1857, 1865, and every ten years thereafter on the basis of which the general court could apportion 40 senatorial districts, "each district to contain, as nearly as may be, an equal number of legal voters, according to the enumeration aforesaid: *provided, however*, that no town or ward of a city shall be divided therefor; and such districts shall be formed, as nearly as may be, without uniting two counties, or parts of two or more counties, into one district."

The essentials of the apportionment system outlined above have been refined and preserved to the present time, the most notable subsequent change consisting of further amendment of the provisions as to the house of representatives, now governed by the provisions of amendment LXXI, as a revision of amendments XXI and XXII, supra. The present constitution thus provides that apportionment of the 240 members of the Massachusetts house of representatives is a legislative function to be accomplished by the general court every ten years. A census is to be taken every ten years from and after 1935, which is to specify the number of legal voters residing in (1) each city and town; (2) each precinct of every town containing over 12,000 inhabitants; and (3) each ward of each city. Reapportionment of representative districts is a two-step procedure. The general court apportions representatives, and county commissioners (or special commissioners appointed by the governor) draw the district lines. The general court at its first session after each enumeration is to apportion the representatives among the counties of the state "equally, as nearly as may be, according to their relative numbers of legal voters, as ascertained by said special enumeration." The boards of commissioners (or special commissioners) in each county are to divide their counties into as many districts as they are allotted representatives "so that each representative in such county will represent an equal number of legal voters, as nearly as may be. . . ."

Amendment XXI, as amended, imposes the following restrictions upon the composition of representative districts: (1) districts must be "of contiguous territory"; (2) towns containing less than 12,000 inhabitants may not be divided; (3) precincts of towns may not be divided; (4) wards of cities may not be divided; and (5) no district may be made which is entitled to elect more than three representatives. In addition, it is an established and accepted custom to grant a representative seat to Dukes County and another to Nantucket County regardless of registered voter strength. The general court may limit the time within which judicial proceedings may be instituted to challenge the apportionment or districting of representatives.

Attorney General v. Suffolk County Apportionment Commissioners, 224 Mass. 598, 113 N.E. 581 (1916) was the first proceeding to test the validity of representative districts created by commissioners. The state attorney general challenged the composition of the 54 districts in Suffolk County as violative of the equal population requirement in the state constitution. The supreme judicial court of Massachusetts held that the "great principle" established by amendment XXI was "equality of representation among all the voters of the Commonwealth." Id. at 604, 113 N.E. at 585. Each voter has one equal voice in the enactment of laws and in the election of officers of the state. The court recognized that absolute equality of representation is not required. "There are other inflexible conditions of apportionment which must be observed and which prevent exactness of equality [contiguity, no division of wards or precincts, no more than 3 representatives per district] . . . . But within these limitations there must be the nearest approximation to equality of representation which is reasonably practicable." Ibid.

Not every deviation from exact uniformity in the ratio between legal voters and representatives justifies resort to the courts; the test is this: "When fair minded men from an examination of the apportionment and division can entertain no reasonable doubt that there is a grave, unnecessary and unreasonable inequality between different districts, the Constitution has been violated and it is the duty of the court so to declare." Id. at 607, 113 N.E. at 586. The districting plan was held invalid when measured against that test.

The test laid down in *Attorney General v. Suffolk County Commissioners* has been applied in later cases challenging commissioners' redistricting plans: *Donovan v. Suffolk County Apportionment Commissioners*, 225 Mass. 55, 113 N.E. 740 (1916) (disparity of 71 per cent held excessive); *Brophy v. Suffolk County Apportionment Commissioners*, 225 Mass. 124, 113 N.E. 1040 (1916) (redistricting of Suffolk County upheld despite some inequalities which could not be readily avoided; "But inequalities alone are not enough to make void an apportionment. The inequalities must be unnecessary and incompatible with reasonable effort to conform to the requirements of the constitution." Id. at 126, 133 N.E. at 1041); *Merrill v. Mitchell*, 257 Mass. 184, 153 N.E. 562 (1926) (plan exhibiting a three to one disparity voided); *Graham v. Special Commissioners of Suffolk County*, 306 Mass. 237, 27 N.E.2d 995 (1940) (districting plan of Suffolk County which contained disparities up to 57 per cent upheld because inequality was unavoidable without combining wards of the city); *McGlue v. Essex County Commissioners*, 225 Mass. 59, 113 N.E. 742 (1916) (only legal voters living in districts wherein the number of representatives

is incorrect have standing to attack the commissioners' plan).

More recently, in *Fishman v. White*, No. 555329 (Mass. Super. Ct., Suffolk County 1963) the plaintiff, a legal voter of Middlesex County, alleged that the failure of the Massachusetts general court to apportion members of the house of representatives in accordance with the special enumeration of legal voters made in 1955 had caused a diminution in the effectiveness of plaintiff's vote, thus depriving him of the equal protection of the laws. The superior court of Suffolk County, on March 27, 1963, held that plaintiff had been denied the equal protection of the laws; but the question as to what action the court should take was reserved for decision by the supreme judicial court. The plaintiff requested that the court retain jurisdiction until its November 1963 sitting because the general court was considering a reapportionment act. That act was approved August 20, 1963, and took effect upon passage. Mass. Gen. Laws 1963, c. 666. (The supreme judicial court, in *Opinion of the Justices*, 191 N.E.2d 779 (Mass. 1963), had ruled on July 8, 1963, that it was not constitutionally competent for the general court to make an apportionment act effective in 1967. Amendment XXII requires prompt reapportionment after each special enumeration, thus ruling out reapportionment to become effective in 1967 after another enumeration.)

Interestingly enough, the 1963 act, in substitution for the last apportionment act (Mass. Gen. Laws 1947, c. 182), reduced the representation in Suffolk County (Boston), which had been overrepresented. The range is now from 1 representative each in Dukes and Nantucket Counties to 28 for each of Essex and Worcester Counties, 40 for Suffolk County, and 55 for Middlesex County.

The Massachusetts senate consists of 40 members. The special enumeration of legal voters required for the apportionment of representative districts is also the basis for determining senatorial districts. Apportionment is a legislative function to be performed by the general court at its first regular session after the return of each special enumeration. Each senatorial district is to contain "as nearly as may be, an equal number of legal voters"; provided, however, that (1) each district must contain contiguous territory; (2) no town or ward of a city may be divided; and (3) "such districts shall be formed, as nearly as may be, without uniting two counties, or parts of two or more counties, into one district." Mass. Const., Amend. XXII.

The most recent apportionment of senatorial districts was made in 1960 (Mass. Gen. Laws 1960, c. 57, § 3), after it was held in *Lamson v. Secretary of the Commonwealth*, 341 Mass. 264, 168 N.E.2d 480 (1960) that the constitutional duty to apportion under amendments XXI and XXII is continuous until it is discharged. To hold otherwise, the court said, would permit a single session of the general court, by inaction, to impose an apportionment on the people for another ten years. Id. at 270, 168 N.E.2d at 484. See also *Attorney General v. Secretary of the Commonwealth*, 306 Mass. 25, 27 N.E.2d 265 (1940).

Amendment XLVIII of the Massachusetts constitution contains the provisions relating to the initiative and referendum.

The state is divided into 12 congressional districts. Mass. Gen. Laws 1960, c. 57, § 1. The population disparity between the most populous and the least populous district is 102,626.

REFERENCES

O'Reilly, John D., Jr. 7 Annual Survey of Massachusetts Law 106. Boston: Boston College. 1960.

Morison, Samuel Eliot. Constitution of Massachusetts, 40 Mass. L. Q. 1 (1955).

MICHIGAN

The commonwealth of Virginia, the original claimant of the land which ultimately became the state of Michigan, yielded its claim to all land northwest of the Ohio River by act of cession in 1783. Thereafter, in the Northwest Ordinance of 1787 Congress provided for the governance of the Northwest Territory and its future division into as many as five states, guaranteeing that "The inhabitants of the said territory shall always be entitled to the benefits . . . of a proportionate representation of the people in the legislature . . . ." Northwest Ord. of 1787, art. II. The ordinance also provided for a unicameral legislative assembly, apportioned on the basis of one representative for every 500 free, male inhabitants, until the number of representatives should reach 25, after which "the number and proportion of representatives shall be regulated by the legislature." Id., art. I, § 9. In time the Northwest Territory was divided into five territories, which ultimately became the states of Illinois, Indiana, Michigan, Ohio, and Wisconsin. Michigan was given territorial status in 1805 by act of Congress providing for "a government in all respects similar" to that provided by the Northwest Ordinance. But the territory did not become a state until 1837, after a convention in Detroit in 1835, called by the territorial legislative council, had drafted a constitution which was approved by Congress and by the Michigan voters in 1836.

The constitution of 1835 provided for a house of representatives of not less than 48 nor more than 100 members and a senate one third the size of the house, "as nearly as may be." Mich. Const. of 1835, art. IV, § 2. The legislature was to provide for a census in 1837, 1845, and every ten years thereafter, so that the legislature could, at its first session after each state census, and after each federal census, "apportion anew the representatives and senators among the several counties and districts, according to the number of white inhabitants." Id., § 3. Each organized county was entitled to elect at least one representative; and the same was to be true as to any newly organized county unless its population was less than the ratio of representation, in which case presumably it was not entitled to separate representation. Id., § 4. The legislature was charged with division of the state along county lines into from four to eight senatorial districts of contiguous territory, from each of which an equal number of senators, as nearly as possible, should be chosen. Id., § 6. In the schedule of apportionments made until the legislature could act there was established a house of representatives of 49 and a senate of 16 in which counties were cumulated where appropriate, and divided where appropriate, in order to satisfy the equal-population mandate of the constitution.

The legislature was apportioned under the constitution of 1835 in 1838, 1841, and 1845. These apportionments were characterized by "relative population equality in the senate, . . . and by a fairly close adherence to the population standard in the lower house, somewhat modified by the creation of a small number of very sparsely settled districts," particularly in the only two counties in the upper peninsula, which were yet unorganized and together contained barely 1,000 white inhabitants in 1837. White, "Legislative Apportionment Under Three Michigan Constitutions," in Lamb, Pierce, White, Apportionment and Representative Institutions: The Michigan Experience 115, 122 (1963).

In the constitution of 1850 the senate membership was fixed at 32, to be elected from single-member districts. Counties were not to be divided except where population justified two or more representatives. Mich. Const. of 1850, art. IV, § 2. The house of representatives was to consist of not less than 64 nor more than 100 members, each district to contain, "as nearly as may be, an equal number of inhabitants, exclusive of persons of Indian descent who are not civilized or are members of any tribe, and shall consist of convenient and contiguous territory." Id., § 3. But each county "hereafter organized" was authorized a separate representative upon attaining a population equal to "a moiety of the ratio of representation." Ibid. Where townships or cities were entitled to more than one representative, the elections were to be at large for the appropriate number to which the unit was entitled by its population. But counties could be divided, the division to be made by the board of supervisors of the county. Ibid. The provision for reapportionment after each state and federal census was continued. Id., § 4. Reapportionment was carried out periodically, as required by the 1850 constitution, as the population increase throughout the state advanced at a fairly even ratio in rural and urban areas alike.

The constitution of 1908 in general continued the provisions of the constitution of 1850. The only change of consequence in the apportionment provisions was the abandonment of the state census. Reapportionment was made a requirement in 1913 and every tenth year thereafter, based each time on the last preceding federal census. Mich. Const. of 1908, art. V, § 4. The authority of the county boards of supervisors to draw district boundaries in multi-seat counties was retained, although the board could not redistrict in the absence of a statewide legislative reapportionment. Op. Att'y Gen. 1915, p. 103. However, no real reapportionment was ever made as required. The 1913 reapportionment of the house was held unconstitutional in *Stevens v. Secretary of State*, 181 Mich. 199, 148 N.W. 97 (1914); and the house apportionment reverted to the act of 1905 (itself a re-enactment of the 1901 apportionment). In 1925 and 1943 the house was reapportioned, but with scant attention to population. The senate was never reapportioned according to the terms of the 1908 constitution. See White, "Legislative Apportionment Under Three Michigan Constitutions," op. cit. supra, at 131.

In 1952 the Michigan voters approved the so-called "balanced legislature" plan, which provided for apportionment of representatives in accordance with population, increased the senatorial districts from 32 to 34, and froze those 34 districts into the constitution without provision for reapportionment. This reflected the increased tensions between Wayne County, where the proposal was disapproved almost two to one, and the rest of the state where it was carried by substantial margins. Thereafter, for the first time since the beginning of the century the Michigan apportionment was consistent with the state constitution, but only because one house, the senate, was for the first time removed from the previously prescribed adherence to population.

The 1952 amendment to the 1908 constitution was challenged in *Scholle v. Hare*, which went through several stages in the Michigan state courts and twice to the Supreme Court of the United States. The first ruling in the state supreme court was a dismissal in 1960 for lack of jurisdiction, relying on *Colegrove v. Green*, 328 U.S. 549 (1946). *Scholle v. Hare*, 360 Mich. 1, 104 N.W.2d 63 (1960). The United States Supreme Court vacated that decision and remanded "for further consideration in the light of *Baker v. Carr*, 369 U.S. 186," 369 U.S. 429 (1962).

On remand the Michigan Supreme Court, by divided vote, held the 1952 amendment to be invidiously discriminatory for want of a "rational, reasonable, uniform or even ascertainable nondiscriminatory legislative purpose . . . ." 367 Mich. 176, 185, 116 N.W.2d 350, 353 (1962). The court said that "Equal protection . . . does not mean arithmetical equality . . . . It does mean that equality which fairly approximates, by the standards of reasonable minds exercising fair discretion, that which should have been done decennially between 1908 and 1952 and must now be done . . . . [W]hen any apportionment plan provides some elective districts having more than double the population of others, that plan cannot be sustained." Id. at 188, 116 N.W.2d at 355. Finally, in 1964 the Supreme Court refused to review that decision, perhaps because of the new apportionment formula in the subsequently adopted Michigan constitution of 1963, which was also destined for rejection.

On January 1, 1964, the state of Michigan began functioning under the constitution of 1963. The apportionment provisions of that constitution are summarized below.

Article IV, section 2 increased the number of senators to 38, increased the term from two to four years (concurrent with the governor's term), and provided a new formula for the apportionment of senate seats. The formula gave weight to both area and population and established a commission on legislative apportionment to apply the formula. Art. IV, § 6. Each county was to be assigned "apportionment factors" computed as follows: (1) The percentage of the total state population in the county (as shown by the federal decennial census) multiplied by 4; plus (2) the percentage of the state land area in the county. There were thus 500 apportionment factors in the state as a whole — 400 (80 per cent) based on population and 100 (20 per cent) based on area.

Counties were divided into two classes — those having more than 13 apportionment factors and those having less than 13. The apportionment commission was first to assign seats to counties with more than 13 apportionment factors, as a class, in the proportion that the apportionment factors of the class bore to the total apportionment factors of the state, computed to the nearest whole number. "After each such county has been allocated one senator, the remaining senators to which this class of counties is entitled shall be distributed among such counties by the method of equal proportions applied to the apportionment factors." Art. IV, § 2(1).

The apportionment commission was then to arrange the remaining counties having less than 13 apportionment factors into districts, each containing as nearly as possible 13 apportionment factors but not less than 10 nor more

than 16. These districts were to be "compact, convenient, and contiguous by land" (island areas were considered to be contiguous by land to the county of which they were a part (art. IV, § 5)), and as rectangular in shape as possible. Id., § 2(2).

The house of representatives was fixed at 110 members elected for two-year terms from single-member districts consisting of compact and convenient territory contiguous by land, apportioned among the counties on the basis of population. Any county with seven tenths of one per cent of the state population became a representative area entitled to one member, thus modifying the provision for separate representation for each county with one half of one per cent which had been included in some form in each constitution since 1850. Counties with less than seven tenths of one per cent of the population of the state were to be combined with one or more other counties to form a representative area. Art. IV, § 3.

After the state had been apportioned into representative areas in the above manner (each receiving one representative), the remaining seats were to be apportioned among the areas on the basis of population by the method of equal proportions.

Article IV, section 6 of the constitution of 1963 contained a new requirement that both the house and the senate be reapportioned after each federal decennial census by a commission on legislative apportionment, consisting of eight members, four chosen by each of the two political parties receiving the highest vote for governor. One member from each party was to reside in each of the four regions of the state — the upper peninsula, the northern part of the lower peninsula, the southwestern part of the lower peninsula, and the southeastern part of the lower peninsula. If a third party's candidate for governor should poll more than 25 per cent of the votes, that party would be entitled to four members of a 12-man commission.

The commission was directed to reapportion and redistrict house and senate seats in accordance with the provisions of the constitution, and the reapportionment plan approved by a majority was given the force of law when published. If a majority of the members could not agree on a plan, they could, either jointly or individually, submit plans to the state supreme court, which would direct the adoption of whichever plan was thought most consistent with constitutional requirements. Judicial review was provided in the supreme court upon the timely application of any elector.

The apportionment provisions of the 1963 constitution were challenged in *Marshall v. Hare*, 227 F. Supp. 989 (E.D. Mich. 1964), in which the decision of the three-judge federal district court in favor of validity was reversed in June of 1964. Before telling that story, however, it is necessary to report contemporary developments in the apportionment commission and in the state courts. Early in 1964 the Michigan Supreme Court had accepted an apportionment plan offered by members of the apportionment commission for implementation of the "80–20" requirement in the state constitution at the elections in the fall of 1964. However, when the Supreme Court of the United States on June 15, 1964, announced the equal-population principle in the *Reapportionment Cases*, the Michigan Supreme Court issued three orders between June 17 and June 22, 1964. On June 17 it vacated its earlier order approving an apportionment plan and

directed the commission to adopt a new plan that would conform with the decision in the *Reapportionment Cases*. When the commission deadlocked, the court approved one of the plans that had been considered by the commission. See *In the Matter of Apportionment of the Michigan Legislature*, 373 Mich. 247, 250, 128 N.W.2d 721, 722 (1964). The plan has the force of law and is reproduced in Mich. Public and Local Acts, 1964, pp. 603–18. Although this plan satisfied the equal-population standard with almost literal exactness, the state supreme court in November 1965 held it violative of anti-gerrymander provisions of the state constitution.

Also on June 22, 1964, the Supreme Court of the United States reversed the three-judge federal district court ruling in *Marshall v. Hare*, supra, remanding for further proceedings consistent with the opinion in *Reynolds v. Sims*, 377 U.S. 533 (1964). *Marshall v. Hare*, 378 U.S. 561 (1964). Thus, the state and federal courts were brought into agreement on the same day, both concluding that the 1963 constitutional provisions were invalid.

Constitutional amendments may be proposed in either house of the legislature. Amendments agreed to by a two-thirds vote of each house and approved by a majority of those voting at the designated election become part of the constitution. Mich. Const. of 1963, art. XII, § 1. Amendments to the constitution may also be proposed by petition of at least 10 per cent of the total vote cast at the last preceding general election for governor, thereafter to be approved by a majority of the voters at the designated election. Id., § 2. The question of a general revision of the constitution shall be submitted to the voters in 1978 and each sixteenth year thereafter. If a majority favors the calling of a constitutional convention, the delegates are to be chosen in the same numbers and manner as the then-prevailing provisions for selection of senators and representatives. Id., § 3.

The initiative and referendum are available as to ordinary legislation, with certain specified exceptions. The initiative petition requires the signature of at least 8 per cent of the electors last voting for governor, and the referendum petition requires at least 5 per cent of such voters. Laws initiated and adopted by the voters are not subject to gubernatorial veto. Id., art. II, § 9.

Since the 1960 census Michigan has been entitled to 19 congressional seats. In 1963 the legislature drew new district lines. Mich. Act 249, P.A. 1963. After decision of the congressional districting case, *Wesberry v. Sanders*, 376 U.S. 1 (1964), the three-judge federal district court held the Michigan act invalid because of the substantial and unexplained population differentials among the districts. *Calkins v. Hare*, 228 F. Supp. 824 (E.D. Mich. 1964). The average deviation from the population ratio was less than 10 per cent, and only two districts were substantially more than 15 per cent away from the norm. But the court considered them excessive, at least in the absence of any attempted justification. Moreover, the court found it "inexplicable" that there should be a difference of almost a hundred thousand persons between two adjacent districts in Detroit.

New lines were drawn by the legislature in time for the 1964 election. The maximum population deviation was reduced to 13,911. Mich. Act 282, P.A. 1964.

In *Johnson v. Genesee County, Michigan*, 232 F. Supp. 567 (E.D. Mich. 1964) a three-judge federal district court dismissed a complaint in which plaintiffs had sought to restrain county officials from certain official acts, claiming invalid authorization from the malapportioned county board of supervisors.

REFERENCES

Friedman, Robert S. The Michigan Constitutional Convention and Administrative Organization: A Case Study in the Politics of Constitution-Making. Ann Arbor: Institute of Public Administration, University of Michigan. 1963.

Lamb, Karl A. "Michigan Legislative Apportionment: Key to Constitutional Change," in Jewell, Malcolm E. (ed.). The Politics of Reapportionment. New York: The Atherton Press. 1962.

Lamb, Karl A., Pierce, William J., and White, John P. Apportionment and Representative Institutions: The Michigan Experience. Washington: The Institute for Social Science Research. 1963.

Garfinkel, Herbert, and Fein, L. J. Fair Representation: A Citizen's Guide to Legislative Apportionment in Michigan. East Lansing: Bureau of Social and Political Research, Michigan State University. 1960.

Shull, Charles W. Legislative Apportionment in Michigan. Con-Con Research Paper No. 6. Detroit: Citizens Research Council of Michigan. 1961.

Michigan Suit Suggests Reapportionment Guidelines, 20 Congressional Quarterly Weekly Report 1302 (August 3, 1962).

MINNESOTA

Portions of the present state of Minnesota have at various times been within the claims asserted by the commonwealth of Virginia (claims relinquished by legislative act in 1783) and by France (claims relinquished by treaty of purchase in 1803); and successively parts of the present state were within the territorial domain of Indiana, Illinois, Missouri, Michigan, Wisconsin, and Iowa. Not until 1849 did Congress establish the territory of Minnesota as a separate entity. In that act legislative power was initially vested in a governor and a legislative assembly consisting of a 9-member council (which could be raised to 15 "in proportion to the increase in population") and an 18-member house of representatives (which could be increased to 39). Apportionment was to be made for both houses, "giving to each section of the Territory representation in the ratio of its population, Indians excepted, as nearly as may be." The governor was to make the apportionment among the "counties or districts" in accordance with a census to be taken before the first election. Act of 1849, § 4.

By enabling act of 1857 Congress authorized the calling of a constitutional convention, the delegates to be chosen on the basis of two from each existing representative district. In the same year the convention was held and a constitution was framed and approved by the people. In 1858 Congress found the government thus established to be "republican in form" and so approved the admission of Minnesota as a state of the Union. An initial apportionment was made dividing the state into 37 senatorial districts and 80 representative districts, chosen much as they would be today under provisions which have been changed only slightly over the intervening years.

The Minnesota constitution provides that the membership of the senate and the house of representatives "shall be prescribed by law." Representation in the senate is never to exceed one member for every 5,000 inhabitants, and representation in the house cannot exceed one member for every 2,000 inhabitants. Minn. Const., art. IV, § 2. Section 2.02 of the Minnesota statutes, as amended in 1959, provided for a senate of 67 members and a house of 135 members, "until a new apportionment shall have been made." Senators are elected for four years while representatives serve two-year terms. Minn. Const., art. IV, § 24.

"The representation in both houses shall be apportioned equally throughout the different sections of the State, in proportion to the population thereof, exclusive of Indians not taxable under the provisions of law." Art. IV, § 2.

Reapportionment is a legislative function. The constitution requires the legislature to provide for an enumeration of the inhabitants of the state every ten years from and after 1865. At the first legislative session after such enumeration and at the first legislative session after each federal census the legislature "shall have the power to prescribe the bounds of congressional, senatorial and representative districts" in accordance with the provisions of article IV, section 2, just described. Art. IV, § 23.

At the same time and in the same manner in which the members of the house are chosen, senators are elected from "single districts of convenient contiguous territory . . . ." No representative district shall be divided in the formation of a senate district. Art. IV, § 24. Accordingly, the 67 senatorial districts are further divided to form the 135 representative districts to represent "the different sections of the state, in proportion to the population thereof," as required by article IV, section 2, discussed above.

More than a century has elapsed since the Minnesota constitutional convention of 1857, and there were six reapportionments through 1913, at more or less regular intervals. Thereafter, there was no further reapportionment until 1959 (effective in 1962); and that was stimulated by threat of court action when it was charged in 1958 that the 1913 act was invalid. The case was *Magraw v. Donovan*, 159 F. Supp. 901 (D. Minn. 1958), motion to dismiss denied, 163 F. Supp. 184 (D. Minn. 1958), case dismissed on plaintiff's motion, 177 F. Supp. 803 (D. Minn. 1959). Plaintiff asked that the 1913 act be declared invalid because substantial increases in population since that year produced gross inequality among the legislative districts amounting to a denial of equal protection of the laws. The district court held (159 F. Supp. 901) that the question should be decided by a three-judge court. The three-judge court ruled that because of the gross inequality among the districts (the smallest house district contained 7,290 persons and the largest 107,246, a disparity of 14.7 to 1), the court would defer decision on the issues (including the jurisdictional issue) until it was shown that the 1959 legislature had deliberately failed and refused to perform its constitutional duty to reapportion. 163 F. Supp. 184, 187. The 1959 legislature responded by enacting a new apportionment to be effective January 1, 1962, and plaintiff's motion to dismiss the action for mootness was granted. 177 F. Supp. 803.

Disparities continued, however, under the 1959 act. The 1960 federal census showed a Minnesota state population of 3,413,864. The senatorial mean (for 67 senators) was therefore 50,953. However, the largest senatorial district contained 100,520 persons, while the smallest district had a population of 24,428. A majority of the senators could be elected by 40.1 per cent of the voters. The house mean was 26,060 (for 135 representatives), with a population range from 56,076 to 8,343; and 34.5 per cent of the population could elect a majority of the representatives.

The 1959 act was invalidated as to both houses of the Minnesota legislature in *Honsey v. Donovan*, 236 F. Supp. 8 (D. Minn. 1964). The court held that it made no difference that plaintiffs had not shown any legislative design to dilute the vote of the people of any area; the very fact of the substantial inequalities was enough. Having delayed decision until December 1964 in order to avoid interference with the November elections, the court expressed confidence that the legislature would act at its 1965 session. Accordingly, jurisdiction was retained, but no absolute deadline was fixed.

The 1965 legislature redrew the district boundaries to make the maximum deviations from the mean 34 per cent below and 37 per cent above in the house and 23 per cent below and 25 per cent above in the senate. Minn. Laws 1965, Sen. File 102. When the governor vetoed this act, certain legislators brought an action to compel the secretary of state to promulgate the act on the ground that the governor lacks power to veto apportionment legislation. Plaintiffs were successful in state court at the trial level. The appeal to the Minnesota Supreme Court was to be heard in October 1965 under the caption *Duxbury v. Donovan*.

The composition of the county commissioner districts in Hennepin County was challenged in *Hedlund v. Hanson*, 213 F. Supp. 172 (D. Minn. 1962) on the ground of population inequality among the districts. Before decision on the merits the state legislature redrew the district lines. Sufficient equalization among the districts was achieved that the proceeding was dismissed upon motion of the county attorney without objection by the plaintiffs.

Article IV, section 23 empowers the legislature to prescribe the bounds of congressional districts, a power most recently exercised in 1961 when Minnesota was divided into eight congressional districts. Minn. Stat. Ann. §§

2.731–2.811. The congressional mean is 426,733, and the congressional districts range in size from 477,884 persons to 363,731.

Smiley v. Holm, 285 U.S. 355 (1932) presented the question of whether or not the governor could veto a bill which redistricted congressional areas. The legislature had passed a bill which divided the state into congressional districts. The governor refused to sign it. No further action was taken by the legislature. In a suit for declaratory judgment the United States Supreme Court held that in Minnesota the governor could veto congressional districting bills because the Minnesota constitution provided that the governor must be presented with all bills before they became laws and that his veto could be overridden by a two-thirds vote of the legislature. There is nothing in article I, section 4 of the United States Constitution which precludes a state from providing for a gubernatorial veto of bills concerning congressional districting.

The legislature may propose constitutional amendments by a majority of both houses after submission to the people for majority ratification. Art. XIV, § 1. A constitutional convention may be called whenever two thirds of the members of both houses recommend such action to the people and a majority of the electors concur. Id., §§ 2, 3.

There are neither constitutional nor statutory provisions in Minnesota relating to the initiative or the referendum.

REFERENCES

Bond, John. Legislative Reapportionment in Minnesota. Unpublished doctoral dissertation. Minneapolis: University of Minnesota. 1956.

Governor's Bipartisan Reapportionment Commission. Report of January 15, 1965, 49 Minn. L. Rev. 367 (1964).

Minnesota Legislative Research Committee. Legislative Reapportionment. Publication No. 63. St. Paul: October 1954.

Dorweiler, Louis C., Jr. "Minnesota Farmers Rule Cities," 35 Nat'l Munic. Rev. 115 (March 1946).

MISSISSIPPI

In the congressional act of 1798 establishing the territorial government of Mississippi, the President of the United States was authorized to establish government "in all respects similar to that now exercised" in the Northwest Territory (with exceptions not here material), thus including the guarantee in the Northwest Ordinance of 1787 "of a proportionate representation of the people in the legislature . . . ." (Northwest Ordinance, art. II), as well as the provision for appointment by the President, with the advice and consent of the Senate, of "all necessary officers . . . ." Act of Congress of 1798, § 3. The proportionate representation guarantee of the Northwest Ordinance was specifically reaffirmed by act of Congress in 1800, which provided also for a general assembly to be constituted as in the Northwest Territory, consisting of governor, council, and house of representatives. Until the territory should have 5,000 free male inhabitants of full age there were to be not more than nine representatives, four from each of two counties, and one from a single district of two settlements. Act of Congress of 1800, § 2. After the 5,000 number had been reached, the proportionate representation provisions of the 1787 ordinance were to apply. Id., § 6.

In 1817 Congress authorized the call of a constitutional convention to prepare a constitution in preparation for statehood. The 44 delegates were divided among the then 13 counties in numbers ranging from two to eight for each county. The delegates met and formed a constitution which was accepted by Congress as "in conformity to the principles" of the Northwest Ordinance. In the same year, 1817, Mississippi was admitted as a state of the Union.

The constitution of 1817 empowered the general assembly to apportion the representatives to counties which might in turn be divided into districts, also by legislative act. In addition, separate representation was provided for any city or town whose population of free white inhabitants equaled the existing ratio; and special provision was made for representation of any residuum of population above the ratio. Miss. Const. of 1817, art. III, § 8. Initially, the number of representatives was to be not less than 24 nor more than 36; and each county was assured at least one representative. Id., § 9. The number of senators was to be fixed by the general assembly, "and apportioned among the several districts to be established by law, according to the number of free white taxable inhabitants in each," for a total of not less than one fourth and not more than one third the number of representatives. Id., § 10. It was further provided that a senatorial district of two or more counties must satisfy the requirement of contiguity; and no county could be divided in forming a district. Id., § 13. Provision was made for a census of free white inhabitants in 1817 and periodically thereafter at intervals of three to five years. Id., § 9.

The apportionment provisions of the constitution of 1832 were little changed except that the periodic census was to be made at intervals of four to six years until 1845 and thereafter at intervals of four to eight years. Miss. Const. of 1832, art. III, § 9.

The constitution of 1869 was framed by a convention called under the reconstruction acts of Congress. That constitution, although rejected once by Congress and once by the voters, was approved by the voters in 1869. On the basis of a census to be taken every ten years of "the whole number of inhabitants, and of the qualified electors of the State" (Miss. Const. of 1869, art. IV, § 33), the number of representatives was to be apportioned among the counties or districts "according to the number of qualified electors in each" to a total of not less than 100 and not more than 120. Id., § 34. The number of senators was also to be apportioned "according to the number of qualified electors," to a total of one fourth to one third the number of representatives authorized. Id., § 35.

The constitution of 1890, the most recent, made substantial changes in the apportionment provisions, principally in freezing into the constitution the boundaries of the legislative districts.

Article XIII, sections 254 to 256 of the 1890 constitution provided for a house of 133 members and for a senate of 30 to 45 (increased to 49 in 1916), and the constitution prescribed territorial limits for all. Except for the creation of seven new counties and minor changes in legislative districts in 1916, both the house and senate districts remained the same as they were in 1890 until constitutional amendments and statutes were adopted in 1962, as noted below. The legislature had not made a general reapportionment for seventy years despite the provisions in section 256 of article XIII authorizing, but not requiring, a new apportionment of senators and representatives at the first session after the federal census of 1900, and decennially thereafter. Section 256 also established three major apportionment divisions of the state for the house of representatives and assigned each county to one of these three divisions, each of which was assigned 44 representatives. Each county was to have at least one representative. The legislature could reduce the number of representatives only if this was done uniformly in each division. However, the number of representatives could not be less than 100 nor more than 133, and the number of senators could not be less than 30 nor more than 45 (except for enlargement to 140 and 49 with the addition of new counties). Miss. Const. of 1890, art. XIII, § 256.

The Mississippi Supreme Court, in *Barnes v. Barnett*, 241 Miss. 206, 129 So.2d 638 (1961), a case decided while *Baker v. Carr*, 369 U.S. 186 (1962), was pending in the United States Supreme Court, had refused to enjoin a special 1960 election on a constitutional amendment wherein plaintiffs (taxpayers) alleged that the legislature was improperly constituted and apportioned. The court held that apportionment of legislative and congressional districts was a political and not a judicial question and therefore "inappropriate" for judicial consideration. Moreover, the court found that the section 256 provision for reapportionment ("may reapportion") was not mandatory as was the Tennessee constitutional requirement at issue in *Baker v. Carr*.

However, in 1962 a taxpayers' suit against the governor and the election commissioners was brought in a local chancery court to enjoin further elections for the house of representatives. *Fortner v. Barnett*, No. 59,965 (Ch. Ct., 1st Jud. Dist., Hinds Co., Miss. 1962). The court concluded that the existing apportionment of the legisla-

ture (the 1890 districts) was, under the 1960 census, "so inequitable, invidious and disparaging" that it violated the equal protection clause of the fourteenth amendment. The court refused to order at-large elections, ordered the cause of action continued to the November 1962 court session, and requested the governor to call a special session of the legislature to consider the passage of reapportionment statutes. The court also announced a reapportionment formula of its own to be put into effect in the event that the legislature failed to provide a fair apportionment. Furthermore, the court held that a legislative formula of reapportionment which was in fact inequitable, even though ratified by the people, would not be permitted to stand; even the electorate could not ratify that which was unconstitutional.

Section 254 of the 1890 constitution was amended (in December 1962, effective with the 1963 elections) to provide for a 122-member house of representatives. Under the provisions of that amendment 58 counties are allotted one representative; 17 counties are given two; 5 counties are allotted three; and the counties of Harrison and Hinds become entitled to six and nine representatives respectively. The legislature may, within any county having more than one representative, provide for the election of representatives either by dividing such county into election districts or by providing for the election of representatives by posts.

The legislature is the apportioning agent and "may," by a two-thirds vote of all members present and voting in both houses, within ten years after the federal census of 1970 "and within each ten-year period thereafter, make a new apportionment of the House of Representatives, provided that in each apportionment each county shall have not less than one Representative, provided further, that the number of members in the House of Representatives shall never exceed one hundred and twenty-two (122)." Miss. Const. of 1890, art. XIII, § 254, as amended. These provisions do not make mandatory any further reapportionment, and they provide no standards to be applied in any subsequent apportionment. Since there are 82 existing counties, each of which must have one representative, that leaves only 40 seats to be distributed among the rest of the counties. It is implied that they be distributed according to population since the apportionments are to take place, if they take place at all, after each federal decennial census. The method employed in assigning representatives is a matter of conjecture.

Article XIII, section 255 of the 1890 constitution was also amended in 1962 to provide for 52 senators, including specification of the counties to be included in each district. The legislature by a two-thirds vote of all members present and voting in both houses "may" within ten years after the federal census of 1970 and within each ten-year period thereafter make a new apportionment of the senate, "provided that the total membership of the Senate shall not be less than forty-five (45) nor more than fifty-five (55)." Miss. Const. of 1890, art. XIII, § 255, as amended. Section 256 of the 1890 constitution was repealed, eliminating the three grand legislative divisions, making equitable reapportionment possible without constitutional amendment.

As in the case of representative districts, reapportionment of the senate is not mandatory upon the legislature.

That population should be the basis for any apportionment is implied, but not explicit.

Only the legislature by a two-thirds vote of both houses may propose constitutional amendments to be referred to the people for majority ratification. Miss. Const. of 1890, Art. XV, § 273. There are no constitutional provisions relating to the initiative and referendum or to constitutional conventions, although practice has supported the call of conventions, probably based on article III, section 6 of the constitution.

Section 3305 of the Mississippi code, as amended in 1962, divides the state into its present five congressional districts, a reduction of one congressional seat as a result of the changes in population shown by the 1960 census. The population disparity among the districts is from 608,441 to 295,072.

Wood v. Broom, 287 U.S. 1 (1932), reversing 1 F. Supp. 134 (S.D. Miss. 1932), involved a challenge to a 1932 Mississippi statute which redrew the congressional districts because the number of Mississippi representatives had been reduced from eight to seven after the 1930 census. Plaintiffs alleged that the statute was void because the new congressional districts were not composed of compact and contiguous territory, having as nearly as practicable the same number of inhabitants, as had been required by the 1911 congressional reapportionment act. The United States Supreme Court, however, held that since the congressional reapportionment act of 1929 did not re-enact the requirements of contiguity and equal population of districts of the 1911 congressional reapportionment act, those requirements no longer controlled congressional districting after 1929. At least on the equality point this decision can no longer be considered controlling since *Wesberry v. Sanders*, 376 U.S. 1 (1964).

In *Glass v. Hancock County Election Commissioners*, 156 So.2d 825 (Miss. 1963) plaintiffs sought to enjoin county election officials from conducting certain local elections until the district lines for the choice of the five members of the board of supervisors could be redrawn (as they had not been for more than a hundred years) to conform to federal and state constitutional requirements. The Mississippi Supreme Court held that the petition did not state a claim on which equitable relief could be granted because the relevant state statute provided an adequate remedy at law by way of mandamus. The Supreme Court of the United States refused review, presumably because the lower court decision was based on an adequate state ground. *Glass v. Hancock County Election Commissioners*, 378 U.S. 558 (1964).

Meanwhile, other suits were instituted challenging the composition of boards of supervisors in other counties. See Vaughan, Controversy Over County Beats, 11 Pub. Admin. Surv. 1 (July 1964); 12 id. 1 (Sept. 1964).

REFERENCES

Hobbs, Edward H. Legislative Apportionment in Mississippi. State Government Series No. 18. University: Bureau of Public Admin., Univ. of Miss. 1956.

Hobbs, Edward H., et al. Yesterday's Constitution Today. State Administration Series No. 19. University: Bureau of Public Admin., Univ. of Miss. 1960.

Vaughan, Donald S. Mississippi's 1963 Legislative Apportionment, 10 Pub. Admin. Surv. 1 (March 1963) and Every Man — One Vote, *ibid.* (May 1963).

————. Controversy Over County Beats, 11 Pub. Admin. Surv. 1 (July 1964); 12 id. 1 (Sept. 1964).

Wilber, Leon. Reapportionment of the Mississippi Legislature: An Analysis of the Question. Jackson: Mississippi Economic Council, 1956.

MISSOURI

The present state of Missouri was originally part of the land ceded by France to the United States by the treaty of purchase of 1803, to which Congress gave the name Louisiana and provided a district government in 1804 and a territorial government in 1805. The territory was redesignated as Missouri in 1812 by an act of Congress which vested the legislative power in the governor, a legislative council, and a house of representatives. Sec. 4. One representative was to be chosen for each 500 free white male inhabitants of the territory, up to the number of 25, "after which the number and proportion of representatives shall be regulated by the general assembly." Sec. 6. The representatives (originally 13 in number) were to be chosen from the "convenient counties" which the governor was authorized to lay off in those parts of the territory "to which the Indian title hath been extinguished . . . ." Sec. 7. The house of representatives, when thus constituted, was to nominate 18 residents of the territory, nine of whom were to be selected by the President of the United States with the advice and consent of the Senate to serve as members of the council for five-year terms. Sec. 5. In 1816 Congress provided that the members of the legislative council should be chosen by the qualified voters, one from each county. Sec. 1.

In 1820 Congress authorized the calling of a constitutional convention looking toward future statehood. The 41 authorized delegates were divided among the then 15 counties, ranging from one for Wayne County (and a portion of Lawrence County) to eight for St. Louis County. Sec. 3. The resulting constitution of 1820 was approved by Congress, and Missouri was admitted as a state of the Union in 1821.

The constitution of 1820 placed the legislative power in a general assembly consisting of a senate and a house of representatives. Mo. Const. of 1820, art. III, § 1. It was specified that the legislature should make an enumeration of inhabitants at its first session, again in 1822, in 1824, and every fourth year thereafter; and at the next session the legislature was instructed to "apportion the number of representatives among the several counties, according to the number of free white male inhabitants therein." Id., § 4. Although each county was entitled to "at least one representative" and the total number of representatives was not to exceed 100, this was not a significant limitation on the principle of proportionate representation in view of the small number of counties then established. Id., § 2. The senate was to consist of not less than 14 nor more than 33 senators to be chosen from "convenient districts" and "apportioned among the several districts according to the number of free white male inhabitants in each . . . ." Districts including more counties than one were to consist only of adjoining counties, and no county was to be divided in forming a district. Id., § 6. The schedule in the constitution of 1820 provided for a 43-member house of representatives divided according to population among the 15 counties (plus that part of Lawrence County within the state which was attached to Wayne County). Schedule, § 7. The 14 senate districts were also apportioned in accordance with population by various combinations among the 15 counties, ranging from one senator for one two-county district to four senators for another two-county district. Schedule, § 8.

In 1848–49 the constitution was amended to provide a different formula for the election of representatives. The ratio of representation was to be determined by dividing the number of free white inhabitants by 140, giving one representative to each county with a population equal to that ratio or less, two representatives to each county with one and three-quarter ratios, three for three ratios, four for four and one-half ratios, five for six ratios, etc. The legislature was charged with making such reapportionments every fourth year, beginning in 1848.

During the years 1861–63, when Missouri was torn between the North and the South in Civil War loyalties, the constitution of 1820 was in part suspended and in part amended by the members of a constitutional convention which met during several periods in 1861, 1862, and 1863. But the apportionment provisions were not significantly affected until the constitution of 1865 further refined the amendment of 1848–49 and adopted for the house of representatives essentially the pattern that survived until 1965. The ratio of representation was fixed by dividing "the whole number of permanent inhabitants" by 200, allowing one representative to each county with less than three ratios, two representatives for three full ratios, three for six ratios, and "one additional member for every three additional ratios." Mo. Const. of 1865, art. IV, § 2. Counties entitled to more than one representative were to be districted by the county court (an administrative rather than a judicial body), preserving equality of population among the districts "as near as may be." Ibid. The senate was fixed at 34 members to be chosen from "convenient districts" (id., § 4), and apportioned "as nearly as may be, according to the number of permanent inhabitants" in each district. Id., § 6. A state census was provided for every ten years beginning in 1876, to be used as the basis for current apportionment until the next intervening federal census, which should also be used as the basis of reapportionment. Id., § 7.

The constitution of 1875 further changed the details of the formula as it applied to the selection of representatives, but not the essence of the plan (Mo. Const. of 1875, art. IV, § 2); and the senate membership remained fixed at 34. Id., § 5. But the intervening creation of additional counties to a total of 114 made the formula work very differently in a house of 143 in which only eight counties were originally allotted two representatives, and only three were assigned more than two, leaving 103 counties with one representative each. Id., § 8.

The constitution of 1945, the most recent, carries forward the senate of 34 members elected for four-year terms from districts which must be "convenient," "compact," "contiguous," and "as nearly equal in population as may be." In addition, counties cannot be divided in the making of districts composed of more than one county. Mo. Const. of 1945, art. III, § 5. Reapportionment of the senate is an executive function to be performed by a senatorial apportionment commission of ten members appointed by the governor within ninety days after the federal decennial census from lists submitted to him by the state committees of the two political parties casting the highest vote for governor at the last preceding election. Id., art. III, § 7. The commission is to divide the population of the state by 34, "and the population of no district shall vary from the quotient by more than one-fourth thereof." Ibid. Seven commission members must approve the

reapportionment statement filed with the secretary of state. If the statement is not filed within six months after the commission is appointed, the commissioners will be discharged and senators to be elected at the next election will be elected at large, following which a new commission will be appointed in like manner and with like effect. The commission's reapportionment is not subject to the referendum. Ibid. When any county is entitled to more than one senator, the county court, or in St. Louis City the body authorized to establish election precincts, is required to divide the county into districts of compact and contiguous territory and as nearly equal in population as may be. Id., art. III, § 8. The 1951 senatorial redistricting commission allotted seven districts to the city of St. Louis, four to Jackson County (Kansas City), three to St. Louis County, with the remaining 20 districts divided among the other 112 counties of the state. The resulting districts varied in the number of counties included from nine counties in the twelfth and eighteenth districts to the single-county thirtieth district (Greene County) and thirty-fourth district (Buchanan County). Mo. Ann. Stat. § 22.010 (1961).

In *Preisler v. Doherty*, 365 Mo. 460, 284 S.W.2d 427 (1955), the Missouri Supreme Court held the 1952 districting of the St. Louis board of elections commission to be void because of too wide variance in the population of some districts in the city of St. Louis, and for lack of compactness. The court further held that the local board of election commissioners (and county courts) had a continuous duty to make a valid redistricting and that it was mandatory that they follow the constitutional requirements of contiguity, compactness, and equality in population as nearly as can be.

The Missouri constitution of 1945 did not fix the number of representatives but instead provided for the election of members according to a ratio of representation obtained by dividing the whole number of the inhabitants of the state by 200. The following formula was then applied: (1) Each county having one ratio or less was to elect one representative, thus assuring at least one representative for each county; (2) each county having two and a half times the ratio was assigned two representatives; (3) each county with four times the ratio chose three representatives; (4) each county with six times the ratio elected four representatives, and so on above that number so that one additional member was given for every two and a half additional ratios. Mo. Const. of 1945, art. III, § 2. The 1945 constitution also provided for apportionment of the house by the secretary of state, who was directed, after each federal census, to certify to each county (either to the county court or other body authorized to establish election precincts in the cities) the number of representatives to be elected by the respective units. Id., art. III, §§ 2, 10, as implemented by Mo. Ann. Stat. § 22.050. The county court or other body authorized to establish election precincts was then directed to establish districts "of contiguous territory, as compact and nearly equal in population as may be." Id., art. III, § 3. The apportionment effective immediately before 1965 assigned 15 representatives to the city of St. Louis, 14 to the county of St. Louis, 13 to Jackson County, 3 to each of three counties, 2 to each of three counties, and 1 each for the remaining 106 counties.

The city of St. Louis, the county of St. Louis, and Jackson County (Kansas City) have nearly half of the state's population but before 1965 only 42 (26 per cent) of the 163 seats in the Missouri house. The 1960 population, 4,319,813, divided by 163 yields a house population mean of 26,502. However, the largest representative district contained 52,970 inhabitants, while the smallest had only 3,936; and 20.3 per cent of the state's population could elect a majority of the representatives.

In *Jonas v. Hearnes*, 236 F. Supp. 699 (W.D. Mo. 1964) a three-judge federal district court held unconstitutional the provisions of article III, section 2 of the Missouri constitution that guaranteed one representative for each county and allowed increased representation only on the basis of progressively increasing population ratios. The court also invalidated the apportionment formula for the state senate, which permitted variations of 25 per cent each way from the mathematical quotient determined by dividing the total population of the state (4,319,813) by the number of senatorial districts (34). Mo. Const. of 1945, art. III, § 7. The court held this variation too great to comport with the requirement of substantial equality. The court did not, however, invalidate the provisions of article III, section 3 relating to the means of fixing districts within a county or the provisions of article III, section 5 establishing the number of senatorial districts and requiring that the districts be "compact" and as "nearly equal in population as may be." 236 F. Supp. at 699. The state legislature was given until the close of its 1965 legislative session to take corrective action. Id. at 709.

The senate lines are to be redrawn by a bipartisan commission as provided in the state constitution; and the house was reapportioned by statute enacted in July 1965. The legislature also approved a constitutional amendment to reapportion the house on the basis of

168 (rather than 163) members; but this proposal was defeated by the voters in August 1965.

The Missouri constitution can be amended by use of the initiative and referendum. Mo. Const. of 1945, art. III, §§ 49, 50; art. 12, §§ 2(b), 3(a). However, initiative petitions must be signed by 8 per cent of the legal voters in each of two thirds of the congressional districts in the state (seven out of ten). Id., art. III, § 50.

Constitutional amendments may also be proposed at any time by a majority of both houses of the legislature (art. XII, § 2(a)), and must be submitted to the electors for majority ratification (art. XII, § 2(b)).

The calling of constitutional conventions to alter the constitution is governed by article XII, sections 3(a), (b), and (c). Beginning in November 1962, and every twenty years thereafter, the secretary of state shall, or the general assembly may, submit the question of the calling of a constitutional convention to the voters. Id., art. XII, § 3(a). In November 1962 the voters refused to call a constitutional convention by a vote of 519,499 to 295,972.

When the number of representatives to which the state is entitled is certified to the governor after each United States decennial census, the general assembly is required to divide the state into districts "composed of contiguous territory as compact and as nearly equal in population as may be." Mo. Const. of 1945, art. III, § 45. The state is now divided into ten congressional districts, the congressional representation having been reduced from 11 to 10 after the 1960 census. Mo. Ann. Stat. §§ 128.202 to 128.302.

Preisler v. Hearnes, 362 S.W.2d 552 (Mo. 1962) was a declaratory judgment action to determine the validity of the 1961 districting of the state. Plaintiffs alleged violation of the contiguity and equal population provisions of article III, section 45 of the constitution of 1945. Since the 1960 population of the state was 4,319,813 and the congressional mean was 431,981, plaintiffs pointed to disparity between the largest congressional district (506,854) and the smallest districts (378,499). Id. at 554. Plaintiffs also contended that all three districts in St. Louis were above the state quotient in population and suggested that compactness and equality of population could be better obtained by dividing counties. However, the Missouri Supreme Court held the act constitutional.

The congressional districting was challenged again in 1965 in *Preisler v. Secretary of State*, 238 F. Supp. 187 (W.D. Mo. 1965). The court noted the population differentials among the ten districts varying from 378,499 to 506,854, which it described as "presumptive malapportionment." Id. at 190. However, the court deferred final decision to give the legislature a "full opportunity" to take corrective action. Id. at 191.

In *Carroll v. Becker*, 285 U.S. 380 (1932), affirming 329 Mo. 501, 45 S.W.2d 533 (1932) plaintiff tried to file his declaration of candidacy under a bill alleged to have been passed by the house of representatives and senate in April 1931. The secretary of state contended the bill had been vetoed by the governor. The question was whether redistricting of the state was authoritatively complete without the governor's approval, a question decided by the United States Supreme Court on the same day in a Minnesota case, *Smiley v. Holm*, 285 U.S. 355 (1932). The Court held that if the state constitution requires that the governor sign all laws, his signature is needed to validate a congressional redistricting bill despite the fact that the United States apportionment statute requires the "legislature" of the state to redistrict. For that purpose he is part of the "legislature."

REFERENCES

League of Women Voters. Apportionment — Background for Study. St. Louis: Oct. 1963.
Missouri State Chamber of Commerce. Missouri Legislative Reapportionment — The Case for the Present System. Jefferson City: Research Report No. 42, Syst. 9. 1963.
Hadwiger, Don F. Representation in the Missouri General Assembly, 24 Mo. L. Rev. 178 (1959).
Note, Validity of Reapportionment of the City of Saint Louis, 4 St. L.U.L.J. 214 (1956).

MONTANA

Portions of what is now the state of Montana were at various times included within lands claimed by France, Great Britain, and Russia. After the completion of treaties and conventions with those powers, present Montana was variously within the jurisdiction, however loose at times the control may have been, of the territories of Louisiana, Missouri, Oregon, Washington, Nebraska, and Idaho. In 1864 Congress gave Montana its own territorial status, vesting legislative power in a governor and legislative assembly. The assembly was to consist of a council of 7 and a house of representatives of 13 (with provision for increase to 13 and 26 respectively as the population should expand). Apportionment of members of the council and of the house was to be made "as nearly equal as practicable, among the several counties or districts," to be based on a census of the inhabitants and qualified voters to be taken prior to the first election. Sec. 4. By 1889 Congress deemed the territory

ready for statehood (along with Washington and North and South Dakota) and provided for a constitutional convention of delegates who should be chosen "in proportion to the population" of the districts or counties represented. Sec. 3. The constitutional convention completed its work in August 1889, and the President of the United States proclaimed Montana a state of the Union in November of that year.

The Montana constitution of 1889, unlike the congressional acts establishing the territorial legislature and the constitutional convention, did not provide for representation in both houses in proportion to population, and Montana was thus the first state since Vermont to disregard population altogether in even one house. In the house population governed the apportionment of the 55 representatives among the counties. Mont. Const. of 1889, art. V, § 4; art. VI, §§ 2, 3, 6. The initial apportionment allocated representatives in varying numbers from one to ten among the 16 counties and in addition employed three floterial districts to take care of overages from the population ratio, thus providing nearly exact proportionate representation in the house of representatives. However, the 16-member senate included one member from each of the 16 counties without regard to population. Id., art. V, § 4; art. VI, § 5.

The apportionment provisions of the constitution of 1889 have survived to the present without change, although, as permitted there, changes have been made in the apportionment formula to accommodate to population shifts and the creation of new counties. Thus, in 1964 there were 56 senators, one from each county (Mont. Rev. Codes Ann. § 43–101), and 94 representatives divided among the 56 counties without the use of floterial districts (id., § 43-104 (Supp. 1961)).

The 1960 population of Montana, 674,767, divided by 56 yields a senate population mean of 12,049. In 1964 the largest senatorial district contained 79,016 inhabitants and the smallest had 894. Theoretically, 16.1 per cent of the population of the state could elect a senate majority. Ten counties, comprising 57 per cent of the population, had only 18 per cent of the senate seats, while 23 counties, with 10 per cent of the population, had 41 per cent of the seats.

The Montana constitution does not establish a fixed number of representatives. Article VI, section 2 of the constitution of 1889 designates the legislature as the apportioning agent to provide for an enumeration of the inhabitants of the state in 1895 and every tenth year thereafter. At the next session following such enumeration, "and also at the session next following an enumeration made by the authority of the United States," the legislature "shall" reapportion the house "according to ratios to be fixed by law." Section 43-103 of the Montana code, as amended in 1961, allotted one representative to each county and one additional representative for each 8,500 persons or fractional excess of 4,250. Section 43-104 provided for districts electing a total of 94 representatives.

The 1960 population mean for the house of representatives was 7,178. However, in 1964 the most populous house district had a population of 12,537 and the least populous a population of 894. It was thus possible for 36.6 per cent to elect a majority of the representatives. Twenty-three counties with 10 per cent of the population had 24 per cent of the house seats. This disproportion could have been remedied by establishing

multi-county districts, which is constitutionally possible, or by the use of floterial districts as established in the original apportionment in the constitution of 1889.

At its 1965 session the Montana legislature proposed a constitutional amendment for submission to the voters for apportionment of both legislative houses "on the basis of population." Authority to provide the specific apportionment is reserved to the legislature following each federal census. The only requirement specified in the proposed amendment is that the districts be contiguous and compact. This interesting provision is also included: "At such time as the constitution of the United States is amended or interpreted to permit reapportionment of one house of a state legislative assembly on factors other than population, the senate of the legislative assembly shall be apportioned on the basis of one senator for each county." The proposed amendment would modify article VI, sections 2 and 3, and would repeal article V, sections 4 and 45, and article VI, sections 4, 5, and 6. Mont. Laws 1965, c. 273.

Despite the proposed constitutional amendment, a three-judge federal district court held the existing formula invalid and ordered its own reapportionment to control the 1966 elections. Closely related to population, but without crossing county lines, the court's plan provided for a 55-member senate, to be elected from 31 senatorial districts, and a 104-member house, to be elected from 38 representative districts. *Herweg v. Thirty-Ninth Legislative Assembly of Montana*, Civ. No. 1214 (D. Mont. 1965).

Article V, section 1 reserves the initiative and referendum powers to the people, and they may be used to propose constitutional amendments. Eight per cent of the legal voters of the state may initiate a proposal, provided that the signatures include 8 per cent of the voters in each of at least two fifths of the counties. The signature of 5 per cent of the legal voters of the state is required for a referendum petition, again with a requirement of dispersion among two fifths of the counties.

Article XIX, section 8 provides for the calling of a constitutional convention to revise, alter, or amend the constitution, while article XIX, section 9 empowers the legislature to propose constitutional amendments by a two-thirds vote of both houses to be referred to the people for majority approval.

Article VI, section 1 of the constitution empowers the state legislature to divide the state into congressional districts. Section 43-107 of the Montana code divides the state into two congressional districts. The districts have not been revised since 1917 although counties were added to both districts in 1945. In 1964 the larger of the two districts had 400,573 inhabitants and the smaller district only 274,194.

In August 1965 a three-judge federal district court held the congressional districting invalid and specified a new division between the two districts so that the population differential, in terms of 1960 population, would be reduced to 20,682. *Roberts v. Babcock*, Civ. No. 539 (D. Mont. 1965).

NEBRASKA

The land which now comprises the state of Nebraska was originally a portion of the land ceded by France to the United States by treaty of purchase in 1803. Successively thereafter it was within he area governed by the territories of Louisiana and Missouri. In 1854 Nebraska achieved its own territorial status, then including portions of the later-created states of Colorado, Idaho, Montana, North Dakota, South Dakota, and Wyoming; but the boundaries of Nebraska were successively limited by the erection of the territories of Colorado, Idaho, and Wyoming.

The 1854 congressional act which made Nebraska a territory vested the legislative power in a governor and legislative assembly, the latter to consist of a council of 13 (with the possibility of legislative enlargement) and a house of representatives of 26 (also subject to enlargement). Sec. 4. Provision was made for a census of inhabitants and qualified voters to be used as the basis for apportionment of councilmen and representatives among the counties and districts "in the ratio of [the] qualified voters as nearly as may be." Ibid.

Congress in 1864 authorized the inhabitants of the territory to form a constitution and state government as the basis for admission into the Union as a state. Delegates to the proposed convention were to be "apportioned among the several counties in said Territory in proportion to the population, as near as may be, and said apportionment shall be made for said Territory by the governor, United States district attorney, and chief justice thereof, or any two of them." Sec. 3.

The constitution thus authorized was framed by the territorial legislature, and it was approved by the people in 1866. A condition subsequently imposed by Congress was accepted by the legislature in 1867; and the President of the United States proclaimed Nebraska a state in the same year.

The Nebraska constitution of 1866 provided that the legislative authority was to be vested in a general assembly consisting of a senate and house of representatives. Id., art. II, § 1. Initially, the senate was to have a membership of 13 and the house 39 representatives, both subject to enlargement after ten years, but not to exceed 25 in the senate and 75 in the house. Id., art. II, § 8. The legislature was required to provide for a census of inhabitants in 1875 and every ten years thereafter; and at the first session after such census, and after each federal census, the legislature was to "apportion and district anew the numbers of the senate and house of representatives, according to the number of inhabitants, excluding Indians not taxed, and soldiers and officers of the United States Army and Navy." Id., art. II, § 3. Further, senators and representatives were to be chosen "by districts of convenient contiguous territory, as compact as may be, to be defined by law . . . ." Id., art. II, § 5.

The constitution of 1875 continued the provisions as to legislative reapportionment following each state and federal census (thus at five-year intervals) and the requirement of representation in accordance with population. Neb. Const. of 1875, art. III, § 2. To satisfy the requirement of equality, floterial districts were employed in the apportionment of both houses. Id., art. IV. The only significant change in the legislative article was the increase in the size of the house to 84 members (with provision for further enlargement to a maximum of 100) and of the senate to 30 members (with provision for further enlargement to a maximum of 33). Id., art. III, § 3. The constitution of 1919, the most recent, carried forward a similar requirement for the establishment of election districts "as nearly equal in population as may be and composed of contiguous and compact territory." Neb. Const. of 1919, art. III, § 5.

Nebraska adopted the unicameral legislative system by constitutional amendment in 1934. Neb. Const. of 1919, as amended, art. III, § 5. Legislative authority was vested in a single-chamber assembly of not more than 50 and not less than 30 members (id., art. III, § 6), elected for two years (id., art. III, § 7). The 1934 version of article III, section 5 provided for apportionment of the legislative districts upon a population basis (excluding aliens) as shown by the federal census. The legislature was empowered to redistrict the state "from time to time, but not oftener than once in ten years," when it was "necessary to a correction of inequalities in the population of such districts." Forty-three districts were created in 1935. Neb. Rev. Stat. § 5-103. Counties containing population sufficient to entitle them to two or more members were to be divided into separate districts "as nearly equal in population as may be and composed of contiguous and compact territory." Neb. Const. of 1919, as amended, Art. III, § 5.

The legislature did not reapportion between 1935 and 1962, in which latter year the existing formula was challenged in *League of Nebraska Municipalities v. Marsh*, 209 F. Supp. 189 (D. Neb. 1962). That case was a declaratory judgment action attacking the 1935 apportionment, which had fixed the election districts on the basis of the 1930 census. Based on the 1960 census the most populous district (100,-826 persons) was more than five times larger than the least populous (18,824 persons). The 14 least populous districts, with 14 votes, had a total population of 282,309, while the 4 most populous districts, with 4 votes, had a total population of 281,377. Id. at 193.

Plaintiffs asked for an at-large election and for an injunction to restrain the submission at the 1962 general election of a proposed constitutional amendment to article III, section 5. The court took jurisdiction, but denied the relief sought, reasoning that with elections close at hand, and with little time for campaigning, justice would best be served by not taking immediate action. The court made clear that in the event the next legislature did not take action, or in the event the action taken was invidious or arbitrary, the court would not hesitate to devise a remedy. In addition, the hope was expressed that the Nebraska Supreme Court would speak to these issues in the meanwhile. Id. at 196.

The 1962 amendment to article III, section 5 was ratified in November 1962 by a vote of 218,019 to 175,613. Nebraska Blue Book, 1962, compiled by the Nebraska Legislative Council. That amendment changed the 1934 provisions in two ways:

(1) It abandoned the requirement that legislative districts be composed of counties or separate units of counties entitled to more than one representative. County lines are to be followed "whenever practicable but other established lines may be followed at the discretion of the legislature." The basis of apportionment was unchanged from the 1934 version of section 5: population (excluding aliens) as shown by the federal census. "The legislature may redistrict the state from time to time, but not more often than once in ten years."

(2) The other new provision moderated the equal-population emphasis achieved by permitting deviation from county lines, allowing some weight to be given to area. The "primary emphasis shall be placed on population and not less than twenty per cent nor more than thirty per cent weight shall be given to area." The court in *League of Nebraska Municipalities v. Marsh,*

supra, declined to express any opinion on the validity or invalidity of any portion of the proposed amendment.

Pursuant to the 1962 amendment the Nebraska legislature in 1963 reapportioned itself by increasing the membership from 43 to 49 and drawing lines partially based on area. Neb. Laws 1963, cc. 22, 23.

In July 1964, after the Supreme Court of the United States decided the *Reapportionment Cases,* the three-judge federal district court, which had retained jurisdiction in *League of Municipalities v. Marsh,* supra, held invalid the 1962 constitutional amendment and its provision for using area as a partial basis for apportionment of the legislative districts. Accordingly, the 1963 legislation was also held unconstitutional. However, since the 1964 election machinery was already in motion, the court allowed that election to be conducted pursuant to the legislation just invalidated. The court held that the legislature so elected would have de facto status for its session beginning in January 1965, at which time it should fix the size of the legislature (within the constitutional limit of 30 to 50) and divide the state into the appointed number of districts. The court retained jurisdiction and advised that if the legislature failed to adopt a "proper enactment, . . . the court will take appropriate action." *League of Nebraska Municipalities v. Marsh,* 232 F. Supp. 411 (D. Neb. 1964).

On March 30, 1965, the legislature made another attempt at reapportionment, this time increasing the membership of the single chamber from 49 to 50 and giving Douglas County (Omaha) 12 members as compared with 10 (of 49) in the 1963 legislation and 7 (of 43) before that. Neb. Laws 1965, L.B. 628. Again the court found the legislation constitutionally defective, this time apparently because of population deviations caused by the legislature's insistence on adhering to county lines (although the state constitution did not so require), and because the plan appeared to have been drafted to prevent incumbents from having to run against each other. *League of Nebraska Municipalities v. Marsh*, 242 F. Supp. 357 (D. Neb. 1965).

Constitutional amendments may be proposed and adopted by the use of the initiative and the referendum. Neb. Const., 1919, art. III, §§ 1–3. For the initiative, the signatures of 10 per cent of the electors of the state must be procured and these signatures must be distributed so as to include 5 per cent of the electors of each of two fifths of the counties of the state. In *League of Nebraska Municipalities v. Marsh*, supra, the court held that the Nebraska initiative does not constitute an "adequate remedy" for the ordinary voter "to correct inequalities which exist in the apportionment of legislative districts." 209 F. Supp. at 193.

The legislature may propose constitutional amendments by a three-fifths vote to be submitted to the voters for majority ratification, provided that the votes cast in favor are more than 35 per cent of the total votes cast. Neb. Const., art. XVI, § 1, as amended in 1952. By a three-fifths vote the legislature may recommend to the voters the necessity of calling a constitutional convention, subject to ratification by a majority of those voting on the proposition, if those voting amount to at least 35 per cent of the total votes cast at the election. Id., art. XVI, § 2.

Nebraska is allotted three congressional seats. Neb. Rev. Stat. § 5-101. The 1960 population of 1,411,330 divided by 3 yields a congressional population mean of 470,443. In 1964 the most populous congressional district contained 530,507 persons while the least populous had 404,695.

REFERENCES

Clem, Alan L. Problems of Measuring and Achieving Equality of Representation in State Legislatures, 42 Neb. L. Rev. 622 (1963).

NEVADA

Portions of what is now the state of Nevada were at one time a part of Mexico ceded to the United States in the treaty of Guadalupe Hidalgo in 1848. For a time after 1850 Nevada was incorporated into the territory of Utah, but it gained separate territorial status by act of Congress in 1861. That act provided for the vesting of legislative authority in a governor and legislative assembly. The legislative body consisted of a council of 9 members (subject to enlargement to 13) and a house of representatives of 13 members (subject to enlargement to 26). The governor was directed to have a census taken of the inhabitants of the several counties and districts, on the basis of which he was to apportion the members of the council and house "as nearly equal as practicable among the several counties or districts . . . giving to each section of the Territory representation in the ratio of its population, (Indians excepted) as nearly as may be; . . . ." Sec. 4.

In 1864 Congress authorized the inhabitants to form a state government. Apportionment of delegates to the constitutional convention was to be accomplished by the governor "in proportion to the population, as near as may be . . . ." Sec. 3. In the same year, 1864, the convention was held, the constitution was approved, and Nevada was proclaimed by the President of the United States to be a state of the Union.

The constitution of 1864, the present constitution, provides explicitly that "Representation shall be apportioned according to population." Nev. Const., art. I, § 13. The constitution also provided for a census of inhabitants to be completed in 1865, 1867, 1875, and every ten years thereafter; that census plus the federal census "shall serve as the basis of representation in both houses of the Legislature." Id., art. XV, § 13. These provisions were originally implemented by the establishment of 11 election districts, in each of which the constitution specified the number of senators and assemblymen to be chosen to a total of 18 senators and 36 assemblymen. Id., art. XVII, § 6. Although the sections of the constitution requiring apportionment in accordance with population have not been changed, the constitution was amended in 1950 to fix the senate formula at one senator for each of the 17 counties despite extreme differences in population among the counties. Nev. Const., art. IV, § 5, as amended in 1950. See also Nev. Rev. Stat. § 218.050 (Supp. 1963). The 1960 total state population of 285,-278 divided by 17 yields a senatorial population mean of 16,781. In 1964, however, the most populous senate district had 127,016 inhabitants while the least populous had only 568. Hence, it became theoretically possible for 8 per cent of the total state population to elect a majority of the senators. The urban counties of Washoe and Clark had 74 per cent of the population but only 12 per cent of the senate seats.

Article IV, section 5, as amended in 1950, directed that "members of the assembly shall be apportioned on the basis of population; provided, that each county shall be entitled to at least one

assemblyman." It was the "mandatory duty" of the legislature "at its first session after the taking of the decennial census of the United States in the year 1950, and after each subsequent decennial census, to fix by law the number of assemblymen, and apportion them among the several counties of the state, according to the number of inhabitants in them, respectively." By legislative act of 1961 provision was made for 37 assemblymen. The legislature was charged with both the apportioning function and the districting function in counties entitled to more than one assemblyman. Nev. Rev. Stat. § 218.060 (Supp. 1963).

In 1964 the most populous assembly district had 12,525 inhabitants while the least populous had only 568; and 35 per cent of the population could elect a majority of the assemblymen. Clark and Washoe Counties, with approximately 74 per cent of the state's population, had only 57 per cent of the assembly seats.

On September 23, 1965, the federal court ruled, in *Dungan v. Sawyer*, Civ. No. 695 (D. Nev.), that a special session of the legislature must be convened no later than October 30, 1965, to act no later than November 26, 1965.

Constitutional amendments may be proposed by a majority vote of both houses and become effective after approval by a majority of the voters. Nev. Const., art. XVI, § 1. By a two-thirds vote the legislature may at any time recommend to the voters the necessity of convening a constitutional convention, to be called by the legislature if approved by the voters. Id., art. XVI, § 2.

The right of the initiative and the referendum is reserved to the people by article XIX, sections 1-3 of the constitution.

Nevada is entitled to one congressional representative, elected from the state at large.

NEW HAMPSHIRE

Although the rudiments of government in what is now the state of New Hampshire go back to a patent issued by James I in 1620, the earliest significant government for present purposes was provided in the constitution of 1776, a brief instrument drawn to establish a government "to continue during the present unhappy and unnatural contest with Great Britain . . . ." A congress which assembled at Exeter in December 1775, on recommendation of the Continental Congress, continued itself as a house of representatives. That body was authorized in the new constitution to choose 12 freeholders to serve as a council from the several counties as follows: Rockingham 5, Strafford 2, Hillsborough 2, Cheshire 2, and Grafton 1. Contrary to the apparent expectations of the drafters of this instrument that it would serve only for about a year, no further constitution was agreed upon until 1784. That constitution vested legislative power in a body known as the general court of New Hampshire, consisting of a senate and house of representatives.

The senate membership was fixed at 12; "and the general court in assigning the number to be elected by the respective districts, shall govern themselves by the proportion of public taxes paid by the said districts . . . ." N.H. Const. of 1784, pt. II, the senate. No other state, except for a time Massachusetts and North Carolina, has based representation in either house on taxes paid. The practice was abandoned in Massachusetts in 1840, while in North Carolina it

was adhered to only between 1835 and 1868. But in New Hampshire the practice survived judicial examination in the state supreme court as recently as 1962, and was not finally abandoned until a constitutional amendment was approved in 1964, as noted below.

Apportionment in the house of representatives, however, was to be grounded upon "principles of equality: and in order that such representation may be as equal as circumstances will admit, every town, parish, or place entitled to town privileges, having one hundred and fifty rateable male polls, of twenty-one years of age, and upwards, may elect one representative; . . . ." The scale provided for one more representative for each additional 300 "rateable polls" in each town, parish, or place. Towns, parishes, and places with less than 150 were to be "classed by the general-assembly for the purpose of chusing a representative"; and the places of holding elections for such combined districts were to be rotated among the annual town meetings of the included communities, beginning with the most populous. N.H. Const. of 1784, pt. II, house of representatives.

The constitution of 1793 did not change the apportionment provisions in any significant particular, nor were the principles outlined above departed from in subsequent amendments in 1877 and 1902. However, the base number of inhabitants for a town to qualify for a representative was increased to 600, and the "mean increasing number" for additional representation became 1,800. N.H. Const. of 1793, as amended in 1877, pt. II, art. 9. Also, a new feature was added which remained part of the apportionment situation in New Hampshire until 1964. Part II, art. 11, as amended in 1877, provided that any town, place, or city ward with less than

600 inhabitants which could not conveniently be classed with any other like unit should be authorized to send a representative to the general court "such proportionate part of the time as the number of its inhabitants shall bear to six hundred; . . . ." Moreover, a few — those living in unincorporated places — were not represented in the house at all. At the same time the senate was increased from 12 to 24. Id., pt. II, arts. 25, 26.

The constitutional direction for apportionment of the senate "by proportion of direct taxes paid" was carried out by use of equalized valuations. This was determined in 1961, for example, by dividing the total equalized valuation of the state, then $2,618,156,082 (N.H. Laws 1961, c. 159), by 24 (the number of senate districts) to produce an average equalized valuation of about $109,000,000. Geographical areas having approximately this value were then determined. Hence, a proper interpretation required that the districts be so established that the "direct taxes paid" by the towns and unincorporated places in each senatorial district should be in the same proportion as the direct taxes paid by the towns and unincorporated places of any other district or as nearly so as is practicable, having regard to the prohibition against the division of towns and places. *Opinion of the Justices*, 101 N.H. 518, 131 A.2d 818 (1957); 101 N.H. 523, 132 A.2d 411 (1957).

In *Levitt v. Maynard*, 104 N.H. 243, 182 A.2d 897 (1962) petitioner sought a declaratory judgment that the 1961 districting of the state, and the provisions of the New Hampshire constitution prescribing the method of senatorial districting, were violative of the fourteenth amendment, citing the variations in the equalized valuations of the 24 districts. Only one district had a valuation approximating $109,000,000 (the mean), and the remaining districts varied from a low of $96,000,000 in one district to a high of $122,000,000 in another. 104 N.H. at 246, 182 A.2d at 899.

The supreme court of New Hampshire held unanimously that neither the method of districting nor the manner in which it was applied violated the fourteenth amendment. The court held that the state constitution did not require mathematically exact equality among the senatorial districts since article 26 required only that the districts be "as nearly equal as may be." Ibid. The court conceded that the apportionment of senatorial districts on the basis of taxes is unique and may be "quaint" (ibid.), but it found no lack of rational basis for the apportionment formula.

The 1960 population of New Hampshire was 606,921. Dividing that number by 24 yields a senatorial population mean of 25,288. When 1960 population figures are applied to the 1961 districting act, the most populous senatorial district had a population of 41,457 while the least populous had 15,829; 45.3 per cent of the population was theoretically able to elect a majority of the senators.

The house of representatives at the same time consisted of "not less than" 375 nor more than 400 members elected biennially from towns and wards "on principles of equality, and representation therein shall be as equal as circumstances will admit." N.H. Const., pt. II, art. 9. The legislature was required every ten years after 1951 to reapportion according to the last general federal or state census. Ibid. Section 66:6 of the New Hampshire code provided that all towns and wards having 822 inhabitants should be entitled to one representative. To be entitled to additional representatives the town or ward needed twice the number required for the first representative (1,644 under the 1961 laws). In making the apportionment, no town was to be divided nor were the boundaries of the wards of any city to be altered. N.H. Const., pt. II, art. 9.

Small towns and cities not possessing the requisite number of inhabitants required for one representative (822) were authorized representation "such proportionate part of the time as the number of its inhabitants shall bear to the requisite number established for one representative ... provided ... that each town and ward shall be entitled to representation in at least one session in every ten years." Id., pt. II, art. 11. The detailed allocations of the numbers of full-time representatives and of those involved in rotation were fixed by statute. N.H. Rev. Stat. Ann. §§ 66:3–4 (Supp. 1963).

The principal inequality in the house resulted from the stepped-up quota required for towns and wards to qualify for each additional seat beyond the first. In 1964 middle-sized towns and wards (between 822 and 1,644 inhabitants) were overrepresented by 29 per cent; slightly larger towns and wards with a population between 1,644 and 2,466 were underrepresented by 26 per cent; and cities were underrepresented by 7 per cent. Since it was the city wards and not the cities themselves which were represented in the lower house, each city received as many low-quota seats based on 822 inhabitants, instead of the 1,644 inhabitants required for an additional member, as it had wards. Both houses were reapportioned in 1965 in an effort to satisfy the population standard. N.H. Laws 1965, cc. 216, 220.

In accordance with the provisions of article II, section 99 of the constitution, a constitutional convention was called to begin meeting in May 1964. That convention, the fifteenth in New Hampshire, approved 19 amendments to the constitution, 7 for submission to the voters in 1964 and the others for later submission. Among the amendments approved in November 1964 (4 of those recommended by the commission and 1 otherwise proposed) were basic changes in the representation formula in both houses of the general court (the New Hampshire legislature). The voters approved apportionment of senate districts on the basis of population, as equally as possible without dividing any town, ward, or unincorporated place, thus abandoning the last vestige in the United States of representation on the basis of taxable wealth. The change in the house of representatives abolished the constitutional requirement that the population increment for a second representative must be double that required for the first, thus permitting reapportionment on a population basis as elsewhere required in the constitution. The legislature was also authorized to establish districts for towns too small for full-time representation under previous rules. The legislature was permitted to propose constitutional amendments. 53 National Civic Review 437–38 (Sept. 1964); 54 id. 25–26 (Jan. 1965).

New Hampshire is entitled to two representatives in the United States Congress. N.H. Rev. Stat. Ann. § 66:4–8. The districts have not been revised since 1881. The larger district in 1960 had 331,818 inhabitants and the other a population of 275,103.

REFERENCES

Stavert, John L. Senatorial Districting in New Hampshire: Levitt v. Maynard, 5 N.H.B.J. 231 (1963).
Commission to Study the State Constitution. Report to the Fifteenth Constitutional Convention (1964).

NEW JERSEY

The area of the present state of New Jersey was at various times within the claimed domain of Virginia (charter of 1606), the Council for New England (charter of 1620), and the Dutch West India Company (grant of 1622). In 1664, when New Jersey was securely under English control, Charles II made a grant of that area to his brother, the Duke of York, who in turn released his interest to Lord John Berkeley and Sir George Carteret. Those proprietors promptly agreed that a governor appointed by them should have the legislative power with the "advice and consent" of a fixed proportion of 6 to 12 persons to be chosen by the governor as his council. Concession and Agreement of the Lords Proprietors of 1664, item first. Provision was also made for a body of 12 (or occasionally more) freeholders as deputies or representatives "for each respective division, tribe or parish. . . ." Id., item eighth. Together, the governor, council, and representatives constituted a general assembly with enumerated legislative powers.

In 1676 the colony was divided into East New Jersey and West New Jersey, each with separate proprietors and separate governments. East New Jersey, for example, was to be governed by a great council consisting of the 24 proprietors to whom the grant had been made, 24 freeholder representatives (3 from each of the eight towns), and 48 county representatives, making an initial total of 96 subject to later expansion to 144 at the will of the great council, which was to apportion the numbers to be selected from each town and county. East New Jersey Const. of 1683, art. II. In 1702, however, Queen Anne recalled the grants to the proprietors of East and West New Jersey and in 1712 reconfirmed the 1676 grant of New England by Charles II to the Duke of York. Thereafter, the reunited colony was governed by royal governors until New Jersey, along with the other American colonies, declared independence from British rule.

The New Jersey constitution of 1776 was a brief instrument declaring dissolution of the ties to Great Britain, proclaiming certain basic rights of citizens, and establishing a frame of government. Uniquely among all the states, the original 13, as well as the later added 37, New Jersey at first rejected representation in accordance with population in both houses of the legislature. In the council (later designated the senate) each county was represented by one freeholder inhabitant, while in the general assembly three freeholder inhabitants were to be selected from each county. N.J. Const. of 1776, art. III. Even though the disparities in population among the then 13 counties were not nearly so substantial proportionately as today, inequalities did of course exist. There was, however, an apparent awareness that reasonable equality might well be worth preserving as population movements should occur or as new, less populous counties might be added; for this interesting provision was included in the same article of the constitution: "Provided always, that if a majority of the representatives of this Province, in Council and General Assembly convened, shall, at any time or times hereafter, judge it equitable and proper, to add to or diminish the number or proportion of the members of Assembly for any county or counties in this Colony [later State], then, and in such case, the same may, on the principle of more equal representation, be lawfully done; anything in this Charter to the contrary notwithstanding: so that the whole number of Representatives in Assembly shall not, at any time, be less than thirty-nine." Ibid.

The reference in the 1776 constitution to the possibility of statutory change to satisfy "the principle of more equal representation" became a specific requirement of the constitution of 1844, but only as to the general assembly, the senate remaining unchanged with one senator from each of the then 19 counties. N.J. Const. of 1844, art. IV, § II. Article IV, section III of the 1844 constitution provided that the representatives should be "apportioned among the said counties as nearly as may be according to the number of their inhabitants." The application of the population principle was limited somewhat by the assurance of one representative for each county with a limit of 60 on the size of the general assembly. N.J. Const. of 1844, art. IV, § III. Reapportionment in accordance with this formula was made a legislative duty at the first session of the legislature after each federal census. Ibid.

The apportionment provisions of the 1844 constitution were continued without change in the otherwise considerably streamlined constitution of 1947. (Indeed, the law calling for a constitutional convention expressly provided against change of those provisions. N.J. Laws of 1947, c. 8, § 2.) N.J. Const. of 1947, art. IV, § II, ¶ 1 (one senator from each county); id., art. IV, § III, ¶ 1 (60-member general assembly, at least one from each county, the remainder to be selected "according to the number of their inhabitants"). Responsibility for reapportionment after each federal census is placed on the legislature, which in 1961 specified that the allotment of representatives beyond one for each county should be computed by the

method of equal proportions and the results certified by the secretary of state to the several county clerks. N.J. Stat. Ann. §§ 52:10-4 to 52:10-6 (Supp. 1963).

Under the 1960 federal census figures, population inequalities inevitably occurred among the New Jersey senate districts. The 1960 state population of 6,066,782, divided by 21 seats, yielded a senatorial population mean of 288,894. The largest senate district had 923,545 inhabitants (Essex County), while the smallest had but 48,555 (Cape May County). Senators from the 11 smallest counties, who constituted a voting majority in the senate, represented only 19 per cent of the state population. Essex County was 219.7 per cent underrepresented in terms of the relative deviation in population from the mean. Hudson and Bergen Counties were underrepresented by 111.4 per cent and 170.1 per cent respectively, while Atlantic, Cumberland, and Cape May Counties were 44, 63, and 83 per cent overrepresented, in that order.

The general assembly districts also demonstrated substantial population disparities. The 1960 assembly population mean was 101,113, but the largest district contained a population of 143,-913, while the smallest had only 48,555 inhabitants.

New Jersey courts have traditionally taken jurisdiction to consider the validity of acts apportioning the membership of the general assembly. *State ex rel. Morris v. Wrightson*, 56 N.J.L. 126, 28 Atl. 56 (Sup. Ct. 1893); *Smith v. Baker*, 74 N.J.L. 591, 64 Atl. 1067 (Ct. Err. & App. 1906); *Botti v. McGovern*, 97 N.J.L. 353, 118 Atl. 107 (Sup. Ct. 1922); *Asbury Park Press v. Wooley*, 33 N.J. 1, 161 A.2d 705 (1960).

When the state constitutional formula for both houses was attacked on fourteenth amendment grounds, the claims were at first rejected in the lower state court. *Jackman v. Bodine,* 78 N.J. Super. 414, 188 A.2d 642 (Ch. Div. 1963). However, after the decision of the Supreme Court of the United States was announced in the *Reapportionment Cases,* the New Jersey Supreme Court held invalid the provision for one senator to each county. The court declined to pass on the general assembly formula on the ground that the people should be given an opportunity to express their preference for reconstitution of both houses. *Jackman v. Bodine,* 43 N.J. 453, 205 A.2d 713 (1964). The court enjoined the holding of any further elections pursuant to the invalid formula (the next election was due in November 1965); authorized the legislature to adopt interim legislation for the selection of legislators in 1965; declared that proposals to amend the constitution could be submitted by a constitutional convention called by the legislature, so long as the delegates to the convention were chosen in accordance with population; and reserved the question whether amendments to the constitution could be submitted by any other process.

Meanwhile, the legislature sought to accommodate to the equal-population command through a resolution of the state senate providing for a system of weighted voting. The state attorney general moved for a declaration that such a plan would not satisfy the federal or state constitutions; and the state supreme court, without passing on the federal constitutional question, agreed that the action was invalid under the state constitution: "We are satisfied that the vote necessary for the adoption of legislation may not be fixed by an internal rule or regulation of one branch of the Legislature." *Jackman v.*

Bodine, 43 N.J. 491, 205 A.2d 735 (1964).

Thus faced with the necessity for specific and prompt reapportionment action, the legislature established the New Jersey Legislative Reapportionment and Congressional Redistricting Planning Commission, which reported its recommendations in February 1965. Although it proved difficult to secure agreement within the legislature and approval by the governor, the interim apportionment called for by the court was at last achieved on April 12, 1965. The 21-member senate was converted into a body of 29 members to be selected from 14 districts. The most populous counties, Bergen and Essex, were allotted four senators each and Hudson County was given three. Passaic, Union, Middlesex, and Camden Counties were each authorized two senators. The other ten senators were divided among the remaining 14 counties of the state in districts ranging from one senator for two counties to two senators for three counties. No change was made in the assembly districts. N.J. Laws of 1965, c. 19. See R.S. Cum. Supp. 52: 10B-1 to 10B-9.

Within less than two weeks the New Jersey Supreme Court unanimously upheld the plan as a transitional plan, although it cautioned that the variations in population among the senatorial districts would be questionable in a permanent measure. N.Y. Times, April 24, 1965, p. 16, col. 2.

On May 10, 1965, the governor signed a further bill summoning a constitutional convention to draw a permanent reapportionment plan by June 1966. The law provided for a popularly elected convention of 126 delegates with 112 votes to be determined on a rough population basis. That is, each county was given from one to 14 votes. It was also provided that counties with an odd number of votes should have an extra delegate. In those cases two of the delegates were assigned one-half vote each. It provided that delegates should be elected March 1, 1966, for a convention to meet on March 21, 1966. N.J. Laws of 1965, c. 43.

Amendments may be proposed by the legislature by agreement of three fifths of all the members of both houses, to be referred to the people (after a public hearing). N.J. Const. of 1947, art. IX, ¶ 1. The amendment becomes effective if approved at the next general election by a majority of electors voting. Id., art. IX, ¶¶ 4, 6. If an amendment is approved by a majority of the members of both houses, but not by the required three fifths, such proposed amendment shall be referred to the legislature in the next legislative year and, if agreed to by a majority of the members of both houses, it shall be submitted to the people for majority ratification. Id., art. IX, ¶ 1. If a proposed amendment is not approved by the voters, neither such proposed amendment nor one to effect the same or substantially the same change in the constitution shall be submitted to the people before the third general election thereafter. Id., art. IX, ¶ 7.

There are no provisions relating to the call of a constitutional convention, and no provisions relating to the initiative or the referendum. *Jackman v. Bodine,* supra, held that it is not required for the constitutionality of the apportionment of assembly districts to afford the New Jersey inhabitants the right to propose amendments to the state constitution through either an initiative or a referendum. 188 A.2d at 652.

New Jersey is divided into 15 congressional districts by legislative act of 1962. N.J. Stat. Ann. § 19:46-1 (Supp. 1963). The districts vary in population from 585,586 to 255,165.

The State Reapportionment Commission unanimously recommended a plan for congressional redistricting that would have substantially equalized the population among the districts, but would in two cases have put incumbent congressmen in districts with another incumbent. Under the proposed plan Essex, Hudson, and Union Counties would have been reduced from six to five districts, and that seat would have gone to South Jersey. Five districts would be given to Bergen County, and Passaic County would be a single district. Under the plan the cities of Newark and Jersey City would each be completely within a single district instead of divided as had been the case. The severely gerrymandered seventh district, which since 1931 had stretched from the Hackensack River around the northern part of the state to within ten miles of Trenton in the south, would consist solely of Mercer, Hunterdon, Warren, and Sussex Counties. N.Y. Times, Jan. 22, 1965, p. 1, col. 1. The legislature, however, was unable to agree upon a plan acceptable to the governor in its regular 1965 session.

In April 1965 the superior court of New Jersey ruled that the large boards of freeholders governing three counties of the third class are malapportioned and that the statutes regulating their composition are unconstitutional. The court ruled, however, that the citizens of the counties should be given time to determine whether they will thereafter be governed by small boards of freeholders or petition the legislature to reapportion their large boards. *Mauk v. Hoffman,* 87 N.J. Super. 276, 209 A.2d 150 (1965).

REFERENCES

New Jersey Law and Legislative Reference Bureau. New Jersey Legislative Reapportionment: A Summary of Legislative Proposals to Reapportion the Seats of the General Assembly of New Jersey. Trenton: 1957.

New Jersey Legislative Reapportionment and Congressional Districting Planning Commission. Report to the Senate and General Assembly. Trenton: 1965.

Reock, Ernest C., Jr. Population Inequality Among Counties in the New Jersey Legislature. New Brunswick: Bureau of Government Research, Rutgers, The State University. 1963.

Rutgers, The State University. New Jersey Congressional Districts, a Plan for the Sixties. New Brunswick: Bureau of Government Research. 1960. A supplementary report was issued in 1961.

Rutgers, The State University. Statement on Senate Concurrent Resolutions 22 and 23 Before the Committee on the Judiciary, New Jersey Senate, May 22, 1957. New Brunswick: Bureau of Government Research. 1957.

Effross, Harris I. Post-Colonial Counties in New Jersey: Factors Affecting Their Creation, 81 Proceedings of Historical Society 103 (April 1963).

NEW MEXICO

What is now the state of New Mexico was successively claimed by Mexico and Texas. The claims of Texas were settled by an 1850 act of Congress offering ten million dollars in return for the relinquishment of claims (act of 1850, § 4); and the last remaining claims of Mexico were resolved by the Mexican Treaty of Cession of 1853. The territory of New Mexico was established by the congressional act of 1850 (it included at that time the present state of Arizona as well), which also provided a territorial government. Legislative power was vested in a governor and a legislative assembly consisting of a council of 13 members and a house of representatives of 26 members. The governor was directed to arrange for a census of inhabitants and to make an apportionment for both houses on the basis thereof, to be made, "as nearly equal as practicable, among the several counties or districts, . . . giving to each section of the Territory representation in the ratio of its population, (Indians excepted,) as nearly as may be." Sec. 5.

In 1906 Congress authorized the qualified electors of the then separate territories of New Mexico and Arizona to vote on the question whether the two should be united to form a single state (to be called Arizona); and provisions were made for selection at the same time of 110 delegates to a constitutional convention which would have been convened if the answer had been affirmative. The delegates were to be chosen pursuant to an apportionment made "as nearly as may be, equitably among the several counties thereof in accordance with the voting population as shown by the vote cast for Delegates in Congress in the respective Territories in nineteen hundred and four." Sec. 24.

In view of the negative answer to the question, a constitutional convention for the formation of a government for New Mexico as a separate state was authorized and convened in 1910. Article IV of the constitution of 1910 divided the state into 24 senatorial districts and 30 representative districts (from which 49 representatives were to be elected); and "there was a real attempt to apportion the legislature as strictly by population as was possible." Gill, Legislative Apportionment and Congressional Districting in New Mexico 3 (1953). The constitution of 1910 further provided for reapportionment by the legislature after the 1920 federal census and after each subsequent census, "upon the basis of population; provided that each county included in each district shall be contiguous to some other county therein." N.M. Const. of 1910, art. IV.

The legislature failed to act following the census of 1920 and of 1930. In 1941 the legislature offered an amendment (HJR 11, N.M. Laws 1941, p. 509) which would have provided one senator for each county and one representative for each 11,000 persons or major fraction, each county to have one, and no county to have more than five. That amendment was defeated in 1942; but in 1949 a further proposal was accepted by the voters which in general followed the 1910 apportionment formula for the house except in enlarging the size of the house from 49 to 55, dividing the 6 extra seats among four counties. The original senatorial districts were abolished, and each county was given one senator (except Los Alamos, which, as a sixth-class county, was not given separate representation). The 1949 amendment also deleted the provision for decennial reapportionment by the legislature and provided no other means in its place.

A new apportionment provision was proposed by the legislature in 1955 as SJR No. 1 and was adopted by the voters in September 1955. Article IV, section 3 of the constitution was amended to establish a senate consisting of 32 members, one from each county of the state. The 66-member house of representatives was to consist of "at least one [1] member elected from each county of the state," 9 members from Bernalillo County, 3 members from each of nine other counties, and 2 members from each of eight other counties.

In addition, article IV, section 3(d) directed that those counties entitled to more than one representative should not be divided into subdistricts each electing one member, nor should the delegates be elected at large. Instead, the county officer who issues election proclamations was to designate as many "places" as there were representatives to be elected, and one member was to be elected from each "place." "No county shall be geographically divided for the purpose of designating places in the election of such members of the house of representatives. Each candidate shall designate, upon filing his petition, the position number for which he is a candidate ...."

The legislature "may" reapportion the membership in the house of representatives "once" following the publication of the official report of each federal decennial census, provided that each county is entitled to elect one member, and that no member of the house "shall represent or be elected by the voters of more than one county." N.M. Const., art. IV, § 3(f), as amended in 1955.

The provisions of the 1955 amendment to article IV, section 3 were successfully challenged in *Cargo v. Campbell*, Civ. No. 33273 (N.M. Dist. Ct., Santa Fe County, Sept. 6, 1963). The court held that the New Mexico constitutional provision apportioning the 66 members of the house of representatives (one from each county, certain counties to have additional representatives) constituted an invidious discrimination in violation of the equal protection clause of the fourteenth amendment. The court noted that the 1960 population of New Mexico, 951,023, divided by 66, would result in a population mean of 14,409 for each representative. However, Bernalillo County, with 9 representatives, had one representative for every 29,133 citizens while the 1,874 inhabitants of Harding County also had one representative. Other cases of extreme overrepresentation were cited. Seventeen counties with less than one sixth of the total population of the state had one third of the total vote in the house of representatives. One half of the membership of the house of representatives (33 members) represented a population of 685,583 as against the remaining 33 representatives from counties with a total population of only 265,440. Discrepancies were reported in the weight of an individual vote as high as approximately 20 to 1. Accordingly, the court found the existing constitutional apportionment of the house of representatives invidiously discriminatory. The court also specifically held unconstitutional the provision which entitled each county to at least one member of the house of representatives.

Since "reapportionment is a legislative and not a judicial function" the court declared it would undertake to reapportion the districts "only as a last resort and only if the legislature does not do it in a lawful manner and in a reasonable time." It was suggested that counties having a population in excess of the population mean could be divided while the smaller counties could be consolidated. The deadline for legislative action was set at December 1, 1963, and the cause of action was stayed to that date.

Cargo v. Campbell did not consider the constitutionality of the basis of representation in the New Mexico senate, although the population disparities were even greater in that body than in the house. The 1960 senatorial population mean is 29,719. Based on those figures the population of the most populous senate district (Bernalillo County) was 262,199 while the least populous had only 1,874 persons. It was possible for 14 per cent of the population to elect a majority of the senate.

Late in 1963 the New Mexico legislature adopted a system of weighted

voting for its house of representatives, the first to be adopted by any state legislature. N.M. Stat. Ann. §§ 2-7-1 to 2-7-13 (Supp. 1964). In addition, the legislature enlarged the house to 77 members. Id., §§ 2-8-1 to 2-8-17. The 77 members were to cast a total of 700 votes, individual representatives casting from 1 to 10 votes depending on the population of the district from which elected. The plan was thus able to provide for continued representation by at least one representative from each county. However, the plan was promptly struck down before the end of 1963 by Judge Caswell S. Neal of the New Mexico district court. He retained jurisdiction and indicated that if the legislature failed to act at its next regular session, he might effect a reapportionment of his own. 53 National Civic Review 90 (Feb. 1964).

In March 1965 the New Mexico legislature adopted a new apportionment plan. House membership was reduced from 77 to 70, all to be elected from single-member districts. The senate was enlarged from 32 to 37 members, giving Bernalillo County six senators and one to each other county, but weighting the votes on a population basis. N.M. Laws of 1965, cc. 642, 870. See also S. Res. 1.

Amendments to the constitution may be proposed in either house and, if passed by a majority of both houses, are to be submitted at the next regular election for ratification by a majority of the voters voting thereon. N.M. Const., art. XIX, § 1. The calling of a constitutional convention may be proposed by a two-thirds vote of both houses, after which the question is submitted to the electors at the next general election for approval by a majority of the electors voting. Id., art. XIX, § 2.

Article IV, section 1 of the constitution reserves the powers of the referendum to the people, in that they can disapprove and suspend legislation enacted by the legislature (with a few exceptions). However, this process does not apply to amendment of the constitution. There is no provision relating to the initiative.

New Mexico is entitled to two delegates to Congress, both of whom are elected at large.

REFERENCES

Gill, Inez. Legislative Apportionment and Congressional Districting in New Mexico. Albuquerque: Department of Government, Division of Research, University of New Mexico. 1953.

Irion, Frederick C. Reapportionment and Redistricting in New Mexico and Conclusion of Reapportionment and Redistricting. Albuquerque: Division of Government Research, University of New Mexico. 1963.

[New Mexico] Legislative Reapportionment in New Mexico, 2nd Series Government in New Mexico 1 (November 10, 1962).

NEW YORK

Representative government in what is now the state of New York had its origins in the seventeenth century after English control over the area had been secured from the Dutch. Charles II made extensive grants to his brother the Duke of York in 1664 (as reconfirmed in 1674 after the Dutch were finally ousted), including what was to become the colony of New York. In 1683 the Duke of York directed the governor to convene an assembly of not more than 18 representatives to be elected by the colony's freeholders. Later in 1683 the assembly divided the colony into 12 counties and apportioned 23 assemblymen among those counties. Although the act of which that apportionment was a part was vetoed by the king, the apportionment act of 1691 contained similar provisions.

Silva, Apportionment of the New York Assembly, 31 Fordham L. Rev. 1 (1962). During the colonial period four units were used as a basis of representation. "While the county was the most general unit, separate representation was also given to certain manors (Cortlandt, Livingston, and Renselaerwyck), to the borough of Westchester, and to townships or mixed settlements like Schenectady and its dependencies. The assignment of more members to the more populous territorial units indicates that population as well as the territorial subdivision was a factor in distributing assembly seats among the various parts of the Colony." Id. at 1–2.

Despite the limited deference to population in the colonial legislatures, the first constitution of New York as a state, in 1777, relied primarily on population as the basis of apportionment in both houses of the legislature. The constitution provided for a senate of 24 members to be chosen from four senatorial districts in the following proportions: nine from the southern district; six from the middle district; six from the western district; and three from the eastern district. In addition, the constitution provided for the taking of a census seven years after the end of the war; "and if, on such census, it shall appear that the number of senators is not justly proportioned to the general districts, that the legislature adjust the proportion, as near as may be, to the number of freeholders, qualified as aforesaid, in each district." N.Y. Const. of 1777, art. XII. The 70 members fixed for the assembly were apportioned among the then 14 counties with a provision for reapportionment of the numbers after a census so that the assemblymen would be "justly proportioned to the number of electors in the said counties respectively." Id., art. V.

In 1791, following the first census, the senate districts were altered and the seats were reapportioned to a senate now increased in size to 43 members. N.Y. Sess. Laws 1791, c. 4, p. 201. The assembly was also reapportioned in the same year, and in 1796 the assembly was enlarged to a membership of 108. N.Y. Sess. Laws 1796, c. 19, p. 652. In 1801 a constitutional amendment fixed the number of senators at 32 and the number of assemblymen at 100, directing the legislature to apportion the senators among the four districts "as nearly as may be, according to the number of electors qualified to vote for senators" and to apportion the assembly seats among the counties also according to the number of their respective electors. In addition, it was then provided that the number of assemblymen should increase at the rate of two members each year to a total of 150 members.

The constitution of 1821 continued the number of senators at 32, but increased the number of senatorial districts from four to eight. Each district was assigned four seats, and as a result the legislature lost its direct authority to reapportion senators among the districts. N.Y. Const. of 1821, art. I, § 5. However, the legislature was directed to redistrict at the first session after a census to be taken in 1825 and every ten years thereafter, so "that each senate district shall contain, as nearly as may be, an equal number of inhabitants, excluding aliens, paupers, and persons of color not taxed . . . ." Id., art. I, § 6. The constitution of 1821 provided for apportionment of the assembly "among the several counties of the State, as nearly as may be, according to the numbers of their respective inhabitants . . . ." Id., art. I, § 7. The size of the assembly was fixed at 128 (id., art. I, § 2), to include at least one assemblyman

from each county regardless of population; but no new county was to be created unless its population justified an assemblyman. Id., art. I, § 7.

The constitution of 1846 continued the senate of 32 members and the house of 128 members, but now provided for the election of senators from 32 single-member districts into which the 60 counties of the state were divided. N.Y. Const. of 1846, art. III, §§ 2, 3. However, once again the legislature was charged with reapportionment following the census in 1855 and each ten years thereafter, so that "each Senate district shall contain, as nearly as may be, an equal number of inhabitants . . . ." Id., art. III, § 4. Districts were to consist of contiguous territory, and no county was to be divided unless entitled to two or more senators. Ibid. The assembly districts were also to be apportioned according to the number of inhabitants; "but no town shall be divided in the formation of Assembly districts." Id., art. III, § 5. Every county was assured at least one assemblyman (except Hamilton, which was for this purpose joined with Fulton County). Where a county was entitled to more than one assemblyman, the districting was to be done by the county boards of supervisors. Ibid.

Although the 1846 constitution provided that each senatorial district should contain, as nearly as may be, an equal number of representative inhabitants, there were greater population differentials among the districts created by the statutes enacted pursuant to this constitution than under the previous constitutions. See Silva, Apportionment in New York, 30 Fordham L. Rev. 581, 601 n.119 (1962). These differences, however, resulted from districting rather than from malapportionment.

The variations among the populations of senate districts under these early constitutions were not especially severe and did not consistently work to the disadvantage of any one particular area or group of voters. For example, under the apportionments enacted pursuant to the 1821 constitution the ratio between the highest and lowest population-per-seat figure never exceeded 1.2 to 1. The apportionments under the 1846 constitution produced ratios ranging from 1.5 to 1 to 1.8 to 1, as contrasted with 1964 variations of 2.3 to 1. The disparities in the assembly were also less marked under the earlier constitutions than in recent years. Under the apportionment of 1791, for example, the maximum ratio was 2.2 to 1, while the 1964 variations were more than 8 to 1.

The 1894 constitution said that each senate district "shall contain as nearly as may be an equal number of inhabitants, excluding aliens, and be in as compact form as practicable, and shall remain unaltered until [the return of another enumeration], and shall at all times consist of contiguous territory, and no county shall be divided in the formation of a senate district except to make two or more senate districts wholly in such county." N.Y. Const. of 1894, art. III, § 4. The objective of population equality among districts was diluted, however, by other "mandatory provisions" noted below. The size of the senate was subject to variation. A minimum number of 50 seats was fixed, but there was no specified maximum. Id., art. III, § 2. In 1964 there were 58 senators; there would have been 57 if reapportionment had been made on the basis of the provisions of the 1894 constitution and the 1960 census.

Reapportionment of the senate every ten years was to be accomplished in several stages, as a result of which the counties were divided into two categories: (1) those with 6 per cent or more of the state's citizen population (the "populous counties"), and (2) those with less than 6 per cent of the citizen population (the "less populous counties"). Different procedures determined the number of seats apportioned to each group.

First, the total population of the state, excluding aliens, as determined by the last federal census, was to be divided by 50 to produce what was known as the first ratio. All counties with citizen populations of at least three times this ratio (i.e., 6 per cent or more of the state's population, excluding aliens) were assigned seats for every full ratio, disregarding fractions of a ratio. Hence, counties with populations between three and four times the first ratio received three seats; those with populations between four and five times the ratio received four seats; those with populations between five and six times the ratio got five seats; and so on.

The total number of seats assigned to the "first ratio" counties also determined the size of the senate because the next step was to compare the number of seats given each first-ratio county to the number it had in 1894. If any of these counties should be entitled to more seats than in 1894, the total senate membership was increased by that number. Thus, if a county which had two seats in 1894 should be entitled to five under a new apportionment, the senate membership would be increased by three seats over the basic 50, that is, to 53. Consequently, the total number of seats which the populous counties had gained since 1894 was added to the original 50. There were 58 senate seats provided in the 1953 apportionment.

After completion of the above process, the remaining seats were to be divided among the counties with less than 6 per cent of the citizen population (the less populous counties). The remaining number of seats were then distributed according to a second ratio, obtained by dividing the combined citizen population of all the less populous counties by the remaining number of seats (including those newly created). For example, under the 1953 law the eight newly created seats were added to the basic constitutional number for a total of 58. The 27 seats assigned to the populous counties were deducted from 58, leaving 31 seats to be distributed among the less populous counties. The total citizen population of these smaller counties was then divided by 31 to arrive at the second ratio. First-ratio counties qualified for more than three seats only as they attained population sufficient for additional *full* first ratios; but there was no similar requirement for second-ratio seats.

The above formula resulted in the populous counties having markedly less per capita representation in the state senate than the less populous counties. Since the first ratio was larger than the second a less populous county might be entitled to three seats if it had less than three full first ratios but had three second ratios, or even if it had two second ratios and a large fraction of a third. Consequently, the number of citizens per senator in the first-ratio counties was much greater than the number of citizens per senator of the less populous counties. Inevitably, the comparative power of the voters in the more populous counties decreased as those counties' proportionate share of the state population increased. Conversely, the comparative power of the voters in the less populous counties increased.

Further requirements regarding the allocation of senatorial districts were these: (1) The districts must be "in as compact form as practicable"; (2) the districts must consist of contiguous territory; (3) "no county shall be divided ... except to make two or more senate districts wholly in such county"; (4) "[n]o town, except a town having more than a full ratio of apportionment, and no block in a city inclosed by streets or public ways, shall be divided in the formation of senate districts"; (5) "nor shall any district contain a greater excess in population over an adjoining district in the same county, than the population of a town or block therein adjoining such district"; (6) "[c]ounties, towns or blocks which, from their location, may be included in either of two districts, shall be so placed as to make said districts most nearly equal in number of inhabitants, excluding aliens"; (7) no county shall have more than one third of all the senators; (8) no two adjoining counties (or those which are separated only by public waters) shall have more than one half of all the senators (inoperative in the light of population dispersal and trends). N.Y. Const., art. III, § 4.

The constitution of 1894 established an assembly composed of 150 assemblymen, apportioned among the several counties "as nearly as may be according to the number of their respective inhabitants, excluding aliens." Id., art. III, §§ 2, 5. However, the specified equal-population standard could not be satisfied as a result of the requirement that each county be guaranteed one seat (except Hamilton County, which "elect[s] with the county of Fulton"). Sixty-one seats were thus apportioned to the 62 counties. The remaining 89 seats were distributed in accordance with a ratio obtained by dividing the 150 seats into the total citizen population. A county whose population was at least one-and-one-half times the ratio received an additional assemblyman. The remaining seats were then apportioned among those counties whose citizen population was three or more ratios, with any remaining seats being apportioned on the basis of the "highest remainders."

Finally, the counties were divided into assembly districts by the board of supervisors or by an equivalent body where there was no board of supervisors. In dividing the counties entitled to two or more assemblymen into assembly districts the districting bodies were required to meet the following requirements: (1) The districts were to be, as nearly as may be, equal in the number of inhabitants, excluding aliens; (2) they were to be of convenient and contiguous territory and as compact as practicable; (3) each assembly district was to lie wholly within a senate district formed under the same apportionment; (4) "[i]n counties having more than one senate district, the same number of assembly districts shall be put in each senate district, unless the assembly districts cannot be evenly divided among the senate districts of any county, in which case one more assembly district in such county having the largest, or one less assembly district shall be put in the senate district in such county having the smallest number of inhabitants, excluding aliens, as the case may require"; (5) no town, except a town having more than a ratio and a half, and no block in a city inclosed by streets or public ways, could be divided; (6) no assembly district could contain a greater excess in population over an adjoining assembly district in the same senate district than the population of a town or block therein adjoining such assembly district; (7)

towns or blocks which from their location may be included in either of two districts were to be so placed as to make the district most nearly equal in number of inhabitants, excluding aliens. Id., art. III, § 5.

Legislative apportionment is to be accomplished at the first regular session after the year 1940 and every tenth year thereafter (i.e., 1950, 1960, etc.). But, if an apportionment is not made at the time above prescribed, it shall be done by a subsequent session occurring not later than the sixth year of such decade, i.e., 1946, 1956, 1966, 1976, etc. N.Y. Const., art. III, § 4.

Each apportionment by the legislature and each districting by a board of supervisors or other appropriate body within a county entitled to two or more senators or assemblymen is subject to review by the New York Supreme Court upon the suit of any citizen. N.Y. Const., art. III, § 5. In such suits the courts of the state of New York traditionally tested apportionment legislation for compliance with the state constitution, but not the federal. See, e.g., *Sherrill v. O'Brien*, 188 N.Y. 185, 81 N.E. 124 (1907), reversing 186 N.Y. 1, 79 N.E. 7 (1906); *In Re Fay*, 291 N.Y. 198, 52 N.E.2d 97 (1943), reversing 179 Misc. 1062, 43 N.Y.S.2d 787 (1943).

In May of 1961 certain citizens, taxpayers and registered voters associated with Radio Station WMCA, and residing in five of the six most populous New York counties, joined WMCA in instituting a class suit in the federal district court for the southern district of New York. *WMCA v. Simon*, 202 F. Supp. 741 (S.D.N.Y. 1962). The defendants, sued in a representative capacity, were officials charged by law with duties in connection with reapportionment and state elections. Specifically, the complaint charged as violations of the due process and equal protection clauses of the fourteenth amendment those provisions of the New York constitution (art. III, §§ 1–5) which (1) require enlargement of the senate by the number of senators to which the larger counties shall have become entitled since 1894; (2) prohibit any county from having four or more senators unless it has a full ratio for each senator; and (3) require that each of the 62 counties (except Hamilton) shall always be entitled to one assemblyman, particularly in view of the overall membership limitation of 150. Because of these provisions, the complaint alleged, the apportionment formula resulted in a grossly unfair weighting of both houses in the state legislature in favor of the less populated rural areas of the state to the disadvantage of the densely populated urban centers of the state.

It was established that under the 1953 apportionment the citizen population of the senatorial districts varied from a low of 146,666 to a high of 344,-547 and that the citizen population of the assembly districts varied from a low of 14,066 to a high of 115,000. Similar disproportions were sure to result from any apportionment conforming to the state constitution and based on the 1960 census. Id. at 748.

The three-judge court dismissed on the ground that the issue was not justiciable. On appeal the United States Supreme Court vacated the judgment and remanded the cause for reconsideration in the light of *Baker v. Carr*, 369 U.S. 186 (1962). *WMCA v. Simon*, 370 U.S. 190 (1962). Upon reconsideration the district court dismissed the complaint on the merits. The opinion (by Judge Levet) concluded that the plaintiffs had not shown by a fair preponderance of the evidence that there

was invidious discrimination; that the apportionment provisions were rational, not arbitrary; that they were of historical origin; that they contained no improper geographical discrimination; that they could be amended by an electoral majority of the people; and that they therefore were not unconstitutional. 208 F. Supp. 368 (S.D.N.Y. 1962). The case was again appealed to the United States Supreme Court and was argued in November 1963.

On June 15, 1964, the Supreme Court of the United States reversed the order of the district court and remanded the case to the lower court "for further proceedings consistent with the views stated here and in our opinion in *Reynolds v. Sims*." *WMCA, Inc. v. Lomenzo*, 377 U.S. 633, 655 (1964). The Court ruled that neither house of the New York legislature was validly apportioned then and that neither house would satisfy the equal-population principle if reapportioned on the basis of 1960 census figures according to the existing state constitutional formula. "However complicated or sophisticated an apportionment scheme might be, it cannot, consistent with the Equal Protection Clause, result in a significant undervaluation of the weight of the votes of certain of a State's citizens merely because of where they happen to reside. New York's constitutional formulas relating to legislative apportionment demonstrably include a built-in bias against voters living in the State's more populous counties." Id. at 653–54. The lower court was directed to determine, "acting under equitable principles," whether the 1964 election should be conducted pursuant to the provisions declared invalid, in view of the imminence of the election, or whether a new formula should be demanded. Id. at 655. Justices Clark,

Harlan, and Stewart dissented. (The opinions are more fully discussed in chapter V, supra.)

On remand the three-judge federal district court declared, on July 27, 1964, that the New York formula for legislative apportionment violated the fourteenth amendment of the Constitution of the United States. Although the court permitted the 1964 election to be conducted in accordance with that formula, it ordered that "not later than April 1, 1965, the Legislature shall have enacted into law a valid apportionment scheme that is in compliance with the XIV Amendment." That order was summarily affirmed by the Supreme Court of the United States in *Hughes v. WMCA, Inc.*, 379 U.S. 694 (1965).

Meanwhile, on July 12, 1964, the governor announced the appointment of a seven-member Citizen's Committee on Reapportionment to study "the structure of representative government in the Legislative Branch of New York State." Reporting on December 1, 1964, the committee recommended the following proposals, among others: (1) reapportionment by statute on a temporary basis because a constitutional amendment could not become effective before January 1, 1967, at the earliest; (2) continuance of the bicameral principle, although free of the constitutional restrictions on the size of each body (later disagreed with by the court of appeals of New York in *Matter of Orans*, discussed infra); (3) continued respect for county lines to the extent possible; (4) consideration of fractional voting for the recommended temporary legislation. Report to Governor Nelson A. Rockefeller by the Citizens' Committee on Reapportionment (1964).

On December 15, 1964, pursuant to a call from the governor, the state legislature convened in extraordinary session. (This "lame-duck" legislature with a Republican majority in both houses was by then scheduled to be replaced in January 1965 by the legislature elected in November 1964, with a Democratic majority in both houses.) By the time the legislature convened it also had before it the report of the Joint Legislative Committee on Reapportionment proposing a reapportionment statute based in part on the recommendations of the Citizens' Committee. Pursuant to the proposals of the two committees the legislature enacted the Reapportionment Compliance Act on December 22 and 23, 1964, to take effect January 1, 1965. The final legislation consisted of four successive apportionment plans, the basic act and three succeeding amendments. N.Y. Laws 1964, c. 976–79, 981.

The rationale behind the enactment of four plans was interesting: The plan first adopted was the one least preferred by the Joint Legislative Committee, but regarded as the least vulnerable to constitutional attack. The succeeding plans, adopted in reverse order of preference, were believed to raise progressively more serious constitutional questions. All four plans purported to meet the equal-population standard fixed by the Supreme Court of the United States, but they differed substantially.

The first complete plan adopted, known as Plan A, was based on the 1960 census of citizens. It provided for a senate of 65 members and an assembly of 165 members.

Plan B provided for apportionment on the basis of votes cast in the 1962 gubernatorial election instead of citizen population. It contemplated a 65-member senate and a 180-member assembly.

Plan C, based on the census of citizens, provided for the use of fractional votes in the assembly as a means of equalizing the representation of voters in districts of unequal population. Under the provisions of Plan C the vote allowed individual assemblymen would have varied from a whole vote to one sixth of a vote. It contemplated a 65-member senate and a 186-member assembly with 165 votes.

Plan D provided for the use of votes cast in the 1962 gubernatorial election as the basis for reapportionment and also for the use of fractional voting in the assembly. It contemplated a 65-member senate and a 174-member assembly with 150 votes.

By order of January 26 and February 16, 1965, the district court invalidated Plans B, C, and D, but held that Plan A did not violate the Constitution of the United States. Accordingly, the court ruled that a special election must be held in the fall of 1965 for all members of the legislature. The court did not pass upon the claims that some or all of the plans violated the compactness and contiguity requirements of the state constitution or the provision limiting the size of the assembly to 150 members. *WMCA, Inc. v. Lomenzo*, 238 F. Supp. 916 (S.D.N.Y. 1965).

On April 14, 1965, the court of appeals of New York ruled on the question thus left open, holding that the provision in Plan A for an assembly of more than 150 members was invalid because in conflict with the provision of article III, section 2 of the state constitution providing for a 150-member assembly. *Matter of Orans*, 15 N.Y.2d 339, 206 N.E.2d 854 (1965).

As a result of these decisions the state of New York was faced with an order by a federal court for a special election for the fall of 1965 and an order by the highest state court invalidating the only apportionment statute which the federal court had held would comply with the Constitution of the United States. On May 10, 1965, the district court directed that the 1965 election be held pursuant to Plan A as a stop-gap measure, and its order to this effect was entered on May 24, 1965; and on June 1, 1965, the Supreme Court of the United States refused to grant a stay of the order to hold an election in the fall of 1965. *Travia v. Lomenzo*, 381 U.S. 431 (1965).

Subsequently, however, in another state court proceeding the highest court of the state ruled on July 9, 1965, in a four-to-three vote that the election should not be held in 1965 "in the absence of a controlling decision elsewhere commanding that an unconstitutional election be held." N.Y. Times, July 10, 1965, p. 1, col. 8. The federal court promptly picked up the challenge four days later by reaffirming its order that the election should indeed be held in 1965. To make doubly sure, the federal court "forever restrained and enjoined" all persons from interfering with the order thus specifically made final and binding. N.Y. Times, July 14, 1965, p. 1, col. 8. When an application for a stay of that order was refused by the Supreme Court of the United States, it was at last settled that an election would take place in 1965. On October 11, the four appeals then pending in the Supreme Court of the United States were all affirmed or dismissed for want of jurisdiction. *WMCA, Inc. v. Lomenzo*, 86 Sup. Ct. 24 (1965); *Travia v. Lomenzo*, id. at 49; *Rockefeller v. Orans*, id. at 75; *Screvane v. Lomenzo*, id. at 90.

Meanwhile, in August a state court ordered the legislature to enact a new apportionment by February 1, 1966, or face the prospect of a judicial order of reapportionment. N.Y. Times, Aug. 25,

1965, p. 1, col. 2.

After some hesitation the equal-population principle has also been applied in the state of New York to local legislative bodies. Before the decision of the Supreme Court of the United States in the *Reapportionment Cases* several federal and state courts in New York doubted the necessity of population equality among election districts for local bodies. See, e.g., *Blaikie v. Power*, 13 N.Y.2d 134, 193 N.E.2d 55 (1963), appeal dismissed for want of a substantial federal question, 375 U.S. 439 (1964); *Bianchi v. Griffing*, 217 F. Supp. 166 (E.D.N.Y. 1963). But see id., 238 F. Supp. 997 (E.D.N.Y. 1964), appeal dismissed for want of jurisdiction, 86 Sup. Ct. 52 (1965). On July 9, 1965, however, the court of appeals of New York ruled unanimously that the population differential of two to one among the seats on the Binghamton city council did not satisfy federal constitutional requirements. *Seaman v. Fedourich*, 16 N.Y.2d 94, — N.E.2d — (1965).

That decision seemed likely to affect pending litigation challenging the composition of the board of estimate and the city council of the city of New York. The city council had been reconstituted and redistricted in 1965 to create 27 districts of substantially equal population; but no change was made in a provision for the election of two representatives at large from each of the five boroughs despite substantial population disparities among the boroughs.

Constitutional amendments are proposed in the assembly or the senate and referred to the attorney general for a written opinion as to the effect of the provisions on other constitutional provisions. Upon receiving the opinion, if the amendment is agreed to by a majority of the members elected to both houses, it is referred to the next regular legislative session. Upon agreement by a majority of the members elected to both houses of the next session the amendment is submitted to the people for approval by a majority of the electors voting on the amendment. N.Y. Const., art. XIX, § 1. The constitution may also be amended by a constitutional convention. The legislature is required to submit the question of a call of a convention to the people at the general election held in 1957 and at least every twenty years thereafter (or at any other time the legislature may choose). Id., art. XIX, § 2. In 1965 the legislature proposed that a convention call be placed on the ballot for vote in the fall of 1965. The voters approved, and the delegates are to be elected in 1966 for a convention in 1967.

On the basis of the 1960 census New York became entitled to 41 congressional seats instead of the 43 allotted under the 1950 census. Accordingly, in 1961 the New York legislature redrew the district lines. N.Y. Laws 1961, c. 57, §§ 110 et seq. As a result of that act New York has been described as having the most gerrymandered congressional district boundaries of any state in the nation, although the population inequalities among the congressional districts are not as severe as those in many other states. Wells, Legislative Representation in New York State 20–22 (1963).

The constitutionality of the 1961 congressional districting has been unsuccessfully challenged in two suits. In each the claim was made that race was taken into account in drawing congressional district lines, alleging the segregation of eligible voters by race and place of origin.

In the first congressional case, *Wright v. Rockefeller*, 211 F. Supp. 460 (S.D. N.Y. 1962), plaintiffs charged that the congressional district lines in New York County's four districts were drawn to exclude nonwhite citizens and citizens of Puerto Rican origin from the seventeenth district, and that the eighteenth, nineteenth, and twentieth districts were drawn to include the overwhelming number of nonwhite and Puerto Rican citizens. Hence, they alleged deprivation of rights arising from the fourteenth and fifteenth amendments and the Civil Rights Act, 42 U.S.C. §§ 1981, 1983 (Supp. 1963). The seventeenth district contains a population which is 94.9 per cent white non-Puerto Rican and has an irregular 35-sided configuration. The adjacent eighteenth district contains a population which is 86.6 per cent nonwhite and Puerto Rican. The boundary between the two districts is a 13-sided, step-shaped configuration alleged to fence a maximum number of nonwhites and Puerto Ricans out of the seventeenth and into the eighteenth.

Two members of the three-judge federal court concluded in separate opinions that no showing had been made of unconstitutionality. Judge Moore of the majority found no invalidity in the severe racial imbalance among the districts as there was no showing that any "citizen of Manhattan, as a result of the legislative redistricting, has been deprived of his right to vote for the duly nominated candidates of the party of his choice and in the area in which he resides." Id. at 467. Judge Feinberg, concurring, found the case much "closer," but did not feel that the plaintiffs had proved their contention of racial discrimination in the drawing of boundaries. Judge Murphy, dissenting, concluded that "the only available inference from the above uncontradicted picture establishes *per se* a *prima facie* case of legislative intent to draw congressional district lines on the basis of race and origin." Id. at 472–73.

The United States Supreme Court affirmed the lower court's dismissal of the complaint. Justice Black, for the majority of seven, accepted the district court's finding that appellants had not shown "that the challenged part of the New York Act was the product of a state contrivance to segregate on the basis of race or place of origin." 376 U.S. 52, 58 (1964). Justices Douglas and Goldberg read the record to support a finding of legislative intent to draw district lines on the basis of race or place of national origin, and accordingly dissented. Id. at 59.

In the second of these cases, *Honeywood v. Rockefeller*, 214 F. Supp. 897 (E.D.N.Y. 1963), plaintiffs claimed that in changing the old fourth congressional district into the new sixth congressional district in Queens County the legislature had consciously and purposefully excluded approximately 75–80 per cent of the Negro population residing in the old fourth, and that the legislature erected a color line running for about five miles along the southern perimeter of the district. Hence, they alleged such a redrawing of the district lines constituted a violation of the fourteenth and fifteenth amendments and of the Civil Rights Act. The three-judge federal district court held that plaintiffs did not sustain their burden of proving that the act was unconstitutional because they offered no direct proof that the legislature was motivated by racial considerations in the redistricting of the old fourth. The court noted that the relevant legislative reports made it clear that the legislature had made an effort to ensure comparative equality of representation throughout the state by using a statewide average of about 409,000 persons per district with a maximum of 15 per cent variation from that average. Id. at 901. The complaint was dismissed; and the United States Supreme Court affirmed. 376 U.S. 222 (1964).

REFERENCES

Csontos, Mildred B. History of Legislative Apportionment in New York State 1777–1940 with Discussion of Obstacles to Apportionment. Albany: New York State Library. 1941.

Lincoln, Charles Z. The Constitutional History of New York. 5 volumes. Rochester: Lawyers' Co-operative Publishing Co. 1906.

New York State Citizens' Committee on Reapportionment. Report to Governor Nelson A. Rockefeller. New York: 80 Centre Street. 1964.

New York State Constitutional Convention (1846). Debates and Proceedings. Croswell, Sherman, and Sutton, Richard (eds.). Albany: Office of the Albany Argus. 1846.

New York State Constitutional Convention (1867). Proceedings and Debates. Underhill, Edward Fitch (ed.). 5 volumes. Albany: Weed, Parsons and Co. 1868.

New York State Constitutional Convention (1894). Revised Record. 5 volumes. Albany: Argus Co. 1900.

New York State Constitutional Convention (1915). Revised Record. 4 volumes. Albany: J. B. Lyon Co. 1916.

New York State Constitutional Convention (1938). Journal and Documents. Albany: J. B. Lyon Co. 1938.

———. Proposed Amendments. 3 volumes. Albany: J. B. Lyon Co. 1938.

———. Revised Record. 4 volumes. Albany: J. B. Lyon Co. 1938.

New York State Constitutional Convention Committee (1938). Volume 2. Amendments Proposed to New York Constitution 1895–1937. New York: Burland Printing Co. 1938.

New York Temporary State Commission on the Constitutional Convention (1957). Transcript of Public Hearing[s]. 4 volumes. Buffalo, June 4, 1957; Albany, June 5, 1957; New York City, June 14 and 17, 1957 (2 volumes).

New York State Legislature. Executive Session of the Joint Legislative Committee on Reapportionment. Albany: March 13, 1935.

———. Legislative Document. (1935) No. 85; (1935) No. 89; (1942) No. 25; (1942) No. 57; (1942) No. 59; (1945) No. 53; (1950) No. 31; (1951) No. 64; (1953) No. 98; (1961) No. 45.

———. Report (and Supplementary Report) of the Joint Legislative Committee on Reapportionment. Legislative Document (1964) No. 76 (and 76-A).

New York State Library. Population and Assembly Representation in New York 1940–1950. Albany: Legislative Reference. N.d.

Silva, Ruth C. Legislative Apportionment [in New York]. 2 volumes. Staff Report No. 33. New York: State of New York Temporary Commission on Revision and Simplification of the Constitution, April 1960. Copies in New York State Library at Albany and in the New York City Public Library.

Silverman, Morris. The Struggle for Reapportionment in New York State. Unpublished master's thesis. New York: Yeshiva University. 1949.

Wells, David. Legislative Representation in New York State. New York: Political Dept., International Ladies' Garment Workers' Union. 1963.

Asch, Sidney H. Legislative Apportionment in New York State, 1 N.Y.L.F. 285 (1955).

McCaffrey, George H. Proportional Representation in New York City, 33 Am. Pol. Sci. Rev. 841 (1939).

Silva, Ruth C. Apportionment of the New York Legislature, 55 Am. Pol. Sci. Rev. 870 (1961).

———. Apportionment of the New York Senate, 30 Fordham L. Rev. 595 (1962).

———. Apportionment of the New York Assembly, 31 id. 1 (1962).

———. The Population Base for Apportionment of the New York Legislature, 32 id. 1 (1963).

———. Legislative Representation — With Special Reference to New York, 27 Law & Contemp. Prob. 408 (1962).

Tyler, Gus, and Wells, David I. "New York: 'Constitutionally Republican,'" in Jewell, Malcolm E. (ed.). The Politics of Reapportionment, New York: Atherton Press. 1962.

Zanoni, Ronald A., WMCA v. Lomenzo: A Case Study of Politics in Reapportionment Litigation, 1 Colum. J. of Law and Soc. Prob. 1 (1965).

Zeller, Belle, and Bone, Hugh A. The Repeal of P. R. in New York City — Ten Years in Retrospect, 42 Am. Pol. Sci. Rev. 1127 (1948).

NORTH CAROLINA

The land which now constitutes the state of North Carolina was among the earliest for which the English Crown issued royal charters and patents. Originally deeded to Virginia by the Virginia charters of 1606, 1609, and 1612, the province of Carolina was given separate status in the charter of Carolina of 1663, in which the land area was granted to a number of proprietors for development, settlement, and the establishment of government. The Fundamental Constitutions of Carolina of 1669 set out the first systematic government under the rule of the lords proprietors. The provisions, complex and bizarre by modern standards, established a parliament "consisting of the proprietors or their deputies, the landgraves, and casiques, and one freeholder out of every precinct . . . ." Art. 71.

In 1776 North Carolina declared its independence of the Crown and framed a constitution for the new state. Legislative authority was vested in a general assembly consisting of a senate made up of one member from each county and a house of commons of two members from each county plus one member from each of six named towns. N.C. Const. of 1776, §§ 2, 3.

The apportionment formulas for both houses were substantially altered by amendments approved in 1835. It was there provided that the senate should consist of 50 members to be selected from districts laid off by the general assembly at its first session after 1841 and 1851, and every twenty years thereafter, "in proportion to the public taxes paid into the Treasury of the State, by the citizens thereof; . . . *Provided*, That no county shall be divided in the formation of a Senatorial district." N.C. Const. of 1776, as amended 1835, art. I, § i, ¶ 1. Until this time only Massachusetts and New Hampshire had used taxes paid as a basis for apportionment, a practice abandoned by Massachusetts in 1840. The North Carolina house of commons was fixed at a membership of 120, to be apportioned among the counties "according to their Federal population" (that is, the whole number of free persons, excluding Indians not taxed, plus three fifths of all others). Reapportionment was required at the same intervals as senatorial redistricting. The proviso for at least one representative from each county (then

65) was continued. Id., art. I, § i, ¶¶ 2, 3, 4.

In 1861–62 a convention called by the legislature adopted an ordinance of secession and amended the state constitution; but it was not until the constitution of 1868 that further changes were made in the apportionment formula. In that constitution the senate, whose membership remained fixed at 50 (N.C. Const. of 1868, art. II, § 3), was now to be apportioned so that "each Senate district shall contain, as nearly as may be, an equal number of inhabitants, excluding aliens and Indians not taxed . . . ." The districts were also to consist of contiguous territory, and no county was to be divided unless "equitably entitled to two or more Senators." Id., art. II, § 5. The house of representatives was continued at 120, to be chosen according to population, except that each county was entitled to at least one representative. Id., art. II, § 6. The last limitation was by now more significant since in 1868 there were 89 counties. Id., art. II, § 8.

With subsequent changes in the numbering of sections and other slight modifications these provisions have remained constant to the present. Thus, the North Carolina house now consists of 120 members elected for two years "by the counties respectively, according to their population," but each county must have at least one representative, even though it does not contain the "requisite ratio of representation." N.C. Const. of 1868, as amended 1873, art. II, § 5. The "ratio of representation" is ascertained by dividing the whole population (excluding aliens and Indians not taxed, and excluding the population of counties which are so small that they do not contain one 120th part of the state's population) by 120 less the number assigned to the excluded counties. Each county containing the population ratio, but less than twice the ratio, is assigned one representative; each county containing twice but not three times the ratio is assigned two representatives; and so on progressively; "and then the remaining representatives shall be assigned severally to the counties having the largest fractions." Id., art. II, § 6. Since there are now 100 counties in North Carolina, only 20 representatives are left for distribution to the largest counties. See N.C. Gen. Stat. § 120–2 (1964 Repl. Vol.).

The 1868 constitution directed the general assembly to reapportion the house seats at the same time that the senate is reapportioned, that is, at the first session after the return of each federal census. Id., art. II, §§ 4, 5. In 1961 the general assembly proposed an amendment to article II, section 5 to be voted upon at the 1962 general election. The amendment, as approved by the voters, directed the speaker of the house to reapportion the house decennially, giving his action the same force and effect as if accomplished by the general assembly.

There are substantial disparities among the populations of the various house districts. Although the house population mean is 37,968 (4,556,155 divided by 120), the most populous single-member house district has a population of 82,059 while the smallest contains only 4,520. Twenty-seven and one-tenth per cent of the population can elect a majority of the representatives.

The North Carolina senate is composed of 50 members elected from districts containing "as nearly as may be, an equal number of inhabitants, excluding aliens and Indians not taxed." N.C. Const. of 1868, as amended, art.

II, §§ 3, 4. Districts must always consist of contiguous territory. No county may be divided unless that county is "equitably entitled to two or more Senators." The general assembly is directed to alter senatorial districts at its first session after the return of each federal census. Id., art. II, § 4. The North Carolina courts have never been required to decide whether the constitutional command that senate districts "shall" be altered by the general assembly imposes a mandatory duty upon the legislature. In *Leonard v. Maxwell*, 216 N.C. 89, 3 S.E.2d 316 (1939), a civil action to recover sales taxes alleged to have been wrongfully collected under an emergency revenue act of 1937, one of the arguments against the revenue act was that the general assembly of 1937 was improperly constituted because the first session after the 1930 census was the session constitutionally directed to make a reapportionment and failed to do so. Consequently, plaintiffs argued, no other session was competent to make the reapportionment or to enact valid legislation, and no legally constituted general assembly could again be convened under the existing constitution. "Quite a devastating argument, if sound," was the answer of the North Carolina Supreme Court. "The question is a political one, and there is nothing the courts can do about it." 216 N.C. at 99, 3 S.E.2d at 324.

The senatorial population mean based on the 1960 census is 91,123. Until 1963 there were 272,111 inhabitants in the largest district but only 45,031 inhabitants in the smallest district. Theoretically, 36.9 per cent of the population could elect a majority of the senators.

At its regular session in 1963 the North Carolina general assembly was unable to agree on reapportionment legislation, but in a senate resolution requested the governor to call an extra session. At the extra session convened in response to the call of the governor the legislature approved a bill which established a 50-member senate, to be chosen from 36 senate districts with a population range from 65,722 in the coastal district comprising Dare, Tyrrell, Washington, Beaufort, and Hyde Counties, to 148,418 in the one-senator district of Cumberland County. At the same session a constitutional amendment was proposed by the legislature which would have established a 70-member senate rather closely related to population and a 100-member house with one representative for each county. This "little federal plan" was defeated by a vote of 125,334 for and 224,488 against. N.C. Manual 1965, 308–309.

Constitutional conventions may be called when proposed by a two-thirds vote of the members of both houses and approved by a majority of the votes cast thereon. N.C. Const. of 1868, as amended, art. XIII, § 1. The legislature may propose amendments to the constitution by a three-fifths vote of both houses, and they become effective upon ratification by a majority of those voting thereon at the next general election. Id., art. XIII, § 2. There are neither constitutional nor statutory provisions regarding the amending of the constitution by use of the initiative or the referendum.

North Carolina is entitled to eleven congressional representatives. N.C. Gen. Stat. § 163-103 (1964 Repl. Vol.). After the 1960 census the North Carolina delegation was reduced from twelve to eleven. Section 163-104 of the North Carolina code directs that whenever the delegation to Congress is reduced, and the general assembly does not provide for an election, all of the representa-

tives shall be elected at large; if the delegation is increased, the delegates are to be elected from the existing districts with only the added representative to be elected at large.

The 1960 population divided by eleven yields a congressional population mean of 414,196: The largest congressional district consists of 491,461 persons; the smallest consists of 277,861.

The first suit to challenge apportionment and districting in North Carolina since the decision of the 1964 *Reapportionment Cases* was filed on September 10, 1965, challenging the state legislative representation formula and the composition of the congressional districts.

REFERENCES

North Carolina Constitutional Commission. Report. Raleigh: State of North Carolina. 1959.

Sanders, John L. Data on North Carolina Congressional Districts, State Senatorial Districts, and Apportionment of the State House of Representatives. Chapel Hill: Institute of Government, University of North Carolina. 1961.

———. Equal Representation and the Board of County Commissioners. Chapel Hill: Institute of Government, University of North Carolina. 1965.

———. Materials on Representation in the General Assembly of North Carolina. Chapel Hill: Institute of Government, University of North Carolina. 1965.

———. Reapportionment and Redistricting in North Carolina: 1961–1965. Chapel Hill: Institute of Government, University of North Carolina. 1965.

NORTH DAKOTA

The land now included within the boundaries of the state of North Dakota was originally part of the area ceded by France in the treaty of purchase of 1803; and it became successively part of the district of Louisiana and then of the territory of Louisiana. By 1812 the land area was included within the territory of Missouri and later, successively, portions of the land were under the governance of the territories of Michigan, Louisiana, Iowa, Minnesota, and Nebraska. In 1861 North Dakota acquired territorial status of its own in an act of Congress which vested the legislative power in the governor and a legislative assembly consisting of a council and a house of representatives. The council was to have 9 members initially (subject to increase to 13), and the house of representatives was to have 13 members (subject to increase to 26). The governor was directed to have a census taken before the first election, on the basis of which he was to apportion the membership of both chambers "among the several counties or districts . . . , giving to each section of the Territory representation in the ratio of its population, (Indians excepted) as nearly as may be; . . . ." Sec. 4.

In 1889 Congress authorized the convening of a constitutional convention to which delegates should be chosen "in proportion to the population of the counties or districts represented." Sec. 3. The convention completed its work in August 1889; the proposed constitution was approved by the people in October; and the President of the United States proclaimed North Dakota a state of the Union in November of that year.

The North Dakota constitution of 1889 provided for a senate of not less than 30 nor more than 50 members (N.D. Const. of 1889, art. II, § 26) and a house of representatives of not less than 60 nor more than 140 members (id., art. II, § 32). The legislature was authorized to fix the number of senators, dividing the state into as many districts as the number of senators authorized, "which districts as nearly as may be, shall be equal to each other in the number of inhabitants entitled to

representation." Id., art. II, § 29. The representatives were to be "apportioned to and elected at large from each senatorial district." Id., art. II, § 35. Reapportionment was made a legislative function to be completed at the first regular session after each federal census and after a state census to be taken in 1895 and every ten years thereafter. Ibid. The constitution of 1889 provided for an initial senate membership of 31 and a house membership of 63, apportioned not only along county lines (including as many as four counties in some districts), but along township lines as well in the more populous counties which were divided into two or more districts. Apportionment in the house, however, was not strictly based on population, in that representatives were assigned on the basis of the senatorial districts, but in numbers varying from one to four for each district. N.D. Const. of 1889, art. XVIII, § 214.

The apportionment provisions described above were not significantly changed until, by constitutional amendment effective in 1960, the size of the senate was fixed at 49 (N.D. Const., art. II, § 26), and the existing statutory apportionment of senatorial districts (N.D. Code § 54-03-01) was made permanent in the constitution without regard to existing population inequalities among the districts or future population shifts. N.D. Const., art. II, § 29. As a result, senatorial districts with substantial population disparities were frozen into the constitution. In 1960, with a senatorial population mean of 12,907 (1960 population of 632,446 divided by 49), the largest senate district had 42,041 inhabitants and the smallest only 4,698. The minimum percentage of the 1960 population necessary to elect a majority of the senate was 31.9.

The formula for apportionment of the house of representatives was substantially altered by the 1960 amendment. Article II, section 35, as amended, continued the provision for apportionment of representatives within the senatorial districts; it also specified not only that there be at least one representative for each senatorial district, but that "any senatorial district comprised of more than one county shall be represented in the House of Representatives by at least as many representatives as there are counties in such senatorial district." Ibid. Only after the making of these allotments were the remaining seats to be apportioned "according to the population of the several senatorial districts." Ibid.

Failure of the legislature to act in accordance with the apportionment obligation outlined in the constitution imposed a like obligation upon a special commission, composed of the chief justice of the state supreme court, the attorney general, the secretary of state, and the majority and minority leaders of the house of representatives, who are required to act within 90 days; and their proclamation is given the force of law. Ibid.

The 1961 legislature failed to reapportion the membership in the house of representatives. Consequently, the reapportionment group authorized pursuant to section 35 met and effectuated a reapportionment plan. Before the chief justice proclaimed the plan, petitioners in *State ex rel. Aamoth v. Sathre,* 110 N.W.2d 228 (N.D. 1961) asked the supreme court of North Dakota to enjoin the chief justice from issuing the reapportionment proclamation on the ground that it was arbitrarily arrived at. The court refused to do so, holding that such an action was "premature" before issuance of the proclamation by the chief justice. Id. at 230–231.

The chief justice issued his proclamation on May 29, 1961 (89 days following the adjournment of the 1961 legislature), after which the legality of the apportionment plan was again challenged, this time in the federal district court of North Dakota. *Lein v. Sathre,* 201 F. Supp. 535 (D.N.D. 1962). The district court refused to rule on the validity of the apportionment plan, holding that a determination of that specific issue would not be dispositive of the basic questions involved, namely: (1) Was the constitutional authority of the apportionment group finally terminated by the issuance of the proclamation? (2) Was the life of such group limited to the 90-day period following adjournment of the 1961 legislative assembly? (3) Does such group have present authority to reconvene and adopt and proclaim another apportionment plan? Id. at 539.

The federal court decided that the supreme court of North Dakota should have the opportunity of passing on all of the above questions before further proceedings could be maintained in the federal court. Id. at 542. The supreme court of North Dakota, in *State ex rel. Lein v. Sathre,* 113 N.W.2d 679 (1962), answered these questions and considered the validity of the apportionment plan. The constitutionality of the 1960 amendment to section 35 was not questioned, and the court observed that "perfect equality of representation cannot be obtained" (id. at 684); however, it ruled that the apportionment should approach "as nearly as is reasonably possible, a mathematical equality." Id. at 685. Since the apportioning group had not included in their computations the 61 representatives apportioned by the terms of section 35, which required one representative for each county within a senatorial district, the plan was held to violate the constitutional mandate of apportionment according to population. It was also held that "While the power of the group to act on behalf of the Legislature expired at the end of the 90-day period, the duty imposed upon the Legislature to reapportion is a continuing one." Id. at 687. The injunction was denied, the court ruling that the last valid apportionment act (1931) would be continued until superseded by a valid apportionment act pursuant to section 35, as amended in 1960. Ibid.

Plaintiffs went again to the federal district court and asked for an injunction to restrain further elections pending a proper reapportionment. *Lein v. Sathre*, 205 F. Supp. 536 (D.N.D. 1962). The three-judge federal district court held that injunctive relief was not warranted since the supreme court of North Dakota had determined only that the particular apportionment was invalid, and that the duty to reapportion continued in the legislature. Since it did not appear that elections would be conducted under the invalid plan, but rather under the previous unchallenged law of 1931, the court retained jurisdiction to act if the 1963 session of the North Dakota legislature failed to act pursuant to its mandatory duty to reapportion.

After judicial invalidation of the 1961 apportionment of the house of representatives by the apportionment board, the legislature reapportioned the house by statute in 1963. N.D. Cent. Code Ann. § 54-03-01 (Supp. 1963). By that act 109 seats were allotted among the 49 senatorial districts, but

the principle was retained by which each senatorial district would have at least one representative and a total representation no smaller than the number of counties within the district.

The apportionment formulas for both the senate and house were challenged and found invalid in *Paulson v. Meier*, 232 F. Supp. 183 (D.N.D. 1964). The three-judge federal district court was unanimous in its ruling that the existing formulas denied equal protection of the laws and that no prior apportionment law was valid. A majority of the court concluded, however, that the 1964 election processes, which were already in motion, should not be interrupted. Accordingly, the court ruled that the legislature chosen in 1964 should have a de facto status and should promptly devise and enact legislation creating a valid apportionment formula for the North Dakota legislature. The court retained jurisdiction to consider the validity of any such plan.

On the final day of the 1965 legislative session the North Dakota legislature approved a further reapportionment designed to conform to the judicial order. The senate membership was increased to 53 and that of the house reduced to 106, and county lines were in part disregarded. Although the governor stated that he would withhold his signature, he noted that it would become law without his approval. N.Y. Times, March 21, 1965, p. 44, col. 3. See 1965 N.D. Sess. Laws, c. 338, amending N.D. Cent. Code Ann. § 54-03-01.

The legislature also provided for popular approval of the subdistricting in multimember districts (id., §§ 54-03-01.2, 54-03-01.3) and provided for reversion to the act of 1963 if an amendment to the United States Constitution should be approved giving the states the right to fix their own apportionment formulas without regard to population (id., § 54-03-01.4). However, the federal district court held the act invalid and ordered into effect its own plan (a modification of a proposal presented to the legislature by the Legislative Research Committee which had passed the senate but failed in the house). The court-approved plan divided the state into 39 legislative districts, none of which varied as much as 15 per cent from the population ratio. *Paulson v. Meier*, Civ. No. 618 (D.N.D. Aug. 10, 1965).

Amendments may be proposed by either house of the legislature; after agreement by a majority of both houses they are submitted to the electors for majority ratification. Amendments may also be proposed by initiative petitions signed by 20,000 electors at large, and become effective upon ratification by a majority of the electors voting at the election. N.D. Const., art. XV, § 202.

North Dakota is entitled to two congressional representatives. The congressional population mean is 316,223. The larger district has 333,290 inhabitants while the smaller has 299,156.

OHIO

The present state of Ohio was included within the land area bound by the principles of the Northwest Ordinance of 1787, which assured the inhabitants of the territory that they would "always be entitled to the benefits . . . of a proportionate representation of the people in the legislature . . . ." Northwest Ordinance, art. II. In 1802, when Congress authorized the calling of a constitutional convention to prepare for statehood, provision was made for delegates to be "apportioned amongst the several counties . . . in a ratio of one representative to

every twelve hundred inhabitants of each county, according to the enumeration taken under the authority of the United States, ..." The 35 delegates were apportioned among the then six counties, including the selection of several from specially designated floterial districts. Sec. 4. The convention was assembled and completed its work in November 1802, and Ohio was admitted as a state of the Union by act of Congress in 1803.

The constitution of 1802 provided for the taking of a census "of all the white male inhabitants above twenty-one years of age" and apportionment of representatives among the several counties on the basis of that enumeration to a total of not less than 24 and not more than 36. Ohio Const. of 1802, art. I, § 2. The senators were also to be apportioned on the basis of the numbers of white males over 21 years of age to a total membership of from one third to one half the membership of the house of representatives. Id., art. I, § 6. The interim apportionment established until the first census should have been taken created 15 senatorial and 32 representative districts divided among the then nine counties.

The constitution of 1851, which remains the basic law of Ohio, with amendments noted below, provided for apportionment in 1851 and every ten years thereafter to be based ordinarily on the federal census. Ohio Const. of 1851, art. XI, § 1. The size of the senate was fixed at 35 for the first decennial period. Id., art. XI, § 7. Although no provision was made for a specific number of representatives, the constitution provided then, as it does today, for a ratio of representation consisting of the whole population of the state divided by 100. Id., art. XI, § 2. Between 1851 and the adoption of the so-called

"Hanna amendment" (approved in 1902 and effective in 1903) the same section of the constitution authorized one representative for each county with a population equal to one half the ratio, two representatives for each county with one-and-three-fourths ratios, three representatives for three ratios, "and so on, requiring after the first two, an entire ratio for each additional representative." Ibid.

Article XI, section 2 of the 1851 constitution further provided that if a county's population should be greater than one ratio but less than two, or more than two ratios but less than three, or more than three ratios but less than four, etc., that county could receive additional representation in one or more of the five biennial sessions, depending upon the amount of population in excess of one or more full ratios. The legislative sessions in which such additional representation is available depends upon the following mathematical formula. Since there are five biennial legislative sessions in a decade, the fraction of a county's population in excess of one or more full ratios is multiplied by five; if the result is equal to one ratio, the county is entitled to one additional representative in one of the five sessions (the fifth); if the fraction equals two ratios, the county is allotted one additional representative in two sessions (the fourth and fifth); and so on through a maximum "fractional" representation in four of five sessions. Id., art. II, § 3. Consequently, the number of representatives to which a county is entitled may vary from session to session because of the allocation of these additional house members. The total house membership accordingly also varies from session to session.

Under the provisions of the constitution of 1851 as originally adopted, if

a county entitled to separate representation had a decrease in population below the one-half ratio, it was to be attached to the adjoining county having the least number of inhabitants. Ohio Const. of 1851, art. XI, § 5. However, in 1903 article XI, section 2 was amended to assure each county at least one representative, thus effectively nullifying the provision for joinder of counties. The 1903 constitutional amendment is said to have been introduced on behalf of Marcus Hanna, long-time Ohio politician, at a time when the Ohio general assembly elected the members of the United States Senate, in order to ensure his future reelection by the assembly where his margin of victory had been uncomfortably narrow. The amendment added ten seats to the house in 1903, all from rural counties which were politically safe for Hanna. By 1960 more than half of the counties in the state (48 of 88) had been reduced in population to a point of less than one half of a ratio, but the 1903 amendment authorized separate representation for each.

As a result malapportionment of the Ohio house of representatives has been substantial since 1903. The 69 smallest counties, with a combined 1960 population of 2,852,406, constituting 29.4 per cent of the state's population, in 1965 had 69 seats in the house, a majority. The seven most populous counties had 51.9 per cent of the state's inhabitants but only 51 seats, or 37.2 per cent of the Ohio representatives. In the 1963–64 biennial session the smallest county, Vinton, was 589.6 per cent overrepresented in terms of the population mean, while the largest county, Lake, was 109.9 per cent underrepresented.

Representatives are elected at large in each county entitled to more than one, there being no system of subdistricting. Consequently, Cuyahoga County (Cleveland) had the "longest ballot in the world" in 1962—17 house members, 6 senate members, 27 other officers, plus 25 bond issues and other questions. 52 Nat'l Civ. Rev. 5 (Jan. 1963). In the primary there had been more than 100 Democratic candidates for the 17 house seats.

The constitutionality of the provision guaranteeing one representative to each member of the house was questioned in *Nolan v. Rhodes*, 218 F. Supp. 953 (S.D. Ohio 1963), and *Sive v. Ellis*, 218 F. Supp. 953 (S.D. Ohio 1963), both reversed in *Nolan v. Rhodes*, 378 U.S. 556 (1964). Plaintiffs, residents and voters in the two most populous Ohio counties, alleged that the Hanna amendment was violative of the equal protection clause of the fourteenth amendment. Plaintiffs limited their complaint to the house apportionment since the senate is apportioned more nearly on a population basis, as will be noted below.

Despite the fact that plaintiffs alleged disparities in voter ratios of almost 15 to 1, the three-judge federal district court found no invidious discrimination, concluding that it was not irrational to allow one representative for each county.

On June 22, 1964, the Supreme Court of the United States reversed the judgment of the trial court in both Ohio cases and remanded "for further proceedings consistent with the views stated in our opinions in *Reynolds v. Sims* and in the other cases relating to state legislative apportionment decided along with *Reynolds*." *Nolan v. Rhodes*, 378 U.S. 556 (1964). Justice Clark would have reversed on the grounds stated in his opinion in *Reynolds*. Justice Stewart would have affirmed "because the Ohio system of leg-

islative apportionment is clearly a rational one and clearly does not frustrate majority rule." Id. at 556–57. Justice Harlan dissented for the reasons stated in his dissenting opinion in *Reynolds*. (The case is more fully discussed in chapter VI, *supra*.)

On remand the three-judge district court held the Ohio apportionment formula invalid and gave the legislature an opportunity to take corrective action. *Nolan v. Rhodes.* — F. Supp. — (S.D. Ohio 1964).

At a special session the Ohio legislature in December 1964 proposed a constitutional amendment to accomplish the reapportionment demanded by the court. Ohio Special Sess. of 1964, H.J.R. No. 1. The proposal, later defeated by the voters, would have put apportionment, in the words of the statute, "substantially" on a population basis. In effect, this would have nullified the Hanna amendment, although repeal was not specified, presumably because the legislature wanted that provision to remain available in case an amendment to the United States Constitution should later be approved permitting representation on a county basis. Under the proposal the state apportionment board (previously the governor, the secretary of state, and the auditor) would have been expanded to seven members by the addition of a member of the majority and minority parties from each house of the legislature. Also unlike the present board, the proposed board would have considerable discretion in the fixing of district lines to adjust to population equality.

Finally, the new amendment would have allowed subdistricting of multi-member counties by providing that the new congressional districts rather than counties be used as house election districts in the populous areas. For example, the Cleveland area, instead of electing 17 representatives county wide, would elect 24, six from each of the four congressional districts. In May 1965, however, the voters rejected the proposal. N.Y. Times, May 5, 1965, p. 26, col. 1. Under the continuing court order further legislative action remains necessary.

The ratio for senators is to be determined "forever" by dividing the whole population of the state by 35. Ohio Const., art. XI, § 6. The state is divided into 33 senatorial districts each entitled to one senator except that the district of Hamilton (Cincinnati) originally had three seats. Id., art. XI, § 7. Hence, senatorial representation is based more nearly on population than the house.

When any senatorial district has a fraction of the ratio such that, after it is multiplied by five, the result is equal to one or more ratios, additional senators shall be elected by that district for two-year terms to a proportionate share of the several sessions of the decennial period, in a manner similar to the "fractional" representation provisions for the house of representatives. Id., art. XI, § 6(a), as amended in 1956.

The senatorial districts are composed of whole counties. If any county forming part of a senatorial district acquires a population equal to a full senatorial ratio it is to be made a separate senatorial district, but only if a full senatorial ratio is left in the district from which it is taken. Id., art. XI, § 9. This has occurred only once in Ohio's history, in 1901. See *State ex rel. Herbert v. Bricker*, 139 Ohio St. 499, 513–14, 41 N.E.2d 377, 384 (1942). Article XI, section 8 establishes similar primaries where a senatorial district or county previously entitled to separate representation falls below the number required by the new ratio for a senator. In that case such county or district is to be attached to the district adjoining it with the least number of inhabitants. Thus, if one of the existing senatorial districts falls below the stipulated three-fourths ratio requirement, it is to be attached to the adjoining district with the smallest number of inhabitants.

Prior to the 1851 constitution, reapportionment had been accomplished by the general assembly, whose members fought over political power. Article XI was designed to prevent this by placing the power of apportionment in impartial hands and preventing gerrymandering by making the apportionment process as to both the house and the senate solely a matter of mathematics. Therefore, article XI, section 10 contains the clause that "no change shall ever be made . . . in the senatorial districts, except as herein provided." *State ex rel. Herbert v. Bricker*, supra at 509, 41 N.E.2d at 383 ruled that this language implies that the senatorial districts shall continue unchanged from decennium to decennium except insofar as the constitution prescribes a change. Those districts cannot be changed unless counties are to be given separate representation or the district falls below the three-fourths ratio, in which case it would be annexed to the adjoining, least populous county. See also *State ex rel. Gallagher v. Campbell*, 48 Ohio St. 435, 27 N.E. 884 (1891).

The lower court in *Nolan v. Rhodes*, supra, although apportionment of the senate was not at issue, nevertheless stated (in arguing that only one house of the legislature need be apportioned on a population basis) that the senate is apportioned according to population and that the most populous counties control the senate. 218 F. Supp. at 956. The eight most populous senatorial districts, containing 12 counties, elect 58 per cent of the senate and have 57 per cent of the state's population. Yet there remain substantial variations among the districts. The senatorial population mean is 277,326 (9,706,397 divided by 33), but the largest senatorial district contains 439,000, while the smallest has only 228,000 persons.

When the Ohio legislature failed to adopt a reapportionment plan at its 1965 session, the federal court ordered the parties to submit reapportionment proposals on or before October 15, 1965. The court asked for plans for both houses despite its earlier announced opinion that the senate formula was valid.

Article II, section 1 of the Ohio constitution, as amended in 1918, reserves to the people the power to initiate constitutional amendments and to adopt or reject them at the polls by a majority vote. However, the initiative procedure requires the signature of at least 10 per cent of the electors, including at least 5 per cent of the electors in each of at least one half of the counties. Either branch of the legislature may propose amendments. If approved by three-fifths vote in each house, an amendment will be submitted to the electors for ratification by majority vote. Id., art. XVI, § 1.

Two thirds of the general assembly may recommend that a constitutional convention be called (id., art. XVI, § 2, as amended in 1912); and every 20 years the legislature is to submit to the electors of the state the question of whether a constitutional convention shall be called (id., art. XVI, § 3, as amended in 1912). The issue was last submitted (and voted down) in 1952.

Through 1964, 23 of the 24 Ohio congressmen were elected from districts, and one was elected at large. The population differentials among the districts ranged from 726,156 to 274,441, both in terms of 1960 population. In December 1964, in a special session of the legislature, a new districting was approved establishing 24 separate districts and sharply reducing the population differentials among the districts. Ohio Rev. Code § 35 21.01 (Supp. 1964).

REFERENCES

Citizens League of Greater Cleveland. Ohio's Apportionment and Subdistricting. Cleveland: 1963.

Governmental Research Institute. Compendium of Reapportionment and Subdistricting Data, Ohio House of Representatives. Cleveland: 1963.

Auman, Francis R. Rural Ohio Hangs On, 46 Nat'l Munic. Rev. 189 (1957).

Waltzer, Herbert. "Apportioning and Districting in Ohio," in Jewell, Malcolm E. (ed.), Politics of Reapportionment. New York: Atherton Press. 1962.

OKLAHOMA

What is now the state of Oklahoma was originally within the land ceded by France to the United States in the treaty of purchase of 1803. At first part of the district of Louisiana (1804) and then of the territory of Louisiana (1805), portions of the land were later successively within the territories of Missouri, Arkansas, Texas, New Mexico, and the Indian Territory. Not until 1890 was Oklahoma given separate recognition as a territory, in an act of Congress which took from the Indian Territory those portions not occupied by Indian tribes. Legislative authority was vested in a governor and assembly, the latter to consist of a 13-member council and a 26-member house of representatives. The governor was directed to have a census taken and, before the first election, to apportion the seats in the council and house of representatives among the seven counties and districts, "giving to each section of the Territory representation in the ratio of its population (excepting Indians not taxed) as nearly as may be . . . ." Sec. 4.

In 1906 Congress adopted an enabling act to permit the inhabitants of the territory of Oklahoma and of the Indian Territory to adopt a constitution in preparation for statehood. The act provided for the selection of 112 delegates (55 from the territory of Oklahoma, 55 from the Indian Territory, and 2 from the Osage Indian Reservation in the territory of Oklahoma) to be selected from 56 districts, "as nearly equal in population as may be," to be drawn by the governor, the chief justice, and the secretary of the territory of Oklahoma. Sec. 2.

The convention so chosen met and adopted a constitution which was approved by the voters in 1907. That constitution was duly found to be "republican in form," and Oklahoma was proclaimed a state of the Union by the President of the United States in November 1907. The apportionment provisions of the constitution of 1907 provided for division of the state into 44 senatorial districts, each of which was to "contain as near as may be an equal number of inhabitants, such population to be ascertained by the next preceding Federal census, or in such a manner as the Legislature may direct." Okla. Const., art. V, § 9(a). Districts were to "be in as compact form as practicable" and to consist of "contiguous territory." Ibid. It was provided that no county should "ever be divided in the formation of a senatorial district except to make two or more senatorial districts wholly in such county." Id., art. V, § 9(b).

Article V, section 9(a) provided that the senate should "always be composed of forty-four senators, except that in the event that any county shall be entitled to three or more senators at the time of any apportionment such additional senator or senators shall be given such county in addition to the forty-four senators and the whole number to that extent." Two Oklahoma Supreme Court decisions construed this clause to allow a senate of more than 44 members apportioned from 44 districts. *Jones v. Freeman*, 193 Okla. 554, 146 P.2d 564 (1944); *Latting v. Cordell*, 197 Okla. 369, 172 P.2d 397 (1946). In the latter case the court gave reasons: "We are of the opinion that the purpose of the exception clause was to increase the number of Senators in the more populated counties so that the larger counties could be given the number of Senators to which they were entitled without reducing the number of Senators to which the other parts of the state were entitled." Id. at 373, 172 P.2d at 400–01.

The 1907 constitution provided that population should be the primary criterion for apportionment of the house of representatives. Art. V, § 10. A ratio of representation was to be fixed by dividing the population of the state (as ascertained by the federal census, or in such manner as the legislature might direct) by the number 100. Id., § 10(c). Every county with a population equal to one half of the ratio was authorized one representative. Every county with a population equal to one-and-three-fourths ratios was authorized two representatives "and so on, requiring after the first two an entire ratio for each additional representative: Provided, That no county shall ever take part in the election of more than seven representatives." Id., § 10(d).

The above apportionment provisions established an imbalance in favor of the inhabitants of the less populous counties and were therefore held to be invidiously discriminatory in *Moss v. Burkhart*, 207 F. Supp. 885 (W.D. Okla. 1962). The three-judge federal district court stated that the ceiling of seven representatives for any one county should be disregarded because it was "constitutionally intolerable." After numerous stays the court reapportioned the Oklahoma legislature, as discussed below, 220 F. Supp. 149 (W.D. Okla. 1963).

Article 5, section 10(e) provided for "flotorial" representation in the house — a representative elected from a county or district with an excess of population over that for its regular representation, but not enough to justify another full-time representative. Sec. 10(e) directed that "When any county shall have a fraction above the ratio so large that being multiplied by five the result will be equal to one or more ratios, additional representatives shall be apportioned for such ratio among the several sessions of the decennial period. If there are two ratios, representatives shall be allotted to the fourth and third sessions, respectively; if three, the third, second, and first sessions, respectively; if four, to the fourth, third, second, and first sessions, respectively."

However, a county having a population of less than one half of a ratio (a population of less than 11,641 under the 1960 census) was not entitled to separate representation and was to be "attached to a county adjoining it and becomes part of such representative district." Okla. Const., art. V, § 10(g).

Finally, article V, section 10(h) forbade division of towns, wards, and counties except to make two or more wholly contained representative districts.

The legislature for some years failed in apportioning the house of representatives to combine counties with less than a half ratio of population with adjoining counties, as required by article V, section 10(g), supra, thus leading to the chief discrepancy among districts in disregard of the state constitution. The first two apportionment bills of 1911 and 1921 followed the constitution in this respect. But each apportionment statute between 1921 and 1963 allocated at least one seat to each county regardless of population. On the other hand, the maximum limit of seven for any county was adhered to. Counties were also permitted to retain "flotorial" representatives without limitation of their service to only some of the sessions.

The Oklahoma legislature has never reapportioned the senate as intended by the constitution. The constitution of 1907 had established 33 senatorial districts (22 to elect one senator and 11 to elect two senators for a total of 44) to remain in effect until a reapportionment was made after the next decennial census in 1911. Until 1963, however, no comprehensive senate reapportionment bill was passed. The legislature in 1919, 1937, and 1941 passed acts which effected minor shifts in the composition of a few districts and created three new districts over the original 33. See The New Perspective of Legislative Apportionment in Oklahoma, supra, at pp. 17, 20.

Beginning in 1943 the Oklahoma Supreme Court several times ruled emphatically that the existing reapportionment statutes failed to comply with the requirements of the state constitution; but in each case the court declined to grant relief on the ground that the apportionment mandate was addressed solely to the legislature and that the court was not empowered to "revise or correct" the apportionment when the legislature refused to act.

Jones v. Freeman, 193 Okla. 554, 146 P.2d, 564 (1944) was an original mandamus action in the state supreme court in which plaintiff, a voter, sought to require that the next election be held under a constitutional apportionment. The court enunciated the principle of equality which pervaded the constitutional apportionment provisions and held it "plain" that the statutes did not comply with the equality requirements of the constitution, which "require at least as close an approximation to exactness and equality as is reasonably possible." Id. at 559, 146 P.2d at 569. The court held, however, that it would not, by mandamus or otherwise, require the legislature to enact proper apportionment statutes. The reason given was that, although article V, section 10(j) provides that "An apportionment by the Legislature shall be subject to review by the Supreme Court at the suit of any citizen," the framers of the constitution did not use the word "review" to mean "revise." Id. at 561–62, 146 P.2d at 571. Nevertheless, the court went on to hold that the duty to apportion is continuous and devolves upon each successive legislature until it is performed, and that only one valid reapportionment law may be enacted during the period between federal censuses. Id. at 563–64, 146 P.2d at 573. See also *Latting v. Cordell*, 197 Okla. 369, 172 P.2d 397 (1946); *Romang v. Cordell*, 206 Okla. 369, 243 P.2d 677 (1952); *Jones v. Cordell*, 197 Okla. 61, 168 P.2d 130 (1946); and *Grim v. Cordell*, 197 Okla. 144, 169 P.2d 567 (1946).

Attempts were later made in federal court to overturn the Oklahoma apportionment statutes, but these efforts were also unsuccessful before 1962. See *Radford v. Gary*, 145 F. Supp. 541 (W.D.

Okla. 1956), aff'd per curiam, 352 U.S. 991 (1957). Relief was denied on the basis of *Colegrove v. Green*, 328 U.S. 549 (1946), ruling the question nonjusticiable.

The 1961 reapportionment of the house was challenged in the state supreme court, and again the court concluded that the current act did not comply with the constitutional requirements, but refused to enjoin filings and elections for the house, noting that elections under the pre-existing law would result in far greater inequalities of representation than under the 1961 act. *Jones v. Winters*, 369 P.2d 135, 137–38 (Okla. 1961). Nevertheless, the state elections board issued a "policy statement" that it would not accept filing of 1962 candidates for election to the house because the act had been deemed invalid, whereupon the supreme court ordered the secretary of the board to conduct the house of representatives elections pursuant to the 1961 act since there was no other apportionment scheme in operation. *Brown v. State Elections Board*, 369 P.2d 140, 151 (Okla. 1962).

In 1961 the legislature also attempted to reapportion the entire state for senatorial purposes, but *Reed v. State Elections Board*, 369 P.2d 156, 160 (Okla. 1962) declared the senate apportionment act invalid and ordered the state elections board to conduct the 1962 election pursuant to the senatorial apportionment act of 1941.

Complaining voters next returned to the federal district court, where it was again alleged that the existing apportionment acts were violative of the equal protection clause of the fourteenth amendment. The three-judge federal district court denied temporary relief to afford the 1963 session of the Oklahoma legislature an opportunity to enact a constitutionally acceptable system of apportionment and elections. *Moss v. Burkhart,* 207 F. Supp. 885, 892 (W.D. Okla. 1962). The court also took into consideration a pending initiative proposal which would have vested the duty of reapportionment in an independent apportionment commission. The court stated that numerical inequality of voting strength does not necessarily prove a deprivation of voting rights, but that "a disparity of ten to one in the voting strength between electoral districts makes out a prima facie case for invidious discrimination, and calls for strict justification." Id. at 891. The court indicated that it would only undertake to reapportion the legislature "as a last resort." Id. at 892.

The facts revealed that a majority of the house could be elected by 26 per cent of the total population. In the senate nine members represented 52 per cent of the people while the other 35 senators represented 48 per cent. Under the Oklahoma constitution, the court said, the principle of numerical equality is the rule, and any deviation is the exception. "There may be relevant counter-vailing factors, such as geography, economics, mass media and functional or group voting strength. But none of these factors, whether considered separately or collectively, can overcome the basic principle underlying the right of an individual to cast an effective vote." Id. at 893. Among the guidelines and standards established by the court in the *Moss* case was a statement that the seven-member ceiling on representatives from populous counties should be disregarded. Jurisdiction was retained until March 8, 1963.

At the November 1962 election the initiative petition to create a reapportionment commission received a ma-

jority of the votes cast on the petition, but not a majority of the votes cast during the entire general election. Accordingly, the initiative was held not to have been validly adopted. *Allen v. Burkhart,* 377 P.2d 821 (Okla. 1962). (The federal district court had referred the matter to the Oklahoma Supreme Court to decide the question of whether the initiative petition had become the law of the state.)

On March 7, 1963, the legislature reapportioned both houses of the legislature. Okla. Stat. Ann. §§ 78.1–78.11 and §§ 100–106 (1964 Supp.). The senate reapportionment provided for a 47-member senate to include four senators from Oklahoma County and three senators from Tulsa County, but allowed no more than one senator for any other county. The house reapportionment provided for a 112-member body during the second legislative period (1964–1966), to be reduced to 91 members by the fifth legislative period (1970–1972).

The three-judge federal court held the 1963 apportionment legislation null and void as violative of the fourteenth amendment because it provided little or no relief from malapportionment under the antecedent laws. *Moss v. Burkhart,* 220 F. Supp. 149 (W.D. Okla. 1963). For example, representative districts varied in population from 11,700 to 62,800; 30.2 per cent of the people could elect a majority of the house as a result of adherence to the "arbitrary ceilings" on the number of representatives to be elected from the most populous counties, under section 10(d), and through skillful manipulation of the "floats" pursuant to section 10(e). The senate disparities between districts ran from 115,300 to 24,400, a ratio of 4.73 to 1. Id. at 153.

The court "reluctantly" decided to reapportion the Oklahoma legislature by judicial decree, because "the Legislature, as now constituted, is either unable or unwilling to reapportion itself, in accordance with our concept of the requirements of the equal protection clause of the Fourteenth Amendment." Id. at 155.

A proposed constitutional amendment (S.J. Res. No. 4) was also passed by the 1963 legislature. It provided for a reapportionment of both houses in accordance with new formulas and directed a reapportionment commission to apportion the legislature upon failure of the legislature to do so. The state supreme court was also required to order the commission to act. The pendency of this amendment was not raised as an appropriate remedy in the July 17, 1963, decision in *Moss v. Burkhart*. However, the court took judicial notice of it (it was to be voted upon on the date of the next primary election) and concluded that in view of the improbability of its adoption and of its doubtfulness as a remedy, a stay of the *Moss* proceedings would not be justified. Id. at 154–55.

The court divided the senate into 44 districts—Oklahoma, Tulsa, and Comanche Counties, receiving eight, seven, and two senators respectively, while the remaining 74 counties were combined to constitute the other 27 districts. The house was apportioned among 109 members for two legislative periods and 107 for the next two. "Flotorial" members were assigned for specific legislative sessions and the ceiling on the number of representatives each county could receive was abolished. Id. at 157–60.

Pending review by the Supreme Court of the United States of the judgment of the three-judge district court an original action was brought in the supreme court of Oklahoma to review the validity of the 1963 legislation. That court held that reapportionment to be valid if adjusted in certain particulars to conform to provisions of the Oklahoma constitution. *Davis v. McCarty*, 388 P.2d 480 (Okla. 1964). Accordingly, the federal court standby order of reapportionment was stayed pending appeal.

On June 22, 1964, the Supreme Court of the United States affirmed "on the merits" the judgment of the three-judge federal court and remanded the cases "for further proceedings, with respect to relief, consistent with the views stated in our opinions in *Reynolds v. Sims* and in the other cases relating to state legislative apportionment decided along with *Reynolds*, should that become necessary." *Williams v. Moss*, 378 U.S. 558, 559 (1964). Justices Clark and Stewart concurred, and Justice Harlan dissented. (The case is more fully discussed in chapter VI, supra.)

On remand the three-judge federal district court on August 7, 1964, reaffirmed its earlier ruling that the 1963 legislation was invalid. Meanwhile, however, the voters had approved the constitutional amendment proposed by the legislature in 1963, and primaries had been conducted pursuant to its provisions in May 1964. S.J.R. 4, Okla. Laws of 1963, p. 736, approved as State Question No. 416, Okla. Const., art. V, §§ 9A–11E. The court accepted those portions of the amendment which it found not violative of the federal Constitution and rejected all other portions. Thus, the court approved a 48-member senate and a house of 99 representatives. For the one-member senatorial districts the court substantially accepted the plan proposed by the state attorney general as satisfying the equal-population principle; and for the house the court prescribed its own plan for districts of approximately equal population. *Reynolds v. State Election Board*,

233 F. Supp. 323, 329, 332–68 (W.D. Okla. 1964). Despite the recently conducted primaries, the court held that the new districts should be effective for the elections in the fall of 1964, thus necessitating further primaries in all districts whose borders were revised by the judicial order.

As noted in the court's supplemental order of August 19, 1964, the governor called special elections in accordance with the terms of the court's order of August 7. Id. at 368. In the resulting primaries for 43 senate and 86 house seats, nine state senators were ousted and ten others renominated. Two Negroes defeated white rivals for house seats, and one Negro won a senate nomination over another Negro and two white candidates. N.Y. Times, Oct. 1, 1964, p. 21, col. 2.

Initiative and referendum powers are reserved to the people by article V, sections 1–3. The legislature may propose constitutional amendments (art. XXIV, § 1); and constitutional conventions are provided for (art. XXIV, § 2).

Oklahoma was divided into six congressional districts as of the 1951 census. Okla. Stat. tit. 14, § 1. The most populous district in 1960 had 552,863 inhabitants, while the least populous had 227,692.

REFERENCES

Bureau of Government Research. Oklahoma's Twenty-ninth Legislative Session. Norman: The University of Oklahoma. August 1963.

League of Women Voters of Oklahoma. Reapportionment. Norman: August 1961.

League of Women Voters of Oklahoma. Supplement to Reapportionment. Norman: August 1962.

Mauer, George J. Bureau of Government Research, University of Oklahoma. Resume of Legislative Apportionment in Oklahoma 1961–1963. Norman: 1963.

Pray, Joseph C., and Mauer, George J. Bureau of Government Research, University of Oklahoma. The New Perspective of Legislative Apportionment in Oklahoma. Norman: July 1962.

OREGON

By an unusual arrangement, the land within the present boundaries of the state of Oregon was, in effect, under the joint occupation of the United States and Great Britain between 1818 and 1846. This awkward status was discontinued by treaty between the two powers in 1846, and in 1848 Congress organized Oregon into a territorial government. The legislative power was vested in a legislative assembly consisting of a council of 9 members and an assembly initially of 18 members, but with a provision for enlargement of the assembly "in proportion to the increase of qualified voters," but not to exceed 30. Before the first election the governor was to have a census taken "of the inhabitants and qualified voters," after which he was to make an apportionment, "as nearly equal as practicable, among the several counties or districts, for the election of the council and representatives, giving to each section of the Territory representation in the ratio of its qualified voters, as nearly as may be." Sec. 4.

The territorial legislature called a constitutional convention which met in 1857 and drew up a constitution which was ratified by the people in that same year and approved by congress as "republican" in form in 1859, whereupon Oregon was admitted as a state of the Union.

The constitution of 1857, which as amended remains the present constitution, provided for an initial senate membership of 16 and an initial house membership of 34. From and after 1860 the legislature was empowered to increase the numbers to 30 for the senate and 60 for the house of representatives. Ore. Const. of 1859, art. IV, §§ 1, 2. A census was provided for in 1865 and every ten years thereafter "of all the white population" (id., art. IV, § 5); and at the next legislative session the number of senators and representatives was to be apportioned "among the several counties according to the number of white population in each." Id., art. IV, § 6. In addition, elaborate provisions involving fractional representation on the basis of fractional ratios were put in the same section. These have been retained in the present constitution, as described below.

In the original schedule, made operative until a legislative apportionment could be made after the first census, the constitution utilized the foregoing principles to create 16 senatorial districts out of the 19 counties. The districts varied in composition from one county with two senators to four counties with one senator among them jointly. The representatives were not only divided in varying numbers among the counties, but floterial districts were created as well. Thus, for example, the counties of Washington, Columbia, Clatsop, and Tillamook were allotted one senator jointly. Washington was assigned one representative directly, and in addition shared a representative with Columbia, while Clatsop and Tillamook, neither of which was given separate representation, elected a single representative jointly. Id., art. XVIII, § 5.

Although the specific schedule summarized above was discarded as population shifts became known and as new counties were added to make the present total of 36, the basic principles of apportionment have remained essentially unchanged since the adoption of the constitution in 1859. Thus, the present senate and house are at their constitutional limits of 30 and 60 respectively. The legislature, which is now

required to reapportion at its first session following each federal census, remains bound to apportion the number of senators and representatives "among the several counties according to the population in each." Ore. Const., art. IV, § 6(1), as amended in 1952. The ratio of both senators and representatives is determined by dividing the total population of the state by the number of senators and by the number of representatives. The population of each county and district is then divided by the senate and representative ratios to determine the number of senators and representatives to be allotted to the counties or districts. When this division results in a fraction over one half, such county or district is entitled to an additional member for such fraction. If any county does not have the requisite population to entitle it to one member, "then such county shall be attached to some adjoining county or counties for senatorial or representative purposes." Ibid. The constitution contains no mention of any factor other than population in making the apportionment.

When more than one county constitutes a senatorial district, it must be composed of contiguous counties, and no county may be divided in creating such senatorial districts. "Senatorial or representative districts comprising not more than one county may be divided into subdistricts from time to time by law." Subdistricts must be composed of contiguous territory within the district; and the ratios to population of senators or representatives elected from the subdistricts must be "substantially equal within the district." Id., art. IV, § 7, as amended in 1954.

By an initiated amendment of 1952 original jurisdiction is vested in the supreme court of Oregon (upon the petition of any qualified elector) to review any reapportionment measure enacted by the legislature. If the supreme court determines that the reapportionment law does not comply with article IV, section 6, the supreme court is required to direct the secretary of state to draft a reapportionment and return it for supreme court review. If that draft complies with section 6, it becomes law upon the date it is filed with the governor. If the draft does not comply with those requirements, it must be returned to the secretary of state for correction. Id., art. IV, § 6(2)(b), (c).

If the legislature fails to enact any reapportionment measure by July 1 of the year of the session next following a taking of the United States census, the secretary of state is directed to make a reapportionment of both the house and the senate by August 1. Id., art. IV, § 6(3)(a). The supreme court may review any apportionment made by the secretary of state (upon the petition of any elector, before September 1) and may direct him to correct the reapportionment. Id., art. IV, § 6(3)(b), (d).

The reapportionment formula in article IV, section 6, however, creates a problem in allotting a mathematically equal number of senators and representatives according to the population ratio. If extra representation were given in every case in which "a fraction exceeding one-half results from such division," the resulting apportionment would exceed the constitutional maximum of 60 representatives and 30 senators. In seeking to deal with this problem the 1961 legislative apportionment act first allocated to each district consisting of a small county or a combination of small counties a senator or a representative for each whole number

(the population ratio) and for each major fraction. The number of available remaining seats was thus reduced to the point where it became impossible to allot to the larger counties the full number of seats called for by a strict application of the population ratios. Accordingly, some larger districts were allotted fewer legislators than their population warranted. Upon petitions of electors residing in these large counties, the supreme court of Oregon, in *Review of Chapter 482 of Oregon Laws of 1961*, 228 Ore. 562, 364 P.2d 1004 (1961), declared the 1961 act unconstitutional and directed the secretary of state to draft a reapportionment plan. "The legislature," the court concluded, "does have the power to make some adjustment in representation, but it does not have the power to adjust the [population] ratios to the extent of disregarding a whole number once the districts have been established." Id. at 571, 364 P.2d at 1007.

The subsequent reapportionment plan of the secretary of state was upheld as meeting the constitutional requirements in *Apportionment of Senators and Representatives*, 228 Ore. 575, 365 P.2d 1042 (1961). By that plan the state was divided into 30 senatorial districts and 60 representative districts. However, there remains some inequality among districts composed of more than one county. The 1960 population of Oregon, 1,768,687, divided by 30 and 60 respectively, yields a senatorial population ratio of 58,956 and a representative population ratio of 29,478. One combination senatorial district has a population of 124,715, but 92,237 of these persons also elect another senator. The "average" of the two districts is 62,357. The population of the largest district whose voters are not also in a combined district is 69,634. A similar situation prevails in the lower house. One combination district composed of two counties has a population of 202,055. To achieve near-equality one of the two counties in the combined district elects five additional representatives of its own and the other county elects one representative of its own. The seven-seat "average," however, is 28,865. The population of the largest district whose voters are not also in a combined district is 39,660. The minimum percentage of the 1960 population necessary to elect a majority of the senate is 47.8 and of the house, 48.1.

Constitutional amendments may be proposed by a majority vote of both houses of the legislature and become effective if a majority of the electors voting at a general or special election approve. Ore. Const., art. XVII, § 1. The constitution may also be amended at a constitutional convention, the procedures for which were established by an amendment approved in 1960. Id., art. XVII, § 2.

The powers of the initiative and the referendum are reserved to the people by article IV, section 1 of the constitution as amended in 1902 and 1954.

The state of Oregon has four congressional districts. Ore. Rev. Stat. § 250.290. The 1960 population of the most populous congressional district was 522,813 while the least populous had a population of 265,164, curiously reflecting substantial disparity in a state in which the state legislative districts are relatively equal in population.

When the Oregon legislature failed to reach agreement on a redistricting plan at its regular session in 1965, the governor called a special session which commenced on May 21, 1965. A new districting statute was adopted at that session to lessen the population inequalities among the districts. Ore. Laws 1965 (Spec. Sess.), c. 1, p. 1407.

REFERENCES

Oregon Legislative Council Committee. Legislative Apportionment Do-it-Yourself Kit. Salem: 1961.

Baker, Gordon E. Reapportionment by Initiative in Oregon, 13 Western Pol. Q. 508 (1960).

Schumacher, Waldo. Reapportionment in Oregon, 3 Western Pol. Q. 428 (1950).

PENNSYLVANIA

Parts of what is now the state of Pennsylvania were variously within grants contained in the Charter of Virginia (1606), the Council of New England (1620), the Charter of Maryland (1632), the Charter of Connecticut (1662), and the grants to the Duke of York (1664 and 1674). Claims were also made by the Dutch West India Company from 1621 and by the Swedish South Company after 1626.

In 1681 Charles II of Great Britain granted lands to William Penn to be called Pennsylvania in honor of Penn's father, whose services to the Crown were thus requited. To perfect his title Penn in 1682 purchased by quit-claim deed from the Duke of York lands west of the Delaware contained in the 1664 grant to York.

Penn's celebrated charter of liberties and the frame of government, issued together in 1682, provided for a government to consist of a governor and the freemen of the province, who were to be represented in a provincial council and a general assembly. The council, to be elected by all the freemen of the province assembled together, was to consist of 72 "persons of most note for their Wisdom Virtue and Ability. . . ." Sec. 2. The first general assembly was permitted to include all the freemen of the province (id., § 16), but thereafter to consist of not more than 200 persons chosen by all the freemen from among their number (id., § 14). Provision was also made for enlargement of the general assembly to not more than 500 as the population should increase; and the "Appointment and proportioning" of both houses was to be accomplished "in future times most equally to the Division of the Hundreds and Counties" into which the province should be divided. Id., § 16.

In 1683 Penn issued a new frame of government providing for a council of 18 (three from each county) and a general assembly of 36 (six from each county). Frame of Govt. of Pa. of 1683, art. I. This in turn was modified in 1696, reducing the representation to two from each county in the council and four in the general assembly. Frame of Govt. of Pa. of 1696, ¶ 2. In 1701 Penn revised and reissued his charter of liberties, confirming the legislative power in a general assembly of four representatives from each county, but now dispensing with an elected council as a second chamber. Charter of Privileges of 1701, art. II. Provision was also made for enlargement of the number of representatives upon agreement of the governor and assembly. Ibid. Moreover, if the representatives of the province and territories should not "agree to join together in Legislation," an assembly could be created with eight representatives from each of the three counties in the province, two from the city of Philadelphia, and as many as "requested" from each county in the territories. Id., special proviso. This charter, granted by Penn with the approval of the general assembly, remained in force until the adoption of the revolutionary constitution of 1776.

The Pennsylvania constitution of 1776 was drawn by a convention assembled in Philadelphia at the request of the Continental Congress. That constitution conferred legislative authority upon a unicameral assembly and executive authority upon a president and council. Pa. Const. of 1776, §§ 2, 3. The assembly was originally to consist of six representatives from Philadelphia and each of the counties of the commonwealth. Thereafter, however, representation was to be based on population, for "representation in proportion to the number of taxable inhabitants is the only principle which can at all times secure liberty, and make the voice of a majority of the people the law of the land . . . ." Accordingly, an enumeration of the "taxable inhabitants" was to be taken, after which representation was to be fixed by the legislature, every seven years, "in proportion to the number of taxables in such returns . . . ." Id., § 17. Even the members of the council, 12 in number, were to serve for terms of from one to three years depending on the population of the counties from which selected. Id., § 19.

The constitution of 1790 retained the principle of representation in accordance with population, or determined by a census of the taxable inhabitants to be taken every seven years. The lower house, now designated as the house of representatives, was to consist of from 60 to 100 members, "apportioned among the city of Philadelphia and the several counties, according to the number of taxable inhabitants in each . . . ." Pa. Const. of 1790, art. I, § 4. Each of the then 21 counties was assured at least one representative, but counties later created were not to be given separate representation until their population should equal the representation ratio. Ibid. The upper house, thereafter known as the senate, was also to be apportioned "according to the number of taxable inhabitants," with a total membership of not less than one fourth nor more than one third of the number of representatives. Id., art. I, § 6. The apportionment for the first session of the legislature was fixed in a schedule included within the constitution, 18 senators divided among 12 districts assigned from one to three senators each. Id., Schedule, § 7. The representatives were to continue in the first legislature their former distribution. Id., Schedule, § 6.

The constitutions of 1838 and 1874 continued to place primary emphasis on population as the basis for apportionment in both houses, but with some advantage to the less populous counties and some disadvantage to the urban areas, especially Philadelphia. The constitution of 1838 began the trend by providing that no city or county should be entitled to more than four senators and that neither the city of Philadelphia nor any county should be divided in the formation of a district. Pa. Const. of 1838, art. I, § 7. By amendment in 1857 separate representation (out of a house of 100) was assured after 1864 to each county with a population of 3,500 taxables; no more than three counties could be joined to form a district; and no county could be divided in forming districts. Id., art. I, § 4, as amended, 1857.

The constitution of 1874 is the present constitution, except as limited by judicial rulings noted below. It provides for 50 senatorial districts with a formula of fractional ratios of representation working out to a close approximation of representation by population, except that no city or county could have representation exceeding one sixth of the entire senate membership. Pa. Const. of 1874, art. II, § 16.

The formula for the house of representatives is also closely based on population, except for the proviso that each county should have at least one representative. Id., art. II, § 17.

There is no set number of seats in the Pennsylvania house, but membership is apportioned among the counties on the basis of a ratio determined by dividing the population of the state, as ascertained by the most recent federal census, by 200. Pa. Const. of 1874, art. II, § 17. The 1960 population of 11,319,366 divided by 200 yields a representative ratio of 56,597; half a ratio is 28,298. The 1874 constitution provided for apportionment of the house in accordance with the following rules: (1) Every county was to have at least one representative, regardless of population. (2) Every county containing less than five ratios (5/200ths or 282,984 people when measured by the 1960 census) was to have one representative for every full ratio and another for every fraction of a ratio larger than one half. (3) Every county containing five or more ratios was to be allotted one representative for each full ratio but none for fractions of a ratio. (4) Every city with a population equal to one ratio was to elect separately its "proportion of the representatives allotted to the county in which it is located." Ibid. Therefore, any such city must be a separate district. *Shoemaker v. Lawrence*, 31 Pa. D. & C. 681, 45 Dauph. 111 (1938). (5) Every city entitled to more than four representatives and every county of more than 100,000 people was to be divided into districts of compact and contiguous territory. *Drocher v. Lawrence*, No. 373 Commonwealth Docket, No. 1338 Equity Docket (1937), ruled that the requirement of compactness was not an absolute one, but must be construed to mean "as compact as practicable." The requirement of contiguity (adjoining and not separated), however, was held to be absolute. (6) There is no provision against the division of counties or political subdivisions in article II, section 17 of the constitution. (7) The general assembly, "immediately after each United States decennial census, shall apportion the state" into both senatorial and representative districts. Id., art. II, § 18.

The Pennsylvania constitution calls for the division of the state into 50 senatorial districts of compact and contiguous territory. Pa. Const. of 1874, art. II, § 16. The senatorial ratio is ascertained by dividing the total population by 50. On the basis of the 1960 census figures one senatorial ratio (1/50th of total population) is 226,387. Every county containing between four fifths of a ratio and a whole ratio (i.e., between 181,110 and 226,387) is entitled to one senator. Additional senators may be allotted for surplus population of one or more whole ratios or surplus exceeding three fifths of a ratio; but no county or city is entitled to separate representation exceeding one sixth of the whole number of senators (eight).

Between 1874 and 1964 the general assembly failed to reapportion on a decennial basis despite the requirement of article II, section 18. Thus, immediately prior to the approval of the 1964 act the senate apportionment was governed by legislation enacted in 1921, and the house apportionment was based on 1953 legislation. However, the several attempts to secure judicial relief during this period were uniformly unsuccessful.

In a 1951 suit in federal court, challenging the 1921 senate act, the court held that since the first general assembly after the 1950 census was still in session there was a "want of equity" in the suit; a proper reapportionment act might yet be adopted by the general assembly or a remedy might be found in the courts of the commonwealth. *Remmey v. Smith*, 102 F. Supp. 708 (E.D. Pa. 1951), appeal dismissed, 342 U.S. 916 (1952).

Subsequent suits were brought in the courts of the commonwealth challenging the legislature's failure to redistrict after each federal decennial census. But, until the United States Supreme Court decision in *Baker v. Carr*, 369 U.S. 186 (1962), the Pennsylvania Supreme Court took the position that the general assembly's failure to reapportion was a political matter and therefore not justiciable. See *Butcher v. Rice*, 397 Pa. 158, 153 A.2d 869 (1959), affirming 73 Dauph. 10 (1958); *Costello v. Rice*, 397 Pa. 198, 153 A.2d 888 (1959).

After the *Baker* decision a Pennsylvania lower court in June 1962, *Butcher v. Trimarchi* (consolidated with *Start v. Lawrence*), 28 Pa. D. & C.2d 537 (1962), ruled on a challenge to the constitutionality of the apportionment of both the house and the senate (the 1921 and 1953 acts) as violative of article II, sections 16 and 17 of the Pennsylvania constitution and of the fourteenth amendment to the United States Constitution. The court held the issues justiciable but denied injunctive relief "until the legislature has had an opportunity to reapportion . . . at the forthcoming session . . . ." Id. at 542.

When the general assembly failed to agree upon reapportionment legislation at the regular session in 1963, the governor called a special session in November 1963. During that session a three-judge federal district court agreed with plaintiffs that the constitutional provisions, if faithfully adhered to by the legislature, would produce wide population disparities among the districts. But the court declined to forbid or to mandate any particular legislative action while the general assembly was in session. Jurisdiction was retained to permit examination of any legislation that might be adopted. *Drew v. Scranton*, 229 F. Supp. 308 (M.D. Pa. 1963).

In January 1964 the general assembly enacted, and the governor approved, new legislation consistent with the complained-against provisions of sections 16 and 17 of the state constitution. Pa. Laws of 1964, Spec. Sess., Acts 1 and 2. The matter was promptly referred once more to the federal court, which concluded that the reapportionment of both houses was invalid. *Drew v. Scranton*, 229 F. Supp. 310 (M.D. Pa. 1964). In discussing the senate apportionment the court said: "When it appears, as it does, that the 13 most populous counties of the State are all under-represented and that 50 of the 54 less populous counties are over-represented, 28 of them by more than 25%, the conclusion is inescapable that such discrimination was deliberate and invidious in violation of the Fourteenth Amendment." Id. at 316–17.

The court found that the discrimination against the populous counties in the senate was caused by two provisions of the state constitution which were accordingly unenforceable: (1) The provision that no city or county, regardless of population, should be entitled to more than eight senators — to the specific disadvantage of Philadelphia. (2) The limitation that a county with one or more ratios of population would be given an additional senator only if the population surplus should exceed three fifths of a ratio, whereas application of the rule of major fractions would authorize additional representation for a surplus population of one half of a ratio. This also worked to the disadvantage of the populous counties.

The court also found invalid the apportionment of the house, again involving discrimination against the 13 most populous counties. The court ruled that the applicable constitutional provisions were invalid in three respects: (1) The requirement that each county have at least one representative, even though 13 counties had 1960 populations of less than one half of a ratio, ranging down to 4,485 as compared with the full ratio of population of 56,597. (2) The restriction, applicable only to counties having five or more ratios of population, against being allotted an additional representative for a population surplus exceeding one half of a ratio. This provision deprived the second and third most populous counties, Allegheny and Delaware, of one representative each to which they would have been entitled under the rule of major fractions. (3) The requirement that no county or part of a county be joined with any other county. The court held that, as to counties with less than one half of a ratio, the prohibition was invalid; but it concluded that county integrity could in other cases be respected as provided in the constitution.

Finally, the court held invalid the provisions of the house reapportionment whereby, without apparent pattern, some election districts were single-member while others required the selection of from two to four representatives. "In the absence of any legislative history or other explanation justifying it, and we have found none, we can only conclude that this districting is either the result of gerrymandering for partisan advantage . . . or that it is wholly arbitrary and capricious." Id. at 326.

Accordingly, on April 9, 1964, the federal court enjoined the conduct of further elections under the plan found invalid, expressing the hope that the legislature would act promptly, or in any event by June 1, 1964, when the court asked for the matter to be returned for further consideration.

Meanwhile, the state case was reactivated and, during its pendency, the federal court order was stayed on April 14, 1964, pending appeal to the Supreme Court of the United States. Thereafter, on September 29, 1964, the supreme court of Pennsylvania announced its judgment on essentially the same issues earlier considered by the federal court. The state court found the 1964 reapportionment legislation invalid, as had the federal court, but differed as to the necessity of invalidating the state constitutional provisions. The state court interpreted sections 16 and 17 of article II to permit the division or combination of counties where necessary to satisfy the equal-population principle.

The state court also differed with the federal court as to the timing of relief. In view of the imminence of the November 1964 elections the court ruled that those elections could be held under the invalid system, but that corrective action must be taken before 1966. Recognizing that the federal court had announced a different timetable, the state court said: "In the presence of the demonstrated willingness of the Legislature to act and the willingness of our courts to assume jurisdiction, the federal district court should be relieved of responsibility in this matter for a period sufficient to allow such remedies to become effective." *Butcher v. Bloom*, 415 Pa. 438, 444, 203 A.2d 556, 559 (1964).

On appeal by the state of Pennsylvania from the decision of the federal district court, the Supreme Court of the United States vacated that judgment and remanded "for further consideration in light of the decisions supervening since the entry of the judgment of the district court." *Scranton v. Drew*, 379 U.S. 40, 42 (1964). In view of the intervening decision of the state supreme court, this was taken to mean that the state court's deadline of September 1, 1965, was controlling. By that date it appeared that the legislature was near agreement, so the state supreme court gave additional time to effect a legislative solution, indicating its intent to step in if the legislature failed to act. N.Y. Times, Sept. 5, 1965, p. 49, col. 5.

Although the prospect of conflict between federal and state courts was thus averted, or at least postponed, the matter was not resolved by the end of October 1965. The Pennsylvania legislature continued unable to reach agreement, and the state supreme court continued to extend the time allowed for legislative action.

Amendments to the constitution may be proposed by a majority of the members elected to both houses of the legislature. If such amendments are approved by a majority of the voters voting thereon, they become a part of the constitution. Pa. Const., art. XVIII, § 1.

When the 1960 census showed that Pennsylvania would lose three seats in the 1963 Congress, the general assembly, in order to prevent an at-large election, enacted a redistricting measure dividing the state into 27 districts, at the 1962 executive session. Pa. Stat. Ann. § 2199.1 (Exec. Sess. 1962). The most populous congressional district in 1960 had 553,154 inhabitants, while the least populous had 303,026.

REFERENCES

Pennsylvania Commission on Constitutional Revision. Report. Harrisburg: Commonwealth of Pennsylvania. 1959.

Pennsylvania Department of Internal Affairs. Re-Apportionment in Pennsylvania. Release No. S-8. Harrisburg: April 1961.

Philadelphia Bureau of Municipal Research. Philadelphia and Constitutional Revision. Philadelphia: Pennsylvania Economy League. 1960.

Corter, Lee E. Pennsylvania Ponders Apportionment, 32 Temp. L.Q. 279 (1959).

Korsak, Tadeusz Z., and DiSalle, Richard. Legislative Apportionment in Pennsylvania, 12 U. Pitt. L. Rev. 215 (1951).

RHODE ISLAND

At various times in the early colonization of New England, dominion over the land which became the state of Rhode Island and Providence Plantations was claimed pursuant to the Charter of Virginia (1606), by the Council of New England (1620), and under the 1688 commission to John Andros. Separate identity was first suggested in 1640 when a number of inhabitants of the town of Providence designated four of their number to arbitrate differences which had arisen among them. That arbitration was recorded in the Plantation Agreement of Providence of September 1640. A government of Rhode Island was agreed upon in March 1641, giving to the freemen assembled in a "Generall Court of Election" the power to "make or constitute Just Lawes . . . ."

In 1643, in response to the petition of settlers in the towns of Providence, Portsmouth, and Newport, the Earl of Warwick, who had been designated governor in chief of the islands and other plantations along the American coast inhabited by British subjects, granted "a free and absolute Charter of Incorporation, to be known by the Name of the Incorporation of Providence Plantations, in the Narraganset-Bay, in New England. — Together with full Power and Authority to rule themselves, . . ." After the Restoration in England Charles II, in 1663, granted a charter of Rhode Island and Providence Plantations to a company of residents. In addition to provisions for a governor and deputy governor, initial appointments were made of ten assistants. The system of representation by towns, which has continued to the present, also first appeared in this charter. The freemen in each town were to elect their deputies to participate with the governor and assistants in the general assembly in the following proportions: six from Newport, four each from Providence, Portsmouth, and Warwick, and two from "each other place, towne or city . . . ."

Interestingly enough, Rhode Island operated without further fundamental orders until 1842 when, for the first time, a written constitution was adopted; and that constitution has survived to the present, although substantially amended. The original provisions were for a house of representatives not to exceed 72 (increased in 1909 to a limit of 100), to be "constituted on the basis of population," except that each city and town "shall always" be entitled to one representative, and no city or town could have more than one sixth of the total number (changed in 1909 to one fourth). R.I. Const. of 1842, art. V, § 1. The senate was described simply as consisting "of the lieutenant-governor and of one senator from each town or city in the state." Id., art. VI, § 1. This provision was modified in 1928 to give some recognition to population differentials among the cities and towns. After 1928 any town having more than 25,000 qualified electors was given an additional senator for each additional 25,000 electors, and an additional senator for a fraction exceeding half the ratio (more than 12,500 electors); but no town or city was allowed more than six senators. Towns or cities entitled to more than one senator were to be divided into senatorial districts "as nearly equal in number of qualified electors and as compact in territory as possible." The general assembly "may after any presidential election reapportion the senate in accordance with the foregoing provisions." R.I. Const., art. XIX, § 1.

Operating under this formula, there were 46 Rhode Island senators in 1965, one from each of the 39 towns and cities in the state, except that the city of Providence had five senators and the cities of Pawtucket, Cranston, and Warwick each chose two senators. R.I. Gen. Laws §§ 22-1-2 to 22-1-6. As a result of the representation by towns and cities, notable population inequalities existed among the senate districts. The 1960 census population of Rhode Island, 859,488, divided by 46, yielded a senate population mean of 18,684. The population of the largest senate district, however, was 47,080 while the smallest district had only 486 persons. It was theoretically possible for 18.1 per cent of the population of Rhode Island to elect a majority of the senate.

The apportionment formula for the house of representatives, as modified by constitutional amendment in 1909, and as most recently implemented by statute in 1930, was challenged in *Sweeney v. Notte*, 183 A.2d 296 (R.I. 1962). In that case plaintiffs, residents and voters in the cities of Cranston and Warwick, sought a declaratory judgment that the 1930 reapportionment act had, by virtue of legislative inaction and population increases and shifts, become violative of the state constitution and that the provisions of the state constitution were violative of the fourteenth amendment to the United States Constitution. The 1909 amendment provided that the house of representatives "shall never

exceed" 100 members, "and shall be constituted on the basis of population, always allowing one representative for a fraction exceeding half the ratio; but each town and city shall always be entitled to at least one member; and no town or city may have more than one-fourth of the whole number of members." The general assembly "may," after any federal or state census, reapportion representation. Towns and cities entitled to more than one representative shall be divided into districts "as nearly equal in population and as compact in territory as possible." R.I. Const., art. XIII, § 1.

These provisions were not entirely voided in *Sweeney v. Notte*; but the Rhode Island Supreme Court concluded that the "limitation of one hundred members and the securing of representation to each municipality, taken together, is an apportionment formula which when followed results in a denial of equal protection within the meaning of article XIV of amendments as laid down by the United States Supreme Court." 183 A.2d at 302. In addition, the court found that the 1909 amendment "validly imposes an obligation on the general assembly to reapportion after every federal or state census whenever it appears therefrom that by reason of population shifts the prevailing apportionment no longer reflects reasonably equitable representation. The use of the verb 'may' rather than 'shall' was prompted, it seems reasonable to believe, by the fact that any census taken at a future time or times might reveal no necessity to reapportion. Whenever such a census does disclose drastic population shifts, however, the obligation on the general assembly is mandatory." Ibid.

The court further held that the general assembly was obligated to reapportion conformably to the 1960 census to prevent gross debasement or dilution of an elector's voting franchise (ibid.); and the court posed alternative plans which the court would accept as valid while yet preserving the identity of the 39 cities and towns (id. at 303). But the court cautioned that if the general assembly failed to reapportion the house within a reasonable time, a federal court would probably do so. Ibid.

In August 1962 the supreme court of Rhode Island declared that the 1909 amendment, as modified by the opinion in *Sweeney v. Notte,* was the "valid, organic law of the state," and advised that nine reapportionment proposals then before the legislature were invalid, while three others would comply with federal and state requirements. *Opinion to the Governor,* 183 A.2d 806, 808 (R.I. 1962). The court also reminded the legislature "categorically" that the securing of minimum representation for every municipality regardless of population could not be achieved without a multiple expansion of the number of house members. Id. at 807.

An application filed in federal court in September 1962 to restrain conduct of the November 1962 elections was denied because interference with the election at that date would create "serious public confusion." *Needham v. LaFrance,* Civ. No. 2930 (D.R.I. 1962).

Under the 1930 house apportionment formula, examined in the light of the 1960 census, 11 communities had a combined population of less than 3 per cent of the state's inhabitants but were allotted 11 per cent of the total seats in the house. Moreover, each of these 11 towns had a population less than one half of the 8,594 factor. The city of Providence, with eight times the population of the 11 towns just referred to, nevertheless had only twice their number of seats. The population of the largest house district was 18,977; the smallest contained 486 inhabitants.

The Rhode Island Commission on Revision of the Constitution was formed as a result of a June 1961 general assembly resolution. A subsequent resolution at the 1962 session of the general assembly extended the time within which the commission was to report from March 1, 1962, to January 3, 1963. The principal apportionment changes recommended in its September 1962 report were the following:

(1) Apportionment of the house to be on a straight population basis, with 100 representatives from districts "as nearly equal in population and as compact in territory as is reasonably possible." In addition, it was proposed that districts shall, "as far as is feasible, follow town or city lines." Report of Commission on Revision of the R.I. Const., art. V, § 1.

(2) The members of the commission were equally divided (six to six) on the question of the manner in which the senate should be reapportioned and therefore presented two alternative forms for article VI, section 1. The first alternative proposed apportionment on a straight population basis of 50 districts, each district to "comprise two districts of those fixed for the house of representatives." The second alternative proposed that one senator be elected from each town or city in the state and that each town or city having a population of more than 25,000 or major fraction thereof be given another representative for each additional 25,000 or major fraction thereof. Towns or cities entitled to more than one senator would be divided into senatorial districts by the general assembly.

(3) Reapportionment of both the senate and the house should be required at the first session of the general

assembly convening after every federal census. The governor would be empowered to promulgate an apportionment plan in the event of legislative failure to reapportion within six months after the first session following each decennial United States census. An interesting proposal would give the governor the "authority to appoint a board of qualified electors to assist him in the matter of apportionment." (Three members of the Commission dissented with respect to this section.)

Under the present constitution the general assembly may propose amendments to the constitution by the votes of a majority of all the members elected to each house. Any proposed amendment must then be passed again by a similar vote of the general assembly after a general election. The amendment must then be approved by three fifths of the electors of the state present and voting. R.I. Const., art. XIII.

There are no constitutional provisions relating to the call of a constitutional convention, but it is within the power of the legislature to call one. *In re Constitutional Convention* 55 R.I. 56, 178 Atl. 433 (1935).

On November 3, 1964, the voters of Rhode Island approved the calling of a state constitutional convention and elected 100 delegates from the state's 100 representative districts. The convention met in Providence on December 8, 1964, recognizing that reapportionment was its principal task although the convention was unlimited, the first since 1842. N.Y. Times, Dec. 9, 1964, p. 61, col. 2. In January 1965 the convention chairman, former governor Dennis J. Roberts, recommended approval of a unicameral legislature. John H. Chafee, the present governor, also indicated his support for a unicameral legislature, perhaps of only 70 mem-

bers. 54 Nat'l Munic. Rev. 145 (March 1965).

There are neither constitutional nor statutory provisions relating to the initiative or the referendum.

Rhode Island is divided into two congressional districts. R.I. Gen. Laws, §§ 17-4-1 to 17-4-3. The 1960 population of the larger district was 459,706 and the smaller, 399,782.

REFERENCES

Report of Commission on Revision of the Rhode Island Constitution (Sept. 1962).

Note, Small Town Representation: Invidious Discrimination? The Reapportionment Problem in Rhode Island, Vermont and Connecticut, 43 Boston U.L. Rev. 523 (1963).

SOUTH CAROLINA

South Carolina adopted as its first constitution the revolutionary constitution of 1776, which was soon revised in 1778. Both of these early instruments were perhaps more accurately legislative acts only, for the legislature treated them as subject to amendment like any other piece of legislation, and the courts concurred in that view. The constitution of 1776 vested the legislative power in a chief executive officer (entitled president and commander-in-chief), a lower house entitled the general assembly, and an upper house called the legislative council. S.C. Const. of 1776, art. VII. The general assembly was to have 202 members chosen from the then 28 parishes and districts, each of which was allotted from six to ten members except the combined parishes of St. Philip and St. Michael (the city of Charleston) which had 30 representatives. Id., art. XI. The legislative council was to consist of 13 members elected from the assembly. Id., art. II.

The constitution of 1778 increased the number of election districts to 30 and renamed the lower chamber the house of representatives, but left its size unchanged and the distribution of seats virtually unaltered. S.C. Const. of 1778, art. XIII. A senate of 29, elected by adult male white property owners or taxpayers, replaced the legislative council as the upper house. The district of St. Philip's and St. Michael's Parishes (Charleston) was given two senators; the parishes of All Saints and Prince George, Winyah had to share a single senator, as did the parishes of St. Matthew and Orange; all others had one senator each. Id., art. XII. The constitution of 1778 also provided for reapportionment every seven years "in the most equal and just manner . . . regard always being had to the number of white inhabitants and . . . taxable property." Id., art. XV.

The South Carolina constitution of 1790 reduced the size of the house to 124 (its present size) and increased that of the senate to 37. The allocation of seats among the election districts was specified in the constitution. In the house the number of seats assigned to each election district ranged from 1 (All Saints) to 15 (Charleston, including St. Philip and St. Michael). In the senate Charleston had two members and the district including Marlborough, Chesterfield, and Darlington also had two members; every other district (sometimes including two or three parishes and/or districts) had one senator. S.C. Const. of 1790, art. I, §§ 3, 7.

In 1808 these provisions of the 1790 constitution were amended to provide for reapportionment of the house of representatives every ten years, giving equal weight in each election district to "the number of white inhabitants" and the amount of taxes paid. If the legislature should fail to act during the course of any years specified for reap-portionment, the governor was directed to take corrective action.

When South Carolina seceded from the Union, the legislature called a constitutional convention which in April 1861 revised the constitution to substitute loyalty to the Confederate States of America and to include the amendments since 1790. This constitution was not submitted to the people for ratification, nor was the successor constitution of 1865, which was framed by a convention called by the provisional governor. The most noteworthy change in the constitution of 1865 was the elimination of the low-country parishes as separate election districts and substitution of the judicial districts as election districts. As a result the low-country lost representation in the senate, which decreased in size to 32, and the more populous up-country gained in representation. Since slaves were no longer taxable property, the low-country also lost representation in the house under the formula which retained property as a factor.

The constitution of 1868, called for under the terms of the congressional reconstruction acts, was prepared in convention and ratified by the voters. The membership of the house of representatives was continued at 124, but now to be apportioned simply "among the several counties according to the number of inhabitants contained in each." S.C. Const. of 1868, art. II, § 4. Each of the then 31 counties was assured at least one seat. Id., art. II, § 6. Provision was made for a census in 1869, 1875, and every ten years thereafter, imposing on the legislature the obligation of reapportionment "at the session immediately succeeding such enumeration." Id., art. II, § 4. Apportionment of the senate was continued unchanged with one seat for each county except two for Charleston. Id., art. II, § 8.

The present constitution, that of 1895, is not essentially different in its apportionment provisions from the constitution of 1868. In the senate, however, even the slight advantage earlier given to Charleston was discontinued so that now each county elects one senator for a four-year term. S.C. Const., art. III, § 6. As a result of this rigid formula the population disparities among counties are substantial. The 1960 population of 2,382,594 divided by 46 (the number of counties) yields a senatorial population mean of 51,796. However, the largest district had 216,382 persons while the smallest county has only 8,629; and 23.31 per cent of the state's population can elect a majority of the members of the senate.

"Representation in the House of Representatives shall be apportioned according to population." Id., art. I, § 2. The membership remains at 124 (id., art. III, § 3), except that each county must have at least one member (id., art. III, § 4). After each county is allotted at least one representative and after additional representatives are allotted to the more populous counties, if some of the 124 seats remain unassigned, those counties having the "largest surplus fractions" over the mean (124 divided into the total population) are to be assigned additional representation. Ibid.

As required by the constitution of 1895, the general assembly has reapportioned itself every ten years since 1901.

The latest revision of South Carolina's house districts occurred in 1961. S.C. Act. No. 207, pt. II, §§ 7, 8 (1961). The constitutional provision that each county must have at least one representative necessitates large population disparities among the county districts.

The total population of the state divided by 124 seats yields a house population mean of 19,214. The population of the largest house district is 29,490 and that of the smallest is 8,629; 45.99 per cent of the population may elect a majority of the members of the house.

The first challenge to the South Carolina apportionment was filed in federal court in September 1965. The State, Sept. 24, 1965, p. 1, col. 5.

Amendments to the constitution may be proposed in the senate or in the house; if agreed to by two thirds of the elected members of both houses, they are to be submitted to the electorate at the next general election for representatives. If a majority of the qualified electors voting thereon votes in favor of the amendment, and if a majority of each branch of the legislature, after that election, and before another, ratifies the same amendment, it becomes part of the constitution. S.C. Const., art. XVI, § 1.

Whenever two thirds of the members elected to both houses of the general assembly recommends that a constitutional convention be called to revise or amend the constitution, the electors voting at the next election for state representatives shall consider such a proposal. If a majority of all the electors voting at such an election votes for a convention, it shall be held. Id., art. XVII, § 3.

There are neither constitutional nor statutory provisions regarding the amendment of the constitution by use of the initiative or the referendum.

The general assembly may "at any time" arrange the various counties into congressional districts "as it may deem wise and proper." S.C. Const., art. VII, § 13. South Carolina is divided into six congressional districts. S.C. Code § 23-554 (Supp. 1964). According to the 1960 census, the congressional population mean is 397,099 (2,382,594 divided by six). The largest congressional district has a population of 531,555; the smallest, 302,235.

REFERENCES

Bain, Chester W. Legislative Apportionment in South Carolina, in The University of South Carolina Governmental Review. Vol. IV, No. 3. Columbia, South Carolina. Aug. 1962.

SOUTH DAKOTA

In 1889 Congress authorized a constitutional convention to prepare for the admission of South Dakota as a state. Delegates to the convention were to be chosen "in proportion to the population" of the districts or counties represented. Sec. 3. The constitution adopted by that convention in 1889 has since served as the constitution of the state of South Dakota, with amendments noted below.

In its original form the constitution of 1889 provided for a house of representatives with a membership of 75 to 135 and a senate of 25 to 45. S.D. Const. of 1889, art. III, § 2. The legislature was directed to have a census of inhabitants conducted in 1895 and every ten years thereafter. Reapportionment was to be effected at the first legislative session after each such census and after each federal census, always to be done "according to the number of inhabitants, excluding Indians not taxed and soldiers and officers of the United States army and navy; . . . ." Id., art. III, § 5. Pending the results of the first census, the constitution divided the 50 counties of the state into 41 senatorial districts, from which 45 senators were to be elected, and 50 representative districts, from which 124 representatives were to

be elected in numbers varying from one to eight in each district. S.D. Const. of 1889, art. XIX, § 2. See also Clem, Legislative Power and Reapportionment in South Dakota, in Public Affairs (Bull. No. 6, Aug. 15, 1961, Gov'tal Research Bur., Univ. of S.D.). A major reapportionment act was passed in 1891, reducing the number of house seats from 124 to 83 and the senate seats from 45 to 43. Other major reapportionment acts were passed in 1897, 1907, 1911, 1917, and 1937; and minor adjustments were made in 1903, 1951, and 1961.

Since 1936 the constitution has provided for a maximum senate membership of 35 and a maximum house membership of 75 (S.D. Const., art. III, § 2); and the legislature has remained at that size since. Both houses of the South Dakota legislature are now comparatively small and it is difficult to make an equitable division of the 75 house seats among the present 67 counties, whose populations vary from 1,042 to 86,575. "Equitably dividing the thirty-five senate seats among the same counties is very close to impossible." Clem, Legislative Power and Reapportionment in South Dakota, supra.

Apportionment is a legislative function to be performed by the regular session of the legislature "in 1951 and every ten years thereafter and at no other time," according to the last federal census prior to the legislative session at which such apportionment shall be made. If the legislature fails to reapportion, it is the duty of a group of public officials (the governor, the superintendent of public instruction, the presiding judge of the supreme court, the attorney general, and the secretary of state) to make the apportionment within 30 days after the adjournment of the legislature. Such apportionment has the same force and effect as though made by the legislature. S.D. Const., art. III, § 5, as amended in 1948. The 1948 amendment deleted from the pre-existing section the clause that "the legislature shall apportion the senators and representatives according to the number of inhabitants, excluding soldiers and officers of the United States Army and Navy." Therefore, it can be argued that the basis of representation is no longer that of population.

To understand the particular allocation of seats, it is important to know that there are three major sections of South Dakota (historically created in the days when the state sent three members to the United States Congress): Northeast, Southeast, and West River. When the sectional representation in the two houses of the legislature is compared with the population proportions of those sections, it is found that the 1961 legislative apportionment was almost perfect from the standpoint of the sections. See Clem, Legislative Power and Reapportionment in South Dakota, supra. However, when the 1961 act is studied on a county basis, the malapportionment in both houses becomes evident. The legislative districts were composed of one or more counties, which were never divided in creating these districts. Most of the senatorial districts were composed of two or more counties represented by a single senator. The majority of the house districts contained one county electing one member, although Minnehaha and Pennington Counties, entitled to nine and four representatives respectively, were notable exceptions. The counties suffering the greatest degree of underrepresentation were the counties with the largest population, while overrepresentation was characteristic of the smaller, more rural, counties.

The South Dakota legislature reapportioned both houses without the spur of an adverse court ruling on the existing plan. Under the 1965 act the population differential among house districts ranged between 7,765 and 10,841; in the senate the range was between 16,198 and 22,568. S.D. Sess. Laws 1965, c. 229.

An amendment may be proposed by a majority vote of both houses of the legislature. If the people ratify such amendment by a majority of the electors voting thereon, it becomes a part of the constitution. S.D. Const., art. XXIII, § 1. Two thirds of the members elected to each house of the legislature may recommend that a constitutional convention be called. A majority of the voters voting thereon must approve the proposal. Id., art. XXIII, § 2. The powers of the initiative and the referendum are reserved to the people. Id., art. III, § 1.

The state of South Dakota is entitled to two representatives in Congress. Until 1965 the Missouri River was the district boundary line, dividing the state into two districts that were nearly equal in area but very unequal in population. One district had 497,669 persons, more than twice the number in the other district, 182,845. After redrawing of the lines in 1965 the range was reduced to the difference between 351,901 and 328,613 in terms of 1960 population figures.

On April 1, 1965, a state court held that the existing apportionment of seats for the board of county commissioners in Sioux Falls was in conflict with the fourteenth amendment, including the state statute providing that no city should have more than half of the commissioner seats on a county board. The court thus encouraged new legislation for the apportionment of county commissioners on a population basis. A study published by the Governmental

Research Bureau at the University of South Dakota in November 1964 showed that 191 of the 282 county commissioner districts deviated more than 15 per cent from the average. Forty-five counties have five-member boards, and the remaining 19 have three-member boards. 54 Nat'l Munic. Rev. 264 (May 1965).

REFERENCES

South Dakota State Legislative Research Council. Reapportionment of the State Legislature in South Dakota. Staff Memorandum. Pierre: April 1961.
————. 1965 Reapportionment of the South Dakota Legislature. Staff Memorandum. Pierre: June 10, 1965.
Clem, Alan L. Legislative Power and Reapportionment in South Dakota, in Public Affairs (Bull. No. 6, Gov'tal Research Bureau, Aug. 15, 1961).
————. Problems of Measuring and Achieving Equality of Representation in State Legislatures, 42 Neb. L. Rev. 3 (1963).
————. Distorted Democracy: Malapportionment in South Dakota Government, in Public Affairs (Bull. No. 19, Gov'tal Research Bureau, Nov. 15, 1964).

TENNESSEE

The pioneers in the western part of the originally broad expanse of North Carolina asserted the right to self-government as early as 1772; and the constitution of the "Watauga" government, as it was known, was the first written charter west of the Allegheny Mountains. North Carolina regained control, however, and in 1784 offered to cede the lands west of the Alleghenies to the United States; but the offer was not accepted. The settlers then created what they called the state of Frankland, adopting as a frame of government the constitution of North Carolina in slightly modified form. Finally, in 1790, North Carolina ceded to the United States that portion of her territory west of the mountains. Congress accepted and promptly designated the land as a

territory of the United States "south of the river Ohio . . . ." It was provided that the government should be "similar to that which is now exercised in the territory northwest of the Ohio," presumably including the guaranty that the inhabitants should "always be entitled to the benefits . . . of a proportionate representation of the people in the legislature . . . ." Northwest Ordinance, art. II.

In 1796 a convention framed a constitution which was promptly approved by Congress in admitting Tennessee as a state of the Union. The constitution of 1796 vested the legislative authority in a general assembly consisting of a house of representatives of 22 to 26 members and a senate not less than one third and not more than one half the size of the house. Tenn. Const. of 1796, art. I, §§ 2, 3. The numbers of both were to be apportioned among the several counties and districts "according to the number of taxable inhabitants in each," on the basis of a census to be taken within three years of the first legislative session and every ten years thereafter. Ibid. The representatives were to be chosen from the counties (id., art. I, § 2) and the senators from districts for the election of not more than three senators in each district (id., art. I, § 4). Where two or more counties were joined together to form a senatorial district, the counties were to be adjoining, and no county was to be divided in forming a district. Ibid. Until an apportionment could be made pursuant to the first census, however, section 6 of the constitutional schedule provided simply that "the several counties shall be respectively entitled to elect one senator and two representatives . . . ."

The constitution of 1834 prescribed a requirement of legislative reapportionment in 1841 and every ten years thereafter (Tenn. Const. of 1834, art. II, § 4), "among the several counties or districts according to the number of qualified voters in each . . . ." (id., art. II, §§ 5, 6). The number of representatives was not to exceed 75 until the population of the state should exceed 1,500,000, and thereafter no more than 99. Id., art. II, § 5. The senate membership was not to exceed one third the number of representatives. Id., art. II, § 6. The emphasis on population was limited somewhat by the provision that any county with two thirds of a representative ratio should be entitled to one member (id., art. II, § 5), although "In apportioning the senators among the different counties, the fraction that may be lost by any county or counties, in the apportionment of members to the house of representatives, shall be made up to such county or counties in the senate as near as may be practicable" (id., art. II, § 6). An apportionment was specified in the constitution, to be effective until the census of 1841 should give the basis for a new allocation. The 62 counties in the state were divided into 25 districts, each of which was to elect one senator; and the representatives were to be chosen from single counties and from various combinations of counties, including floterial counties, to a total of 75. Ordinance accompanying Tenn. Const. of 1834, art. V.

The constitution of 1870, which remains the present constitution, provides for a maximum of 99 representatives. Tenn. Const., art. II, § 5. The number of senators may not exceed one third of the representatives (id., art. II, § 6), which is the number now fixed by statute (33). The general assembly is directed to effect an enumeration of the qualified voters of the state every ten years (id., art. II, § 4) and to apportion the representatives and senators among the several counties or districts "according to the number of qualified voters in each" (id., art. II, § 5). From 1870 on the figures used to ascertain the number of qualified voters have been based upon the number of persons 21 years of age and over. *Baker v. Carr*, 369 U.S. 186, 189 n.4 (1962). However, the provision has been continued that "any county having two-thirds of the ratio shall be entitled to one member." Tenn. Const., art. II, § 5. In addition, floterial representatives may be elected from more than one county. Thus, a county may directly elect one or more representatives while also participating in the election of a floterial representative. See Williams, Legislative Apportionment in Tennessee, 20 Tenn. L. Rev. 235 (1948).

Senators are to be apportioned among the counties or districts "according to the number of qualified electors in each." Districts composed of two or more counties must consist of "adjoining" counties; and no county may be divided in forming a senatorial district. The provision for evening out population inequalities between the two houses, first included in the constitution of 1834, is continued: "In apportioning the Senators among the different counties, the fraction that may be lost by any county or counties, in the apportionment of members to the House of Representatives, shall be made up to such county or counties in the Senate, as near as may be practicable." Tenn. Const., art. II, § 6.

Kidd v. McCanless, 200 Tenn. 273, 292 S.W.2d 40 (1956), appeal dismissed, 352 U.S. 920 (1956) raised essentially the same issues as those presented six years later in *Baker v. Carr*, supra, asking that the 1901 reapportionment act be declared unconstitutional.

Baker v. Carr, 179 F. Supp. 824 (M.D.

Tenn. 1959), reversed and remanded, 369 U.S. 186 (1962), on remand, 206 F. Supp. 341 (M.D. Tenn. 1962), 222 F. Supp. 684 (M.D. Tenn. 1963) was brought in May 1959 in the federal district court as a class suit by citizens and qualified voters of Tennessee. Plaintiffs attacked the most recent Tennessee apportionment act, that of 1901. Tenn. Code Ann. § 3-101 to 3-107. The complaint asserted rights under 42 U.S.C. § 1983 (Civil Rights Act of 1871), which provides for suits in equity or other proper proceedings to redress deprivations of federal constitutional rights under color of state authority, and claimed that the district court had jurisdiction under 28 U.S.C. § 1343(3). The plaintiffs further alleged that, despite the mandatory provisions for decennial reapportionment in article II, sections 4–6 of the Tennessee constitution, no reapportionment had been made by the legislature since the act of 1901. Other allegations were that (1) during the period intervening between the acts of 1901 and 1950 the population increased from 2,021,000 to 3,292,000 but the growth had been uneven among the counties; (2) 37 per cent of the voting population of the state controlled 20 of the 33 members of the senate and 40 per cent of the voting population controlled 63 of the 99 members of the house of representatives; (3) a minority ruled in Tennessee by virtue of control of the house and the senate; (4) there had been continuous and systematic discrimination by the legislature against the plaintiffs and those similarly situated, resulting in a denial of the equal protection of the laws guaranteed by the fourteenth amendment.

A three-judge federal district court was convened which dismissed the complaint on the grounds that the court lacked jurisdiction of the subject matter and the complaint failed to state a claim upon which relief could be granted. 179 F. Supp. 824 (M.D. Tenn. 1959).

The Supreme Court of the United States, Justice Brennan for the majority, reversed the lower court and held that (1) the court possessed jurisdiction of the subject matter; (2) a justiciable cause of action was stated; and (3) the plaintiffs had standing to challenge the Tennessee apportionment statutes. *Baker v. Carr*, 369 U.S. 186, 197–98 (1962). Justice Brennan noted that the district court rested its dismissal of the action upon lack of subject-matter jurisdiction and lack of a justiciable cause of action without attempting to distinguish between those two grounds. 369 U.S. at 196. "The distinction between the two grounds is significant. In the instance of nonjusticiability, consideration of the cause is not wholly and immediately foreclosed; rather the Court's inquiry necessarily proceeds to the point of deciding whether the duty asserted can be judicially identified and its breach judicially determined, and whether protection for the right asserted can be judicially molded. In the instance of lack of jurisdiction the cause either does not 'arise under' the Federal Constitution, laws or treaties (or fall within one of the other enumerated categories of Art. III, § 2), or is not a 'case or controversy' within the meaning of that section; or the cause is not one described by any jurisdictional statute." Id. at 198. Since the Court found it clear that the cause of action arises under the equal protection clause of the fourteenth amendment of the United States Constitution, the action could only be dismissed if it was deemed "frivolous" or "unsubstantial." Since the district court obviously did not so regard the action, it should not have been dismissed. Id. at 199.

On the question of standing the majority held that voters who allege facts showing disadvantage to themselves as individuals have standing to sue. They assert a plain, direct, and adequate interest in maintaining the effectiveness of their votes. Furthermore, the Court held it did not have to decide whether the plaintiffs' allegations of voter impairment entitled them to relief in order to decide that they have standing to seek it. Id. at 206–208.

On the question of justiciability the Court held that the challenge to an apportionment statute is not a "political question." "The cited cases do not hold the contrary." The district court had "misinterpreted" *Colegrove v. Green,* 328 U.S. 549 (1946), and other decisions relied upon. Id. at 209.

Justice Douglas, in a concurring opinion, "put to one side" the problem of "political questions," asserting that the question "is the extent to which a State may weight one person's vote more heavily than it does another's." Id. at 242. He reasoned that a state may not require impermissible voting standards, and that the traditional test under the equal protection clause has been whether a state has made an "invidious discrimination." "Universal equality is not the test; there is room for weighting." Id. at 244–45. He further asserted that the right to vote in both federal and state elections was protected by the judiciary long before that right received the explicit protection it is now accorded by federal statute. Id. at 247. As to the problem of remedies to be afforded, Justice Douglas pointed out that the district court need not undertake complete reapportionment. It might possibly achieve the goal

of substantial equality by directing the defendants to eliminate "egregious injustices." Or its conclusion that reapportionment should be made may in itself stimulate legislative action. Id. at 250, n.5.

Justice Clark, concurring, would have decided the case on the merits. He found the overall Tennessee constitutional formula not unreasonable although the statutes enacted pursuant to it were irrational. After comparing the voting strength of the various counties he found that "Tennessee's apportionment is a crazy quilt without rational basis." Id. at 254. Although Justice Clark found the Tennessee apportionment statute offensive to the equal protection clause, he said he would not consider intervention by the Court "if there were any other relief available to the people of Tennessee. But the majority of the people of Tennessee have no 'practical opportunities for exerting their political weight at the polls' to correct the existing 'invidious discrimination.' Tennessee has no initiative and referendum." Id. at 258–259.

In view of the Supreme Court ruling the governor of Tennessee called a special legislative session to consider the question of apportionment. A reapportionment act was passed in June 1962; but the district court, considering *Baker* on remand from the Supreme Court, held the provisions relating to both the house and the senate invalid. *Baker v. Carr,* 206 F. Supp. 341 (M.D. Tenn. 1962). The 1962 act had extended to floterial districts the principle in article II, section 5 of the state constitution, which permitted one representative to any county with two thirds of the voter ratio. While the court did not disapprove the two-thirds principle, the legislative application had produced inequalities which the court found unacceptable. The two-thirds principle was described as designed "to afford a measure of protection to governmental units or subdivisions of the state not having a sufficient number of voters to equal a full ratio but yet having a substantial population and possessing significant and substantial interests in state legislative policy. Such a state plan . . . at least in one house of a bicameral legislature, cannot . . . be characterized as per se irrational or arbitrary. . . . The state has the right, if it sees fit, to assure that its smaller and less populous areas and communities are not completely overridden by sheer weight of numbers." Id. at 345–46.

The senate reapportionment, on the other hand, was found to be "devoid of any standard or rational plan of classification." There was no pretense of equality or substantial equality in numbers of qualified voters. Nor were the districts even remotely equal in area. Id. at 346–47.

The court considered various possible remedies and concluded that the best solution was to permit the general assembly itself to reconsider the problem with the help of certain "minimal standards" required to meet the test of equal protection. "[I]f the two-thirds principle should be applied and used in apportioning seats in the House of Representatives, either by applying it to counties or floterial districts, or to both, then it would follow that the Senate would have to be apportioned on the basis alone of numbers of qualified voters. Contrariwise, if the Senate should be apportioned on an equitable and rational basis not fully related to voting strength, it would be necessary to apportion the House of Representatives on the basis of numbers of qualified voters alone, without regard to the two-thirds principle whether applied to

counties or districts or both. . . . [A]pportionment in at least one house shall be based, fully and in good faith, on numbers of qualified voters without regard to any other factor." Id. at 349.

At its regular 1963 session the general assembly again enacted apportionment legislation. Tenn. Code Ann. §§ 3-101 to 3-107 (Supp. 1963). The plaintiffs filed a supplemental complaint alleging that the 1963 apportionments of both the house and the senate were violative of the equal protection clause, arguing that any substantial departure from numbers is forbidden in both houses and that the court should give effect to the principle that "one person equals one vote." The district court in October 1963 reasserted its conclusion that "equal protection should not be construed in such a way as to deny to a state the right in distributing its legislative strength to give a rational recognition to both geography and population." 222 F. Supp. at 686. The apportionment of the house was held valid, since it eliminated the inequalities of the 1962 act. The senate plan, however, was declared invalid, since the senate committee decided to take factors other than population into account in the 1963 apportionment. In so doing the legislature had deviated from the direction of the court that one house should be apportioned on the basis of qualified voters without regard to any other factor. Instead of allowing the legislature to reapportion the senate once more, the court set forth its own plan (submitted by the plaintiffs). Retaining jurisdiction, the court gave defendants until February 3, 1964, to file objections to the court's proposal or to submit an alternative. 222 F. Supp. at 694–95. In June 1964 the three-judge federal district court directed that the apportionment plan proposed by the plaintiffs would go into effect if the legislature failed to make a valid reapportionment by June 1, 1965.

In May 1965 the legislature reapportioned both houses of the Tennessee legislature, and the governor signed the acts into law on May 28. In disregard of a ruling of the state attorney general that counties may not be divided to form senatorial districts, the legislature divided the five most populous counties into districts for the election of both senators and representatives. It was said that as a result Republicans were assured of increased representation in both houses, and that the election of more Negroes (one in 1965) was probable. N.Y. Times, May 29, 1965, p. 9, col. 2. In September 1965 the federal court heard argument on the validity of the new legislation, but did not immediately decide the issue.

Meanwhile, plans were laid for a constitutional convention to be held in the summer of 1965 to consider comprehensive changes in the constitutional provisions relating to the legislature, including reapportionment. 54 Nat'l Civ. Rev. 199 (April 1965).

A constitutional amendment proposed in the senate or the house must first be approved by a majority of both houses and again by a two-thirds vote of the members of the general assembly next chosen. The proposal is then submitted to the people at the next general election at which a governor is to be chosen. If a majority of the citizens voting thereon approve, the amendment becomes part of the constitution. Tenn. Const., art. XI, § 3, as amended in 1953.

The legislature may submit to the people at any general election the question of whether to call a convention to consider specified proposals. Proposals adopted at the convention do not become effective unless approved by a majority of the qualified voters voting

separately on each proposed change or amendment at an election fixed by the convention. Conventions may not be held oftener than once in six years. Ibid. There is no provision for the popular initiative or referendum in Tennessee. See *Baker v. Carr*, 369 U.S. 186, 258–59 (1962) (Clark, J., concurring).

Tennessee is divided into nine congressional districts. Tenn. Code Ann. § 2-502. The 1960 population of Tennessee was 3,567,089, and the congressional population mean was 396,343. However, through the November 1964 elections the largest district contained 627,019 persons while the smallest had only 223,387 inhabitants.

On May 28, 1965, the governor approved redistricting legislation that reduced the population disparities among the congressional districts to 33 per cent between the largest and smallest districts. To minimize the changes in the districts and to reduce the chance for the election of a Negro, Shelby County (including Memphis), the ninth district, was divided between the seventh and eighth districts, which were expected to remain in control of rural west Tennessee counties. N.Y. Times, May 29, 1965, p. 9., col. 2. A challenge to the act was heard in federal court in September 1965.

REFERENCES

Crane, Wilder. "Tennessee: Inertia and the Courts," in Jewell, Malcolm E. (editor), The Politics of Reapportionment. New York: Atherton Press. 1962.

Nashville, City of. Legislative Apportionment in Tennessee, 1901–1961. Nashville: 1961.

Tennessee State Legislative Council Committee. Legislative Apportionment Study 1962. Final Report, FR 1962-B5. Nashville: 1962.

———. Tennessee Legislative Apportionment and the Courts. Nashville: April 1965.

Tennessee, University of. Memorandum on Legislative Reapportionment in Tennessee. Knoxville: Bureau of Public Administration. 1961.

Williams, Henry N. Legislative Apportionment in Tennessee, 20 Tenn. L. Rev. 235 (1948).

TEXAS

Although what is now the state of Texas has at one time or another been under the dominion of no fewer than six sovereign states, it is here sufficient to begin with the 1836 declaration of independence from Mexico and the recognition of the independence of the republic of Texas by other powers, including the United States in 1837.

The constitution of 1836 provided for a house of representatives of not less than 24 nor more than 40 members (subject to expansion to a maximum of 100 when the population should exceed 100,000), each county to have at least one representative. Const. of Republic of Tex. of 1836, art. I, § 5. The senate was to have not less than one third nor more than one half the membership of the house; and the senators were to be chosen from districts "as nearly equal in free population (free negroes and Indians excepted) as practicable; . . . ." Id., art. I, § 7. Until the completion of the first enumeration, and pending the division of the republic into counties (id., art. IV, § 11), the constitution provided by schedule for the apportionment of 32 representatives and 14 senators among the 23 precincts, as the political units were then known. Id., schedule, §§ 6, 7.

By joint resolution in 1845 Congress offered statehood to Texas, the Texans accepted, and the state was formally admitted to the Union. The Texas constitution of 1845 provided for a house of representatives of not less than 45 nor more than 90 members and a senate of not less than 19 nor more than 33. Tex. Const. of 1845, art. III, §§ 29, 31. The legislature was directed to arrange at its first session for a census, as well as in 1848, 1850, and every eight years thereafter, "of all the free inhabitants (Indians not taxed, Africans and descendants of Africans excepted)"; and the representatives were to be apportioned "among the several counties, cities, or towns, according to the number of free population in each; . . . ." Id., art. III, § 29. The senators were to be apportioned "according to the number of qualified electors . . . ." Id., art. III, § 31. Until the first census should be taken the constitution apportioned 66 representatives and 21 senators among the then 36 counties, giving each county from one to five representatives, but using multiple-county districts and one floterial district in the senate. Id., art. III, §§ 30, 32.

In 1861 an ordinance of secession was adopted by a "people's convention" and ratified by the people; but the changes in the constitution, which survived until 1866, were not submitted to the people. The constitution of 1866 continued the provisions of the 1845 constitution without significant change except that the census, now to be taken in 1875 and every ten years thereafter, was to include "all the inhabitants (including Indians taxed) of the State, designating particularly the number of qualified electors and the age, sex, and color of all others . . . ." Tex. Const. of 1866, art. III, § 28. "White population" was maintained as the basis for the apportionment of the house of representatives and "qualified electors" as the basis for apportionment of the senate. Id., art. III, §§ 28, 30.

The constitution of 1869, framed by a convention called pursuant to the congressional reconstruction acts and approved by Congress in 1870 as the basis for readmission of Texas to representation in the Union, required reapportionment by the legislature at its first session after each census authorized by law, retaining the concept of apportionment "according to the number of qualified electors . . . ." Tex. Const. of 1869, art. III, § 34. "Until otherwise provided by law," the then 153 counties were divided into 30 districts consisting of from one to 21 counties, from which 30 senators and 90 representatives were to be elected. Id., art. III, §§ 39, 40.

The present Texas constitution, framed at a convention in 1875, was ratified by the people in 1876. That constitution provided originally (and currently) for a house of representatives of 93 members which could be enlarged with population growth to a maximum of 150. Tex. Const. of 1876, art. III, § 2.

Representation in the house is to be apportioned among the counties according to the total population of the state, "as nearly as may be." The unit of representation is a "ratio obtained by dividing the population of the State, as ascertained by the most recent United States census, by the number of members of which the House is composed." (The population of the state is divided by 150.) The constitutional limitations are: (1) Whenever a single county has sufficient population to be entitled to a representative, that county must be made a separate district. (2) Counties not having the required population must be joined to another contiguous county or counties. (3) Counties with populations in excess of the ratio must be given additional representation. (4) Where a county has a surplus of population beyond the ratio for one or more representatives, but short of another ratio, it may be joined with a contiguous county or counties in a representative district and is permit-

ted to elect a floterial representative as a means of providing representation for the extra population. Id., art. III, § 26. However, this rule of equality was undermined in 1936 by a constitutional amendment limiting to seven the number of representatives from any one county unless that county's population should exceed 700,000, in which event an additional representative is allowed for each 100,000 additional persons residing therein. Id., art. III, § 26(a), as amended in 1936. The interpretive commentary to article III, section 26 states that "This amendment [§ 26(a)] shows the continuation of the old rivalry between rural and urban areas, and is a discrimination in favor of the former. As such, it aids in permitting the rural areas to maintain their supremacy in the House of Representatives."

Although the constitution of 1876 required the legislature to reapportion after each decennial census, as of 1948 there had been no reapportionment since 1921. Under the doctrine of separation of powers, the courts did not intervene to compel the legislature to perform a legislative duty. Therefore, there was no method to force the legislature to reapportion even though it had violated a constitutional duty. Tex. Const., art. III, § 28, interpretive commentary. With this in mind, a new method of enforcement was added by constitutional amendment in 1948. Now, if the legislature fails to reapportion at its first regular session after the publication of the United States decennial census, reapportionment is to be accomplished by a legislative redistricting board, composed of the lieutenant governor, the speaker of the house of representatives, the attorney general, the land commissioner, and the comptroller. The board is required to meet 60 days after the adjournment of the legislature which failed to reapportion, and is to reapportion by majority vote. Such apportionment, when executed, has the force and effect of law. Jurisdiction is given to the supreme court of Texas to compel the board to perform its duties. Tex. Const., art. III, § 28, as amended in 1948.

Membership in the senate shall "never be increased" above 31 members. The state must be divided into senatorial districts composed of contiguous territory, according to the number of qualified electors, "as nearly as may be." However, the population basis is limited by the proviso that "no single county shall be entitled to more than one senator." Id., art. III, § 25.

Between the years 1961 and 1965 30 per cent of Texas voters could elect a majority of the senators. The population of the state (9,579,677) divided by 31 yields a senatorial population mean of 309,022. The largest senatorial district (No. 6) had a population of 1,243,158 and the smallest (No. 16) a population of only 147,454. A vote of citizens in the essentially urban senatorial districts (Nos. 6, 8, 10, 26 and 29) was worth less than one half the vote of the citizens in the 21 smallest districts.

Disparities were also present in the representative districts. The smallest district was composed of 33,987 persons, while the largest had 105,725. Thirty-eight per cent of the population could elect a majority of the house.

In *Kilgarlin v. Martin*, Civ. Action No. 63-H-390 (S.D. Tex. 1964) the "one county" senatorial restriction of article III, section 25 of the Texas constitution was challenged, as was the provision in article III, section 26(a)

that no county may have more than seven representatives unless its population exceeds 700,000 people. The three-judge federal district court upheld these challenges to require reapportionment to meet the constitutional standard of reasonable equality.

In May 1965 the legislature responded by reapportioning both houses in approximation of equality among the election districts. County lines were crossed in several instances, and floterial districts were again used in the house. Tex. Laws 1965, cc. 342, 351. In addition, an amendment was proposed to sections 2 and 25 of article III of the state constitution, calling for a senate of 39 and a house of 150, and providing specifically that the state should be divided into senatorial districts "of contiguous territory according to population, as nearly as possible." Id., S.J.R. No. 44.

The legislature, by a two-thirds vote of all members elected to each house, may propose a constitutional amendment. Ratification is effective by a simple majority of all voters who cast votes on the question; and the amendment becomes operative on the proclamation of the governor. Constitutional amendments cannot be proposed at special sessions of the legislature. Tex. Const., art. XVII, § 1.

There are no provisions requiring or forbidding the call of a constitutional convention, nor are there provisions concerning the initiative and referendum.

Of the 23 congressmen to which Texas is currently entitled, until 1965 22 were elected from statutory districts and one was elected at large. Tex. Election Code Ann. art. 197(a). This act was held unconstitutional in *Bush v. Martin*, 224 F. Supp. 499 (S.D. Tex. 1963), affirmed, 376 U.S. 222 (1964). The three-judge federal district court found the population disparity among the Texas congressional districts "indeed spectacular" in its extreme variations from a low of 216,371 to 951,527. Marked underrepresentation was "not surprisingly" found in the metropolitan areas. But the disparity was not confined to the cities. 224 F. Supp. at 505. Only once since 1933 has Texas made any redistricting, and this was done in 1957 (the act under attack) with only one significant change. The 1963 legislature failed to pass, after considerable debate, a congressional redistricting bill. However, the trial court found that even the rejected proposals did not "begin to provide a reasonably equal reapportionment." Id. at 507.

The lower court held that plaintiffs established a clear case of invidious discrimination. Consequently, the whole of article 197(a) was held unconstitutional, and its enforcement was enjoined. The court also observed that if the legislature failed to redistrict, all congressmen would have to be elected at large. Id. at 516. The United States Supreme Court affirmed the judgment on the authority of *Wesberry v. Sanders*, 376 U.S. 1 (1964), but continued the stay previously granted by Justice Black "in light of the present circumstances including the imminence of the forthcoming election and 'the operation of the election machinery of Texas'. . . ." 376 U.S. 222, 223 (1964).

In May 1965 the legislature redrew the district lines to meet the federal court's demands, now providing that all 23 should be elected from single-member districts. In several instances county lines were crossed. The most interesting was Bexar County (San Antonio) in which the center city becomes the 20th district while the remainder of the

county is divided between the 21st and 23d districts. Tex. Laws 1965, c. 349.

REFERENCES

Cherry, H. Dicken. "Texas: Factions in a One-Party Setting," in Jewell, Malcolm E. (ed.). The Politics of Reapportionment. New York: Atherton Press. 1962.
MacCorkle, Stuart A. Texas Apportionment Problem, 34 Nat'l Munic. Rev. 540 (1945).

UTAH

The territory of Utah was created by act of Congress in 1850 to encompass the present states of Utah and Nevada as well as parts of Colorado and Wyoming. Legislative power was vested in the governor and a legislative assembly consisting of a 13-member council and a 26-member house of representatives. The governor was directed to have a census of the inhabitants taken before the first election, after which he was to make an apportionment for both houses "as nearly equal as practicable, among the several counties or districts . . , giving to each section of the Territory representation in the ratio of its population, Indians excepted, as nearly as may be." Sec. 4.

In 1894 Congress adopted an enabling act for the preparation of a constitution with the prospect of statehood upon its approval. The act provided for 107 delegates to the constitutional convention, to be chosen in numbers of from one to 29 from each of the then 26 counties. The convention so authorized met and in 1895 drafted the constitution which has ever since served the state. The President of the United States found the constitution "republican in form" and proclaimed the admission of Utah into the Union in 1896.

The constitution of 1895 provided originally for an 18-member senate and a 45-member house of representatives, but authorized the legislature to enlarge those numbers to a total senate membership of no more than 30, and a number of representatives never to be less than twice nor more than three times the number of senators. Utah Const., art. IX, § 3. The legislature was directed to provide for a census of the inhabitants of the state in 1905 and every tenth year thereafter. At the session next following such state enumeration, and at the session next following a federal census, the legislature is now directed to reapportion both the senatorial and the representative districts "on the basis of such enumeration according to ratios to be fixed by law." Id., art. IX, § 2. However, the population basis for apportionment is limited by the provision that each county is to be allotted at least one representative. Senatorial districts composed of more than one county must be contiguous. No county may be divided in the formation of senatorial districts unless that county contains sufficient population within itself to form two or more districts. Parts of counties may not be united with any other county in forming any senatorial district. Id., art. IX, § 4.

The most recent reapportionment of legislative districts before 1965 was in 1963. The house of representatives then consisted of 69 members elected from 29 districts (each representative district is a county) on the basis of a house ratio of one representative to each 16,000 inhabitants residing within the representative district. Utah Code Ann. § 36-1-2 (Supp. 1963). This ratio somewhat distorted the population basis for representation in view of the fact that the 1960 population of Utah (890,627) divided by 69 yields a representative

population mean of 12,907, substantially below the ratio of 16,000 fixed by the legislature.

The senate consisted of 27 members elected from 18 districts on the basis of one senator for the first 20,000 inhabitants or major fraction thereof, and one additional senator for each additional 61,000 inhabitants, or major fraction thereof, residing within the senatorial district. Utah Code Ann. § 36-1-1 (Supp. 1963). Thus, in order for a district to be entitled to an additional senator, it must have had approximately three times the ratio needed for one senator. The 1960 population (890,-627) divided by 27 yielded a senatorial population mean of 32,986. But under applicable law more than twice that number was needed in order for a senatorial district to qualify for two senators (20,000 plus 61,000), while 142,000 inhabitants were needed to qualify a district for three senators, and so on. It is evident that, as a result, the Utah senatorial districts were substantially unequal in population, in each case to the disadvantage of the most populous counties. (Salt Lake County had seven senators; Weber, Utah, and Davis Counties had two senators each; and the rest of the districts had one senator each.)

A 1955 act with similar provisions (a first ratio of 19,000 and a second ratio of 55,000) was upheld by the supreme court of Utah in *Parkinson v. Watson*, 4 Utah 2d 191, 291 P.2d 400 (1955), relying in part on a decision of the supreme court of Colorado upholding similar legislation on which the Utah act had been modeled. *Armstrong v. Mitten*, 95 Colo. 425, 37 P.2d 757 (1934).

Under the provisions of the 1963 apportionment each county entitled to more than one member in the house of representatives and/or in the senate was to be divided into legislative districts by a committee consisting of five voters from that county. Two members were to be appointed by the county Republican party executive committee and two by the county Democratic executive committee; one was to be elected by a majority vote of the other four. In dividing the county into districts, the committee was to "take into consideration the population and physical features of the county and shall make the districts as near equal in population as may be most practicable; provided, that representative districts shall not be divided in the formation of senatorial districts." Utah Code Ann. § 36-1-4 (Supp. 1963).

In *Petuskey v. Clyde*, 234 F. Supp. 960 (D. Utah 1964) a three-judge federal district court held unconstitutional the 1963 reapportionment of both houses of the legislature and the constitutional provisions on which the 1963 act was based. The court found it "unnecessary to elaborate upon the obvious and simple fact" that neither house satisfied the constitutional standard; and it concluded that "the restrictive provisions of the Utah Constitution are in irreconcilable conflict with the Constitution of the United States . . . ." Id. at 963–964. While retaining jurisdiction pending legislative correction, a majority of the court thought it neither necessary nor desirable to suggest any particular plan. Judge Ritter, however, disagreed on this point and offered a specific plan which, if adopted, would provide near-equality among the election districts in each house. Id. at 968–977.

In May 1965 the Utah legislature reapportioned both houses of the legislature and provided that in each county entitled to multiple representation an apportionment committee for that county (constituted as before) should draw the district lines to insure that both senatorial and representative district lines should be "as nearly equal as possible in population." Utah Laws 1965, c. 72, § 4. In the basic act of reapportionment the senate was fixed at 28 and the house of representatives at 69. The adjustments to population authorized 11 senators and 28 representatives for Salt Lake County; 3 senators and 8 representatives for Weber County and for Utah County; and 2 senators and 5 representatives for Davis County. Corresponding adjustments were made elsewhere, including two senatorial districts in each of which five counties were cumulated to make a single district. No county lines were crossed. Id., §§ 1, 3. The effective date for the election of senators was delayed until the 1968 elections; but the federal court ordered it into effect in 1966. *Petuskey v. Rampton*, 243 F. Supp. 365 (D. Utah 1965).

Amendments may be proposed by two thirds of the members elected to both houses of the legislature. If a majority of the electors voting thereon approve them, such amendments become part of the constitution. Utah Const., art. XXIII, § 1.

Two thirds of the members of both houses may recommend to the voters that a constitutional convention be called. A majority of the electors voting must approve the proposal. Id., art. XXIII, § 2. Amendments adopted by the convention must be approved by a majority of the electors voting at the next general election. Id., art. XXIII, § 3.

The powers of the initiative and the referendum are reserved to the people. Id., art. VI, § 1.

The district lines for Utah's two congressional districts were drawn in 1913. In terms of 1960 population, the more populous district has 572,654 inhabitants and the smaller has only 317,973 inhabitants.

REFERENCES

Note, Utah Law Providing a Double Ratio for Reapportionment of the Senate Held Constitutional, 5 Utah L. Rev. 112 (1956).

VERMONT

As late as the American Revolution the present state of Vermont was claimed not only by the British, but by Massachusetts, New Hampshire, and New York. Massachusetts relinquished her claims in 1781, as did New Hampshire in 1782; but it was not until 1790 that New York assented to the admission of Vermont into the Union. Accordingly, the first constitution of Vermont, framed in 1777 shortly after the citizens of Vermont declared it a free and independent state, included in its preamble a recital of complaints against New York. The governmental structure established in that first constitution was retained almost without change in the successive constitutions of 1786 and 1793, all providing that "the supreme legislative power Shall be vested in a House of Representatives . . . ." Vt. Consts. of 1777, 1786, 1793, c. II, § 2.

The concept of representation by towns in the lower house appeared first in the constitution of 1777 (c. II, § 16) and was continued in each successor constitution. Vt. Const. of 1913, c. II, § 13. The predecessor of the present senate, however, was essentially an arm of the executive branch and thus quite different from its modern counterpart. The supreme executive council was to consist of the governor, the lieutenant governor, and a 12-member council of safety, all to be chosen by the freemen of the various towns in Vermont. Vt. Const. of 1777, c. II, § 17; Vt. Const. of 1786, c. II, § 10; Vt. Const. of 1793, c. II, § 10. Finally, these early Vermont constitutions, drawing upon Pennsylvania experience, provided for a 13-member council of censors to be chosen by vote of the freemen in the various towns. The council's function was to insure "that the freedom of this Commonwealth may be preserved inviolate, forever, ..." To achieve that objective the council was directed to ascertain whether the legislative and executive branches were faithful in performance of duty, to determine whether taxes were justly laid and collected, and to inquire into the expenditure of public monies. Given the subpena power, they were authorized to bring impeachments, to recommend repeal of laws, and to call constitutional conventions, all for "the preservation of the rights and happiness of the people; . . . ." Vt. Const. of 1777, c. II, § 44; Vt. Const. of 1786, c. II, § 40; Vt. Const. of 1793, c. II, § 43. (The conventions which approved the constitutions of 1786 and 1793 were both convened at the call of the council of censors and simply approved or rejected proposals of that body. A number of changes during the nineteenth century were initiated by the council of censors until its functions were given to the legislature by amendments adopted in 1870 and 1913.)

Through constitutional amendment adopted in convention in 1836 the legislature became bicameral, thereafter consisting of a house of representatives (without change in composition) and a 30-member senate. It was provided that each of the then 13 counties should be entitled to at least one senator, and the remainder should be "apportioned to the several Counties according to their population," taken from the last federal census. The functions of the now-discontinued council of safety were principally committed to the governor and, in minor respects, to the newly created senate. Vt. Const., arts. of amendment 2-11 of 1836.

The apportionment provisions until 1965 were, with minor changes, the same as those which had been formulated by the time of the 1836 amendments. Under the provisions of that formula each inhabited town in Vermont, regardless of its population, chose one representative to the house of representatives. Vt. Const. of 1913, c. II, § 13. Severe malapportionment was the inevitable result. The smallest town, with 38 inhabitants in 1960, was represented equally with the largest city, with a 1960 population of 35,531. Consequently, 11.8 per cent of the population was able to elect a majority of the 246 members of the lower house. Unwieldy though this number may seem to non-Vermonters, a proposal to reduce the number of representatives from 246 to 100 was handily defeated at the 1961 session. Similarly, until 1965 every proposal to apportion the house in accordance with population had failed.

The 30 senators were apportioned among the 14 counties according to population, "regard being always had, in such apportionment, to the counties having the largest fraction, and each county being given at least one Senator." Vt. Const. of 1913, c. II, § 18.

Reapportionment is made a legislative obligation after each federal census or any census taken for this purpose under state authority. Ibid. However, there was no revision of senatorial districts between 1941 and 1965.

In *Mikell v. Rousseau*, 123 Vt. 139, 183 A.2d 817 (1962) plaintiffs claimed that the legislative failure to reapportion after 1941, as required by chapter II, section 18 of the state constitution, resulted in an unconstitutionally constituted state senate. The Vermont Supreme Court agreed, but allowed the legislature additional time to reapportion the senate. The court also found it "apparent" that a senatorial apportionment could not be effected on an exact population basis because of the constitutional limitation on membership to 30 senators and the assurance of at least one senator for each of the 14 counties. 183 A.2d at 821. "The constitutional concern is representation in the Senate according to population. The constitutional result is the one which achieves the least disparity in the number of persons represented by each Senator." Id. at 822.

Minor adjustments in the senate apportionment were made in a special session of the legislature in 1962. V.S.A. Title 17, c. 17.

In *Buckley v. Hoff*, 234 F. Supp. 191 (D. Vt. 1964), modified and affirmed sub. nom. *Parsons v. Buckley*, 379 U.S. 359 (1965), the reapportionment provisions of the Vermont constitution were directly challenged for the first time. The three-judge federal district court, in an opinion announced a few weeks after the Supreme Court decision of the *Reapportionment Cases*, held invalid the apportionment formula for both houses of the state legislature. The court enjoined the relevant state officials as parties defendant from proceeding with further elections under the invalid formula after 1964. However, the court further provided that if the legislature to convene in January 1965 was chosen by the invalid method, its authority to legislate should be "limited to the devising of a constitutional method of reapportionment and redistricting, and that the terms of such members shall expire on March 31, 1965." 234 F. Supp. at 201.

On appeal to the Supreme Court of the United States all parties agreed by stipulation to a modification of the order of the lower court, and the Supreme Court adopted the terms of the stipulation on January 12, 1965. 379 U.S. 359 (1965). Under the terms of the modified order the legislature was allowed to conduct its normal legislative functions so long as a specified timetable of reapportionment steps was satisfied, the aim of which would be reapportionment of the legislature either by legislation or by convention, all to be completed in time for a validly constituted legislature to be convened in January 1966.

After some hesitation the legislature complied with the order, meeting the judicial deadline of July 1, 1965, for the fixing of elections in the fall of 1965 on the basis of a new formula. As a temporary measure the legislature reapportioned the house, creating single- and multimember districts for the election of 150 members allocated on the basis of registered voters. A second measure established an apportionment board to apportion the senate on the basis of population after each federal census and to apportion the house on the basis of registered voters following each second presidential election after 1964. No house district may deviate from the population ratio by more than 15 per cent. Review is authorized in the state supreme court by five or more "freemen of the state." The court promptly approved the plan for both houses provided the elections were held in accordance with that formula. *Buckley v. Hoff,* 243 F. Supp. 873 (D. Vt. 1965).

Changes in the constitution of Vermont may ordinarily be made only once every ten years. (The changes in apportionment formula are an exception prompted by federal constitutional necessity.) The senate, by a two-thirds vote of its members, may propose a constitutional amendment. If such an amendment is concurred in by a majority of the members of the house, it is referred to the next session of the general assembly. If a majority of both houses at the next session approves such amendment, it may then be referred to the people for majority ratification. Vt. Const., c. II, § 68.

Vermont elects only one United States representative, but provision is made for a division of the state into two congressional districts in the event that the state should ever be entitled to two representatives. V.S.A. § 1561.

VIRGINIA

The first permanent English settlement in North America was made in what is now the Commonwealth of Virginia. Acting under the authority of the first Charter of Virginia (1606), in which James I of England made extensive grants to a group of adventurers formed into the London Company, the expedition landed at Jamestown in 1607 and thereafter established a number of plantations along the James River. The London Company, and thus the new colony, was originally governed by a crown-appointed council of 13 through successive reissues of the charter in 1609 and 1612, each reconfirming the grant of authority and defining more precisely the territorial limits of the colony. By 1619 the first representative assembly in North America had been established, the Virginia House of

Burgesses, which was essentially a meeting of planters to assist the governor and council. In 1621 the London Company was granted authority to appoint the governor and council, while the colonists annually chose delegates to the House of Burgesses from their counties, towns, hundreds, and plantations.

By the time the Declaration of Independence was issued by the Continental Congress, Virginia freeholders had already assembled in convention to draft a new constitution. One proposal, containing universal suffrage, proportional representation, and religious freedom, was offered by Thomas Jefferson, but rejected. Instead, the constitution of 1776 set forth a representation formula which allowed the older counties a large majority in the new legislature, on the theory that the preponderance of property (slavery) in that section required such security against the rising democracy in the "new west."

The constitution of 1776 provided for a general assembly consisting of a house of delegates and a senate. The house of delegates was to include two representatives from each county, two from the district of West-Augusta, and one each from Williamsburg, Norfolk, and "such other cities and boroughs, as may hereafter be allowed particular representation by the legislature . . . ." Va. Const. of 1776 (sections unnumbered). The senate was to consist of 24 members to be elected from single-member districts into which "the different counties shall be divided . . . ." Ibid.

The constitution of 1830 made more specific the practice of representation in the house of delegates by areas of the state. The 134 delegates were divided into four regions of the state: 31 to be chosen from the 26 counties west of the Allegheny Mountains; 25 from the 14 counties between the Allegheny and

Blue Ridge mountains; 42 from the 29 counties east of the Blue Ridge Mountains and above tidewater; and 36 from the 37 counties and three separately represented municipalities in the tidewater area. The constitution further specified the number of representatives allotted to each county, city, town, and borough within the enumerated areas. Va. Const. of 1830, art. III, § 2. Similarly, the 32 members of the senate were apportioned among the counties, but with an area differentiation which specified that 13 should be assigned west of the Blue Ridge Mountains and 19 east of that dividing line. Id., art. III, § 3. The legislature was directed to reapportion in 1841 and every ten years thereafter, provided "That the number of delegates from the aforesaid great districts, and the number of senators from the aforesaid two great divisions, respectively, shall neither be increased nor diminished by such reapportionment." Id., art. III, § 4.

The constitution of 1850 enlarged the house of delegates to 152 and specified the apportionment by county and city. The range was from three representatives for each of two counties and for the city of Richmond to one representative for a multiple-county district of four counties. Floterial representation was also established, and provision was made for rotation of representation in the house of delegates between two counties with population beyond the representative ratio in alternating sessions. Va. Const. of 1850, art. IV, § 2. Representation in accordance with population was also sought in the senate, now increased to 50 members, by providing 50 senatorial districts consisting of varying numbers of counties, and also employing the floterial principle to equalize population differentials. Id., art. IV, § 3. An interesting addition to the provision for decennial reapportionment from and after 1865 was a requirement that, in the event of legislative failure to act, the governor should propose to the voters which of the following apportionment formulas should be adopted: (1) representation in both houses on a "suffrage basis," according to the number of voters; (2) representation in both houses on a "mixed basis," with equal weight given to the number of white inhabitants and the amount of taxes paid; (3) representation solely on the basis of taxes paid; and (4) representation in the senate on the "mixed basis" and in the house on the "suffrage basis." Id., art. IV, § 5.

An ordinance of secession was adopted by convention, and the constitution was amended in 1861. That constitution was further amended in 1864 to reduce the number of delegates to not more than 104 and the senate to 34. Va. Const. of 1864, art. IV, §§ 2, 5. The apportionment among the then 101 counties, and the cities of Norfolk, Petersburg, Richmond, and Williamsburg, was made in the constitution (id., art. IV, §§ 4, 5); and reapportionment was made a legislative duty in 1870 and every ten years thereafter "from an enumeration of the inhabitants of the State" (id., art. IV, § 6).

The constitution of 1870 was framed by a convention called pursuant to the congressional reconstruction acts as a condition of readmission of Virginia to congressional representation. Population was given scant attention in the apportionment among the 101 counties and several cities of 132 delegates into 96 districts, of which only two were entitled to more than three delegates. Va. Const. of 1870, art. V, § 2. The senate, which was to be divided into not more

than 40 districts, probably provided a closer approximation to representation in accordance with population although there was no specific requirement to that effect. Id., art. V, § 3. However, these provisions lasted only until 1876 when they were supplanted by a constitutional amendment providing that after 1879 the house should have not more than 100 and not less than 90 members, while the senate should be fixed at not more than 40 and not less than 33 members, leaving the reapportionment itself to the legislature not later than 1879, again in 1891, and every ten years thereafter. Va. Const. of 1870, art. V, §§ 2–4, as amended in 1876.

The provisions were carried over into the constitution of 1902 and have been controlling ever since. Va. Const. of 1902, art. IV, §§ 41–43. Thus, what had been one of the most detailed constitutional prescriptions became as short as any, leaving the apportionment to the legislature with no constitutional guidance at all.

By statute the number of senators has been fixed at 40 and the number of delegates at 100. Although the constitution specifies that reapportionment is required decennially, there are no express standards to guide the general assembly in apportioning the senators and the delegates into various districts. The establishment of districts is implicitly left to the discretion of the legislature. (The constitution does, however, impose limits on legislative discretion in forming congressional districts, which must be contiguous, compact, and contain as nearly as practicable an equal number of inhabitants. Va. Const., art. IX, § 55.)

Since 1900 the Virginia general assembly has consistently followed the constitutional mandate to reapportion decennially, including the 1962 reapportionment. Va. Code Ann. §§ 24-12, 24-14 (Supp. 1963). In a 1961 report by the commission on redistricting to the governor and the general assembly, which had preceded the 1962 act, the commission stated that it had attempted, in its proposal, to keep in mind the factors of compactness, contiguity, ease of access and communication, community of interest, and a "reasonable degree of equality of representation." In addition, the commission reasoned that since an occasional district which may be underrepresented in the house may be overrepresented in the senate, "the combined representation of the House and Senate should be considered in determining the extent of over or under-representation in the area." Virginia Commission on Redistricting, Report on Reapportionment of the State for Representation, pp. 7–8 (1961).

The 1962 apportionment statutes established 36 senatorial districts, among which the 40 senatorial positions were distributed, and 70 delegate districts for the 100 delegates. The act was challenged by voters residing in Arlington and Fairfax Counties and in the city of Norfolk. They complained that the 1962 apportionment reduced the value of votes in their districts below that of the votes in other senatorial and delegate districts. It was shown that the legislation produced disparities in terms of voter representation of more than two to one in the senate and more than four to one in the house of delegates.

The three-judge federal district court held that this inequality amounted to invidious discrimination for the reason that the "Equal Protection Clause of the Fourteenth Amendment . . . demands that this apportionment accord the citizens of the State substantially equal representation." Moreover, the court found that population has historically been the principal factor in redistricting in Virginia, although never the exclusive criterion. *Mann v. Davis,* 213 F. Supp. 577 (E.D. Va. 1962).

The majority of the court found "no rational basis for the disfavoring of Arlington, Fairfax and Norfolk." Id. at 585. A judgment was entered declaring the acts invalid and enjoining further proceedings thereunder, but staying operation of the injunction until January 31, 1963, to allow corrective action by the general assembly in a special session, or to allow the defendants to appeal to the United States Supreme Court. On December 15, 1962, this stay was further extended by Chief Justice Warren.

The Supreme Court of the United States affirmed the judgment of the lower court and remanded the case to that court "for further proceedings consistent with the views stated here and in our opinion in *Reynolds v. Sims.*" *Davis v. Mann,* 377 U.S. 678, 693 (1964). The Court also observed that it would be inappropriate to consider specific remedies since the next session of the Virginia legislature would not occur until 1965, thus allowing ample time for legislative action. (The opinion is more fully discussed in chapter V, supra.)

On remand the three-judge district court held that the general assembly elected in 1963 under the invalidated statute must expire as to both houses not later than the second Wednesday in January 1966. Meanwhile, the court ruled that the legislature should first enact a constitutionally valid reapportionment plan, after which it could turn to other regular legislative business. The legislature was given from the date of the opinion (September 28, 1964) until December 15, 1964, to act. *Mann v. Davis*, 238 F. Supp. 458 (E.D. Va. 1964), aff'd, 379 U.S. 694 (1965).

Early in December 1964 the legislature in special session approved a reapportionment almost exactly in the form recommended by a legislative study committee. In the 40-member senate two seats went to the Hampton Roads area and one to northern Virginia, while in the 100-member house northern Virginia was awarded five more seats and Hampton Roads three more. The losers were the less populous sections of Virginia in the mountainous southwest, the tobacco-growing Southside, and the Shenandoah Valley. N.Y. Times, Dec. 6, 1964, p. 70, col. 1. See Va. Code Ann. §§ 24-12, 24-14 (Supp. 1964).

One feature of the new plan was greeted with some dissatisfaction and a judicial challenge. The city of Richmond and the adjoining urbanized Henrico County were combined into a single district sharing eight senators. Some legislators were quoted as having said privately that the dual representation for county and city was designed to dissipate the power of Richmond's Negro voters. However, when the issue was presented to the federal court in the form of a petition to intervene in the original judicial proceeding (of which the court had retained jurisdiction), the court refused to require separation of the eight-member district into single-member constituencies. At the same time the court rejected efforts by Henrico County to obtain representation in the house independent of Richmond. Thereupon, the apportionment was upheld with only a relatively minor change. *Mann v. Davis*, 245 F. Supp. 241 (E.D. Va. 1965). An appeal to the Supreme Court of the United States

was taken by the Negro intervenors whose claims of discrimination had been rejected. However, the Supreme Court denied review. *Thornton v. Davis* and *Burnette v. Davis*, 34 U.S.L. Week 3141 (U.S. October 25, 1965).

An amendment to the constitution may be proposed by a majority vote of the members of both houses. If the proposed amendment is agreed to by a majority of the general assembly meeting after the next general election for the house of delegates, the amendment is submitted to the people for approval by a majority of electors voting thereon. Va. Const., art. XV, § 196.

A majority of the members of both houses may vote to submit to the voters the question whether to call a constitutional convention. If a majority of the electors voting thereon vote in favor of a convention, the general assembly, at its next session, shall provide for the election of delegates to the convention. Id., art. XV, § 197.

There are no provisions relating to the initiative or the referendum.

Virginia is entitled to ten United States representatives. The general assembly is required to divide the state into districts which must be "composed of contiguous and compact territory containing as nearly as practicable, an equal number of inhabitants." Va. Const., art. IV, § 55. With that standard in mind the Virginia Supreme Court, in *Brown v. Sanders*, 159 Va. 28, 166 S.E. 105 (1932), upset the congressional reapportionment act of 1932 because it allowed too great a variation in population among the districts, although the court noted that some variation was inevitably necessitated in Virginia by the custom of refraining from dividing any county or city into separate districts."

The 1952 congressional districting in Virginia left population differentials among the ten districts ranging from 539,618 to 312,890. Nevertheless, the commission on redistricting reported in 1961 its view that it would be impractical and unnecessary to make further changes to produce substantial equality. After the decision by the Supreme Court of the United States in *Wesberry v. Sanders*, 376 U.S. 1 (1964), the legislature made some changes. Va. Laws of 1964, c. 536. However, this was held insufficient by the Virginia supreme court of appeals in *Wilkins v. Davis*, 205 Va. 803, 139 S.E.2d 849 (1965). The court warned that the legislature must complete the redistricting before another election or face the prospect of an election at large. Moreover, the court ruled that the districts must be composed of contiguous and compact territory, containing as nearly as practicable equal numbers of inhabitants. So far as possible without impairing substantial equality, the legislature was directed to give effect to the community of interest within the districts.

In September 1965 a new congressional districting act was approved, with population variations ranging from 377,000 in the least populous to 419,000 in the most populous district.

REFERENCES

Virginia, State of. Reapportionment of the State for Representation. Report to the Governor and the General Assembly of Virginia. Richmond: Commission on Redistricting. 1961.

Eisenberg, Ralph. Legislative Apportionment: How Representative is Virginia's Present System? News Letter. Bureau of Public Administration, University of Virginia. Charlottesville: April 15, 1961.

WASHINGTON

The northwest coast (now Oregon and Washington) was settled in the late eighteenth and early nineteenth centuries principally by British and Americans. By a unique arrangement between the United States and Great Britain there was in effect a joint occupation of the land by the two powers between 1818 and 1846 when the boundary between the two was fixed by treaty. In 1848 Congress organized a territorial government under the name Oregon, and in 1853 Congress created out of that territory the new territory of Washington. Legislative power was vested in a 9-member council and an 18-member house of representatives, the latter subject to enlargement to a maximum of 30. On the basis of a census to be taken before the first election the governor was directed to make an apportionment, "as nearly equal as practicable, among the several counties or districts, for the election of the Council and Representatives, giving to each section of the Territory representation in the ratio of its qualified voters, as nearly as may be." Sec. 4.

Congress adopted an enabling act in 1889 to authorize the calling of a constitutional convention in preparation for statehood. The constitution drawn by that convention was ratified by the people and made the basis for a proclamation admitting Washington as a state of the Union in the same year.

The constitution of 1889, which remains the present constitution except as amended, vests legislative power in a house of representatives of not less than 63 and not more than 99 members (initially fixed at 70) and a senate not more than one half nor less than one third the membership of the house (initially fixed at 35). Wash. Const. of 1889, art. II, § 2. The legislature is directed to have a census taken every ten years from and after 1895; and at the first session after each such census, as well as after each federal census, such an apportionment is to be made of both houses "according to the number of inhabitants, excluding Indians not taxed, soldiers, sailors and officers of the United States army and navy in active service." Id., art. II, § 3. In addition, senators are to be elected from single districts of convenient and contiguous territory and no representative district may be divided in the formation of a senatorial district. Id., art. II, § 6.

Pending the taking of the first census the 35 senatorial positions were apportioned among the then 34 counties divided into 24 districts. The districts ranged from King County's five-senator allotment to the single senator allotted in some cases to as many as four counties. The principle of floterial representation was also recognized in several of the districts. Id., art. XXII, § 1. The 70 representatives were divided among the counties in numbers ranging from one to eight for each county. Id., art. XXII, § 2.

Reapportionment and redistricting acts were passed by the legislature in 1890 and 1901. However, the legislature did not in either case conform to the article II, section 3 requirement that apportionment be "according to the number of inhabitants," since at least one representative was given to each county regardless of its population. Brief for Respondent, p. 30, *Meyers v. Thigpen*, 378 U.S. 554 (1964).

Between 1901 and 1965 the legislature neither reapportioned nor redistricted the house or the senate on its own; and in 1916 the supreme court of Washington held that the legislature could not be compelled to redistrict the state as required by the constitution. *State ex rel. Warson v. Howell*, 92 Wash. 540, 159 Pac. 777 (1916). In 1930 the state was redistricted by an initiative measure providing for an increase in state senators from 42 to 46 and of representatives from 97 to 99. Representative district boundaries were also made to coincide with senatorial district boundaries and each legislative district was given a minimum of two representatives. Initiative No. 57, Wash. Laws of 1931, c. 2, p. 31.

In November 1956 the voters of the state again reapportioned by means of the initiative. Initiative No. 199, Wash. Laws of 1957, c. 5, p. 11. In 1957 the legislature amended initiative 199 to such an extent that it substantially reestablished the apportionment existing prior to the adoption of the 1956 initiative. Wash. Laws of 1957, c. 289, p. 1147. The constitutionality of this act was questioned in *State ex rel. O'Connell v. Meyers*, 51 Wash. 2d 454, 319 P.2d 828 (1957), in which relator claimed that the legislative amendment to initiative 199 caused significant disproportion in the various districts in violation of the equality requirement in article II, section 3. The Washington Supreme Court held, however, that the legislature had unlimited power to establish methods of redistricting and to alter, modify, take away, add to, or change the various districts as it saw fit. Id. at 464, 319 P.2d at 832.

In November 1962 initiative 211, which would have redistricted the state legislative districts according to 1960 population figures, was defeated by the voters. Meanwhile, in June 1962 a class action had been instituted in the federal district court of Washington to compel the legislature to reapportion both the legislative and the congressional districts. The three-judge court, in December 1962, dismissed the action as to congressional districting, as more fully noted below, but found that the existing legislative apportionment was invidiously discriminatory. The court took notice of the convening of a new legislature in January 1963 and continued the cause to permit the legislature to act. *Thigpen v. Meyers*, 211 F. Supp. 826 (W.D. Wash. 1962).

The district court held that under the Washington constitution "the principle of numerical equality is the rule," citing *State ex rel. O'Connell v. Meyers*, supra, and that both representative and senatorial districts "must be reasonably proportionate according to the number of inhabitants, in order to stand the test of the constitutional mandate." The court noted that the equal protection clause does not demand absolute equality, "but a rational basis for the legislative distinctions [in population among districts] is necessary . . . . There may be relevant countervailing factors, such as geography, economics, mass media and functional or group voting strength. But none of these factors, whether considered separately or collectively, can overcome the basic principle underlying the right of an individual to cast an effective vote . . . . The test is whether a state has made an invidious discrimination." Id. at 831–32.

In support of the finding of invidious discrimination the court cited the following evidence of malapportionment: (1) If each district had the same population as every other district, the number of persons per state representative would be 28,527 and the number of persons per state senator would be 57,-636; (2) however, only one legislative district approximated the norm: others ranged from 57 per cent below the norm to 102 per cent above the norm as to population per state representative, and from 65 per cent below the norm to 152 per cent above the norm as to population per state senator; (3) furthermore, 38 per cent of the population could

elect a majority of the house, while 35.6 per cent could elect a majority of the senate; (4) "The lines of inequality run the length and breadth of the State." Id. at 830–32.

The Washington legislature met in regular session and in special session in the early months of 1963 but failed to enact any reapportionment legislation. The cause was again heard by the federal court in April 1963. A decree entered in May 1963 declared the 1957 reapportionment act unconstitutional as to both the house and the senate. In effect, the decree provided that the only alternative to reapportionment by the legislature would be an at-large election, unless the state should be redistricted by the time of the 1964 election (although the court did not specifically order such an election). The Supreme Court of the United States affirmed that judgment "on the merits" and remanded the case "for further proceedings, with respect to relief, consistent with the views stated in our opinions in *Reynolds v. Sims* . . . ." *Meyers v. Thigpen*, 378 U.S. 554 (1964). Justice Clark would have affirmed on the grounds stated in his opinion in *Reynolds*; Justice Stewart would have remanded for further proceedings consistent with his dissenting views in *Lucas v. Colorado General Assembly*, 377 U.S. 713, 744 (1964); and Justice Harlan dissented for the reasons stated in his opinion in *Reynolds*. Id. at 554–55. (The case is further discussed in chapter VI, supra.)

On remand the three-judge federal district court deplored the two-year delay since the suit was first filed and the continuing absence of corrective action. However, believing the time for judicial reapportionment too short before the elections to be held in the fall of 1964 (it was then July 23), the court encouraged a special legislative session.

Withholding any immediate action, the court suggested the possibility that a judicial order for weighted voting might be entered if the legislature failed to act by August 31, 1964. *Thigpen v. Meyers*, 231 F. Supp. 938 (W.D. Wash. 1964).

After the legislature failed to act the court reconsidered its threat to order weighted voting but instead decreed (1) that the legislators' terms should be limited to one year and (2) that no legislation except internal "housekeeping" measures could be enacted until a satisfactory reapportionment had been adopted.

At the 1965 regular session of the Washington legislature the issue of how to effect the reapportionment produced acrimonious disputes between Republicans and Democrats, between legislature and governor, and a 47-day deadlock. On February 26, 1965, an act passed both houses which the governor approved after vetoing two previous bills. Wash. Laws of 1965, c. 6. The new act retained the existing senate and house membership at 49 and 99 respectively. It apparently satisfied the provisions of the state constitution, and the federal district court promptly held that it also satisfied the requirements of the Constitution of the United States. Accordingly, the court dismissed the three-year-old litigation. N.Y. Times, March 10, 1965, p. 26, col. 1.

An interesting feature of the 1965 legislation is that the 99 representatives are to be chosen in November 1966 from 14 single-member districts, 41 two-member districts, and one three-man district. The 49 senators are to be chosen, partly in 1966 and partly in 1968, from 49 single-member districts, as required by the state constitution, in each case the same as the representative districts except that the 14 single-

member representative districts are divided into seven senatorial districts. Wash. Laws of 1965, c. 6, §§ 51, 53.

Constitutional amendments may be proposed by either branch of the legislature and, after ratification by a two-thirds vote of the members of both houses, are to be submitted to the electors for approval by a majority of the electors voting thereon. Wash. Const., art. XXIII, § 1.

Two thirds of the members elected to both houses may recommend to the electors that a constitutional convention be called. If a majority of all the electors voting at the election concur, the legislature is to provide for calling a convention at its next session. Id., art. XXIII, § 2.

The powers of the initiative and the referendum are reserved to the people by amendments 7 (1912) and 26 (1952) to article II, section 1. The people may initiate legislative reapportionment acts. *State ex rel. Miller v. Hinkle*, 156 Wash. 289, 286 Pac. 839 (1930).

Washington elects seven congressional representatives. Wash. Rev. Code Ann., §§ 29.68.005 to 29.68.066. The congressional reapportionment statutes were unsuccessfully attacked in *Thigpen v. Meyers*, 211 F. Supp. 826, 830 (W.D. Wash. 1962), where the federal district court held that the population variance among the congressional districts of 1.5 to 1 was not "so invidiously discriminatory as to amount to a denial of equal protection." In terms of 1960 population the most populous district contains a population of 510,512, while the smallest district has 342,540 inhabitants.

REFERENCES

Baker, Gordon E. The Politics of Reapportionment in Washington State. New York: "Eagleton Foundation Case Study," Holt, Rinehart & Winston. 1960.

WEST VIRGINIA

When the commonwealth of Virginia seceded from the Union in 1861, the western counties of Virginia did not join their parent state, but instead, in convention in 1861, declared their separate existence. In 1862 Congress consented to the formation of the new state (on the condition of one change being made in the constitution), and the President of the United States issued a proclamation admitting West Virginia to the Union in 1863.

That first constitution vested legislative power in an 18-member senate and a 47-member house of delegates, both subject to enlargement with increase in population. W. Va. Const. of 1863, art. IV, §§ 2, 4. The constitution provided for initial division of the state into nine senatorial districts from each of which two senators were to be elected, "but after the first election both shall not be chosen from the same county." It was specified that "The districts shall be equal, as nearly as practicable, in white population, according to the returns of the United States census. They shall be compact, formed of contiguous territory, and bounded by county lines." Id., art. IV, §§ 4, 6. The constitution further provided that the delegates should be apportioned in accordance with a ratio determined by dividing "the whole white population" by the number of delegates. Each county with a white population of less than half the delegate ratio was to be attached to a contiguous county or counties to form a delegate district, while counties with white population in excess of the ratio were to be assigned as many delegates as merited by their population. Additional delegates to make up the whole number in the house were to be assigned to the

counties or districts with the largest unrepresented fractions. Id., art. IV, §§ 7–9. Initial apportionment of delegates was also made pending the first census, and provision was made for the representation of additional counties as they should later be added to the state (the final addition was made in 1895 to the present total of 55 counties). Id., art. IV, §§ 10–14.

The constitution of 1872, the present constitution, continued in essential part the apportionment provisions of the 1863 constitution. The constitution provides for the division of West Virginia into 12 or more senatorial districts, "as nearly as practicable, equal in population," each to elect two senators to four-year terms. Senatorial districts must be "compact," "formed of contiguous territory," and "bounded by county lines." When districts are composed of more than one county, both senators may not be chosen from the same county. W. Va. Const., art. VI, § 4. Thus, 34 senators are elected from the present 17 senatorial districts. West Va. Code Ann., art. 2, § 5 (Supp. 1963).

Representation in the West Virginia house of delegates is also based on population. The ratio of representation for the house is ascertained by dividing the whole population of the state (1,860,-421 in 1960) by the number of seats in the house (106 in 1963, but 100 since 1964) and rejecting any resulting fraction of a unit. W. Va. Const., art. VI, § 7. Every county with a population of less than three fifths of the ratio must be attached to some contiguous county or counties to form a delegate district. Id., art. VI, § 6. The population of each delegate district and of each county not included in a delegate district (counties containing more than three fifths of the ratio) is then divided by the ratio and is assigned a number of delegates equal to the resulting quotient, excluding the fractional remainder. Any additional seats remaining are then distributed to counties and delegate districts having the largest fractions unrepresented. Id., art. VI, § 7. The present house of delegates consists of 100 members. West Va. Code Ann., art. 2, § 6 (Supp. 1964). For the earlier history, see Ross, House of Delegates Apportionment in West Virginia, p. 35 (mimeo., Bur. for Gov't Research, W. Va. Univ. 1961).

The legislature is directed to reapportion both the house and the senate districts "as soon as possible after each succeeding" United States census. W. Va. Const., art. VI, §§ 4, 7, 10. Legislative apportionments continue in force until the next succeeding reapportionment based on the next census. Id., § 10. See *Harmison v. Ballot Commissioners*, 45 W. Va. 179, 181, 31 S.E. 394, 395 (1898), in which the court also held that the constitutionality of a reapportionment act is a justiciable issue. Id. at 180, 31 S.E. at 395.

In *State v. Thornberg*, 137 W. Va. 60, 70 S.E.2d 73 (1952) the West Virginia Supreme Court took jurisdiction of a case arising out of the apportionment act of 1951 in which it was alleged that the 1951 act apportioned delegates to counties with populations below the three-fifths ratio of representation, as demonstrated by the fact that each county of the state was apportioned at least one delegate. The court held that it would not question a "finding of fact" (as to population) by the legislature. This practice of assigning one delegate to each county, the court found, was a "long practice," which had not been questioned for fifty years. "Whether this long practice results from actual findings of fact by the Legislature, whether it resulted from a legisla-

tive interpretation of what appears to be a possible conflict between the provisions of Sections 6 and 7 of Article VI, or whether the provisions of Section 6 were intended to apply only to delegate representation prior to the taking of the first census after the adoption of the Constitution, we need not say. In the more than 50 years such legislation has been in effect, no question has been raised as to its validity." Id. at 74, 70 S.E.2d at 80–81.

In the 1963 apportionment each county was again allotted at least one delegate (West Va. Code Ann., art. 2, § 6 [Supp. 1963]), although in the 1960 census the population of 11 counties fell below three fifths of the required ratio of representation. In February 1964 the supreme court of appeals of West Virginia held that the 1963 reapportionment of the house of delegates violated sections 6 and 7 of article VI of the state constitution. *Robertson v. Hatcher*, No. 12306. Later in the same month the legislature, in extraordinary session, again reapportioned the lower house, reducing the number of delegates to 100 and specifying delegate districts, ranging from three counties for one delegate to 14 delegates for one county (Kanawha). Enrolled H.B. No. 2, 1st Extra. Sess. 1964, W. Va. Code Ann., art. 2, § 6 (Supp. 1964). The changes made were intended to satisfy the requirements laid down by the state supreme court of appeals; but no further legislative adjustment was made to conform both houses to the equal-population principle announced later that year by the Supreme Court of the United States in *Reynolds v. Sims*, 377 U.S. 533 (1964).

At the 1965 legislative session the West Virginia legislature, acting pursuant to article XIV, section 1 of the state constitution, agreed to submit to the voters in November 1965 the question whether a constitutional convention should be called for 1966. If agreed to by the voters, 106 nonpartisan delegates would be chosen on March 29, 1966, and the convention would meet on July 20, 1966. 54 Nat'l Civ. Rev. 314 (June 1965). However, in September 1965 the West Virginia Court of Appeals held invalid the proposed apportionment of delegates to the convention, which was comparable to the provisions for selection of delegates to the lower house of the state legislature, previously held invalid. The governor indicated his intention to call the legislature into special session to redesignate the means of selection for convention delegates.

Amendments to the constitution may be proposed in either house of the legislature and, if agreed upon by two thirds of the members elected thereto, such amendments are submitted to the voters for ratification. They become effective upon ratification by a majority of the electors voting on the question. W. Va. Const., art. XIV, § 2, as amended in 1960. There is no provision for the initiative or referendum.

The West Virginia constitution provides that congressional districts must be "compact," "formed of contiguous counties," and "contain as nearly as may be, an equal number of population." W. Va. Const., art. I, § 4. West Virginia is at present entitled to five congressmen, a loss of one as a result of the 1960 federal census. West Va. Code Ann., art. 2, § 7, as re-enacted in 1963. While the requirements of article I, section 4 of the state constitution have been violated more than once by the West Virginia legislature, the state supreme court of appeals has never ruled on a challenge to such an act. Throughout the history of congressional redistricting in West Virginia, all districts

have consisted of contiguous counties. However, the other two requirements — compactness and equality of population — were violated by the legislature as late as the last redistricting act. The congressional population mean is 372,084 (1,860,421 divided by 5). The largest district has 422,046 inhabitants; the smallest, a population of 303,098.

REFERENCES

Davis, Claude J. Congressional Redistricting in West Virginia for the 'Sixties. Morgantown: Bureau for Government Research, West Virginia University. 1960.

Ross, William R. House of Delegates Apportionment in West Virginia. Publication No. 33. Morgantown: Bureau for Government Research, West Virginia University. 1961.

Heyman, Victor K. "West Virginia: Tradition and Partisan Advantage," in Jewell, Malcolm E. (ed.), The Politics of Reapportionment. New York: Atherton Press. 1962.

Note, Legislative Reapportionment: Baker v. Carr, 65 W. Va. L. Rev. 129 (1963).

WISCONSIN

Wisconsin was originally part of the Northwest Territory and thus governed by the congressional act of 1787 which guaranteed that "The inhabitants of the said territory shall always be entitled to the benefits of ... proportionate representation of the people in the legislature . . . ." Northwest Ordinance of 1787, art. II. Thereafter, modern Wisconsin was successively within the territorial jurisdiction of Indiana, Illinois, and Michigan before Congress established a separate territory of Wisconsin in 1836. (That territory included a substantially larger area than the present state of Wisconsin; in 1838 the territory of Iowa was created out of the territorial limits of Wisconsin.) That act vested the legislative power in the governor and legislative assembly, the latter to consist of a 13-member council and a 26-member house of representatives. Previous to the first election the governor was directed to have a census taken of the inhabitants of the several counties; and on the basis of those figures he was to make an apportionment, "as nearly equal as practicable, among the several counties for the election of the council and representatives, giving to each section of the Territory representation in the ratio of its population, Indians excepted, as nearly as may be; . . . ." Sec. 4.

In 1846 Congress adopted an enabling act authorizing the formation of a constitution looking to statehood for Wisconsin. A constitutional convention framed a constitution for the proposed new state in 1848; the proposed government was approved by Congress in the same year as republican in form; and Wisconsin was admitted as a state of the Union.

The constitution of 1848 vested the legislative power in an assembly of not less than 54 members nor more than 100, and a senate to consist of not more than one third nor less than one fourth of the membership of the assembly. Wis. Const. of 1848, art. IV, §§ 1, 2. A census was to be taken in 1855 and every ten years thereafter. At the first legislative session after each such census, and after each federal decennial census, the legislature was directed to "apportion and district anew the members of the Senate and Assembly, according to the number of inhabitants, excluding Indians not taxed, and soldiers and officers of the United States Army and Navy." Id., art. IV, § 3. The only further general guidance for the apportionment function were provisions that assembly districts "be bounded by county, precinct, town, or ward lines, to consist of contiguous territory, and be in as compact form as practicable," and that senators "shall be chosen by single districts of convenient contiguous territory, . . . and no Assembly district shall be divided in the formation of a Senate district." Id., art. IV, § 5. Pending the results of the first census, the senatorial and assembly districts were specified in article XIV, section 12 of the constitution.

Although the constitution of 1848 remains the present constitution, the apportionment provisions were amended in several respects in 1881, 1910, and 1962. The present provisions are summarized below.

The legislature of Wisconsin is directed to reapportion and redistrict the members of the senate and the assembly at the first legislative session after each federal decennial census is taken, "according to the number of inhabitants, excluding soldiers, and officers of the United States army and navy." Wis. Const., art. IV, § 3. Membership in the assembly may never be less than 54 nor more than 100, and the senate consists of not more than one third nor less than one fourth of the number of the members of the assembly. Id., art. IV, § 2. Assembly districts must be bounded by county, precinct, town, or ward lines; and they must consist of contiguous territory and be in as compact form as practicable. Id., art. IV, § 4. Senatorial districts must be composed of "convenient contiguous territory," and "no assembly district shall be divided in the formation of a senate district." Id., art. IV, § 5. These provisions have been construed to require that "an assembly district must either comprise one or more entire counties or must consist of only a portion of a single county." *State ex rel. Reynolds v. Zimmerman*, 22 Wis.2d 544, 570, 126 N.W.2d 551, 566 (1964), reaffirming the standards established in 1892 in the case next discussed.

State ex rel. Attorney General v. Cunningham, 81 Wis. 440, 51 N.W. 724 (1892) involved a challenge to the 1891 senatorial and assembly reapportionment act as violative of the equality-of-inhabitants clause of article IV, section 3 of the state constitution. Original jurisdiction over the subject matter of the suit was taken by the supreme court of Wisconsin on the theory that the matter was publici juris (within the highest public interest) and that the attorney general represented the whole state and the people therein. The act was voided because on its face the disparities in population among the districts were excessive. "[P]erfect *exactness* in the apportionment according to the number of inhabitants is neither required nor possible. But there should be as close an approximation to *exactness* as possible, and this is the utmost limit for the exercise of legislative discretion." Id. at 484, 51 N.W. at 730.

In *State ex rel. Lamb v. Cunningham*, 83 Wis. 90, 53 N.W. 35 (1892), when the attorney general refused to apply for a writ to enjoin state officers from acting pursuant to an allegedly invalid apportionment act, the supreme court of Wisconsin ruled that it could take jurisdiction of the matter in the name of the state on the relation of a private citizen. The court voided the 1892 act for glaring inequalities, quoting the test of *State ex rel. Attorney General v. Cunningham*, supra. In addition, the court held the equality requirement applicable to two or more assembly districts in a single county as to an assembly district composed of two or more counties. The act was voided principally because the equality of population standard was not met in many subdistricts.

The 1931 reapportionment act was upheld in *State ex rel. Bowman v. Dammann*, 209 Wis. 21, 243 N.W. 481 (1932). However, in *State ex rel. Martin v. Zimmerman*, 249 Wis. 101, 23 N.W.2d 610 (1946) the attorney general claimed that the 1931 reapportionment act, enacted on the basis of the 1930 census, became unconstitutional by virtue of the failure of the legislature to reapportion the state in 1941 pursuant to the constitutional mandate. The supreme court of Wisconsin denied any remedy on the ground that the court is powerless to compel the legislature to enact reapportionment legislation since the constitutional mandate to reapportion runs exclusively to the legislature. Id. at 104, 23 N.W.2d at 611.

Reapportionment was next achieved in 1951 (with minor adjustments in 1961) by a bill popularly known as the Rosenberry act. Sections 1 and 2 apportioned the senate and assembly according to population, based on the 1950 federal census; but section 3 of the act provided for an advisory referendum, to be held during the general election of November 1952, on the question of whether the apportionment of either house of the Wisconsin legislature should be based on area as well as on population. Section 3 further provided that sections 1 and 2 of the act would become operative on January 1, 1954, only if the voters rejected the area apportionment concept in the referendum. Section 4 of the act was a nonseverability clause directing that the entire act should become inoperative in case the courts should hold any one of the preceding sections invalid.

Less than a year later the referendum provision of the Rosenberry act was challenged in *State ex rel. Broughton v. Zimmerman*, 261 Wis. 398, 52

N.W.2d 903 (1952). Petitioners alleged that the legislature's apportionment of the senate and assembly in accordance with the latest federal census had exhausted its apportionment function and that the apportionment could not be made contingent on a referendum. The Wisconsin Supreme Court disagreed, however, and denied the petition, holding that "while the Legislature may not delegate its power to make a law, it can make a law to become operative on the happening of a certain contingency . . . upon which the law makes or intends to make its own action depend." Id. at 414, 52 N.W.2d at 911. The fact that the effective date for the act was postponed until 1954 in case the 1952 referendum should make the act operative was held not to void the act. The court held that the duty to reapportion is a continuing one so that "if the legislature fails to apportion at the first general session after the census it may do so in a subsequent session. . . ." Id. at 416, 52 N.W.2d at 912. Hence, the court likened the situation to one in which the legislature fails to reapportion at its first biennial session following the publication of the federal census.

Pursuant to section 3 of the Rosenberry act, the question of whether the constitution should be amended to provide for the establishment of either senate or assembly districts on an area as well as on a population basis was submitted to the voters in the November 1952 election. In a heavy turnout the proposition was rejected by a vote of 753,092 "No" to 689,615 "Yes." Rejection of the area apportionment proposition fulfilled the conditions for the execution of the Rosenberry act, which accordingly became operative on January 1, 1954.

The defeat of the 1952 area apportionment referendum did not end the attempts to make area a factor of legislative apportionment in Wisconsin. A constitutional amendment to article IV, section 3 was proposed by the legislature and submitted to the voters at the election of April 7, 1953. The proposal provided in general terms for senate apportionment on an "area and population" basis (specific implementation was vested in the legislature), permitted assembly districts to cross county lines, and senate districts to split assembly districts. The people adopted the amendment, 433,043 "For," and 406,133 "Against."

The Rogan act of 1953, enacted to implement that amendment, apportioned the senate approximately 30 per cent on area and 70 per cent on population, and adopted mainly the Rosenberry provisions in apportioning the assembly districts. After the secretary of state (Zimmerman) announced he would not use the 1953 Rogan act, but would call the 1954 elections in accordance with the 1951 Rosenberry act, the attorney general instituted a suit to compel the secretary of state to act pursuant to the later act. *State ex rel. Thomson v. Zimmerman*, 264 Wis. 644, 60 N.W.2d 416 (1953), rehearing denied, 264 Wis. 663, 61 N.W.2d 300 (1953).

The supreme court of Wisconsin held the constitutional provisions to have been incorrectly ratified and thus inoperative. Although the court did not reject altogether the possibility of constitutional amendment to require use of area as an apportionment factor, it did note the following: "While we hold that it is not beyond the power of the people to establish area as a factor in determining representation in the legislature, the legislature may not apportion the state in such a manner that practical equality of representation on the chosen basis is destroyed." Id. at 652, 60 N.W.2d at 419.

State v. Zimmerman, 205 F. Supp. 673, 209 F. Supp. 183 (W.D. Wis. 1962) was instituted by the attorney general as parens patriae for the people of Wisconsin, to compel the secretary of state to refrain from conducting the legislative elections pursuant to the Rosenberry act of 1951, and to refrain from conducting the congressional elections under the provisions of the 1959 congressional apportionment act. The three-judge federal district court first suggested that the Wisconsin legislature reconvene and enact a fair apportionment act. 205 F. Supp. at 676. The special legislative session called from June 18, 1962 to July 31, 1962 approved a reapportionment act but the governor's veto was sustained. The action was reopened, whereupon five citizen-voters intervened as party plaintiffs in a class capacity. The court found that 40 per cent of the population elected a majority of the assemblymen and 42.5 per cent elected a majority of the senators. 209 F. Supp. 183, 186 (W.D. Wis. 1962). However, the court did not at that time decide whether the disparities amounted to invidious discrimination, believing that relief should not be given so shortly before the November elections. The court expressed the "hope" that the 1963 legislature would carry out its constitutional mandate to make a fair reapportionment. Id. at 187–188.

Senate bill 575S seeking to reapportion the legislative districts passed both houses of the legislature in June 1963, but was vetoed by the governor, who had been attorney general during the litigation of *State v. Zimmerman,* supra.

Thereafter, in June 1963 the governor petitioned the state supreme court to enjoin the 1964 legislative elections and to compel the secretary of state to conduct the elections either (1) at large, on the grounds that the present reapportionment was violative of both the Wisconsin and the federal constitutions, or (2) pursuant to such plan as the court might direct. In August 1963 both houses of the legislature passed joint resolution 49, purporting to reapportion the legislative districts. This resolution was nearly identical to the bill which had been vetoed by the governor. In October 1963 leave was granted to permit the president pro tem of the state senate and the speaker of the assembly to intervene in the action for the purpose of seeking a declaration from the court that joint resolution 49 was a proper reapportionment act.

In an opinion of February 28, 1964, the court held that the governor of the state had standing to challenge the constitutionality of an apportionment under the provisions of either the state or the federal constitution. Joint resolution 49 was held invalid because it was not signed by the governor. *State ex. rel. Reynolds v. Zimmerman,* 22 Wis. 2d 544, 126 N.W.2d 551 (1964).

The Rosenberry act was held invalid as violative of the standard contained in article IV, section 3 of the Wisconsin constitution that legislative districts shall be apportioned according to the number of inhabitants. The *Cunningham* rule was reiterated: "[A] valid reapportionment 'should be as close an approximation to *exactness* as possible, and this is the utmost limit for the exercise of legislative discretion.'" Id. at 565, 126 N.W.2d at 563. An application of the per capita equality of representation standard to the Rosenberry apportionment scheme showed sharp deviations from the norm of both the senate and the assembly districts. "A reapportionment plan which permits a deviation from an equal population norm of 100, ranging from 221.3 (largest district) to 49.7 (smallest district) in assembly districts, and a similar deviation in senate districts from 173.9 (largest district) to 62 (smallest district), does not conform to the standard of per capita equality of representation." Id. at 569, 126 N.W.2d at 565.

In fashioning its remedy the court pointed out that under the state constitution it is impossible to devise any plan under which every assembly district will have exactly the same number of people, or even approximately the same number, because of the Wisconsin constitutional requirement that an assembly district must either comprise one or more entire counties or must consist of only a part of a single county. There are situations where a choice must be made between fairly substantial overrepresentation and fairly substantial underrepresentation. "[T]hese choices should be made in the legislative process rather than in the judicial process, and the court should make these choices only when it becomes absolutely necessary to do so." Id. at 571, 126 N.W.2d at 566. Finally, the court promised that if a valid legislative apportionment plan should not be enacted by May 1, 1964, the court would promulgate a plan by May 15, 1964, to govern the 1964 legislative elections.

When the legislature and the governor failed to agree on any apportionment act after that warning, the Wisconsin Supreme Court, on May 14, 1964, announced its own plan to be effective for the 1964 elections. County lines were held inviolable so that each of the 100 assembly districts consisted either of a whole county, several whole counties, or a part of a single county. For no assembly district did the 1960 population exceed by more than one third the statewide average population of assembly districts: 39,528. Similarly, each of the 33 senate districts consisted of whole assembly districts; and for no senate district did the 1960 population exceed by more than one sixth the statewide average population of senate districts: 119,780. *State ex rel. Reynolds v. Zimmerman*, 23 Wis. 2d 606, 128 N.W.2d 16 (1964). Under the revised plan Milwaukee County increased its assembly representation by one seat; suburban Waukesha County went from two to four members; and rapidly urbanizing Outagamie County increased its representation from two to three. The four seats came from the sparsely populated areas of northern and northwestern Wisconsin that had been declining in population.

Constitutional amendments may be proposed in either house of the legislature and, if approved by a majority of the members elected to each house, are submitted to the legislature next chosen to be agreed to again by a majority of the members elected to each house. The proposal becomes part of the constitution if ratified by a majority of the electors voting on it. Wis. Const., art. XII, § 1.

A majority of the senate and the house may recommend to the voters that a constitutional convention be called. Id., art. XII, § 2.

Wisconsin is allotted ten congressmen. Prior to 1963 the congressional districts were last wholly reapportioned in 1931. A 1959 law changed descriptions of two districts to conform to the revision of ward boundaries, but did not affect the district boundaries. In terms of 1960 population the most populous district was 530,316 inhabitants and the least populous had 236,870. The 1963 act made substantial changes, creating ten congressional districts with an average deviation of plus or minus 1.5 per cent. The population of the districts varied only between 408,667 and 382,818. County lines were observed throughout, a fact made possible by creation of three whole congressional districts in the combined area of Milwaukee and Waukesha Counties. Wis. Stat. Ann. §§ 3.01–3.11 (Supp. 1963). For a history of earlier congressional reapportionment in Wisconsin see Wisconsin Legislative Reference Library, Congressional Reapportionment in Wisconsin (mimeo. Research Bull. 126 March 1960).

Wisconsin became in 1965 one of the first states to apply the equal-population principle to local governmental bodies with legislative functions as well as to the state legislature. In *State ex rel. Sonneborn v. Sylvester*, 26 Wis. 2d 43, 132 N.W.2d 249 (1965), the Wisconsin Supreme Court held invalid the state statute providing for the selection of all county board members (except in Milwaukee and Menominee Counties). The invalidated system had provided that each county board should consist of the chairman of each town board, a supervisor from each city ward or part thereof in the county, and a supervisor from each village or part thereof in the county, all without regard to population. The court ruled further that if appropriate action should not have been taken by November 1, 1965, application could be made to the court to fix a date by which invalidly constituted county boards "shall no longer be validly in office, to enjoin elections of members of county boards pursuant to said statute, or for other ap-

propriate relief." Id. at — , 132 N.W.2d at 258. In April 1965, however, the state legislature responded with new legislation providing for division of counties into supervisory districts with populations varying no more than 15 per cent from the norm. The total size of the county boards may vary from 21 to 47 depending on population. Wis. Laws 1965, c. 20.

REFERENCES

League of Women Voters of Wisconsin. Problems of Reapportionment. Madison: August 1962.

Pommerening and Pommerening. A Study of the First Step of Wisconsin Legislative Redistricting Based Upon the 1960 Federal Census. Milwaukee: 1961.

Wisconsin Legislative Council. Research Bulletin to the Reapportionment Committee, Summary of Conclusions of 1959–1961 Reapportionment Committee. Research Bulletin 63-1. Madison: June 1962.

Wisconsin Legislative Reference Library. Congressional Reapportionment in Wisconsin. Research Bulletin 126. Madison: March 1960.

——. Legislative Apportionment in Wisconsin: The Development Between 1950 and 1960. Information Bulletin No. 198. Madison: December 1960.

——. Reapportionment of the State Legislature in Wisconsin. Information Bulletin No. 130. Madison: March 1954.

——. Wisconsin Legislative Apportionment: Background, 1960 Census, and the Measures Considered by the Legislature During the 1961 Regular Session. Information Bulletin No. 217. Madison: June 1962.

WYOMING

Wyoming was originally within the lands ceded to the United States by treaty of purchase with France in 1803. Thereafter, the land, largely unsettled until after the Civil War, was successively under the claimed dominion of several foreign nations and within the designated limits of a number of American territories. Finally, in 1868, Congress established a temporary government for Wyoming as a separate territory, vesting legislative power in the governor and a legislative assembly consisting of a 9-member council (subject to enlargement to 13) and a 13-member council (subject to enlargement to 27). The governor was directed to have a census of all inhabitants taken before the first election and, on the basis of those returns, to make an apportionment, "as nearly equal as practicable among the several counties or districts for the election of the council and house of representatives, giving to each section of the Territory representation in the ratio of their population, (excepting Indians not taxed,) as nearly as may be, ..." Sec. 4.

In 1889 the people of the territory, by a constitutional convention, framed a constitution which was ratified and adopted by the people in the same year. In 1890 Congress found the constitution "republican in form" and declared Wyoming a state of the Union.

The constitution of 1889, which remains the present constitution, vests legislative power in a senate and house of representatives. The constitution provided that at the first election the senate should consist of 16 members and the house of 33 representatives (Wyo. Const., art. III, § 3), which were divided among the then ten counties in numbers allotted to each county varying from one to three senators and from two to six representatives (id., art. III, § 50). However, the constitution did not then, and does not now, establish the number of members for each house beyond the time of the first census of inhabitants, which was to be taken in 1895, and every ten years thereafter. Id., art. III, § 48. The legislature was directed to reapportion both houses at its first session after each state census and after each federal census (ibid.), always to be "apportioned among the said counties as nearly as may be ac-

cording to the number of their inhabitants." Id., art. III, § 3. In addition, the legislature is directed to observe the following standards: "Each county shall have at least one senator and one representative; but at no time shall the number of members of the house of representatives be less than twice nor greater than three times the number of members of the senate." Id., art. III, § 3. Thus, each county is a senatorial and a representative district at the same time. "It [a county] cannot be a senatorial and at the same time not a representative district." *State ex rel. Sullivan v. Schnitger*, 16 Wyo. 479, 512, 95 Pac. 698, 704 (1908). See also Note, Possible Action to Force the Wyoming Legislature to Reapportion, 11 Wyo. L.J. 136 (1957).

Despite the constitutional requirement of legislative reapportionment after each census, the legislature took no action between 1933 and 1963 when the state supreme court invalidated the earlier act. *State ex rel. Whitehead v. Gage*, 377 P.2d 299 (Wyo. 1963). The 1933 apportionment had been based on the 1930 census, providing that each county "shall have one senator for every 11,000 inhabitants, or major portion thereof" and that each county "shall have one representative for every 4,150 inhabitants, or major portion thereof . . . ." Wyo. Stat. §§ 28-9, 28-10 (1957). In terms of 1960 population substantial disparities had developed under the 1933 act. The largest senate district contained 30,074 persons; the smallest, only 3,062. The largest house of representatives district contained 10,024 persons; the smallest, only 2,930.

State ex rel. Whitehead v. Gage, supra, was a taxpayer suit instituted in June 1962 to compel reapportionment of the Wyoming senatorial and representative districts. Plaintiffs sought a writ of mandamus to compel the secretary of state and the attorney general to certify to the counties the number of senators and representatives to be elected in 1962 by applying to the 1960 federal census the ratios fixed under the existing 1933 apportionment laws, namely, one senator for every 11,000 inhabitants and one representative for every 4,150. In the alternative, plaintiffs asked for an at-large election. The state supreme court denied the issuance of the writ of mandamus, noting that since the commencement of the action a new legislature had been elected, which had not yet had the opportunity to act upon reapportionment. Furthermore, there was no clear constitutional basis for directing the secretary of state or the attorney general to perform the acts which the petition sought to compel. 377 P.2d at 300–301.

One month later, on February 6, 1963, the legislature reapportioned in light of the 1960 federal census figures. Each county was allotted one senator for every 30,000 inhabitants or major fraction thereof and one representative for every 5,400 inhabitants or major portion thereof. Wyo. Stat. Ann. §§ 28-9, 28-10 (Supp. 1963). The resulting apportionment established a 25-member senate (one senator for each of 21 counties, and two for each of 2 counties) and a 61-member house (from one to 11 representatives for each county). Id., § 28-11 (Supp. 1963).

The 1963 apportionment was challenged in an action instituted on May 20, 1963, in federal court. *Schaefer v. Thomson,* 240 F. Supp. 247 (D. Wyo. 1964). The plaintiffs (citizens and taxpayers in a class action) argued that the 1963 apportionment act failed to produce a senate and a house of representatives apportioned among the counties as nearly as may be according to

the number of their inhabitants, as constitutionally required. (1) Under the 1963 act each of the two senators from Laramie County (60,150 inhabitants) would represent ten times as many people as the senator from Teton County (3,062 inhabitants); and each of the 11 representatives from Laramie County would represent 1.78 times as many people as the representative from Teton County; (2) 24.2 per cent of the total population of the state would be able to elect a majority in the senate, actually a worsening of the previously existing situation under which a majority of the Wyoming senate could be elected from counties with 27.8 per cent of the total population.

The three-judge federal district court found the imbalance in the house of representatives not excessive but ruled that the senate must be reapportioned to meet the equal-population standard. The court advised the legislature that it could disregard limiting provisions of the state constitution. The court also indicated that, if no action should be taken in the 1965 legislative session, the court itself would reapportion the senate. Despite this warning the Wyoming legislature failed to agree on reapportionment in its regular session in 1965. 54 Nat'l Civ. Rev. 206 (April 1965). As a result the federal court again considered the matter; a decision was expected in the fall of 1965.

Amendments to the Wyoming constitution are proposed by a two-thirds vote of both houses of the legislature. Ratification must be by a majority of the electors voting in the particular election, and not merely a majority of those actually voting upon the amendment. Wyo. Const., art. XX, § 1. See also *State ex rel. Blair v. Brooks,* 17 Wyo. 344, 99 Pac. 874 (1909).

Two thirds of the members of both

houses of the legislature may recommend to the electors the calling of a constitutional convention. Wyo. Const., art. XX, § 3. Any constitution adopted by the convention becomes effective upon ratification by the people. Ibid.

There are neither constitutional nor statutory provisions relative to the enactment of constitutional amendments by use of the initiative or referendum.

Wyoming has only one congressional representative, who is elected at large. In the event that the state should be allotted another representative, "the legislature shall divide the state into congressional districts accordingly." Wyo. Const., art. III, § 47.

REFERENCES

Wyoming Taxpayers Association. How Many Shall Be Seated? Report No. 326. Cheyenne: August 1962.

Note, Possible Action to Force the Wyoming Legislature to Reapportion, 11 Wyo. L.J. 136 (1957).

Note, Wyoming Legislative Reapportionment in the Light (?) of Baker v. Carr, 18 Wyo. L.J. 23 (1963).

LEGISLATIVE REPRESENTATION FORMULA IN THE CONSTITUTION OF EACH STATE AT ITS ORIGIN AND MAJOR REVISIONS THROUGH OCTOBER 1965

The information in this tabulation is intended to permit comparison of the development of representation formulas in the fifty states. The formulas summarized are those contained in the state constitutions; occasionally, in order to make the developments more intelligible, legislative action — or inaction — is noted. In general, no attempt has been made to report restrictions on the franchise such as limitation of the vote to white persons, males, citizens, or registered voters. Those refinements and qualifications upon the right of franchise are noted to the extent relevant to the present study in the individual state summaries that precede this tabulation. For the original thirteen states the date of ratification of the Constitution of the United States has been entered in the first column as the "date of entry into the Union."

State (and date of entry into the Union)	Original Formula		Date of Significant Change	Revised Formula	
	Upper House	Lower House		Upper House	Lower House
Alabama (1819)	Population, but until first census schedule was 1 from each county.	Population, but at least 1 from each of 22 counties in 44-member body.	1901	Primarily population.	Population, but at least 1 from each of 66 counties in 105-member body.
Alaska (1959)	Area and population.	Primarily population.	1965	Primarily population.	Primarily population.
Arizona (1912)	1 from each of 14 counties in 19-member body, remaining 5 by population.	1 from each of 14 counties in 35-member body, remaining 21 by population.	1953	2 from each of 14 counties.	1 from each of 14 counties in 80-member body, remaining 66 by number of votes in last gubernatorial election.
Arkansas (1836)	Population.	Population, but at least 1 from each of 34 counties in 54-member body.	1956	Districts based on then-population distribution written into state constitution.	1 from each of 75 counties in 100-member body, remaining 25 by population.
California (1850)	Population.	Population.	1926	Population, but no county allowed more than 1 senator.	Primarily population.
Colorado (1876)	Population.	Population.	1950	1 for first 19,000 population plus 1 for each additional 50,000.	1 for first 8,000 population plus 1 for each additional 25,500.
Connecticut (1788) (Fundamental Orders of 1638–39 until 1818.)	Population (elections at large for 12-member body).	2 from each town or city.	1955 (Gradual change by amendments after 1818.)	Primarily population, but limitations on division of counties and towns.	2 from each town or city with population over 5,000 and for most others.
Delaware (1787)	3 from each of 3 counties.	7 from each of 3 counties.	1897	7 for New Castle County and 5 from each of the other 2 counties.	15 for New Castle County and 10 from each of the other 2 counties.

| Formula in January 1962 | | Formula in October 1965 | | |
Upper House	Lower House	Upper House	Lower House	Comments
Population.*	Population, but at least 1 from each of 67 counties in 106-member body.*	Primarily population.	Primarily population.	*No reapportionment between 1901 and 1962.
Area and population.	Primarily population.	Primarily population.	Primarily population.	
2 from each of 14 counties.	1 from each of 14 counties in 80-member body, remaining 66 by number of votes in last gubernatorial election.	Primarily population, but at least 1 from each of 14 counties in 31-member body.*	1 from each of 14 counties in 80-member body, remaining 66 by number of votes in last gubernatorial election.*	*Challenge to both houses pending in federal court.
Districts frozen into state constitution since 1956.	1 from each of 75 counties in 100-member body, remaining 25 by population.	Primarily population.	Primarily population.	
Population, but no county allowed more than 1 senator.	Primarily population.	Primarily population.	Primarily population.	
1 for first 19,000 population plus 1 for each additional 50,000.	1 for first 8,000 population plus 1 for each additional 25,500.	Primarily population.	Primarily population.	
Primarily population, but limitations on division of counties and towns.	2 from each town or city with population over 5,000 and 1 for most others.	Primarily population.	Primarily population.	
7 for New Castle County and 5 for each of the other 2 counties.	15 for New Castle County and 10 for each of the other 2 counties.	Primarily population.	Primarily population.	

461

State (and date of entry into the Union)	Original Formula		Date of Significant Change	Revised Formula	
	Upper House	Lower House		Upper House	Lower House
Florida (1845)	Population.	Population, but at least 1 from each of 20 counties in a 41-member body, remaining 21 by population.	1924	Primarily population, but 38 districts must be made up of whole counties.	3 members from 5 most populous counties, 2 from each of next 18, and 1 from each of remaining counties.
Georgia (1788) (Unicameral legislature until 1789.)	1 from each county.	From each of 11 counties 2 to 5 representatives in 34-member body.	1865	44 districts of 3 counties each.	2 members from 37 most populous counties and 1 from each of remaining 95 counties.
Hawaii (1959)	Area.	Registered voters, but each of 4 basic areas to have at least 1 representative in 51-member body.	No significant change.	....	....
Idaho (1890)	Primarily population through use of floterial districts.	Primarily population through use of multimember districts and floterial districts.	1911	1 from each county.	At least 1 from each county.
Illinois (1818)	Population.	Population.	1954	Fixed districts primarily based on area.	Primarily population.
Indiana (1816)	Population.	Population.	No significant change.*	....	....

Formula in January 1962		Formula in October 1965		
Upper House	Lower House	Upper House	Lower House	Comments
rimarily opulation, but 8 districts must e made up of hole counties.	3 members from 5 most populous counties, 2 from each of next 18, and 1 from each of remaining counties.	58-member body with substantial population disparities.	109-member body with substantial population disparities.	
2 three-county istricts, 1 two-ounty district, nd 1 one-ounty district.	3 members from 8 most populous counties, 2 from next 30, and 1 from remaining 121.	Primarily population, but substantial deviations.	Primarily population, but substantial deviations.	
rea.	Registered voters.	8 districts, from which 1 to 4 senators to be elected at large.*	Registered voters.*	*U.S. Supreme Court accepted review of apportionment for 1966 decision.
from each of counties.	1 from each of 44 counties in a 63-member body, remaining 19 apportioned in rough relation to population.	Essentially on the basis of 1 from each county, although 44 senators divided among 9 districts.	Primarily population, each district consisting of 1 to 4 counties represented by from 1 to 9 representatives in 67-member body.	
xed districts imarily based area.	Primarily population.	Primarily population.	Primarily population.	
opulation.	Population.	50 divided among 38 districts, using both multi-county and floterial districts.‡	100 divided among 58 districts of 1 to 4 counties, each district to elect 1 to 15 representatives.‡	*Inequalities primarily due to legislative failure to reapportion between 1921 and 1963. ‡1965 act held invalid by federal court in September 1965, giving legislature until December 1, 1965, for valid act.

State (and date of entry into the Union)	Original Formula		Date of Significant Change	Revised Formula	
	Upper House	Lower House		Upper House	Lower House
Iowa (1846)	Population.	Population.	1904 and 1928	No more than 1 from any county in 50-member body.	1 from each of 99 counties plus 1 from each of 9 most populous counties.
Kansas (1861)	Population.	Population, but at least 1 from each of 40 counties in 75-member body.	1873	Primarily population.	At least 1 from each of 105 counties in 125-member body, remaining 20 by population.
Kentucky (1792)	Primarily population (from 1799).	Population.	No significant change.	. . . .	. . . .
Louisiana (1812)	Population and area.	Primarily population.	1921	Population, but prohibition against division of parishes (except New Orleans).	80 seats in 100-member house allotted to 17 wards in New Orleans and 63 parishes outside New Orleans, remaining 20 by population.
Maine (1820)	Primarily population.	Primarily population.	No significant change.	. . . .	. . . .

	Formula in January 1962		Formula in October 1965		
	Upper House	Lower House	Upper House	Lower House	Comments
	No more than 1 from any county in 50-member body.	1 from each of 99 counties plus 1 from each of 9 most populous counties.	Primarily population, with some limitations to preserve county lines where possible.	Population.	
	Primarily population.*	At least 1 from each of 105 counties in 125-member body, remaining 20 by population.*	Population.	1 from each of 105 counties in 125-member house, remaining 20 by population.‡	*No substantial reapportionment between 1886 and 1963 despite requirement for reapportionment every 5 years. ‡Held unconstitutional by state supreme court in 1964.
	Population.*	Population.*	Primarily population.	Primarily population.	*House became malapportioned after 1918 from legislative failure to join more than 2 counties in single district. Senate malapportionment arose out of legislative failure to reapportion between 1942 and 1963.
	Population, but prohibition against division of parishes except New Orleans.	80 seats in 100-member house allotted to 17 wards in New Orleans and 63 parishes outside New Orleans, remaining 20 by population.	Population, but prohibition against division of parishes (except New Orleans).*	80 seats in 100-member house allotted to 17 wards in New Orleans and 63 parishes outside New Orleans, remaining 20 by population.*	*Challenge pending in federal court.
	Population, but at least 1 from each of 16 counties in 34-member body, remaining 18 apportioned on rough population basis.	Population, but at least 1 from each of 16 counties in 151-member body, remaining 135 by estimates of population at mid-point between apportionments.	Population, but at least 1 from each of 16 counties in 34-member body, remaining 18 apportioned on rough population basis.	Population, but at least 1 from each of 16 counties in 151-member body, remaining 135 by formula closely related to population.	

State (and date of entry into the Union)	Original Formula		Date of Significant Change	Revised Formula	
	Upper House	Lower House		Upper House	Lower House
Maryland (1788)	Indirect election of 9 senators from Western Shore and 6 from Eastern Shore.	Four delegates from each county and 2 delegates from Annapolis and 2 from Baltimore.	1837	1 from each county and 1 from city of Baltimore in 21-member body.	82 delegates allotted to counties and cities in rough approximation to population.
Massachusetts (1788)	In proportion to taxes paid.	Primarily population.	1840 and 1857	"Legal voters" except for limitation on division or union of counties.	Primarily population.
Michigan (1837)	Population.	Population, but at least 1 from each of 19 organized counties in 49-member body.	1952	34 senatorial districts written into constitution.*	Population.*
Minnesota (1858)	Population.	Population.	No significant change.	. . . .	. . . .
Mississippi (1817)	Population, but prohibition against division of any of 14 counties in 8-member body.	Population, but at least 1 from each of 14 counties in 24-member body.	1890	Primarily area.	Primarily area and each county assured at least 1 representative.

| | Formula in January 1962 | | Formula in October 1965 | | |
---	Upper House	Lower House	Upper House	Lower House	Comments
	...from each county and 6 from city of Baltimore in 29-member body.	In 123-member body 36 from city of Baltimore, 6 from each of 7 counties, 4 from each of 4 counties, 3 from each of 5 counties, and 2 from each of 7 counties.	1 from each county and 6 from city of Baltimore in 29-member body.*	In 142-member body each county and each district of city of Baltimore assured 2 delegates for total of 58, remainder on basis of "relative population."*	Apportionment held invalid; legislature approved, and governor signed, two plans, leaving choice to federal court.
	"Legal voters" except for limitation on division or union of counties.	Primarily population.	"Legal voters" except for limitation on division or union of counties.	Primarily population.	
	...4 senatorial districts written into constitution.	Population.	Population.	Population.	*Between 1900 and 1952 constitutional requirement of reapportionment in relation to population disregarded.
	...opulation.*	Population.*	Primarily population.‡	Primarily population.‡	*1913 reapportionment not consistent with population standard, and no further substantial reapportionment until 1959. ‡Challenge to governor's right to veto 1965 act pending in state court.
	...rimarily area.	Primarily area, and each county assured at least 1 representative.	Population and area.	Each of 80 counties given from 1 to 3 representatives, and 2 counties given 6 and 9 respectively.	

State (and date of entry into the Union)	Original Formula		Date of Significant Change	Revised Formula	
	Upper House	Lower House		Upper House	Lower House
Missouri (1821)	Population, but prohibition against division of counties.	Population, but at least 1 from each of 15 counties in 43-member body.	1865	Primarily population.	1 from each county, with additional representation on the basis of progressively increasing population ratios.
Montana (1889)	1 from each of 16 counties.	Population.	No significant change.	. . . .	. . . .
Nebraska (1867)	Population.	Population.	1934	Unicameral legislature, with 43 population-based districts.	
Nevada (1864)	Population.	Population.	1950	1 from each of 17 counties.	Population, but at least 1 from each of 17 counties in 37-member body.
New Hampshire (1788)	Representation in relation to "public taxes paid" in each of 12 districts.	1 from each town with 150 "rateable polls" with increase for each additional 300.	No significant change.	. . . .	. . . .
New Jersey (1787)	1 from each of 13 counties.	3 from each of 13 counties.	1844	1 from each of 19 counties.	Population, but at least 1 from each of 19 counties in 60-member body.
New Mexico (1912)	Population.	Population.	1949 and 1955	1 from each of 32 counties.	1 from each of 32 counties in 66-member body, remaining 34 allotted in constitution in rough relation to population.

Upper House	Lower House	Upper House	Lower House	Comments
imarily pulation.	1 from each county, with additional representation on the basis of progressively increasing population ratios.	Primarily population.	1 from each county, with additional representation on basis of progressively increasing population ratios.*	*In August 1965 voters rejected plan providing population formula, but including objectionable features.
rom each of counties.	Population, but at least 1 from each of 56 counties in 94-member body.	Population (by federal court order).	Population (by federal court order).	
nicameral legislature — 80% pulation, 20% area in 43 stricts.*		Unicameral legislature with 50 districts based on population and area.‡		*No reapportionment between 1935 and 1962. ‡1965 act held invalid by federal court.
rom each of counties.	Population, but at least 1 from each of 17 counties in 37-member body.	1 from each of 17 counties.*	Population, but at least 1 from each of 17 counties in 37-member body.*	*In September 1965 federal court ordered calling of special legislative session, court to act if legislature should not do so.
presentation relation to ublic taxes id" in each of districts.	1 representative for first 822 inhabitants with increase for each additional 1,644.	Population.	Population.	
rom each of counties.	Population, but at least 1 from each of 21 counties in 60-member body.	Primarily population in 29-member body selected from 14 districts consisting of entire counties.*	Population, but at least 1 from each of 21 counties in 60-member body.*	*Plan approved on "transitional" basis by federal court; constitutional convention to be held in 1966.
rom each of counties.	1 from each of 32 counties in 66-member body, remaining 34 allotted in constitution in rough relation to population.	1 from each of 31 counties and 6 from Bernalillo plus weighted voting to even out population differentials.*	Primarily population.*	*1965 constitutional amendment to become effective if approved by voters in 1966.

469

State (and date of entry into the Union)	Original Formula		Date of Significant Change	Revised Formula	
	Upper House	Lower House		Upper House	Lower House
New York (1788)	Primarily population.	Primarily population.	1894	Population and area in complex formula.	1 from each of 61 of 62 counti₋ in 150-member body, remainin 89 allotted by ratios related t₋ population.
North Carolina (1789)	1 from each county.	2 from each county and 1 from each of 6 towns.	1835	In proportion to taxes paid.	1 from each of 65 counties in 120-member body, remainin 55 by popula-tion.
			1868	Population.	Same formula for then 89 co₋ ties.
North Dakota (1889)	Population.	Primarily population.	1960	Existing statu-tory apportion-ment fixed in constitution without regard to population inequalities.	1 from each of 53 counties in 113-member body, remainin 60 by popula-tion.
Ohio (1803)	Population.	Population.	1903	Primarily population.	1 from each of 88 counties, with additiona representation (of variable number) roughly by population.
Oklahoma (1907)	Population, but limitation on division of counties.	Population, but additional rep-resentation for counties de-pended on progressively higher popula-tion ratios.	No significant change.	. . . .	. . . .
Oregon (1859)	Population.	Population.	No significant change.	. . . .	. . . .

Formula in January 1962		Formula in October 1965		
Upper House	Lower House	Upper House	Lower House	Comments
Population and area in complex formula.	1 from 61 of 62 counties in 150-member body, remaining 89 allotted by ratios related to population.	Population.*	Population.*	*1964 plan held to violate state constitution requiring modification in 1966.
Primarily population.	1 from each of 100 counties in 120-member body, 20 by population.	Primarily population.*	1 from each of 100 counties, 20 by population.*	*Formula challenged by suit filed in September 1965.
Existing statutory apportionment fixed in constitution without regard to population inequalities.	1 from each of 53 counties in 113-member body, remaining 60 by population.	Population (by court order).	Population (by court order).	
Primarily population.	1 from each of 88 counties in 137-member body.	Primarily population.*	1 from each of 88 counties in 137-member body.*	*Federal court ordered parties to submit proposed reapportionment plans by October 15, 1965.
Population, but limitation on division of counties.*	Population, but additional representation for counties depended on progressively higher population ratios.*	Primarily population.	Primarily population.	*Between 1907 and 1963 legislature failed to apportion senate as required by state constitution; same as to house after 1921.
Population.	Population.	Population.	Population.	

State (and date of entry into the Union)	Original Formula		Date of Significant Change	Revised Formula	
	Upper House	Lower House		Upper House	Lower House
Pennsylvania (1787)	Unicameral from 1776 to 1790, with each county and city of Philadelphia each choosing 6.		1838 and 1874	Population, but no city or county to have more than 1/6 of membership.	Population, but at least 1 from each county.
	Primarily population from 1790.	Primarily population from 1790.			
Rhode Island (1790) (Charter of 1663.)	10 "assistants" elected at large.	2 from each town or city except Newport (6), Providence (4), Portsmouth (4), and Warwick (4).	1842	1 from each town or city.	1 from each town or city in 72-member body, remainder by population, but no city to have more than 1/6 of membership.
South Carolina (1788)	1 from each parish and district, with stated exceptions in adjustment to population.	Allocation of 202 seats among 28 parishes and districts in rough relation to population.	1865, 1868, and 1895	1 from each of 46 counties.	Population, but at least 1 from each of 46 counties in 124-member body, remaining 78 by population.
South Dakota (1889)	Population.	Population.	1948	Population standard removed; 35 seats divided among 67 counties.	Population standard removed; 75 seats divided among 67 counties.
Tennessee (1796)	Population, but no county to be divided.	Population.	1834 and 1870	Population, but no county to be divided.	Population, but at least 1 from each county with 2/3 of ratio; floterial representation permitted.
Texas (1845)	Population.	Population.	1875	No county entitled to more than 1 in 31-member body.	Population.

Formula in January 1962		Formula in October 1965		
Upper House	Lower House	Upper House	Lower House	Comments
opulation, but ▯ city or ▯unty to have ▯ore than ⅛ ▯ membership.	Population, but at least 1 from each county.	Population, but no city or county to have more than ⅛ of membership.*	Population, but at least 1 from each county.*	*Legislature under court order to act in fall of 1965.
▯t least 1, but ▯ more than 6, ▯om each of 39 ▯wns or cities ▯ 46-member ▯dy.	At least 1 from each of 39 towns or cities in 100-member body, but no city to have more than ¼ of membership.	At least 1 but no more than 6, from each of 39 towns or cities in 46-member body.*	At least 1 from each of 39 towns or cities in 100-member body, but no city to have more than ¼ of membership.*	*Apportionment commission to recommend plan for 1966, and constitutional convention to propose permanent plan.
▯from each of ▯ counties.	Population, but at least 1 from each of 46 counties in 124-member body, remaining 78 by population.	1 from each of 46 counties.*	Population, but at least 1 from each of 46 counties in 124-member body, remaining 78 by population.*	*Federal court challenge filed in October 1965.
▯ seats divided ▯nong 67 coun-▯es with some ▯gard to ▯pulation.	75 seats divided among 67 counties with some regard to population.	Primarily population.	Primarily population.	
▯pulation, but ▯ county to ▯ divided.*	Population, but at least 1 from each county with 2/3 of ratio; floterial representation permitted.*	Primarily population.‡	Primarily population.‡	*Requirement for decennial reapportionment disregarded from 1890 to 1963. ‡Constitutional convention on apportionment convened in July 1965.
▯o county en-▯led to more ▯an 1 in 31-▯ember body.	Population, but no more than 7 representatives to a county unless population over 700,000, then 1 for each extra 100,000.	Population.	Population.	

State (and date of entry into the Union)	Original Formula		Date of Significant Change	Revised Formula	
	Upper House	Lower House		Upper House	Lower House
Utah (1896)	Population, but no county to be divided unless entitled to 2 or more senators.	Population, but at least 1 from each county.	No significant change.	. . . .	. . . .
Vermont (1791)	Unicameral legislature with representation by towns.		1836	Population, but at least 1 from each of 13 counties in 30-member body.	1 from each inhabited town.
Virginia (1788)	24 single-member districts based on population estimates.	2 from each county and 1 each from West Augusta, Williamsburg, and Norfolk, as well as other cities, later established.	1830	In 32-member body, 19 from east of Blue Ridge Mountains, and 13 from the west.	State divided into 4 regions which received allocations for 134-member house.
Washington (1889)	Population.	Population.	No significant change.	. . . .	. . . .
West Virginia (1863)	Population, but no county to be divided.	Population, but each county with more than ½ ratio to be represented.	No significant change.	. . . .	. . . .
Wisconsin (1848)	Population.	Population.	No significant change.	. . . .	. . . .
Wyoming (1890)	At least 1 from each of 10 counties in 16-member body.	At least 1 from each of 10 counties in 33-member body.	No significant change.	. . . .	. . . .

| | Formula in January 1962 | | Formula in October 1965 | | |
Upper House	Lower House	Upper House	Lower House	Comments
pulation, but dditional representation ven only for gher popula- n ratios.	Population, but at least 1 from each of 29 counties in 69-member body.	Population without cross-ing county lines.	Population without cross-ing county lines.	
pulation, but least 1 from ch of 13 unties in 30-ember body.	1 from each inhabited town.	Population.*	Population. (Lower house reduced in size from 246 to 150.)*	*Federal court approval withheld for failure to provide for required election.
scretion in gislature to lines for 40-ember body, population a ctor.	Discretion in legislature to fix lines for 100-member body, population a factor.	Primarily population.	Primarily Population.	
pulation.*	Population.*	Population.	Population.	*State constitutional requirements for decennial reapportionment in relation to population disregarded until 1965.
imarily popu-tion in 34-ember body; t when any of senatorial stricts in-des more an 1 county, nators must me from dif-rent counties.	Primarily population (but legislature gave at least 1 seat to each of 55 counties in 106-member body).	Primarily population in 34-member body; but when any of 17 senatorial districts includes more than 1 county, senators must come from different counties.*	Primarily population.*	*Special legislative session to fix population basis for choice of delegates to constitutional convention.
pulation.*	Population.*	Primarily population.	Primarily population.	*Malapportionment prior to 1964 arose out of legislative failure to comply with state constitution.
ch county to ve 1 senator r each 11,000 population 930 census).	Each county to have 1 representative for each 4,150 population (1930 census).	At least 1 from each of 21 counties in 25-member body.*	At least 1 from each of 21 counties in 61-member body.*	*Legislative failure to reapportion in 1965 reopens federal court ruling that house apportionment is invalid.

Selected Bibliography

BOOKS AND MONOGRAPHS

Baker, Gordon E. Rural Versus Urban Political Power. New York: Random House. 1963.

——. State Constitutions: Reapportionment. New York: National Municipal League. 1960.

Beth, Loren P. *See Havard, William C.*

Bickel, Alexander M. The Least Dangerous Branch. New York: Bobbs-Merrill Co. 1962.

Boyd, William J. D. Patterns of Apportionment. New York: National Municipal League. 1962.

Bromage, Arthur W. American County Government. New York: Sears Publishing Co. 1933.

Butler, P. E. The Electoral System in Britain: 1918–1951. Oxford: The Clarendon Press. 1953.

Carpenter, William S., and Stafford, Paul T. State and Local Government in the United States. New York: F. S. Crofts & Co. 1936.

Cooke, Jacob E., ed. The Federalist. Middletown, Connecticut: Wesleyan University Press. 1961.

The Council of State Governments. The Book of the States. Chicago: Annual.

——. Legislative Apportionment in the States. Chicago: Issued at irregular intervals.

Dahl, Robert A. A Preface to Democratic Theory. Chicago: University of Chicago Press. 1956.

——. Who Governs? New Haven: Yale University Press. 1963.

David, Paul T., and Eisenberg, Ralph. Devaluation of the Urban and Suburban Vote, 2 vols. Charlottesville: Bureau of Public Administration, University of Virginia. 1961–62.

——. State Legislative Redistricting. Chicago: Public Administration Service. 1962.

De Grazia, Alfred. Essay on Apportionment and Representative Government. Washington: American Enterprise Institute for Public Policy Research. 1963.

De Tocqueville, Alexis. Democracy in America. London: Oxford University Press. 1953.

Eisenberg, Ralph. *See David, Paul T.*

Farrand, Max. The Framing of the Constitution of the United States. New Haven: Yale University Press. 1913.

Farrand, Max, ed. The Records of the Federal Convention of 1787, 4 vols. New Haven: Yale University Press. 1911–1937.

Goldberg, Edward M. The Constitutional Law and Politics of Legislative Apportionment. Unpublished Ph.D. dissertation, University of Pennsylvania. Philadelphia: 1965.

Grimes, Alan P. Equality in America. New York: Oxford University Press. 1964.

Hacker, Andrew. Congressional Districting: The Issue of Equal Representation, rev. ed. Washington: The Brookings Institution. 1964.

Handlin, Oscar, and others. Harvard Guide to American History. Cambridge: Belknap Press. 1954.

Harris, Robert J. The Quest for Equality. Baton Rouge: Louisiana State University Press. 1960.

Hartz, Louis. The Liberal Tradition in America. New York: Harcourt, Brace and World, Inc. 1955.

Havard, William C., and Beth, Loren P. The Politics of Misrepresentation. Baton Rouge: Louisiana State University Press. 1962.

Jennings, Sir W. Ivor. The Approach to Self-Government. Boston: Beacon Press. 1963.

———. Party Politics. Vol. I: Appeal to the People. Cambridge: Cambridge University Press. 1960.

Jewell, Malcolm E., ed. The Politics of Reapportionment. New York: Atherton Press. 1962.

Johnson, Claudius O. (and associates). American State and Local Government, rev. ed. New York: Thomas Y. Crowell Co. 1965.

Keefe, William J., and Ogul, Morris S. The American Legislative Process: Congress and the States. Englewood Cliffs: Prentice-Hall, Inc. 1964.

Key, V. O. Politics, Parties and Pressure Groups. New York: Thomas Y. Crowell Co. 1952.

Larson, James E. Reapportionment and the Courts. Tuscaloosa: Bureau of Public Administration, University of Alabama Press. 1962.

Lobingier, Charles Sumner. The People's Law or Popular Participation in Law-Making. New York: The Macmillan Co. 1909.

McKay, Robert B. Reapportionment and the Federal Analogy. New York: National Municipal League. 1962.

National Municipal League. Compendium on Legislative Apportionment. New York: 1962.

———. Court Decisions on Legislative Apportionment, 13 vols. New York: 1962–1965.

———. Model State Constitution, 6th ed. New York: 1963.

Nevins, Allan. The American States During and After the Revolution. New York: The Macmillan Co. 1924.

Ogul, Morris S. *See Keefe, William J.*

Rossiter, Clinton. Seedtime of the Republic. New York: Harcourt, Brace and World, Inc. 1953.

Schubert, Glendon. Reapportionment. New York: Charles Scribner's Sons. 1965.

Sears, Kenneth Craddock. Methods of Reapportionment. Chicago: University of Chicago Law School. 1952.

Stafford, Paul T. *See Carpenter, William S.*

Thorpe, Francis Newton, ed. The Federal and State Constitutions, Colonial Charters and Other Organic Laws, 7 vols. Washington: Government Printing Office. 1909.

Twentieth Century Fund. One Man — One Vote. New York: 1962.

United States. Advisory Commission on Intergovernmental Relations. Apportionment of State Legislatures. Washington: 1962.

————. Department of Commerce, Bureau of the Census. Governing Boards of County Governments: 1965. Washington: 1965.

————. ————. County and City Data Book. Washington: 1962.

————. The Library of Congress. Guide to the Study of the United States of America. Washington: 1960.

————. The Library of Congress Legislative Reference Service. Action With Respect to Apportionment of State Legislatures and Congressional Districting. Washington: 1964, 1965.

————. ————. Apportionment of Local Political Subdivisions and Judicial Districts. Washington: 1965.

————. ————. Apportionment of State Legislatures. Washington: 1965.

————. ————. Congressional Districting and the Wesberry Case. Washington: 1965.

————. ————. Initiative and Referendum — with Particular Reference to Apportionment of State Legislatures. Washington: 1965.

————. ————. Legislative Apportionment — A Study of the Issue. Washington: 1965.

————. ————. Legislative Apportionment — Statistics. Washington: 1965.

————. ————. Methods for the Measurement of Legislative Apportionment Systems. Washington: 1965.

————. ————. State Constitutional and Statutory Provisions for Popular Initiative and Referendum With Particular Reference to Legislative Apportionment. Washington: 1964.

————. ————. State Conventions as Instrumentalities for Considering Ratification of Constitutional Amendments. Washington: 1964.

————. ————. State Petitions and Memorials to Congress on the Subject of Apportionment of State Legislatures. Washington: 1965.

————. ————. Withdrawal of Jurisdiction of Federal Courts Over Questions of State Legislative Apportionment. Washington: 1965.

————. Senate. Hearings Before the Subcommittee on Constitutional Amendments of the Committee on the Judiciary of the United States Senate (Reapportionment of State Legislatures). 89th Cong., 1st Sess., on S. J. Res. 2, 37, 38, 44. 1965.

Wheeler, John P., ed. Salient Issues of Constitutional Revision. New York: National Municipal League. 1961.

Wood, Robert C. 1400 Governments: The Political Economy of the New York Metropolitan Region. New York: Doubleday & Company, Inc. 1964.

ARTICLES

Abram, Morris B. A New Civil Right, 52 Nat'l Civ. Rev. 186 (1963).

Atleson, James B. The Aftermath of Baker v. Carr — An Adventure in Judicial Experimentation, 51 Calif. L. Rev. 535 (1963).

Auerbach, Carl. The Reapportionment Cases: One Person, One Vote — One Vote, One Value, 1964 Supreme Court Rev. 1.

Auerbach, Carl A. Proposal II and the National Interest in State Legislative Apportionment, 39 Notre Dame Law. 628 (1964).

Baldwin, Fletcher N., Jr., and Laughlin, Stanley K., Jr. The Reapportionment Cases: A Study in the Constitutional Adjudication Process, 17 U. Fla. L. Rev. 301 (1964).

Banzhaf, John E., III. Weighted Voting Doesn't Work: A Mathematical Analysis, 19 Rutgers L. Rev. 317 (1965).

Bebout, John E., and Wheeler, John P. After Reapportionment, 51 Nat'l Civ. Rev. 246 (1962).

Bickel, Alexander M. The Durability of Colegrove v. Green, 72 Yale L.J. 39 (1962).
———. Reapportionment & Liberal Myths, 6 Commentary 483 (1963).

Black, Charles L., Jr. Inequities in Districting for Congress: Baker v. Carr and Colegrove v. Green, 72 Yale L.J. 13 (1962).

———. The Proposed Amendment of Article V: A Threatened Disaster, 72 Yale L.J. 957 (1963).

Bone, Hugh A. States Attempting to Comply with Reapportionment Requirements, 17 Law & Contemp. Prob. 387 (1952).

Bonfield, Arthur Earl. Baker v. Carr: New Light on the Constitutional Guarantee of Republican Government, 50 Calif. L. Rev. 245 (1962).

———. The Guarantee Clause of Article IV, Section 4: A Study in Constitutional Desuetude, 46 Minn. L. Rev. 513 (1962).

Caruso, Lawrence R. The Proper Role of the Federal Courts in the Reapportionment of State Legislatures, 36 Miss. L.J. 300 (1965).

Celler, Emanuel. Congressional Apportionment — Past, Present, and Future, 17 Law & Contemp. Prob. 268 (1952).

Chafee, Zechariah, Jr. Congressional Reapportionment, 42 Harv. L. Rev. 1015 (1929).

Clem, Alan L. Guidelines for Solving the Representation Riddle, 8 S.D.L. Rev. 109 (1963).

———. Problems of Measuring and Achieving Equality of Representation in State Legislatures, 42 Neb. L. Rev. 622 (1963).

De Grazia, Alfred. General Theory of Apportionment, 17 Law & Contemp. Prob. 257 (1952).

———. Righting the Wrongs of Representation, 38 State Gov't 113 (1965).

Dixon, Robert G., Jr. Apportionment Standards and Judicial Power, 38 Notre Dame Law. 367 (1963).

———. Legislative Apportionment and the Federal Constitution, 27 Law and Contemp. Prob. 329 (1962).

———. New Constitutional Forms for Metropolis: Reapportioned County Boards; Local Councils of Government, 30 Law and Contemp. Prob. 57 (1965).

———. The Reapportionment Amendments and Direct Democracy, 38 State Gov't 117 (1965).

———. Reapportionment in the Supreme Court and Congress: Constitutional Struggle for Fair Representation, 63 Mich. L. Rev. 209 (1964).

———. Reapportionment Perspectives: What is Fair Representation? 51 A.B.A.J. 319 (1965).

Durfee, Elizabeth. Apportionment of Representation in the Legislature: A Study of State Constitutions, 43 Mich. L. Rev. 1091 (1945).

Edwards, Charles P. Theoretical and Comparative Aspects of Reapportionment and Redistricting: With Reference to Baker v. Carr, 15 Vand. L. Rev. 1265 (1962).

Emerson, Thomas I. Malapportionment and Judicial Power: The Supreme Court's Decision in Baker v. Carr, 72 Yale L.J. 64 (1962).

Engle, Robert H. Weighting Legislators' Votes to Equalize Representation, 12 W. Pol. Q. 442 (1959).

Farrelly, David G., and Hinderaker, Ivan. Congressional Reapportionment and National Political Power, 17 Law & Contemp. Prob. 338 (1952).

Freidelbaum, Stanley H. Baker v. Carr: The New Doctrine of Judicial Intervention and Its Implications for American Federalism, 29 U. Chi. L. Rev. 673 (1962).

Freund, Paul. New Vistas in Constitutional Law, 112 U. Pa. L. Rev. 631 (1964).

Goldberg, Arthur L. The Statistics of Malapportionment, 72 Yale L.J. 90 (1962).

Hacker, Andrew. Votes Cast and Seats Won, Trans-Action 7 (Sept.–Oct. 1964).

Hagan, Charles B. The Bicameral Principle in State Legislatures, 11 J. Pub. L. 310 (1962).

Hanson, Royce. Courts in the Thicket: The Problem of Judicial Standards in Apportionment Cases, 12 Am. U.L. Rev. 51 (1963).

Harvey, Lashley G. Reapportionment of State Legislatures — Legal Requirements, 17 Law & Contemp. Prob. 364 (1952).

Hess, Sidney W. *See Weaver, James B.*

Hinderaker, Ivan. *See Farrelly, David G.*

Israel, Jerold. Nonpopulation Factors Relevant to an Acceptable Standard of Apportionment, 38 Notre Dame Law. 499 (1963).

———. On Charting a Course Through the Mathematical Quagmire: The Future of Baker v. Carr, 61 Mich. L. Rev. 107 (1962).

Jewell, Malcolm E. Minority Representation: A Political or Judicial Question? 53 Ky. L.J. 267 (1964–65).

Kauper, Paul G. Some Comments on the Reapportionment Cases, 63 Mich. L. Rev. 243 (1964).

Kennedy, Cornelius B. The Reapportionment Decisions: A Constitutional Amendment Is Needed, 51 A.B.A.J. 123 (1965).

Klain, Maurice. A New Look at the Constituencies: The Need for a Recount and a Reappraisal, 39 Amer. Pol. Sci. Rev. 1105 (1955).

Krastin, Karl. The Implementation of Representative Government in a Democracy, 48 Iowa L. Rev. 549 (1963).

Lancaster, Robert. What's Wrong with Baker v. Carr? 15 Vand. L. Rev. 1247 (1962).

Larson, James E. Awaiting the Other Shoe, 52 Nat'l Civ. Rev. 189–93 (1963).

Laughlin, Charles V. Proportional Representation: It Can Cure Our Apportionment Ills, 49 A.B.A.J. 1065 (1963).

Laughlin, Stanley K., Jr. *See Baldwin, Fletcher N., Jr.*

Lerner, Richard E. The Role of the State Judiciary in Redistricting and Reapportionment, 18 N.Y.U. Intra. L. Rev. 79 (1963).

Lewis, Anthony. Legislative Apportionment and the Federal Courts, 71 Harv. L. Rev. 1057 (1958).

Lucas, Jo Desha. Legislative Apportionment and Representative Government: The Meaning of Baker v. Carr, 61 Mich. L. Rev. 711 (1963).

———. Of Ducks and Drakes: Judicial Relief in Reapportionment Cases, 38 Notre Dame Law. 401 (1963).

McCloskey, Robert G. Foreword: The Reapportionment Case, 76 Harv. L. Rev. 54 (1962).

McKay, Robert B. Court, Congress, and Reapportionment, 63 Mich. L. Rev. 255 (1964).

———. Don't Amend the Constitution, 38 State Gov't 121 (1965).

———. Political Thickets and Crazy Quilts: Reapportionment and Equal Protection, 61 Mich. L. Rev. 645 (1963).

———. The Federal Analogy and State Apportionment Standards, 38 Notre Dame Law. 487 (1963).

———. Reapportionment Decisions: Retrospect and Prospect, 51 A.B.A.J. 128 (1965).

Merrill, Maurice H. Blazes for a Trail Through the Thicket of Reapportionment, 16 Okla. L. Rev. 59 (1963).

Mitchell, Stephen R. Judicial Self-Restraint: Political Questions and Malapportionment, 39 Wash. L. Rev. 761 (1964).

Nagel, Stuart S. Applying Correlation Analysis to Case Prediction, 42 Tex. L. Rev. 1006 (1964).

————. Simplified Bipartisan Computer Redistricting, 17 Stan. L. Rev. 863 (1965).

Nahstoll, R. W. The Role of the Federal Courts in the Reapportionment of State Legislatures, 50 A.B.A.J. 842 (1964).

Neal, Phil C. Baker v. Carr: Politics in Search of Law, 1962 Supreme Court Review 252.

O'Brien, F. William. Baker v. Carr Abroad: The Swiss Federal Tribunal and Cantonal Elections, 72 Yale L.J. 46 (1962).

Paschal, Joel F. The House of Representatives: "Grand Depository of the Democratic Principle"? 17 Law & Contemp. Prob. 276 (1952).

Perin, Noel. In Defense of Country Votes, Yale Rev. 23 (Fall 1962).

Pollak, Louis H. Judicial Power and "The Politics of The People," 72 Yale L.J. 81 (1962).

Roeck, Ernest C., Jr. Measuring Compactness as a Requirement of Legislative Apportionment, 5 Midwest J. Pol. Sci. 70 (1961).

Rudolph, W. M. A Conservative Defense of Individual Rights, 43 Neb. L. Rev. 854 (1964).

Sandalow, Terrance. The Limits of Municipal Power Under Home Rule: A Role for the Courts, 48 Minn. L. Rev. 643 (1964).

Scanlan, Alfred L. Problems of Pleading, Proof and Persuasion in a Reapportionment Case, 38 Notre Dame Law. 415 (1963).

Schattschneider, E. E. Urbanization & Reapportionment, 72 Yale L.J. 7 (1962).

Schmeckbier, Laurence F. The Method of Equal Proportions, 17 Law & Contemp. Prob. 302 (1952).

Short, Lloyd M. States That Have Not Met Their Constitutional Requirements, 17 Law & Contemp. Prob. 377 (1952).

Shull, Charles W. Political and Partisan Implications of State Legislative Apportionment, 17 Law & Contemp. Prob. 417 (1952).

Silva, Ruth C. Compared Values of the Single- and Multi-Member Legislative District, 17 W. Pol. Q. 504 (1964).

Sindler, Alan P. Baker v. Carr: How to "Sear the Conscience" of Legislators, 72 Yale L.J. 23 (1962).

Srb, Hugo F. The Unicameral Legislature — A Successful Innovation, 40 Neb. L. Rev. 626 (1961).

Swindler, William F. Reapportionment: Revisionism or Revolution, 43 N.C.L. Rev. 55 (1964).

Tabor, Neil. The Gerrymandering of State and Federal Legislative Districts, 16 Md. L. Rev. 277 (1956).

Taylor, William L. Legal Action to Enjoin Legislative Malapportionment: The Political Question Doctrine, 34 So. Cal. L. Rev. 179 (1961).

Todd, James E. The Apportionment Problem Faced by the States, 17 Law & Contemp. Prob. 314 (1952).

Tyler, Gus. Court Versus Legislature, 27 Law & Contemp. Prob. 390 (1962).

Velvel, Lawrence R. Suggested Approaches to Constitutional Adjudication and Apportionment, 12 U.C.L.A. L. Rev. 1381 (1965).

Vickery, William. On the Prevention of Gerrymandering, 76 Pol. Sci. Q. 105 (1961).

Weaver, James B., and Hess, Sidney W. A Procedure for Nonpartisan Districting: Development of Computer Techniques, 73 Yale L.J. 289 (1963).

———. Districting by Machine, 53 Nat'l Civ. Rev. 293 (1964).

Wechsler, Herbert. The Political Safeguards of Federalism: The Role of the States in the Composition and Selection of the National Government, 54 Colum. L. Rev. 543 (1954).

Weinstein, Jack B. The Effect of the Federal Reapportionment Decisions on Counties and Other Forms of Municipal Government, 65 Colum. L. Rev. 21 (1965).

Weiss, Jonathan. Analysis of Wesberry v. Sanders, 38 So. Cal. L. Rev. 67 (1965).

Wheeler, John P. *See Bebout, John E.*

Willcox, Walter F. Last Words on the Apportionment Problem, 17 Law & Contemp. Prob. 290 (1952).

NOTES AND COMMENTS

Apportionment and the Courts — A Synopsis and Prognosis, 59 Nw. U.L. Rev. 500 (1964).

The Apportionment Cases: An Expanded Concept of Equal Protection, 1965 Wis. L. Rev. 606 (1965).

Baker v. Carr and Legislative Apportionment: A Problem of Standards, 72 Yale L.J. 968 (1963).

Baker v. Carr — Malapportionment in State Governments Becomes a Federal Constitutional Issue, 15 Vand. L. Rev. 985 (1962).

Beyond Wesberry: State Apportionment and Equal Protection, 39 N.Y.U. L. Rev. 264 (1964).

Challenges to Congressional Districting: After Baker v. Carr Does Colegrove v. Green Endure? 63 Col. L. Rev. 99 (1963).

City Government in the State Courts, 78 Harv. L. Rev. 1596 (1965).

Congressional Apportionment: The Unproductive Search for Standards and Remedies, 63 Mich. L. Rev. 374 (1964).

Congressional Reapportionment: The Theory of Representation in the House of Representatives, 39 Tul. L. Rev. 286 (1965).

Courts and Legislative Reapportionment after Baker v. Carr, 1963 U. Ill. L. Forum 75 (1963).

The Equal-Population Standard: A New Concept of Equal Protection in State Apportionment Cases, 33 U. Cinc. L. Rev. 483 (1964).

Legal Problems of Ward Realignment in Philadelphia, 38 Temp. L.Q. 174 (1965).

Legislative Apportionment: A Judicial Dilemma? 15 Rutgers L. Rev. 82 (1960).

Nonpolitical Remedies of the People, 20 N.Y.U. Intra. L. Rev. 274 (1965).

Report of the Governor's Bipartisan Reapportionment Commission, January 15, 1965, 49 Minn. L. Rev. 367 (1964).

Small Town Representation: Invidious Discrimination? The Reapportionment Problem in Rhode Island, Vermont and Connecticut, 43 B.U.L. Rev. 523 (1963).

State Reapportionment — the Wake of Reynolds v. Sims, 45 B.U.L. Rev. 88 (1965).

Wesberry v. Sanders: Deep in the Thicket, 32 Geo. Wash. L. Rev. 1076 (1964).

Wright v. Rockefeller and Legislative Gerrymanders: The Desegregation Decisions Plus a Problem of Proof, 72 Yale L.J. 1041 (1963).

BIBLIOGRAPHIES

Boyd, William D., and Silva, Ruth C. Selected Bibliography on Legislative Apportionment and Districting. New York: National Municipal League. 1963.

Tompkins, Dorothy C. State Government and Administration (A Bibliography). Berkeley: Bureau of Public Administration, University of California. 1954.

United States. The Library of Congress Legislative Reference Service. Congressional Districting and Legislative Apportionment: Selected References. Washington: 1965.

———. ———. Legislative Apportionment — A Study of the Issues: Bibliography on Political Representation (following appendix E). Washington: 1965.

University of Chicago Law School Library. Federal and State Legislative Apportionment; a Selected List of References. Chicago: 1962.

Table of Cases

Subject Index

About the Author

Robert B. McKay, Associate Dean and Professor of Law at New York University, long an authority on constitutional law, has been in the forefront of the effort to achieve fair apportionment. In addition to extensive writing and lecturing on the topic, he prepared for the American Civil Liberties Union, the American Jewish Congress, and the NAACP Legal Defense and Educational Fund, Inc. their brief *amici curiae* in four of the six Reapportionment Cases before the Supreme Court in 1963. He is a member of the citizens' commission to draft a new state reapportionment plan for New York.